5-20-76

THE NEWSPAPER AND
THE HISTORIAN

Théophraste Renaudot

THE NEWSPAPER AND THE HISTORIAN

BY

LUCY MAYNARD SALMON

"Is there anything in the paper, Sir?"
"Anything in the paper! All the world is in the paper.
Why, Madam, if you will but read what is written in
the *Times* of this very day, it is enough for a year's
history, and ten times as much meditation."—*Thackeray.*

OCTAGON BOOKS

A DIVISION OF FARRAR, STRAUS AND GIROUX

New York   1976

Copyright, 1923 by Oxford University Press
American Branch

Copyright renewed 1951 by Vassar College

Reprinted 1976
by special arrangement with Oxford University Press, Inc.

OCTAGON BOOKS

A DIVISION OF FARRAR, STRAUS & GIROUX, INC.

19 Union Square West

New York, N.Y. 10003

Library of Congress Cataloging in Publication Data

Salmon, Lucy Maynard, 1853-1927.
    The newspaper and the historian.

    Reprint of the ed. published by Oxford University Press, New
York.

    Includes bibliographical references and index.
    1. Newspapers—History.   2. Periodicals—History.   3. Histori-
ography.   I. Title.

PN4801.S28   1976   070   75-43836
ISBN 0-374-97020-3

Manufactured by Braun-Brumfield, Inc.
Ann Arbor, Michigan
Printed in the United States of America

1909114

PREFACE

Peccavi should be the opening word of many prefaces. A consciousness of much left undone that ought to have been done, and of much done that ought not to have been done, detracts from the pleasure that otherwise might have been felt in passing from one piece of work to another. But the delinquent and offender may at least be heard in his own defense, and state what his object has and has not been.

The object of writing this book has been to discover if possible the advantages and the limitations of the periodical press, especially the newspaper, considered as historical material, and thus to determine the extent of its usefulness to the historian in his efforts to reconstruct the past. It therefore attempts to give an analysis of the component parts of the press, with a sufficient number of examples to illustrate or to justify the conclusions that have been deduced.

It is not the object of the book to give a history, even a fragmentary one, either of the newspaper or of journalism. It is not to be considered a brief for the press, or an indictment of the press, or "a presentation of both sides of the case"; in a sense, it does not concern itself at all with the press, since the person ultimately in mind has been the student of history. But while it shows the pitfalls the historian must encounter in his use of the newspaper, it may also incidentally indicate how unnecessary has been the alarm constantly raised through the blanket arraignment of the press, and how inherent are the dangers found in the general statement.

The present volume considers the essential characteristics of the newspaper as they affect the historian and as they are made known by the newspaper itself, unaffected by official control. It considers the press only on its esoteric side. If in the discussion of the relations of the newspaper and the historian the newspaper has occupied the foreground, it is hoped that it will be found that all lines have converged on the historian in the background.

Many extracts from the newspapers themselves have been given since the newspaper is both consciously and unconsciously its own best record of its aims and its methods of attaining them. Since it is essential to the purpose of the book to consider testimony, to weigh evidence, and to arrive at decisions, it is necessary to hear the evidence given by the press itself. A large number of the citations have been taken from the New York City papers, in part for reasons of convenience, and in part because news-collecting associations have standardized news, and advertising clubs and fashion have in a measure standardized advertisements. Illustrative newspapers, however, from practically every state in the Union, and many from other countries, have been examined, and it is thus hoped that no undue basis will be found for the charge of generalizing from insufficient data.

A companion volume now in press is entitled *The Newspaper and Authority*. This considers the advantages and the limitations of the press considered with reference to external control. The questions of regulation of the press, all forms of censorship of the press, freedom of the press, libel laws, press bureaus, press publicity, and press propaganda suggest conditions where the press is limited by an authority outside of itself. This exoteric side of the press and all its relations to external authority must be examined by the historian as well as the limitations arising from conditions within the press itself.

My obligations to others seem out of all proportion to the results visible in the book. They include a group of colleagues and friends, V. Barbour, L. F. Brown, E. Ellery, I. C. Thallon, and C. M. Thompson, all of whom have read the manuscript wholly or in part, and have at all times lent a listening ear as each new interest in the subject has developed. A group of friends, M. L. Berkemeier, R. L. Lowrie, H. Rottschaefer, and E. M. Rushmore, have given untiring help in the collection of material. Friends have sent to the Vassar College Library special copies of newspapers from all over the world; they can not all be named individually, but special gratitude goes to K. B. Béziat for newspapers from France covering a wide range of interests and localities during 1914–1915; to Charles Upson Clark for copies of Italian papers during the war; to Burges Johnson for the material collected for the Vassar College Library in 1918; and to A. L. Walker for many consecutive numbers and special copies of Greek newspapers. H. M. Bartlett and M. Newcomer have contributed copies of inscriptions in London in memory of British war correspondents. C. Saunders has been a friendly adviser.

Special acknowledgment must gratefully be made to L. F. Brown for the preparation of the Biographical Notes and to Henry S. Fraser for making the Index and reading the proof. My obligations to F. G. Davenport, M. Relf, E. Rickert, Frank G. Royce, A. Underhill, B. C. Wilcox, and President Henry Noble MacCracken have been great and constant.

The courtesy of librarians in arranging inter-library loans has made possible the use of books loaned the Vassar College Library from the libraries of Columbia, Cornell, Harvard, and Yale Universities, the New Bedford Free Public Library, the New York State Library, and the Library of Congress. Frequent use has also been made of the important collections of the New York Public Library. An abiding sense of appreciation for such kindnesses must remain with every one who has had similar opportunities.

All those to whom acknowledgment has directly or indirectly been made are absolved from all responsibility for errors of omission or commission; the ultimate liability for such errors must rest with the writer alone. The closing word must be *peccavi*.

L. M. S.

Poughkeepsie, New York,
April 23, 1923.

CONTENTS

INTRODUCTION

CHAPTER I

THE DEVELOPMENT OF THE NEWSPAPER

CONTENTS

CHAPTER II

THE NEWSPAPER AS A PERSONALITY

CONTENTS

CHAPTER III

GUARANTEES OF PROBABILITY

CHAPTER IV

THE PRESS AND OTHER ACTIVITIES

CHAPTER V

NEWS-COLLECTING AND NEWS-DISTRIBUTING ORGANIZATIONS

CHAPTER VI

THE GENERAL REPORTER

CHAPTER VII

THE OFFICIAL REPORTER

CHAPTER VIII

THE SPECIAL CORRESPONDENT

CHAPTER IX

THE WAR CORRESPONDENT

CHAPTER X

THE INTERVIEW

CHAPTER XI

THE EDITOR AND THE EDITORIAL

CHAPTER XII

CRITICISM AND THE CRITIC

CHAPTER XIII

THE ADVERTISEMENT

CHAPTER XIV

THE ILLUSTRATION AND THE GRAPHIC PRESS

CONTENTS

CHAPTER XV

Authenticity of Newspapers

CHAPTER XVI

THE AUTHORITATIVENESS OF THE PRESS

CHAPTER XVII

How Far Can the Past Be Reconstructed from the Press?

ILLUSTRATIONS

INTRODUCTION

"Subordinate persons were employed to note down the events of the day and news of the city for the absent men of quality; and Caesar as early as his first consulship took fitting measures for the immediate publication of an extract of the transactions of the senate. From the private journals of those Roman penny-a-liners and these official current reports there arose a sort of news-sheet for the capital (*acta diurna*), in which the *résumé* of the business discussed before the people and in the senate, and births, deaths, and such like were recorded. This became a not unimportant source for history, but remained without proper political as without literary significance."—*Theodore Mommsen.*

"Interprète fidèle des temps qu'il a traversé, le journal en reproduit la physionomie exacte; il est pour le moral des peuples ce que l'invention de Daguerre est pour les formes matérielles. C'est seulement en interrogeant ces mille échos de l'opinion publique, ces témoins imperturbables des événements, en les confrontant et les contrôlant les uns par les autres, qu'on peut arriver à la vérité."—*E. Hatin.*

HISTORIANS were some years ago surprised, even perplexed, by the appearance of the first volume of an unheralded history dealing with America. The surprise was not altogether due to its unusual title, for this was evidently an adaptation of that of a well-known English work, nor was it explained by the fact that the author was not known to be one of the guild,—Grote had been a banker, Hodgkin a merchant, and Stubbs a clergyman, and a history written by an instructor in civil engineering was conceivable. The surprise was in large measure to be ascribed to the material on which the work was apparently based,—an examination of the foot-notes showed references, not to the conventional authorities, but to newspapers, pamphlets, dodgers, and every variety of ephemeral material. That old newspapers were interesting reading had always been appreciated, but no historian had hitherto ventured to use them as a main authority for his work. Was it possible that the stone which the builders refused had become the head stone of the corner?

During the forty years that have elapsed since the appearance of the first volume of McMaster's *History of the People of the United States from the Revolution to the Civil War*, the newspaper has become a familiar historical source, although its legitimacy as such does not even yet pass unquestioned. The historian has found much to commend in the use of periodical and even of ephemeral literature in his study of the past, but during this period he has attached an ever-increasing importance to the reliability of the material he uses. He knows that before everything else this material must be both authentic and authoritative; if the sources he uses are defective in either particular, the history that he writes rests on shifting sands and his work collapses with the first breath of criticism that discloses the weakness of its foundations. In the use of books and of documents of every kind it is comparatively easy to determine the authoritativeness of the statements made, but in the use of the newspaper this has seemed almost impossible. The responsibility for the tidings spread abroad can not be assigned to any single person, but must be divided among several large groups of individuals, and each group in its turn must be resolved into its constituent parts. Every issue of a great newspaper represents the work of scores, hundreds, possibly thousands of persons all over the world and it seems obviously impossible for the historian to investigate the truth of even a small proportion of the statements made by the press. He recognizes the manifest usefulness that the newspaper might have in his work, yet he hesitates to accept a form of material the authoritativeness of which has not been thoroughly established.

The historian has at hand a mass of official documents,—constitutions, charters, laws, treaties, court decisions, and similar material. He accepts its authoritativeness without question and recognizes that it is indispensable in writing a history of the state. Creeds, papal bulls, decisions of religious bodies must be accepted as authoritative sources in dealing with all questions of religious belief and of ecclesiastical organization.

But while the press touches every human interest, it has no standards by which its authoritativeness may be judged, it has no Magna Charta or Apostles' Creed to which appeal may be made, it has no formulated laws governing its policy, and no court decisions to which resort may be made. Such external laws as directly affect it, as libel laws, are purely negative and prohibitory and in no sense afford a standard of belief or of conduct. Collectively it is a mass of shapeless material that can not be made amenable to the forces of order and reason.

The historian perhaps also shares the current opinion in regard to the credibility of the newspaper. This seems to be equally divided between those who dismiss the whole question by saying, "You can't believe anything you read in the papers," and those who aver with equal emphasis, "I know it's so, I read it in the paper." But the historian can not follow the golden mean so often advised in other quandaries and say that he will trust one-half of the newspapers and reject the other half of them, or that he will believe one-half of every newspaper and disbelieve the other half,—he must know very definitely just what part is to be accepted and what part is to be rejected. Since this in its turn has seemed a difficult matter to determine, he has at times been tempted to include the newspaper in his wholesale condemnation of all material that is unreliable, inaccurate, and sensational. If at other times he has tolerated its use by others, it has been with the blanket warning, "newspapers must be used with great care and discretion,"—an injunction that in its turn becomes difficult of application.

The old proverb "familiarity breeds contempt" must also be applied to the newspaper since its very accessibility becomes in the eyes of the public the best of reasons for ignoring it. Unconsciously this same idea has been the basis of the procedure of the historian since he has often apparently believed that the more difficult it is to find material the more worthy of credence it is when found. This is in a measure counterbalanced by the lavish use made by the press of the telegraph, the cable, and the wireless and the importance unconsciously attached to all messages received by these means, but this only in part brings from the historian a hesitating recognition of the value of the newspaper for his work.

But while these doubts still prevail there has been a noticeable change of attitude on the part of historians towards the newspaper. Even before McMaster had placed so great a reliance on newspapers as a source for his work, von Holst had shown something of the possibilities inherent in this class of material and had made effective use of it, though in a limited way, in his *Constitutional and Political History of the United States*. Since that time historians have come to accept the latent serviceableness of the newspaper to the fraternity. In 1908 an entire session of the annual meeting of the American Historical Association was given to the discussion of the use of the newspaper by historians, and there are everywhere evidences of an increasing appreciation of the important place the newspaper occupies in the equipment of the historian. Yet there are still misgivings in the minds of many, citations from the press are made with a semi-apology, and the newspaper as an historical source still needs the support of distinguished historians like James Ford Rhodes to convince the rank and file of students of history that it holds an honorable place in the study of the past.[1] As long as the historian must concern himself primarily with the question of evidence, with testing the truth of statements made, with determining the authoritativeness of all the material that he uses, he feels that he must reject in large part the newspaper as a source for his work. Such use as he makes of the press is confined to those portions of it that will lend color and vivacity to the past and aid him in giving a graphic description of society and especially of the external manoeuvres of political society. Before the historian is ready to admit the newspaper into the inner circle of his friends and allies, he must have unimpeachable assurance of its veracity and trustworthiness. What grounds of confidence can be given the student of the past that the greater part of the newspaper can be taken at its face value, what tests can be applied that will enable him to separate the wheat from the chaff, what principles can be deduced that will qualify him to detect falsehood and discern truth, what guarantees can be given that will absolve him from the necessity of testing the accuracy of every statement made,—these and similar questions must be answered before the historian is justified in accepting

[1] "Newspapers as Historical Sources," *Atlantic Monthly*, May, 1909, 103: 650–657; reprinted in *Historical Essays*, chap. IV.

the newspaper as an important source in the reconstruction of the past and in the study of the evolution of the present from that past.

To answer these questions involves an analysis of the newspaper into its component parts, an inquiry into the source of the statements of each part, and the application to each of such tests as will determine the authenticity and the authoritativeness of the various parts considered separately and collectively. If the newspaper stands the tests, some of the justifiable doubts of the historian are answered.

But the question of how far the newspaper can be of service to the historian is but half answered even if it can be determined what parts of the press are presumably reliable and what are the regions where danger lurks. The historian uses the newspaper in his effort to reconstruct the life of the past and he may therefore find both the authoritative and the unauthoritative parts of value to him; the authoritative parts are necessary in giving a connected account of past events, while the unauthoritative parts may be of value in determining ideals and standards, in gauging collective ignorance or intelligence, and interpreting the spirit of a time or of a locality. Not only must tests be applied to determine how far the statements of the press can be accepted at their face value, but it is equally important to submit the newspaper to those tests that will determine how far it unconsciously records, for better or for worse, the interests of the day, how far material that is in itself absolutely and obviously untrue may yet have value in ascertaining the real conditions of past life. For the historian is concerned not simply with the accounts of material events, he is equally interested in the interpretation of the spirit of a time or locality. This spirit is revealed both by the true and by the false accounts given by the press. The numerous advertisements of patent medicines, for example, that were once announced as cures for every ill known to the body or the mind are to the historian in themselves wilful attempts to deceive an ignorant public, and while obviously false they are records of the baser elements in men; of the proneness of the ignorant to grasp at straws; of the general lack of information in regard to hygiene, sanitation, and the general welfare of the

human body, and of right living; of the low standards of the press
that lends itself to such advertising and of the low standards
of a community that tolerates such advertising in its press.
Advertisements giving fictitious valuations of articles that their
owners desire to sell are, for the historian, unimpeachable records
of prevailing low business standards.

The historian is ceasing to write history in the flat, to be
content with a study of the superficial area of a period and with
a belief that what men have done expresses to the full the interests that have occupied men's thoughts. In his endeavor to
write history in the round the historian must read the records
of contemporary interests if he is to understand and to interpret
the spirit of an age, and he may quite as often find these records
in material that in and of itself is trivial, unreliable, exaggerated
or grossly untrue as in material that has borne every test submitted for authenticity and authoritativeness.

The historian may accept the conclusions of a distinguished
author who in writing of "the waning power of the press,"[2]
discriminates between the direct influence that the press wields
"through its definite interpretation of current events" and its
indirect influence that "radiates from the amount and character
of the news it prints, the particular features it accentuates, and
its methods of presenting these." He may agree that the direct
influence of the press may be trifling and harmless while its
indirect influence may be large and pernicious, or *vice versa*, and
yet he knows that both conditions give him records that are
equally important to him in his reconstruction of the past.

Periodical literature must therefore be considered by the historian with reference to those general parts whose authoritativeness may be guaranteed and to such other parts as those in
which errors are most likely to abound. It must also be considered
with reference to those parts that consciously and by design
give an account of the events of the day, and the other part that
unconsciously and unintentionally records the spirit of the age.
Two processes are involved for the historian. The first is the
narration of events that have happened, a narration based on

[2] Francis E. Leupp, "The Waning Power of the Press," *Atlantic Monthly*,
February, 1910, 105: 145–156.

the material available after the rejection of what proves to be unauthoritative. The second process involves the interpretation of the life and interests of a community, of a nation, of an age, as these are unconsciously revealed through the columns and pages of periodical literature.

In their use of newspapers and similar materials, McMaster and von Holst submitted them to all the critical tests necessary to determine their value for their own work, but it was foreign to their purpose to elaborate these principles. The very nature of their work precluded giving their readers an analysis of their own methods of writing history, although these methods could be reconstructed from the histories themselves. The architect who plans a house does not give and can not be expected to give his working plans to the passerby who may admire the results without understanding or even questioning the methods by which they have been achieved. Yet the working plans may be of value and interest to other architects, and a knowledge of the principles used in developing these working plans is absolutely essential to those beginning the study of architecture.

What then is the newspaper and to what extent can it serve the historian?

CHAPTER I

THE DEVELOPMENT OF THE NEWSPAPER

"Now sing, my Muse, what various parts compose
These rival sheets of politics and prose.
"First, from each brother's hoard a part they draw,
A mutual theft that never fear'd a law;
Whate'er they gain, to each man's portion fall,
And read it once, you read it through them all:
For this their runners ramble day and night,
To drag each lurking deed to open light;
For daily bread the dirty trade they ply,
Coin their fresh tales, and live upon the lie:
Like bees for honey, forth for news they spring—
Industrious creatures! ever on the wing;
Home to their several cells they bear the store,
Cull'd of all kinds, then roam abroad for more."

"These are the ills the teeming press supplies,
The pois'nous springs from learning's fountain rise;
Not there the wise alone their entrance find,
Imparting useful light to mortals blind;
But, blind themselves, these erring guides hold out
Alluring lights to lead us far about;
Screen'd by such means here Scandal whets her quill,
Here Slander shoots unseen, whene'er she will;
Here Fraud and Falsehood labour to deceive,
And Folly aids them both, impatient to believe."—*Crabbe.*

"This folio of four pages, happy work
Which not even critics criticise; that holds
Inquisitive attention, while I read,
Fast bound in chains of silence, which the fair,
Though eloquent themselves, yet fear to break;
What is it but a map of busy life,
Its fluctuations, and its vast concerns?"—*Cowper.*

"A newspaper is an adviser who does not require to be sought, but who comes of his own accord, and talks to you briefly every day of the common weal, without distracting you from your private affairs."—*De Tocqueville.*

"Ivrybody is inthrested in what ivrybody else is doin' that's wrong. That's what makes th' newspapers."

"D'ye think people likes th' newspapers iv th' prisint time?" asked Mr. Hennessy.

"D'ye think they're printed f'r fun?" said Mr. Dooley.—*F. P. Dunne.*

"THE desire to know the events of the day," says J. B. Williams, "to be told what distant friends are doing, and to hear of occurrences in far-off countries is an instinct implanted in human nature." Accepting the truth of this dictum, it must follow that instincts implanted in human nature will always find some channel through which they can be satisfied. The instinct to know the events of the day and to hear of occurrences in far-off countries has always found some vehicle for the exchange of news and for the formation of public opinion. Among the early Greeks poetry and every other form of literature became the medium of exchange.[1] The Greek agora gave similar opportunity and St. Paul in speaking of the Athenian Areopagus tells us that "all the Athenians, and strangers who were there, spent their time in nothing else, but either to tell or to hear some new thing."

"If the ancients," says Gaston Boissier, "did not feel like ourselves the need of newspapers, it was because they had something else which took their place." These substitutes, he goes on to say, were first of all placards. The Romans had not much taste for home life, but strolled abroad and spent most of their time in the Forum. The placard never grew into a newspaper, but remained the medium of publicity until the end of the Empire. The Roman *Corpus* with more than 200,000 inscriptions indicates the extent to which these placards were a medium of communication between those wishing to give and to receive news. Literary publicity, newsmongers and news-letters, the *Acta Senatus* and *Acta Diurna* were all means among the Romans for gratifying this instinct for news.[2]

The Roman baths gave a similar opportunity, and Jebb finds in the oracles, common both to the Greeks and the Romans another organ of public opinion. Juvenal does not name the journal when he speaks of a Roman lady passing the morning reading the paper,[3] but Mommsen, presumably an anti-feminist,

[1] R. C. Jebb, "Ancient Organs of Public Opinion," *Essays and Addresses*, pp, 127–163.

[2] Gaston Boissier, "The Roman Journal," *Tacitus and Other Roman Studies*, pp. 195–229; "Le Journal de Rome," *Revue des Deux Mondes*, November 15, 1895, 132: 284–310.

[3] This statement has been repeatedly attributed to Juvenal, but it is impossible unhesitatingly to substantiate it. The various passages so interpreted have received quite different explanations from different editors.

would perhaps have judged it to be Cicero's, in spirit, for he considers that "Cicero was a journalist in the worst sense of the term, over-rich in words as he himself confesses, and beyond all imagination poor in thought."

Caesar had already found on the Roman frontier that a characteristic of the Gauls was "their habit of stopping travellers on the road, and, in spite of protest, of closely questioning them on any facts or rumours concerning any event of passing interest each may have gathered on the way. The same thing is done to traders on reaching a town; the crowd surrounding them and compelling them to give a clear and full account, both of the district they have come from and of the news they found current in it." [4]

The Gaul of a later day ran true to type and traveller and trader developed into the *nouvellistes* whose occupation it was to know every day the most recent news. The wars of Louis XIV gave them their great opportunity, for all hung on their lightest word and they were then in their element. They grew in numbers and importance until "every body became a newsmonger" and "even women shared in the general desire to collect and disseminate news,"—so comments one of their historians who anticipated the speedy arrival of the time when the common greeting on the street would be, not "how do you do," but "what's the news." The *nouvellistes* specialized not only on military information, but on political news, travels, literature, art, the theater, music, the ballet, and jokes, even carrying with

---

The lady, who while her slaves were being whipped, read over "*transversa diurna*" (Juvenal, IX, 84), may have read the *Acta Diurna*, but Escott thinks it improbable and interprets it as "household accounts" which were written across the page as well as down. The phrase *Quis dabit historico, quantum daret acta legenti*, (VII, 104) Klein says refers to Acta Diurna; Escott says "Petronius mentions that the *actuarius*, who copied out the *acta*, read them aloud at table to amuse the company." But in Petronius it was the household accounts that were read. Other passages are omitted altogether by some editors. In the multitude of interpreters there is confusion. The statement that "Juvenal speaks of a Roman lady passing her morning in reading the paper, so that it appears private copies [of *Acta Diurna*] were in vogue" (H. Chisholm, "Newspapers," *Encyclopaedia Britannica*, XIX, 544) seems a somewhat free translation of disputed passages, while the concluding inference can only be regarded as a pleasantry of speech.

[4] *Commentaries*, IV, 5. Translation of F. P. Long.

them paper and carbons that they might by sketches make their news the clearer. They frequented all public places in Paris,— the gardens of the Tuileries and the Luxembourg, the Palais Royal, Pont-Neuf, convent cloisters and cafés,—and pressed into their service all who would gather news for them.

The professional newsmonger known to Paris has disappeared from modern society and his place is taken by the daily news-paper, but, sighs Funck-Brentano, "quelle n'était pas son importance sous l'ancien régime!" [5] Yet to Montesquieu he had seemed to have his origin in an idle curiosity to which nothing was sacred and to find his end in an overweening self-confidence that led him in advance of Providence to anticipate the future of mankind. Montesquieu can not help adding that during fifty years the influence of the *nouvelliste* had really been no greater than a silence equally long would have been.[6]

But origins are everywhere somewhat similar. The news was at first cried aloud in France, but later the most important items were written out by hand and copies were circulated in Paris. Each circle had its editorial bureau, its correspondence in the provinces, and the manuscript gazettes had many subscribers. It is natural to think that they would disappear with the coming of printed journals, but both in France and in England the *nouvelles à la main* and the news-letters circulated contemporaneously with the printed news-sheet and it was long before they were entirely supplanted by it. What made their fortune in France was not so much their greater freedom, as was the explanation in England, but their satiric character and their dissemination of scandals that really were of libellous nature. But this ultimately led to their undoing. The secret gazettes were constantly persecuted by the police, decrees against them were

---

[5] For a full and authoritative account of this part of the subject see F. Funck-Brentano, *Les Nouvellistes*, 1905, and *Figaro et ses devanciers*, 1909.

Important contemporaneous material is found in De Bachaumont, *Mémoires*, 18 vols., and in the selection from them edited by A. Van Bever under the title *Mémoires secrets de Bachaumont*, 2 vols. This gives "La Jeunesse de Bachaumont," an autobiographical fragment, II, 219–288, and specimens of *nouvelles à la main*, II, 289–318.

An earlier famous *nouvelliste* was "le bon homme Métra," of whom Funck-Brentano gives an extended account, *Les Nouvellistes*, pp. 185–194.

[6] *Lettres Persanes*, Lettre CXXX.

LES NOUVELLISTES

frequently issued, and individual writers were conspicuously punished—Hatin gives an account of the punishment by whipping on the Pont-Neuf of a man who had suspended from his neck a placard reading *"gazetier à la main."* Although sending the writers to the Bastille by the dozen "had not made them wiser," they flourished for a time and the Prince of Condé wrote, "the evil is without a remedy," but in the end they disappeared.[7]

Contemporaneously in England it was the coffee-houses through which news circulated and that became in London the chief organ of public opinion. They had been started in London in 1652 and speedily acquired such influence that the Earl of Danby attempted to suppress them in 1676 on the ground that they were centers of political agitation and the resort of disaffected persons "who devised and spread abroad divers false, malicious and scandalous reports, to the defamation of His Majesty's government, and to the disturbance of the peace and quiet of the nation." But they were too firmly entrenched in public life to make it wise to prosecute them and efforts against them were abandoned. Since English judges decided in 1679 that the temporary suspension of the licensing act did not cover the newspaper press, the coffee-houses were given a still greater impetus and "every man of the upper or middle class went daily to his coffee-house to learn the news and to discuss it," and "every rank and profession, and every shade of religious and political opinion, had its own headquarters." [8]

What the coffee-house was to the metropolis the news-letter was to the provinces. It was the only means through which persons living at a distance could be regularly informed in regard to affairs in the capital [9] and thus "To prepare such letters became

[7] An important and interesting account of the *gazettes à la main* is given by Hatin in *Les Gazettes de Hollande et la presse clandestine aux XVIIe et XVIIIe siècles.* Copies of these gazettes that have been preserved show that they contained analyses of dramatic pieces, reports of literary meetings, notices of new books,—especially of clandestine and prohibited books, —unpublished poems, anecdotes and bon mots, and social items.

Funck-Brentano gives several reproductions of the *gazettes à la main*, as well as an exhaustive account of them.—*Figaro et ses devanciers.*

[8] T. B. Macaulay, *History of England*, I, chap. III.

[9] An exceptionally interesting collection of news-letters illustrating this point is found in the manuscripts of S. H. Le Fleming of Rydal Hall, Westmoreland. They date from 1667 to 1691 and were in part supplied by friends

a calling in London, as it is now among the natives of India. The newswriter rambled from coffee-room to coffee-room, collecting reports, squeezed himself into the Sessions House at the Old Bailey if there was an interesting trial, nay, perhaps obtained admission to the gallery of Whitehall, and noticed how the King and Duke looked. In this way he gathered materials for weekly epistles destined to enlighten some country town or some bench of rustic magistrates." [10]

In Edinburgh news-letters were prepared by writers hired by groups of country magnates to send them weekly intelligence of the capital, "just as the coffee-houses of the city undertook to provide news-letters from the southern metropolis, which were read immediately on the arrival of the mails. These letters passed from hand to hand in the country districts and circulated among the houses of the gentry. Their lives were extended and their usefulness increased by judicious copying. They ceased only when newspapers had obtained such a hold upon the community as made them no longer necessary." [11]

As early as 1652 the town council of Glasgow had a regular correspondent in Edinburgh and the service was kept for nearly fifty years; other cities had similar correspondents in the northern capital.[12]

In its "paper criers" or "caddies" Scotland made connection with the newsmongers of Paris. "We sometimes wonder," says Robert Chambers, "how our ancestors did without newspapers. We do not reflect on the living vehicles of news which then

---

and relatives in London, but oftener, according to a regular agreement, by clerks in the office of Sir Joseph Williamson. They contain such items of political and military news in London as would naturally at that time have interested an important provincial.—Historical Manuscripts Commission, *Twelfth Report*, Preface, and Appendix, Part VII.

An interesting series of news-letters in America, somewhat comparable to these, were the nine news-letters written to Governor Fitz John Winthrop by John Campbell, from Boston, dated variously from April to October, 1703.—Massachusetts Historical Society, *Proceedings*, IX, 485–501.

[10] T. B. Macaulay, *History of England*, I, chap. III.

[11] W. J. Couper, *The Edinburgh Periodical Press*, I, 71–72.

[12] Couper states that a minute of the town council of Glasgow, September 2, 1681, authorized the payment to the Provost of "ten marks which he gave Donald McKay for half a barrel of herring which was promised him for sending the news-letter and gazettes extraordinary quhilk half barrell of herring is ordained to be given yeerly for that end." *Ib.*, p. 73, *Note*.

existed: the privileged beggar for the country people—for towns-folk, the caddies." [13] Not only were the caddies the criers who sold newspapers but they were also "news-providers and gossip-mongers on their own account." [14] At the close of the seventeenth century, they were incorporated in Edinburgh with a constitution that made them in a sense a benefit society and among other clauses was one providing that authorized news-carriers should be identified by a badge. The society quickly became a nuisance and was dissolved in 1710, reappearing in 1771 as "The Running Stationers of Edinburgh" and finally disappearing prior to 1806.

Contemporaneously with all these substitutes for the press, there grew up and still continues the broadside, in all of its pro-tean forms of poster,[15] placard, circular, handbill, dodger and other "wall" or hand literature. Its name coming from the simultaneous discharge of guns on one side of a ship of war, the broadside focuses attention on a single item of news or informa-tion and it conveys it in impressive form. Royal mandates, church manifestoes, political agitation, party information, charitable appeals, poetry and art all have been or are the sub-ject of the broadside. In times of political crises, in places where no newspaper press has been available, the broadside has reason-ably well met the need. Immediately preceding the English Reform Bill of 1832, no newspaper was published in Arbroath, but its place was taken fairly well by the broadsides and posters that came from the local press.[16] The place of the broadside in affecting as well as in recording public opinion in Massachusetts during the Civil War has been convincingly shown.[17] These are but illustrations showing that even though the broadside may be

[13] Cited by Couper from R. Chambers, *Traditions of Edinburgh*, p. 194.
[14] W. J. Couper, in *The Edinburgh Periodical Press*, I, chap. XII, gives an important account of the paper criers.
[15] "*Affiches* just then and afterwards, played as large a part in the life of Brussels as had newspapers before the war. They might not always provide news but they could provide sensation."—B. Whitlock, *Belgium*, I, 247.
[16] J. M. M'Bain, *Bibliography of Arbroath Periodical Literature and Political Broadsides*, p. 59.—This has an account of an important collection of political and municipal broadsides preserved in Arbroath in 1888.
[17] E. E. Ware, *Political Opinion in Massachusetts during Civil War and Reconstruction, passim*. Two collections are described, pp. 215–216.
W. C. Ford has edited an important check list of broadsides. 1922.

a substitute for the press, it has not been superseded by it.[18]
An ephemeral rival of the broadside to-day is found in the bulletin
board that many newspapers keep in their street windows for
the benefit of the passerby, but the bulletin board does not record
public opinion, it makes no appeal to the public or on behalf of
it, and its value even as a business asset has been seriously
questioned.

The news-letter may also be said to be continued to-day in
another form through the various news services that are rendered
by commercial agents to private clients needing special news, or
more particularly, the interpretation of special kinds of information.

Even the town crier is continued in remote or backward districts. "In the small Bohemian town the newspaper is a crier
who summons the people by a vigorous roll on his drum,
and when the curious townsfolk are assembled he proceeds to
impart the latest news to them." [19]

Hospitality was a virtue on a Southern plantation, as well as
in ancient Greece, and it was rewarded by the guests who brought
news from distant parts. The New England town meeting and
the intermissions between sabbath services were favorable times
for learning of the events that concerned absent neighbors. The
country postoffice, the corner grocery, the church sewing circle,
and the fashionable city club have each in its turn served as a
medium for exchange of news as well as for the discussion of new
ideas. There have thus been many forerunners of the newspaper
that in an incomplete way have served this time-old and universal
desire for "news." [20]

The somewhat meager histories of the press on the continent,[21]
outside of France, seem to indicate that the first stage in its
history concerned the collection of news, and that early news-

---

[18] The long and extensive use of broadsides is indicated in the catalogues
announcing auction sales of significant collections.

[19] L. S. Kirtland, "The Obstacle Race in Central Europe," *Travel*, May,
1921, 37: 5–10, 34.

[20] The predecessors of the press are discussed by E. Hatin, *Bibliographie
de la presse périodique française*, pp. xlii–lxii, and *Histoire de la presse
en France*, I, Preface and pp. 3–60.

[21] See, however, Ludwig Salomon, *Geschichte des Deutschen Zeitungswesens*, 3 vols., 1899–1905.

The new tydings out of Italie are not
yet com.

Out of Weenen, the 6 November.

THe French Ambassadour hath caused the
Earle of Dampier to be buried stately at
Presburg In the meane vvhile hath Bethlem
Gabor cited all the Hungerish States , to com
together at Presburg the 5. of this present , to
discourse aboute the Crovvning & other causes
concerning the same Kingdom.

The Hungarians continue vvith roveing
against these Lands. In like manner those of
Moravia , vvhich are fallen upon the Cosackes
yester night by Hotleyn, set them on fire , and
slaine many dead , the rest vvill revenge the
same.

Heere is certaine nevves com , that the Cra=
bats , as also the Lord Budean , are fallen unto
Betlem Gabor.

The Emperour sends the Earle of Altheim as
Ambassadour to Crackovv in Polen, to appeare
upon the same meeting-day.

Novv comes tidings, that Betlem Gabor is at
Thurna, there doe gather to gether great store of
States

The Emper. Maj. hath appoynted heere a
meeting-day vpon the 1. of Decemb. thereupon
should appeare the 4. Proclaimed States The
appoynted taxing shall bring up a great som of
money.

Out of Prage , the 5 of November.

Three dayes agone are passed by, 2 mile from
this Cittie 6000 Hungarians (chosen out Soldiers) under the General Rediferens, vvhich are
gon to our Head-camp, & the Enimie lieth yet
neare unto ours by Rackonits , though the crie
goeth, that the enimie caused all his might to
com togither, to com this vvayes against Prage,
if that comes to passe, it shall not run of vvith-
out blovves, the vvhich might be revealed vvith
in sevv dayes.

It continues , that in the Satser Crais are gathered togither 10000 Contrie-men, most high-
dutch-men, against Meissen, & no Bohemians ,
they vvill help the King, to drive the enimie out
of the Land. In like manner som certaine 1000
Contrie-men rebel in the Lentmaritscher Crais,
but it is feared that those Countrie-men are
starred up , through practise of the Adversarie ,
that the enimie in the meane vvhile might com
to Prage. Wee understand, that Bucquoy hath
not been in the Camp, but by the Duke of Saxen
som certaine dayes , therefore vve are to looke
to our selves, for feare of Trecherie. And it is
thought that the Emperour vvill leave Austria
to the Hungorians, & see to effect his intention
only uppon Praghe.

Out of Ceulin, the 21. Novemb.

Writing from Marpurg in Hessen , that the
Earle of the same Land, doth cause the foresaid
Cittie to be strongly fortified , there on doe
vvorke many 100 men dayly , and there is mustered in the Earlesship Zigenheym not long
since 1.Governement of foote-men , & 6.Cor-
nets of horse-men , the foote-men are sent to
Marpurg & Rijnfels. But the horse-men are lodged in the Villages about the Cittie , & thereafter are also mustered the Duke of Saxen Lau-
vvenburgs Governement in Tries-Zigenheym,
novv further vvhere they shalbe laid & used, is
yet unknovvn. The sames Brothers Governement, there quarter is laid by Cassel , the Souldiers vvhich are taken on about Hamburg, Lu-
beck, in the Dukeship of Holsteen , & Mecke=
lenburg, should also be mustered about Cassel ,
& be used vvhere neede shall require.

Since the last vve cannot enquire, that there
is any thing of any importance passed bervvixt
the Marquis Spinola & the Vnited Princes. We
understand that the foresaid Spinola vvil lay his
Souldiers in Garnison vvith the first , & deale
them unto divers places, on part to Oppenheym,
Altzey, Ingelheym & Cruitsnach, the other part
at Summeren & Bacharacht , the speech goeth
that there shalbe layed vvith in Ments a good
Company in Garnison.

The Bishop at Halberstadt, Duke Christiaen
at Bruynsvvyck, doth cause to be taken on 2000
Musquetters, to send to the Vnited Princes.

Heere is tydings , that bervveen the King of
Bohemia & the Emperours folke hath beene a
great Battel about Prage , but because there is
different vvriting & speaking thereuppon , so
cannot for this time any certainety thereof be
vvritten, but must vvayte for the next Post. As
also of the Cittie Pilsen , vvhich the Earle of
Mansvelt (so the speech goeth) should have delivered into the Emperours hands.

From Cadan in Bohemia , 4 mile from
Racunits, the 12. November.

From Solts is certaine advise that the Emperours folk have made them selves vvith all
theire might out of theire Camp, & taken their
vvay to vvards Praghe, like as they vveare then
com to the long mile , but as the King understand such , he is broken up vvith his armey, and
com to the log mile beforen the enimie, vvhere
they have had a very strong Battelle & on both
sides more then 6000 men slaine , though most
on the Kings side , also hath the enimie gotten
of the King som peeces of Ordenuaunce and
vvaggens vvith amunitie, so that the King must
retire back to Praghe , and the enimie to the
Weissenberg , there he lies yet and roves from
thence to the Leut Maritscher Crais unto Brix,

THE FIRST ENGLISH NEWSPAPER, DECEMBER 2, 1620

hath taken in, Trebnits, Pielan & Dux, also laid folk upon Leutmarischer Slainer, and Launer passages, that the Passage upon Prage is vvholy taken avvay, and this day is com heere in a certain Person that brings tydinghs unto our Magistrat, that betvvixt Sonnevveid and Patronit, vvhere the enimie hath lien are found som certaine 1000 dead Bodies, & on the other side there King lay also som certaine 1000. dead bodies, vvhat is com to passe betvvixt both vve shal shortly heare.

Out of Amberghe, in the Upper-Pallatine, the 17. dito.

Here hath beene a greate crie, that the Duke of Beyeren should have taken in Praghe, and beaten our King out of the helde, but is not certaine, for the Carle of Solms vvrites out of Waltsaxsen of the 14 of this present, that the Duke of Beyeren vvas broken up vvith his camp very stil, & marched in al hast to Prage, though they had left som 100 men vvhich lay in theire quarter soom houres, vvhich made fires there in, that on vvoulde not have thought but that the vvhole Armay had layen there still, but as ours understood that they vveregon follovved they them presently, though the Beyerens vverd com to Weissenberge before but the 8 of this present have ours sett upon the Beyerens by force, and fought the vvhole day togither, that on both sides are slaine aboute 8000 men, and very many should be hurt. Our King, vvith the Lord General the Earle of Hohenlo, also the vvhole army are rvvith in Prage, .& the Duke of Beyeren upon the Weyssenbergh & Stern; vve hoope that they shall shortly be driven from thence. Whatfurther is done betvvixt them, vve look for every houre to enquire further thereof & it seemes none can com from Prage, becaufe the passages are every vvhere shut.

Out of Cenlen, the 24 of November.

Letters out of Neurenburghe of the 20 of this present, make mention, that they had advise from the Borders of Bohemia, that there had beene a very great Battel by Prage, betvveen the King & the Duke of Beyeren, & many 1000. slaine on both sides, but that the Duke of Beyeren should have any folke vvith in Prage, is yet uncertaine, there uppon under the Merchants vvith in Neurenberge are laid many 100 Florins that the Emperour, nor the Duke of Beyeren have no folke vvith in Prage. The cause that here comes no certainty thereof, is this, That all passages are so beset, & so dangerous to travaile, that it is to vvondered at, & not enough to be vvritté of, vvhat roveing, spoyling and killing is done dayly uppon all vvayes.

Vppon the Schanse Priests cap is strongly buileed, & buy dayly much vvood lime & stone, to make houses there upon, and so provide them selves for the vvhole vvinter. And are not long since in the night 500 Souldiers passed by Dure out of Gulik, so the speech goeth, there meaning shoulde be to build a nievv School.arse by Flammersheym, to take avvay the passag. from the Marquis Spinola.

Imprinted at Amsterdam by George Veseler, A₀. 1620. The 2. of Decemember.

And are to be soulde by Petrus Keerius, dvvelling in the Calverstreete, in the uncertaine time.

sheets were distributed through semi-annual fairs, and later through stage coaches. Since the time of issuing and the frequency of issue depended on the opportunities for distribution, monthly periodicals were unknown and the semi-annual leaped at a bound to the weekly.[22] It was long, however, before there was any development of a newspaper in the present usage of the word, and its place was supplied by other media of communication.

The genesis of the newspaper in England, as known to-day, has been traced to the letters written in time of war to friends and relatives at home.[23] "Until the year 1641," says J. B. Williams, "the corantos were nothing more than a running history of the Thirty Years' War, then in progress on the Continent." These letters were presumably concerned primarily with personal matters, but their narrations were naturally supplemented by accounts of events of the day and by descriptions of the country where they were written. The modern newspaper first came into existence when progress in the technique of printing made possible the multiplication of copies of these letters, and improvement in means of communication facilitated their distribution. It was long, however, before the printed newspaper supplanted the written news-letter, owing to the stringent regulations enforced by the Government against all printed periodicals.[24]

It was Théophraste Renaudot, a physician, who, in 1631,

---

[22] Carl Bücher, "The Genesis of Journalism," *Industrial Evolution*, pp. 215-243. Chapter VI gives a brief but excellent historical sketch of the development of the newspaper on the continent.

A contemporary account written in Latin of the Russian invasion of Poland in 1563 was published at Douay as a news-sheet. This was republished in facsimile in London, in 1874, and probably illustrates fairly well the early continental news-sheet.

[23] It is important to note that the attribution of the origin of newspapers in England to the corantos has not passed unchallenged. Recent investigators have raised the question whether the *Diurnall Occurrences*—"the culmination in the development of news-letters"—may not be "almost as significant in the origin of English journalism as the corantoes. May one possibly say that the English newspaper has one of its origins in the custom, in use as early as 1628, of sending out résumés of parliamentary news in manuscript form?"—W. Notestein and F. H. Relf, *Commons Debates for 1629*, p. liv.

[24] These facts apply specially to England and they have been taken from J. B. Williams, *History of English Journalism to the Foundation of the Gazette*, chap. I. Similar conditions apparently were found in other countries.

founded the *Gazette de France* [25] and proclaimed, "In one thing only will I yield to nobody—I mean my endeavour to get at the truth. At the same time I do not always guarantee it, being convinced that among five hundred despatches written in haste from all countries it is impossible to escape passing something from one correspondent to another which will require correction from Father Time." Both here and in his discrimination between history and the press—"History is the record of things accomplished. A *Gazette* is the reflection of feelings and rumours of the time which may or may not be true"—Renaudot showed himself far in advance of his day and generation.

The newspaper thus did not spring full armed from the head of Zeus, but as far back as human history can be traced it had its beginnings in the various expedients that provided partial equivalents for gratifying a desire for news, as well as the early awakenings of a desire for an expression of public opinion. It has seemed important to note these antecedents of the modern newspaper since many of its features have their lineage in these primitive types. King's herald and town crier gave the news deemed essential that the public should know and they were the crude prototypes of modern news-collecting and news-distributing agencies. The pasquinade seems the forerunner of the "colyum." The carbon and the paper of the *nouvelliste* were the ancestors of the modern illustrator. Thus from these modest beginnings of the written news-letter, supplemented by the printed newspaper, has been developed the great metropolitan daily of to-day that may reach in size one hundred and fifty pages, that may have a daily circulation of more than a million copies,[26] that has on its pay-roll eighteen hundred or more persons,[27] and that has become one of the great industries of the world.[28]

This development of the newspaper has been largely made through the accretion of new interests. Beginning with the

[25] E. Hatin, *Histoire de la presse française*, I, 63–192, 463–472; J. Macintyre, "Théophraste Renaudot," *Nineteenth Century*, October, 1893, 34: 596–604; F. Roubaud, *Théophraste Renaudot.*

[26] The average net daily sale of the London *Daily Mail* for the first half of April, 1921, was 1,365,256.—F. A. McKenzie, *The Mystery of the Daily Mail*, p. 128.

[27] Elmer Davis, *History of the New York Times*, pp. 389, 411–428.

[28] *Ib.*, pp. 310–330; 370–403.

circulation of news concerning persons temporarily in foreign countries, the newspaper has added domestic and local news,[29] comment on the news made by the editor, headlines to attract attention, official notices, advertisements, the interview, special correspondence, occasional correspondence, letters to the editors, answers to correspondents, book reviews, dramatic news, art news, musical criticism, a humorous column, a weather chart,[30] a woman's page,[31] a society page, a sporting page, school news, college news, church news, choir news, news from the army and navy, financial reports, market reports, genealogical columns, health columns, legal columns, special articles, syndicated articles, clippings from exchanges, "fillers," illustrations, the illustrated supplement, the comic supplement; supplements designed to interest special industries or occupations, as those of building, real estate, oil, automobiles, trade with Japan, South America, Australia, or the Orient; special interests, as fire protection, vital conservation; bureaus to give advice on financial investments, on the choice of schools or colleges, on travel at home or abroad,— every great daily vies with its competitors in discovering and developing some new interest or device that will increase its circulation and attract advertisers, and thus increase its returns on the capital invested in the plant.

At one time the newspaper relied on "the scoop" to give this new interest, but this was only a passing phase. To-day the great news-collecting agencies may be said to have eliminated "the scoop," although it would be more nearly true to say that while they have not eliminated it, they have changed its character. The newspaper of to-day finds an outlet for its enterprise and activity, not in securing "a beat" from its rival when both are interested in obtaining the same piece of news, but in devising

[29] G. S. Strong says that the Syracuse *Journal* in 1846 was the first paper to establish a local column.—*Early Landmarks of Syracuse*, p. 93.

[30] The weather chart was started in 1848 by the *Daily News*. It had its origin in the bad harvests of that year and ceased with the occasion, but was soon taken up by the Astronomer Royal in co-operation with the railway companies.—J. C. Francis, *John Francis*, I, 155–156. See also H. Leach, *Fleet Street from Within*, chap. XIII, "Some Specialists on Duty."

[31] This has been almost entirely discontinued in American papers, but the London *Daily Mail* "recognizes that women readers exist."—F. A. McKenzie, *The Mystery of the Daily Mail*, pp. 16–17.

some new activity not thought of by others. It may finance an expedition to Africa, or to the North Pole; it may promote a "without stop" aeroplane flight between two distant cities, or between two continents; it may secure interviews with great potentates who have never before been interviewed; it may for the nonce become a detective bureau and ferret out crimes the existence of which was unsuspected by the police; it may avail itself of work done by the Associated Press and secure for publication in its own columns in the same issue the editorial comment of a hundred papers in every part of the country on important public measures; it may summarize the views of a thousand foreign-language newspapers printed in America; it may carry on a postal card canvass to ascertain public opinion on every conceivable subject; it may print weekly editions in Braille for the use of the blind; it may become a publisher and put on the market a great encyclopaedia, a popular dictionary, an important atlas, a history of the war, or sets of standard authors;—there is no limit to the creative activities of the modern journal in its efforts to improve on the now dishonored scoop. "Journalism busies itself now with everything that affects the public welfare" said the New York *Tribune*, as far back as February 11, 1873 in an editorial, "A new field for journalism."

It is of interest to compare these activities as they have been developed collectively by the press, with the activities that have been accumulated on a large scale by a single newspaper like the London *Daily Mail*.[32] This has been considered to have reached the farthest goal in newspaper enterprise, yet a study of the activities organized, fostered, and assisted to a successful issue by the *Athenaeum* in its early days might lead a newspaper of to-day to speak of its own achievements with becoming modesty. Among them were the Sir John Franklin relief expedition, the establishment of the Public Record Office in 1847, hygienic and sanitary reforms as a result of the cholera epidemic in 1849, penny banks, mechanics' institutes, postal reform, prison reform, reform of the criminal laws, housing of the London poor, the

[32] W. E. Carson, *Northcliffe: Britain's Man of Power*, "A Wonderful Newspaper," chap. V; W. D. Newton, "The Practical Vision," *The Bookman* (London), January, 1917, 51: 124-126; F. A. McKenzie, *The Mystery of the Daily Mail*, 1896-1921.

great exposition of 1851 and the Crystal Palace at Sydenham, ragged schools, provident institutions for the trades and professions connected with journalism, and reforms necessary for Ireland.[33]

The success of the press in collecting funds in 1863 for the relief of the Lancashire sufferers was praised by contemporaries, especially since it was in striking contrast with the failure of the imperial government to relieve the distress caused by the French cotton famine.[34] The American press plumed itself, when the Livingston relief expedition was sent out by the New York *Herald*, in setting an example to the London press, since soon after this the *Daily Telegraph* sent out George Smith, the keeper of the British Museum, to search for Assyrian antiquities to supplement and explain those already in the Museum. The *Tribune* rejoiced that newspapers were pioneers in learned exploration, that not satisfied with the dissemination of knowledge collected by learned men, they were themselves making their own investigations and explorations.[35]

It seems indeed a far cry from the early seventeenth century weekly with its meager intelligence to the powerful twentieth century daily, with its "unequalled ability for raising money;" with its own offer of $200,000 in cash prizes for aviation; $5,000 in prizes for the best sweet peas, and $3,000 in prizes in egg-laying competitions; its promotion of a standardized loaf of bread; its advocacy of patriotism through the collection of "smoke funds" for troops; and a thousand other activities through which it enters intimately into the domestic life of a nation while at the same time making and overturning great ministries. There is evident truth in the significant comments that "people are as a rule more interested in what the *Daily Mail* does than in what it thinks," and that in politics "it affects elections rather than political thought."[36]

Imposing as is this array of bustling activities undertaken by

[33] J. C. Francis, *John Francis*, I, xxvi–xxvii.

[34] "The British Newspaper: the Penny Theory and its Solution," *Dublin University Magazine*, March, 1863, 61: 359–376.

[35] New York *Tribune*, February 11, 1873.

[36] Sydney Brooks, "Lord Northcliffe and the War," *North American Review*, August, 1915, 202: 185–196.

a modern newspaper it may after all be said to represent only the type of mind to which the founding of a newspaper has always appealed. Théophraste Renaudot founded, in 1631 at La Maison du Grand-Coq, the *Gazette de France*, the first newspaper printed in Paris, and in 1884 an inscription commemorating that event was placed on the building erected on the site of the earlier structure. To M. Hatin it seemed inexcusable that the inscription did not enumerate the other services of Renaudot,— the establishment of an employment office, an information bureau, an auction market, a dispensary, the *mont-de-piété*, and other "simple inventions" as their originator termed them,— and in various brochures he has done honor to the memory of this greatest forerunner of modern journalists.[37]

But at least the eighteenth century periodical in England had tried the plan of stimulating interest and increasing its circulation through prize-giving and other devices held to be modern. *The Gentleman's Magazine* in 1734 offered a prize for poems and soon after for epigrams,[38] but it was doubtless an appreciation— perhaps unconscious—of the failure of such prizes to conform to the principles subsequently laid down by Pebody,[39] that led Samuel Johnson, in 1738, to write Cave, who had offered a prize for the best poem on the Divine Attributes, "I shall engage with little spirit in an affair, which I shall *hardly* end to my own satisfaction, and *certainly* not to the satisfaction of the parties concerned." [40]

It is at least significant that the most recent step in the evolution of prize-giving in connection with the press has been the conferring of prizes and medals on newspapers in addition to the

[37] E. Hatin, *La Maison du Grand-Coq; Théophraste Renaudot et ses innocentes inventions; A propos de Théophraste Renaudot. L'Histoire, la Fantasie et la Fatalité.*

E. T. Cook says of Delane that "he was a pioneer in the journalism which does things as well as says things."—*Delane of "The Times,"* p. 89. But Delane had been anticipated on the continent by more than two centuries.

[38] J. Nichols, *The Rise and Progress of the Gentleman's Magazine*, pp. xi–xii.

[39] To all newspaper enterprises of this character the one condition is "that the work shall be work that appeals to the imagination, to national sentiments, or to national pride."—C. Pebody, *English Journalism and the Men Who Have Made It*, p. 184.

[40] Boswell's *Life of Samuel Johnson*, Dent ed., I, 76.

awarding of prizes by them, and that the Pulitzer School of Journalism has annually awarded a prize to the newspaper deemed to have contributed the most signal service to the press.

This enormous and rapid increase in the activities connected with the press has been greatly facilitated by the extraordinary development of inventions of the age. The telegraph, the cable, the telephone, wireless telegraphy, leased wires, and pneumatic tube mail service have greatly facilitated the reception of news,[41] although the fact that news is transmitted by these means often gives it a factitious importance. Stenography [42] and the typewriter have increased the speed with which the news received is transmitted into "copy," while at the same time they reduce to a minimum the danger of error from undecipherable chirography. The linotype and the Morkrum printer increase the speed with which "copy" is in turn transmuted into the newspaper. The folder, which made the web-perfecting press a possibility, the rotary press, and the multiple press in all its forms expedite the printing of the newspaper.[43] In turn, again, the very fact that news is printed, and that the press has at its command all the inventions of an inventive age tends to give news an importance often out of all proportion to its real value. The substitution of esparto grass,[44] and later of straw and of wood pulp for cotton rags in the manufacture of paper has reduced the price of the newspaper and thus increased its circulation,—it is indeed impossible to estimate the enormous extension of the press that

[41] F. W. Scott gives an interesting table showing how closely the establishment of daily newspapers in Illinois followed the opening of new telegraph lines.—*Newspapers and Periodicals of Illinois, 1814–1879*, p. lxx.

[42] Alfred Baker, *The Life of Sir Isaac Pitman.*

[43] R. Hoe, in *A Short History of the Printing Press*, gives a full account of the inventions that have made possible the enormous increase in the production of newspapers and a corresponding decrease in the time and labor demanded.

T. Catling gives an account of the interest aroused by the introduction of the Hoe press into Europe.—*My Life's Pilgrimage*, pp. 50–55.

J. C. Francis cites from the *Athenaeum*, March 17, 1849, an account of an American printer who had died in Paris leaving £40,000 as a premium to any one who would construct a press capable of striking off 10,000 copies of a newspaper an hour.—*John Francis*, I, 155.

[44] Thomas Routledge made paper from this grass in 1860 and it was gradually adopted by other papers, *Lloyd's News* being among the earliest to do so.—J. C. Francis, *Notes by the Way*, p. 194.

has resulted from the discovery of the process of making paper from wood pulp.[45]

Increase in circulation has been followed by the demand for increasing facilities in distribution and this has been met by the perfecting of great distributing agencies, as those of the English house of W. H. Smith and Son and the American News Company.[46]

All of these inventions and improvements in the collection of copy, in its transmutation into the newspaper, and in the facility with which the newspaper is placed in the hands of the reader have made the newspaper a great business enterprise and at the same time they have thereby increased enormously its sphere of influence. It is on this business side that the greatest development of the press is being made to-day. Works are constantly appearing on newspaper management, newspaper book-keeping and accounts, the publication of weeklies, book-keeping for weeklies, newspaper efficiency, on advertising in all its forms, and on every phase of the newspaper as a business enterprise.[47] So much in evidence is this side of the newspaper that many persons have been apprehensive lest it constitute a real danger to freedom of the press. If the content of the newspaper is to be subordinated to the business management concerned only in efficiency for the sake of larger circulation, more advertising, and

[45] The ability to control the supply of print paper through the control of pulp mills has been an element of power in the hands of certain representatives of the press. See H. W. Steed, *The Hapsburg Monarchy*, pp. 190–191; W. E. Carson, *Northcliffe*, pp. 130–133; F. A. McKenzie, "The Transformation of Newfoundland," *The Mystery of the Daily Mail*, pp. 41–48.

[46] H. Maxwell, *Life and Times of the Right Honourable William Henry Smith*, 2 vols., 1893.

The American News Company unfortunately does not print any description of its work nor has apparently any descriptive article relating to it found its way into any American periodical.

In striking contrast with these methods of distribution is the account of E. S. Thomas, a nephew of Isaiah Thomas, who writes of the effort of his father who lived in Lancaster, Massachusetts, to get subscribers to newspapers at the close of the Revolutionary War. He secured fifty-two subscribers who took turns in going sixteen miles to Worcester for them. When his father's turn came, the boy, eight years old, was mounted on horseback and sent for the papers, the journey there and back taking two days.—*Reminiscences of the Last Sixty-five Years*, II, 4–5.

[47] This side of the question has been comprehensively put forward by Jason Rogers, in *Newspaper Building*, 1918.

larger circulation, in an ever-widening circle, the fear for the independence of the press is well grounded. If a nice balance is preserved between the business side of the newspaper that relieves editors from personal care and anxiety, and the editorial side that prepares material worthy of the best efforts of business managers, then the perfect circle is achieved.

But the very extent to which invention has promoted speed in production and cheapness in distribution makes it necessary for the historian to take them into account. Speed may be attended by inaccuracy, and the newspaper sold for a cent may cater to those who value a commodity by the low price paid for it. The historian must understand the possible limitations for his purposes of the newspaper that has a daily circulation of half a million copies; he may find that the newspaper of restricted circulation and higher price has for him the greater value.

This enormous increase in circulation has been both a result and a cause, it has both met a demand and created a demand. The rapid and wide extension of free systems of education carrying with them compulsory features has created a new and ever-widening circle of readers. Special times of crises at home and abroad, like Parliamentary reform bills, political and industrial revolutions, the Crimean War, the Civil War, and similar events have all given an impetus to the circulation of the press, and its influence has not stopped with the consideration of the news that gives it its increased circulation. Through these influences the weekly has often grown into the daily, the rural free delivery has extended the demand for the daily, and thus the newspaper in ever assuming new interests extends the area of its own influence.

The newspaper has ceased to be a personal organ and has become a social product; it no longer represents the interests of an individual, but it represents rather a group activity. The press groups society and unifies each group, as Scott-James has pointed out.[48] It unifies society on national lines and thus the press of each country has developed in its own characteristic direction. It unifies the groups interested in religion, in politics, in business, in automobiles, in sports, in education, or in

[48] R. A. Scott-James, *The Influence of the Press*, pp. 208–209.

fashion,[49] and from these groups having unified interests there has developed the press that ministers to each specialized group.

Religious journalism groups every special sect, however large or small it may be. Political parties are ranged on opposite sides and their support of ruling authorities or opposition to them is organized through the press. Trade journals consolidate and promote business interests.[50] Amateur journalism binds together as well as represents the interest developing in growing youth. The city press unifies the undistinguishable masses in metropolitan areas; the country press unifies individuals whose interests have never been merged into those of a larger group. The early newspapers were almost exclusively issued for grown men; later, newspapers introduced features for the groups of women and children; present day newspapers abandon the special pages or columns for women and children and make a new alignment based on community of interests among men, women, and children.[51]

When different groups have become unified, the press again may exploit group hostility among different groups. When one group has been unified by the press representing the dominant interest of the group, new interests may arise and a new type of newspaper be demanded for the same group. Interest in ama-

[49] In some instances the unification of a group extends to those speaking a foreign language,—a prominent fashion journal issues an edition in French and in Spanish as well as a third for the British Islands.

[50] Trade journalism was started in America in 1846 by William Burroughs and Robert Boyd who issued the *Dry Goods Reporter and Commercial Glance.*—C. T. Root, "The History and Development of Industrial Journalism," *Industrial Journalism*, pp. 9–27.

The trade journals published in Chicago in 1922 numbered 450.—List compiled by the Chicago Association of Commerce,—W. H. Harper, editor of *Chicago Commerce.*

A later development has been the store papers now apparently found in every business,—clothing, hardware, grocery, florist, druggist, to note but a few of the very many found.—T. A. Bird, "Store Papers," *Sales Plans*, pp. 98–115.

Extreme specialization of newspapers representing the multifarious industries of modern days is probably best illustrated in Germany where trade periodicals like the *Schornsteinfeger* for chimney sweeps and the *Allgemeine deutsche Käseblatt* for cheese-workers record the extent to which this specialization has prevailed.—R. H. Fife, Jr., *The German Empire between Two Wars*, pp. 359–388.

[51] Congratulations on discontinuing its fashion page were sent to the New York *Tribune*, June 15, 1918.

teur journalism yields to the unifying influences of sports or of war; the "little urchin in knickerbockers" who brought out in manuscript *The Schoolboy's Punch* [52] has now become a boy scout and his activities are unified vicariously through the regular press.

The religious press becomes so highly specialized that it represents every variation of religious opinion, and then a recombination ensues. The Catholics did not support Lord Acton, and the Church of England did not support Frederick Denison Maurice. Lord Acton desired to have a periodical press that should be the organ of the Catholic laity, and have " 'entire and resolute independence' of all powerful interests, public parties, or knots of private friends." [53] He kept this attitude by ignoring the divisions among the Catholics, rather than by criticising them. In stating the principles that should govern the *Rambler* in its relation to Rome, it seemed to him that "the best way to fight authorities is to convert their subjects, and this not by doing battle against power, but for the principles of the *Rambler*," [54]—"the principle of independent inquiry, within the bounds, and for the promotion, of the Catholic faith, it is our pride and our duty to maintain." [55] The leading Catholic *Review*, he felt, occupied too narrow a ground, since when new ideas and new wants arose it could not meet them and instead of leading, it fell behind and soon looked with increasing jealousy upon all who did not accept the same limitations.[56] This opinion expressed with reference to the position of a prominent religious periodical indicates with exceptional clearness some of the limitations the historian must find in his use of the religious press.

Difficulties of a different nature were opened up to Frederick Denison Maurice. His "Letters to a Quaker" [57] "contained an

[52] H. Furniss, *Confessions of a Caricaturist*, I, 7.

[53] Abbot Gasquet, *Lord Acton and his Circle*, p. xxv.

[54] Letter of Lord Acton from Munich, October 6, 1861.—*Lord Acton and his Circle*, pp. 206–210. Abbot Gasquet gives in the *Introduction*, ix–lxxxviii, an admirable summary of the place taken in religious journalism by the *Rambler*, the *Home and Foreign Review*, the *Chronicle*, and the *North British Review*, with all of which Lord Acton was associated either as part-owner, editor, or contributor.

[55] "The Catholic Press," *The Rambler*, February, 1859, 11: 73–90.

[56] The article on *The Catholic Press* is one of the best discussions noted of the failures and the possible successes of the religious press.

[57] Frederick Maurice, *The Life of Frederick Denison Maurice*, I, chap. XV.

an open proclamation of war against all the religious newspapers of every sort whatsoever. It was an internecine war to be continued henceforth without intermission throughout his life." The war grew out of the habit of the religious press of stating the doctrines of its own denomination and attacking those of others. Maurice was ever ready to be the champion of a cause he thought had been misrepresented even if he did not agree with it himself. He objected to the anonymous attacks of the religious press, and others as well as Maurice realized the lack of effort on the part of the religious press to state truthfully the actual nature of the views they were opposing. Maurice's "battle against what he believed to be the immoral and godless domination of anonymous religious journalism, for long an all but solitary fight, was solitary no longer," [58] for many, both defendants and opponents, rallied to his support in demanding a fair interpretation of the views of adversaries.

The wars of the religious press in America have been no less vigorous, and orthodoxy and heterodoxy have from the beginning had their pronounced champions. *The Panoplist*, or *The Christian's Armory*, "conducted by an association of friends to evangelical truth," announced in its first number, July, 1805, that nothing could ever be admitted into it "manifestly inconsistent with the Doctrine of the Reformation as recognized in the articles of churches of evangelical faith."

The religious press also illustrates the changing tendencies towards early extreme representation of small factions, later protests against rigid points of view on the part of the press, and still later re-groupings that give opportunity for a wider horizon.[59] The protests of both Lord Acton and of Maurice against the religious press of their day in England were the same in character that later impelled Harvey W. Scott on the Western coast of America to protest against the rigid sectarianism of still another denomination. The religious press through all of these and

[58] F. Maurice, *Life of Fredrick Denison Maurice*, II, pp. 368–369, 370.

[59] "The easiest way to kill the true spirit of a religious journal is to make it the mere bulletin of the denominational organizations."—*Christian Register*, September 4, 1919, 98: 842.

A summary of "The Religious Press" is given in the *Dublin Review*, July, 1881, 37: 1–29. It is based on *The Newspaper Press Directory* for 1881.

similar protests has everywhere taken on new aspects and at the same time religious intelligence and religious inspiration have been more widely diffused than ever before through the secular press. The circumference of the circle enlarges as the radius is prolonged.

The religious press illustrates how different are the problems presented to the historian by it and by the political press. Political newspapers represent organized parties with definite politics. The election barometer may indicate a rise or fall in the tariff temperature,—Brand Whitlock speaks of Joseph Medill's low tariff editorials in the Chicago *Tribune* becoming high tariff editorials during national campaigns, "the percentage of protection rising like a thermometer in the heat of political excitement." [60] But there is never a shade of variation in the determination of the "outs" to get in and of the "ins" to stay in. The religious press, on the other hand, represents not simply two but scores of warring factions and of divisions within sects each actuated by a missionary zeal for converting every one to its own particular tenets.

The political press has shown the same tendencies towards the establishment of local organs representing the political views of individual owners, new political alignments involving press combinations, and still again the individual owner looking upon the press as a business enterprise with the resulting chain of newspapers and periodicals of every description, together with the control of pulp mills and other activities concerned in their publication. [61] The newspaper can not live longer than the special

[60] *Forty Years of It,* p. 48.

[61] The "string" of English newspapers controlled by the "Amalgamated Press"—the stock company under the presidency of Lord Northcliffe— and of American newspapers belonging to W. R. Hearst are the most conspicuous illustrations of this principle.

A recent writer comments on this tendency: "Perhaps, as there were once too few newspapers, there are now too many, and I should be in favour of a law forbidding any one to own more than one hundred and fifty newspapers."—J. A. Bridges, "Country Editors in the Past," *Victorian Recollections,* pp. 90–101.

J. S. Buckingham started the *Athenaeum* in January, 1828; he was already the proprietor of the *Sphynx,* "a journal of politics, literature, and news;" of the *Oriental Herald* that dealt with Indian affairs; of the *Verulam,* a weekly scientific periodical; and in May he started the *Argus,* an evening newspaper.—J. C. Francis, *John Francis,* I, 20–21, 30–31.

object which it was founded to promote, and it is often shorter
lived. The merging of two or more papers in one, and the control
of several papers by a single owner is not a new tendency
although specially pronounced at the present time.[62]

Every new controlling interest that arises in any group of
persons quickly finds expression through a new type of periodical.
In England in the first third of the nineteenth century the legislative restrictions placed on the press a century before gave rise
to radical newspapers that protested against these restrictions.
When the conditions giving rise to this class of newspapers were
altered, the newspapers themselves disappeared. If society has
been honeycombed with slander, intrigue, and scandal, a dis-
reputable press has appeared that has purveyed to all these evil
tendencies. Protests against these tendencies have in turn found
expression through the press. The *People's Review*, says McCabe,
in writing of one of Holyoake's ventures, "was a novel departure
even for an age that seemed to have exhausted the possibilities
of journalism. Speaking somewhere of the monthly apparitions
of new journals, and their frantic vicissitudes of form, color, size,
price, etc., he [Holyoake] says: 'Like flags carried in battle, they

---

The Globe was started in 1803 by London booksellers and in the course
of years it "absorbed a whole crop of journals."—J. C. Francis, *Notes by
the Way*, 179–180.

The consolidation of two or more newspapers in America has long been
a custom and its frequency is evident in the hyphenated names of many
papers. The Louisville *Courier-Journal* represents the consolidation of
three dailies.—"*Marse Henry*," I, 175.

Different newspapers in different cities are sometimes controlled by
members of the same family.

In 1913 it was asserted that two Berlin firms controlled five-sixths of
Berlin's total output in daily and weekly papers, and that these were the
medium for semi-official utterances.—About the same time, shares in the
Lokal-Anzeiger were transferred to a group of firms representing the Kaiser's
interests.—New York *Sun*, November 30, 1913.

See especially John Mez, "The Portent of Stinnes," *Atlantic Monthly*,
April, 1922, 129: 547–555; H. Brinckmeyer, *Hugo Stinnes*, pp. 102–108.

[62] O. G. Villard, "Press Tendencies and Dangers," *Atlantic Monthly*,
January, 1918, 121: 62–66.

J. A. Spender, writing in the *Westminster Gazette* on "The Editor *versus*
the Proprietor," notes the present tendency towards few newspapers with
enormous circulations and these few controlled by still fewer proprietors.
While there has been a great increase in the number of newspapers sold,
it has in reality meant but the multiplication of the same things, without
corresponding increase in brains and ability.—Cited by the *Literary Digest*,
April 13, 1918, 19: 29–30.

were made out of such material as happened to be available in the exigencies of forced marches, and were often shot into tatters by the enemy.'" [63]

A society that has lost interest in the fundamental questions of life, or that has never had such an interest, demands amusement and entertainment and this is provided in the gossip of the modern society journal.[64] A society that loves a sparkling jest, a piquant phrase, a refined witticism, and a clever parody, on "a foundation of very sound information" finds expression in periodicals like *The Owl* that for some years amused and informed English society with its entertaining comments on normal life in the upper circles.[65]

Education as it is provided through normal, conventional channels has often been inadequate for satisfying the demands of alert boys and girls and, especially before the recent development of interest in sports, athletics, and all forms of physical recreations, they have found an outlet for their mental energies in establishing everywhere amateur journals that record both their present interests and their future ambitions.[66]

[63] J. McCabe, *Life and Letters of George Joseph Holyoake*, I, 160.

[64] Edmund Yates in his *Recollections and Experiences* gives a full account of the establishment of *The World*, sometimes spoken of as "the pioneer of modern Society journalism."—II, 305-336.

A Journalist, in *Bohemian Days in Fleet Street*, chap. V, gives a sketch of "Society Journalism."

[65] *The Owl* owed its existence to Algernon Borthwick and a group of clever young Englishmen who from sheer joy of living carried it on for more than five years (April 27, 1864-July 28, 1869). Its founder says of its close, "So ended an adventure, entered upon in jest, pursued not with serious intent, and successful enough to leave behind it lasting memories; unlike all other journalistic enterprises in that it was unconcerned with financial aims, yet the pioneer of a great commercial enterprise and of a new element in our social life."—R. Lucas, *Lord Glenesk and the "Morning Post*," 195-218; H. Drummond-Wolff, *Rambling Recollections*, II, 38-42; A. I. Dasent, *John Thadeus Delane*, II, 116-118.

[66] The extent of amateur journalism both in time and in place is indicated by the remarkable collection of such journals deposited in the School of Journalism, Columbia University; T. J. Spencer, *A Cyclopaedia of the Literature of Amateur Journalism;* H. H. Billany and C. A. Rudolph, *The Amateurs' Guide for 1875* (with bibliography and list of amateur editors); G. M. Huss, *A History of Amateur Journalism;* T. G. Harrison, *The Career and Reminiscences of an Amateur Journalist;* J. C. Nixon, *History of the National Amateur Press Association.*

R. Chambers, writing in 1838 of "Playing at Newspapers," gives an account of the publication of two numbers of the *Inveresk Gazette* by boarding school boys.—*Select Writings*, II, 91-106.

College journalism has for more than a hundred years recorded the interest of student life,[67] imitated in a measure the features of the contemporaneous press,[68] and to-day is one of the leading representatives of the so-called "non-academic" activities of American colleges and universities.[69]

The recent war has been prolific in the number and variety of the newspapers that issued from camp and trench and field and cruiser. The German government and the French government issued bulletins of the war for the troops in the trenches, but quickly the troops themselves, especially those of the Allies, began the publication of their own papers, and their collected issues better than any other source interpret one side of the spirit behind the great struggle.[70]

This expedient, however, has not been recent,—it dates at

A characteristic article by Kipling, in answer to a request for a contribution, is given in *The Budget*, published by the Horsmonden School, Kent, and a caricature of Kipling by Max Beerbohm. These two numbers for May 14 and May 28, 1898, were reprinted in New York in 1899.

[67] S. S. McClure, *ed.*, *A History of College Journalism*, lists 224 college journals in 1882. See also J. F. McClure, *History of American College Journalism*. 1883.

[68] An interesting MS. copy of a school journal of 1837 shows that the subjects of its articles and editorials tallied almost perfectly with the subjects discussed at that time in the printed press.

The Smith Street Gazette and Institutional Review, a four-page journal published monthly from December, 1849 to November, 1851 "by a knot of young men for the most part utterly unskilled in the mysteries of magazine publication" but connected with the Westminster Institution, also illustrates this point.

[69] "College Journalism," *Scribner's Monthly*, October, 1878, 16: 808–812; L. G. Price, "American Undergraduate Journalism," *Bookman*, March, 1903, 17: 69–82; M. S. Stimson, "The Harvard Lampoon," *New England Magazine*, January, 1907, n. s. 35: 579–590; a series of articles on the leading college undergraduate publication in eight different colleges appeared in the *Bohemian* in 1907–1908; J. Bruce and J. V. Forrestal, *eds.*, *College Journalism*, 1914.

An interesting, but probably unique, illustration of the connection between the newspaper and the official side of education has been the *Moscow Gazette*, the property of the University of Moscow that published it under the privilege granted by the Empress Elizabeth about the middle of the eighteenth century.—H. S. Edwards, "Mr. Katkoff and the Moscow Gazette," *Fortnightly Review*, September, 1887, n. s. 42: 379–394.

[70] Gelett Burgess, "The Magazines of the Trenches," *Century*, September, 1916, 70: 641–658; A. M. Schlesinger, "The Khaki Journalists," *Mississippi Valley Historical Review*, December, 1919, 6: 350–359; *The Wipers Times*, a facsimile reprint of trench magazines; *The B. E. F. Times*, a companion volume; *The Hatchet* of the United States Ship "*George Washington;*" *Stars and Stripes*, February 8, 1918–June 13, 1919.

least as far back as 1815 when Metternich instructed "la librairie Herder," in Freiburg im Breisgau, to publish a journal "à l'intention de l'armée autrichienne qui marchait sur Paris. Herder installa ad hoc une imprimerie de campagne dont sortirent, chemin faisant, les exemplaires d'une *Deutsche Feldzeitung*." [71]

During the war in the Transvaal two journals were published for the troops, "un petit journal amusant la *Lyre*, rendit moins longues les heures des assiégés de Lady Smith," and *The Friend*. The latter was begun in March, 1900, at the request of Lord Roberts for the entertainment and the information of the troops at Bloemfontein, and was in charge of several well-known young writers.[72]

The interests of women were long assumed to be peculiar, apart from the interests of the world in general, and consequently to demand journals especially for them. But here as elsewhere women came quickly to develop newspapers owned, edited, and published by themselves and these continued until the weakening of the artificial barriers that had separated the interests of men and women, and new alignments have ranged together all having a common cause.[73] Madame Adam in *La Nouvelle Revue* has well shown that a common cause unites the interests of men and

[71] C. Rieben, "Les Journaux et la guerre," *Bibliothèque universelle et revue suisse*, November, December, 1919, 96: 241–258, 408–428.

[72] Julian Ralph, *War's Brighter Side*, pp. 1–14. The volume gives a history of the paper and includes a number of the contributions made to it.

[73] One of the earliest women editors was Anne Royall whose *Life and Times* has recently been written by Sarah H. Porter. Mrs. Royall bought a second hand printing press, hired a printer, "adopted the editorial 'We' and with a full set of principles on hand began her journalistic career." She published in Washington the first number of *Paul Pry*, December 3, 1831, and the last number November 19, 1836. It was followed at once by *The Huntress* that continued from December 2, 1836 to July 2, 1854.— *Life and Times*, pp. 146–191, 223–226.

Her editorial policy was indicated in her refusal to print a personal scandal concerning a man prominent in the church, in part because "it is against *a private man*. Public men are fair game." P. 150.

D. C. Bloomer in *The Life and Writings of Amelia Bloomer* gives a full account of the work of Mrs. Bloomer who owned, edited and published *The Lily*, devoted to the interests of women. Its first number appeared January 1, 1849.

The Woman's Journal under Lucy Stone and Henry B. Blackwell began in 1870 and was devoted especially to securing suffrage for women. The greater its success in advocating this cause the more inevitably it ultimately declined. When the goal was practically reached it was merged with *The Woman Citizen*.

women on a higher plane than when these interests are separated by arbitrary barriers.[74]

There has recently been an extraordinary increase in America in the number of newspapers and other periodicals published by or in the interests of labor and industry. A bulletin of the Library of the United States Department of Labor, Washington, D. C., 1919, lists nearly five hundred such journals, exclusive of general economic and statistical periodicals.

The foreign language press has met the needs of new arrivals in a foreign country, it has existed until familiarity with the language of the country has made it unnecessary, and then it re-appears in another locality to meet the needs of a new group of prospective citizens. Long as is the list of foreign language newspapers in a country, the individual papers have as a rule an uncertain tenure of life; their very success often the more quickly hastens their dissolution.[75] In great metropolitan centers, however, it is the clientele that constantly changes, while the same newspapers continue.

Somewhat similar is the class of newspapers that show the tentative efforts of partly undeveloped groups "to stand on their own feet" and the change in point of view and in direction of effort with the development of experience and of maturity.[76]

Prison journalism has had a fluctuating development, beginning apparently in 1799, with the *Forlorn Hope*, a weekly published by convicts in the New York State Prison,[77] and continuing

[74] W. Stephens, *Madame Adam*, 1918.
[75] Much important information in regard to the German-American press and the work of press correspondents, reporters, and editors is given in the *Memoirs of Henry Villard*, 2 vols., in the *Reminiscences of Carl Schurz*, 3 vols., and in *Carl Schurz: Speeches, Correspondence and Political Papers*, 6 vols.
A. Belisle, *Histoire de la Presse Franco-Américaine*, 1911, and A. O. Barton, "The Beginnings of the Norwegian Press in America," from the *Proceedings of the State Historical Society of Wisconsin*, 1916, illustrate this point.
R. E. Parks, in *The Immigrant Press and Its Control*, gives a general survey of the subject.
[76] I. G. Penn, *The Afro-American Press;* W. E. B. DuBois, *ed., The Crisis;* R. T. Kerlin, *The Voice of the Negro;* F. G. Detweiler, *The Negro Press in the United States.*
[77] I. N. P. Stokes, *The Iconography of Manhattan Island*, II, 419.— The Library of Congress has a partial file of the *Forlorn Hope*,—from May 3 to August 23, 1800; one number is in the library of the Wisconsin State Historical Society.

intermittently to the present. At one time prison journals were sheets giving the inmates such news from the outside world as it was thought wise for them to have, while the new prison journalism has given the outside world news from behind the bars.[78] Modifications in the name of a single prison journal may be significant of changes in the policy of control.[79]

The newspaper, when unaffected by external control, becomes everywhere a barometer indicating the fluctuating interests of society and the changing expedients in ministering to them. "The Oldest Sporting Journal" that in 1793 [80] ministered to the interests of sportsmen in England reappears in essence on the "Sporting page" of innumerable dailies everywhere in America and England. It is possible that the newspaper for beggars established in Paris,[81] with its lists of centers where begging could be pursued most profitably, may have been re-incarnated in the columns and pages devoted to "drives," that since 1914 have so flourished in aristocratic circles.

The *Mercurius Gallobelgicus* that annually informed English readers of the seventeenth century concerning events on the continent; the *Annual Register* that since the middle of the eighteenth century has faithfully chronicled political and literary news; the gift annuals that in the nineteenth century probably seemed to their originators the final word in periodical miscellany;[82] the newspaper almanacs that for many years subordinated chronology and weather to a mass of heterogeneous information on important subjects;[83] the Sunday newspaper that "might well be called a literary dime museum;" [84] all these classes of periodi-

[78] "The New Prison Journalism," *Literary Digest*, January 22, 1916, 52: 179–180; "Prison Journalism," *Bookman*, November, 1903, 18: 281–290.

[79] The prison journal at Sing Sing was for some years called *The Star of Hope*, it then became the *Star Bulletin*, and in 1920 was renamed *The Sing Sing Bulletin*.

[80] H. Maxwell, *Rainy Days in a Library*, pp. 23–32.

[81] New York *Evening Post*, January 6, 1911.

[82] A. A. Watts, *Alaric Watts*, I, chaps. xv, xix, xiii, *et seq.*

[83] The almanac was at one time issued by many local newspapers, but as thus issued it was necessarily slight in form and in matter; the local almanac yielded the field to that of the metropolitan press and the *World Almanac* is now the most important survivor, and represents in more extended and more authoritative form the earlier attempts at almanac making.

[84] Frank Foxcroft has discussed "The American Sunday Newspaper," in the *Nineteenth Century and After*, October, 1907, 62: 609–615.

cals illustrate the effort of the periodical press to reach out beyond a restricted circle and to supply the needs of a wide class of readers.

Similar in object has been the syndicated article that in its present form, so says S. S. McClure, was in the air about 1884, but that has been protean in form and that has had numerous kith and kin.[85]

These changes in the purpose of the newspaper have been accompanied by radical changes in its character. Interest in the nature of the news presented often seems subservient to the speed with which news is disseminated;[86] events that are abnormal or unusual seem to have priority of claim over those that are normal or usual,—such normal events are indeed not regarded as news; trivialities are magnified, as news, out of all proportion to their relative importance;[87] news becomes important not through

[85] S. S. McClure gives a full account of his own connection with the syndicate in *My Autobiography*, pp. 42–44, 164–192; L. Klopsch, in 1885, began syndicating the sermons of Dr. Talmage.—C. M. Pepper, *Life-Work of Louis Klopsch*, pp. 6–7.

The forerunner of the syndicated article was the paper in small towns printed at a central office. The Joliet, Illinois, *Phoenix* printed the *Phoenix* for six other towns; at least three pages were alike, the rest of the paper gave the distinctive local news of each place.—F. W. Scott, *The Newspapers and Periodicals of Illinois*, p. c.

The bar sinister is found in the press that does not join a syndicate but prefers to appropriate the news collected by others. R. H. Fife, Jr., says that in Germany much pirating of news from the larger journals is carried on by all the provincial papers, "in a way that is absolutely conscienceless, possibly because, . . . the reading public seems less eager for news than for editorial comments thereon."—*The German Empire between Two Wars*, p. 362.

[86] The adoption of the Declaration of Independence was first recorded in a Philadelphia newspaper ten days afterwards, and in a Boston newspaper twenty-two days afterwards.—H. F. Harrington and T. T. Frankenberg, *Essentials in Journalism*, pp. 193–194.

The *New York Evening Post* published the news of the battle of Waterloo forty-four days after the battle was fought; the London papers did not know of it for three days. The *Evening Post* had no editorial comment on it,—"editorials were not a great factor in that period of American journalism."—*Evening Post*, August 2, 1915.

It seems reasonable to infer that to-day no news would be published if received forty-four days after the event.

[87] This is not a new criticism. The *Athenaeum*, February 2, 1856, in writing of the *Globe*, remarks: "Rich in its vein of solemn respectability, it discourses on everything with judicious gravity, and in a spirit of unimpeachable Whiggism. It can, however, condescend to the assumed tastes of its readers; and it handles little matters as an evening journal must do, though always with great seriousness and dignity. Only a few days ago it

its inherent character but because it concerns an individual who is important or for the moment prominent;[88] the very definition of "news" seems indeed to be constantly changing and this change is either the cause or the result of marked changes in the newspaper. It is to the philosopher of Archey Road that the student of history must really turn for a characterization of news as it is regarded to-day:

"An' that's all th' news," said Mr. Dooley. "There ye ar-re jus' as if ye cud read. That's all that's happened. Ain't I a good newspaper? Not a dull line in me. Sind in ye'er small ads."

"Sure, all that's no news," said Mr. Hennessy, discontentedly. "Hasn't there annything happened? Hasn't anny wan been— been kilt?"

"There ye ar-re," said Mr. Dooley. "Be news ye mane misfortune. I suppose near ivry wan does. What's wan man's news is another man's throubles. In these hot days, I'd like to see a pa-aper with nawthin' in it but affectionate wives an' loyal husbands an' prosp'rous, smilin' people an' money in th' bank an' three a day. That's what I'm lookin' f'r in th' hot weather."

"Th' newspapers have got to print what happens," said Mr. Hennessy.

"No," said Mr. Dooley, "they've got to print what's diff'rent. Whiniver they begin to put headlines on happiness, contint, varchoo, an' charity, I'll know things is goin' as wrong with this counthry as I think they ar-re ivry naytional campaign." [89]

examined and settled, with the most patient impartiality, an interesting discussion between a parson and his curate, as to who should have the hatbands presented at a funeral. These are just the kind of problems which one has strength to enter on in the hungry hour before dinner, and we may be glad to have them handled so soberly and discreetly."—J. C. Francis, *Notes by the Way*, pp. 203–204.

[88] It was news, for example, to cable from Paris the breakfast prison menu of a prominent woman who was the defendant in a murder trial; that at a Swiss winter resort the wife of a prominent public official had worn Turkish trousers at a fancy dress ball; that King George and Queen Mary breakfasted on buckwheat cakes while visiting an encampment of American troops; to report, not the points in an address on the League to Enforce Peace made by a former president of the United States, but his winter rule for keeping down his weight.

[89] "Newspaper Publicity," *Observations by Mr. Dooley*. pp. 237–244.

Fisher Ames wrote in the *Palladium*, October, 1801, "A newspaper is pronounced to be very lean and destitute of matter, if it contains no account of murders, suicides, prodigies, or monstrous births. . . . Is this a reasonable taste? or is it monstrous and worthy of ridicule? Is the History of Newgate the only one worth reading? Are oddities only to be hunted? Pray tell us, men of ink, if our free presses are to diffuse *information*, and we, the poor ignorant people, can get it no other way than by newspapers,

This present conception of news and the keen competition for news has led to the rapid increase in personal journalism with its emphasis on the private life, the personal appearance, the public affairs of every individual in any way conspicuous. The result is often a complete reversal of the essential position of many individuals,—those who are naturally or inevitably in the public eye shrink from the press exploitation of their personal characteristics and private or public expenditures, while those who are in no way pre-eminent in the community are often most solicitous to have their comings and their goings chronicled by the press. Personal journalism thus often results in magnifying the infinitesimal and in minimizing the importance of what is truly great.

It is this insistent desire for news and also the desire to be the subject of news that has given rise to the so-called yellow press. Its origin has been somewhat superciliously laid at the door of America, and it has at times aroused apprehension among the friends of the press lest its baneful influence should affect all members of the guild. But the press has always been of rainbow hues and the yellow press was in existence before the periodical press was established here. It is easily recognized and in and of itself it does not concern the historian since he naturally does not consult it for the records it gives. But the yellow press collectively is itself a record that can not be ignored since it has been but one of many symptoms that have indicated a diseased, morbid state of society,—a condition that the press itself has done much to restore to health and well-being. Yet this change has been partly attributable to the general improvement in the moral tone of society. The influence of the yellow press may seem pronounced at a given time, but it is one that has been greatly deprecated by prominent leaders of the press itself, and it is probable that Scott-James is correct in saying that

" Just when the aforetime reputable Press has learnt the lesson of indecency, the controllers of the popular Press have learnt the market-value of decency. They have discovered that accurate information pays; that an irresponsible sensational manner no longer makes a sensation; that news must be news; that authority

---

what knowledge we are to glean from the blundering lies, or the tiresome truths about thunder storms, that, strange to tell! kill oxen or burn barns."
—*Works*, II, 406–407.

is still authoritative—that the largest newspaper audience in the world is not destitute of common sense. This is the amazing discovery which has recently been dawning upon the world; and it emanated, not from 'respectable' England, which had discarded the idea, but from the Press which had once been called the "Yellow Press'." [90]

The desire for news has been universal and it has been ministered to in multiform ways. The newspaper of to-day has been the most recent result of this desire and it has come to be both a purveyor of news and an accumulator of a thousand and one activities that have reached out far beyond its original circumference. Combinations and recombinations, progress and reaction, dangerous tendencies and constructive policies, vision and creative imagination, sordid aims and crass ignorance, have at all times been characteristic features of the newspaper in the abstract, although never all found in concrete form in any single paper or group of papers. It must suffice to note here a few other tendencies, not necessarily the most important or the most conspicuous, but tendencies somewhat general in scope that have characterized a changing press.

The relative importance of the editorial has undergone a change. When it was the rule that a newspaper was edited by its owner, it was the excellence of the newspaper, and especially of its editorial, that determined the success of the paper. With the transference of the ownership from an individual to that of a stock company the relative importance of the editor and of the editorial has apparently declined while that of the business manager is in the ascendant. Individual newspapers often change

[90] R. A. Scott-James, *The Influence of the Press*, p. 201.
The pros and cons of the yellow press may be found in L. K. Commander, "The Significance of Yellow Journalism," *Arena*, August, 1905, 34: 150–155; C. Whibley, "The Yellow Press," *Blackwood*, April, 1907, 181: 531–538; A. Brisbane, "Yellow Journalism," *Bookman*, June, 1904, 19: 400–404; S. Brooks, "The Significance of Mr. Hearst," *Fortnightly Review*, December, 1907, n. s. 82: 919–931, and "The American Yellow Press," *Fortnightly Review*, December, 1911, n. s. 90: 1126–1137; E. L. Banks, "American 'Yellow Journalism'," *Nineteenth Century*, August, 1898, 44: 328–340; A. Brisbane, "William Randolph Hearst," *North American Review*, September 21, 1906, 183: 519–526; G. Harvey, "Mr. Brisbane's Eulogy of Mr. Hearst," *ibid.*, pp. 569–572; A. M. Low, "The Yellow Press in Japan," *North American Review*, August 16, 1907, 185: 837–847; S. W. Pennypacker, "Sensational Journalism and the Remedy," *North American Review*, November, 1909, 190: 587–593.

their policy with change of owners or of editors, and even the theory of journalism held by an editor may not be the same at all stages of his career, as was apparently the case with Samuel Bowles.[91]

This shifting of the importance of the editor has led to a change in the form of writing; "the modern tendency has been," says Chisholm, "to make journalism less literary and at the same time literature more journalistic,"—a tendency recorded in the coining of the word "journalese."

One farther change in the newspaper may be considered both an internal and an external change. Its very name implies that its chief, indeed its only interest lies in questions of the hour or even of the moment, and a writer on journalism has recently said, " 'Yesterday' has almost ceased to exist for the newspaper man." [92] Yet however strong may be its insistence on its obligation to reflect the present through the presentation of "news," the newspaper is more and more anchored in the past. No newspaper could live for a week if it omitted from its columns everything that went back of the date of publication,—its main strength comes from the strong rope it twists of the news of the past and the news of the day. In news and in editorial, in special correspondence and in advertisement it is the past to which appeal is made and it is the past that gives stability to the present. The present can not be understood—the facts concerning it may be learned, but it can not be understood—without the knowledge that only a study of the past can give.

It by no means follows that these tendencies make the press of any less value to the historian. It does follow that the center of gravity changes its position as new elements are added and old interests decline in importance and that therefore the relative importance of the press shifts from time to time. The tendencies of the press differ at different times in different countries and to such an extent that it is impossible to make any statement concerning the press that is true at all times, or of all countries, or of any country at any one time. If, at the moment,

[91] Review of *The Life and Times of Samuel Bowles,* by George S. Merriam.— *The Nation,* December 31, 1885, 41: 553-554.
[92] W. G. Bleyer, *Newspaper Writing and Editing,* p. 19.

the controlling interest in the press of America is in the news it presents; if in France it has been in the criticism it contains; if in England the two-party political organization has given a predominance of interest to party organs; and if in Germany the influence of the government has given opportunity for wide use of the press for propagandist purposes, these varying tendencies do not diminish the value of the press to the historian, but they do make his use of it infinitely more complicated. His own unconscious tendency may be to judge the press collectively by the press of the country with which he is most familiar, and to judge the press of his own country by the conditions under which he personally knows it. But even here he must be on his guard since in no country has the press had a continuous development. In England its utterances, and therefore its influence, were long restrained by the taxes on knowledge, though even before their removal discriminating critics have found that new influences were at work. "The appearance of The Craftsman at the end of 1726," says Percival, "marked the beginning of a new era in the history of journalism. At that time the newspaper press was playing a very minor rôle in politics." [93] But the *Craftsman* became the organ of those opposed to Walpole and the Ministry and it thus made its influence felt although it was in no sense the influence of an independent press.

At the end of the eighteenth century, the time was ripe, Scott-James believes, for the appearance of a new daily,—a literate public was waiting for it, the French Revolution and the career of Napoleon had stimulated thought, and the age of mechanical invention was making it possible. *The Times* filled this need,— it appealed to the more solid element of the middle class, and "it was the first paper in the world that really organized a universal news service." It sent Henry Crabb Robinson to Germany and to Spain and later it made him its foreign editor. It had its agents and correspondents everywhere searching for news. "What *The Times* said on any important matter was listened to, all over Europe," and through *The Times* "the daily press emerged as an intermediary between those who were really the

[93] Milton Percival, *Political Ballads Illustrating the Administration of Sir Robert Walpole*, p. xiii.

rulers of the country, and those who, according to the Constitution, were supposed to be." [94]

"The development of the Press as an independent political power," says Pebody, "dates from the Reform Bill in 1831. Till then newspapers had never thought of discussing the principles of Government in their broadest sense. They attached themselves to this or that Minister, attacked or defended this or that treaty, this or that policy. But in 1831 the Press struck out a bolder line. It, so to speak, set up for itself." [95]

This independence gained after long struggle has, in the opinion of some, been threatened by masterful editors or proprietors. "If there was ever anything in English public life," says a recent writer, "that could properly be called a 'herd', it was that shepherded by the crook labeled *The Times*," while "each uses journalism to his own patriotic ends, feeling that patriotism consists in his having his way." [96]

Yet these very conditions have been to some a reason explaining why the *Daily Mail* was, to them, as inevitable at the end of the nineteenth century as *The Times* had been a hundred years before,—a vast literate public had been created by the Act of 1870, the working classes were appealed to by the press, political conditions growing out of the Boer War had fostered discussion, and speed and business efficiency rendered it possible to fill the need. [97]

The function of the newspaper has radically changed from the practically passive one of transmitting news to the active one of reflecting public opinion and of so influencing it that it has won for itself the title of "the fourth estate." But even this statement can not pass unchallenged. The question as to whether the press reflects public opinion, guides public opinion, or forms public opinion may be deemed "purely academic," yet the historian

[94] R. A. Scott-James, *Influence of the Press*, pp. 92–109. See also S. V. Makower, *Some Notes upon the History of the Times;* A. I. Shand, "The Centenary of 'The Times'," *National Review*, February, 1888, 10: 841–856; James Creelman, "The London 'Times'," *McClure's Magazine*, October, 1895, 5: 387–397.

[95] C. Pebody, *English Journalism and the Men Who Made It*, p. 178.

[96] J. M. Robertson, "The Press Fetish," *Contemporary Review*, January, 1916, 109: 49–56.

[97] R. A. Scott-James, *The Influence of the Press*, pp. 175–199.

who uses the newspaper as a record must at least attempt to answer it and if convinced that its work falls under all three heads, he may also find it necessary to attempt to apportion the different measure of each.[98] **1909114**

In all of these changes in the purpose of the newspaper it has thus seemed to be repeating the experience of the museum of natural science. This once had as its aim the collection of curiosities, monstrosities, and every form of abnormal life, and in their arrangement within the museum formal and artificial principles were adopted,—birds were mounted on stiff perches, shells were arranged according to the prevailing ideas of what "looked well," and stuffed skins of the larger animals were placed wherever convenience of space demanded. But the museum to-day seeks whatever represents normal life in its own native locality and with infinite pains its collections are arranged in the manner natural to them in their own habitat. The public library once had similar methods, arranging its books on its shelves according to sizes and loaning them out for periods that also corresponded to their dimensions. The historian himself was once interested in the unusual and even the abnormal,—religious inquisitions, the executions of kings, reigns of terror, filled his pages. To-day his interest lies in the study of normal life, he seeks the typical, not the isolated experiences of the past.

[98] The question often asked, "Was *The Times* of Delane a mirror, a guide, or an initiator?" is answered by Sir Edward Cook, "it was all three." Since Delane was independent personally, was independent of the Government of the day, and was independent of party ties, the answer in this case is a simpler matter than it sometimes is. See an admirable discussion of the whole subject in *Delane of "The Times,"* chap. X, "The Influence of Delane."

A variant of the same question has often been raised in regard to *The Nation*, and it has been answered by Rollo Odgen who says: "*The Nation's* influence in shaping the American press was out of all proportion to the mere numbers of its readers. It did not strive nor cry. The effects it wrought were subtle and insinuated, never clamorous. A virtue went out from it which was unconsciously absorbed by many newspaper writers. They could scarcely have said where they got their new impulse to exercise a judgment independent of party. All can raise the flowers now, for all have got the seed. To-day the most powerful newspapers in the United States are those which have the reputation of being already ready, on a question of real principle, to snap the green withes with which politicans would bind them. But until twenty years after *The Nation* was founded, how few they were, how sneered at, how disliked!"— Gustav Pollak, *Fifty Years of American Idealism*, p. 81.

The newspaper, therefore, abnormal as it in itself may seem with its flaring headlines, its blurred and smudgy pages of splashy cartoons and illustrated advertisements, its lack of a sense of proportion when one paper may give twelve columns of one issue to a murder trial and another paper of the same date in the same city give twelve lines to the same case,—the newspaper in all of these stages of its development is but recording the spirit of the times as it has been disclosed in other and corresponding activities. Like them also it gives evidence of the changes in purpose and in method that are already on the way.

These illustrations have been suggested to indicate that the task of the historian is often not to ascertain what the press says, but to go behind the face of the returns and to determine why it says what it says, when it says it, and what is the effect of what it has said. Back of the newspaper are the conditions that have made it what it is,—the sources from which its news has been derived; the reporters who have gathered from the four quarters of the globe the material for its columns; the men who have written its editorials, its special articles, and its correspondence; Bohemia and the school of journalism; the personal and professional relations of members of the press. All of the conditions affecting the press have produced an infinitely complex result that have made the work of the historian in dealing with it as historical material one of enormous difficulty.

The press itself records in a measure the influences that have made it what it is,—yet only in part. It does not fully record its relation to governmental authority that by censorship, regulation, and control of news service has from time to time laid a heavy hand on the periodical press; it can not always record the existence of a public opinion that has made it what it is, or the absence of a public opinion that has prevented it from becoming what it might otherwise have been.[99] To understand the value of the press as historical material it is necessary to know the records the press gives of itself; the legislation that has modified it and the degree to which in some countries it has controlled it; the lives of those who have so largely made it what it is. And

[99] F. V. Keys, "The Great Illusion about Germany," *North American Review*, March, 1918, 207: 345-353.

when all of these conditions have been understood, it must still remain true that but one general conclusion can be safely drawn concerning the press and that is that all general statements concerning it collectively are untrue.

These are but suggestions of the internal changes that have been developed in the newspaper partly as a cause, partly as a result of the changes that have come in the purpose and the function of the newspaper,—changes that in themselves form an important record for the use of the historian.[100] In and of themselves they have added enormously to the complexity of the newspaper and have to the same degree increased the difficulties of the student of history in dealing with it as historical material. They have been suggested to make evident the statement that in the use of the newspaper as historical material the historian must first of all consider the time at which the newspaper was published and understand the transformations through which it has passed. The world has been enlarged through the steamboat, the railroad, the telegraph, the telephone, the trolley, and the automobile,—the personal letter no longer is adequate to meet the needs of a world thus enlarged. The newspaper has adapted itself to meet this expansion of interests. The transformation also includes the variations that have been developed in the press of different nationalities.[101] The historian who uses the newspaper must be familiar with the history of the press, and conform his use of it to the conditions under which it arose.

It must also be remembered that the enumeration made of the accumulated interests of the newspaper applies chiefly to

[100] "And if anything is plain in newspaper history of recent years, it is the fact that the political, militant phase of the newspaper artist's work has been steadily receding before what we may characterize as the commentative, social phase. The spirit of the Home Page, with its absorption in the simple norms and simple oddities of the every-day life, has penetrated the first page also and the editorial page. Men and women in the home, the man in the office, the child in the home and on the playground, landlords, employers, commuters, theatres, fashions—these are the topics that now absorb the newspaper draughtsman."—New York *Evening Post*, May 3, 1912.
This is written specifically of the illustration, but it describes perfectly the changes that are coming in the newspaper as a whole.
[101] "The power of the newspaper in France differs from that of the English newspaper, in that it seems to act more on the government and the parliament than on public opinion."—H. Chisholm, "Newspapers," in *Encyclopaedia Britannica*, XIX, 577.

the great metropolitan dailies,—outside of this relatively small class of newspapers no paper can carry on all of the activities enumerated, or even more than a small part of them. The historian, in his use of the newspaper in reconstructing the past must test the papers used for their completeness as well as for their authoritativeness, and must submit the great daily of a large city to one set of tests and the weekly paper of a small village to quite other tests.

Different tests must also be applied to the general newspaper that reaches a wide and diversified constituency, and to the organ of a special political party, religious faith, or industry. Different tests must be applied to the various parts of the same newspaper, as well as to the same newspaper at different stages of its history. Different tests must be applied to the newspapers of different countries.

The words *newspaper*, *periodical*, and *press* are often used interchangeably, as indeed is the case in this discussion of the subject, yet it must again be remembered that the frequency or the infrequency of the appearance of a periodical gives it certain characteristics that modify at different times and in various ways its use as historical material.[102] It is also essential to discriminate clearly between *journalism*, the technical process by which articles for the press are produced, and the *press*, the completed product of this process. The historian must concern himself primarily with the press, rather than with journalism.

The question presented to the historian is therefore a two-fold one. The first concerns the authoritativeness of the material found in its pages; the second concerns the value of all this material, both authoritative and unauthoritative, in any attempted reconstruction of the past. What principles can be deduced that will guide the historian in his use of periodicals; what guarantees does the press carry in itself that will absolve the historian from the necessity of investigating the truth of every statement made by the newspaper; how far can he accept at its face value the material presented in the reputable press;

[102] "The prospectus of *The Nation* laid stress upon the advantages of a weekly over a daily newspaper in respect of leisure for ascertainment of the facts and deliberation in comment."—Wendell Phillips Garrison, cited by Gustav Pollak, *Fifty Years of American Idealism*, p. 58.

to what extent has the regulation of the press by public opinion and by different authorities and organizations made it unnecessary for him to reject *in toto* all forms of periodical literature as a source for his work; what tests can be applied that will determine not only the authoritativeness of the newspaper but also its advantages and its limitations as historical material,—all of these and similar questions vitally affect the student of history in his use of the press.

It is impossible to give a definite and final answer to all, perhaps to any one, of these questions, but at least the conditions to which they give rise must be recognized before the historian is justified in using the periodical press as authoritative historical material.

CHAPTER II

THE NEWSPAPER AS A PERSONALITY

"They were passing through the Strand as they talked, and by a newspaper office, which was all lighted up and bright. Reporters were coming out of the place, or pushing up to it in cabs; there were lamps burning in the editors' rooms, and above where the compositors were at work: the windows of the building were in a blaze of gas.

" 'Look at that, Pen,' Warrington said. 'There she is—the great engine—she never sleeps. She has her ambassadors in every quarter of the world—her couriers upon every road. Her officers march along with armies, and her envoys walk into statesmen's cabinets. They are ubiquitous. Yonder journal has an agent at this minute, giving bribes at Madrid; and another inspecting the price of potatoes in Covent Garden. Look! here comes the Foreign Express galloping in. They will be able to give news to Downing Street to-morrow: funds will rise or fall, fortunes be made or lost; Lord B. will get up, and, holding the paper in his hand, and seeing the noble Marquis in his place, will make a great speech; and—and Mr. Doolan will be called away from his supper at the Back Kitchen; for he is foreign sub-editor, and sees the mail on the newspaper sheet before he goes to his own.' "—*Thackeray*.

THE authoritativeness of the press as historical material is to a large degree determined by its personality. If "personality" is a baffling, elusive term defying definition when applied to an individual, it may seem equally so when applied to a newspaper. Yet many characteristics easily recognizable enter into the personality of a newspaper and these often determine in large measure its reliability and its consequent importance from the historian's point of view. The historian must recognize and understand the personality of every periodical he uses, for only through this understanding can he appreciate the value and the limitations of the newspaper as historical material.

The most obvious elements that disclose the personality of a newspaper are its external features. These often predispose its readers in its favor or prejudice them against it, and under normal conditions weigh for or against it when its authoritativeness is tested.[1] Its external dress, like that of an individual, determines

---

[1] Newspapers printed on wrapping paper or on the back of wall-paper when printing paper can not be obtained because the town where they

somewhat its standards, and it indicates the class of readers to which it appeals, and these factors must in turn affect its reliability. Its form, its size, the quality of the paper, the color of the ink, the width of the columns and the number of the columns to the page, the varieties of type used, the appearance of headlines, the use or the lack of illustrations, the nature and the place of advertisements, the place of telegraphic news and of editorials,—all these and other external characteristics give a newspaper an appearance that to a certain extent predicates its real character. The historian does not look for reliable information in a newspaper printed on paper of inferior quality, or on colored paper for special sheets, as pink paper for the sporting sheet; or in newspapers that use black ink that "smuts;" red ink, or green ink conspicuously used about the seventeenth of March; or in newspapers that have cheap pictures, inferior type, flaunting headlines, and sensationally displayed "features." These characteristics are not simply an affront to good taste,—they are warnings that the columns of such newspapers presumably do not contain unimpeachable historical evidence. Slovenly or flaunting attire usually indicates that mental processes are untrustworthy.

The personality of a periodical is indicated not only by its external appearance but also by its beliefs and opinions. The newspaper, like the individual, is radical or conservative in its tendencies; it is independent in the formation of its opinions and fearless in its expression of them, or it is evidently controlled by some outside influence in the expression of its judgments; if it is independent, it may be aggressively independent, or negatively independent; in its spirit it is exclusive and aristocratic, or it is free and democratic; it has its political, religious, and economic convictions, or it may be a time-server, an opportunist, or a coward; it may be "up-to-the-minute" in its encouragement of a style of writing that borders on slang and its language may be not only infelicitous but even incorrect and ungrammatical, or its editorials may be couched in classic English and its reporters called sternly to account if they sin against the literary canons of the office.

are printed is in a state of siege are obviously not printed "under normal conditions." Other abnormal features due to exceptional circumstances are manifestly excluded in any discussion of the external appearance of a paper as conditioning its authoritativeness.

This internal spirit of a paper is often perfectly reflected by its external appearance.

The business habits of a periodical in conducting its own affairs are something of an index to its personality. If it is prompt and efficient, the statements made in regard to its business policy indicate at least its business ideals, while if it is slack or negligent in its business management this is often betrayed by the announcements of its policy.

These business habits concern the publication of its office hours and information as to the means of communication with it at these or at other times either by local or long-distance telephone, information as to the precise hour of publication and the hour when the paper will be on sale in other cities, the time when communications should reach the office to insure insertion, and the hour of morning delivery.

It publishes its subscription rates, and often states that subscriptions must invariably be paid in advance; it gives warning that names are not entered until payment has been received; it gives a receipt for subscription through a printed label; it discontinues the paper if the subscription is not renewed; and cautions its subscribers that it is not responsible for advance payments made to out-of-town local carriers, dealers, or agents; it states that extra copies needed must be ordered in advance, and it usually expresses a willingness to change the address of subscribers as often as desired; more lax business methods are indicated in the statement not infrequently found, "Our terms are $1.00 a year if paid in advance; otherwise $1.50."

The newspaper is often equally firm in stating its intention to secure the prompt delivery of papers to its subscribers and it promises to give immediate attention to all complaints made of carriers, though stating at the same time that carriers are not allowed to receive complaints or notices to stop subscriptions. It asks for information from its readers if the paper can not be bought at news stands or on railway trains, announces the hours for the closing of the mails that carry the paper to near-by towns, gives rates of postage for its issues having a varying number of pages, warns its readers that "the laws of the postal department are strict and newspapers insufficiently prepaid can not be forwarded," and gives information as to the best methods of forwarding money by domestic or foreign subscribers.

Advertising rates are often given in great detail, the location of advertising bureaus in America and in Europe stated, advertisers are informed that unusual time should be given on large space advertisements, and the statement made, "All bills payable on demand. Advertisements unless ordered for a definite time will be continued until ordered out."

All of these business methods of the most reputable papers indicate a desire to give prompt and efficient service and thus point to a personality that commands the respect of other members of the business community. To the degree that it shows opposite characteristics, it fails, as does the individual, to maintain its business standing.

The ideals of a newspaper are a part of its personality and these ideals are often expressed in its motto. If the chief ambition of a paper is to supply its readers with the news, that ambition is indicated in its motto,—"All the news the day it happens," "To-day's news to-day," "The news of the week as told by the man on the street," "*The Times* leads in news—both local and telegraph. That's the mission of a REAL newspaper." If it recognizes limitations placed on the publication of news by the character of the news itself, the motto chosen recognizes that limitation,—"All the news that's fit to print," "All the news that's worth reading," "First of all the news—clean and correct." And if again its chief concern is with the accuracy of the news published, the motto records that ideal,—"It's all here and it's all true," "If it's sent by the Associated Press, it's so." But if the newspaper conceives that its chief function is, not to supply news, but to represent public opinion, or to influence public opinion, the motto indicates this belief,—"The only daily newspaper in Newburgh not obligated to anybody but the people for its existence," "*The Times-Union* is the people's paper first, last and all the time," "Without fear or favor we stand for the people's interest," "The people's newspaper," "With a mission and without a muzzle." It even goes farther than this and through its motto often points out how this should be done,—"Neutral in nothing," "*Tros Tyriusque mihi nullo discrimine agetur*," "Open to all parties but influenced by none," "*Fiat justitia, ruat coelum,*" "*Vérité sans peur,*" "Nothing extenuate, nor set down aught in malice." A paper sometimes tries several mottoes or creeds before it finds one to its liking. *Niles' Register* had as the motto for the issues of its first volume a passage from Shakespeare's Henry VIII:

> "I wish no other herald,
> "No other speaker of *my living actions,*
> "To keep mine honor from corruption
> "But such an honest chronicler."

With the second volume, it changes to "*Haec olim meminisse juvabit,*" and with the thirteenth volume it becomes and continues, "The past—the present—for the future." It does not seem possible to find a statement of the functions of a journal that more perfectly expresses the idea of the historian on this point than does the motto finally selected for *Niles' Register.*

The motto setting forth the ideals of a newspaper shades imperceptibly into the statement giving the basis of its appeal to readers or advertisers. Age is one appeal,—"New York's oldest newspaper. Established 1797;" youth another,—"The Twentieth Century newspaper;"—local pride a third,—"Boost White Plains," "Success is yours in Amsterdam," "The leading newspaper of a leading Connecticut town," "Pasadena and suburbs first, the world afterwards," "The first seven-day newspaper in the Southwest north of Dallas, south of Kansas City, east of Denver, and west of St. Louis;" and the industry of the staff still another,—"Keeping everlastingly at it brings success." An appeal is made on the score that the paper is an excellent family newspaper,—"An evening journal for the fireside," "A family journal devoted to local news, literature, art, science, and general intelligence," "A home newspaper for all the people," "The paper with pictures," "Clean in news and clean in advertising," "The magazine that entertains," "More fascinating than fiction," "The liveliest magazine in America." Others attempt to square the circle in the assertion of their principles,—"Independent but not neutral," "Progressive but not radical," "An impartial newspaper, democratic in politics," "Clean but not dull." The appeal may be directed to the business interests of the community, with the emphasis placed on circulation,—"The daily *Times-Demo-crat* has a larger prepaid circulation than any other daily news-paper south of the Potomac and Ohio rivers," "Circulation grow-ing at the rate of 1,000 per week;" or on excellence as an adver-tising medium,—"The paper that gets results," "This paper has a circulation larger than that of any other evening paper in the United States. Its value as an advertising medium is apparent;" or on the special kind of business news or information presented, —"Full market reports," "Wall Street news complete," "Com-plete stock market reports," "Home trade advocate," "Encour-age national industry;" or the individual interests of the small advertiser,—"We specialize on small ads," "Quick returns from 'rent' and 'sale' ads," "Low terms for small ads," "Advertise your property for sale with us;" or statements as to the nature, source, and variety of the general news presented,—"Full Asso-ciated Press report," "Exclusive Associated Press service," "Member of the United Press and Newspaper Enterprise Asso-ciation," "Full leased wire," "One hundred correspondents."

Many newspapers show their personality in an external atti-tude towards life that is disclosed in the gentle observations that daily appear at the head of their editorial columns,—observations that may show a helpless pessimism before conditions they can not change, or a cheerful optimism that all's well with the world, or that indicate that they are colorless spectators of the interests of others,—"The blessings of government, like the dews of heaven, should descend alike upon the rich and the poor," "The world is governed too much," "First the blade, then the ear, then the full corn in the ear," "An independent press is the bulwark of liberty," "Fair and free discussion will ever be found the primal friend of truth," "*La nuit porte conseil.*" The melancholy Jaques has his chair in many a sanctum.

A variant of these standing observations is the "thought for the day," the "daily greeting," the "good-morning" comment, or the general sentiment, either original or expressed by classic writers in prose or poetry,—a quotation that changes with each issue.[2]

[2] These mottoes and appeals are of great interest in the study of the history of the press, recording, as they do, the interest of the day. At the time of

The formal journalistic creed is occasionally found and it becomes a permanent feature of the paper. The Prospectus of the *Evening Post*, dated November 16, 1801, states: "The design of this paper is to diffuse among the people correct information on all interesting subjects, to inculcate just principles in religion, morals, and politics; and to cultivate a taste for sound literature."

The World, as established by Joseph Pulitzer, May 10, 1883, has carried this creed at the head of its editorial columns: "An institution that should always fight for progress and reform, never tolerate injustice or corruption, always fight demagogues of all parties, never belong to any party, always oppose privileged classes and public plunderers, never lack sympathy with the poor, always remain devoted to the public welfare, never be satisfied with merely printing news, always be drastically independent, never be afraid to attack wrong, whether by predatory plutocracy or predatory poverty."

The Evening Mail goes back to the civic oath of the young man of Athens and it states as its creed: "We will never bring disgrace to this our city by any act of dishonesty or cowardice, nor

---

the American Revolution, and immediately after it for example, the mottoes frequently used were "Freedom and unity," "E pluribus unum," "For the country," "Our country, and our country's friends," "Join or die," "Appeal to Heaven: Independence," "Liberty and Independence."

An exceptionally interesting collection has been made of the Latin and Greek mottoes of the *Spectators*, *Tatlers*, and *Guardians;* the second edition added the mottoes of the *Freeholders*. They were translated into English and both originals and translations published in London, the second edition, in 1737.

The *Spectator* itself says, No. 370, "Many of my Fair Readers, as well as very gay and well-received Persons of the other Sex, are extremely perplex'd at the Latin Sentences at the Head of my Speculations; I do not know whether I ought not to indulge them with Translations of each of them."—The translations given in the collected edition are for the most part quite different from the English lines that accompany, but do not always translate, the original mottoes.—In the 1247 numbers of the four publications, nearly 30 Latin authors are represented in the mottoes and about a dozen Greek authors, while only six mottoes are cited from English writers.

No greater contrast can be found than is that between the selections made by Addison from the Latin and Greek classics and their modern up-to-date counterparts that head the newspaper of the day.

Among the most modern as well as the most characteristic of these remarks were probably those used by the London *Daily Mail* during the recent war,—"The Paper that Persistently Forewarned the Public about the War," "The Paper that is Trying to Drag out the Truth," "The Paper that secured 'Single Men First'," "The Paper that Helped to get the Shells," "The Paper that Developed Airmanship."

ever desert our suffering comrades in the ranks. We will fight for the ideals and sacred things of the city, both alone and with many; we will revere and obey the city's laws and do our best to incite a like respect and reverence in those above us who are prone to annul or set them at naught; we will strive unceasingly to quicken the public's sense of civic duty. Thus in all these ways we will transmit this city not only not less but greater, better and more beautiful than it was transmitted to us."

In considering the motto or the creed of a paper as an index to its personality, it must be recognized that they are not necessarily the paper's own selection. If a newspaper does not always live up to the rule of action indicated by them, possibly chosen for the paper years before and never changed, their value as historical material is not thereby necessarily vitiated.

The name of a newspaper, like its motto, is often an indication of its historic, if not of its present personality. These names may denote important questions that were uppermost in the public mind when the papers were established and the position of the papers towards these questions,—*Patriot, Republic, Commonwealth, Union, Constitution, Citizen, Statesman, Liberator, Squatter Sovereign, Democrat, Republican*; they may record the time-old interest of man in nature and in natural phenomena,—*Sun, Sunbeam, Moon, Star; Evening, Morning*, or *Rising Star; Eastern Star, Western Star, Meteor, Comet, Planet; Zenith, Eclipse, Crescent, Globe, Cosmos, World; Blizzard, Tornado, Avalanche, Breeze, Lake Breeze, Ocean Breeze;* as also his friendly relationship with animal life,—*Bee, Bee Hive, Hornet, Wasp, Eagle, Eagle Eye, Pelican, Cricket, Black Cat, Buck, Elk, Tiger, Rooster, Hawkeye.* They may indicate the natural resources or the geographical location of the place where the paper is published,—*Gem, Diamond, Nugget, Emerald, Pearl; Surf, Wave, Anchor, Buoy, Coast Watch, Pilot, Lookout, Search Light, Lighthouse, Inter Lake, Inter Ocean,* as also the probable conditions of life under which the paper was started,—*Frontier, Pioneer, Path Finder, Log Cabin, Plow Boy, Landmark, Guide, Guide Post, Scout.* They may show a once universal familiarity of the newspaper-reading public with classical mythology, language, and literature,—*Aegis, Apollo, Argo, Argonaut, Argus, Athenaeum, Atlantis, Atlas, Iris, Mercury,*

Palladium, Phoenix, Psyche, Sphynx. They may indicate a confidence in sound, or in sight, to attract attention to itself,—*Bugle, Bell, Chimes, Harp, Phonograph, Tocsin, Town Crier, Trumpet, Voice, Warbler; Beacon, Light, Torch.* At other times the same object is secured through names indicating some form of military or of patriotic endeavor,—*Arrow, Tomahawk, Lance, Free Lance, Scimitar, Cannon Ball; Minute Man, Volunteer, Pilgrim, Crusader, Standard, Banner, Flag, Herald, Signal.*

The names chosen indicate still more often what the newspaper believes its function to be. To one this function may seem to be the perfect reflection of the times,—*Kodak, Mirror, Portrait, Reflector;* to another, leadership,—*Advance, Chief, Chieftain, Forward, Leader, Progress, Vanguard;* to others activity,—*Alert, Hustler, Push, Rustler;* to others the transmission of news,—*Courier, Messenger, Mail, Post, Express, Telegram, Telegraph, Telephone, Cablegram;* while other names emphasize the presentation of news,—*Chronicle, Index, Informer, Intelligencer, Record, Register, Reporter, Tidings, Times.* One group of names suggests the attitude of self-satisfaction,—*Climax, Eureka, Excelsior, Favorite, Hub, Nonpareil, Optimist, Oracle, Success, Summit;* another the New England conscience,—*Plain Talk, Plain Speaker, Plain Dealer, Truth, Square Deal;* still another an active responsibility, that in another group becomes aggressive responsibility,—*Advocate, Vindicator, Champion, Defender, Monitor, Agitator, Awakener; Call, Gridiron, Muck Rake, Hot Blast, Crank, Critic, Boomerang.* Far different are the names that suggest the attitude of detachment or that of the on-looker devoid of all personal responsibility,—*By-stander, Observer, Watchman, Survey, Outlook;* even an appreciation of humor is disclosed in the names of otherwise serious papers,—*Acorn* (Burr Oak, Mich.), *Epitaph* (Tombstone, Arizona), *Eye* (Needles, Cal.), *Réveille* (Rifle, Cal.), *Twiner* (Woodbine, Iowa). But it is in the organs of special trades, industries, and occupations that the personality of a newspaper is most unequivocally conveyed through its name,—*Bit and Spur, Farm and Garden, Profit and Loss, Case and Comment, Ores and Metals, Square and Compass, Barrel and Box.*[3]

[3] The extent to which the names of periodicals reflect current interests is indicated in the names given in N. W. Ayer and Son, *American Newspaper*

The recent war has been prolific in newspapers published in camp and trench and on shipboard and their names have been specially appropriate,—*The Periscope, Over the Top, The Fusillade, The Hatchet of the George Washington, Speed Up, The Dry-Dock Dial.*

Change of name may be an interesting illustration of the personality of a newspaper. After rigorous censorship, M. Clemenceau changed the name of *L'Homme Libre* to *L'Homme Enchaîné*, but after he became premier, the paper reverted to its former name. Many years before in Paris, *La Lune*, after it was suppressed, reappeared under the name *L'Eclipse*.[4] Change in point of view may bring an equally interesting change in designation; *The Forlorn Hope* was the name of a weekly published in 1799 by the convicts in the New York State Prison,[5] while the corresponding paper later was called *The Star of Hope.*

A newspaper may change its name many times and yet, like the leopard, not change its spots. Richard Carlile brought out papers bearing the various names of *Republican, Deist, Moralist, Lion, Prompter, Gauntlet, Christian Warrior, Phoenix, Scourge, Church,* and yet apparently the character of the paper never changed with change of name.[6]

Annual and Directory; Paul Bluysen, *Annuaire de la presse française; Sell's World's Press;* W. E. Connelley, *History of Kansas Newspapers;* A. T. Griswold, *Annotated Catalogue of Newspaper Files in the Library of the State Historical Society' of Wisconsin;* D. C. Haskell, *Check List of Newspapers and Official Gazettes in the New York Public Library;* J. V. N. Ingram, *A Check List of American Eighteenth Century Newspapers in the Library of Congress;* A. Matthews *Bibliographical Notes on Boston Newspapers, 1704–1780;* F. W. Scott, *Newspapers and Periodicals of Illinois, 1814–1879;* L. H. Weeks and E. M. Bacon, *An Historical Digest of the Provincial Press.*

The names of many papers begun in France during the years 1848–1852 are especially significant in recording contemporaneous conditions not only in France but elsewhere,—*La Californie Agricole, Le Courrier de San-Francisco.* See E. G. Swem, ed., *French Newspapers of 1848–50* in the Virginia State Library; E. Hatin, *Bibliographie historique et critique de la presse périodique française; Curiosités révolutionnaires. Les Journaux rouges.*

Napoleon I had earlier protested against the name *Citoyen français* as being too democratic and it became the *Courrier français; Les Debats* became the *Journal de l'Empire.*—H. Welschinger, *La Censure sous le premier Empire,* pp. 88, 93.

[4] J. A. O'Shea, *Leaves from the Life of a Special Correspondent,* I, 258.

[5] I. N. P. Stokes, *Iconography of Manhattan Island,* II, 419.

[6] Theophila Carlile Campbell, *The Battle of the Press,* p. 5.

The name of a paper varies in different countries at different times. The early English newspapers were most frequently named *Mercury*, with some qualifying appellation. During the French Revolution, the favorite French name for a newspaper was *Journal*, while *Zeitung* is the most common name in Germany. Again, it is its desired clientele that determines the name of a periodical,—the *Gentleman's Magazine* appealed to the reading public, the *Athenaeum* to those who wished counsel, and the *Knickerbocker* and the *New England Magazine* to sectional interests.

Not only does the newspaper have its own business name, but it does not escape the tendency of acquiring from external sources the nickname that to others describes its personality. The London *Times* was for many years synonymous with "The Thunderer," in allusion to an editorial by Edward Sterling; the *Daily Telegraph* became "Jupiter Junior;" the London *Morning Post* was long known as "Jeames," from the importance it attached to news in high life; the *Morning Herald* and the *Standard* when owned by the same proprietor used to appeal to each other as independent authorities and were spoken of as "Mrs. Harris" and "Sairy Gamp." *Fraser's Magazine* was called "Regina" by its admirers, as *Blackwood's* became "Maga" to its owners and contributors. Disraeli in *Vivian Grey* nicknamed the *Quarterly* "The Attack-All Review," while the *Edinburgh* scarcely lived up to the name he gave it of "Praise-All Review." C. D. Warner dubbed *The Nation* "The Weekly Judgment Day," while the *Vossische Zeitung* has been aptly called "Aunt Voss." *The Reporter*, started in Kilmarnock about 1831, was quickly called by the public *The Wee Cannon* "in consequence of the noise and effect of its report." [7] In college journalism the *Daily Princetonian* was called the *Printsanything*, and the *Harvard Crimson* was dubbed the *Crimesown* by the rival comic papers of Princeton and Harvard.

The counterpart is found in the names given by the press to different sets of men whose interest in the public welfare has not been unquestioned. *The Nation* began referring to the members of the old Republican machine as "the Boys," later they were designated as "Johnnies," "Jakes," and "Mikes," and still later

---

[7] J. Paterson, *Autobiographical Reminiscences*, p. 109.

reference was made to them as "engaged in their Jakery and Mikery,"—a course "most effective in bringing that kind of political activity into disrepute." [8]

The emblem of a newspaper in still another way indicates its personality. These emblems may illustrate the name of the paper, as the *World*, the *Globe*, or the *Sun;* or a characteristic occupation or feature of the locality, as hunting and fishing equipment become the emblem of the *Boonville Herald* and *Adirondack Tourist*, and miners' tools for a Pennsylvania paper, or the mission belfrey that belongs appropriately to the *Daily News* of Santa Barbara, and a view of the surf to the Santa Cruz *Surf*. The products of the country, prairie scenes, characteristic city buildings, the building in which the paper is published, or the printing press are all utilized as emblems. Often these emblems represent abstract ideas, as the scales of justice, the horn of plenty, the American eagle, a national, state, or municipal shield or coat of arms, or they may be scenes that never were on land or sea. Whatever form the emblem may take, it adds one more noteworthy feature to the personality of the press.

The headline in the American newspaper is perennially discovered by foreign travellers and is deemed by them the most striking feature of the American press.[9] Yet it is not necessary to turn to visiting tourists from Europe to realize how essentially the headline measures the good taste or the bad taste of the press. The headline may be a space filler, as where twelve lines of headlines are placed over two lines of news; it may be absolutely misleading, as when it reads, "Say women sold votes" while the item it heads states that three women and 1100 men were indicted for vote-selling; it may feature the least important part of a political victory, as when it proclaims the election of a certain governor—a foregone conclusion—but does not mention the passage of a hard-fought-for amendment to the Constitution; it may feature doubtful items as certain; it may be "question-begging;" it may wilfully misrepresent, it may misinterpret, it may be dubbed "scare," "screaming," or "screeching;" headlines may

[8] J. B. Bishop, "Personal Recollections of E. L. Godkin," *Century Magazine*, September, 1902, 64: 694–700.
[9] Stephane Dubost, letter to Marcel Complans, quoted in full in the New York *Evening Post*, November 21, 1908.

be so exchanged as to place the account of a dignified Friends' meeting under a "scare" movie headline, while a flippant movie story appears under the headline of a religious service; the headline may commit unnumbered sins of inaccuracy, but it is, after all, its sins against good taste, correct spelling, grammar, and syntax, and its general cruelty to language that make the headline so important an index of the personality of the newspaper. The chief virtue of the headline from the point of view of the press itself is not, indeed, accuracy, but ability to catch the attention of the reader; it is affected by the conditions under which it is read, and it is in part explained by the physical conditions of its readers; it is read in the subway or on the elevated road, probably by readers standing in an uncomfortable position after a wearying day; the evening edition has headlines in larger type and in blacker ink than those of the morning edition of the same paper.[10] This must explain, although not excuse, the flauntingly bad taste of the headline, and it indicates that the headline, like every other part of the newspaper, has its own history.[11] But the headline, whatever apologies may be made for its bad manners and its offences against good taste, remains one of the clearest illustrations of the temper of a newspaper,—of its sensational character or of a restrained desire to indicate the nature of the news beneath it but without exploiting it.

The price of a newspaper is something of an index to its personality. The paper may be aristocratic in its tendencies and like the London *Times* in its earlier days seek its clientele only among those influential through birth, wealth, or intellect. Its price may correspond to its social ideals,—the London *Times* was at first 5*d*; the abolition of the newspaper stamp duty in 1855 caused the price to be lowered to 4*d*; later it was reduced to 3*d*; in 1914 to 1*d*; but it has returned to 3*d*. G. A. Sala reports that objec-

---

[10] Suggested by E. M. Rushmore.

G. K. Chesterton says that editors print everything possible in large capital letters, not because it is startling, but because it is soothing,—as children are taught to read through the use of large letters.—"The Mildness of the Yellow Press," *Heretics*, pp. 113–117.

Burges Johnson has a good word for the headline in "Impression and Expression," *The Well of English, and the Bucket*, pp. 53–82.

[11] Morris Van Vliet, "Fifty Years of War Headlines," New York *Evening Post*, August 8, 1914.

tion was made to his frequenting an informal club of newspaper men because he was known to be connected with a penny paper, and that for the same reason his presence was protested against in the room where men connected with the aristocratic high-priced papers met to write up their notes after the speeches made at public dinners.[12] Reduction in price may indicate a desire for a larger circulation or a wish to reach a different class of readers. The business manager may fall far short of paying for the cost of production with the receipts of circulation and therefore depend unduly on advertisements to make up a threatened deficit, or he may secure a nice balance of forces between all the factors of income and outgo and maintain at the same time the lowest price, the largest circulation, and the largest dividends.

A sense of proportion or a lack of it enters into the personality of the newspaper, and this affects both the amount of space given to the questions of the moment and the position in the paper accorded them. One paper may give twelve columns to a scandal and another dismiss it in twelve lines. One paper may feature the latest discovery in science, and another a wedding in high life or below stairs. "A Scripps newspaper has in [the preferred] position an account of a working men's strike in Sweden, a Hearst newspaper a breach of promise suit, an Ochs newspaper a railway merger." [13] Times may also change and the same papers may within a comparatively short period show an increase in the proportion of space given to gossip, scandal, and sport and a proportionate decrease in news concerning religion, science, literature, and art.[14]

Changing standards of conventionality affect the personality of a newspaper. Edward Dicey tells us that among the unwritten laws of early journalism were those that every leading article should have three paragraphs, that it should be not less than one and one-fourth columns in length or more than one and one-half columns, that under no pretence should the name of another

---

[12] *Life and Adventures*, I, 333–334.
[13] Will Irwin, *Collier's Weekly*, April 1, 1911.
[14] J. G. Speed, "Do Newspapers Now Give the News?" *Forum*, August, 1893, 15: 705–711.—The author gives tables showing the comparative amount of space given thirteen selected subjects in 1881 and in 1893 by the New York *Tribune, World, Times*, and *Sun*.

paper be mentioned, and the repetition of the same word in the same sentence was a grave literary offense.[15] "The new type of paper," says the London Correspondent of the New York *Evening Post*,[16] "belongs to the era of 'breakfast foods'." The London morning papers, sold at a penny, are well arranged to give the gist of the news to the clerk who goes to the city every morning and spends about half an hour on train or street car,—he can read the important news in that time and leave nothing demanding further attention.

The cartoon or the photograph may fill a large part of the front page when there is a dearth of telegraphic news. When the office force is "short," plate matter may be used, or an interview sought with some person of local prominence. The various expedients used in the presence of the emergencies that arise in every occupation indicate the range of the paper's versatility and adaptability.

These are certain external features of the press that like the dress of an individual indicate the crudities or the refinements of taste that repel or attract different classes of readers.[17] But other elements enter into the personality of a newspaper that are comparable in the individual to good manners and an ability to be "a good mixer." With all the discordant elements in the press to-day there is a courtesy evident that was often lamentably lacking in the press of an earlier date. "If there was ever a Yellow Press in England," says Scott-James, "in the vilest sense of the term, it was not in the twentieth century, but in the years between the death of Cromwell and the accession of Charles II, when a disorganized public opinion was being played upon and exploited by the most scandalous journalism which this country has ever known."[18]

The Covent-Garden Journal was bitterly attacked by its opponents and in the prolonged controversy that ensued it was almost literally a case of "Fielding against the field," and reasonableness in controversy was flung to the winds.[19] At a much

---

[15] Edward Dicey, "Journalism New and Old," *Fortnightly Review*, May, 1905, n. s. 77: 904–918.

[16] New York *Evening Post*, January 28, 1911.

[17] See E. S. Grew, "The Physiognomy of Newspapers," *Anglo-Saxon Review*, June, 1901, 9: 222–231.

[18] R. A. Scott-James, *The Influence of the Press*, p. 64.

[19] Henry Fielding, *The Covent-Garden Journal*, edited by G. E. Jensen, 2 vols., 1915.

later date Vizetelly gives an account of the ribald press of London about 1840 dealing "with the shadiest subjects, including some which no publication of to-day would even hint at." [20] The correspondence of many journalists shows much plain speaking of each other's sins on the part of newspapers and magazines and a lack of those personal and professional amenities fortunately found in the periodical literature of to-day.[21]

It was long the fashion to charge pre-eminence in this personal abuse to the newspapers of America, and Albany Fonblanque wrote in 1842, "Our Press is just now ringing with attacks upon the Americans for supporting a trade in slander, and with what consistency can we throw the stone of this vulgar vice, the foul appetite of the craftiest minds, while so much of it exist in our community? It is as much the policy of Society to protect the reputations of its members as to protect their lives, their persons, and their properties." [22] This sentiment provoked from Dickens the heated comment, "I was very sorry to see in the postscript to the last 'Examiner' something that careless readers (a large class) will easily twist into a comparison between the English and American newspapers. Bad as many of our journals are, Heaven knows, they cannot be set against each other for a moment, and decency is not befriended by any effort to excuse the transatlantic blackguardism, which is so intense that I seriously believe words cannot describe it." [23]

De Tocqueville found that "The characteristics of the American journalist consist in an open and coarse appeal to the passions of the populace; and he habitually abandons the principles of political science to assail the characters of individuals, to track them into private life, and to disclose all their weaknesses and errors." [24] To the fastidious Matthew Arnold the personality of the American press seemed most repellant,—"their badness and ignobleness are beyond belief." "They are the worst feature in

[20] H. Vizetelly, *Glances Back Through Seventy Years*, I, chap. IX.

[21] Illustrations may be found in *Passages from the Correspondence of Rufus W. Griswold*, edited by W. M. Griswold.

[22] *The Life and Labours of Albany Fonblanque*, edited by E. B. de Fonblanque, p. 447.

[23] *Idem.*

[24] Alexis de Tocqueville, *Democracy in America*, I, 200.

the life of the United States," he says, and he writes from Stockbridge, apropos of his speedy return to England, "the great relief will be to cease seeing the American newspapers." [25] It was apparently only Edward Dicey among English readers of the American press that found that "one great merit" was its "comparative freedom from private personality." [26]

But even American journalists themselves deprecated, as did Walt Whitman, the tone of the American press, the presence of petty personalities in it, and the assumption that it was a matter of moment "whether A eats roast beef or Graham bread, or whether he understands a given Scripture text this way or that way." [27]

The newspaper often yields to ill temper and vindictiveness and relentlessly persecutes men and measures to such an extent that the persecution acts as a boomerang against the newspaper itself. The personal attack may be against Gladstone or Disraeli, Asquith or Lloyd George, Roosevelt or Bryan, free trade or protective tariff, prohibition or equal suffrage, but whatever the object of the attack the temptation, not always resisted, has been to deal in personalities that infallibly record the bad manners of the attacking newspaper.

The newspaper may have a personality characterized by a narrow provincialism or sectionalism that merges into jealousy. The first number of the *Southern Literary Messenger* asks in its first article, August, 1834, "Are we to be doomed forever to a kind of vassalage to our northern neighbor—a dependence for our literary food upon our bretheren, whose superiority in all the great points of character,—in valor, eloquence and patriotism, we are no wise disposed to admit?" and Southern writers constantly complained that the Northern papers did not notice their works. [28]

Newspapers may be characterized by independence of views,—an independence either real or simulated. They may be fairly independent in politics, but six weeks before the November elec-

[25] *Letters of Matthew Arnold*, edited by G. W. E. Russell, II, *passim*.
[26] *Six Months in the Federal States*, I, 47.
[27] Walt Whitman, Brooklyn *Eagle*, February 26, 1847, cited by C. Rodgers and J. Black, in *The Gathering of the Forces*, III, 253-255.
[28] See numerous letters in *Passages from the Correspondence of Rufus W. Griswold*.

tions they may become uncompromisingly Democratic or Republican. It has been pointed out by Horace White that "independent journalism" is a phrase "sometimes used to signify mere neutrality between political parties. A newspaper of this kind aims to offend neither party, so that it may gain patronage from both. That is not independence. An independent journal must offend both parties, and all parties, or must hold itself ready to offend when they go wrong." [29] It is a pseudo-independence that sometimes explains the effort of the press to square the circle,—a paper may make much of its having discarded all liquor advertisements, but it may give entire pages to showing the evil results of prohibition.

Another feature of the newspaper that forms an element in its personality is found in "letters to an editor." [30] If it is not the ambition of every man to be known as the one "who has written more letters to *The Times* than any other living person," at least a large number of readers at one time or another write to the press, usually in approval or adverse criticism of its policy. These columns and pages "given up to 'letters to the editor' have come to be considered as among the most useful and interesting in any newspaper." [31] Sir Charles Walston goes still farther and considers the "Letters to The Times"—the occasional publication of discussions by those qualified to deal with important questions— "one of the characteristic and undying achievements of the paper." [32] They are, to the student of history, one of the most accurate gauges of the development of the press, and he agrees with Walter Besant when he says, "The student of London middle-class opinions in the year 1892 can best learn them from the

[29] Address at the complimentary luncheon tendered the editorial staff of the *Evening Post*, November 16, 1901.
This address should be compared with the review of G. S. Merriam, *Life and Times of Samuel Bowles, The Nation*, December 31, 1885, 41: 553-554.
[30] *The Gentleman's Magazine* opened its volume for 1737 with many "letters to the editor."
[31] The New York *Evening Post*, March 27, 1915.
[32] Charles Walston, *Truth*, p. 147.
Among the numerous letters appearing in the London *Times* that have had historic interest may be cited those of Lord Acton, Gladstone, and Archbishop Manning on the Vatican Decrees and the question as to how far Roman Catholics owed allegiance to the State when the doctrines of the State and the Church were at variance.—*The Times*, November 9, 24, December 12, 1874.

daily correspondence of two London papers." And "it is still, too, in letters to the editor of *The Times* that one finds the most important questions discussed by leading men of affairs for which the correspondence columns of no other paper have an equal attraction." [33]

If at one time "the old rule was to see that the Whig dogs got the worst of it, in letters as well as editorials," the principle to-day is to consider that these columns "furnish a kind of forum in which men of diverse views can meet and produce their arguments." The press itself often invites letters from prominent men when questions of great moment are brought before the public and it thus is able to record public opinion that in turn may be interpreted through the editorial columns. Even the so-called "correspondence dodge" has had its uses, and special papers, like the London *Daily Telegraph*, have been very successful in finding a subject that appeals to large numbers of persons, as, "What shall we do with our boys?" and opening its columns to those who wish to discuss it. These letters to the editor have not only proved a happy expedient for arousing interest during the proverbial "silly season" of the newspaper, but they become an important record of current opinion as well as of the personality of the newspaper.

The newspaper is fast disappearing that prints only the letters that are agreeable to the editor or that reflect his personal views, since the press realizes that it "would be striking at its own life if it were to seek to discourage or repress the fullest expression of opinion;" by adopting this policy the press has become in a sense undreamed of in its early days a genuine organ of public opinion.[34]

These letters to the editor have become a regular feature of the American and the English press and hence are one element in their personality that differentiates the press of these countries from that of France and other Continental countries.

[33] London correspondent of the New York *Evening Post*, January 28, 1911.
[34] One of the most marked changes noted in the method of dealing with these letters has been the change that has taken place in the captions under which they are printed. Unfailing good humor now characterize them, even when the letters are most virulent in their attacks on the paper where they are printed. A particularly vitriolic attack on the New York *Evening Post* was printed by it under the caption "He Doesn't Like The Post." Countless illustrations of this change have been noted.

Akin to letters to the editor are the "answers to correspondents," the prototype of which Jebb finds to be the oracles of ancient days. "Any one," he says, "who reads the columns of Answers to Correspondents in a prudently conducted journal will recognize the principal types of oracle. . . . In editing an oracle, it was then, as it still is, of primary importance not to make bad mistakes." [35]

But the more immediate and direct ancestor of the "answers to correspondents" was *The Athenian Gazette*, a publication that originated in the fertile brain of the versatile John Dunton. The idea seemed to him of such importance that he remarked to his friends who were with him when it occurred to him, "Well, Sirs, I have a thought I will not exchange for fifty guineas." [36] The paper was intended to answer all questions asked it by those thirsting for information in regard to love and marriage, history and philosophy, religion and politics, nature and science, and all other subjects on earth, in the heavens above, and in the waters under the earth. It evidently met the long-felt want, for Dunton says, "We were immediately overloaded with *Letters;* and sometimes I have found several hundreds for me at Mr. Smith's Coffeehouse in Stocks Market, where we usually met to consult matters."

The name of the paper was soon changed to *The Athenian Mercury*, later the questions and answers were collected in four volumes under the title *The Athenian Oracle. Being an Entire Collection of All the Valuable Questions and Answers in the Old Athenian Mercuries*, and a still later selection in one volume,[37]—so perennial is the curiosity in regard to the curiosities of the past.

Imitation is the sincerest flattery and Dunton soon quarrelled with Defoe saying, "This man has done me a sensible wrong, by interloping with my 'Question-Project', Losers may have leave to speak; and I here declare, I am 200*l* the worse for De Foe's clogging my 'Question-Project'. His answering Questions Weekly

[35] R. C. Jebb, "Ancient Organs of Public Opinion," *Essays and Addresses*, p. 157.
[36] *The Life and Errors of John Dunton*, I, 188. Dunton's own naïve account of his "darling Project" should be read in order to appreciate fully the conditions that made the questions and answers so popular.
[37] *The Athenian Oracle*, edited by John Underhill, 1892.

put a stop to my 'Monthly Oracle': for, though his answers were false and impertinent, (and for that reason his interloping continued but a few weeks) yet, being published every Tuesday, they ruined my 'Monthly Oracle'." [38]

These facts have been stated to indicate that almost as old as the newspaper itself is that part of it that makes special claim to wisdom. The first Harmsworth paper, called *Answers to Correspondents* (and later *Answers*), was dated June 2, 1888, and the first number of *The Athenian Gazette*, March 17, 1689-90. The very nature of the newspaper lends itself most readily to this most pronounced element in its personality,—omniscience.

Omniscience is the twin of infallibility and this is another characteristic of the newspaper's personality. "In America apology in journalism is unknown" is the somewhat flippant remark of a visiting journalist,[39] ignoring the fact that its very nature may prevent an apology not only in the American newspaper, but in the newspaper of every country and of every time. "The demands of individuals," says Munroe Smith, "for the correction of misstatements or for the withdrawal of misjudgments are unreasonable demands which the newspapers are compelled to resist. Any considerable concessions to these demands would be distinctly injurious to the essential interests of journalism." [40] And he further sums up the situation in saying, "It is well known that doctrines expressing policies tend to harden into dogmas presented as truths. With this tendency every student of government or of law or of religion is familiar. To this peril journalism has also succumbed. The Dogma of Journalistic Inerrancy converts a maxim of policy into a tenet of faith."

It is, however, very obvious that a great change has of late years taken place in the press, and that if it does not yet acknowledge its errors on questions of public policy, it is at least ready to apologize for incorrect statements made with reference to individuals. The New York *Tribune*, for example, now carries the statement that it "will be glad to receive and publish corrections of inaccuracies in its columns." Such corrections it often publishes.

[38] *Life and Errors of John Dunton*, II, 423.
[39] Harry Furniss, *The Confessions of a Caricaturist*, I, vii.
[40] "The Dogma of Journalistic Inerrancy," *North American Review*, February, 1908, 187: 240-254.

The newspaper, like the individual, has its own sense of humor that changes from generation to generation and that undergoes a sea change in passing from one country to another. The early type was largely that of the joke, and Charles Lamb, writing in 1831 of "Newspapers Thirty-Five Years ago," says that "In those days every Morning Paper, as an essential retainer to its establishment, kept an author, who was bound to furnish daily a quantum of witty paragraphs. Sixpence a joke—and it was thought pretty high too—was Dan Stuart's settled remuneration in these cases. The chat of the day, scandal, but, above all, *dress*, furnished the material. The length of no paragraph was to exceed seven lines. Shorter they might be, but they must be poignant."

Of his own efforts at sixpenny joke-making, he writes ruefully: "No Egyptian taskmaster ever devised a slavery like to that, our slavery. . . . Half a dozen jests in a day (bating Sundays too), why, it seems nothing! We make twice the number every day of our lives as a matter of course, and claim no Sabbatical exemptions. But then they come into our head. But when the head has to go out to them—when the mountain must go to Mahomet—

Reader, try it for once, only for one short twelve-month." [41]

"But the fashion of jokes, with all other things, passes away," and the joke was in large part superseded by the professional humorist who through literary form or through cartoon has lent his own individuality to that of the newspaper. Artemus Ward and Bill Nye, Josh Billings and Doesticks, Nasby, Alden, Mr. Dooley, Mark Twain and Lowell, Nast, and the galaxy of *Punch* humorists have all been teachers and with more or less seriousness of purpose have attempted through humor of pen or pencil to convey truths unacceptable in other form.

The individual humorist has been followed by the "colyumist" who, with many of his contemporary cartoonists, becomes not a teacher but an entertainer.[42] The jokemaker, the humorous writer

[41] *Works*, Edited by W. Macdonald, II, 136–147.
[42] Different origins of the humorous column have been noted. Julian Street thinks it probably began in 1885 in the Chicago *Tribune* where H. T. E. White called a column "Lakeside Musings." Five years later this column was taken over by Eugene Field.—*Abroad at Home*, pp. 156–163.
The fullest discussions of the humorous column noted are those of A.

or illustrator, the editor of the "colyum" may each in turn change from teacher or entertainer to the passive onlooker who records the pleasantries of every-day life; the paragraph develops into the column, the column into the page, the page into the syndicated article; and this in turn degenerates into the colored supplement that "reduced to first principles, therefore, is not humor, but simply a supply created in answer to a demand, hastily produced by machine methods and hastily accepted by editors too busy with other editorial duties to examine it intelligently." [43] But in whatever form the element of humor enters into the newspaper, whether it relies on misspelled English, or on dialect, or on its own innate qualities; whether it creates a Mr. Dooley or a Hennessy, a Senator Sorghum or a Farmer Corntossle, a Mrs. Partington, or a Dulcinea, it is an important contributory factor to the personality of a newspaper.[44]

A still further development of the column must be noted. It has been during the recent war, and it is to-day, the part of the newspaper where a writer can in seriousness, without the cloak of a jest, and without fear or favor express opinions quite at variance with the conventional opinions held by the public or possibly by the newspaper itself.[45]

The personality of a newspaper is further disclosed by the emphasis it places on various questions or by omission of them. Its column of original, contributed or clipped jokes and humorous articles appeal to one class of readers, its pages of society news appeal to others; while special attention to education, to real estate transactions, to the theatre, to art, to music, to sports, to various other permanent public interests indicates an apprecia-

---

McD. Stoddart, "Journalism's Radium, the Colyum," *Independent*, February 16, 1918, 93: 274, 289–293; C. L. Edson, *The Gentle Art of Columning*, with four prefaces written by four well-known "colyumists;" and editorial, "The Art of Columning," *Literary Review*, May 14, 1921.

[43] R. Bergengren, "The Humor of the Colored Supplement," *Atlantic Monthly*, August, 1906, 98: 269–273.

[44] The personality of a humorous paper like *Punch* is so strong that none of its numerous imitations has had more than a brief existence. M. H. Spielmann notes the *Punch à Paris*, Berlin *Punsch*, Munich *Punsch*, Y *Punch Cymraeg*, Shanghai *Punch*, Japan *Punch*, Japanese *Punch*, Parsee *Punch*, Sydney *Punch*, Queensland *Punch*, *Mac Punch*, and the *Manx Cat.*— "The Rivals of 'Punch'," *National Review*, July, 1895, 25: 654–666.

[45] See C. Morley on Bouck White, *New York Evening Post*, June 2, 1921; "The Conning Tower" conducted by F. P. A. has also illustrated this.

tion of the importance of these interests and a desire to promote them. It is true that occasionally such interest is a factitious one and is feigned only with the ulterior object of increasing its circulation among those concerned with these questions, but even this indicates in itself another side of the personality of the newspaper.

"Special editions" issued by women, or by an educational institution, or in the interests of the Red Cross movement, or a new tuberculosis hospital, or some local charity all throw side lights on the personality of the newspaper.

Essential differences are found between the country and the metropolitan press. Not more than one-tenth of the newspapers published in America are said to be published in the larger cities.[46] The country weekly, whose editor is probably the leading man in the community and whose general attitude is one of kindliness and affectionate goodwill towards his fellow-citizens, is far different from the great city daily with its impersonal, coldly critical, masterful personality. Even in small ways the differences are marked. The metropolitan papers disclose an exoteric interest in life and give news in regard to what prominent citizens of their communities are doing elsewhere, where they are traveling, and the social attentions shown them. Special correspondents are assigned to summer resorts, winter resorts, watering places, and other localities sought by the leisure class, and the social life there is reported for the stay-at-homes. The opposite attitude is taken by the provincial press and this serves as a medium of communication among the neighboring places and as a clearing house for the local news of all the surrounding country villages where it maintains a large staff of local correspondents.

The suburban newspaper is often disclosed by its omission of many subjects that are discussed in full by the neighboring metropolitan dailies and presumably read by the entire community.

Marked contrasts are found between the daily, the weekly, the monthly and the quarterly, and between the representatives of these classes in the different countries. No more important illustration of this can be found than becomes evident in examining long runs of periodicals, or extended files of newspapers. The

[46] H. F. Harrington, and T. T. Frankenberg, *Essentials in Journalism,* p. 210.

varying personality of the German newspapers has been signifi-
cantly described by Gowans;[47] Massingham has pointed out the
differing characteristics of the representatives of the London
press;[48] Goldwin Smith has felicitously described the *Saturday
Review* in saying that "Its tone during its palmy days was epi-
curean and this was the source of its popularity in the circles by
which it was chiefly supported. It was said by us that whereas
with the generation of the Reform Bill, everything had been new,
everything had been true, and everything had been of the
highest importance, with us nothing was new, nothing was true,
and nothing was of any importance." [49]

Something of the personality of the editor himself or of his
immediate ancestors may enter into the personality of the newspaper and unconsciously color its general attitude towards questions of the day,—high courage and fearlessness must be the
expected characteristic of one paper, conventionality and respect
for established authority is looked for in another.

But the personality of the paper as a whole is not to be confused with that of its editor,—it has a personality of its own
quite apart from that of any individual connected with it. It is
the personality of the paper as a whole that undoubtedly appeals
to that of its readers, or alienates them from it, even when the
editor becomes the scapegoat;—Earl Gower wrote to C. K.
Sharpe under date of January 28, 1809, "I hear that two hundred
copies of the 'Edinburgh Review' [have] been countermanded in
consequence of the democratical principles of Mr. Brougham in

---

[47] A. L. Gowans, *A Month's German Newspapers: Being representative
extracts from those of the memorable month of December, 1914.*

[48] H. W. Massingham, *The London Daily Press,* 1892.

The New York *Nation* in 1880 published an interesting series of nine
articles on the characteristics of English journals at that time.—July 22,
1880—October 28, 1880, vol. 31. A difference of opinion in regard to the
characterization of the London *Times* was expressed by "An Ex-Member
of the 'Times' Staff" in *The Nation,* September 9, 1880, 31: 185.

Somewhat later J. Reinach drew up "a guide to the French press" in
which he characterized for the English its leading representatives.—"Parisian Newspapers," *Nineteenth Century,* September, 1882, 12: 347–360.

A clever parody on the English press of the day is found in *All the Papers.
A Journalistic Revue* (1914).

[49] *Reminiscences,* p. 166.

W. L. Cook treats a cognate phrase of the subject in "Character in
Newspapers," *University of Iowa Extension Bulletin,* No. 62. 1920.

the last number," [50] an interesting illustration that the impulse to "stop my paper" is not of to-day.

The consideration of the personality of a newspaper also includes the question as to how far the paper as a whole is normal and how far it must be deemed eccentric or abnormal. A long list could be made of newspapers like "the lonesomest newspaper in America,"—published thirty-five miles from the nearest railroad station; the smallest daily newspaper in America; a freak newspaper printed with ink containing phosphorus so that the paper could be read in the dark; a paper printed with non-poisonous ink on thin sheets of dough which could be eaten; papers published by the patients of hospitals for the insane; newspapers in the extreme north that are published once a year; newspapers for theatre-goers that go to press at 10:30 P. M.; the "continuous-per-formance" newspaper published "at all hours of the day and night that conditions and the development of news may warrant;" newspapers of the Cherokees, "said to be the only Indian tribe in the world whose language has been developed to a point where its own characters can be used;" papers printed on yellow silk as was the oldest Chinese newspaper,—all these are but a few of the variants from the conventional that have been noted.[51] The historian may have a passing interest in these peculiar issues, recording as they do the existence of peculiarities in the human mind that find expression through these channels, but he must regard them only as curiosities having a psychological rather than an historical value.

Anonymity as an element in the personality of the press usually centers around the question of the signed or the unsigned review,

[50] *Letters from and to Charles Kirkpatrick Sharpe*, I, 359. The number referred ·to contained an article on "Don Cevallos on the Usurpation of Spain."

[51] One of the most interesting of these unusual papers is the first number of the *Sitka Times*, September 19, 1868. It was written by hand, nearly all of it in red ink. Reduced in size, it is reproduced in *The Pahasapa Quarterly* (Rapid City, S. D.), April, 1916.

The London *Sun* printed in letters of gold an account of the coronation of Queen Victoria in 1838.

The New York *Independent* printed a limited but sumptuous edition on white silk in honor of its twenty-first anniversary, December 2, 1869. Presentation copies were sent to the crowned heads of Europe, and at least two of them have found their way back to America.

but it reaches far beyond this region. The newspaper was at first entirely unassociated with the name of any individual except that of the printer. Nearly a hundred years after the appearance of the first English newspaper, Swift was horrified because in a bill concerning the press "there was a clause inserted, (whether industriously with design to overthrow it,) that the author's name and place of abode should be set to every printed book, pamphlet, or paper; to which I believe no man, who has the least regard to learning, would give his consent." [52]

It is a far cry from the anonymity of Swift's time to a condition that Burges Johnson has aptly termed "the 'star' development in the press as well as on the stage." Columns and pages of articles and contributions of every description are signed by the name of special correspondents, and special reporters. The name of the local country reporter heads the items he sends in to the press of the nearest small city. Even advertisements are not infrequently signed by the name of the writer. Newspapers advertise their own claims to superiority over their rivals on the ground that certain well-known authors are under contract to write exclusively for their columns, that a prominent sportsman will edit their sporting page, that eminent critics will furnish the dramatic and musical criticism, and a professional humorist will be in charge of the "colyum." Practically the only parts of the paper that are not signed are the editorial, the despatches of the Associated Press, and the contributions of the local reporter.

The result of the change is that "the writer of signed articles is really a pamphleteer, who uses the newspaper as a vehicle just as in other days he would use a publisher," [53] while the personality of the newspaper as a purveyor of news is dissipated through the increasing importance attached to the individual news gatherers. Signature emphasizes the importance of the journalist and explains why in France the query is always, "What does a certain writer say", while anonymity tends to increase the importance of the journal and in England for so many years led to the question, "What does *The Times* say?"

Different and somewhat opposing influences have brought

[52] "History of the Four Last Years of the Queen," *Works*, V, 149–150.
[53] G. B. Dibblee, *The Newspaper*, p. 104.

about this change. The personal ambition and the material welfare of authors have been the strongest of them—motives pressed by Émile Zola in his address in favor of signature before the Institute of Journalists in London, September, 1893. "To my thinking," he urges, "when a writer does not sign his work, and becomes a mere wheel in a great machine, he ought to share the income earned by that machine. Have you retiring pensions for your aged journalists? After they have devoted their anonymous labour to the common task, year after year, is the bread of their old age assured them? If they signed their work, surely they would find their reward elsewhere; they would have laboured for themselves. But when they have given their all, even their fame, strict justice demands that they should be treated like those old servants whose whole life has been spent in the service of the same family." [54]

The subordination of the press to the welfare of the individuals connected with it has seemed to many a case of "putting the cart before the horse" and to be less an argument for signature than a plea for old age pensions. In truth, the French law requiring that every article on politics, philosophy or religion should be signed and prescribing heavy penalities for its violation had been aimed, not at the welfare of individual journalists, but at the suppression of the press. When the Marquis de Tinguy proposed the "law of hate" in 1850, he replied to its opponents by saying, "You tell me my plan will mutilate the Press, destroy its influence, take from it its individuality? But that is precisely what I want." M. Laboulie seconded it and said, "We must finish with journalism, as we have finished with barricades." [55]

That this end was in a measure achieved is evident from Nassau Senior who asked M. Beaumont how the law prohibiting anonymous journalism was received. "Better than was expected," replied M. Beaumont. "In the first place, it is much eluded. Every journal has some confidential subaltern whose

[54] E. A. Vizetelly, Émile Zola, Novelist and Reformer, pp. 330–331. An authorized translation of the paper is given in the London Times, September 23, 1893.

[55] James Macintyre, "Théophraste Renaudot: Old Journalism and New," Nineteenth Century, October, 1893, 34: 596–604; E. Hatin, Histoire de la Presse en France, VIII, 630–632.

name is affixed to articles which the reader sees to be the work of a different hand. So far, indeed, as it is obeyed, the object of those who framed it, the diminution of the influence of the newspaper press, has been effected. The oracle loses half its force by losing its mystery. The world is glad to see weakened a power which has been so much abused. Many writers, too, are pleased to see their names in print." [56] While the "*loi Tinguy*" has now become obsolete, in the opinion of many the blight it brought on the French press still remains.[57]

The tendency towards signature and away from anonymity has evidently been to weaken the personality of the press, but it is less clear how far this weakening of personality has affected the authoritativeness of the press. Governments have sometimes compelled signature in order to regulate and therefore to weaken the authority of the press. Newspaper proprietors have encouraged signature for the sake of increasing circulation through the éclat given by distinguished names and to this extent they weaken the authoritativeness of the press. Journalists have almost unanimously come to favor signature but their reasons have apparently been very diverse. The early advocates of signature urged in its favor that in every other field anonymous information, counsel, or judgment was disregarded; that the press itself rejected anonymous communications; that the part taken by the press had come to be that of a judge rather than that of an advocate; [58] that it fostered a greater sense of responsibility on the part of writers; and that anonymity simply prolonged "the reign of the mighty 'we'." [59] Its later advocates have apparently been influenced by a desire for personal recognition of their work, but this very desire has carried "its besetting temptations of personal vanity" and has led journalists like

[56] *Journals in France and Italy*, I, 273, written from Paris, October 26, 1850.

[57] M. Biré says that the greater part of the French press vigorously opposed a law that they believed "blessait la presse au coeur."—But the law was defended by M. Nettement in *L'Opinion publique* where he first signed his name, July 25, 1850, and thereafter many times in each number. —E. Biré, *Alfred Nettement, sa vie et ses oeuvres*, p. 388.

[58] J. B. Kinnear, "Anonymous Journalism," *Contemporary Review*, July, 1867, 5: 324-339.

[59] T. Hughes, "Anonymous Journalism," *Macmillan's Magazine*, December, 1861, 5: 157-168.

Brodrick to accept with hesitation and with many qualifications the tendency away from anonymity.[60] Reinach also deprecated the effect of signature on the character of the journalist himself, believing that it developed individualism and *amour propre* and led to exaggeration and scandal, and that the press should encourage anonymity.[61]

It must also be remembered that many persons prefer to publish their articles anonymously because they write "to free their minds," rather than to influence public opinion. They realize that articles without a name attached to them are often not read and seldom attract notice, but since their object is attained by publication, this, to such writers, is immaterial.

To Schopenhauer the *status quo* was always black and he held that "Anonymity is the refuge for all literary and journalistic rascality. It is a practice which must be completely stopped. Every article, even in a newspaper, should be accompanied by the name of its author; and the editor should be made strictly responsible for the accuracy of the signature. The freedom of the press should be thus far restricted; so that what a man publicly

[60] G. C. Brodrick, *Memories and Impressions, 1831 to 1900*, pp. 135–142.
The special reasons that he gives seem to sum up the question particularly well. "I felt a satisfaction," he says, "in knowing that no reader, lighting upon an article of mine, could put it aside as the work of a young man with little experience or authority, but that, if he cared to read it at all, he must needs judge it upon its merits. This is, in my opinion, the supreme advantage of anonymous journalism. It seems to me quite right that periodicals should admit signed articles, and I now prefer myself to write under my own name; but when I remember all the rubbish which I have read with an eminent signature attached to it, probably commanding a fancy price and an immense audience, I realize how much is gained by compelling the public to read the comments of the Daily Press with a more or less open mind." While he was not so free to set forth every shade of his own innermost convictions as if he had been writing under his own name, he was not sure that his articles lost much in force by this limited suppression of individuality, with its besetting temptations of personal vanity, especially since "it is not always one's best thoughts which clamour most loudly for expression."
Edward L. Bulwer gives all the arguments used for anonymity and, by refuting them all, favors signature.—*England and the English*, II, 15–26.
Dibblee maintains that writers who prefer signature "are not permanently destined for journalism" and he favors anonymity both for the sake of the journalist himself and for the newspaper as well.—*The Newspaper*, pp. 102–104.
[61] J. Reinach, "Parisian Newspapers," *Nineteenth Century*, September, 1882, 12: 347–360.

proclaims through the far sounding trumpet of the newspaper, he should be answerable for, at any rate with his honor, if he has any; and if he has none, let his name neutralize the effect of his words. And since even the most insignificant person is known in his own circle, the result of such a measure would be to put an end to two-thirds of the newspaper lies, and to restrain the audacity of many a poisonous tongue." [62]

The varying opinions have been affected by national and political conditions to which the press has from time to time been obliged to conform, and they have also varied with the nature of the periodical. The daily and the weekly periodical press have accepted and favored signature only in part, while the monthly and quarterly magazines and reviews have come to accept it wholly. John Morley in his Valedictory as editor of the *Fortnightly Review* says that one of the chief experiments in founding this review had been that of the signed article, but that the change had "followed the course of most changes. It had not led to half either of the evils or of the advantages that its advocates and its opponents foretold." [63] Frederick Harrison also emphasized later the value of the principle of the signed article for which the *Nineteenth Century* had always stood, since it had thus afforded opportunity for free public discussion of important questions.[64] The compromise experiment was tried by *The Unpopular Review* of withholding the names of authors until the succeeding number, but after a trial of somewhat more than five years it was abandoned in favor of immediate signature.

This general acceptance of signature by the monthlies and the quarterlies has done much to dispel the somewhat pharisaical spirit shown by those who favored either side towards those who adopted the opposite custom. *Blackwood's Magazine* showed something of this "holier than thou" attitude when it wrote that "one of the superficial peculiarities of American Magazines is that the names of *all* contributors are generally paraded conspicuously on the cover, very few seeking even the guise of a pseudonym.

[62] *Essays*, Translated by T. B. Saunders, p. 347.
[63] "Valedictory," *Fortnightly Review*, October, 1882, n. s. 32: 511–521.
[64] Frederick Harrison, "The Nineteenth Century, No. D: A Retrospect. The First Fifty Volumes: 1877–1901," *Nineteenth Century and After*, October, 1918, 84: 785–796.

The number of 'most remarkable' men and women who thus display themselves in print is surprising." [65] It was Anthony Trollope who later found that while signature was good for the journalist himself, anonymity was better for the public.[66]

Yet if fame is sought by the journalist, it must never be forgotten that signature alone has never gained for articles the enduring fame that has been that of the author of the Letters of Junius.[67]

The question remains as to how far all of these many minds of many men, these varying practices of the press in different countries and of the press in a single country at different times affect the authoritativeness of the press from the point of view of the historian. The historian must prefer the signed article whenever the identification of the article adds authoritativeness, but when signature has encouraged the reporter or the correspondent to roam far afield and to add to his report of news his own interpretation of news he must prefer anonymity. No general principle can be deduced from the mass of conflicting opinions and customs, —each case must be decided on its merits. Even Zola, strongly as he urged signature as a personal advantage to the individual journalist, admitted "that the practice of signing political articles in France had undermined the authority of the press there, and tended to the destruction of parties; but at the same time, said he, it had to be recognized that much of the inspiriting ardor of the political battle sprang from that same practice. On the other hand, as it was the custom for English political journalists to write anonymously, it might be well if they continued to do so, in order to preserve the power and authority of their press." [68]

The question really in the last analysis resolves itself into one of national differences. "In France the modern newspaper press is what journalists have made it, in England it is a reflection of the public mind," [69]—a situation regarded with complacency by

[65] "The Periodical Literature of America," *Blackwood's Magazine*, January, 1848, 63: 106–112.

[66] "On Anonymous Literature," *Fortnightly Review*, July 1, 1865, 1: 491–498.

[67] See Byron, "The Vision of Judgment," stanzas 74–84.

[68] Résumé of address to the Institute of Journalists, E. Vizetelly, *Émile Zola*, p. 330.

[69] J. Macintyre, "Théophraste Renaudot: Old Journalism and New," *Nineteenth Century*, October, 1893, 34: 596–604.

Trollope who says that "in France the periodical press of the country is not allowed to guide public opinion." [70] In Germany where the derogatory ideas of Bismarck in regard to journalists have prevailed and where the government has long regulated the press, anonymity has for the most part prevailed,—the pen has been held by "the man higher up" and the name of the individual writer has mattered little. The historian must recognize the habit of signature in the French press, of anonymity in the English newspaper press and the early quarterlies and of signature in the later quarterlies and the monthlies, of an extreme tendency towards signature in all American periodicals, and of an inconspicuous anonymity in the German press. In each country, the place of the press varies and signature or anonymity varies with it.

It is also this question of the place of the press that must determine whether the press is an organ or a forum. If it is an organ, anonymity must be the rule; if it is a forum, signature is essential. Frederick Harrison in the five hundredth number of the *Nineteenth Century* emphasizes the value of the principle for which that review has always stood—the signed article, that has permitted "free public discussion by writers invariably signing their own names." He substantiates his claim that it is a forum by long classified lists of both Englishmen and foreigners distinguished in all fields who have written for it on different and opposing sides.[71] The question of the signed article in a periodical that aims to present all sides of disputed subjects is very different from the same question as it is presented to an organ of a particular political faith like the *National Review*. All of these phases of the subject are inherent in the press and all must be reckoned with.

These irreconcilable differences between writers who, for personal reasons, urge the signature of articles, and newspapers that, for the maintenance of authority, prefer anonymity affect materially the personality of the press. One element in its personality

[70] A. Trollope, "On Anonymous Literature," *Fortnightly Review*, July 1, 1865, 1: 491–498.
[71] "The Nineteenth Century, No. D: A Retrospect. The First Fifty Volumes: 1877–1901," *Nineteenth Century and After*, October, 1918, 84: 785–796.

vanishes into thin air as the individual writers emerge from the mass, yet to some the loss of this element is not without its compensations. Sir Wemyss Reid finds that worse than the egotism of journalism is its "wegotism"—a word said to have been invented by Sir William Harcourt. "No priesthood was ever more arrogant than this priesthood of the press," [72] he affirms, and yet the vanishing anonymity leaves a regret in the minds of many.[73]

Signature, in its relation to the press, may be compared to a bunch of grapes and anonymity to an orange. Each has its advantages and the historian must there rest the question.

"Have Papers Souls?" was a question once raised by Edmund Garrett.[74] His answer is inferential, but that newspapers have personality admits of no doubt. Efforts have been made to indicate the personality of the newspaper, and therefore to determine the character of its influence, by tabulating the relative proportions that various selected newspapers give to different classes of material, as news, opinion, crime, advertisements, or illustrations.[75] But since so many other elements are involved in the personality of the newspaper, this proportion, in and of itself,

[72] T. Wemyss Reid, "Some Reminiscences of English Journalism," *Nineteenth Century*, July, 1897, 42: 55–66.

[73] Thomas Arnold held an unusual view in regard to anonymity. He wrote to Sir Culling E. Smith, February 14, 1840: "It seems to me that the mischief of our newspapers mainly arises from the virulent language which men use while writing anonymously, and that, as far as example goes, this is better reproved by temperate writings which are also anonymous." He argues at some length that "no man, writing with his name, would allow himself to write in the style which newspaper writers often use;" that if moderate men write with their names, it is not strange that they write moderately; but if others observe the courtesies that their incognito would enable them to cast aside if they so desired, their letters have a salutary influence since "their moderation could scarcely be ascribed to anything but to their real disapprobation of scurrility and unfairness."—*Life and Correspondence*, II, 178–179.

[74] *The Cape Times*, February 18, 1896, cited in E. T. Cook, *Edmund Garrett*, p. 84, Note.

[75] *America and the Americans from a French Point of View*, pp. 267–285; F. Fenton, *The Influence of Newspaper Presentations upon the Growth of Crime and Other Anti-Social Activity;* J. E. Rogers, *The American Newspaper;* D. Wilcox, "The American Newspaper: A Study in Social Psychology," *Annals of the American Academy of Political and Social Science*, July, 1900, 16: 56–92; H. R. Elliot, "Ratio of News," *Forum*, March, 1888, 5: 99–107; T. R. Garth, "Statistical Study of the Contents of Newspapers," *School and Society*, January 22, 1916, 3: 140–144.

does not seem necessarily conclusive either as to personality or influence.

Matthew Arnold had a true appreciation of what is involved in personality, and while he may have been wrong in his interpretation of the personality of *The Times*, yet no clearer indication of its personality, as he understood it, can be found than his identification of it as a character in literature. "What is *The Times*," he asks, "but a gigantic Sancho Panza, to borrow a phrase of your friend Heine;—a gigantic Sancho Panza, following by an attraction he cannot resist that poor, mad, scorned, suffering, sublime enthusiast, the modern spirit; following it, indeed, with constant grumbling, expostulation, and opposition, with airs of protection, of compassionate superiority, with an incessant byplay of nods, shrugs, and winks addressed to the spectators; following it, in short, with all the incurable recalcitrancy of a lower nature, but still following it?"[76]

The historian can not evade the responsibility of at least attempting to understand the personality of the newspaper if he is to make use of it as historical material, for upon the personality of the newspaper as a whole largely depends its power for good or for evil.

[76] *Friendship's Garland*, p. 159.

CHAPTER III

GUARANTEES OF PROBABILITY

"Delane's Printing House Square period was coming to an end when, in 1875, his Paris correspondent, Blowitz, sent him news of the Prussian plan for reopening the war against France. Not till after a fortnight of the letter's arrival did its contents see the light. In the interval Delane had personally investigated the whole matter, had sent Chenery on a secret inquiry to Paris. The sensation known as the war scare of 1875 was thus only flashed upon the world when the editor and his aides-de-camp had sifted every statement in connection with it."—*T. H. S. Escott.*

NEWSPAPERS, when tested for evidences of their authoritativeness, show that their pages carry large numbers of general and of specific guarantees of their reliability that, with certain limitations, may re-assure the doubting historian in his contemplated use of them.

The first guarantee provided the student of American history is that given by the first amendment of the federal constitution that forbids Congress to make any law that shall abridge the freedom of the press,—a guarantee that is re-enforced by a similar statement made in the constitution of every state in the union. This secures to every periodical, at least in theory, under normal conditions, absolute freedom in the publication of news and in the expression of opinion so far as each periodical chooses to exercise this freedom. The guarantee is, it is true, a negative one. No editor is compelled to publish all the news received or to express an opinion on any and every subject, or to take sides in any controversy, but if he chooses to do so, no condign punishment follows. The guarantee does not protect the historian from a colorless, negative press, but it should protect him from a fawning subservient press that truckles to authority.

These federal and state provisions that guarantee freedom of the press throughout the country have their counterpart in laws restraining the press from printing false or malicious statements. It must be assumed not only that the press as a whole wishes to publish only trustworthy information, but that even the most sensational member of it hesitates to incur the notoriety and the expense involved in becoming the defendant in a suit for libel, yet these laws are necessary to afford an effective guarantee that all possible care has been taken not to make statements that are wilfully untrue. Libel laws, however, carry with them no guarantee of the wisdom of printing articles that may be true in themselves, but nevertheless may convey a wrong impression.[1] The historian may be reasonably sure of the truth of what he reads but he has no assurance that he has read the whole truth, or that the truth printed is in fair proportion to the truth not printed.

Laws concerning freedom of the press and libel laws are of necessity very general in character and they form only the first, outer breastworks that protect the historian from the concealment of truth on the one hand and from deliberate falsehood on the other hand.

The federal government furnishes still more specific guarantees by which the historian profits. The federal law that went into effect October 1, 1912, provides that all periodicals that pass through the federal mails shall file with the postmaster-general a sworn statement of their circulation, the names and post office addresses of their editors, business managers, owners, and stockholders. The historian thus shares with the general public the knowledge of the ownership of all newspapers and of the influences that may exert a control over editors and journalists.

This federal legislation had been anticipated by state laws that now in nearly every state of the union secure the publication by every paper in the state of the name and address of editor and business manager. This legislation is not as a rule so detailed as is the federal law, but it serves to determine the responsibility for the general conduct of a paper and thus it provides a guarantee that the newspaper on its business side may by law be held accountable for its contents.

[1] A newspaper itself sometimes gives this supplementary guarantee. The Brooklyn, N. Y., *Daily Times* prints this "Notice to the Public" at the head of its editorial columns: "Any erroneous reflection upon the character, standing or reputation of any person, firm, or corporation which may appear in the columns of The Brooklyn Daily Times will be gladly corrected upon request at the main office, 24 and 26 Broadway, Brooklyn." It must be noted that no evidence is demanded that the reflection was erroneous.

Registration in the federal post office as second class matter carries with it the privileges of the mails and therefore this becomes a guarantee that the periodical contains no advertisements of lotteries or other forms of business prohibited in any state. Registration also assures regularity of appearance. Copyright legislation protecting authors and artists benefits the historian in so far as it assures him that the articles and illustrations are the property, if not the actual work, of the person holding the copyright, and thus he is able to decide who is responsible for at least a part of the literary and the art columns.

The federal government not only gives certain guarantees through its constitution and its laws, but it becomes itself responsible for the authoritativeness of no small or unimportant part of what appears on the pages of the press. The weather reports and forecasts, the times of sun and moon and tides, the arrival and departure of domestic and foreign mails, shipping news, regulations affecting the army and navy, the time and place for holding examinations for the federal civil service, the calendars of federal courts and summaries of court decisions, the names of persons admitted to practice in these courts, signed proclamations of the chief federal executive, reports of the regular federal administrative departments as well as those appointed for times of emergencies, and a mass of official announcements and reports are made with the sanction and approval of the federal government.

In a similar way the state governments are directly or indirectly responsible for the publication of state laws, proclamations of governors, the calendars of state courts, the notices of the incorporation of stock companies, election notices, change of personal name, reports of state bureaus or commissions charged with the oversight of state educational, charitable, reformatory, and penal institutions, and with the direction of all efforts to conserve food and fuel, and for other large classes of legal and public matters.

County, town and municipal governments are responsible for calendars of cases arising in criminal, civil and surrogates' courts; for all notices concerning the administration of the estates of deceased persons, for notices concerning recorded transfers of property, recorded, satisfied, and assigned mortgages, and mechanics' liens; for the publication of permits for new buildings and the alteration of old ones; for notices of bankruptcies and business reverses and of the sale of property for unpaid taxes; for notices of bids for city contracts and of assessments for pavements and for water and sewerage improvements; announcements of permanent and temporary assignments in the police department, as also the transfers, leaves of absence, fines, reprimands and dismissals of charges in the department, and similar notices concerning the fire department, when this is under direct civic control; and for all legal advertisements that concern the local government.

It is thus seen that the government, in some form, either federal, state, or local, is the source of no small part of the daily paper and it thus becomes the guarantor of the reliability of such parts as it itself furnishes. It is true that even here errors may creep in,—weather forecasts may be disturbed by extraordinary atmospheric conditions, violent storms may delay the arrival and the departure of mails, and the fallibility of typesetters may change the meaning of reports and announcements. But it can at least be assumed that the guarantee of the government reduces to an irreducible minimum the element of errancy in those parts of the newspaper for which it is responsible.

It is true that some of these guarantees have been modified during times of war or social upheaval, but they must be understood as the guarantees that may be relied upon under normal conditions.

The newspaper on its part stands ready to assume much more responsibility than is formally demanded by the law. If it does not actually print, it is at all times ready to give the name of the person in charge of the various special departments demanded by its readers, or engaged to increase its circulation.

Much space is given in the press to the letters of regular correspondents concerning foreign and domestic affairs. These are as a rule signed with the name of the writer, or with his initials and thus easily identified. The larger papers have their columns or pages for games, sporting news, and athletic contests, and these are in charge of an editor usually named. The art editor, the musical and dramatic critic, and the literary editor often sign their names or their initials to their contributions, and thus indicate their willingness to assume the responsibility for their part of the newspaper.[2]

The newspaper makes its own regulations for its own protection as well as for that of its readers. The occasional correspondent must give his name and address, "not necessarily for publication but as a guarantee of good faith," and this regulation is frequently re-enforced by the statement that the paper will pay no attention to anonymous communications. In large cities, all notices of marriages and of deaths must be accompanied by the name and address of the sender, although no regulation seems to have been devised that will prevent a person from sending a false notice of his own marriage.

It sometimes places at the head of its "lost and found" column the section of the penal code warning the public of the penalties incurred in not making reasonable effort to find the owner of lost property and restore it to him. In every possible way the newspaper uses its authority to avert the publication of false statements sent it by those who are not members of its staff but who seek to shield themselves under its panoply.

The large number of persons connected with the press is not in itself a guarantee that statements are correct,—no reporter sees more than if he were the sole reporter, but the large number on a metropolitan press becomes an unconscious check on the way a person sees.

Not only the date of appearance, but the volume, number of issue, and number of pages in the issue are stated,—items that have more than once been important factors in determining the forgery of newspapers.

There is a somewhat general assumption that the main object of a paper is to hoodwink the public, yet even a cursory examination must show that the newspaper and other periodicals give their own explicit guarantees that they have used every known means to guarantee the reliability and the authoritativeness of the definite statements made by them, in the ways that have been

[2] The Concord, N. H., *Evening Monitor* states that "political and other communicated reading matter will be designated by a star at the conclusion of the article and will ordinarily appear on page five of the *Monitor*."

enumerated, and that they are to the best of their knowledge true and unimpeachable.

The newspaper as a business enterprise offers certain guarantees through the information it publishes concerning itself. It often prints facts concerning its own history, such as the year when it was established, its press ancestors,[3] consolidations, and consequent change of name, and this pride in ancestry or of a long and honorable journalistic career has a tonic effect. It states its membership in one or more of the great co-operative news-supplying associations, such as the Associated Press, the United Press, the New York Associated Dailies, or that it has received the news service of the New York *Sun*, or of the International News Service, thus guaranteeing a far-reaching collection of news and availing itself of the guarantee afforded by these great organizations.

It states the necessary facts in regard to the frequency of its appearance,—whether it appears daily, semi-weekly, or tri-weekly, whether it has a Sunday issue, publishes a magazine section or an illustrated or comic supplement, and it sometimes gives the hours when different editions appear.[4] It states the number of pages or of sections appearing with each issue, and it often furnishes information in regard to combination subscriptions with other newspapers or magazines. It gives terms of subscription, sometimes announcing higher rates when the subscription is not paid in advance and sometimes stating that the subscription must invariably be paid in advance; it states where papers are on sale locally, in other American cities, and in foreign cities, and in what foreign hotels and offices the paper may be read; and it often names its branch offices, as also newsdealers, postmasters, and other agents authorized to receive subscriptions. It states that it has complied with the federal law requiring registration as second class mail matter. It gives its business

---

[3] The Philadelphia *North American* states at the head of its editorial column that it was founded in 1771, that it is the oldest daily newspaper in America, and that it is the descendant of the *Weekly Pennsylvania Gazette*, founded by Benjamin Franklin in 1728.

[4] The Boston *Evening Transcript* gives the special features that appear in it by separate days. It is interesting to note that genealogical features are listed for two days in the week.

address and sometimes the home address of its editor,[5] its various telephone numbers and its cable address. It publishes the statement that it is the official paper of the city, or of the county, or of both, and at least one paper claims to be "the official paper for all the people." It often publishes in full its advertising rates for regular, classified, displayed, or illustrated advertisements or states that it will give them on request; it announces when and where advertisements may be submitted and where its representatives for foreign advertisements may be found; it may state that "editorial notices, when admissible at any price, the effect of which is to promote private interests [are charged at the rate of] ten cents per line. No notice inserted for less than One Dollar," and that "the privilege of advertisers by the year is limited to their own immediate business and to the particular business which is the subject of the contract, and advertisements concerning any other matter will be charged for at the usual rates." [6] It makes a distinction between news and business, and while often publishing free, as news, notices of births, marriages, and deaths as well as certain classes of church notices, it prints at specified rates per line all resolutions, cards of thanks, obituary notices, obituary poetry, unsolicited poetry, and also all notices of suppers, socials, or sales where admission is charged or articles are sold. It often states that its circulation books, press room and mailing room are open at all times day or night to advertisers or their representatives; it gives its net circulation, after deducting the number of copies used for exchange or by the employees, and the number of unsold or returned papers; and it frequently makes affidavit before a notary public of all facts affecting its circulation. In the case of papers having an unusually large circulation, the guarantee is given their advertisers that the circulation stated has been attested by a responsible organization.[7]

[5] "The editor resides at 45 Prospect Street, and if there should be any one desiring to get in touch with him they may ring Phone 674, outside of office hours, night or day. The real newspaper man never has any license to sleep if there is need to be awake. There is no fixed time for quitting in all the bright lexicon of journalistic accomplishment."—Port Chester, N. Y., *Record*.

[6] *Yates County Chronicle*, Penn Yan, New York.

[7] This service was for some time rendered by the Association of American Advertisers. The Association in its turn protected itself by stating that it

The press thus guarantees on the one hand protection to its readers from advertisers seeking to promote their own selfish ends, and on the other hand it guarantees its advertisers a reliable circulation. It sometimes goes even farther than this and gives its readers a guarantee that all goods advertised in its columns are what they purport to be; if they are found to be otherwise than as advertised, the newspaper will itself refund the money paid if the advertiser does not do so.[8]

It gives its subscribers much information in regard to domestic and foreign postal rates for newspapers, and in regard to the best ways of remitting money for subscriptions or advertising. It informs its contributors, actual or would-be, of the best way of preparing manuscript, warns them against anonymous contributions, but sometimes asserts with vehemence and even asperity that "all unsolicited manuscripts, articles, letters and pictures sent to *The Tribune* are sent at the owner's risk and *The Tribune* company expressly repudiates any liability or responsibility for their safe custody or return." [9]

Newspapers often state the various forms of printing and kindred enterprises carried on in connection with the publication of a paper, including commercial printing, ruling, binding, occasional book publishing, and job printing of every description. This information in regard to its business activities becomes, especially in the case of the paper with a necessarily small circulation, a guarantee of its independence in a financial way of both its circulation and its advertising.

The newspaper itself thus presents on its business side a wide range of guarantees as to its credibility and reliability. Many of these guarantees may seem to the casual reader of minor im-

---

guaranteed only the figures of circulation contained in the report of the Association.

This Association discontinued service May 21, 1914, and its place has been taken by the Audit Bureau of Circulations.

[8] The New York *Tribune* at the head of its editorial columns carries this guarantee: "You can purchase merchandise advertised in THE TRIBUNE with absolute safety—for if dissatisfaction results in any case THE TRIBUNE guarantees to pay your money back upon request. No red tape, no quibbling. We refund promptly if the advertiser does not."

The *Good Housekeeping Magazine* has for some years carried a similar guarantee.

[9] New York *Tribune*, January 1, 1911.

portance, but they can not be ignored by the student of history who inquires how far the newspaper is an authoritative source for the reconstruction of the past.

The columns of the periodical press also carry other guarantees. Many forms of business whose activities are reported by the press or whose advertisements are carried in its columns become themselves a guarantee of the accuracy of the statements made. One of the most significant of these guarantees is connected with the advertisements carried in 1916 by the Metropolitan Trust Company of New York City. The Company gave instances of carelessness or of actual dishonesty in the administration of different estates, gave the points at issue in the suits at law that followed, the decisions of the Court, and the explicit reference to the legal reports giving these decisions.

The reports of the transactions of the stock exchange, of dividends declared on bank deposits and on corporation stocks, of real estate transfers, of market sales and purchases must all be accepted as authoritative. Moreover, newspapers often expressly disclaim all responsibility for the accuracy or authenticity of curb market quotations.

The business management of entertainments like operas, theatres, and concerts in effect guarantees that the entertainments advertised will be given at the place, hour and price stated in the advertisement, and, with limitations, that the programme will be given as announced.

The Church in its various branches becomes responsible for the official announcements of its religious services, for information in regard to the increase or decrease in its membership, for facts concerning its missionary and charitable undertakings, and for the published programmes of its stated local, state and national meetings.

Educational authorities are responsible for official information in regard to school buildings, school organization, school curricula, and all extra-school activities carried on under their auspices, such as playgrounds and school gardens; for official statements concerning expenditures needed for school buildings, salaries, and general operating expenses; and for the names of persons appointed to the teaching staff.

Public and private hospitals publish the vital statistics that come under their jurisdiction, and boards of health and health officers are in their turn responsible for other information in regard to health conditions.

These are but suggestions of the large number of responsible organizations and individuals that in effect guarantee the authoritativeness of much that is published by the press. The material thus guaranteed by the nature of its source does not lie in the field generally denominated "news," nor is it in the assignments given reporters, nor is it found in editorial columns, nor does it lend itself always to the writing of a "story." Nevertheless, this guaranteed material forms a large part of every newspaper and it can be readily separated from other parts where the guarantee is less in evidence. It is also obvious that while the greater part, if not all, of the newspaper that has behind it an absolute guarantee can not in any sense be considered *news*, yet its inherent value in reconstructing the past may be far greater than the published news of the hour.

It is thus evident that the newspaper always contains certain features permanent as regards the source from which they are derived. The superficial details may vary, but the source remains the same, and hence the responsibility is a constant one. These permanent elements are those furnished by federal, state, county, town, and municipal governments; by other official organizations of a public or a private character; by business associations whose credit in the eye of the public depends on their contributing to the press only absolutely trustworthy information; and by many elements of the newspaper itself considered as a business enterprise.

The responsibility for these permanent features of the newspaper is thus readily recognized and it becomes as absolute as lies within the range of human responsibility. Error may be found in these portions of the newspaper,—permanent as to their source and as to their responsibility,—but every possible precaution to avoid them has been taken by their guarantors. The student of history may accept at its face value this permanent element in the press and be assured that in so doing he has not been led into avoidable inaccuracies of statement. The errancy of the press, if such there be, must lie elsewhere.

CHAPTER IV

THE PRESS AND OTHER ACTIVITIES

'The newspaper is parent, school, college, pulpit, theatre, example, councelor, all in one."—*Wendell Phillips.*

"The modern newspaper literally has its fingers reaching out toward every quarter of the globe, and every finger is sensitive, and every nerve brings back the treasures of the intellectual wealth that are stored up there, and a photograph of the occurrences of life that are there taking place."—*C. D. Warner.*

The functions of a newspaper "are practically those of a middleman between the public and matters of public interest."—*H. W. Steed.*

THE press is a living exemplification of the truth of the Biblical phrase "none of us liveth to himself, and no man dieth to himself." Probably more than any other single agency it touches every other activity in human society, and in this lies its great value in a reconstruction of the past. As long as history was interpreted as meaning a chronicle of the deeds of individual heroes, or of the events that concerned kings and courts, or of the acts of armies, or a description of the ceremonies of the Church, the historian could confine himself to the comparatively few classes of sources immediately connected with his subject,—the material demanded for a history of one dimension was simple and easily obtainable. But a history of four dimensions demands an infinite variety of sources, and the connection of the press with a vast range of human interests places it in the forefront among the sources that claim the attention of the historian. A bare enumeration of some of these interests must show that the newspaper can not be neglected by him, while an examination of the connection thus made is essential in determining how far the relation of the press to other activities is a guarantee of its authoritativeness, and to what extent its authoritativeness is thereby limited.

The newspaper and the government are connected primarily through the general questions of freedom of the press and censorship of the press. But many specific questions bring the two into

intimate relationship. It is important for the press to publish
as news both the important and the trifling transactions of the
government, while the government needs and sometimes seeks
the support of the press. This mutual dependence explains the
large number of reporters congregated in every capital city, as it
also explains why executive messages, legislative acts, speeches,
documents of every description, are sent to the press in advance
to be released at a specified hour. Reporters are often taken into
the confidence of governmental authorities and given important
information, although permitted to print only a specified amount,
and this confidence has almost never been violated.[1]

Many of the specific questions involve the press in a very
direct way. The press is intimately connected with the post
office department, where shortage in postal revenues is prone to
be attributed to carrying second class mail at too low a rate; the
transmission of so-called "incendiary literature" whether issued
by abolitionists or anarchists, the closing of the mails to all
newspapers advertising lotteries, or immoral occupations, and
more recently intoxicating liquors, all indicate the wide range of
connection between the government and the newspaper; they
must at the same time indicate the limitations on the authoritativeness of the greater part of the press in the discussion of all
these measures that so vitally concern it.

The press plays an important part in the conduct of political
parties and in all political campaigns, and at various times it has
accepted, if it has not openly sought, the rewards of such political
service. Editors have frequently been appointed to postmasterships, they have held diplomatic and consular posts, they have
been elected to Congress, they have been nominated for important
state and municipal offices, and they have filled various other
appointive and elective offices,—in apparent return for services
rendered to a political party. The biographer of Thomas Ritchie
finds that "from the very beginning [May 9, 1804] the [Rich-
mond] *Enquirer* fell under the influence of party patronage. . . .
Without official patronage it could not have lived in so strong a

---

[1] One instance of this violation of confidence occurred during the administration of President Roosevelt with the result that the reporter was forbidden the White House.

Federalist atmosphere as Richmond and in competition with a well established and popular press. From the first Ritchie did not disguise his purpose to speak for the administration and his expectation of compensation for such service." [2]

In the early days in America postmasters had the franking privilege and newspaper publishers therefore sought postmasterships in order to distribute their papers free of charge,—Franklin was for nearly forty years connected in some capacity or other with the post office department.

Joseph Hume clearly recognized the double-edged character of this connection between the press and the government in England, and said in the House of Commons in 1822 that if the Government wished to give publicity to its advertisements, it ought to send them to the papers having the largest circulation, but it did not send a single one to *The Times*, although it had a greater circulation than any other two papers in England. On the other hand, he feared that the same system would grow up as in Ireland, where some papers had been set on foot solely with the view of making profit by the government advertisements. Government advertisements had been inserted in some favored Irish papers two years and seven months after the transactions to which they related had been settled and he moved for a return of the amount of all sums paid to different English newspapers for advertisements of all descriptions from public offices.[3]

To the more open co-operation sometimes found to-day no objection can be made,—Secretary Wilson publicly announced in 1918 a plan by which seven hundred and thirty-six daily newspapers were made branch offices of the United States Employment Service and offers of co-operation were made to newspapers in cities having a population of over 20,000.[4] Much more questionable must be deemed the action of one branch of the Government in asking the aid of the New England press in reporting disloyalty.[5]

In France, journalism has apparently been the great highway leading to political office. Joseph Reinach once said that in

[2] C. H. Ambler, *Thomas Ritchie*, pp. 19–20.
[3] *Hansard*, May 7, 1822.
[4] New York *Evening Post*, March 22, 1918.
[5] New York *Times*, June 12, 1918.

France every one had been, was, or was about to be a journalist, and that every politician wrote for the papers.[6] The journalistic activities of Napoleon have recently been made the subject of an exhaustive study.[7] The interest in the press shown by Napoleon I and by Napoleon III seems indeed but the culmination in imperial circles of the desire of every Frenchman to have his own newspaper. "M. Thiers prompted a dozen articles, &c. every day," is Reinach's comment, and he notes that Louis Napoleon never ceased during his entire reign writing articles and brochures. In 1895, from thirty-five to forty journalists had seats in the Chamber of Deputies, and a smaller but still important number in the Senate. The professional politician wishes an organ and the professional journalist wishes a seat in the legislative body to enforce his opinions and to aid in his advancement.[8]

In England, gifts have been made to newspaper owners and editors of peerages and of other lower orders of nobility.[9] In the distribution of birthday honors a goodly proportion has fallen to the lot of provincial and colonial editors. But this connection has not escaped criticism. Cobden, in 1857, was much concerned over "the illicit and secret connection between the Government and the Press," [10] and Peel, aware of similar criticism, once wrote Edward Sterling thanking him for avoiding "every species of intercourse which could throw a suspicion upon the motives by which he was actuated." [11] Lord Palmerston's dinner parties, where Delane was a frequent guest, did not escape the eagle eye and caustic pen of John Bright. Canning had earlier much resented Jerdan's request for office for his son and through his secretary wrote that it was absolutely necessary that he should have it in his power to deny in the House of Commons that the influence of the Government had been employed to induce the

[6] J. Reinach, "Parisian Newspapers," *Nineteenth Century*, September, 1882, 12: 347–360.

[7] A. Périvier, *Napoléon Journaliste.*—L. Salomon, *Geschichte des deutschen Zeitungswesens*, gives much information in regard to Napoleon's relation with the German press, especially in "Die Napoleonische Zeit," II, 83–264.

[8] A Resident in Paris, "French Journalism," *National Review*, September, 1895, 26: 74–82.

[9] Henry Bate, created a baronet in 1813, is said to have been the first journalist to receive a title.—*Dictionary of National Biography*, 16: 102.

[10] J. A. Hobson, *Richard Cobden the International Man*, p. 213.

[11] T. Carlyle, *The Life of John Sterling*, pp. 306–307 (Boston ed., 1851).

Press to support it.[12] That success had been slight in avoiding even the semblance of connection between the English Government and the press seems evident from a later judgment that "journalism is not an independent fourth estate, as it is sometimes described; it is a 'mere appendage of the House of Commons'." [13] Recent writers have pressed the point still farther and have found a still more ominous development in the controlling influence the prime minister has come to exert in the House of Commons and in his consequent heirship to a controlling influence over a large part of the press.[14]

The gift of conspicuous honors to members of the press has not been confined to the governments of the West. Titles and orders of nobility have been the coin of the realm with which the Sultan has in Turkey secured immunity from criticism.[15]

The financial, as well as the official and the social, rewards that come to the press through party support can not be ignored. The thick and thin supporters of party issues often openly seek and are awarded printing contracts and political advertising.[16] Edward Porritt has shown how in Canada the patronage of the Dominion Government has been bestowed on the newspapers that supported the Liberal Party. This patronage has been specially lucrative in the advertising of the Intercolonial Railway, of the Departments of Agriculture and of Immigration, and in the printing of official notices.[17]

This desire for party favor must check the authoritativeness of the press in so far as it prevents a newspaper from criticizing adversely any action of the political party to which it is indebted for political preferment, or leads it to suppress facts, the publica-

[12] The letters of both Canning and his secretary are given in the *Autobiography of William Jerdan*, IV, 159–164.

[13] "Politics and the Press," *Fraser's Magazine*, July, 1875, 92: 41–50.

[14] A. G. Gardiner, "The Twilight of Parliament," *Atlantic Monthly*, August, 1921, 128: 248–255.

[15] Ahmed Emin, *The Press in Turkey*, p. 83.

[16] "The country press in Republican territory has been, from the time of the Civil War, tied fast to the party machine by the county printing contracts and by cessions of county postmasterships to the editor."—G. K. Turner, "Manufacturing Public Opinion," *McClure's Magazine*, July, 1912, 39: 316–327.

[17] E. Porritt, "The Value of Political Editorials," *Atlantic Monthly*, January, 1910, 105: 62–67.

tion of which would react unfavorably on the party. Yet even here general statements must be qualified. In the early history of a comparatively undeveloped country, the value of government printing is very great and is eagerly sought, since without laws to be printed and politicians to have organs, newspapers could hardly be kept alive.[18]

The thorough-going party organ is probably less frequently found to-day than it has been in times past, it is probably less influential than it formerly was, its authoritativeness on all questions outside of political ones may be unquestioned, yet its publication of political news and its editorial expression of opinion on party questions can not pass unquestioned by the historian. Even the independent political press may have its political animosities towards individuals or specific political questions, and on these special points its opinions and its statement of facts must be discounted. The names of Mr. Bryan and of Mr. Roosevelt have been anathema to more than one otherwise independent newspaper; free trade and protection are antagonistic and the support of one by the press implies the condemnation of the other. The specific question of the admission of wood pulp free of duty, a matter of vital interest to the newspaper on its business side, had the support of the press in 1908 and this must have vitiated the authority of press opinions on the tariff at that time.

The intimate association of the press with government and with political parties must warn the historian that he can not invariably accept at face value all that every newspaper prints either for or against the government or the political party temporarily in power. He must go behind the face of the returns and determine how far the value of these statements is impaired by the favors the individual paper has received at the hands of those having political authority. The press may not be openly subsidized by the government, yet this result may be practically accomplished by the low postal rates granted it, by the awards of public printing and political advertising, by appointments to office, or by other favors shown. The "caution" signal always

[18] F. W. Scott, *Newspapers and Periodicals of Illinois, 1814–1879*, pp. xxxvii–xl.

confronts the historian when he seeks information and opinions from the press concerning governmental and political activities.

The newspaper maintains an intimate relationship with the Church as an organization and with the leading persons connected with it. The Church indeed has for many years maintained its own denominational organs that have often been identified by name with the special denomination represented.[19] But the denominational press is becoming each year a less important factor in the field of the historian. This is in part explained by the breaking down of the barriers that have separated denominations and even religions, in part by the growing secularization of the Church, in part by the growing interest of the secular press in the affairs of the Church.

This growing interest of the press has in a measure had a mercenary origin. The verbatim report of the sermons of popular preachers has increased the circulation of newspapers, as has the publication of the Sunday-school lessons, the reports of Sunday services, and the columns given to church music. The announcements of church services, of church fairs, suppers, dinners, breakfasts, and socials, of personals relating to clergymen of local or national reputation all help in establishing friendly relationships between the press and the Church, increasing friendliness means growing circulation, and growing circulation means expansion of advertisements. Thus it must be frankly recognized that the secular press has been interested in religion less from a desire to promote the cause of religion than from a wish to further the interests of the press.[20]

[19] *The American Baptist, Catholic Witness, The Churchman, The Congregationalist, The Methodist, The Universalist,* are a few illustrations.

Probably the first issue of the first distinctly religious newspaper was that of the *Herald of Gospel Liberty,* September 1, 1808. It was published at Portsmouth, New Hampshire, and was edited by Elias Smith. It is interesting to note the emphasis the paper placed on the idea of liberty,—in the first one hundred and forty-six numbers, fifty-three articles were on "Liberty," apparently all written by the editor.

J. Pressley Barrett has written *The Centennial of Religious Journalism* (1808–1908).

[20] G. H. Hepworth wrote regularly sermons for the New York *Herald,* they were cabled to the Paris edition of the *Herald,* and they were brought out weekly in the Chicago *Record-Herald,* and in many other journals in the West and South and in Canada.—S. H. Ward, *George H. Hepworth,* chaps. X, XIV.

It must be recognized with equal frankness that certain religious denominations are everywhere advocating the use of the press as a means of increasing their membership, their church attendance, and their Sunday collections. Church activities are made known not only through news items, but through paid advertisements; clergymen not only do not avoid but seek the interview; the bestowal of church printing becomes an important feature in the alliance between church and press; the camera is a medium of connection, and illustrations of church buildings, group pictures of church associations, and press reproductions of illustrated posters all cement the union.[21] Even a church "rose service" is made possible through the promise of a daily paper to pay for the roses and the mutual advantage follows in the first page publicity given both donor and recipient.[22] The alliance of Church and press is not weakened when the demand is made that the Sunday-school lessons be removed from the sectarian press because their editor is a pacifist.[23]

At two points the press and the Church have been antagonistic, —the press has upheld and the Church has opposed the Sunday edition and the comic supplement. The present result of the controversy apparently shows that the Church has lessened its opposition to the Sunday issues of morning papers, while many representatives of the press have been disposed to yield to the opposition to the comic supplement and to substitute for it

---

The sermons of T. De W. Talmage had similarly wide circulation through the secular press, as had those of H. W. Beecher, Joseph Cook and other notables of the pulpit.

De Witt McMurray, under the title *Religion of a News-Paper Man*, has collected the "religio-philosophical editorials which appeared in the Sunday issues of *The Dallas Morning News* and *The Galveston Daily News*."

An earlier, but very eccentric series of sermons was published in the New York *Sunday Mercury* under the title of *Short Patent Sermons* by "Dow, Jr." They were collected in book form and in 1857 reached a four-volume edition.

[21] The extent of the use the Church makes of the press is indicated in Charles Stelzle, *Principles of Successful Church Advertising;* W. B. Ashley comp., *Church Advertising;* C. F. Reisner, *Church Publicity.*

It is significant that Roman Catholics and Hebrews advertise their charities but not their religious services. The advertisements of Protestant churches are rather of the social side of the church as an organization than of the religious beliefs held.

[22] C. F. Reisner, *Church Publicity*, p. 282.

[23] See the controversy in the daily press, March, 1919.

something more artistic and less morally pernicious. The clergyman to-day receives regularly his Sunday morning paper and mass meetings protesting against the comic Sunday section of the press have had their effect.[24]

Yet this friendly relationship between the press and the Church may constitute a serious obstacle in the path of the historian.[25] The press, because of this very friendliness, may hesitate to attack a powerful denomination in any community, even though its secular acts may justly expose it to unfavorable criticism; it is unwilling to question the wisdom of the methods used by the Church in raising money, and thus fishponds, grab-bags, raffles, prizes, and lotteries under various other names all pass unnoticed by the press, although condemned in other organizations; it does not report small audiences, or dull sermons, or execrable music,—in its columns all Sunday audiences are large and appreciative, all sermons are eloquent or timely, all church music is beautiful and harmonious. In general, this over-generous attitude towards the Church matters little,—it is understood and discounted, but in large and vital questions it must lead the historian astray, unless he supplements the records of the press by sources found elsewhere.

Where the Church is intimately connected with the State, a somewhat different relationship between the press and the Church is found, and therefore somewhat different conditions are presented to the historian. "The Church and the Press have much to say about each other; but they are not upon speaking terms," wrote an Englishman in 1893.[26] "There is between the two an air of suspicion and stand offishness,"—the mechanical relations are on a satisfactory footing, but beneath the surface a real cleavage is apparent. While it is recognized that the press

[24] New York *Evening Post*, March 30, 1911.

[25] The increased attention given the pulpit and its work by the press has been deprecated in the interests of the Church itself; it "is interesting as a tacit recognition that the pulpit is a force, and a force of very different kind from that which is suggested by the correspondence on the decay of preaching. . . . But there are dangers lurking in it, especially to the preacher himself."—J. G. Rogers, "The Pulpit and the Press," *The Ancient Faith in Modern Light*, pp. 353–391.

[26] J. T. Bunce, "Church and Press," *National Review*, November, 1893, 22: 387–393.

has tempered the Church "in political, ecclesiastical, and educational conflicts; it has helped towards stimulating criticism, liberalizing theology, and moderating sacerdotalism," and that it has also "rendered incalculable service in enlarging and defending the freedom of the laity," the Church still finds that the tone of the press "is too often distasteful to the clergy." This may or may not be due to the tendency of the clergy "to do unwise things in the assertion of their own position, and to regard as direct acts of enmity the frank and not unfrequently the crude discussion of Church principles, and of topics which immediately affect Church interests; especially those of an external character, such as questions of discipline, of disestablishment, of legislation, and generally of the relations of the Church with the State." [27] Whatever the cause, it seems to an outsider that the organic character of the Church of England and its relation to the State give it a cohesion that makes it independent of the press and that fosters aloofness on the part of the press towards the Church. The press recognizes its relation to the State and its obligation to support or to censure it according to circumstances, but the Church is in effect separated from the press by the intervening State and thus each practically goes its own way. The press finds affairs of state more interesting than those of the Church, it feels free to "talk about the Church," especially about its relations with the Church, but it neither asks favors of the Church nor gives them. The Church does not advertise through the press, the efforts of the daily press to issue a seven-day paper have not as yet succeeded and Press and Church live side by side in a state of armed neutrality.[28]

In America, the splitting up of the Church universal into innumerable bodies makes its relations with the press more intimate

---

[27] J. T. Bunce, *National Review*, November, 1893, 22:387–393.

[28] General statements are always dangerous and involve exceptions as numerous as the instances on which they are based. The Nonconformist press has for years been powerful and independent,—its critics have also been numerous. Its early beginnings may be understood through Arthur Miall, *Life of Edward Miall;* Edward Baines, *Life of Edward Baines;* more radical phases are suggested by W. A. Smith, *"Shepherd" Smith the Universalist;* criticisms of the later press are given by the Editor in "The Cocoa Press and its Masters," and "Cocoa and Cant," *National Review*, May, July, 1910, 55: 402–416; 761–775; criticisms of all except the Roman Catholic press are given by T. W. Marshall in *Protestant Journalism*.

as well as more friendly than is the case in England. In France, the alliance of the Church with royalty makes the republican press distinctly hostile to the Church. Conclusions drawn in regard to the relationship between the press and religious activities must differ when in one country this relationship is cordial and intimate, in another it is one of more or less detachment, and when in another the relationship is conditioned by political affiliations.

The newspaper is intimately connected with all questions of public health and its effective aid in promoting it is everywhere recognized. "Printer's ink is saving more lives than any other single agency employed by modern health workers," was the statement made at the forty-third annual meeting of the American Public Health Association in 1915. "You may cure individuals of their ills in the privacy of a sickroom, but to cure the public of its ills you must get into the newspaper," sums up the question. The press reports health congresses, announces medical and surgical discoveries, publishes vital statistics, and hospital reports; it is coming to reject advertisements of patent medicines and of quack doctors;[29] it carries on campaigns against flies, mosquitoes, rats, caterpillars, impure milk, contaminated drinking water, and exposure of food to dust; it opens a column for giving free advice on matters of health,—"the health column in newspapers is as indispensable as the joke column,"—and in every way it records the growing interest in all questions of private and public health. In its turn, the department of public health often takes the press into its confidence and thus secures its co-operation in the presentation and circulation of information bearing on the subject.

In the consideration of public health, the press is not so much divided against itself as it is divided with reference to the parts of the subject itself. The press has a free hand in some of its campaigns for public health,—flies, rats, mosquitoes, and caterpillars are not commercialized and campaigns against them are

[29] Evidences of a recrudescence of patent medicine advertising were found in 1921, but there were also evidences of a recognition that the acceptance of such advertising was for the press a "penny-wise, pound-foolish policy." More than one newspaper discovered that reputable advertisers were repelled by patent medicine advertisements and that they placed their advertising in newspapers that did not carry them.

universally popular. But the press suffers a heavy handicap
when it attempts to improve other conditions that militate
against the health of the public. Efforts to secure pure milk
may run counter to milk dealers and to the Grange; proposals to
improve the water supply come into collision with the taxpayers; epidemics must not be reported because they reflect on
the board of health and diminish out-of-town trade;[30] news of
the bubonic plague must be suppressed because its publication
will interfere with travel; disgraceful living conditions in con-
gested districts must be ignored because the tenement houses
are the property of wealthy residents; the results of accidents
must be minimized because they reflect on the railroads, or on
important local manufacturing industries, or on the large department store; danger from fire in buildings where many persons
are employed must not be dwelt upon because the owners are
influential citizens; advertisements of patent cure-alls must not
be rejected because they make widely known the home town
where they are manufactured; a "clean-up-week" must not be
urged because it is opposed by the board of public works; exposure
of filthy conditions behind the scenes in restaurants will result in
boycotting the restaurants by the public and in boycotting the
exposing newspapers by the restaurants; advocacy of free clinics
may incur the displeasure of the medical profession; the premature announcement of discoveries in medicine or surgery may
bring only ridicule on a paper over-zealous to publish news.[31]

In all matters pertaining to the public health as reported by
the press the inquiries of the historian must be specially directed
towards discovering how far conditions that interfere with the

[30] The American Historical Association had planned to hold its annual
meeting in Cleveland, Ohio, during Christmas week, 1918. The meeting
was at the last moment abandoned on the advice of the health officer, but
residents of the city report that no Cleveland paper noted that the meeting
had been given up, although the press had in advance given wide publicity
to it.

[31] In a dearth of important news, a reporter is said to have remarked to
his fellow reporters, consulting as to what could be done, "We have revolutionized medicine a half a dozen times the past month and we can't do it
again just now." Like many another serious jest, the reputed remark was
a volume in itself.

The wide-spread publicity given the Friedmann serum in 1913 and the
resulting derision of the more conservative press is but one illustration of
this danger of excessive zeal in announcing medical "discoveries."

good health of the public are commercialized and how far they are free from those outside influences that tend to limit the press in its discussion of them.

The newspaper is a large factor in the industrial world. It faces the question of union or non-union labor,—many newspapers to-day bear the union label,—of strikes, of hours of work, of night work, of the employment of women and children, and of the introduction of machinery. In its advocacy of the protection of workmen from dangerous machinery it has sometimes incurred the bitter enmity of mill owners and manufacturers,—Alaric Watts, in the *Leeds Intelligencer*, was one of the first to urge such protection and the immediate result was that "he received as many letters discontinuing subscription to it as filled a breakfast tray," though he subsequently won back his subscribers, states his biographer.[32] In strikes the weekly press seems often more dependent on industrial conditions than does the daily, but it is usually able to rise above defeat and by its resourcefulness adapt itself to adverse conditions.[33]

In Australia and New Zealand a minimum wage for journalists has been established through statutes representing an agreement made in September, 1913, between the Australian Journalists' Association and the Proprietors of the Metropolitan Daily Newspapers and Weekly Newspapers in regard to the classification of

[32] A. A. Watts, *Alaric Watts*, II, 159–160.
[33] The disagreements between publishers and compositors in October, 1919, led to the issuing of various weeklies by entirely different methods. The successful experiment of the *Literary Digest* in typewriting and photographing its regular edition and other experiments by other weeklies led some to anticipate that "the whole future of magazine publication may be revolutionized by the elimination of what has hitherto been its costliest operation—the type-setting."

This resourcefulness was not new and it had led the *Publishers' Weekly* to remark: "Journalists are said to be much sought after by the British army authorities because they make good officers, by reason of the initiative and resource that they have to show constantly in their civil occupation. One London newspaper has forty-eight members of its literary staff holding commissions."—August 4, 1917, p. 410.

A serious strike among the printers in Paris in November, 1919, resulted in fifty-three papers collaborating to bring out temporarily a joint paper called *La Presse de Paris*.

The Manchester, England, *Evening Chronicle*, issued a typewritten, one-page edition, 8 x 13, during the printers' strike in Manchester, September, 1920.

journalists and consequent questions of hours, wages, duties, vacations, and similar matters.[34]

In America, since the close of the war, there has been an evident tendency on the part of some newspapers to minimize the importance of the question of unemployment.

The newspaper is concerned with questions of mail trains, of automobile stage routes, and of railway rates. As a business enterprise it is called on to meet every question that confronts every other occupation while recording the situation in the business world as regards all other industries. These facts must be taken into consideration by the historian and must put him on his guard against a too implicit reliance on the press when he turns to it for facts and discussions of industrial situations, especially those that affect the newspaper industry.

The press and social welfare are intimately associated. The newspaper raises fresh air funds for city children and vacation funds for working girls; it investigates and reports "the one hundred neediest cases" in the city, collects funds to alleviate their necessities, and distributes them through its own agencies; it receives and publishes subscriptions to aid sufferers from fire and flood, war and pestilence;[35] it starts sunshine societies, and finds homes for motherless children; it entertains orphans at the theaters; it opens up undeveloped woodlands into communities of bungalow homes;[36] it starts back-yards gardening movements, and it persuades real estate agents to offer vacant lots for gardening purposes.

In its own special field it is concerned with the Newspapermen's Benevolent League, with clubs and lodging houses for

[34] W. Williams, *The Press Congress of the World*, University of Missouri, Bulletin X, January, 1918. The full text of the statute is given.

[35] *The Christian Herald* under Louis Klopsch in eighteen years collected nearly three and a half million dollars for eighty-four different major and minor charities and funds, in addition to much relief work for individuals.— C. M. Pepper, *Life-Work of Louis Klopsch*, pp. 345-357.

The London *Times* in the first six months of the recent war raised £1,000,000 for the sick and wounded and during the war a total of more than £10,000,000 for the Joint War Committee of the British Red Cross and the Order of St. John.—New York *Evening Post*, February, 1915, May 18, 1918.

[36] The New York *Tribune* frankly stated, May 14, 1916, that this was done "as a means of stimulating circulation."

newsboys, with the age at which newsboys should be licensed,[37] with the question of allowing newsgirls at the stands of subway stations, and with that of giving the preference for news stands at the elevated stations to those incapacitated for more active employments. Newsboys have specially enlisted its interest and it promotes summer camps for them, it invites them to see baseball games, gives them dinners, and entertains them at moving picture shows. It organizes a newsboys' detachment of boy scouts, advertises extensively the efforts made by private individuals to raise funds for newsboys' homes through theater benefits and hippodrome entertainments. It notes with patriotic pride the service flag with 2520 stars in front of the Brace Memorial Newsboys Home.[38]

The newspaper press undertakes welfare work among its own employees and establishes lunch rooms, rest rooms, and smoking rooms; it installs shower baths for stereotyping and press room employees, and the most recent machinery for securing perfect ventilation; it encourages and contributes to benefit associations organized by its employees.[39]

Familiar as has much of this work become as it has been conducted by American and European newspapers, it has been apparently surpassed both in extent and in variety by the welfare work and general community service rendered in Buenos Aires by *La Prensa*. This maintains for its employees a restaurant, a gymnasium, opportunities for recreation, and an emergency hospital. It has its own electric light and power plant with every mechanical device for facilitating work, and incidentally for

[37] A. Y. Reed, in *Newsboy Service*, presents the problem of the newsboy in relation to the work of the public school.

John Morrow, a newsboy, told his own story in *A Voice from the Newsboys* (1860).

See also J. E. Gunckel, *Boyville*; *A History of Fifteen Years' Work among Newsboys*. Toledo, Ohio, 1905.

[38] Charles Loring Brace gives the history of the formation of the newsboys' lodging house in *Short Sermons to Newsboys*, pp. 5-52.

[39] See *Bulletin of Labor Statistics*, Washington, September 11, 1913, for special account of the welfare work connected with the *Evening Post*, New York City.

A. I. Shand gives an account of the London *Times*,—"the first to break with the sordid old practices and set a generous example of wise liberality" in the matter of making "the premises a comfortable club."—"The Centenary of the 'Times,'" *National Review*, February, 1888, 10: 841-856.

sterilizing all drinking water used by its employees. As part of its community service, it gives the public free of cost the use of legal and medical consultation bureaus and also bureaus for matters concerning chemistry, agriculture, and stock raising; and it maintains a show room for the display of objects relating to these branches. It conducts a school of music, gives prizes for unusual instances of self-denial and heroism, and encourages popular education. It sets aside finely appointed rooms for public meetings, lectures, plays, and concerts for charitable purposes. It provides a public library and reading-room and it has a suite of luxuriously furnished apartments for the entertainment of distinguished foreign visitors. Its magnificent building provides an observatory on the roof that furnishes information about the state of the weather, a searchlight shows the location of fires and flashes the news of important events, while a siren whistle directs attention to most unusual news.[40]

In all of these general welfare and community activities, the reports given of them by the press presumably need not be discounted,—they are often reported as news items from other cities and are to be accepted as authoritative except where allowance must evidently be made for the exaggeration possibly used by the reporting paper in regard to its own part in promoting social welfare.

It is often said that much of the welfare work carried on by the press, particularly that of collecting funds for charitable causes, is done with an eye to publicity. But the historian can not go into the question of motive, except in so far as the press itself announces the reasons for its course. The fact remains that much has been done by the press that has served the community irrespective of the ulterior object of the press in rendering the service.

Another side of the social service carried on by the press is found in its correspondence columns. In 1916, a popular woman's magazine listed over twenty-five hundred different topics that it had treated by letter, the greater part of them involving the

[40] W. R. Shepherd, *Latin America*, pp. 221–223; I. Goldberg, "What South Americans Read: The Newspapers. A Survey of Editors, Press and Policies," *Bookman*, July, 1915, 41: 478–489; *"La Prensa" of Buenos Aires, 1869–1914.* Pamphlet. 107 pp.

consideration of serious life problems. The appeal for help and advice is often made to the newspaper and the magazine through fear of betrayal of confidence, if counsel is sought from local advisers, and undoubtedly the press in such cases has rendered aid and comfort.[41]

But it is interesting to note that this relationship between the press and welfare work is apparently not reciprocal. "The case reading for this book," says the author of the most significant work yet published on social welfare, "brought to light no illustrations of the use of newspaper files and news indices to establish the date of one event by associating it with another, or to discover the notice of an accident, an arrest, an award, a death, a disappearance, or any of the thousand and one happenings that are recorded in the daily press,"[42]—an omission difficult to understand since newspaper indices make such information easily accessible.

The newspaper both encourages an interest in all educational matters and also profits by this interest. It publishes advertisements of colleges and private schools, it frequently maintains a bureau to help parents in the selection of schools for their children, it reports changes of personnel in the teachers of the private schools, and it announces the comings and the goings of the teachers in the public schools. It reports the meetings of boards of education and publishes the annual reports of school superintendents and principals. It takes an active interest in the selection of sites for school building and in the letting of contracts for their erection and equipment. It opens its columns for the discussion of the curriculum and questions of general educational policy, and it frequently maintains a department for settling among its subscribers their disputed questions of grammar, orthography, pronunciation, and similar vexing subjects. It even enters the field itself and announces that it has organized free courses "of nine lessons" in French, and that it will give in its columns "a free business education" by publishing a complete course in shorthand, business arithmetic and bookkeeping. It rents assembly halls and provides free lectures for citizens

[41] *Survey*, November 3, 1917, 39: 124.
[42] M. E. Richmond, *Social Diagnosis*, pp. 268–269.

of foreign birth. When new educational methods are agitated, it secures special correspondents and contributors who set forth the pros and cons of the Montessori system, the Gary plan, the educational survey, vocational training, night schools for foreigners, and other mooted questions. It encourages the study of current events in schools, gives reduced rates to school classes, and offers prizes to school children in innumerable contests.

Education on its side establishes schools for the training of journalists and introduces courses in journalism into educational curricula. It maintains generally amicable relations with the press, except when it is under criticism by it. These criticisms it resents as coming from a source it deems incompetent to pass judgment on the work of experts, yet it is at a distinct disadvantage in all controversies with the press since educational organs are comparatively few in number, they are published at infrequent intervals, they are little read outside of the profession, and their opinions receive scanty approval when transferred to the columns of the ordinary press.

But in its general relation to education, the press is between Scylla and Charybdis. Boards of education and the teaching staff wish better school buildings and better equipment, but this demands money from the taxpayers, and the taxpayers demur. School superintendents and teachers are anxious to maintain discipline in the schoolroom, but the parents of undisciplined children insist on the sacred rights of parenthood and protest. Specialists in educational theory and practice advocate the introduction of new subjects into the curriculum, but the constitutional objector condemns them as "fads." Eminent scholars and successful teachers prepare new textbooks based on their studies and their classroom experience, but the conservative finds "the old ones good enough." Taxpayers, parents, constitutional objectors, and conservatives are all subscribers and advertisers, and they form the numerical majority in every community,— what attitude is the press to take? Probably in every community the press is divided against itself on all disputed educational questions and thus the historian must also steer between opposing dangers in his efforts to reconstruct from the press alone the intelligent public opinion on education.

The newspaper and literature have inseparable associations,—indeed, Boynton finds that "between literature and 'the higher journalism' the partition is extremely thin," [43] while Shaw regards them as identical,—"journalism is the highest form of literature; for all the highest literature is journalism." [44] These judgments seem justified when it is remembered how many men of letters have gone into journalism and have carried with them the high standards of writing that in many cases still prevail, how many journalists have developed into littérateurs, how many have made permanent contributions to both fields of writing. [45] From the time of Defoe, Addison, and Steele to that of Bryant, Lowell and Curtis, Aldrich and Howells,—to name no more—many writers distinguished in literature have brought literary distinction to the periodicals with which they were connected.

In the early colonial period in America, literature was largely ecclesiastic, secular literature received little encouragement, the news-sheets were crude, inter-colonial communication was irregular, European news arrived six months late, "criticism of the government was not in order," homilies were not needed

[43] H. W. Boynton, *Journalism and Literature*, p. 19.
[44] "Nevertheless, journalism is the highest form of literature; for all the highest literature is journalism. The writer who aims at producing the platitudes which are 'not for an age, but for all time' has his reward in being unreadable in all ages; whilst Plato and Aristophanes trying to knock some sense into the Athens of their day, Shakspear peopling that same Athens with Elizabethan mechanics and Warwickshire hunts, Ibsen photographing the local doctors and vestrymen of a Norwegian parish, Carpaccio painting the life of St. Ursula exactly as if she were a lady living in the next street to him, are still alive and at home everywhere among the dust and ashes of thousands of academic, punctilious, archaeologically correct men of letters and art who spent their lives haughtily avoiding the journalist's vulgar obsession with the ephemeral."—G. B. Shaw, *The Sanity of Art*, p. 4.
J. S. L. Strachey answers negatively the question, "Are Journalism and Literature Incompatible?"—*Fortnightly Review*, April, 1909, n. s. 85: 734–742.
The subject is also considered by T. H. S. Escott, "Literature and Journalism," *Fortnightly Review*, January, 1912, n. s. 91: 115–130.
[45] A writer in the New York *Nation* once noted that the *Saturday Review* at first intended to have as writers, not professional journalists, but university scholars, lawyers, clergymen and others of similar tastes and qualifications. While it was impossible to keep up the plan in its entirety, since a journal must be edited by a journalist, it has always had a large infusion of writers not distinctively newspaper men.—"The London Weekly Newspapers," *The Nation*, October 14, 1880, 31: 270–271.

since they were supplied by the pulpit, and editors, "cribbed, cabined, and confined," wrote essays on English models,—Addison, Pope, and Dryden. It was much of an innovation when "Benjamin Franklin deliberately entertained his readers with his own literary efforts, in preference to stale news from Hungary or Poland."[46] The change in the choice of literary subjects in the newspaper press has since then been rapid and it has recorded the changing interests of society. Classical models long prevailed, literary interests gave way to "human interest" subjects, as these have been supplanted by the commercial type, and these in turn were temporarily superseded by military influences.

The change in literary style has been equally pronounced. R. G. White once complained, and with reason, of "this silly bombast, this stilted nonsense" that infests journalism.[47] To-day the wide-spread use of the word "story" by journalists and reporters records the present influence of short story writing on the press,[48]—even in the ostensible news column, news proper is subordinated to the "story," or it acquires a factitious importance because it appears in this guise. It is more nearly true to say that mutually repellent influences have long prevailed in the connection between literature and the press. One tendency has been towards the use of "newspaper English,"—not a mere pleasantry of speech, but one that often connotes slovenliness, over-emphasis, crudeness of expression together with the phonetic spelling of language imperfectly acquired by foreigners. This crudeness is in part due to the haste with which all newspaper material is necessarily prepared; in part to the college graduate who in increasing numbers has gone into journalism and has taken into the profession the college slang he has affected,—W. T. Arnold once complained, "it really seems as if every Greats man needed a year in a newspaper office to unlearn his

---

[46] E. C. Cook, *Literary Influence in Colonial Newspapers*, chap. I. The book is an excellent exposition of the subject.

[47] "Newspaper English. Big Words for Small Thoughts," *Words and Their Uses*, pp. 28–43.

[48] "The journalistic use of the word 'story' indicates the case of a transition which is not a wandering from fact to falsity, but an upward shift from the plane of simple registry to the plane of interpretation."—H. W. Boynton, *Journalism and Literature*, p. 13.

journalese;"[49] in part to the stilted, grandiose language that has often been fashionable, in part to the ambition of reporters to create a new dialect,—the descriptions of baseball games have partially created a language that many read even though not particularly interested in the game itself; in part to the fashion of the hour and an eagerness to be "up to the minute;"[50] and again in part to the enthusiastic but untrained reporters still found on the smaller papers.[51] Somewhat in the nature of a by-product of this influence is the tendency to-day towards the elimination of unnecessary words, coupled with a multiplicity of facts that in themselves may add confusion since they are the result of excessive imagination on the part of the reporter and thus leave no scope for imagination on the part of the reader.[52]

This aspect of newspaper activity in and of itself need give the historian little concern. As one phase of a newspaper's personality it only repels him and leads him to seek his material in more congenial form, but however repellent it may be in it-self, it does not necessarily vitiate the accuracy or truthfulness of the accounts presented.

But the opposite tendency is indicated by Dr. Arnold who wrote more than eighty years ago, "A newspaper requires a more condensed and practical style than I am equal to."[53] W. C. Bryant kept an *index expurgatorius* in the office of the *Evening Post*, solely for office use, and although many of the prohibited words and phrases included in it have since passed into reputable usage, it stands as an enduring example of the ideals in language maintained by a great editor.[54] To-day the journalist writes of

[49] Mrs. Humphry Ward and C. E. Montague, *William Thomas Arnold, Journalist and Historian*, pp. 82–83.

[50] The climax of newspaper English is perhaps to be found in A. H. Lewis' *Richard Croker* (1901).

[51] In an important work dealing with the press, recently published, the word "stuff" was used twenty-six times in thirty-five pages, and the use of the word records fairly well the attitude of many young reporters towards their work.

[52] F. N. Scott finds a partial explanation in the apparent effort to write with children in mind. The funny page, the illustrated sporting page, "sob" stories, the crimes of children as well as of adults, all appeal to the unde-veloped mind.—"The Undefended Gate," *The English Journal*, January, 1914, 3: 1–14.

[53] Letter to Mr. Platt, December 6, 1837, *Life and Correspondence of Thomas Arnold*, ed. by A. P. Stanley, II, 96.

[54] G. C. Eggleston, *Recollections of a Varied Life*, pp. 209–214.

the opportunity for exact thinking afforded by the newspaper, while recognizing the reasons why journalism is popularly considered "the field in which loose and inexact thinking is most at home." [55] These opposing tendencies indicate the line of cleavage in the press between the newspapers that are ephemeral and those that contain genuine literature.

For much that is to-day classed as literature appeared first in the columns of the newspaper press,—Robinson Crusoe was published as a newspaper serial, Uncle Remus' songs and fables were printed first in the *Atlanta Constitution*, Kipling's "Recessional" appeared in the London *Times*, Drake's "American Flag" came out in the New York *Evening Post*, Holmes' "Old Ironsides" was first published in the Boston *Advertiser*,[56] and many of the volumes of collected humor on every library shelf ran first in newspaper columns,—the *Biglow Papers*, and the numerous volumes of Mr. Dooley, Petroleum V. Nasby, and practically every other well-known humorist were contributed first to the press. It is eminently true that "the newspaper has not only monopolized the news—its proper field—but it has drawn to itself the best of literature. Both magazines and publishers of books complain that the newspapers are more attractive to writers and pay more than they can afford, while their cheapness appeals to the readers. To the future historian the point is not without interest." [57]

Yet the question can not be summarily dismissed. Empson praised the newspaper articles of Albany Fonblanque, collected under the title *England Under Seven Administrations*,[58] but his praise greatly displeased Lord Brougham who wished "the *Newspaper* had not been flattered so much." [59] But to Macaulay it

[55] F. Franklin, "Newspapers and Exact Thinking," *People and Problems*, pp. 1–10.

[56] B. Matthews, "Literature as a Profession," *The Historical Novel*, pp. 193–213.

[57] W. C. Ford, Report of the Council, *American Antiquarian Society*, 1918. In a somewhat similar spirit, H. W. Boynton writes: "The popularity of journalism in America has reacted upon most of our magazines so strongly that they are distinguished from the better daily journals by exclusion of detail and modification of method rather than by essential contrast in quality."—*Journalism and Literature*, pp. 22–23.

[58] "Newspaper Literature," *Edinburgh Review*, July, 1837, 65: 196–213.

[59] Macvey Napier, *Selection from the Correspondence of the late Macvey Napier*, 199–200.

seemed a grave mistake to collect and reprint these *Examiner* articles that "were extolled to the skies, and not without reason, while they were considered merely as leading articles; . . . People said it was a pity that such admirable compositions should perish,—so Fonblanque determined to republish them in a book. He never considered that, in that form, they would be compared, not with the rant and twaddle of the daily and weekly press, but with Burke's pamphlets, with Pascal's letters, with Addison's Spectators and Freeholders. They would not stand this new test for a moment." [60]

The services rendered to literature by the periodical press, as they have been appraised by a French writer, must not be forgotten. M. Des Granges has given warm appreciation of these services rendered the history of romanticism. He finds that many authors who later became famous began their careers through publication in periodicals. Thus the original texts are preserved and they show, by comparison with later collected editions, the many variations through which poems and essays often pass after their first publication. The periodical is also helpful in understanding and in reconstructing contemporaneous criticism. When criticism is read later, especially since the critic often omits explanation of what is well understood at the time, it may seem altogether lacking in the essentials of criticism, but when read in its original setting it becomes replete with meaning.[61]

When all has been said on the side of the identification of journalism with literature, it still seems clear that various subtile differences distinguish the two. Literature must always emphasize the artistic side of writing and transcends rules, while journalism is controlled by the space at command and by unwritten laws. In the news columns and the correspondence columns of the newspaper, the carefully arranged climax of the essayist becomes the anti-climax. The most important items must come first and the items following must trail off into the one of least importance so that the closing paragraphs can be

[60] Macaulay to Napier, June 24, 1842, *Napier Correspondence*, p. 394.
[61] Ch. M. Des Granges, *La Presse Littéraire sous la Restauration, 1815–1830*, pp. 7–34.
    T. R. Davies gives an admirable discussion of the press and romanticism in *French Romanticism and the Press*. The Globe. 1906.

lopped off if space requires. The most carefully prepared news articles and letters to the editor seem often foreordained to become journalistic amoebae. Writers sometimes find a news article sent in to the press distributed through different columns, one portion appearing as news, perhaps one paragraph as a short editorial, and a third coming out as a letter to the editor.

The old rule of the English press that the leader must contain three and only three paragraphs and each paragraph elaborate a single idea applies to journalism a procrustean measure that would be fatal to literature. However "little distinction can be made between a piece of journalism and a piece of literature on the ground of external subject-matter alone;" and however well it may be recognized that the product of the same incidents may in one instance "be interesting as news, in the other, as it bears upon some universal principle or emotion of human life," it may assume the creative and interpretative function of literature;[62] yet, the limitations of journalism from which literature is free, must be accepted.

The headline defies classification, yet it is rapidly transforming current English "as she is read" into a new and surprising language; the exigencies of space demand the use of the shortest, though not necessarily the clearest word.[63]

This result is seen in such words as flat (apartment), gems (jewelry), hit (criticize), knife (surgical operation), loot (plunder), lore (wisdom), nab (arrest), pact (treaty), probe (investigation), quiz (investigate), rap (censure), score (rebuke), show (exhibition), waifs (children), wed (marry), zone (territory),—an almost endless list could be made. It seems as if the desire to put a story into a headline practically eliminates all parts of speech except the noun and the verb.[64]

[62] H. W. Boynton, *Journalism and Literature*, pp. 1–23.

[63] Much of the telescoping of words was many years ago charged to the manifolder of the Associated Press,—Frisco, Rio, Orleans, and numerous other syncopated words were all laid at its door. The Associated Press is held to a rigid accountability for "pouring a stream of cold poison into the English language every morning."—W. Aplin, "At the Associated Press Office," *Putnam's Magazine*, July, 1870, 16: 23–30.

[64] See a column contributed by J. L. Lowes to the New York *Evening Post*, February 21, 1913.

See also a diverting editorial on "Headlines," New York *Evening Post*, November 21, 1908.

Spelling is also affected by the headline. The city of Cleveland, Ohio, named in honor of Moses Cleaveland, it is said varies in spelling from the name of its chief founder owing to the exigencies of the headline of the first newspaper printed there.[65]

The net effect of the headline as it appears to a prominent journalist is well stated by Catling in saying:

"The professor of journalism who periodically tells us all about newspapers, has failed to notice a comparatively modern and a very important feature of the newspaper, namely, the headlines. This is a department of the paper which has steadily conquered for itself an influence which every newspaper manager—sometimes inadequately—recognises. It often happens that the ingenious artist in this department is really editing the paper. He can convey an impression which the writers of ponderous leaders are endeavouring to avoid. He can create a doubt or awaken suspicion by a single artfully-chosen word, or sow broadcast an opinion which it may take columns of writing to show is unfounded. Suggestions that are buried in the body of the articles may attract no attention, but the flaming headline takes the eye at once, and its diagnosis of the matter which it criticises may be very wide of the mark without the average reader applying any correction. The headline largely regulates the emphasis that is given to the report of current events. Small matters in this way may be magnified and mere conjectures invested with nearly the dignity of facts." [66]

Headlines, as regards their content, need not concern the historian since they serve merely as "bulletins giving the substance of the articles to which they are attached," [67] and he naturally passes on to the articles below them. He need not question their guarantees of accuracy and truthfulness of impression,—they are intended for the hurried reader rather than for the student, they are used by the press of large cities for the benefit of commuters, and by the newspapers of small cities anxious to emulate the metropolitan press.

But inasmuch as "headlines," in the opinion of an authority

[65] Rufus King, *Ohio*, p. 228.

[66] Thomas Catling, *My Life's Pilgrimage*, p. 362.
But Catling has also failed to notice that in American schools of journalism the construction of the headline receives much attention from the professor of journalism.

[67] W. G. Bleyer, *Newspaper Writing and Editing*, p. 271.

on the subject, "as developed by the American press during the last half-century have come to be, next to the news itself, the most important part of our newspapers," [68] the historian is actively interested in them for their own sake. He finds in them a record of a new and surprising development of successful efforts to catch the reader's eye, of the ideals and standards of the press, of newspaper management, of the tastes of newspaper readers, and he is interested in the light they unconsciously throw on contemporary conditions of thought. The headline is one of the newspaper's own activities, rather than an allied activity, yet as one of the ramifications of language and literature it forms a footnote in the consideration of that part of the subject.

Credit must at least be given to the press for keeping language in a fluid state. The chief agency in the coinage of words is to-day the newspaper, and this is especially seen in the transformation of proper names into common nouns, adjectives and verbs. These give records of passing interests of society often left in no other way and of the permanent impression made on their own times by men of inventive genius or of pronounced characteristics. Sometimes the words thus coined become a definite contribution to language, while often they pass with the day's work.[69] They are at all times successful in conveying through a single word a meaning otherwise understood only through a circumlocution.[70]

The newspaper and the library, both public and private, have intimate affiliations. The press records the growing interest in the establishment of new libraries, it publishes the accessions of new books, through book reviews it gives information in regard to their contents and value, and it publishes statistics of library circulation; it publishes annotated bibliographies of important subjects and it prepares lists of books available for various trades and occupations; it notes the public activities of libraries and

[68] W. G. Bleyer, *Newspaper, Writing and Editing*, p. 271.

[69] Marconigram, silhouette, rooseveltism, wilsonize, baedecker, chautauqua, boycott, gerrymander.

[70] The expansion of an unauthenticated news item gave rise to the pleasantry, "The result of creeling is something less than a whopper. It is something more than a fib."—New York *Tribune*, August 18, 1918.

librarians both at home and abroad, it establishes its own library and puts it in charge of a special librarian, and in its office equipment it adopts many of the devices first introduced by the library.

The library on its part is specially interested in the newspaper on its material side,—in the quality of the paper used, in the color and the permanency of the ink, in the size and legibility of the type, and the nature of the illustrations; it must choose the papers for the reading-room use and those for binding; it must decide for or against the binding of advertisements with periodicals; it is confronted with the serious problem of the storage of long files of bound newspapers; and it is often handicapped by the lack of newspaper indices.

The problem of the material preservation of the newspaper as it confronts the library has been best stated by W. C. Ford when he says:

"As to newspapers there can also be no doubt on the point of policy, but to carry it into effect involves difficult and costly problems of management. The papers of the colonial period were of excellent quality, homely in color, but strong and lasting, some that have seen little usage being as bright and crisp as on the day of issue. Even if they have suffered modern methods of treatment will renew their lives with no damage to texture. The newspapers of the first half of the nineteenth century are also of good quality, and when bound are as permanent as printed matter can well be. But those issued after 1870 have steadily degenerated in quality of paper and have long presented insuperable difficulties in the way of preservation. These difficulties need not be here repeated. Every librarian has met them, and in our Society, with its immense newspaper collections, it constitutes a true problem involving a continuance of its shining preeminence among collecting institutions. Today the situation is more acute than it ever was, and the solution of the problem is as distant." [71]

[71] Report of the Council, *American Antiquarian Society*, 1918. The Report is so important in presenting a question that concerns alike the newspaper, the library, and the historian that these specific points presented by it must be added:

"Yet this great treasury of information rests upon a foundation almost as light as air, for it is recorded on a paper which rapidly disintegrates whether used or not, whether bound or in sheets, whether sealed or exposed. A few hours in the sunlight irreparably injures the texture; exposed to sun and air a neglect of a month reduces it to a condition in which it cannot be handled. And such it must be the chief task of this Society to collect and,

The early indifference of the library to the preservation of newspaper files and of the press to the preservation of its own files has often caused embarrassment to the historian, as has the wanton, or necessary, destruction of files that have been carefully collected and preserved. Jerdan, writing about 1850, exclaimed, "I do not think there is one perfect set of a London newspaper in the National Repository! . . . Of provincial journals there are only few irregular fragments." [72] Applications at newspaper offices for permission to consult their files have been granted,—only to find that their files are incomplete. A complete set of *Godey's Ladies' Book* was somewhat recently destroyed because its owner regarded the contents as "frivolous," and a box of jams and jellies was recently sent North,—wrapped in priceless Confederate newspapers. War and revolution are no respecters of libraries or of presses and the recent war has been no exception. [73]

---

if possible, preserve. Our American newspapers were offenders in this direction before the war, and war conditions have led to a further deterioration in quality. The same may be said of foreign journals, where the reduction in size has not compensated for the increasing difficulties in obtaining paper. The mere statement of the situation measures its acuteness and the obstacles to betterment. To the ordinary reader so much of the daily sheets seems unnecessary, the pages of advertisements, the discussions by the inexpert and the local items of small note gathered from the world as news. If only the vital parts of the journal could be concentrated upon two or three pages, and not strung over pages, broken and buried by the advertisements or other necessities of the "make-up." Such pages mounted on manila paper would outlive the ordinary usage of a century; but who would undertake to select the matter to be thus preserved? Who could have the time, the patience and intelligence? To reinforce the newspaper with crêpeline would be too costly and unsatisfactory. Perhaps the photostat offers a remedy, for the essential parts could be reproduced by it and on a paper which still uses a percentage of rag high enough to make it lasting. It is useless to ask the newspaper publishers to improve the quality of print paper; that quality is fixed by conditions beyond their control. The problem is one for this Society and its fellow societies, and we cannot pretend to be able even to suggest as yet a positive solution."

See also H. M. Lydenberg, "Saving the Newspaper Files for Posterity," *New York Evening Post*, April 2, 1921, and New York *Times*, August 12, 1921; C. Hemstreet, "The Times War News," New York *Times*, August 13, 1921.

[72] William Jerdan, *Autobiography*, I, 156-157.

[73] A tragic result of revolution was the destruction, when the Russians entered Tabriz in December, 1911, of a unique collection of files of Persian newspapers and magazines that the owner had been collecting during fourteen years,—necessarily destroyed by his family during the "Reign of Terror under which no one suspected of sympathy with Liberal ideas was safe."—E. G. Browne, *The Press and Poetry of Modern Persia*, pp. 1-2.

These mutual interests of the press and of the library may seem to be of a somewhat routine, conventional character, and apart from the reviews of new books, to affect little the question of authoritativeness with which the historian is primarily concerned. Yet neither can afford to neglect the other and the historian is equally dependent on both.

This partial enumeration of the manifold relationships of the press and other activities must indicate that it is a source for the study of any period and of presumably any question, and that therefore it can not be ignored by the historian. Yet while all of these ramifications of the newspaper must make it clear that the historian can not ignore periodical literature if the history written is to be the result of a study of the development of the present from the past, it is this very inter-relation of the press and all of these other activities that becomes one of his greatest perplexities in judging of the authoritativeness of the material presented. He has an absolute legal guarantee for a large part of the matter appearing in every newspaper; he has a probable guarantee of the reliability of the mass of material furnished by the great news-collecting agencies; he has no effective guarantee of what is provided by the local reporter; in the large, vaguely-defined territory where other occupations and interests share with the newspaper overlapping claims, the historian has and can have no fixed permanent guarantee of the authoritativeness of the material presented. All of this he must test by the laws of evidence used in the examination of other classes of records, and only that part that stands the test can be accepted by him.

An effort has been made to indicate the general lines along which these tests must be applied, and to suggest the special dangers connected with some subjects, and the comparative immunity from danger of others. But to a large extent every individual question must be decided on its own merits and it must be decided by every individual historian who uses the newspaper as historical material.

CHAPTER V

NEWS-COLLECTING AND NEWS-DISTRIBUTING ORGANIZATIONS

"And I have hope to erect a Staple for News ere long, whither all shall be brought and thence again vented under the name Staple-news."—Ben Jonson, *News from the New World discovered in the Moon*, *1621*.

> "An office, sir, a brave young office set up:
> . . . Newly erected
> Here in the house, almost on the same floor,
> Where all the news of all sorts shall be brought,
> And there be examined, and then register'd,
> And so be issued under the seal of the office,
> As Staple News; no other news be current."
>
> "This is the outer room, where my clerks sit,
> And keep their sides, the register in the midst;
> The examiner, he sits private there, within;
> And here I have my several rolls and files
> Of news by the alphabet, and all put up
> Under their heads."
> "But those too subdivided?"
> "Into authentical, and apocryphal—"
> "Whereto, beside the Coranti, and Gazetti—"
> "I have the news of the season—"
> "As vacation news,
> Term-news, and christmas-news."
> "And news of the faction."
> "As the reformed-news; Protestant-news;—"
> "And pontifical-news; of all which several,
> The day-books, characters, precedents are kept,
> Together with the names of special friends—"
> "And men of correspondence in the country—"
> "Yes, of all ranks, and all religions.—"
> "Factors and agents—"
> "Liegers, that lie out
> Through all the shires of the kingdom."
> "This is fine,
> And bears a brave relation!"
>
> Ben Jonson, *Staple of News*, 1626.

CORANTE, OR, NEVVES FROM
Italy, Germanie, Hungarie, Spaine and France. 1621.

From Lyons the 6 of Iune 1621.

OVr King in perſon lies before S Iohn Dangely, wherein the Duke of Roans brother is gouernour: whereof the Towne iſſued out 2. mile towards their enemie : Firſt Beaumont regiment, and after them a company of light horſemen, after that a truce for 8. dayes was made therein to intreate for peace : In the meane time preparation is made to beſiege Rochell, and the Duke de Guiſe is gon to Marſellis, there to prepare an armie by Sea, to beſiege Rochell by water, Monſieur Ladignier is not permitted to goe from the Court, it may be, becauſe they feare, that he being a Souldier of great experience might ſeeke to aide thoſe of the religion; it is ſayd that there ſhalbe a new gouernour choſen to his place of gouernment in Daulphinois.

In Parris in regard of certaine marſhall matters, the ſpiritualtie aſſembled together, and as the Biſhop of Bollonia deſired to haue obedience before the Parliament, as he begunne to frame his Oration, his ſpeach beganne to faile him, and when he would haue giuen it in writing, he could not doe it, but within three houres after he died ſpeachleſſe.

From Venice the 21 of Iune 1621.

From Millane it is written, that although there hath 2. commiſſions already bin ſent out of Spaine to reſtore Valtelina againe; the gouernour to the contrarie ſends more men thether, the like doth the Arch Duke Leopoldus, and ſee that 14 companies of Switzers entred into Leopoldus gouernement; and therein burne an Abby the reſtitution is ſtayed, yet the Spaniards were forced to giue backe, who wonder much, that the Duke of Sauoy muſters many Souldiers, and they know not his intent.

From Conſtantinople it is written that the great Turke with his principall officers, is gon to Adrianopolie, with a great number of Iannizaries and Spaggyans his armie, beſides the Tartarians being 300 thouſand ſtrong, that haue taken 4. millions and a halfe of Suldanes out of the treaſurie with them to pay their Souldiers, and he hath deliuered 4 hundred thouſand Suldanes to his generall of the Seas, who with 70. ſhippes or gallies is gon into the blacke Sea, to keepe the Coſſackers backe, that with their gallies, vſed to goe almoſt to Conſtantinople, and other letters certifie, that the great Turke, will goe into Polonia with 150. thouſand men, and will ſend 100. thouſand into Moldauia, and as many into Hungaria, to withſtand the Emperor of Germanie if he attempeth any thing.

From Leniſch in Hungarie the 4 of Iune. 1621.

Heere is great trouble, there are 400 Dutch ſouldiers in the Towne, and there ſhall 1200. more come, which will trouble vs much.

The 6 of Iune at Eperies there ſhall an aſſemblie be holden without doubt, becauſe Bethlem Gabor is deſirous to know of the Nobilitie there ſmall reſolution, whether they will hold with him or not; it is thought, that the 15 of Iune he will march forward with all his forces, and that the Marquis of Iagernedors will ioyne with him ſtrange things will ſhortly be heard of, whoſoeuer liues to ſee them; ſeeing he can doe nothing in the treatie of peace, becauſe they ſought to betray him: it is ſayd that 30 thouſand Turkes, and 20 thouſand Tartarians are marching forward, that are to fall vpon Krain and Kaeneten God be mercifull vnto vs, if it comes to that, that the Turkes and Tartarians ſhould deſtroy this goodly Countrie, God turne it all to the beſt.

From Leniſch the 10 of Iune 1621.

To morrow the generall aſſembly of the States is to begun at Eperies, and this day there are certaine letters come, one from the Emperor, wherein he writes very friendly vnto the States, another from the Lords Palatine, and the third from Setſcbt Georgen, with all in a manner are ſent vnto Bethlem Gabor as there King. What anſwere ſhall be giuen them,

and this aſſemblie will effect, we ſhall heereafter know.

From Neis the 13 of Iune 1621.

On Whitſonday his grace let Balthaſer Hoffman Van Gorlitz that was agent for the Emperor heere, vntill this preſent, goe out of priſon, who was forced to deliuer the key of his Maſtle. and it was opened to ſee what was therein.

Lieutenant Lohane hath a good number of men by him againe, yeſterday cauſed 10. barrels of beere, and ſome wine to be ſent into his quarter, a great number of men come to him with his grace, entertained es, and the money giuen them in hand is payd in Bethlemiſh ſuckets, and Rheins golde Nobles; he giues a horſe man 15. Florins in hand; it is thought that they will ſhortly goe to Otmachaw a mile and a halfe from hence, which for that it is a ſtrong Fort, therefore they intend to fortifie themſelues therein : Leſchwitz was yeſterday more then halfe burnt by fire that fell in a Malt houſe.

From Nns the 20 of Iune 1621.

It is ſaid 6. or 700 of theſe ſtubee Souldiers horſemen ſhall come hether, yeſterday about 2. of the clocke at night there came 3. Poſts hether to what end we know not, but all the Captaines that were here in the Towne, were ſent for to the Marquis, and preſently poſts were ſent into the quarter, and the people willed to come. The Towne-gates were kept ſhut till nine of the clocke in the morning, and at laſt none but the gate vnder the toll ſowre was ſet open, and all the company that lay in the new Towne, ſtood ſtill in armes about 10. of the clocke, the ſame company came in hether and were ſet before the lanet Captaines houſe, with commandement to charge there peeces, after that they were ſent into the Caſtle, and therein alſo are ſome of the Burgers with them that lay therein before, while this company went into the Caſtle, the Lorrehouſe company, ſtood ſtill behind the Caſtle, which procured no ſmall feare.

Yeſterday it was reported, that Bruten belonging to the Marquis was burnt by the Polanders, and Iagerenwelder taken by the Emperors forces, whether it be ſo or not, by the next we ſhall know : Since the gilders are daily caried by the Captaines and Commaunders into the quarter to pay the Sileſian Souldiers.

From Vianna the 25 of Iune 1621.

Although Steneral Tuerſo is in treatie with Bucquay, the Hungarians in Newheuſel will not grant to yeild, but will rather cut Tuerſo in peeces, then graunt to yeild : Therefore great ſtore of great Ordinance, bullets and powder are this weeke ſent thether to batter the Towne; there is likewiſe 600 thouſand Florins in money, and 200. thouſand Florins in iewels ſent, to giue euery one of our Souldiers 3 moneths pay : in the meane time the Hungarians daily skirmiſh with our men, and it is ſayd that Bethlem at Caſchew prepares a great ſtreegth to releiue Newheuſel, and that Setſchy George ſeekes to ſtop his paſſage.

On this ſide the Earle of Colaldo hath gotten the Budianers goods out of the inuincible Caſtle called Giſſingen, where he himſelfe is, whereof there is a deale of corne and wine come, which is ſent backe to Papa and the comfeſtien borders.

In Morauia, there are more principall Lords and Burgers committed to priſon, whoſe expectation, as alſo in Prague of the priſoners ſhall this weeke be done, and Eraſmus & George Van Landaw ſhall be brought priſoners hether.

The Emperors iourney to Prague ſhall begin the fift of Iulie, and the Rickes day at Regenſpurg ſhall begin the 1. of Semptember.

From Prague the 26 of Iune 1621.

The ſeuenth of this moneth, as 8. daies ſince it was written, old Strenuin, one of the impriſoned directors, in the night time threw himſelfe headlong out of the white Tower into the ditches and there died, his body was yeſterday cut in 4.

quarters.

...atters,and hange in 4.places of the high way, his head and hand nailed vpon the Gibet in the Towne, and it is fayd that the execution of the rest next Monday or Tuesday shall be done: It is said that Silesia the Souldiers are discharged, and that there are certaine Captaines sent thether with gold to take vp men for the Bohemian states; who at their owne charges will raise an other Regiment of Souldiers for the Emperor; it appeares that the Marquis of Iagerendorf, makes great preparation for warre, and that with him is the young Earle of Thorne, the barron *Van Lumpenburgh*, Colonell *Stubrewell*, *Tschereten* and others.

Thabor holds out still, and daily make sallies out, and neither side holds quarter; but if on either side they take any Souldiers, they straight hang them vp, and Colonell *Francke* is still heere.

This *Fronlichnam* feast, was holden by the Catholickes in the presence of the Prince of Liechtensteen and others, principall Lords, with a stately Procession, and in the old Towne, or by the old Bohemians or Hussites held by two banners of handicrafts men.

From Reinhousen the 22.of Iune 1621.

This day the Rheingrates Ottains 10. corner of horse, being well armed & mounted by Lycence of his grace lodged in the Bishop of Speres Territories.

Thursday next at Crentznach, and Sunday after at Openheim there shall be an open Procession made, and all the inhabitants that are not Catholikes, and will not goe with the Procession are commanded to be quiet and not to stir vpon paine of death.

From Bergstrassen the 24.of Iune 1621.

The Rhingrate 1Ottains horse men that are discharged, that serued the Vnion goe from hence to Wetteraw, and the Kniphausche Souldiers are come into the Territories of Wurtzburg, and 1000.horses ioine with them, which robe and rantsancke all about the Countrie, and while the Souldiers that are taking vp Continewes; they imbolden themselues to goe in troupes together.

Out of the vpper Palatinate the 19.of Iune 1621.

The Earle of Mansfields souldiers doe great hurt by robbing, rantsacking and burning of houses, and for that the Towne of Weyden that should haue giuen 4000. Florins refuse it, the Earle of Mansfield will lay his campe betweene Weyden and the new Towne on the Walduab, what the Duke of Newburg or Sultzbach will say to that, we shal hereafter know, and for that the Lords of Weymar haue ioined their forces with his, the Earle of Mansfield is about 15 thousand horse and foote men strong, and still more Souldiers come to him, it is thought hee will breake vp his campe at Thaus, and goe further into Bohemia, and leaue 2.Regiments of souldiers in the Palatinate, and if Pilsen Eelenbogen and Eger were with him he would goe towards prague: this day there hath bin iustice done among all the Colone s.Captaines of horsemen, and Captaines touching Colonell *Franckenstand*, or *Malefirz*, who was cited to appeare, and if he did not, to be prescribed Doctor *Leiminger*, did much complaine of him, saying that he was the cause that Pilsen gaue ouer: The Bauiain souldiers spoile all about Elenboghen and Romigsweeret, and many runne away: They want prouant, and many of them die and so doe Mansfields men: *Thabor, Klingenburgh*, and *Wittengaw* hold strong still, if they had good Garrisons.

From the Hage the 28 of Iune 1621.

By the last out of France it is written, that they of S.Iben

Dangely haue issued out vpon the Kings forces, and haue slaine some hundreds of them, and that the Prince of Gunuille and other Lords were hurt, whereby the Kings forces were forced to retire 4.miles backe; in the meane time the Duke of Roan in Langedor, Guienne, and those places here abe uts, raiseth a great armie for those of the religion, and euery day more Colonels ioyne with him, and make great preparation for the warre, while they see it will be no otherwise, God helpe them in their iust cause, and send them good issue. The King, that is still incited and moued by the Priests & Iesuites, to hold war, and contribute to the same, takes vp 10.or 12000.men more, whervpon not onely they of the religion but also some peaceable Papists wggle strangely of such and the like counsellers.

Yesterday a Polish Ambassador (that had bin in France, and Braboo and there long frequented with the Spaniards) cam hether and was according to the maner stately receiued, on Saturday he had audience giuen him in the generall states counsell being present, who as I vnderstand, spake to them to this effect, that for as much as the Turke prepared great forces to inuade, Poland and other Christian Countries, that they would graunt some aide, to direct him from thence, and due their best therein, as a so that they would graunt to a long time with the Spaniards, that so the house of Austria might employ all their forces against the Turke, what answere he had, is not yet knowne.

That the Zelands men of warre haue brought in 5.Spanish shippes laden with all kinde of wares, and that ship of warre for the States are layd before all the Sea hauens of Portugall and Spaine.

For that they of Hertogenbuske, did take the gouernour of the Graues watch and horses, he sent out certaine Souldiers to enter into a Village belonging to the Bush called Osy: Where as then there was a Fayre, which he rantsackt and spoiled, and his Souldiers with great bootie and many prisoners came home to the Graue againe.

To morrow the States Proclamation touching preparation to be made for the Armado, to goe to the West Indes at euery mans costs and charges shall be proclaimed.

From Ben the 1.of Iuly 1621.

By our last we haue newes out of Fraunce, that they of the religion prepare a great armie, to that end gathering great troupes together, and many resort vnto them, to aide themselues in their iust cause.

Two dayes since the Lords and Officers of Bohemia that are come out of the Countrie, and now in the Netherlands, had audience first of his Excellencie and after of the generall States, and by the chiefe Chauncelor, were much commended (that made a long Oration vnto them to that end) for their fidelitie, and most friendly welcomed, and so conuaied to their lodgings, and there when the King goes to Church or to the Court, honorable attend him.

This day an Arminian preacher who apparelled like a souldier, preached at Gouda, was committed prisoner.

The Bishop of Collens Ambassadors haue once had an expedition, and haue moued the Newtralyte there, to appoint a certaine time when they would take order for reparation to be made for the Turkes deteriments.

The Zeland is haue brought in 3.shippes more besides 5. others, Spanish ships laden with Oyle, Suger, and other wares, and not long since there is a great Zeland ship come thether called Wallacher, out of the East Indes richly laden, and 2.others are comming to Amstelredam.

The west Indian Marchants patent is proclaimed euery where

Printed at Amstelredam by Broer Ionson, dwelling on the new side behinde Borchwall in the siluer Can, by the Brewery, the 9. of Iuly. 1621.

"Is there anything whereof it may be said, See, this is new? it hath been already of old time."

BEN JONSON'S plan for "a staple of newes," even though purporting to emanate from the moon, must have been realized and been practically coincident with the beginnings of the newspaper in England. The marriage of the daughter of James I with Frederick, the Elector Palatine, had involved England, sympathetically, in the Thirty Years' War, and there was great demand for news of the war as well as for tidings from friends. Impecunious English volunteers on the continent translated the current accounts of the war and these quickly developed into the weekly "corantos;" [1] and soon the civil war in England gave rise to the "diurnal," and to the "mercurius," with various descriptive terms. The extraordinary development of "newsbooks,"—"all the main features of the modern newspaper being found in them within seven years," [2]—and of their successors undoubtedly made necessary the realization in some form of Ben Jonson's description of the "office of the staple of newes," with its governor, emissaries, examiner, register, and clerks who

"manage all at home, and sort, and file,
And seal the news and issue them."

[1] It is clearly evident from Williams' *History of English Journalism* that the author believed that these "war correspondents" gave England its first newspapers. The titles of the corantos in the Burney collection, from May to November, 1622, indicate the receipt of news from Italy, Germany, Hungary, Austria, Bohemia, the Palatinate, France, the Low Countries, and "most parts of Christendom."—J. B. Williams, *History of English Journalism to the Foundation of the Gazette*, Appendix C, pp. 215–217; J. B. Williams, "The Beginnings of English Journalism," *Cambridge History of English Literature*, VII, 389–415.

These corantos in the Burney collection have been held to be the earliest English newspapers known. But they are antedated by a collection of eighteen newspapers printed in English at Amsterdam, including one at the Hague, running in time from December 2, 1620, to September 18, 1621. The first five were "to be soulde by Petris Keerius, dvvelling in the Calverstreete, in the uncertaine time." "A faithful reproduction made from the originals, acquired in 1913 by the British Museum, London, and published on the occasion of the International Exhibition of Graphic Art, Leipzig, 1914," has been edited by W. P. Van Stockum, Jr., and was published at The Hague in 1914.—For an account of these see J. B. Williams, "The First English Newspaper," *Nineteenth Century and After*, March, 1914, 75: 514–525.

[2] J. B. Williams, *History of English Journalism to the Foundation of the Gazette*, p. 30.

Ben Jonson, however, was but anticipating the *nouvellistes* who during the wars of Louis XIV organized crude forerunners of news-collecting agencies in the *bureaux et pelotons* formed that each news-gatherer might report specially in regard to a particular city and then share his news with his associates.[3]

It seems, however, to have been Edward Cave who, about 1725, began the exchange of news between the country newspapers and the London press, selling the country news for a guinea a week. He held the office of inspector of the franks and thus had facilities for securing intelligence from provincial towns and country newspapers. This was in embryo the news-collecting organization of to-day as operated for gain by private agencies.

It was again many years before Alaric Watts applied the same idea to the exchange of literary intelligence that Cave had used in the exchange of political news. He seems to have originated the idea of getting free notices of the magazines into the London and provincial newspapers through publishing in them "a regular train of quotation at the beginning of each month." As he finds, so he writes to Blackwood, that "some of the London gentlemen of the press are most willing to quote clever papers from your work," but are unwilling to spoil their magazines to get the extracts, he begs Blackwood to obviate "this weighty difficulty" by sending him a "parcel of waste sheets every month." This scheme, Watts argues, would enable him "to organize a plan by which you can be very extensively quoted."

He writes insistently to Blackwood of the advantage it would be to his magazine to have these extracts appearing in the twenty papers he has in training and the ten others he is sure would voluntarily copy from these, and he urges him to have in the magazine "something perfect in itself of a reasonable length for quotation." But the publisher seems not to have yielded to Watts' repeated solicitations, as he also rejected a somewhat similar plan urged on him fifteen years later by A. Mallalieu.[4]

But Watts was indefatigable as well as versatile and he was

[3] F. Funck-Brentano, *Les Nouvellistes*, pp. 83–102.
[4] The correspondence on this subject is interesting as showing the sharp contrast in the business methods of newspapers and magazines about 1820 and those of to-day. It is given in Mrs. Oliphant, *Annals of a Publishing House: William Blackwood and His Sons*, I, 495–510; II, 201–202.

quickly, in the words of Dr. Maginn, "head nurse of a hospital of rickety newspaperlings, which breathe but to die,"—as his captious critic characterized the string of Conservative papers of which Watts was in charge about 1832. These, with the title and leading articles set up, were printed in Fleet Street and the local news and local politics subsequently added in the country by the local printers. This was apparently the origin of "partly-printed newspapers." [5]

It was not, however, until 1863 that the germ of the idea of Cave and of Watts took form in the largely amplified plan of William Saunders and Edward Spender for the organization of the Central Press. They proposed to send daily to subscribing local papers throughout the country eight columns of matter classified under twelve different heads ranging from "topics of the day" to literary and religious intelligence. The office when opened included an editorial staff, the members of which acquainted themselves with the contents of the London, country, colonial, and foreign papers, and thus gave a complete service of general and foreign news.[6]

"These arrangements," says Hunt, "admirable as they were, were not at first used to the extent that had been expected." Perhaps an explanation may be found in a letter written at the time by James Macdonell, apropos of the sale of the Newcastle-upon-Tyne *Express*, of which he was editor, to one of the proprietors of the Central Press. He describes the London establishment "in which a staff of journalists prepare the news of the day, and write leaders on the principal current topics. The matter thus obtained is put in type; then stereotyped three, four, or five times; and then the blocks are sent by afternoon train to Plymouth, Hull, and other places in which the firm have papers of their own, or an arrangement for supplying the papers of others with stereotyped matter." He protests, however, that under such a system "The *Express* will every morning be an exact copy of other journals, except in having one, two, or at most three

[5] A. A. Watts, *Alaric Watts*, II, chap. XIV.
[6] W. Hunt, *Then and Now*, chap. VII, "Co-Operation in Newspaper Work—The Central Press." This gives in full the circular letter issued by the organizers.

columns of local news." He, therefore, refused to continue connection with the paper under this system.[7]

It was out of this Central Press, organized for supplying on an extensive scale partly printed papers to the provincial press, that later was developed the great Press Association of England, now corresponding to the Associated Press of America. The immediate occasion of its organization was, however, the relation of the newspaper to the telegraph and cable companies whose system was a monopoly, whose service was unsatisfactory, whose tolls were excessive, and whose manners left much to be desired,—so thought the journalists.[8]

The foundation of the English Press Association had been antedated a few years by the now universally-known *Reuter's*. As early as 1849, on the completion of the first telegraph line between Germany and France, Paul Julius Reuter had started a news-collecting agency, bridging one gap in the line by means of a pigeon-post. In 1851 he established himself in England and became a naturalized British citizen. He strove, unsuccessfully for some years, to persuade the English press to publish his foreign news telegrams, but in 1858 *The Times* published matter forwarded from Paris by a Reuter agent. After that, since "the telegram is necessarily the backbone of the news service of the daily paper," he directed his efforts largely to securing concessions for the use of the telegraph and cable lines and to securing the recognition of his agents at important points. Before his death in 1899 he had transformed his business into a limited liability company whose operations covered the world, and in February, 1915, the fiftieth anniversary of the founding of the Reuter Telegram Company was celebrated in London.[9]

The formation of great news-collecting associations has everywhere been inevitable. As long as local news is the chief interest

---

[7] W. R. Nicoll, *James Macdonell*, pp. 107–113.

[8] W. Hunt, in *Then and Now*, chap. X, "The Electric Telegraph," includes a full account of the organization of the Press Association.

[9] The press of that date gives accounts of the establishment of *Reuter's*. Brief statements are found in G. B. Dibblee, *The Newspaper;* F. M. Thomas, *Fifty Years of Fleet Street*, pp. 165–166; H. Simonis, *The Street of Ink*, pp. 157–182; J. D. Symon, *The Press and its Story*, chap. VI, "Press Telegrams."

The London *Nation*, April 24, 1915, after the death of the second Baron Reuter, gave an appreciative account of the service rendered by *Reuter's*.

of the newspaper, it is possible to collect such news without special difficulty, but when the horizon widens conditions are changed. If at one time each paper gathered its own news and there was no collective responsibility for its reliability, such as is furnished to-day by the great news-gathering agencies, it must be remembered that the field from which news was gathered was much more restricted than is the case to-day.

But with the increase in the number of periodicals of all kinds, with the growth in size of each individual copy, with the enormous expansion in their circulation, and with the consequent development of the periodical as a business enterprise, there has followed the upbuilding of intricate, complicated machinery that on the one hand controls and regulates the output of the press and on the other hand facilitates its further extension.

The first real beginnings of associations of newspapers for mutual benefit in securing foreign news were made in America about 1827. At that time "there existed a combination of the leading newspaper establishments of the city [New York] for obtaining foreign intelligence; but it appears to have been rather a combination of laziness than of enterprise—the object being not so much to obtain news promptly as to insure that no one should obtain news to the disadvantage of the rest." [10]

The *Journal of Commerce* had been jealously excluded from this association, but its new owners had known of a rowboat that had prowled around Boston Harbor and collected news from incoming European packets and they quickly transferred the idea to New York where they built a yacht, named it the *Journal of Commerce*, erected a semaphore telegraph to which their news was signalled and which through various relays reached the publication office.[11]

The forerunner of the Associated Press had been organized in America when several New York papers joined forces with the telegraph company and established "a staple of news." Other newspapers gradually were admitted to membership, an offensive and defensive alliance was formed with the Reuter

[10] J. P. Thompson, *Memoir of David Hale*, pp. 54–55; *Memoirs of James Gordon Bennett*, pp. 134–135.
[11] M. E. Stone, "Newsgathering as a Business," *Century Magazine*, June, 1905, 70: 299–310; *Fifty Years a Journalist*, pp. 204–207.

agency, subsidiary associations were formed, mutually advantageous agreements were made with the Western Union Telegraph Company, rival associations sprang up, reorganization was effected, and through various changes the Associated Press has developed into the most important news-collecting agency in existence.[12] In 1921 it had a membership of nearly 1,300 daily papers, the basis of membership was that of mutual association, and its day service and its night service commanded nearly 65,000 miles of leased wire. In 1917 it had 52,000 special correspondents in its service, it had graduated from its affiliations with the Reuter service of London, the Wolff service of Berlin, the Havas service of Paris, and the smaller agencies of other countries, into the maintenance of its own bureaus in all the great capitals of the world, as well as in the leading American cities. Unlike all other news-collecting organizations, which are proprietary, the Associated Press is organized on a mutual basis,—it makes no profits, pays no dividends, has no stock ownership and sells no news, but gathers news on joint account and distributes it to its members in amount varying from 500 to more than 60,000 words daily. "It is the greatest and most successful co-operative enterprise in the world." [13]

It has been necessary to revert to these historical facts in order to understand what is the function of a news-collecting

[12] In 1892, various recombinations "threw the practically absolute control of the telegraphic news service of the United States into the hands of three individuals," with all that such proprietary control menaced. This was averted by the formation of the new association, "democratic in control, disinterested in motive, and co-operative in method and management."—J. P. Gavit, "Melville E. Stone," "M. E. S." His Book, pp. 1–56.

[13] These facts have been taken from the annual reports of the Associated Press; from articles by M. E. Stone, Century Magazine, April, May, June, August, 1905; F. B. Noyes, "The Associated Press," North American Review, May, 1913, 197: 701–710; the general press reports of legal decisions where the Associated Press has been either a plaintiff or a defendant; the clippings filed in the Columbia University School of Journalism, and in the Vassar College Library; from "M. E. S." His Book, A Tribute and a Souvenir of the Twenty-Five Years, 1893–1918, of the Service of Melville E. Stone as General Manager of the Associated Press, and from M. E. Stone, Fifty Years a Journalist (1921).

The Library of Congress, Division of Bibliography, issued in May, 1914, in typewritten form, a List of References on the Associated Press and Other Press Agencies.

Special information in regard to the "News Machinery of Wall Street" is given by F. J. Rascovar, The Nation, March 8, 1917, 104: 292–293.

organization from the standpoint of the historian. He is not immediately concerned with the questions as to whether the Associated Press is a monopoly; whether "the United Press scored an epochal scoop" in announcing the death of Pius X in advance of its rivals, how far it was responsible for the false dispatch sent November 7, 1918, prematurely announcing the signing of the armistice, and whether "it has revolutionized journalism;" whether the International News Service should be coerced into giving up the field; or whether the *Sun* Printing and Publishing Association was justified in protesting against the course of action taken by other associations. But he is deeply concerned to know whether news-gathering associations furnish reliable news, whether they suppress such information as they do not wish to have circulated, whether the news reported is biased, distorted, juggled, falsified, or misrepresented, or whether it is fair and truthful. The historian is indebted to news-collecting organizations more than to any other single source for the information published in the press,—what guarantees do they afford that this information can be accepted without question and that important news is not suppressed?

The Associated Press, as the oldest, largest, and most far-reaching of these agencies in America, has been most in the public eye and the greatest number of criticisms have been directed against it. These charges have been that it is a monopoly, that it caters to a capitalistic press, that it suppresses the news, and that its reports are biased or unfair.

The charge that the Associated Press is a monopoly is a confusing one since it may imply that it is a commercial monopoly in the sense of making excessive profits through controlling the news, or it may imply that it is a monopoly through controlling the market for news and preventing the formation of other news-collecting organizations. That the Association is not a commercial monopoly must be self-evident since it makes no profits whatsoever and they can not therefore be "excessive." The contention that the Associated Press has been a violator of the Federal Anti-Trust Act was held to be unwarranted by Attorney-General Gregory in an opinion given March 12, 1915, after a careful and exhaustive scrutiny of the object and scope of the

Association.[14] He held that a group of newspapers had the right to associate for the exchange of news, if no attempt was made to prevent the formation of rival associations, or to prevent its own members from getting news from other associations. The charge, therefore, that the Associated Press is a monopoly must be dismissed on both counts.

But even were it otherwise, it must be evident that the question whether news-gathering agencies are "news trusts" or not does not in the slightest degree affect their credibility, although an understanding of the organization of such associations must make it evident that the very term "monopoly" is incompatible with the very existence of such associations. They are formed to collect and to distribute news and all their members receive as much as or little news as they wish and as they pay for. But even were they monopolies of the most extreme character, that fact would not in and of itself militate against their absolute reliability,—the question that most concerns the historian.

It is sometimes charged that the Associated Press is controlled by "capital." The expression "a capitalistic press" is frequently heard and the implication may be that the press is owned by so-called capitalists and managed by them in their own interests, —a charge easily made but less easily proved. The press assuredly can not be called capitalistic in the usual sense of the word. A few large metropolitan dailies are owned in the main by a single individual or family, and the object of the paper, as of other forms of business enterprise, is to make money. But the element of speculation does not enter into the conduct of the business, the very nature of the business is in itself a guarantee against monopoly, and no lobby is maintained to secure or to prevent the passage of legislation in its interests. As a business enterprise it has the temptations of other forms of business, but it can not be said that these temptations are those of what is usually denominated a capitalistic industry. That the Associ-

[14] The letter is given in full in the New York *Evening Post*, March 17, 1915.—The same charge in a different form had been met by F. W. Lehmann in 1898 in an address, "Is the Associated Press a Trust?"—"*M.E.S.*" *His Book*, pp. 76–84.—The Associated Press "monopoly" was ably, but probably not finally, disposed of by the New York *Evening Post* in an editorial, February 5, 1914.

ated Press or any other news-gathering agency could be "bought" by a capitalist is as unthinkable as the converse,—that a capitalist could be bought by any press organization.

The implication in the charge that the Associated Press is "capitalistic" may also be understood as meaning that its selection and presentation of the news are influenced by so-called "big business." If it is true that the great mass of its members are primarily interested in "big business," then it is the news concerning it that is reported. In all selection of news, the ultimate decision in regard to that selection is made by the members of the Associated Press, not by the persons or interests wishing to be selected. Whatever the decision made it must meet the wishes of the members and in turn the wishes of the readers of the newspapers represented in the Associated Press. If the news that is selected and presented is favorable to "big business," it is because the great mass of readers all over the country are interested in that subject, not because "big business" has chosen to be reported to the exclusion of other interests. But that these interests have the right of way is not evident. No daily paper of general scope could survive a month if its news concerned only a limited element in society. The newspaper holds the interest of the public largely because of the variety of the news it presents, because the news is selected from every quarter of the globe, because the appeal it makes to its readers is universal.[15]

It is sometimes charged that the Associated Press suppresses the news.[16] To this charge the somewhat blunt reply has been

[15] This was recognized in the announcement made by the New York *World* that it had added the *Manchester Guardian's* entire news service to the work of its own bureaus and staff correspondents abroad.—*The World*, May 28, 1921.

[16] E. A. Ross, "The Suppression of Important News," *Atlantic Monthly*, March, 1910, 105: 303–311; Editorial, "In Justice to the 'A. P.'," *Collier's Weekly*, June 6, 1914; An Observer, "The Problems of the Associated Press," *Atlantic Monthly*, July, 1914, 114: 132–137.

A conclusive reply to these charges was given by M. E. Stone in a letter to *Collier's Weekly* and published by it in its issue of July 11, 1914, and in a letter, under date of August 1, 1914, to the *Atlantic Monthly*, but apparently not published by it. The letter was subsequently included in the volume edited by W. G. Bleyer, *The Profession of Journalism*, pp. 124–132. This volume was published by the Atlantic Monthly Press in 1918.

The example of "suppression of the news" most frequently cited is that of the West Virginia coal strike in 1909; the Associated Press was charged with suppressing the facts, and that in consequence the public did not know

made, "It takes courage to tell the reader that plenty of things happen every day which are none of his business." [17] It may also take a comprehension of the organization of the Associated Press to appreciate that whatever its shortcomings may be, suppression of news by it is absolutely unthinkable. It exists to collect and to disseminate news,—to suppress news is to commit suicide. Not all of the news it supplies is presumably printed by a single member of the Associated Press,—its members are free to pick and choose what they publish. If news is "suppressed," it is not at the fountain head.

So keenly has the Associated Press felt this criticism that comes so trippingly from the tongue that in 1913 it welcomed the opportunity of bringing a suit for criminal libel against the editor and the cartoonist of a monthly magazine which had charged it with the suppression of facts. Previous charges of this nature had been made on the floor of Congress where those making them had been immune, or they had been so carefully made as to permit escape from the penalties of libel, or they had been voluntarily retracted. After two years, however, the case was dismissed by the court.[18] As far as the contention of the Associated Press has been concerned, not a single case of alleged wilful suppression of the news has been proved.

That the correspondents of the Associated Press commit errors of judgment the Association itself is the first to recognize. It is possible for all persons to be wise after the event, and in one or two conspicuous cases the small beginnings of what subsequently proved to be important matters were not noted in the Associated Press dispatches. Questions that at the time were believed to have only a local import afterwards proved to be of

---

of the trouble. In reality, the Associated Press had sent more than 93,000 words concerning it to the New York press and about sixty columns in regard to it were printed.—Letter of M. E. Stone to the *Atlantic Monthly*, August 1, 1914, "*M. E. S.*" *His Book*, pp. 273–279, and W. G. Bleyer, *supra*.

The pros and cons of the Associated Press are considered by Gregory Mason, "A Criticism," and by George Kennan, "A Defense," in *The Outlook*, May 30, 1914, 107: 237–240, 249–250; an editorial defense is given in *The Outlook*, July 18, 1914, 107: 631–632.

[17] W. P. Hamilton, "The Case for the Newspapers," *Atlantic Monthly*, May, 1910, 105: 646–654.

[18] The indictment was filed December 2, 1913, and the case dismissed December 1, 1915.

national importance. Local correspondents sometimes fail to see events in true perspective. "But it is one thing to charge it [the Associated Press] with not coming up to the full measure of an extremely high and arduous responsibility, and an altogether different thing to accuse it of wilful and systematic suppression." [19]

It is charged that the news supplied is partisan. This also is incredible. The newspapers making up its membership represent every shade of political, industrial, economic, social, and religious opinion,—the furnishing of partisan news would mean the instant disintegration of the Association. The charge undoubtedly has its basis in the headlines under which the news appears, but these are written by the receiving office, not by the news-supplying Association. These captions as found in different papers may be quite contradictory, even for the same account, but whatever of partisan tinge they may have has been acquired in the local office, not through the Associated Press.

The charge that inaccurate, sensational, and exaggerated news is sent out is equally incredible. Not infrequently brief statements of minor events are sent out by the Associated Press; these may be embroidered by local reporters and appear all over the country in accounts that bear little relation to what actually occurred;[20] they may appear under sensational headlines out of all proportion to the relative importance of the dispatches themselves. But the Associated Press can not be held responsible for the accounts written by irresponsible reporters connected with the papers constituting its membership.

Over against these somewhat irresponsible, wholesale charges, the fundamental points of which have not as yet been proved in a single instance, the historian must put the very nature of the organization of the Associated Press as the best guarantee that could be desired of the general authoritativeness of its

[19] "The Associated Press," *The Nation*, March 12, 1914, 98: 256–257.

[20] At one time a slight accident occurred in the chemical laboratory of a college. It was due to the haste of a student who, in heating alcohol for a very simple experiment, had not followed instructions. An account of it, giving every fact, was written in six lines by the president of the college and sent to the press. This brief statement was expanded by some papers into a column of description filled with harrowing details and everywhere it assumed various forms.

dispatches. He must recognize the elaborate and careful preparations made for the receipt and transmission of all important news,—two years before the presidential election of 1916 it began its preparations for giving the returns of the elections. He must give credit to its desire to guarantee its statements wherever and whenever and by whom questioned. A statement was questioned that had been made by one of its correspondents in France in December, 1917. The Associated Press promptly cabled for definite information as to the source of his statement; the correspondent cabled in reply that it was copied from the official communication issued by the general commanding the division concerned and that a copy of the original order was in his possession;—this is but one instance of the many that could be given to illustrate the care taken to secure unimpeachable evidence.

That in spite of every precaution against sending out incorrect news, the Associated Press sometimes does send out such news is inevitable, but wherever possible the wrong is redressed. It reported Senator La Follette as saying in a speech, September 20, 1917, that "we had no grievances against Germany" when in fact he had said precisely the reverse. When eight months later the error of its reporter was shown the Associated Press, it immediately explained its probable source and apologized, but it could hardly be held responsible for the injustice done Senator La Follette during the intervening months when error had travelled on wings and the Associated Press had been ignorant of its escape.

It has been inevitable, however, that various special interests should feel that they have not been given as full publicity as their merits have deserved and therefore they have organized special news-collecting agencies to disseminate information concerning particular subjects. The Federated Press was organized in 1919 and is "a co-operative, non-profit making association of editors with a membership in America and abroad of approximately two hundred and fifty. It is established on four continents with Bureaus in Paris, London, Berlin, Vienna, Rome, Sydney, Mexico City, Ottawa, Pekin, Washington, New York, Chicago, Boston and elsewhere. . . . The design of the organization is to report the news dispassionately and to maintain the service absolutely free from propaganda." [21] The objects of the Federated Press, as stated more fully in its by-laws, are as follows:

"Being unable to obtain unbiased news service from the existent press associations, certain persons, owners of or representing newspapers and other publications, hereby unite in a mutual and co-operative organization for the collection and interchange of intelligence, telegraphic and otherwise, for publication in the newspapers or other publications owned or represented by them. . . . This association is not to make any profit and is not to make or declare any dividends. It shall be the general policy of this association that its news service must be handled without bias for or against the principles of the several groups represented by the membership." [22]

This statement of principles does not vary materially from that made by other co-operative, non-profit making associations organized to collect and to distribute news. But a self-imposed handicap has seemed to be its motto, "The news in spite of the newspapers." Since it restricts its reports to "the news of the labor and political movements" and to "all matters of interest to the workers everywhere," the scope of its activities seems limited. Moreover, since it recognizes that "while it is not possible to eliminate all opinion from news reports, since every person who writes, necessarily writes of events as he sees them, the Federated Press adheres strictly to the *principle* of reporting events objectively," [23] it does not in its statement of principles differ from other organizations that also aim to report events objectively.

The Industrial News Bureau Service is a proprietary business "that goes out each week to five thousand newspapers in fourteen western states, more than half the area of the United States, three to five sheets to each paper. Sheet marked four is gotten up separately for each state. We get more matter published for industries and against radicalism, or socialist schemes that are against private ownership, than any publicity organization in the West." [24]

[21] Letter of Clark H. Getts, March 22, 1921.
[22] Cited in the Constitution of the Federated Press League, Article II.
[23] Folder issued by the Federated Press, n. d.
[24] Letter from the proprietor.

It has been inevitable that as the large news-collecting organizations have grown still larger and waxed more powerful, other organizations should grow up, less as competitors than as supplementary associations or business enterprises formed to furnish news to special interests. It has been equally inevitable that it quickly becomes difficult to distinguish such news agencies from publicity bureaus pure and simple.[25]

Three forms of news-collecting agencies have been organized, and this must be realized in appraising their comparative value in collecting material the historian is subsequently to use. One is the proprietary association where, as in the case of *Reuter's* as first organized, the newspapers "lost control of their sources of information so far as foreign countries were concerned" and although "the originator of the new system did his best to secure impartial news, that system put enormous power in the hands of correspondents, whose messages were beyond the wholesome influence of competition."[26] It would seem inevitable that any news-collecting agency in private hands must be in danger of having this limitation on its usefulness, yet after fifty years of service, the London *Nation* could say, "The head of such a business has an enormous power in his hands, but we can not recollect that it was ever used to further individual views or policies."[27] Its real limitation is of an entirely different character. "The news that comes through *Reuter's*," continues the *Nation*, "is made up to such an extent of official documents, reports of speeches, debates, trials, and the unbiassed doings of nature in time of flood and earthquake that we had grown into the way of regarding it as something nearly as mechanical as 'the tape'."

[25] Private news service "offers to a select clientele, in letter form, intimate information, chiefly of a sort that under modern world conditions has its source in Washington. It is designed to visualize a field which is not covered by newspapers, and to supplement the press reports, which, admirable as they are, are frequently incomplete, inaccurate, and otherwise unsatisfactory, because of the difficult conditions under which they are assembled and printed."—Statement of a private news service bureau.

News-collecting agencies formed to distribute intelligence in regard to foreign countries are especially in danger of unconsciously merging into publicity bureaus.

[26] F. M. Thomas, *Fifty Years of Fleet Street*, p. 166.

[27] "*Reuter's*," The London *Nation*, April 24, 1915, 17: 108–109; see also A. Meister, *Die deutsche Presse im Kriege und später*, pp. 34–37.

But "it is the progressive parties," rightly says the *Nation*, "who suffer most in their way of thinking by the dominance of a colorless but invariably conservative agency." [28]

Reuter's has been a proprietary organization controlled by those who have no personal or immediate connection with the press. But a proprietary news service organized, widely extended to other papers, and controlled by a single newspaper has infinite possibilities for mischief. Such a service extended to several hundred subscribers has more than once been in the hands of a powerful editor. "He is in constant telegraphic communication with all these publications; he has engaged their editors in business relations with himself; and consequently his version of the story and his views are bound to receive more or less favorable consideration." [29] Such a proprietary service assuredly tends to become "cunning propaganda."

Even more serious is the limitation on the usefulness of the second form of organization where the collection of news is controlled or influenced by the action of government, since at any time news may be delayed or entirely suppressed by government order. In 1914, five days after Serbia had replied to Austria, the Russian chargé d'affaires in Berlin reported to his government, "The Wolff Bureau has not published the text of the Servian response which was communicated to it. Up to this moment this note has not appeared *in extenso* in any of the local journals, which, according to all evidence, do not wish to give [it] a place in their columns, believing that the publication of it would bring a feeling of calmness upon German readers." [30]

[28] "*Reuter's*," The London *Nation*, April 24, 1915, 17: 108–109.

[29] "The Press as a Big Stick," *The Nation* (New York), September 10, 1908; 87: 228–229.

Several of these news agencies started by different newspapers sprang up during the war. One announced under date of May 12, 1917, "The A. B. has inaugurated a news service with headquarters at Washington. It aims to furnish the American press with studies, editorials, news letter and Sunday feature stories, dealing with important stories about war conditions and war items about the trend of public opinion. . . . We are seriously engaged in the endeavor to keep the American people accurately informed on a multitude of vital problems which have been suddenly thrown upon us all."

[30] Russian Orange Book, No. 46.

Somewhat similar embarrassments have existed in the case of the semi-official news agency and page of dispatches arranged for in connection with

Many illustrations of this limitation are found. A more fundamental one is suggested by the London *Nation* in saying that the Wolff Agency "at least realized something of the dizzy possibilities of its position, and made a nation's thinking by a bold and adventurous handling of fact."[31]

Only in the third form, a co-operative association like that of the Associated Press, does it seem possible to reduce these dangers to a minimum,—they can never be absolutely eliminated. Even in a co-operative association, the highest type that has as yet been developed or that it seems possible to develop, there lurks the question how far an association in its selection of news unconsciously becomes a means of influencing public opinion and to that extent becomes a propagandist.

Before the question of the authoritativeness of news-collecting organizations can be finally dismissed, another side must be considered. All such associations have their own difficulties, as well as serious obstacles to overcome, in their efforts to serve the press. They must surmount not only the initial difficulties involved in collecting reliable news, but they later encounter the obstacles of censorship; the exigencies of reaching telegraph and cable stations through the dangers inherent in war conditions; the congestion of telegraph and cable lines; the dangers to their own morale through merciless criticism and entire lack of appreciation of the difficulties under which their work is done; the piracy of rival organizations and the prolonged litigation that ensues; the growing embarrassment of securing important items of news from those in a position to give them; the tempta-

the Holy See. In 1890, the *Osservatore Romano* was bought by the Pope, and M. Casoni, the director, was told "that nations and governments should be scrupulously respected, especially those which maintained good relations with the Holy See,"—a difficult provision, said Casoni, "in view of the amount of consideration to be observed towards governments in friendly intercourse with the Holy See, even when they deserved the severest censure."—Granvelle, "The Vatican and the Press," *Contemporary Review*, December, 1908, 94: 650–665.

[31] April 24, 1915, 17: 108–109. For the Wolff Agency, see A. Meister, *Die deutsche Presse im Kriege und später*, pp. 38–41.—The author gives in chapter 3, "Die Organisation des Nachrichtendienstes," a full account of the Havas, as well as of the Reuter, Wolff, and other national agencies.—An excellent survey of press agencies is given in Paul Eltzbacher, *Die Presse als Werkzeug der Auswärtigen Politik*, especially on the side of their opportunities for circulating propaganda.

tion of correspondents to camouflage and the dangers of camou-
flaging; at times the necessity of placating both governmental officials and the public when the interests of the two are antagonistic;
the troubles with distant correspondents who may sometimes
prove irresponsible; the exuberance of reporters who may
metamorphose a cable "Vesuvius grows" into a "story" of
eighty-eight words describing a conventional volcanic erup-
tion.[32] · · · · · · · · · · · · · · · · · ·

It must also not be forgotten how often the Associated Press
may be confronted by embarrassing situations, even though they
may seldom take such positive form as they did when in the
Spanish-American war the press was asked to announce the
departure of the American fleet for Spain,—a *ruse de guerre*.[33]

Some of these hindrances and trials have ultimately cleared
the air and thus proved beneficial. When the news collected by
the Associated Press was pirated by the International News
Service, the decision handed down by Judge C. M. Hough from
the United States Circuit Court was to the effect that news is
property, that the distribution of news not gathered by the
sender is unfair competition, and that the law protects property
rights in news,—thus upholding every contention that had been
made by the Associated Press.[34] A decision on appeal to the
United States Supreme Court was given in favor of the Associated Press, December 23, 1918,[35] and a final decree in its favor
entered May 19, 1919.[36]

The war brought about international complications that could
scarcely have been anticipated by news-collecting agencies.
Early in the war, the Havas Agency was the victim of a false
report industriously circulated to the effect that it had agreed
to furnish news concerning Germany only if supplied by the
Wolff Bureau,—a report whose truthfulness it indignantly
denied.[37] Agencies were soon established to give certain neutral

[32] W. Aplin, "At the Associated Press Office," *Putnam's Magazine*, July,
1870, 16: 23–30.
[33] New York *Evening Post*, December 29, 1917.
[34] The text of the decision is given in full in the New York *Times*, June
22, 1917.
[35] The text is given in the New York *Times*, December 24, 1918.
[36] New York *Evening Post*, May 19, 1919.
[37] New York *Times*, September 6, 1914.

countries authoritative information concerning the war,[38] or to promote "a better understanding between the Central Powers of Europe and North America," and in addition to telegraphic reports, incidentally, newspapers were to be supplied with mail contributions dealing with important political, economic, and art events and also with literary articles.[39] In 1914, the Krupps Munitions Company formed the Overseas News Agency to disseminate pro-German propaganda through American newspapers and early in 1917 it acquired a control of the Wolff Bureau.[40] Propaganda masquerading under the guise of telegraphic reports of news to promote a better understanding between nations has been one of the most dangerous, because insidious, enemies of proprietary news organizations.

Serious international misunderstandings are inevitable when a news agency suppresses passages in important official communications, as was the case when the Wolff Agency omitted passages from President Wilson's address to Congress April 2, 1917,—a suppression defended by the German government.[41] The situation was not improved when a German press association adopted, though by a narrow majority after a sharp debate, the resolution that German newspaper reports of speeches delivered by alien statesmen should be confined to the abbreviated summaries circulated by the Wolff Telegraph Bureau,—a decision apparently unqualifiedly censured by the *Frankfurter Zeitung*, the *Berliner Tageblatt*, *Vorwärts* and in general by liberal, radical, and socialist papers. The *Frankfurter Zeitung* frankly disapproved of the plan because of the general lack of confidence in the Wolff Bureau, especially in translating; because the suspicion would be inevitable that when condensation of speeches was authorized, something had intentionally been omitted; and because compression of speeches could best be done by each paper, and thus no essential passage would be omitted simultaneously in every newspaper.[42]

A contrasting policy was that of the Havas Agency in whose

[38] New York *Evening Post*, October 7, 1914.
[39] New York *Evening Post*, January 29, 1917.
[40] New York *Tribune*, February 4, 1918.
[41] New York *Times*, November 4, 1917.
[42] *Christian Science Monitor*, November 26, 1917.

Paris office had been placed for publication in France and in the French Colonies the message of President Wilson to Congress December 3, 1917. The Havas Agency was also asked to send it out verbatim to all of its correspondents in Italy, Spain, Portugal, and Switzerland, and it was also entrusted with sending it verbatim from Buenos Aires to Rio de Janeiro.[43]

How serious are the responsibilities of all foreign news-collecting agencies is indicated by the action of the Associated Press, the English Reuter's Telegram Agency, and the Havas Agency in severing their connection with the Swedish Telegram Bureau on account of its pro-German activities.[44]

A somewhat similar situation existed when the British and the French governments refused mail and cable privileges to the International News Service because the Hearst papers that subscribed to this service had violated the censorship and had published exaggerated or false dispatches purporting to have been cabled to the United States from Europe. The ban was subsequently removed and mail and cable privileges restored on all lines controlled by Great Britain, its colonies, and its allies, but the removal of the ban applied only to the International News Service as an agency, and not to the Hearst newspapers.[45]

The gravity of the responsibilities of news-collecting agencies in collecting, selecting, and distributing news can not be overstated. The ramifications of these agencies extend to every part of the globe and it seems clear that the historian finds these responsibilities best understood and met by co-operative newspaper agencies rather than by those controlled by private or governmental organization.

Closely allied in object with the news-gathering associations that furnish news to the city dailies are the news-distributing organizations that supply country weeklies with reading matter and illustrations. This service is of two kinds, "boiler-plate" and "ready-print." Plate service is furnished in the form of

[43] *New York Evening Post*, December 5, 1917.
[44] R. C. Long, New York *Evening Post*, June 21, 1918.—The Swedish press bureau was proprietary, in the hands of a single individual. A new independent agency was reported as about to be founded.—Daily press, June 21, 1918.
[45] New York *Times*, February 16, 1918.

metal plates that can be cut into pieces and as much or as little used as may be desired; ready-print service furnishes sheets printed on one side, on two or more pages, by or through the distributing organization, the remaining pages being printed in the office of the paper receiving the service.[46] Plate service does not carry advertising, but ready-print service carries advertising and derives its greatest revenues therefrom, the newspapers receiving nothing from it. In 1912, it was estimated that 16,000 newspapers in America received either plate service or ready-print service, and that these newspapers were read by 60,000,000 persons.[47] Thus practically two-thirds of the population of the country depend on these news syndicates for information in regard to the larger world and for knowledge of the articles advertised through them. As this service is rendered without charge to not fewer than 16,000 newspapers of all shades of opinion and by its very nature does not lend itself readily to the manipulation of headlines, it may be assumed that its statements are reliable. Moreover, it must be said that much of the material furnished is not in any sense news, but consists of humorous articles, jokes, fashion notes, "anything that may interest, amuse, or thrill," and thus it plays no important part in the work of the historian. Its chief interest for him lies in the existence of the syndicate itself as a means of purveying somewhat harmless information to an extraordinarily large number of persons.[48]

[46] Newspapers receiving this kind of service were at one time said to have "patent outsides" or "patent insides." The custom apparently originated in America at the time of the Civil War and grew out of the difficulty in printing newspapers since so many journeymen had enlisted. A. N. Kellogg, of the Baraboo, Wisconsin, *Republic*, ordered half-sheet supplements from the Madison *Daily Journal*, and issued his first "patent inside" July 12, 1861. The idea spread rapidly.—F. W. Scott, *Newspapers and Periodicals of Illinois, 1814–1879*, p. lxxxix.

[47] These facts are given by Charles A. Brodek in connection with a decision rendered by Judge Landis, August 3, 1912, that involved the American Press Association and the Western Newspaper Union. These news syndicates were enjoined by the decree from selling below cost or otherwise unfairly competing.—Daily press of August, 1912.

An account of the important use made of plate service in distributing agricultural news is given by R. L. Slagle in "The Development of the College and Station News Service," *Proceedings of the Twenty-sixth Annual Convention of the Association of American Agricultural Colleges and Experiment Stations* (1913), pp. 150–154.

[48] How widely the use of plate matter has been extended was made apparent in October, 1919, when certain weeklies printed the text in type-

Yet as no field can be absolutely free from dangerous germs, the "ready-print" matter may have danger concealed beneath an apparently innocuous exterior. If "eternal vigilance is the price of liberty" in the state, it is equally the price the historian must pay for truth, and the advertising carried with "ready-print" matter may be less innocent than the unwary suspect. Under the caption "A Real Case of Tainted News" an account is found of the testimony given before a United States Senate Committee by George A. Joslyn, President of the Western Newspaper Union that supplied "ready-print" matter. This testimony was to the effect that plate matter was furnished the Union by persons who desired to further a particular cause, paid for by the persons interested, distributed to the newspapers free of charge, printed without marking it "advertisement," and with no means of informing the public that the matter had been paid for by persons interested in its circulation. The Western Newspaper Union had in this way received from the Canadian Government about $42,000 annually for twelve years to print in American country newspapers glowing descriptions of the agricultural resources of Canada, thus promoting a propaganda under the guise of honest news. There is no way of estimating how large a proportion of the 800,000 farmers who had emigrated to Canada had been influenced to do so by this "ready-print" matter.[49]

The counterpart of ready-to-print papers is found in the "ready-made" notices of books, the "literary notes," and the "reading notice" sent out by publishing houses and used everywhere by newspapers that would scorn the use of ready-to-print matter. "There is a firm in New York at the present time," says Bliss Perry, "which agrees to place simultaneously in a chain of syndicated newspapers both reviews and advertisements of the books reviewed."[50] The historian must find criticism atrophied whenever these "ready-made" notices are used.

Closely affiliated with the collection and distribution of news

written form while the advertisements were printed in regular type because it was supplied in plate form by the advertisers.—*Literary Digest*, November 1, 1919, p. 63: 11.

[49] *Collier's Weekly*, June 6, 1914.

[50] "The American Reviewer," *Yale Review*, October, 1914, 4: 3–24.

is the question of the distribution of the newspaper itself. The crude beginnings of distribution go back more than a hundred years. The great difficulty of getting trustworthy news from the continent during the latter part of the Napoleonic wars led John Walter, Jr., of *The Times* to write, May 9, 1811, to J. W. Croker, then Secretary to the Admiralty, to the effect that no French journals whatsoever could be procured except through smugglers. He therefore proposed a plan by which a French officer, then engaged in this contraband traffic, should exchange it for that of supplying French papers only to the English; he could then be granted Admiralty protection to his vessel, upon the sole condition that no smuggled goods should be transported by him.[51] The request was apparently granted by Croker.

The problem has been definitely met and best met by a central distributing agency. In England the repeal of the stamp duties led to a reduction in the price of newspapers and an enormous increase in the demand for them. The somewhat primitive methods that had been used to distribute newspapers were no longer adequate to these demands and it was not long before the control of newspaper distribution was in the hands of the firm of W. H. Smith and Son that has supplied railway stations and the sub-distributing companies all over the country.[52] A similar distribution is made in America by the American News Company.

The question of the distribution of newspapers may not seem to concern the historian, yet how vitally it does concern him is evident from the controversy precipitated when the news companies in New York City, due to the insistence and threats of the city dailies, refused to deliver the New York *Tribune* to any newsdealer who on patriotic grounds, or for any other reason, refused to handle and sell the Hearst papers. The *Tribune* therefore installed its own delivery system and, through supplying the newsdealers directly, enabled citizens to understand both the *Tribune*, and the Hearst side of a great public question.

[51] L. J. Jennings, *ed.*, *The Correspondence and Diaries of John Wilson Croker*, I, 32–33.
[52] H. Maxwell gives an important account of newspaper distribution, especially of the distribution of *The Times.—Life and Times of William Henry Smith*, I, chap. III.
W. J. Couper gives an account of "The Distribution of Edinburgh Periodicals" in *The Edinburgh Periodical Press*, I, 124–130.

The student of history therefore finds one great source of information used by the press to be the various news-collecting agencies; he finds that these necessarily differ among themselves as regards their authoritativeness and that this must be gauged by their own form of organization and the measure of their dependence on external authority. Even if the news received from the source is free from suspicion, the press itself may distort it by partial omissions, pervert its meaning by the use of exaggerated headlines, and embroider simple facts beyond recognition. Happily, while all this is possible, the materialization of these dangers seldom occurs. In the great news-collecting agencies, organized on a co-operative basis and serving the best representatives of the press, is found one of the most reliable parts of the newspaper.

CHAPTER VI

THE GENERAL REPORTER

"This thing was not done in a corner."

"See men's divers opinions! It is the printing of 'em makes 'em news to a great many who will indeed believe nothing but what's in print."—*Ben Jonson.*

"L'essentiel était d'avoir des informations toutes fraîches et d'être le premier à les faire connaître. 'Ils donneraient tout ce que l'on voudrait pour avoir une nouvelle que personne ne sût encore.'"—*Funck-Brentano.*

"The same republican Hands who have so often since the Chevalier de St. George's Recovery killed him in our publick Prints, have now reduced the young Dauphin of France to that desperate Condition of Weakness, and Death itself, that it is hard to conjecture what Method they will take to bring him to Life again. Meantime we are assured, by a very good Hand from Paris, That on the 20th Instant, this young Prince was as well as ever he was known to be since the Day of his Birth."—*The Spectator*, No. 384, May 21, 1712.

"I fancy," said I, "that post brings news from Scotland. I shall long to see the next Gazette." "Sir," says he, "I make it a rule never to believe any of your printed news."—*The Freeholder*, No. 22, March 5, 1716.

"He [the reporter] is without the borrowed dignity of magnificent ecclesiastical vestments, without soldier's epaulets, the prestige of the lawyer's robe, the doctor's parchment and mystic language. He is just a chiel takin' notes."—*The Nation.*

"I take all th' pa-apers an' read thim fr'm end to end. I don't believe a bad thing they print about anny iv me frinds but I believe ivirything about anny body else."—*Mr. Dooley.*

STUDENTS of history may be reasonably sure that they may accept at their face value the statements of the press that carry with them the evident guarantee of accuracy and truthfulness. These sections are first the part that is permanent as to the guarantee behind it but that can not properly be classed as news, and second the part that is strictly news and that has behind it the collective guarantee of a news-collecting organization. In addition to these somewhat definite guarantees, the newspaper through its own personality and through its connection with other activities carries prima facie evidence of its probable reliability or of the extent to which its statements must be discounted.

The tests for authoritativeness must next be applied to that very large section of the newspaper that carries with it no visible guarantee of a faithful portrayal of current events and that is evidently the work of the local reporter, or the local correspondent. Here the historian finds a mass of material that bears evidence of haste and inaccuracy. Fortunately for him, many of these errors are quickly detected, and it is possible to classify them according to their source and thus be prepared to recognize other errors of the respective classes.

It may be thought that many of the errors found in the press are connected with the source from which the information is derived, yet this is probably true only to a slight extent. Reporters are assigned the work of collecting the local news and they obtain it from various well-recognized sources of information. Every intelligent, responsible reporter to-day intends to indicate in some way in his report the source of his authority for the information or news given the public.[1] This is done not only because reporters are themselves becoming more responsible, but because of the growing demand on the part of the reading public that all news must be authoritative. The reporter who thus includes in his report the source of his information has a near kinship with the historian who supports his statements with a footnote.

The first important source of information for the local reporter comes from the group made up of the court houses, the police courts, hospitals, the morgue, the undertaker, places of amusement, hotel registers, and steamboat offices. These form a regular, well-recognized supply of news that differs each day as regards the names of the individuals involved but that after all remains in essentials a somewhat stable element in the day's work. No new crimes are committed; the decisions in civil suits are based on precedent; the emphasis may shift from theatre to moving

[1] "Mr. A. is registered at the Commodore;" "Lord B. was seen by a representative of the *Times* on the tug that met the Caronia;"—the illustrations are innumerable in which the reporter in very definite, although in inconspicuous ways, indicates the source of the report made.

picture and from vaudeville to cabaret, but the thirty-six plots possible in dramatic action are not increased in number. The interest in the news secured from all of these and similar sources is the interest that attaches to individuals. From the standpoint of news, it matters little whether it concerns a hardened criminal, an unknown man who is the victim of an accident, or a distinguished visitor whose presence is disclosed by hotel register or steamer passenger list. Everything that relates to an individual in unusual circumstances is news, and a tale about such an individual is important whether it concerns one person or another.

An occasional source of news is afforded by clergymen, physicians, charity organization societies, and other semi-public individuals and organizations. In this class also it is the individual that is in the limelight,—the extraordinary marriage, the distressing accident, the mysterious death, the man once rich who is now an object of charity,—all of these afford "copy" that the reporter considers of unusual interest and importance.

Special sources of news are found in the meetings of local legislative bodies and of different executive boards, as the board of education, of public works, of public health, and of police commissioners; of the boards of trustees of museums, art galleries, universities, and other privately endowed institutions. In information derived from such sources the interest concerns mainly platforms, policies, activities, endowments, and the extension or contraction of work already undertaken.

All these sources of information may be unimpeachable, and yet the resulting "story" may, from the historian's point of view, leave much to be desired. This may be explained by the conditions under which the reports are written out. Charles Dickens, in an address at the second annual dinner of the Newspaper Press Fund in 1865, gives a vivid account of his experiences as a reporter:

"I have pursued the calling of a reporter under circumstances of which many of my brethren here can form no adequate conception. I have often transcribed for the printer, from my short-hand notes, important public speeches in which the strictest accuracy was required, and a mistake in which would have been to a young man severely compromising, writing on the palm of my hand, by the light of a dark-lantern, in a post-chaise and four,

galloping through a wild country, and through the dead of the
night, at the then surprising rate of fifteen miles an hour. The
very last time I was at Exeter, I strolled into the castle-yard
there, to identify, for the amusement of a friend, the spot on
which I once 'took,' as we used to call it, an election-speech of
Lord John Russell at the Devon contest, in the midst of a lively
fight maintained by all the vagabonds in that division of the
country, and under such a pelting rain that I remember two
good-natured colleagues, who chanced to be at leisure, held a
pocket-handkerchief over my note-book, after the manner of a
state canopy in an ecclesiastical procession. I have worn my
knees by writing on them on the old back row of the old gallery
of the old House of Commons; and I have worn my feet by
standing to write in a preposterous pen in the old House of Lords,
where we used to be huddled together like so many sheep,—kept
in waiting, say, until the woolsack might want restuffing. Returning home from exciting political meetings in the country to the
waiting press in London, I do verily believe I have been upset
in almost every description of vehicle known in this country.
I have been, in my time, belated on miry by-roads, towards the
small hours, forty or fifty miles from London, in a wheelless
carriage, with exhausted horses and drunken post-boys, and have
got back in time for publication, to be received with never-
forgotten compliments by the late Mr. Black, coming in the
broadest of Scotch from the broadest of hearts I ever knew.
These trivial things I mention as an assurance to you that I
never have forgotten the fascination of that old pursuit. The
pleasure that I used to feel in the rapidity and dexterity of its
exercise has never faded out of my breast."[2]

With change of scene, these are the conditions under which reports
to-day must often be written.

It is possible that an explanation may be found in the words of
an experienced editor,— "'The case of the reporter' is to a considerable extent a question of moral education,"[3] or the older explanation of Addison's may hold good to the effect that sensations
must be manufactured if not found at hand. He says:

"It is an old observation that a time of peace is always a time
of prodigies; for, as our news-writers must adorn their papers
with that which the critics call *the marvellous*, they are forced
into a dead calm of affairs, to ransack every element for proper

[2] John Forster, *Life of Charles Dickens*, I, 99–100.
[3] W. L. Cook, "The Press in its Relation to History," *History Teacher's
Magazine*, January, 1914, 5: 3–8.

amusements, and either to astonish their readers, from time to time, with a strange and wonderful sight, or be content to lose their custom. The sea is generally filled with monsters, when there are no fleets upon it, mount Aetna immediately began to rage upon the extinction of the rebellion: and woe to the people of Catanea, if the peace continues; for they are sure to be shaken every week with earthquakes, till they are relieved by the siege of some other great town in Europe. The air has likewise contributed its quota of prodigies. We had a blazing star by the last mail from Genoa; and, in the present dearth of battles, have been very opportunely entertained, by persons of undoubted credit, with a civil war in the clouds, where our sharpsighted malcontents discovered many objects invisible to an eye that is dimmed by Whig principles." [4]

Whatever the cause, it can not be gainsaid that much of the criticism of the press is directed towards that part supplied by the local reporter, and many will agree with Godkin, when in writing of a not-remote past he says,

"Everything, however trifling, was considered worth printing, and the newspaper finally became, what it is now, a collection of the gossip, not only of the whole world, but of its own locality. Now, gossip, when analyzed, consists simply of a collection of actual facts, mostly of little moment, and also of surmises about things, of equally little moment. But business requires that as much importance as possible shall be given to them by the manner of producing each item, or what is called 'typographical display.' Consequently they are presented with separate and conspicuous headings, and there is no necessary connection between them. They follow one another, column after column, without any order, either of subject or of chronology." [5]

This seems a somewhat depressing situation into which the reporter has brought the press, yet it is after all not so hopeless. The reporter writes much gossip and he makes many errors in so doing, but it is possible to make an analysis of these errors, based on the nature of the error, and to show that they fall into a few well-defined classes.

Many erroneous statements are attributable to ignorance and hence they are easily exposed and rejected. A prominent local paper made the statement after the census of 1910: "When the

[4] *The Freeholder*, No. 27, March 23, 1716.
[5] E. L. Godkin, *Unforeseen Tendencies of Democracy*, p. 199.

House of Representatives was first organized there was one congressman for every 30,000 people."—Reference to the Constitution would have shown the phrase, "The number of representatives shall *not exceed* one for every thirty thousand;" the number of representatives assigned the different states by the same section of the Constitution would have shown that at the time there was one representative to approximately forty-five thousand persons.

A local paper recently stated, "Postmaster A. of the neighboring village of X. was re-instated March 2 on a petition sent to Washington signed by one hundred and sixty-five patrons of the office, after having been removed on a complaint said to have been made by Mr. B. who accused Mr. A. of being in a saloon." This was contradicted by the postmaster of the village in question who stated that Mr. A. had never been postmaster of that village and therefore could not have been either removed or re-instated.

In 1911 the press from New York to California copied the statement, "Miss A., principal of B. College which was opened in 1867 says 'no graduate of B. College ever has obtained or been involved in a divorce.'" Reference to the B. College catalogue would have shown that no person was connected with the college bearing the name given, that it had no officer with the title of "principal," and that the College was not opened in 1867; reference to the register of graduates would have shown that the statement attributed to the mythical principal had no foundation in fact.

A local paper announced one morning that the previous night a man had disregarded the signals and had driven his horse over a pavement just laid in fresh cement, thereby causing damage to the pavement to the amount of nearly $1,000. An evening paper of the same date described the affair and stated that damage to the amount of several hundred dollars was reported to have been done and added that five signal lanterns had also been destroyed. Two days later the same evening paper announced that there was no serious damage to the pavement and that the driver agreed to pay the city for the damage done the red lights along the pavements. The morning paper next announced that no actual damage was done to the pavement and that the driver had settled for the breaking of one lantern and the globes of four others, the total damage amounting to two dollars. Thus ended the incident reported to have caused "damage to the amount of nearly a thousand dollars."

A few years ago a distinguished gentleman lectured in a small city during the Christmas holidays. A few days later a gentleman, who had not himself heard the lecture, wrote to the local morning papers protesting against certain statements he had heard it said the lecturer had made. Although both papers published the letter, they accompanied it with a statement that the lecturer had said precisely the opposite of what was attributed to him. The press far and wide, however, copied the letter without the explanation of the local papers, enlarged on the statements, transferred the lecture from the city to a neighboring college, and added that "the college students gasped at the advice,"—all this when the lecture was given two miles and a half from the College, it was given during the vacation when not a student could have heard it, and the lecturer said exactly the opposite of what a person who did not hear him reported on hearsay had been said.

The love of jesting is behind many statements that unless subsequently explained, must be puzzling to the historian. *The Nation*, April 1, 1909, published a letter from a correspondent who quoted a eulogy of the art of printing, said to be from the Latin of Cardelius, and then inquired, "Who was Cardelius?" Two correspondents proffered detailed but differing accounts of Cardelius, and were then followed by a letter from the author of the eulogy, who wrote, "All the truth about him is told in this letter of mine. Cardelius is a child of the imagination; rather, he was born of the union of a printer's composing-stick and a font of 60 point Cheltenham;" and he then gives a long account of "the evolution of Cardelius" from his own experiments with a printing press and types.

The illustrations are almost endless of the jokes played through the press on persons not well-known in the community but on friendly terms with jesting reporters. One may be represented as receiving a $5,000 touring car from his employer, or the quiet home marriage of another in a distant city may be described as having taken place in the cathedral in the presence of a large and fashionable gathering.

New York City papers one day contained an elaborate detailed account of the marriage of a wealthy young man in a neighboring city. The local papers copied the account,—to learn afterwards that no marriage had taken place and that the description had been written by the young man himself, "as a joke," he explained.

Jesting in its turn is next of kin to deliberate hoaxing, an excellent illustration of this being the mass of reports in connection with Dr. F. A. Cook's reputed discovery of the North Pole.

Other errors are to be charged to the plain carelessness of reporters. One recently stated that at a public dinner "papers were read by Mr. A. and Miss B." In fact, after-dinner speeches were made by Mrs. A. and Miss B. Another reports the connection of Professor Maria Mitchell with Vassar College as being that of a "model student," calls the chairman of a college faculty elected by themselves "the acting president," reports a newly-appointed professor as "returning after a year's leave of absence," and states that a college president who had been in office six months and in that time had delivered many public addresses "delivered yesterday a speech in public for the first time since becoming president." There is much in this type of reporter that seems to justify the caustic description given by G. B. Shaw of one of his characters:

"A cheerful, affable young man who is disabled for ordinary business pursuits by a congenital erroneousness which renders him incapable of describing accurately anything he sees, or understanding or reporting accurately anything he hears. As the only employment in which these defects do not matter is journalism (for a newspaper, not having to act on its description and reports, but only to sell them to idly curious people, has nothing but honor to lose by inaccuracy and unveracity) he has perforce become a journalist." [6]

The love of sensation explains many misstatements. A New York paper of June 16, 1910, announced "the members of the graduating class of X. College to the numbers of 118 occupied seats in the orchestra of the Academy of Music last night and enjoyed the production given. This was one of the features of

[6] G. B. Shaw, *The Doctor's Dilemma*, Act IV.

commencement week with the graduating class. Roses in profusion were tossed over the foot lights to the leading woman of the play who was a member of the class of '03, of X." As the commencement exercises had occurred eight days before the above notice, the members of the graduating class were scattered far and wide rather than attending the theater in New York City, while the leading actress, who was stated to be a graduate of the college, had never been even enrolled as a student there.

The advertiser is sometimes a brother of the reporter in carelessness. One advertiser recently ran a daily advertisement for two months after his store had been burned out. Another advertiser ran for two months an undated advertisement of a "great sacrifice of automobiles for five more days only," followed by a list of cars for sale and the statement "prices quoted above limited to five days only."

The proof reader must also share the errors of the reporter. It is difficult to locate a prominent citizen and his wife when one page of a local paper states that they are at their summer home in Massachusetts and the next page that they are motoring in the Pyrenees; an important chamber concert was recently reported as one where "several selections from C. Hopin were played." [7]

A local account of a Christmas celebration recently read: "Last night the college met for the annual signing of Christmas cards. At half past nine the choir descended to the library bower. Here under the stairs they sang the well-known Christmas carols to the college waiting below. At ten o'clock the choir came down and all went home." Translated, this meant, "The college met for the annual singing of Christmas carols. The choir ascended the library tower and under the stars sang carols to the college waiting below." The account as published in a local morning paper was copied verbatim by a local evening paper.

Carelessness merges imperceptibly into blundering and this in its turn is responsible for innumerable errors. A local paper of April 6 announces that C. College "opens for the short term," meaning that it re-opens after the spring vacation,—the academic

---

[7] H. B. Wheatley gives many illustrations of the blunders found in newspapers,—amusing in themselves, yet lending color to the general impression of the untrustworthiness of the press.—*Literary Blunders*, chap. II.

year being divided into two semesters; also, that "there was a large attendance at the chapel this morning," although chapel service is held in the evening; that "a reception has been given to a thousand freshmen," although the entire student body numbers only a thousand; that Miss X. is vice-president of the C. College Club, although Miss X. has never attended the C. College and there is no C. College Club in the city; that "between two and three hundred students reached here to-day by every train," although seventy-five trains stop in the city every day and the number of college students is limited to one thousand.

Exigencies of publication must be the explanation of another large class of errors. An important item of news comes in just as a paper is going to press and a hurried account is written but the statements made can not be verified. The editor takes the chances and publishes accounts that not infrequently are corrected on the following day by his rival editor. A fire alarm may be sounded as the evening paper is going to press, and in startling headlines it announces that a general alarm has been sent out, that a disastrous fire is threatening an entire business block, and that the loss will be heavy.—The morning paper, with ample time to ascertain the facts, states that no general alarm was sounded, that at no time was there danger of a general conflagration, that the total loss did not exceed $3,000, and it virtuously rebukes its evening rival as a journal of yellowest dye. *Mutatis mutandis*, such accounts are of almost daily occurrence in the papers of the smaller cities all over the country.

Still another source of error comes from the habit of turning in copy written by one reporter and leaving the headlines to be written by a member of the office. This often results in wide discrepancy between the headlines and the "story" that follows,— a discrepancy that sometimes results in absolute contradiction of statements. A leading New York daily of June 27, 1914, had a headline reading "Yankee Duchess Indorses Militants," while the interview given below contained the statement, "I am a suffragist but not a militant."

Two rival morning dailies somewhat recently had contradictory headlines announcing the decision of the court on the result of local option,—one headline read "Town of Beekman is to remain

Wet," while the other headline read "Beekman Town will be Dry." Inasmuch as one of the papers, in addition to the error of the headline, reversed the figures of the vote on the question, both a careful reading of the decision and a knowledge of local conditions were required in order to determine the actual situation in Beekman.

Other errors may be classified as those coming from taking information at second hand or from the imperfect information gained over the telephone. The reporter is often at the mercy of seekers for publicity and may inadvertently be betrayed by the telephone into an exaggerated report of insignificant events.

Still other errors are to be classed as "tricks of the trade." Bussey gives many illustrations of the devices used by reporters to manufacture news in a dull time, or to save themselves the trouble of going personally to the scene of an important meeting, or to gain entrance to a meeting from which all strangers were supposedly excluded.[8]

The "temperament" of a distinguished man must be the caption under which to classify errors of omission erroneously attributed to the reporter.[9]

Errors of a deliberate nature are sometimes made through a desire to connect an unimportant or local incident with some occurrence of national interest or with some person of national fame. The daily papers of October 6, 1915, reported: "Speaker Champ Clark and his son were in a posse that dispersed a band of twenty men which to-day attempted to lynch Harrison Rose, a negro charged with murdering a farmer. The mob attacked the jail, broke the outer doors, and were pounding with sledge hammers on the inner door when the sheriff appeared with the posse." Often these statements may be strictly correct as regards specific details, yet the account as a whole may give an erroneous emphasis to unimportant incidents, it may show a wrong perspective, it may deduce a conclusion from insufficient data. In any

[8] H. F. Bussey, *Sixty Years of Journalism*, "Journalists' Tricks," pp. 254–266.
  C. A. Cooper gives many examples of the manufacture of news by industrious though unscrupulous penny-a-liners.—*An Editor's Retrospect*, pp. 86–95.
[9] *Infra*, p. 380, Note 13.

case, the effect is to create a wrong impression, even though the facts have been stated accurately.

Somewhat akin in spirit is the temptation of the reporter, after describing a local incident, to add, "This reflects the feeling of the entire community [or state or country, as the case may be]."

Related to these errors of general impressions are those that grow out of the meager facts furnished the reporter and the apparent necessity, as he sees it, of supplementing these with accounts padded by his own imagination. The result is that a column is often spun from a very slender basis of fact and it may in the future be difficult to disentangle the basis of fact from the attenuated description. Often the reporter is not present at the events he describes and hence draws on his imagination for the details needed and thereby again falls into error. A reporter once described a college commencement dinner at which a silver bowl was presented to the college from the Mikado of Japan and stated, "It was presented to the college by the Baroness Uriu herself in a clever speech, in the deliberate English which marks her delivery." But the Baroness made no public address on the occasion, the presentation of the gift being announced by the president of the college.

The reporter sometimes yields to the temptation to "feature" an insignificant episode, thus distorting all sense of proportion and in effect falsifying the news. At a great public meeting called in New York in 1915 to consider a massacre of the Armenians, a slight disturbance was caused by the necessity of putting a man out of the theater. This was "featured" by four New York dailies that therefore gave "only a fraction of their valuable space to a true report of the meeting and of the massacre it was called to consider." [10]

A variant of this is the proneness to exaggerate the trifling news connected with important persons,—"only the rich man is interesting" once said a prominent newspaper man in an address on journalism to college students. On the other hand, events important in themselves but connected with an individual

[10] "The Falsification of the News," The Independent, December 13, 1915, 84: 420.

unknown in the community are passed over by the reporter,—
"Who cares?" is the somewhat contemptuous question of the
reporter.

The reporter is sometimes compelled to be forehanded and
he may send in a provisional account with a later confirmation
or alteration and thus occasional errors arise. But an over-
elaborate forehandedness may give rise to a class of errors that
may cause the future historian the greatest perplexity. It is
often necessary for the descriptions of important events to be
written long in advance of the events themselves, yet it not
infrequently happens that the events do not take place either at
the time or in the manner described. The coronation of Edward
VII of England was arranged to take place June 26, 1901, and a
London weekly not only wrote but also printed an elaborate
account of the ceremony, and included in it an adverse criticism
of an opera at Covent Garden that was never given. The illness
of the King made it necessary at the last moment to defer the
ceremony until August 9 but the paper giving the account of
the ceremony that did not take place is retained and prized by
its owners "as probably the most stupendous and artistic fake
in history." It is, however, not just to label as "fakes" all
accounts thus written in advance,—the very fact that they are
so written, if revised in the light of the events themselves, is often
a guarantee of the accuracy and faithfulness of the description,
and to that extent the custom is to be commended rather than
condemned. The difficulty of the historian in using such accounts
arises from the frequent failure of the reporter to check up his
account with the event itself and he thereby falls into error.
In 1907, November 5–9, the Association of Collegiate Alumnae
celebrated the twenty-fifth anniversary of its formation. A
leading weekly in New York City published in its issue, dated
November 2, a long and complimentary account of the celebration. It was written by a special correspondent and evidently
was intended for the issue of a date two weeks later than the one
in which it appeared.

The weather is the cause of many variations between the events
and published accounts of them. Public lectures, concerts, entertainments, sermons, social engagements, ice carnivals, church

festivals,—all are often written up in advance and the accounts published, yet the events themselves have been postponed or given up altogether on account of conditions of weather. Marriage ceremonies are described as having taken place in a church, while sudden illness has made necessary a change in plans and the ceremony has been performed in private. Obituary notices are published of prominent citizens said to be at the point of death, yet they have recovered and sometimes lived for years after these notices appeared.

Another fertile source of error is found in mistranslation, although it is one that does not belong particularly to the local reporter. Errors are almost inevitable when reports are transmitted through an unfamiliar language, or when seemingly unnecessary words are omitted and have to be filled in. Conscious mistranslation may explain other errors, as was possibly true when in September, 1914, a dispatch was received in English in New York City quoting an English naval officer who, when the Kaiser was a child, had once carried him on board a British warship. He was quoted as often saying, "If I had dropped the little fellow overboard, what a lot of trouble would have been saved to Europe and the world."—The New York *Staats-Zeitung* of September 29, 1914, translated the remark, "Ich wollte, ich hätte ihn über Bord geworfen"—"I wish I had thrown him overboard." [11]

If the reporter is sometimes censured for fostering a sense of disproportion in news values, he, in his turn, may retort that he is himself the victim of this perverted sense. Macaulay once exclaimed, "A broken head in Coldbath Fields produces a greater sensation than three pitched battles in India," [12] and it is the broken head that the reporter often feels obliged to report. [13]

Yet here again the report may be conditioned by time and place. In a sparsely settled country, where there is little to break

[11] New York *Times*, October 2, 1914.
See also translation of *le presbytère* as "the Presbyterian School [in Belgium]."—New York *Times*, February 8, 1918.
[12] Cited by M. Macdonagh, "In the Sub-Editor's Room," *Nineteenth Century*, December, 1897, 42: 999–1008.
[13] *The Monthly Chronicle* in its third volume, 1730, announced that it would give special place to "observable domestick occurrences, honours and preferments, ecclesiastical promotions, marriages and births, and deaths,"—a list of subjects that affords an enlightening comparison with the local occurrences on which reports were demanded a century later.

the monotony of frontier life, it is usually true, as the historian of its early newspapers found in Illinois, that "the remoteness of the event seemed to increase its importance, and one finds more often an account of the hop yield in Silesia than of the wheat crop in Illinois. It was easier to reset items from the eastern papers, when they arrived, than to gather facts and compose original matter." [14] In this the beginning of the newspaper on a frontier settlement but duplicates the experience of early newspapers everywhere; the special eagerness has been for news from abroad and there has been no demand for local news.

In reality, the reporter is here the victim of two antagonistic instincts representing two clearly defined types of mind,—one type is specially interested in the things and events near at hand and the other is most interested in whatever is remote. It is the function of the newspaper, through the reporter, to attempt to gratify both instincts, but the success is not always equally divided between the two and the reporter sometimes seems predestined to at least partial failure.

The reporter may be handicapped by other conditions that he does not or can not control. One of these may be a large circle of acquaintances. While his intentions may be the best, he may unconsciously have his reports colored by a desire to spare the feelings of his friends or by a wish to promote their interests.[15]

Circulation is sometimes knowingly given to false statements, as when detectives send word through the press that search for criminals has been abandoned and thus are enabled to secure them by putting them off their guard.

In some schools of journalism and in some textbooks on journalism a disproportionate amount of time and space may seem to

[14] F. W. Scott, *Newspapers and Periodicals of Illinois, 1874–1879*, p. xxxiii.

[15] E. W. Townsend, "The Reporter," *Bookman*, August, 1904, 19: 558–572.

For the effect of the work of the reporter on the reporter himself, see the observations of N. Hapgood, who finds that the reporter tends to become cynical. "He cares for the outcome of nothing. He says to the politician, 'Go on and stir things up. I do not care what you do, so you do something. It is all good for me.'"—"The Reporter and Literature," *Bookman*, April, 1897, 5: 119–121.

See also "Confessions of a 'Literary Journalist,'" *Bookman*, December, 1907, 26: 370–376.

an outsider to be given to the work of the reporter. But since attention is directed mainly to the "story" element in the news, little appreciable improvement in the work of the reporter can be traced directly to this source, and the young reporter can not always be held strictly accountable for over-emphasizing the manner of the telling of the "story" rather than what is told. If the cardinal sin of a reporter is held to be dullness rather than inaccuracy, he conforms to what he believes to be the standards of his profession.

It must be remembered, too, that the reporter, on the other hand, is sometimes in the hands of "the man higher up" who "improves" or "elaborates" his report and thus introduces inaccuracies. "Speed the day of the fact-loving, truth-serving, intelligent reporter!" cries the reader impatient with the sins of the press.[16] The long-suffering reporter, writhing under criticism he deems unjust, replies that his copy is doctored by the re-write man to make it flashy,[17] and that he is called a poor newspaper man when he refuses to invent stories. "A reporter's success on the average newspaper," he affirms, "depends on how skilfully he can weave ordinary facts into a story that shall be topped by bold-faced headlines."[18] If the reporter gives too many details, he may involve his paper in litigation; if he gives too few, he may be reminded that he is not on a weekly paper.

The reporter has also been influenced by the general conditions of the press. The reporting of news long suffered because the work was ill organized. "The reporting profession," says O'Brien, "was still in the statusless condition in which the reporter, within one circuit of the clock, might be fawned upon by the very highest and snubbed by the very lowest."[19]

"Still an obscure pressman," writes Edmund Garrett, "I have written reports and paragraphs, leaders and skits, verses and

[16] E. A. Fitzpatrick, "The Lost Art of Reporting," *New Republic*, May 27, 1916, 7: 93.
[17] Two news items were recently sent to the office of a local paper where they were changed beyond recognition. When the "re-write man" was reproached with having so altered the copy as to make it absolutely untrue his retort was, "But I made the stories interesting."
[18] H. P. S., "In Defense of Reporters," *New Republic*, June 10, 1916, 7: 147.
[19] William O'Brien, *Recollections*, p. 186.

parodies, reviews and stage *critiques*, interviews and special correspondence—to-day making acquaintance with a prima donna, to-morrow with a Cabinet Minister, and, in between, turning a ready hand to any trivial, dull little piece of drudgery which happens to need doing." [20]

But specialization affects the work of the reporter and not only divides it into the great classes of the general and the official reporter, but each class becomes specialized. The general reporter develops into the one who specializes on financial news, or on reporting crime, or society news, or on the shipping trade, or any one of the multifarious activities and interests of a great city. The specially able reporter may develop into a free lance and without being attached to any special paper, may be sent out to get reports where special tact, knowledge, and experience are necessary, and thus have a connection with all the papers in the community.

All these changes in the work of the reporter are both a cause and a result of the change in his social status. In 1808, the benchers of Lincoln's Inn adopted a by-law excluding all persons who had written for hire in the daily papers from being called to the bar, and while the other Inns of Court refused to accede, and it was afterwards rescinded,[21] it indicates probably only too well the early contemptuous attitude towards the reporter that prevailed in England. It was one of the guild who wrote that "newspaper men have a gipsy-like habit of shifting their quarters —they are veritable members of the 'tribe of the wandering foot.'" [22] This reputation for uncertainty of tenure, whether well or ill deserved, has long discredited their work. Even to-day, an English writer makes one of his characters, a conjuror, say, "I have thought out everything by myself, when I was a gutter-snipe in Fleet Street, or, lower still, a journalist in Fleet Street." [23] In America, a prominent weekly can say, "The type has become fixed in common thought . . . [it] has become as definite as that of the stage Irishman." [24]

[20] E. T. Cook, *Edmund Garrett: A Memoir*, p. 19.
[21] Lord Colchester, *Diary*, II, 240.
[22] D. Croal, *Early Recollections of a Journalist, 1832–1859*, p. 26.
[23] G. K. Chesterton, *Magic*, Act II.
[24] "The Man with the Note-Book," *The Nation*, February 19, 1914, 98: 179–180.

The reporter, as he sees himself crushed between the upper and the nether millstone, is indeed far different from the reporter as he is sometimes believed to be. "To the Parisian imagination," says *The Nation*, "the reporter is the man who makes and unmakes Ministries, drives financiers to suicide, cements or disrupts international alliances, beats open the doors of the Théâtre Français for ambitious vaudeville artists, and has writers and painters eating out of his hand." [25] To himself, he may seem to be a person whose ideals and beliefs have been shattered by the inexorable, relentless tasks demanded by the cry "copy." [26]

It thus seems possible to "isolate" one fertile source of error and find it in the region controlled by the local reporter. Moreover, it must be evident that these errors are apparently more frequent in the newspapers published in small towns and cities than they are in the great metropolitan dailies, and this in spite of the apparent ease with which the truth of the statements received can be known or verified. A reasonable explanation of many of these errors can be found in the necessarily small force of reporters attached to the smaller papers and to their presumable lack of special training for reportorial work. That the press itself often realizes these difficulties is evident from the publicity not infrequently given to various measures attempting to correct at least a part of the difficulty. Some of these efforts have taken the form of proposed or enacted legislation. Somewhat recently, a bill was introduced in the Vermont legislature that was intended to guard newspapers against "lying informants" and carrying a fine of from $5.00 to $20.00 for each offense of giving false news to a newspaper with intent to deceive.[27]

"There is a popular impression," is the comment of a newspaper man, "that all is grist that comes to the mill of a newspaper; that the editor will publish, and does publish, everything brought into the office, whereas, the truth is, that what is tendered for publication is carefully scrutinized as to its authenticity

[25] "The Man with the Note-Book," *The Nation*, February 19, 1914, 98: 179–180.

[26] "Confessions of a 'Literary Journalist,'" *The Bookman*, December, 1907, 26: 370–376.

The conflict between the ambitious essayist and the necessitous reporter is portrayed by Philip Gibbs, *The Street of Adventure*.

[27] New York *Evening Post*, December 8, 1908.

in the necessarily limited time obtainable between one day's publication and the next. In spite of all precautions, untruths are unintentionally given circulation from time to time. Until some such law as the proposed Vermont statute is enacted, the victimized editor or publisher has no recourse or redress. A law such as the Vermont Legislature suggests would rob newspaper work of most of its terrors. Nothing happier could be devised to protect newspaper readers than a law which would permit newspaper correspondents and editors to bring into court men who have deceived them by disseminating false news."

But the reporter is often cheerful under fire and is sometimes disposed to take these errors not too seriously, as is evident from the jests the press itself collects and publishes on its own shortcomings. This may be illustrated by the varying accounts of an address given in Buffalo by a former governor of New York that were collected by the Columbia, S. C., *State*:

"New York *Times*—'Twelve Thousand Persons Hear Him Speak.'

"New York *World*—'Twenty Thousand Cheer as Sulzer Opens His Primary Campaign.'

"New York *American*—'Fifteen thousand cheering, militant citizens . . . greeted Gov. Sulzer.'

"New York *Tribune*—'An audience of 7,500 persons.' At any rate, we suppose all are agreed that the meeting was in Buffalo, and that Gov. Sulzer spoke." [28]

He doubtless goodnaturedly contemplates that remote time in the future when "the advance of the newspaper towards exact reporting will go hand in hand with the exact organization of human affairs." [29]

That it is the sum total of these errors, greatly magnified and equally misunderstood, that has brought unwarrantable discredit on the press, especially the American press, seems clear. While it is not possible to accept literally the criticisms made on the American press by European travelers, especially by those who came during the nineteenth century, the abounding small errors of the local reporter as read daily in the morning

[28] New York *Evening Post*, May 29, 1913.
[29] D. Wilcox, "The American Newspaper: A Study in Social Psychology," *Annals of the American Academy of Political and Social Science*, July, 1900, 16: 56–92.

paper give at least a sympathetic understanding of these criticisms.

It must also be evident that these innumerable errors of statement are in themselves often of trifling importance, that for the moment some of them may add to the gaiety of the nations, although others are, to the last degree, irritating and annoying to those concerned. Nearly all of them are quickly forgotten, and the number is extremely small of those that will discomfort the future historian. These he can for the most part quickly detect and either correct or omit them as unnecessary in his reconstruction of the past. He cheerfully agrees with the editor who writes:

"When we consider that Hudson did not discover New York Bay, but that Verrazzano did; when we consider that Fulton did not invent the steamboat, but that Fitch did; when we consider that Bell did not invent the telephone, that Morse did not invent the telegraph, that Gutenberg did not invent the printing-press, that Morton did not discover anaesthesia, that Darwin did not discover evolution, that Shakespeare did not write 'Hamlet,' that Homer did not write the Iliad, that Galileo did not say 'And still it moves,' that Wellington did not say 'Up guards and at them,' that Washington did not win the battles of the Revolution, that Robespierre did not create the Reign of Terror, that Nero was not a monster, that Cleopatra was not beautiful—when we reflect that history is emblazoned with the titles of usurpers and that true merit lies unchronicled in the grave, let us address a word or two of apology to that much-berated enemy of the truth, the newspaper. If history, with a thousand years' leisure at her disposal, cannot find out just who set up a new throne or pulled down an old one, let us forgive the reporter if he misspells the Christian name of the prominent citizen who was thrown from his automobile at 2:30 A. M." [30]

It must finally be evident that the errors are found, not in the region reached by libel laws, but in the apparently harmless districts where inaccuracy is of comparatively small moment. But it must also be clear that it is the sum total of these errors that is magnified out of all due proportion to its importance and that in every community forms the basis of the charge, "You can't believe anything you read in the papers."

[30] New York *Evening Post*, October 8, 1909.

CHAPTER VII

THE OFFICIAL REPORTER

"No circumstance in the history of our country,—not even parliamentary reform,—has done more for freedom and good government, than the unfettered liberty of reporting. And of all the services which the press has rendered to free institutions, none has been greater than its bold defiance of parliamentary privilege, while laboring for the interests of the people."—*T. E. May.*

"The Reporters' Gallery is an elaborate organization for the spreading of news of the Imperial Parliament to all the ends of the earth."—*Macdonagh.*

THE official reporter of legislative and legal proceedings has been a comparatively recent development of the press. As long as the news sheet was simply a means of communication between those absent in foreign wars and friends at home, the conduct and the actions of public officials were of no concern to readers; as long as public officials regarded their conduct and actions as sacrosanct, they considered any report of their proceedings an unwarranted interference with their public work. With the enlargement of the sphere of the press, and with the development of the theory that the public has a right to know what is said by its political representatives, the parliamentary reporter made his surreptitious entrance.

Yet the way had been long prepared for him. Sir Symonds D'Ewes in the early seventeenth century was restless under the admonitions of the Speaker of the House of Commons that the Members should not discuss its affairs out-of-doors and should give no note of its proceedings to "any person or persons whatsoever, not being members of this House." [1] During the reigns of Elizabeth and of James I, "strangers who had found their way into the House were held in custody of the sergeant-at-arms until they had sworn at the bar not to disclose what they heard within

[1] *The Journals of all the Parliaments during the reign of Queen Elizabeth both of the House of Lords and House of Commons,* pp. 432, 433.

the Chamber."[2] Moreover, the careless way in which the records of the House of Commons were kept had aroused Sir Symonds D'Ewes and he notes in 1629 "the beginning of a memorable and great work" which he afterwards finished and of which he says: "This work contained all the journals both of the Upper House and the House of Commons, of all the Parliaments and Sessions of Parliament during all Queen Elizabeth's reign; gathered out of the original journal-books of both the Houses, which I had the most free use of . . . Into which, in the due places (unless in some few particulars where I was fain to guess) I inserted many speeches and other passages, which I had in other private journals and manuscripts and in loose papers. I added also many animadversions and elucidations of mine own where occasion served."[3]

How the work of these "collectors and antiquaries and historians of seventeenth century parliaments, whose researches although a little obscured in this latter age do live after them,"[4] prepared the way for the official and semi-official legislative reports of to-day has recently been convincingly shown. The editors of *Commons Debates for 1629* have by diaries, letters, note-books, and "parliamentary compilations;" by news-letters and "separates;" by the Book of Notes and the Clerk's Book kept in the House of Commons; by the Jottings and the finished Journal prepared by the clerk of the Commons; by the various efforts made to meet "a desire on the part of members to have their speeches circulated and so to bid for public approval" and on the other hand to adhere to the "old practice of keeping proceedings in Parliament secret,"—by the use of all of these fragmentary parts of the parliamentary report the editors have shown the evolution of the report as it is available for the first third of the seventeenth century. The study made also shows the existence at this time of the very modern devices of publishing speeches that were supposed to be delivered in secret; of editing speeches after they were

[2] E. Porritt, "The House of Commons and the Press," *The Unreformed House of Commons*, I, 584–596.

[3] *The Autobiography and Correspondence of Sir Simonds D'Ewes*, I, 409–410.

[4] Wallace Notestein and Frances Helen Relf, *Commons Debates for 1629 critically edited and an Introduction dealing with Parliamentary Sources for the Early Stuarts*, Dedication, p. iii.

made; of circulating speeches that were never delivered; of attributing to members speeches "which they never spake." It must be remembered, however, that the stationers, rather than the reporters, were often the ones responsible for some of these short-comings, since to stationers and printers all such parliamentary material had a commercial value.[5]

These "separates," or parliamentary documents or speeches "to be found in a single manuscript," when combined with the news-letter, "a daily or weekly narrative of parliament, a narrative that was sent out in many manuscript copies," gave the constituents of members all the information in regard to Parliament that escaped the vigilance of the authorities.

By the time the Long Parliament met the news-letter had "become a regular feature in connection with Parliament. It satisfied a real demand." Yet in spite of this the Commons were ordering "their Printing Committee to 'suppress the Printing or Venting in manuscript, the diurnal Occurrences of Parliament.' " But suppression was impossible and the "*Diurnall Occurrences* in print was the successor of Diurnall Occurrences in manuscript news-letter."

Later in the century the professional news-letter writers "flourished exceedingly," says Porritt, largely through the eagerness of the county families for Parliamentary news, and "between the Restoration and the Revolution, [they] had more subscribers to their letters from London than at any time in the history of the news-letter writing calling." [6] But the more these writers flourished the more vigorously were they prosecuted by Parliament,— a controversy that was kept up for half a century. The news-letters as such had disappeared before the middle of the eighteenth century, but their spirit was perpetuated through the magazines and newspapers that gave wider circulation to reports concerning Parliament and that in their turn inherited the old quarrel that had been waged against the news-letters.

It was Edward Cave who introduced the idea of circulating the reports of what was done in Parliament. Having a post office situation, he had been able to supply his London friends with the

    [5] W. Notestein and F. H. Relf, *Commons Debates*. "Introduction," pp. xi–lxvii.
    [6] E. Porritt, *The Unreformed House of Commons*, I, 588–589.

provincial papers and to give country printers the written minutes of the proceedings in Parliament that John Nichols says within his remembrance were regularly circulated in the coffeehouses before the daily papers were tacitly permitted to report the debates.[7] In 1728, Cave had supplied Robert Raikes with the minutes of the House of Commons for the use of the Gloucester *Journal*,—a proceeding that resulted in reprimands and heavy fines for both Cave and Raikes. With the founding of the *Gentleman's Magazine* in 1731, Cave began tentatively publishing the reports of parliamentary debates. He first cautiously gave the King's Speech in the May number, and later gave a few harmless communications. In 1732, after the July prorogation of Parliament, he printed the proceedings and debates, with the initial and final letters of the names of the several speakers. The reports quickly grew in length and interest, so much so that they evoked a storm of protest in Parliament and in 1738 the House of Commons resolved, "That it is an high indignity to, and a notorious violation of, the privileges of this house, for any news-writer, in letters, or other papers, (as *minutes*, or under any other denomination,) or for any printer or publisher of any printed newspaper, of any denomination, to presume to insert in said letters or papers, or to give therein, any account of the *debates*, or other proceedings of this house, or any committees thereof, as well during the recess, as the sitting of parliament; and that this house will proceed with the utmost severity against such offenders." [8]

But the resourceful Cave and his rivals [9] quickly found ways of

---

[7] *Rise and Progress of the Gentleman's Magazine*, p. vii. The author gives a full account of the difficulties of Edward Cave in securing the reports.

[8] *Hansard*, XXIII, 148.

[9] So popular had the publication of the debates become that the *London Magazine* quickly entered the lists, and the *Gentleman's Magazine* as quickly showed the asperity of one whose supremacy has been threatened. In March, 1739, it comments: "At length, determining to be no longer debarred from a share in so beneficial a project, a knot of them combined to seize our whole plan; and, without the least attempt to vary or improve it, began with the utmost vigour to print and circulate the *London Magazine*, with such success, that in a few years, while we were printing the fifth edition of some of our earliest Numbers, they had SEVENTY THOUSAND of their Books returned unsold upon their hands."—*Gentleman's Magazine*, March, 1739, IX, 111.

circumventing Parliament.[10] The Debates were prefaced with the statement, "An Appendix to Captain Lemuel Gulliver's Account of the famous Empire of Liliput," or they appeared as "A Letter from a member of Parliament to his country friend;" or as the "Proceedings of the Political Club;" only the first and final letters of speakers' names were printed, names were given through anagrams, or the names of eminent Romans were attached to the various speakers,—various expedients were used since "Parliament then kept the Press in a kind of mysterious awe, which made it necessary to have recourse to such devices."

With reporters forbidden to report and printers forbidden to print, the authoritativeness of the accounts of parliamentary debates may well be questioned.[11] It was the custom of Cave and one or more friends to gain access to the House of Commons, secretly to take a few notes giving the substance of the arguments, and then to compare notes in a neighboring tavern. This crude material was then reduced to a form suitable for the *Gentleman's Magazine*, by William Guthrie, or later by Samuel Johnson.[12] It was in this reduction that opportunities existed for the

[10] "It was no part of Cave's original design to give the debates in either house of parliament, but the opposition to the minister, and the spirit that conducted it, had excited in the people a great eagerness to know what was going forward in both, and he knew that to gratify that desire was to encrease the demand for his pamphlet. Indeed the experiment had already been made, for the speeches in parliament had for some time been given in the Political State of Great Britain, a publication above spoken of, and though drawn up by persons no way equal to such an undertaking, were well received. These for the most part were taken by stealth, and were compiled from the information of listeners and the under-officers and door-keepers of either house; but Cave had an interest with some of the members of both, arising from an employment he held in the post-office, that of inspector of the franks, which not only gave him the privilege of sending his letters free of postage, but an acquaintance with, and occasions of access to many of them.

"Of this advantage he was too good a judge of his own interest not to avail himself."—Sir John Hawkins, *Life of Samuel Johnson*, p. 85.

[11] Cave himself agreeably explained the situation: "The candid Reader, who knows the difficulty, and sometimes danger, of publishing Speeches in Parliament, will easily conceive that it is impossible to do it in the very words of the Speakers. With regard to the major part, we pretend only to represent the sense, as near as may be expected in a summary way; and therefore, as to any little expression being mistaken, which does not affect the scope of the argument in general, we hope, as not being done with design, it will be favourably overlooked."—John Nichols, *The Rise and Progress of the Gentleman's Magazine*, p. xiii; *Gentleman's Magazine*, 1737.

[12] Sir John Hawkins, *Life of Samuel Johnson*, pp. 85–87.

greatest divergence from the speeches as actually delivered. Sir John Hawkins reports Dr. Johnson as saying that he never entered the House of Commons and Arthur Murphy says that he was there but once,—the difference is immaterial. The secret of the authorship of the debates was divulged by Dr. Johnson at a dinner given by Samuel Foote where he stated that he had himself written them in a garret in Exeter Street.[13] The result of the disclosure was that "the company was struck with astonishment" and bestowed lavish encomiums on him; one, in particular, praised his impartiality; observing, that he dealt out reason and eloquence with an equal hand to both parties. "That is not quite true," said Johnson; "I saved appearances tolerably well; but I took care that the Whig dogs should not have the best of it."

One of his biographers much extols these reports of Dr. Johnson since he

"had the art to give different colours to the several speeches, so that some appear to be declamatory and energetic, resembling

[13] The dinner is fully described by A. Murphy, *Essay on the Life and Genius of Dr. Johnson*, pp. 43–45. The author says in part: "That Johnson was the author of the debates during that period was not generally known; but the secret transpired several years afterwards, and was avowed by himself on the following occasion: Mr. Wedderburne (now Lord Loughborough), Dr. Johnson, Dr. Francis, (the translator of Horace), the present writer, and others, dined with the late Mr. Foote. An important debate towards the end of Sir Robert Walpole's administration being mentioned, Dr. Francis observed that 'Mr. Pitt's speech, on that occasion, was the best he had ever read.' He added, 'That he had employed eight years of his life in the study of Demosthenes, and finished a translation of that celebrated orator, with all the decorations of style and language, within the reach of his capacity; but he had met with nothing equal to the speech above-mentioned.' Many of the company remembered the debate; and some passages were cited, with the approbation and applause of all present. During the ardour of conversation Johnson remained silent. As soon as the warmth of praise subsided, he opened with these words: 'That speech I wrote in a garret in Exeter-street.' The company was struck with astonishment. After staring at each other in silent amaze, Dr. Francis asked, 'How that speech could be written by him?' 'Sir,' said Johnson, 'I wrote it in Exeter-street. I never had been in the gallery of the House of Commons but once. Cave had interest with the door-keepers. He, and the persons employed under him, gained admittance; they brought away the subject of discussion, the names of the speakers, the side they took, and the order in which they rose, together with notes of the arguments advanced in the course of the debate. The whole was afterwards communicated to me, and I composed the speeches in the form which they now have in the Parliamentary Debates.' To this discovery Dr. Francis made answer: 'Then, Sir, you have exceeded Demosthenes himself; for to say that you have exceeded Francis's Demosthenes, would be saying nothing.'"

the orations of Demosthenes; others like those of Cicero, calm, persuasive; others, more particularly those attributed to such country-gentlemen, merchants, and seamen as had seats in parliament, bear the characteristic of plainness, bluntness, and an affected honesty, as opposed to the plausibility of such as were understood or suspected to be courtiers: the artifice had its effect; Voltaire was betrayed by it into a declaration, that the eloquence of ancient Greece and Rome was revived in the British senate, and a speech of the late earl of Chatham when Mr. Pitt, in opposition to one of Mr. Horatio Walpole, received the highest applause, and was by all that read it taken for genuine; and we are further told of a person in a high office under the government, who being at breakfast at a gentleman's chambers in Gray's Inn, Johnson being also there, declared, that by the style alone of the speeches in the debates, he could severally assign them to the persons by whom they were delivered." [14]

Dr. Johnson himself declared "that the only part of his Writings which then gave him any compunction, was his account of the Debates in the Gentleman's Magazine; but that, at the time he wrote them, he did not think he was imposing on the world. The mode, he said, was, to fix upon a Speaker's name; then to make an argument for him; and to conjure up an answer. He wrote those Debates with more velocity than any other of his productions; often three columns of the Magazine within the hour. He once wrote *ten pages* in a single day, and that not a long one, beginning perhaps at noon, and ending early in the evening." [15]

Having once revealed the secret, Dr. Johnson "was free, and indeed industrious, in the communication of it, for being informed that Dr. Smollett was writing a history of England, and had brought it down to the last reign, he cautioned him not to rely on the debates as given in the Magazine, for that they were not authentic, excepting as to their general import, the work of his own imagination." [16]

But the ability of reporters so much lauded by their contemporaries becomes the discomfiture of the historian. All of the

[14] Sir John Hawkins, *Life of Samuel Johnson*, pp. 112–116. A. W. Hutton gives a summary of "Dr. Johnson and the 'Gentleman's Magazine'" in *Johnson Club Papers*, pp. 93–113.

[15] J. Nichols, *Rise and Progress of the Gentleman's Magazine*, p. xxxi.

[16] Sir John Hawkins, *Life of Samuel Johnson*, p. 117.

early parliamentary reporting that appeared in the *Gentleman's Magazine* and in its rival, the *London Magazine*, must be dismissed as having little or no historic value, however great its biographical value may be. That Samuel Johnson's reports "should have so long passed current shews how unacquainted people were at that time with real debating." [17] But it was not only that the reports were often figments of the reporters' imagination that make them untrustworthy,—many specific charges against them must discredit them. Samuel Johnson himself knew nothing of debating, he wrote the reputed speeches equally well with or without notes, the reports were published months after the debates, they were published irregularly, several discussions of the same subject might be thrown into one report,[18] speeches were attributed to the wrong member, a debate in the House of Lords was reported at length, but condensed in the House of Commons "lest we should disgust our readers by tedious repetitions," [19] a debate in the time of Cromwell was eighty-four years later published in the *Gentleman's Magazine*,[20] after it had been "abridged, modified and digested" by Dr. Johnson,—an examination of the *Gentleman's Magazine* and of its rival the *London Magazine*, especially from November, 1740, to November, 1743, when Dr. Johnson was writing the debates,[21] is an experience fraught with mixed sensations.[22]

With the fervid eulogy of Dr. Johnson's biographer all must agree:

"The debates penned by Johnson were not only more methodical and better connected than those of Guthrie, but in all the ornaments of stile superior; they were written at those seasons when he was able to raise his imagination to such a pitch of fervour as bordered upon enthusiasm, which, that he might the

[17] *Boswell's Johnson*, edited by G. B. Hill, I, 586.
[18] *Gentleman's Magazine*, 1742, 12: 676.
[19] *Ib.*, 1744, 14: 125.
[20] 1741, 11: 93–100, 148–154.
[21] An admirable comparison is given by M. Macdonagh, *The Reporters' Gallery*, chaps. XIV–XVIII.
[22] G. B. Hill gives interesting parallel versions of the debates as reported by Dr. Johnson and by other reporters for different periodicals. They are scarcely more dissimilar than are the variations in some of the speeches made by Macaulay as reported in Hansard and as given in his collected works.—*Boswell's Johnson*, I, Appendix A, pp. 581–593.

better do, his practice was to shut himself up in a room assigned him at St. John's gate, to which he would not suffer any one to approach, except the compositor or Cave's boy for matter, which, as fast as he composed it, he tumbled out at the door. . . . In the perusal of these debates, as written, we cannot but wonder at the powers that produced them. The author had never passed those gradations that lead to the knowledge of men and business: born to a narrow fortune, of no profession, conversant chiefly with books, and, if we believe some, so deficient in the formalities of discourse, and the practices of ceremony, as in conversation to be scarce tolerable; unacquainted with the stile of any other than academical disputation, and so great a stranger to senatorial manners, that he never was within the walls of either house of parliament. That a man, under these disadvantages, should be able to frame a system of debate, to compose speeches of such excellence, both in matter of form, as scarcely to be equalled by those of the most able and experienced statesmen, is, I say, matter of astonishment, and a proof of talents that qualified him for a speaker in the most august assembly on earth." [23]

Considered as historical material, the verdict must be that "as records of the speeches in the period they cover, they are practically worthless" [24] and that "they are 'dramas' which may be perused for amusement rather than for instruction." [25]

These illustrations have been given to suggest not only the unreliability of the early reports of Parliament, but even more the obstacles placed in the way of reporters that made these subterfuges necessary. It was long before members of Parliament realized that by allowing their speeches to be reported they were multiplying their power, and therefore, long before there was even a tacit relaxation of the stringent regulations against the presence of reporters.[26] The beginning of the open controversy over the admission of press representatives to the House of Commons is found in a plot laid by John Wilkes in 1771. He had long encouraged newspaper proprietors to publish parliamentary debates and, as a result of a ruse to bring about a quarrel between the City

[23] Sir John Hawkins, *Life of Samuel Johnson*, pp. 90, 111.
[24] M. Macdonagh, *The Reporters' Gallery*, p. 163.
[25] *Id.*, p. 164, cited from A. Murphy.
[26] An interesting account of the efforts to exclude reporters is given in M. Macdonagh, *The Reporters' Gallery*, chaps. XLIII, XLVI, "Clearing the Reporters' Gallery" and "'Mr. Speaker, I Espy Strangers.'"

of London and the House of Commons, "with a few occasional interruptions, the newspapers were [thereafter] allowed to publish parliamentary debates." The victory thus became "the most conspicuous incident in the history of the freedom of the Press." [27]

The gradual change came with the slowly developing changes in the organization of the British government until the theory that the representatives of the Fourth Estate are also the representatives of the other estates had been built into the new Houses of Parliament in the provisions made for reporters' galleries. But it is still theoretically possible for any member to "espy strangers" therein and by vote of the House to clear the galleries.

The gulf between toleration and cordial welcome is wide and deep. William Jerdan describes the difficulties of parliamentary reporting when the work was ill organized, there were no conveniences, no telegraph, no opportunities, but many obstacles and much disfavor.[28] Samuel Bamford had other troubles outside of Parliament and he gives an account of the reporters from several London papers being excluded from an inquest at Oldham because they persisted in furnishing daily reports to several London journals contrary to the coroner's order and therefore a strict supervision was kept over other reporters.[29]

The provincial press had its own special grievance in that its representatives were barred from the galleries. As late as 1867, Lord Charles Russell, the Sergeant-at-Arms, said he had repeatedly been urged to allow representatives of the Scotch and Irish to have seats in the gallery, but he had always fought against it. "I considered," he says, "that the best way to serve the interests of the public in the Reporters' Gallery was to give every accommodation to the London Press, and to restrict it entirely to the London Press." [30] Not until 1879 was provision made in the galleries for the accommodation of representatives of the provincial press,—a welcome change from the difficulties under which they had worked at an earlier time. Thomas Frost has well described these difficulties as well as the secret favors shown the favored

[27] The story is told in full in H. Bleackley, *Life of John Wilkes*, pp. 260–263.
[28] *Autobiography*, I, chap. XI.
[29] *Passages in the Life of a Radical*, II, 201–212.
[30] M. Macdonagh, *The Reporters' Gallery*, p. 412.

provincial papers.[31] Justin McCarthy had more than one trying experience in attempting to report for a provincial paper.[32] Wemyss Reid bartered his services to the *Morning Star* in exchange for the coveted gallery ticket that enabled him to send parliamentary news to the Leeds *Mercury* and he describes the "two wretched little cabins, ill-lit and ill-ventilated, which were used for 'writing out,' " one occupied exclusively by *The Times* staff, "and the other so small that it could not accommodate a quarter of the number of reporters." [33] W. H. White gives a depressing picture of the work of a sketch writer for the provincial press in the Reporters' Gallery in the House of Commons.[34]

Since these days of disfavor, restraint, and multifarious obstacles put in the path of the reporter, there has been developed an elaborate organization of reporters comprising the stenographic or verbatim reporters, the sketch writers who describe the speakers and the effects of their speeches,[35] and the lobbyists who gather up political gossip and official communications and write in brief paragraphs reports that appear as the "London Letter" or as "Political Notes." [36] All of this development is in itself an assurance of the authoritativeness of Parliamentary reporting as at present carried on. Yet even in the earlier days, when all note-taking in Parliament was absolutely prohibited visitors, an occasional prodigy like "Memory Woodfall" was able to report the debate so perfectly as to be "popularly supposed to be endowed as a reporter with powers somewhat akin to the supernatural," [37] and to win recognition in fields outside of parliamentary reporting. John Taylor writes that:

[31] *Forty Years' Recollections*, chap. XV, "Provincial Journalism and Journalists."

[32] *Reminiscences*, I, chap. II, "First Glimpses at Parliament."

[33] S. J. Reid, *Memoirs of Sir Wemyss Reid*, chap. VI, "Life in London."

[34] *Mark Rutherford's Deliverance*, chap. I, "Newspapers."

[35] The delightful sketches of Parliament written by H. W. Lucy have been collected in three volumes,—*Sixty Years in the Wilderness; Sixty Years in the Wilderness—More Passages by the Way; Nearing Jordan;* the somewhat satirical sketches of E. M. Whitty are entitled *St. Stephen's in the Fifties*.

[36] M. Macdonagh, *The Reporters' Gallery*, chapters on "The Reporter and the Speech," "The Sketch-writer," and "Lobbying."

[37] "Such was his fame that the first trembling question of the awestricken visitor from the country, on entering the House of Commons was: 'Which is Memory Woodfall and which is Mr. Speaker?'"—M. Macdonagh, *The Reporters' Gallery*, p. 269.

"Upon one occasion some observations were made upon one of Mr. Woodfall's reports in the Court of King's Bench, when Lord Kenyon was Chief Justice. In consequence of what the counsel had said on the report in question, in which a fact of some importance was involved, Lord Kenyon desired to see the newspaper, which was handed to him. After perusing the passage referred to, his lordship enquired if the journalist was the gentleman who was so distinguished for accuracy in reporting debates, and being answered in the affirmative, he said, that he had been so frequent a witness of that gentleman's surprising correctness in reporting debates in the House of Lords, that he was disposed to give implicit credit to his precision in the present instance, and therefore no more was said on the subject." [38]

Until a comparatively recent period, the parliamentary reporter apparently shared with his fellow journalists outside of St. Stephen's the reputation of being something of an outcast from society. On a memorable occasion in 1810 when Sheridan had in an impassioned speech favored greater freedom for parliamentary reporters as well as general freedom of the press, William Windham had sneeringly objected to reporters on the ground that "persons should make a trade of what they obtained from the galleries, amongst which persons were to be found men of all descriptions; bankrupts, lottery-office keepers, footmen and decayed tradesmen." "He did not know any of the conductors of the press; but he understood them to be a set of men who would give into a corrupt misrepresentation of opposite sides." [39]

Later, in 1867, Wemyss Reid found that "In those days a gulf that was regarded as impassible divided the members of the Press from the members of the House." . . . The caste of reporters neither had, nor wished to have, any relations with the Brahmins of the green benches below them." But he found compensation in the thought that "our very aloofness from the inner side of parliamentary life, with its personal interests and its incessant intrigues, strengthened our position as independent critics and observers." [40] The social cleavage long remained,[41]

[38] *Records of My Life*, II, 245–246. The author gives a number of illustrations showing Woodfall's tenacious memory and ability as a reporter. Macdonagh gives chap. XXXI to "Memory Woodfall" and discusses the value of his reports.

[39] *Hansard*, VI, 330.

[40] S. J. Reid, *Memoirs of Sir Wemyss Reid*, pp. 123, 124, 156.

[41] An anonymous writer in 1877 described the reporters as being "com-

perhaps still remains, in spite of "honors" conferred on representatives of the press, though apparently its direction is changing; a recent writer on "Journalism for University Men" says that "the aristocracy of this branch of journalism [short hand reporting] are the reporters in the Gallery of the Houses of Parliament,"[42] thus tacitly acknowledging that a university man may join the ranks at least of parliamentary reporters without losing social caste.

The historian must see possible limitations on the results of the parliamentary reporter's work in the early legislation against his presence in Parliament, in the obstructions put in his way after he had gained an entrance, in the long exclusion from Parliament of the representatives of the provincial press and in the present exclusion of representatives of the foreign press and of women reporters, in the somewhat contemptuous attitude towards them of "the Brahmins of the green benches." But what of the reporter himself,—how far has he been able to overcome limitations of condition and rise superior to opposition, supercilious disregard,[43] difficulty of hearing or seeing the speaker, rapid or indistinct delivery, poor light, bad air, crowded quarters, lack of all the accommodations to-day held to be indispensable for him?

All of these difficulties the reporter may overcome, but he always has to reckon with the speakers. Few have altogether ignored them as did Dr. Johnson. But they have found stumbling-blocks in their after-thoughts, as did Vizetelly in editing an edition of Macaulay's speeches taken "verbatim from 'Hansard' which in those days was commonly accepted in the House of Commons as an unimpeachable authority." "In an edition," says Vizetelly, "which Mr. Macaulay himself subsequently prepared of his speeches, which he professed to have merely revised while materially altering them to suit his more recent opinions, he took

---

monplace men," but charitably explained it on the ground that newspapers did not lay so much stress as formerly on the fulness of their reports of parliamentary debates.—"Parliamentary Reporting," *Contemporary Review*, June, 1877, 30: 165–167.

[42] F. S. A. Lowndes, *Contemporary Review*, December, 1901, 80: 814–822.

[43] When speeches reported have unexpectedly aroused animosity against the speaker, he is prone to ignore the reporter and to take refuge in the statement that "he has been incorrectly reported." This is one of the greatest trials of a parliamentary reporter.

special exception to the report published in 'Hansard' of a speech he had delivered on the Dissenters' Chapel bill, and put forward an amended version of his own;[44] justifying this mode of dealing with speeches, the accuracy of which for twenty or thirty years had passed unchallenged, by the following ingenious piece of special pleading:

'I do not pretend to give with accuracy the diction of these speeches which I did not myself correct within a week after they were delivered. Many expressions, and a few paragraphs linger in my memory. But the rest, including much that had been carefully premeditated, is irrevocably lost. . . . My delivery is, I believe, too rapid. Able shorthand writers have complained that they could not follow me, and . . . as I am unable to recall the precise words which I used, I have done my best to put my memory into words which I might have used.'" Vizetelly can not refrain from adding the comment, "I am unaware whether Mr. Macaulay spoke as rapidly in private—where, as is well-known, he commonly monopolised all the conversation—as he here represents himself as doing in Parliament, but I remember that Lord Brougham, who was sufficiently loquacious himself, spitefully compared Macaulay's incessant flow of talk to the chatter of ten parrots and a chime of bells." [45]

If "many members of Parliament had cause to be amazed at their own eloquence whilst Dr. Johnson was reporter for the *Gentleman's Magazine*, between 1740 and 1743," other speakers both in and out of Parliament may have been somewhat similarly amazed. G. J. Holyoake, in a chapter called "Reporting Speeches which never were Made," gives an account of the speeches made

---

[44] A parallel column arrangement of Macaulay's speech on the Dissenters' Chapel Bill, June 6, 1844, as given in Hansard and in his collected works published in 1866, shows not only much elaboration of phraseology, but genuine emendations. Louise Fargo Brown's intimate knowledge of the Anabaptists has led her to detect the evident irritation of the various divisions of the Baptists over Macaulay's statement as reported in Hansard— "If . . . it were a Bill in favor of Catholics, or the Wesleyan Methodists, or the Baptists . . ." In the collected works the passage reads, ". . . or Wesleyan Methodists, or General Baptists, or Particular Baptists." The two versions of the speech may be found in Hansard, Third Series, 75: 338–351, and *Collected Speeches*, "Dissenters' Chapels Bill," pp. 385–403.

[45] H. Vizetelly, *Glances Back Through Seventy Years*, I, 386.—The version of Macaulay is given in his *Collected Speeches*, Preface, pp. 12–18.

at the laying of the foundation stone of a new town building and
at the banquet that followed. The banquet was prolonged and
boisterous. The proprietor of the newspaper who had asked
Holyoake to come from London went over the toast list with him.
Holyoake inquired concerning the characteristics of the speakers,
manner of mind, peculiarities of expression, antecedents and family, public service and other particulars. "By eleven o'clock I had
sent out speeches for them all, and by midnight their orations
were all in type, and the paper was out in the early morning." [46]

Parliamentary reporters have themselves, however, pointed
out the curious circumstance that the verbatim report may, at
least in spirit, be less accurate than other forms. G. J. Holyoake
found that the stenographic, literal, verbatim reporters often
lacked the faculty of bringing into focus the genius of a speech
and that often the summary reporter was better "able to measure
the mind and discern the purpose of the speaker." [47] Reporters
learn that speakers often repudiate their own words,—"they
make all sorts of muddles and then stand aghast to see themselves in black and white." Sometimes reporters "doctor" the
speeches of very inferior speakers until little is left of the original,
but they are praised by the speakers for the "accuracy" of the
report,—commendation that once led to the caustic comment,

---

[46] *Sixty Years of an Agitator's Life*, II, 157–158.

J. D. Symon gives an account of a speech in praise of the Irish potato
purporting to have been made by Mr. Wilberforce during a nap taken by
an Irish reporter. A friend had promised to take notes for him and dictated
this speech which was reported in every newspaper of note, except the
Morning Chronicle to which the jesting friend was attached.—*The Press
and Its Story*, pp. 80–81.

[47] *Sixty Years of an Agitator's Life*, II, p. 156.

"Every day the Parliamentary reports of speeches present them in a
more effective form than the hearer was sensible of during the delivery.
When *The Times* sought to destroy the popularity of Orator Hunt of a
former day, it reported his speeches verbatim. There are many speakers
in Parliament who would suffer in public estimation if their repetitions and
eccentricities of expression were recorded. On one memorable occasion the
Morning Star reported a passage from a speech of Mr. Disraeli's, with all
its bibulous aspirates set forth, which few forgot who read it."—*Id.*, II, 159.

"If a reporter has a grudge against a Town Councillor, a Poor Law
Guardian, or a Borough Magistrate, and if he is really vindictive, the most
effective course of vengeance that he can adopt is to record verbatim all
that his enemy utters in public . . . 'Oh that mine enemy were reported
verbatim' would assuredly be the modern equivalent of the bitter cry of the
patriarch."—F. F. Moore, *A Journalist's Note-Book*, p. 179.

"Our advice to intelligent reporters who wish to be credited with accuracy, *when they report quite ordinary men,* is this—*Avoid* accuracy, and cook the speeches." [48]

Another phase of "accuracy" is presented by the habit of reporters of comparing notes. If the comparison has resulted in error, it is difficult for the member misreported to set himself right and to disabuse the public of the belief that if all reports agree, they must be correct and the member wrong. "Any report appearing in a score or a hundred newspapers, if it has a common origin may and often does lead to mischief. Independent reports correct each other." [49]

This perfected system of parliamentary reporting that "reached its zenith of fullness in the sixties and seventies" carried with it the seeds of dissolution. If an important speech by a great statesman was scheduled for a certain evening, the morning papers were given the choice of a verbatim report, a full report, or a summary of a column in length; the verbatim and the full reports were given in the first person, the summary report in the third. But there came a sharp decline in the demand for verbatims. "Verbatim reports are as dead as the Dodo," emphatically states one reporter.[50]

This decline in interest in the verbatim parliamentary report is in part explained by the conditions suggested,—a summary report may give a truer idea of the intent of the speaker than do his own words literally set forth. But it is still more explained by the unnecessary duplication of reporting maintained by many newspapers and the obvious advantage of division of labor and reduction of expense. Press agencies have for the most part superseded the verbatim reporters formerly maintained by all the great London and provincial dailies and "the agencies have captured

---

[48] "Parliamentary Reporting," *Contemporary Review,* June, 1877, 30: 165–167.

[49] C. A. Cooper, *An Editor's Retrospect,* pp. 80–81. The author has a word of sympathy for the unhappy reporter whose faithful account may be "corrected" by the printer into an impossible version, as was the case when Lord Palmerston, in allusion to Gulliver's Travels, began a speech, "We have all heard of the battles of the Big-Endians and the Little-Endians." The printer altered it into the battle of "the big Indians and the little Indians;" and thus it appeared in the *Morning Star.*

[50] A. Kinnear, "The Trade in Great Men's Speeches," *Contemporary Review,* March, 1899, 75: 439–444.

the gallery." The reporters themselves disagree as to the comparative advantages of the two systems,[51]—from the point of view of the historian there seems little choice as regards real authoritativeness.

The explanation of the prolonged and obstinate opposition of Parliament to the presence of reporters during their sessions must be found in the theory that lies behind the English government,—it has been a government by classes instead of by the masses. It was long before the tug-o'-war between the sticklers for parliamentary authority and those who desired publicity for the sake of the public was decided in favor of publicity. But in time even opponents of the reporters were won over. G. O. Trevelyan notes that Charles James Fox had been one of the most formidable among the ancient enemies of the parliamentary reporters, yet in 1778 he declared that "the only method of preventing misrepresentation was by giving more publicity than ever to the debates and decisions of the House, since the surest recipe for killing a lie was to multiply the witnesses to the truth." [52] No similar problem has been presented to the American federal government and hence the members of the press have had free access to Congress except during the executive sessions of the Senate. Congress, rather than the press, has arranged for the reports of its proceedings. These have been verbatim reports, and not a word or a sign of approval or of disapproval of the words spoken on the floor has escaped the note books of the stenographers. So keen have been members of Congress to make sure that they have received good measure, pressed down, shaken together, and running over, that they have added to the official reports of legislative proceedings a mass of material having its origin in times and places far removed from legislative halls.

The same theory that the public has a right to know how its business is conducted pervades all classes and is applied to legislative bodies, however small or comparatively unimportant.[53]

[51] A. Kinnear, "Parliamentary Reporting," *Contemporary Review*, March, 1905, 87: 369–375; A. P. Nicholson, "Parliamentary Reporting: A Reply," *Contemporary Review*, April, 1905, 87: 577–582.
[52] G. O. Trevelyan, *The Early History of Charles James Fox*, p. 347.
[53] Francis Lieber notes an illustrative case in Columbia, S. C., where two reporters were sued. They subsequently published a report of the trials

Three general systems of legislative reporting have been used. The British Parliament has come to tolerate, but it does not officially recognize the reporter and therefore all reporting has been in the hands of the press itself and it has been carried on either through the reporters of individual newspapers or through press agencies. *Hansard's Debates* were long made up of the various newspaper reports carefully collated and since no official report is authorized by Parliament itself, if the newspapers are compelled to suppress a debate, it is lost forever.

This system has had in it so many elements of confusion that in 1874 the House of Commons instituted an inquiry in regard to parliamentary reporting in foreign countries and in the colonies. The resulting report brought together much valuable information and showed that the prevailing method was for reporting to be the work of private enterprise. But Austria, France, Germany, Italy, and the United States at that time used the system of official reporting, while several of the smaller British provinces provided for their legislative reporting through a contract system.[54]

Excellent as was the report in itself, it brought no immediate relief for a troublesome situation in England. But a few years later, in 1878, a *Report from the Select Committee on Parliamentary Reporting* presented the results of an elaborate inquiry concerning the comparative merits of official reports and reports made by private enterprise. The inquiry on which the Report was based showed conclusively the existence of two radically different ideas in regard to the use to be served by parliamentary reports. Certain representatives of the press wished reports that would interest their readers, while the Parliamentary Committee was concerned with the question of what constitutes an official record. During the inquiry the superintendent of the reporters on *The Times* was asked: "Do you never elaborate a little personal encounter and pass over more solid discussions?" And he replied:

---

under the title "Rights of Corporations and Reporters." It contained letters from nearly thirty American mayors, testifying that reporters could not be denied admission to the deliberations of the councils of their cities, even though there were an appointed printer to the board.—"Publicity," *On Civil Liberty and Self Government*, pp. 127–142.

[54] *Reports on the Subject of Parliamentary Reporting in Foreign Countries and in the Colonies.* 1874.

"Doubtless that is always interesting; that is a matter not only interesting to the Members, but it is interesting to outsiders. Anything of a personal character is sure to attract attention." Is it strange that he thought the necessity of an official report was obviated by the very full reports given in *The Times?*[55] It was the manager of the Press Association—a co-operative association that supplied one hundred and seventy-two members and one hundred and one newspapers not members of the Association—who realized that, over and above the reports given in the press, Parliament should have "some record of its transactions for historical purposes, or for the purposes of the Members themselves."

The inquiry had made it obvious that two things were equally necessary,—a supply of daily reports to be used by the newspapers, and the establishment of a parliamentary record, but the report was made to the House of Commons too late in the session for definite action to be taken on it.

The House of Lords was also concerned with parliamentary reporting and in 1880 it conducted an exhaustive inquiry on the subject, although the inquiry largely turned on the question of how to provide more adequate accommodations in the House of Lords for the increasing number of reporters.[56]

To these diverse systems of parliamentary reporting the line of Pope may well be applied: "Man never is, but always to be blest." Samuel Whittaker favored official reports of parliamentary debates since "the first essentials of any system of reporting must ever be accuracy and absolute impartiality. These essentials are, in a great measure, neutralized, so far as the work of Parliamentary Reporting is undertaken by the Press, by the political bias which is inseparable from newspaper enterprise."[57]

The American Congress authorizes its own stenographic verbatim reports and these are published as the *Congressional Rec-*

---

[55] When it was brought out in the inquiry that the reports given in the press could "not be sufficient for the House of Commons as a source of reference, or a record of their transactions," the representative of *The Times* replied, "I can not conceive what use it can be to the House to have a fuller report of such a matter."—*Report on Parliamentary Reporting*, 1875, p. 52.

[56] *Report from the Select Committee of the House of Lords on Reporting.* 1880.

[57] Samuel Whittaker, *Parliamentary Reporting in England, Foreign Countries, and the Colonies*, Manchester, 1877.

ord. For extreme verbal accuracy, which may or may not be a virtue in the eyes of the historian, the advantage lies with the plan adopted by Congress; for correct interpretation of spirit, the advantage lies with the press reports of Parliament. Incidentally, *Hansard* is of consuming interest, the *Congressional Record* is deadly dull.

The opposition of legislative bodies to having their proceedings reported seems inherent, certainly in their early history. The same hostility that long persisted in the English Parliament, Godkin found in Hungary during the revolutionary period. "Whether from the jealousy of the government," he writes, "or the apathy of the Magyars, no printed reports of the parliamentary proceedings had ever yet [1832] been published, so that the people remained without any intelligence of the sayings and doings of their representatives, except such as was afforded them by rumour or hearsay. To supply this defect, Kossuth resolved to devote the time, which would otherwise have been wasted in idle listening, to carefully reporting everything that took place, and circulated it all over the country on a small printed sheet."

And again similar conditions led to similar results. Kossuth found that "the importance of the proceedings which then occupied the attention of the diet caused it to be read with extraordinary eagerness," and he therefore "rendered it still more attractive by amplifying, and often even embellishing the speeches. The Cabinet, however, soon took the alarm, and although the censorship was unknown to the Hungarian law, prohibited the printing and publication of the reports."

Kossuth, however, was not to be thwarted and he quickly collected a group of young men who, as secretaries, wrote out large numbers of the journal which circulated in manuscript throughout Hungary. After the diet closed, he reported the meetings of the county assemblies,—a proceeding that angered the Government who stopped the journal at the post office, but could not stop its circulation by messengers among the villages.[58]

---

[58] E. L. Godkin, *The History of Hungary and the Magyars*, pp. 305–306. This account is apparently based on E. de Langsdorff, "La Hongrie en 1848 Kossuth et Jellachich," *Revue des Deux Mondes*, 1848, new series, 24: 252–279.

The question of official reporting does not end with the right of reporting the proceedings of representative legislative bodies, although it has involved more bitter controversy than have other branches of the subject. The right of the press to report court trials was early disputed and obstacles were put in the way of reporters scarcely less troublesome than awaited them at the doors of Parliament. Even in the early nineteenth century, newspapers were forbidden under heavy penalties to publish reports of unfinished cases in the law courts,—a rule, however, that was set at naught in the case of at least one enterprising newspaper.[59]

The hostility of the courts towards press reporters was no less in evidence during the same period in America. In 1830, J. G. Bennett went from New York to Salem, Massachusetts, to report a murder trial, where he found the court much opposed to reporters. The judges waived jurisdiction for one day over the press from other states, and then forbade all from taking notes for immediate publication,—Bennett wrote, July 10, 1830, that the court gave notice that "if any person was *detected* in taking notes of the evidence in the Court House, for the purpose of sending them out of the State for publication, previous to the conclusion of the trial, he would be proceeded against by the court as for a contempt." [60]

But the reporter may often render a very real service to the cause of justice. It has been noted more than once that a trained reporter may sometimes brush away the obscurities of the law and see the point at issue more clearly than the court, bound to give decisions in accordance with the law. The reporter may see more clearly the point of justice than the judge who sees only the law, "and often bad law." This at least has been the opinion of a former court reporter.[61]

The historian is indeed not dependent on the press for verbatim reports of trials and decisions of courts, but he may be misled by the "stories" given by it. If a newspaper is for any reason specially interested in securing the conviction of a person wrongfully charged with violation of the law, its reporters may skil-

[59] H. Vizetelly, *Glances Back through Seventy Years*, I, 154.
[60] *Memoirs of James Gordon Bennett*, pp. 119–120.
[61] F. F. Heard, *Curiosities of the Law Reporters*, 1871.

fully suppress testimony in favor of the person accused, use qualifying adjectives as "alleged," "professed," while giving great prominence to accusation, — and in other ways give an erroneous impression. But such errors are not those of the official reporter and they must not be charged to his account.

More or less unreliability has in times past been attached to the work of the official reporter, but it has been an unreliability for which the reporter himself can not be held strictly accountable. Almost unsurmountable obstructions have blocked his way and that in the beginning he made any headway against them is surprising. The value of his reports must be estimated by the success he has had in overcoming collective opposition, in understanding the idiosyncrasies of individual speakers, and in securing such freedom from the letter as enables him to preserve the spirit of what he reports. If the work of the reporter has been confused with that of "the fanciful writer of parliamentary debates," it is well to remember that there has been but one Dr. Johnson. And if the work of the reporter has in a measure been nullified by the after-thoughts of speakers, it is also well to remember that there have been many Macaulays who have made of Hansard "an embarrassing monument of the vanity of our senators." [62] "The press gallery is the height of reportorial ambition" and to the press gallery in every country the historian is indebted not only for the official reports of legislative proceedings, but also for an insight into the legislative Johns and Thomases as, in more humble circles, they have been described by Oliver Wendell Holmes.

[62] J. D. Symon, "The Press Gallery in the House of Commons," *The Press and Its Story*, pp. 75–86.

CHAPTER VIII

THE SPECIAL CORRESPONDENT

"Much have I seen and known; cities of men
And manners, climates, councils, governments,
Myself not least, but honor'd of them all;
And drunk delight of battle with my peers,
Far on the ringing plains of windy Troy.
I am a part of all that I have met;
Yet all experience is an arch wherethro'
Gleams that untravell'd world, whose margin fades
For ever and for ever when I move.
How dull it is to pause, to make an end,
To rust unburnish'd, not to shine in use!"

Tennyson, *Ulysses*.

SPECIAL correspondence is the chameleon of the press. Its ancestors have been numerous, and its own forms are protean. In the early seventeenth century it grew out of the letters concerning the Thirty Years' War. In the eighteenth century in England, it was in form the political pamphlet or tract. At the close of the century, its highest type is represented by the *Letters of Junius* and its importance at that time is best described by John Wade when he says, "Newspaper correspondence had an authority and interest in the time of Junius which it no longer possesses, and the Miscellaneous Letters derive a value from the illustration they afford of this antecedent phase of journalism. At this period existed none of those leading articles or elaborate commentaries on public questions, which now occupy so prominent a place in our daily papers. The correspondents of the press were then the only writers of political communications which bore the character of leaders; and, as reports of the debates were not permitted, members of either house suffered equally with the people in possessing no common channel by which the one could learn, and the other convey, their sentiments. In consequence of this restrictive system, the correspondence of newspapers formed the most talented portion of their contents, influential men of all parties adopting this medium as the best for giving publicity to their opinions." [1]

Somewhat similar conditions were found in America during the same period. Newspapers were small, unattractive, and inadequate, and the overworked editor, who probably was also the printer, at important times had the assistance of unpaid contributors; the clergyman, the lawyer, the scholar were glad to write special letters to the press and thus have a channel for the expression of their individual opinions. [2]

If at an early period it was the special correspondent that developed into the pamphleteer, at a later period it was the reporter that developed into the special correspondent,—a fact recorded in the term "*grand reportage*" applied in France to special correspondence. Again, it has been the interview that has grown into special correspondence, as on the other hand special correspondence leads to the interview.

The functions of special correspondence have come to be even more various than have been its origins. Special correspondence has given rise to war correspondence that during war overshadows that branch of the press from which it has been developed. In time of peace, the ebb and flow of the tide brings again special correspondence into the more important place, and its various branches are distinctly classified. The staff correspondent is the regularly appointed resident representative of the press at home and foreign capitals. He lives in the shadow of foreign courts and describes the events in the daily life of high potentates or of those below stairs. He lives at national capitals and reports political policies and conditions. [3] "Our own correspondent" travels hither and yon and describes great public functions, as coronations, royal marriages, christenings, or funerals, and the general pageantry of life; the inaugurations of presidents of great republics or of small colleges; the national meetings of bankers, dry goods merchants, or of learned societies; the calamities in the wake of fire, flood and earthquake. He travels abroad and describes the unusual scenes, customs, and habits of countries little known to

[1] *Letters of Junius*, edited by John Wade, II, iii.
[2] M. C. Tyler, *The Literary History of the American Revolution*, I, 19.
[3] T. C. Crawford, "Special Correspondents at Washington," *Cosmopolitan*, January, 1892, 12: 351–360.

outsiders, and he carries with him the prestige of the newspaper he represents. [4] The occasional correspondent is not regularly attached to the press, but sends to it letters on subjects which he is specially well qualified to treat.

The historian must first of all ask what have been the qualifications demanded of those who cover so large a part of the world's activities. From the standpoint of the editor, they may be best given in the words of James Gordon Bennett, when he says:

"The Special Correspondent of a great newspaper possesses for the time being something of the influence of an Ambassador from one nation to another. Now, according to an axiom of Machiavelli, an Ambassador should endeavor to make himself *persona grata* with those to whom he is accredited, if only thereby to gain the best opportunities for obtaining every possible information and to be able to report events in a broad impartial spirit. The correspondent should give his sources wherever possible, and allow the reader to form his own opinion on the facts submitted. The views of the paper itself should be found in the editorial columns. The correspondent is to take no side, and to express no opinions of his own. In many cases it would appear that the matter sent to the papers by their correspondents in Turkey is biased against the Turks. This implies an injustice against which even a criminal on trial is protected." [5]

But his own list of qualifications, from the standpoint of the special correspondent himself, may vary materially from those of the editor; if the editor emphasizes the needs of the newspaper, the correspondent does not forget the correspondent *propria persona.*

"The special correspondent must be 'to the manner born'. He may or may not have creative ability. He must have such a temperament as to be new-born every morning, and to look on all that he is to write about with new eyes and fresh interest. He must have a made-to-order sort of a soul, that will suffer itself to be thrown into whatever he does as a boy's soul enters into what games he plays at college. He must have at once the broadest and the finest power of observation, and the vocabulary and facility that are the bases of expression and freedom with his pen. He must be as sanguine as a songbird, and as strong and

---

[4] W. Beatty-Kingston, "Our Own Correspondents," *A Journalist's Jottings*, II, 339–368.

[5] Cited by Sidney Whitman, *Turkish Memories*, pp. 11–12.

willing as a race-horse. Above all, he must love his work better than his comfort, his club, his home, or his friends. He must have a personality all vigor to keep on past every hindrance, and with much candor and sweetness to win and keep men's confidence, so that they will admit him everywhere and talk to him unrestrainedly; but his personality must be of a kind that does not intrude itself too rigidly at many points. . . . The special correspondent must be so constituted as to remain poor, and willingly, so long as he sticks to newspaper work. . . . The correspondents of to-day must be and are welcome at the houses, clubs, and business places of the men who lead in public affairs. They must be men of parts and of good appearance and behavior." [6]

Lord Salisbury more briefly and more cynically defined the ideal special correspondent as "a man who combines the skill of a first-rate steeple chaser with the skill of a first-rate writer." [7]

The London *Times* long had, if not an additional, definite requirement, at least a strong preference for foreigners as its chief correspondents, and it numbered on its staff men of American, Czech, Hungarian, and Italian birth who rendered it signal service. This was a peculiarity that distinguished its foreign correspondence, as was also the entire independence in which it left its correspondents in the expression of their opinion, even when, as often happened, these opinions were radically opposed to the editorial tone. [8]

But however high the standards set for special correspondents and however successfully they may meet them from the editor's standpoint as well as their own, the all-important question for the historian is,—how authoritative is that part of the newspaper that appears under the caption "special correspondence"?

[6] Julian Ralph, "The Newspaper Correspondent," *Scribner's Magazine*, August, 1893, 14: 150–156.
Somewhat similar, though more serious qualifications, are enumerated, from the English point of view, by W. Beatty-Kingston, "Foreign Correspondents," *Fortnightly Review*, March, 1886, n. s. 39: 371–387.
[7] S. T. Sheppard, "In Memoriam: William Howard Russell. The Genesis of a Profession," *United Service Magazine*, March, 1907, 155: 569–575.
The apparently casual way in which a man may become a special correspondent is graphically described by H. Labouchere in "How I became the Besieged Resident," *The Daily News Jubilee*, by Justin McCarthy and John R. Robinson, pp. 94–98.
[8] An Ex-Member of the "Times" Staff, "The London Times," *The Nation*, September 9, 1880, 31: 185.

The question may in part be answered by noting the sources of his news.[9] In London, these are the lobby of the House of Commons, the alleys near the Bank of England, the National Liberal Club and other prominent London clubs, the smoking-rooms of the leading London hotels, the various embassies, and perhaps the British Foreign Office, and the large business houses with which the correspondent must establish connection. He has a wide personal acquaintance and shares the fashionable life of the city; he is a good conversationalist, he entertains and is in turn entertained, he gives "tips" to inferior officers in exchange for "tips" on news.[10]

But the very multiplicity of authoritative sources of information becomes in itself a handicap. The special foreign correspondent, especially in Europe, is bound by unwritten regulations that often prevent him from availing himself of these opportunities; he must not give the names of his informants;[11] he must conceal the source of his news; he must not give official news without the consent of officials; he may be expected to color the news so as to give a good impression; he may chafe under restrictions and conditions where, like the diplomat, "he must get as much as possible and give as little as possible." A foreign correspondent is under more or less suspicion, and not unreasonably, since he is often a secret agent of the government, and he therefore works at a serious disadvantage. Officials regard him as an easy prey and may mislead him; all information that is important is given him under the stipulation that he must not disclose it; the editorial office is anxious to emphasize the authoritativeness of the information, while the more the source is unimpeachable the greater is the reluctance to have it disclosed. The information given may carry with it the permission to print, but later be semi-officially contradicted; journals that are utilized by govern-

---

[9] T. C. Crawford says: "Almost the entire worth of a piece of information depends upon the person who furnishes it."—"Special Correspondents at Washington," *Cosmopolitan*, January, 1892, 12: 351–360.

[10] E. A. Dithmar, "The European Correspondent," *Bookman*, May, 1904, 19: 244–257.

[11] "The American newspaper correspondent in Europe in time of peace can not get used to the fact that he can not quote the names of his informants." —W. von Schierbrand, "Confessions of a Foreign Newspaper Correspondent," *World's Work*, April, 1903, 5: 3355–3358.

ments may deny or may ridicule the revelations made.[12] On the continent there has been more or less supervision of what is written and the correspondent inevitably adopts a "read-between-the-lines-style." Bismarck was said "to keep the foreign press in order" because the special correspondent was at his mercy,—if his letters displeased the Chancellor, he was refused all information.[13]

But even with absolute authoritativeness as to source of news and with no restrictions on communicating the news received, errors may arise for which neither press nor correspondent can justly be held responsible, as when they are due to the necessary expansion of skeleton messages.[14] The errors may be deliberate on the part of the press, as when a correspondent sends a dispatch,—to find that only the place-and-date line has been kept, while the dispatch that follows has been written from the New York office,[15] or dispatches may be credited to non-existent staff correspondents,[16] or the correspondent assigned to a certain side may be told, "Don't be too hard on them if they are unlucky." [17]

The correspondent himself may be responsible for at least false impressions, as when a journalist told W. H. Russell, soon after his arrival in America, that he had himself created the office of Washington correspondent to the New York papers. "At first," the journalist said, "I merely wrote news, and no one cared much; then I spiced it up, squibbed a little, and let off stories of my own. Congressmen contradicted me—issued cards—said they were not facts. The public attention was attracted, and I was told to go on; and so the Washington correspondence became a feature in all the New York papers by degrees." [18]

[12] W. Beatty-Kingston, "Foreign Correspondents," *Fortnightly Review*, March, 1886, n. s. 39: 371–387.

[13] "The Change of Government in Germany," *Fortnightly Review*, August, 1890, n. s. 48: 282–304.

[14] W. J. Chamberlin, *Ordered to China*, 231–232. H. Leach, *Fleet Street from Within*, chap. IX, "Occasional Fallibilities."

[15] Isaac Russell, "Hearst-Made War News," *Harper's Weekly*, July 25, 1914, 592: 76–78.

[16] H. D. Wheeler, "At the Front with Willie Hearst," *Harper's Weekly*, October 9, 1915, 61: 340–343.

[17] J. A. O'Shea, *Leaves from the Life of a Special Correspondent*, II, 235–236.—The author says this is the only hint he ever received during his whole career as a special correspondent that could be construed into instructions.

[18] W. H. Russell, *My Diary North and South*, pp. 24–25.

An account of the new form of Washington correspondence is given by C. G. Miller, *Donn Piatt His Work and Ways*, pp. 215–223.

Yet other correspondents have protested against this conception of the special correspondent's work. Labouchere, under date of December 24, 1870, wrote with great emphasis, "Had I been M. Jules Favre, I confess that I should have turned out all foreign journalists at the commencement of the siege. He, however, expressed a wish that they should remain in Paris, and his fellow-citizens must not now complain that they decline to endorse the legend which, very probably, will be handed down to future generations of Frenchman as the history of the siege of Paris." [19]

On the other hand, the absolute truth as conveyed by correspondents may lead to international controversies, ministerial complications, and personal disaster to the correspondents. Frederick Boyle, the correspondent of the London *Standard*, was expelled from Russia because certain phrases, the truth of which was not denied, were offensive to the government.[20] In 1902, the correspondent of the London *Times* in Russia was expelled for too truthfully reporting one of the many organized persecutions of the Jews.[21] Valentine Chirol, who represented the London *Times* in Berlin, was expelled for speaking plainly in regard to the Kaiser's dispatch to President Krüger anent the Jameson raid.[22] Robert Dell, long the Paris correspondent of the Manchester *Guardian*, was expelled by the French Government because his political comments seemed objectionable.[23] The not infrequent expulsion of foreign correspondents seems to have been due not to false statements but to truthful letters when the truth has been embarrassing to the government concerned.

The special foreign correspondent is always in a peculiarly trying position as well as in one involving serious responsibility. Not only are his own government and his own newspaper concerned as well as the foreign capital where he resides, but he has a

[19] *Diary of the Besieged Resident*, pp. 262–263.

[20] *Narrative of an Expelled Correspondent*, pp. v–xxiv. The volume gives much information concerning the status of newspaper correspondents during the Russo-Turkish War.

[21] G. M. Royce, in New York *Times*, July 15, 1917.

[22] Wolf von Schierbrand, "Confessions of a Foreign Newspaper Correspondent," *World's Work*, April, 1903, 5: 3355–3358.

[23] *Dial*, June 6, 1918, 64: 547–548; foreign comment on the expulsion, *Dial*, July 18, 1918, 65: 56–57.

responsibility to the thousands of readers whose only knowledge of foreign affairs is derived from his letters. He may even have a responsibility towards the citizens of the country where he temporarily resides. During the Second Empire, when the French press was under galling restrictions, it was in the correspondence of the representatives of the foreign press that the French had "the unique source of information about their own affairs." [24] The long list of special correspondents from Henry Crabb Robinson to the present time shows men who have appreciated and lived up to these responsibilities. Speaking of the Civil War, E. L. Godkin once said: "There never was a war which afforded such materials for 'special correspondence' of the best kind as this one—no matter in what way we look at it." [25] The special correspondent has for the most part not only lived up to his responsibilities, but he has appreciated his opportunities.

The truth of this statement is not invalidated by another patent fact,—that the special correspondent has been at times prone to magnify his office. If he is sent abroad by a great newspaper to report to it, for example, the effects of the Pasteur treatment on four children sent from America to Paris to receive it, and he writes that "in the newspaper world the taking of a leading part in the burning subject of the day, and being the first to ventilate it, plays a very important rôle," [26] the historian accepts the spirit of the work, without necessarily accepting the value placed upon it by the writer.

But these very opportunities are fraught with danger. It is not alone in Great Britain that it has been possible to say, as does Greenwood, that "The most difficult and least satisfactory service of the Press in Britain is the Foreign Correspondent's." [27] The influence of the correspondent may be used for good ends, but he may be in turn under the influence of the man higher up. Greenwood gives an account of a visit in the early days of the *Pall Mall Gazette* from a German official coming directly from

[24] Theodore Child, "The Paris Newspaper Press," *Fortnightly Review*, August 1885, n. s. 38: 149–165.
[25] Rollo Ogden, *Life and Letters of Edwin Lawrence Godkin*, I, 204–205.
[26] Aubrey Stanhope, *On the Track of the Great*, p. 56.
[27] F. Greenwood, "The Newspaper Press: Half a Century's Survey," *Blackwood's Magazine*, May, 1897, 161: 704–720.

Bismarck who stated how much the Chancellor admired the *Pall Mall Gazette* and that he wished to supply it occasionally with really good information on foreign affairs. Bismarck, it was represented, wished to send both news and letters of observation and comment. When his representative was told that only news would be desired, he said that no doubt this could be arranged, and left, but nothing further was heard from him. Not alone in the press of Great Britain has danger lain concealed in "letters of observation and comment," offered by admiring chancellors.

But the press has not always refused proffered letters from royal correspondents even when made "with a view to influencing opinion." Sir Roland Blennerhassett has somewhat recently disclosed the efforts of Napoleon III in this direction. "It is a curious fact," he says, "not known to half a dozen individuals even at the present moment, that most important communications were sent by Napoleon III to the *Times* during the last ministry of Lord Palmerston. These contributions were made with the utmost secrecy, and no human being was aware that the Emperor of the French was writing in the *Times* except Mr. Delane, editor of the leading journal, and Lord Palmerston, the Prime Minister. The correspondence between Mr. Delane and Lord Palmerston on this subject was until lately in the hands of my recently departed friend, Mr. Evelyn Ashley. The communications were made by Napoleon III with a view to influencing opinion both in England and France, and Lord Palmerston was able to get from them true insight into the policy of the Emperor." [28]

While, however, governments have not been averse to acquiring true insight into the policy of emperors, they have chafed under the "true insight" of themselves that foreign correspondents have ostensibly given. Charles Lowe much resented the misrepresentations of England given to the German press by its correspondents in London [29] and it was in England a long-standing grievance.

Sir William F. Butler has given an interesting and enlightening

[28] "The Foreign Policy of Queen Victoria," *National Review*, January, 1908, 50: 811–825.
[29] "The German Newspaper Press," *Nineteenth Century*, December, 1891, 30: 853–871.

account [30] of the work of the press correspondents in South Africa in influencing the public there and in England against the Boers; the editor of the *Cape Times* was also the special correspondent at Cape Town of two important London dailies, while "the editors of the leading Johannesburg journals had been specially imported from England" to carry out the policy of Mr. Rhodes. The result, Sir William wrote a high government official, was his conviction that "the small and noisy group of men who had got all the telegraphic and most of the press power into their hands are steadily intent upon the production of friction, and nothing but friction, in this country." He again writes, under date of May 3, 1899: "We are getting our South African news from London as we get much of our meat and all our drink from it. But there is a difference between the mental and bodily sustenance thus received. The news is first made up here by the syndicate for the transmission of false information, which has such enormous resources at its disposal, and is then cabled to London to produce alarm on the Stock Exchange or unrest in the Cabinet. Here nothing is known about this alarming state of things, and in Johannesburg it is even less apparent. Our Johannesburg has more prosperity in it . . . than any place in the world. . . . But your *London* Johannesburg is quite another place." [31]

Even lords of high degree have not scrupled to write as did Sir A. Henry Layard of his success in securing the support of the English and European press for Sir Stratford Canning in his policy as the ambassador of Great Britain at Constantinople. "For sometime I had under my control," he writes, "the Constantinople correspondence of the most influential journals in England and on the Continent. I succeeded at the same time in obtaining a small subsidy for the *Malta Times*—a newspaper published in the island and conducted with some ability, and which was then widely circulated in the Levant." "I learnt by experience," he continues, "how much the success and reputation of a diplomatist may depend upon his skill in obtain-

[30] *Autobiography*, pp. 376–455.
[31] *Autobiography*, pp. 424–425.
There must be put with this, "Editor of the *Cape Times*," *Edmund Garrett* by E. T. Cook, chap. VII.

ing the support of the newspaper correspondents and their incessant and exaggerated approval of all he says and does." [32]

It is probably experiences of this character that have led to the judgment that "one of the banes of an editor's life, [is] the foreign correspondent who lives in his own set abroad and reflects only their opinions without regard to the views of the paper at home." [33] At least one journalist has found foreign correspondents inveterate grumblers,—probably because they feel themselves exiles and can not keep in touch with affairs at home.

A form of occasional correspondence long in vogue was that of the traveller who wrote to his home paper descriptions of European scenery, and of European capitals with their art treasures. Much of this was enthusiastically received at a time when comparatively few persons went abroad, [34] but it was necessarily superficial and lacking in perspective. The letters even of the most famous among these correspondents are to-day almost forgotten, yet the impression made on their own time can not be overlooked. [35] The correspondence of this character has almost disappeared from the press owing to the great increase in the use of the cable, [36] the enormous expansion of foreign travel in times of peace, and the multiplicity of authoritative guidebooks to European cities.

The place of this early correspondence has in time of war been taken by "letters from the trenches" sent usually to local papers

[32] A. H. Layard, *Autobiography and Letters*, II, 102–103.
[33] G. B. Dibblee, *The Newspaper*, p. 240.
[34] Representative letters may be found in *Letters from Three Continents* by the Arkansas correspondent of the *Louisville Journal* (1849); *Letters of Travel* written by David Grey for the *Buffalo Courier* (1865–1868); *Letters from Europe* by J. W. Forney (1867).
Since negative results are often quite as significant as are positive ones, it is of interest to note that these letters from abroad rarely, if ever, concern the press of foreign countries. Even editors, when traveling abroad, have seldom written of the press in the countries visited.
The extent attained in America by special correspondence prior to the Civil War has been described by Allan Nevins in the *New York Evening Post*, August 10, 1921.
[35] A. Shadwell, "Journalism as a Profession," *National Review*, August, 1898, 31: 845–855.
[36] "Foreign correspondence, especially foreign political correspondence, has been reduced by the cable to a humble and vanishing rôle."—Rollo Ogden, "The Press and Foreign News," *Atlantic Monthly*, September, 1900, 86: 390–393.

by men describing the daily life of the troops. This can not in any way be classed as war correspondence, but it has had a prominent place in the press. Much of it, however, has been distrusted and to counteract the incorrect, exaggerated reports contained in such letters a "truth tour" was arranged in May, 1919, and the "A. E. F. Press Special" carried two hundred former newspaper men then in the army to show them the Army Headquarters, the entire service of supplies, and the Army of Occupation. The object was to forestall the "whoppers" that had been written home and that had returned to confound the regular representatives of the press in France. These "whoppers" had been due to imagination, to ignorance, to credulity, to a desire for notoriety, and to a necessarily limited point of view. The "truth tour" gave a perspective all had lacked and must favorably affect the occasional correspondence that for years to come will fill the columns of the local press.[37]

What then are the limitations of special correspondence as historical material? The limitations are primarily the official relations that have been already suggested, but they tend to become crystallized when the usefulness of correspondents is recognized by the governments of the countries where they temporarily reside. In May, 1918, "With the approval of the American Government," there was formed the "Association of Foreign Press Correspondents in the United States." [38] The authorities placed at the disposal of the new organization "special facilities for an examination of the war activities of the United States in all directions, facilities which include talks with leading statesmen, inspection of military and naval work, and visits to the centers of war industries in various parts of the country." But since nothing indicates that facilities for seeing normal conditions were placed or to be placed at the service of the foreign correspondents, the opportunities accorded them must be classed as efforts on the part of government officials to influence foreign opinion through press correspondents. These facilities offered must seem near of kin to those presented by the German government in 1914 to foreign press correspondents,—facilities that

[37] W. Forrest, "The Truth Tour," New York *Tribune*, May 21, 1919.
[38] New York *Evening Post*, May 20, 1918.

have been so graphically and so naïvely described by Sven Hedin in *With the German Armies in the West*.

A second form of official limitation on foreign press correspondence is found in the censorship that even months after the signing of the armistice prevented letters from accomplishing their end,—a double censorship that has opened letters on the frontier and again examined the surviving remnant at their destination,[39] and has thus prevented the circulation of information concerning revolutionary movements. Even at the Peace Conference, the foreign press correspondents were effectively prevented from acquiring special knowledge essential to their work and from receiving information from America that would have shown the attitude of the country towards some of the questions under consideration.[40] If the foreign press correspondence has at times seemed to the editor the least satisfactory part of the product of the newspaper press, at least a partial explanation may be found in the mutual relations of press correspondents and governments.

It often happens that special correspondence is written "for home consumption." When the first American troops arrived in France in 1917, some of the American press correspondents wrote of the enthusiastic greeting they received on landing, while the troops themselves were said to view the landing otherwise,—the landing had been made early in the morning, the day was wet, the peasants were weary, they had seen many troops land, troops of all nationalities looked much alike to them and they did not appreciate the significance of the landing of American troops. The enthusiasm felt to be noticeably lacking in the reality was abundantly supplied by some of the press correspondents. At a later time one woman socially prominent in America was recognized among the war workers by a crowd of troops and given a great ovation that was fully described by the press correspon-

[39] "Freedom of the Press in France," *The Nation*, February 22, 1919, 108: 305–306.
[40] H. P. Stokes, "Colonel House [is] Correspondents' Stand-By," New York *Evening Post*, May 26, 1919.
    An interesting description is given of "the erection of a wire barrier in the courtyard [of the Royal Palace at Versailles], from behind which the multitude of newspaper correspondents will be permitted to witness the arrival and departure of the plenipotentiaries."—New York *Tribune*, April 28, 1919.

dents. Soon after another woman equally prominent at home was not recognized by the crowd and therefore received no ovation,—except in the columns of the press. "It would never do at home," it was explained, "to let Mrs. X. have great public appreciation here and give none to Mrs. Y."

Another limitation is found in the work of the free-lance special correspondent who goes forth to see what is to be seen. He may go to Mexico on behalf of the owners of oil wells and presumably he decides that intervention in Mexico is necessary. He may be sent to a foreign country whose language he neither understands nor speaks and again presumably he hears and sees and reports what his interpreter wishes to have heard, seen, and reported, and thus absolutely contradictory letters concerning the same situation may be sent by different correspondents to their respective papers. He may visit the offices of various public utilities and decide that the agricultural districts are opposed to daylight saving. He may have his orders "to pitch into" public officials and he does not miss the opportunity of so doing.[41] The line that divides the special correspondent from the propagandist is at times invisible.

But some of the limitations on the work of the special correspondent may be personal rather than official. If his life at the capital tends to be drab and dull,—"the foreign correspondent under the Second Empire had a most uninteresting time;" if he is not received at Court as was the case during the Empire in Germany; if time hangs heavy,—he yields to temptation and

---

[41] "A correspondent once brought me a dispatch he had prepared, requesting me to look it over and see whether it contained anything strictly libellous. It proved to be a forecast of the course of the secretary of the treasury in a financial crisis then impending. 'Technically speaking,' I said, after reading it, 'there is plenty of libellous material in this, for it represents the secretary as about to do something which, to my personal knowledge, he has never contemplated, and which would stamp him as unfit for his position if he should attempt it. But as a matter of fact he will ignore your story, as he is putting into type to-day a circular which is to be made public to-morrow, telling what his plan really is, and that will authoritatively discredit you.'

"'Thank you,' he answered, rather stiffly. 'I have my orders to pitch into the secretary whenever I get a chance. I shall send this to-day, and to-morrow I can send another saying that my exclusive disclosures forced him to change his programme at the last moment.'"—Francis E. Leupp, "The Waning Power of the Press," *Atlantic Monthly*, February, 1910, 105: 145–156.

becomes a social lion in circles without the official pale, where "he is much courted by aspirants and much hated by rivals." If he is a man of engaging personality and fulfills all the requirements prescribed for special correspondents and is admitted to social circles deemed the highest, temptation also lies in that direction. More than one eminent special correspondent has succumbed to the insidious allurements of social life and his work has thereby become dogmatic in temper, superficial in its interpretations, and lacking in vigor of expression. The historian can not hope to find his best perspective through the eyes of petted social favorites.

Yet in spite of all these generally recognized limitations on the authoritativeness of special correspondence, the correspondent himself is "a fine fellow" who is often not responsible for the limitations that hamper his work. "What most extraordinary men are these reporters of newspapers in general, I mean English newspapers!" exclaims George Borrow when viewing an insurrection in Madrid from behind a bolted door in company with the correspondent of the *Morning Chronicle*. "The activity, energy, and courage which they occasionally display in the pursuit of information, are truly remarkable." [42] The high type of men who have been special correspondents on five continents at the behest of the greatest newspapers in the world is a guarantee that as far as is humanly possible they will overcome these limitations inherent in the position. It must rest with the historian to separate the writer from his work and to give to the one his due meed for his efforts that have often been thwarted by forces outside of himself.

[42] *The Bible in Spain*, chap. XIV.

CHAPTER IX

THE WAR CORRESPONDENT

"It was the reactionary Tory Xenophon who had retired from public life, civil, or military, before instituting the alliance, since so fruitful, of the writer with the fighter."—*Escott*.

"On quitting school I boldly undertook to write and relate the wars."
—*Froissart*, 1357.

"They sent us back the news which greatly rejoiced the whole army."—*Philippe de Comines*, 1492.

"How should younger brothers have maintained themselves, that have travelled, and have the names of countries and captains without book as perfect as their prayers? . . . It has been a great profession; a peace concluded is a great plague unto them, and if the wars hold, we shall have store of them; oh, men worthy of commendations; they speak in print."—*Shirley*, 1631.

"Our own war with Spain seemed to be waged by and for the newspapers."—New York *Evening Post*, August 1, 1914.

THE first war correspondent of modern times may be said to have been Julius Caesar who, happily for posterity, combined with his duties as war correspondent those of censor and editor. The uncensored letters of the Crusaders gave the Western Europe of that day its first real knowledge of the Orient, and the by-products of the correspondence, in the descriptions of the country and of the life of that time, have had a more permanent value than have the descriptions of assaults and sieges. Froissart was the great war correspondent of the fourteenth century and the by-products of his accounts have been the interesting picture he unconsciously gives of himself and of life at the courts he visited. Successive correspondents and chroniclers followed until the seventeenth century when "war correspondents" appeared in the Low Countries. These were penniless English soldiers who translated from the High Dutch or the Low Dutch and wrote "relations" for booksellers. The relations or "corantos" soon were issued at frequent intervals and thus news of the Thirty

Years' War and the countries involved became familiar in England, and incidentally they perhaps led to the first regular English newspaper.[1]

The functions of the early war correspondents were not indeed the same as those of the war correspondent of a later day, yet the steps in the evolution of the one from the other are clearly seen and to his long career may perhaps be in part ascribed the continued activity of the war correspondent in the field of journalism.[2] His speedy disappearance has often been predicted and

[1] J. B. Williams, *History of English Journalism to the Foundation of "The Gazette,"* pp. 12–13

The titles of the corantos in the Burney collection, from May to November 1622, indicate the receipt of news from Italy, Germany, Hungary, Austria, Bohemia, the Palatinate, France, the Low Countries, and "most parts of Christendom."—*Ibid.,* Appendix C, pp. 215–217.

See also, J. B. Williams, "The Beginnings of English Journalism," *Cambridge History of English Literature,* VII, 389–415.

These "relations" sent to England had been preceded on the Continent by the *Mercurius Gallo-belgicus.* The first volume was published in 1594 and it contained a summary of important events from 1588 as they had occurred in France, Belgium, Spain, Italy, England, Germany, Poland and neighboring places. The volumes were issued until 1635 and they resemble more an annual register than a daily or weekly periodical.

[2] Henry Crabb Robinson writes in his *Diary, Reminiscences and Correspondence,* I, chap. XI, that in January, 1807 he received a proposal from Mr. Walter that he should go to Altona and become *The Times* correspondent. He "was to receive from the editor of the *Hamburger Correspondenten* all the public documents at his disposal, and was to have the benefit also of a mass of information of which the restraints of the German press did not permit him to avail himself." The offer was accepted and his letters from Altona ran from March to August, 1807, and were followed by three from Sweden. On his return to London he served some months as foreign editor of *The Times,* and in July, 1808, went to Spain where for nearly six months he again served as war correspondent for *The Times.*

This seems to have been the beginning of definite war correspondence, although S. T. Sheppard finds precedent for it in the *Swedish Intelligencer* which contained, he says, an entertaining correspondence about the army of Gustavus Adolphus. See his interesting article, "In Memoriam: William Howard Russell. The Genesis of a Profession," *United Service Magazine,* March, 1907, 155: 569–575.

"The real beginning of newspaper correspondence was the arrival of 'Billy' Russell with the English army in the Crimea," says E. L. Godkin. "He was a welcome guest at every mess-table, from the moment of his arrival in the camp. In his hands correspondence from the field really became a power before which generals began to quail." He considers that the most important result of the Crimean war was the creation and development of the "special correspondents" of newspapers.—R. Ogden, *Life and Letters of E. L. Godkin,* I, 100, 101–102.

This is the view generally accepted and a memorial to Sir William Howard Russell in the crypt of St. Paul's, London, bears the inscription:

collectively he has found a place in the newspaper "morgue." [3]
His work has called forth the satire of writers for the press in
other lines,[4] and he has repeatedly been told that the public has
ceased to be interested in his work.[5] Yet with each recurring
conflict between warring nations he finds a place and his letters
appear in the daily press.

The position of the war correspondent has indeed always been
a most difficult one, and one that has been growing increasingly
complicated, since so many different and warring factors are

"The first and greatest of War Correspondents." This is reproduced in
J. B. Atkins, *The Life of Sir William Howard Russell*, II, 388.

This statement, however, is challenged by F. Lauriston Bullard who says
that the first war to be adequately and comprehensively reported in the
daily press was the conflict of 1846 and 1847 between the United States
and Mexico. *Famous War Correspondents*, pp. 5, 6, 9.

See also Allan Nevins, "Newsgathering in the Forties," *New York Evening Post*, August 10, 1921.

[3] "Since the days of the Crimean war we have seen the business of war
correspondence run its full course and sink perhaps into comparative insignificance. Owing to the vastly increased range of modern weapons and
extended sphere of military operations, on the one hand, and owing, on
the other, to the extreme severity of the censorship, the opportunities even
of the most enterprising correspondents are greatly restricted. All are
placed very much in the same position—a position generally in the rear of
actual operations; and, except when enterprise takes the form of fiction,
the correspondent becomes, so far as any immediate publication is concerned,
little more than an official chronicler."—Sir Edward Cook, *Delane of
"The Times,"* p. 82.

Winston Spencer Churchill, in one of his books on the Boer War, laments:
"Alas! the days of newspaper enterprise in war are over. What can one
do with a censor, a forty-eight-hour delay, and a fifty-word limit on the
wire?"— Cited by F. Lauriston Bullard, *Famous War Correspondents*, p. 3.

[4] "Dr. Russell, of the *Times*, was preparing to mount his war-horse.
You know the sort of thing,—he has described it himself over and over
again. Bismarck at his horse's head, the Crown Prince holding his stirrup,
and the old King of Prussia hoisting Russell into the saddle. When he was
there, the distinguished public servant waved his hand in acknowledgment,
and rode slowly down the street, accompanied by the *gamins* of Versailles,
who even in their present dejection could not forbear a few involuntary
cries of 'Quel homme!'"—Matthew Arnold, *Friendship's Garland*, pp.
313–314.

The friends of Matthew Arnold also much deprecated the tone taken in
Friendship's Garland towards G. A. Sala.

[5] "It is a plain fact that the public at present takes less and less interest
every year in either foreign or war correspondence."—G. B. Dibblee, *The
Newspaper*, p. 71.

"The public is so infatuated with the early stages of a war and so bored
and incapable of serious interest in it after a few weeks, that the proper
treatment of war news is the most serious problem which a newspaper
manager has to face."—*Ib.*, pp. 69–70.

concerned in his work. The war correspondent is never too insignificant to escape the notice of the government; the war office regards him as its arch enemy; army officers deem him an interloper; the troops complain that they are not adequately noticed by him; the censor wields his blue pencil and mercilessly strikes out his most telling paragraphs; the general public is prone to consider him omniscient while criticizing him for not providing on tap fresh and important news; to his own newspaper he is a valuable but expensive asset; to himself, the war correspondent would not be worth sending to the front if he did not consider his work sufficiently important to justify all the attention it receives from all the circles that it touches. The problem of squaring the circle is not more hopeless than is that of harmonizing all these mutually contradictory elements in the work of the war correspondent.

It is easy to understand why the war correspondent seems everywhere to be *persona non grata* to those in authority. His letters are not desired by the government because "in informing the public, the newspaper informs the enemy." As early as 1807, the Duke of Wellington had protested against the freedom allowed Henry Crabb Robinson, sent out by the London *Times* as its first special war correspondent,[6] and he lost no opportunity of inveighing against all of the tribe. In 1810 he found one of his great difficulties in "the babbling of the English newspapers, from whose columns the enemy constantly drew the most certain

---

[6] "The Duke had never held the newspaper press in much respect. The information which it conveyed to the public during the Peninsular War, although of the deepest interest to the British community, was offensive to him, because the same information reached the enemy whom it was of importance to keep in ignorance of the operations of the English camp and the disposition of the troops. Moreover, the press libelled him without mercy, giving publication to the grossest falsehoods, and assigning the worst motives to those acts which proved to be the result of the most consummate judgment, the most profound forethought, and the purest patriotism. But he took no steps to procure the punishment of the libellers. He despised, or affected to despise them—he found a safety-valve for his wrath in calling them 'rascally,' 'licentious,' and so forth; and upon one occasion he wrote to Sir Henry Wellesley, 'What can be done with such libels and such people, excepting to despise them, and continuing one's road without noticing them?' It had been well for his renown if he had continued this lofty policy, leaving to time the assertion of truth and the confusion of his maligners."—J. H. Stocqueler, *The Duke of Wellington*, II, 152.

information of the strength and situation of the army," [7] and in 1812 he bewailed that he was constantly hampered by the mischief occasioned by the English newspapers, "For the latter," he said, "while deceiving the public with stories of victories never gained, battles never fought, enthusiasm and vigor which had no existence, did most assiduously enlighten the enemy as to the numbers, situation, movements, and reinforcements of the Allies." [8] In the following year he found a new grievance in that "Discourses and writings against the British abounded in Lisbon and Rio Janeiro, and were re-echoed or surpassed by the London newspapers, whose statements overflowing with falsehood, could be traced to the Portuguese embassy in that capital." [9] The troubles in the Portuguese situation he indeed charged to the English newspapers that "did much mischief by their assertions, but he never suspected they could by their omissions alienate the Portuguese nation and government. The latter complained that their troops were not praised in parliament, nothing could be more different from a debate within the house than the representation of it in the newspapers;—the latter seldom stated an event or transaction as it really occurred, unless when they absolutely copied what was written for them; and even then their observations branched out so far from the text that they appeared absolutely incapable of understanding much less of stating the truth on any subject. The Portuguese people should therefore be cautious of taking English newspapers as a text of the estimation in which the Portuguese army was held in England, where its character stood high and was rising daily." [10] The situation in Spain was no better, for the vexatious disputes with it were increasing daily, and if the omissions or assertions of newspapers were to be the causes of disagreement with the Portuguese, the Iron Duke could only hurl at the offending papers the dire threat, "*I will quit the Peninsula for ever!*" [11]

[7] W. F. P. Napier, *History of the War in the Peninsula*, II, 366.
[8] *Ib.*, IV, 125.
[9] *Ib.*, IV, 461.
[10] *Ib.*, IV, 464–465.
[11] *Ib.*, IV, 465.
The contemptuous attitude of the Duke of Wellington towards the press is well illustrated in Napier, IV, Appendix VIII B, which gives two letters written by the Duke of Feltre, Minister of War, to King Joseph. These

The hostility of the Duke of Wellington towards newspapers was not confined to war correspondents in the Spanish peninsula and to editors in London, but was all embracing in extent and character. Nor again was it a temporary feeling growing out of irritation with Henry Crabb Robinson. As early as 1810 he had written to Croker stating with much emphasis his entire and absolute disapproval of the English press and of newspapers in general. "The licentiousness of the press," he writes, "and the presumption of the editors of the newspapers, which is one of the consequences of their licentiousness, have gone near to stultify the people of England." "Nothing will suit editors (friends and foes are alike) but that the enemy should be swept from the face of the earth." [12]

The Spanish peninsula under the Duke of Wellington was not a fertile soil for the development of war correspondents and the representative of *The Times* after a few months returned to London.

It has been said that the Crimean War was the first in which newspaper correspondents were in the field. Yet how unwelcome they were to the government officials at home and to the commanding officers in the field is abundantly evident from all the contemporaneous records. William Howard Russell had been sent by *The Times* to the Crimea in February, 1854, to report the operations of the English expedition and on leaving he had been told by Delane, "You will be back by Easter, depend upon it, and you will have a pleasant trip." [13] Of the character of this "pleasant trip" the letters of Russell to *The Times* give abundant proof.[14] The effect of these letters can best be understood by a

were dated Paris, October 8, and November 19, 1812, and enclosed extracts from the London *Courier*, *Morning Post*, *Times*, *Statesman*, and *Morning Chronicle*, containing minute details in regard to the numbers, situation, and destination of the Sicilian, Spanish, and Anglo-Portuguese armies, and the most exact account of the reinforcements sent from England. One of the letters is endorsed by Wellington—"Advantage of English newspapers."

[12] L. J. Jennings, *ed.*, *The Correspondence and Diaries of John Wilson Croker*, I, 36–38; from Cartaxo, December 10, 1810.

[13] J. B. Atkins, *The Life of Sir William Howard Russell*, I, 124.

[14] W. H. Russell, *The War: from the Landing at Gallipoli to the Death of Lord Raglan; The War: from the Death of Lord Raglan to the Evacuation of the Crimea*. These two volumes contain the letters written by Russell to *The Times* from the seat of war in the East.

study of the official correspondence of that time. The papers of Lord Panmure indicate, page after page, the constant hostility of the war office to *The Times* and to its special correspondent at the front, because of his criticism of the conduct of the Crimean War, and a resentment of this criticism,—criticism that the very letters of Lord Panmure to Lord Raglan show was abundantly justified.[15] Russell was repeatedly accused of "hounding Lord Raglan to death" by his strictures on the conditions under which the war was carried on, although Kinglake who "set out to write an epic with Lord Raglan for his Achilles" put the ultimate onus on the *owners* of *The Times* for not restraining Delane to whom he accorded more blame than to Russell. The critics of Russell have upheld the cause of Lord Raglan on the ground of his popularity among his officers and also on the ground that the war correspondents were meddlers who should not have criticized military conditions.[16]

"The king never dies," and the sensitiveness of the English commanding general in the Crimea to the criticisms of *The Times* correspondent and his hostility to the press in general may, at least in part, be explained by his having served on the staff of the Duke of Wellington and having married his niece.[17]

The tug of war between the Government and *The Times* during the period of the Crimean War ended for the time being in favor of the press. "These were the golden days of *The Times*,"

Even more impressive is the volume of W. H. Russell, *The Great War with Russia: A Personal Retrospect.* It was published in 1895 and is a masterly account of the difficulties of an early war correspondent as described behind the scenes.

[15] *The Panmure Papers*, 2 vols., 1908.

[16] The controversy in regard to the justice of the criticism of the war office and the management at the front can be found in A. W. Kinglake, *The Invasion of the Crimea*, IV, chap. IX; J. B. Atkins, *The Life of Sir William Howard Russell*, I, chap. XIX; A. I. Dasent, *John Thadeus Delane*, I, 154–208. Kinglake, IV, 360–365, gives under a veiled description of the Company a bitter description of the great power wielded by *The Times* at the time of the Crimean War. His chapter on "The Demeanor of England" is mainly a discussion of Russell's letters to *The Times* and the effect of their disclosures on the English people.—IV, chap. IX.

How prolonged and how bitter this controversy has been is indicated by the articles of F. A. Maxse, "Lord Raglan's Traducers," *National Review*, March, 1899, 33: 62–73, and "The War Correspondent at Bay," *National Review*, April, 1899, 33: 246–253.—W. H. Russell's version is given in *The Army and Navy Gazette*, February 11, 1899.

[17] A. W. Kinglake, *Invasion of the Crimea*, IV, 169.

says Charles Pebody. "*The Times* was king, *The Times* and its special correspondent; and the public believed far more in the men of Printing House Square—in their sagacity, in their military capacity, and even in their patriotism—than it believed in the men of Whitehall." [18]

The same hostility towards the press was subsequently maintained by Lord Wolseley who complained, "Without saying so directly, you can lead your army to believe anything; and as a rule, in all civilized nations, what is believed by the army, will very soon be credited by the enemy, having reached him by means of spies, or through the medium of those newly-invented curses to armies—I mean newspaper correspondents." In no uncertain terms he continues, "Travelling gentlemen, newspaper correspondents, and all that race of drones, are an encumbrance to an army; they eat the rations of fighting men, and do no work at all. Their numbers should be restricted as much as possible." And concerning retreats, he bewails, "An English general of the present day is in the most unfortunate position in this respect, being surrounded by newspaper correspondents, who, pandering to the public craze for 'news', render concealment most difficult. However, . . . he can, by spreading false news among the gentlemen of the press, use them as a medium by which to deceive an enemy." [19]

The antipathy of General Sherman to the war correspondents of the American Civil War was no less pronounced. In 1861 he "looked on them as a nuisance and a danger at headquarters and in the field, and acted towards them accordingly." Later, "his hostility to the press had become more and more pronounced. . . . In one letter to a publisher he had said that he thought praise from a newspaper was contamination, and he would willingly agree to give half his pay to have his name kept out of the public prints." [20] His letters to his brother are filled with denun-

[18] *English Journalism, and the Men Who Have Made It,* pp. 182–183.

[19] General Viscount Wolseley, *The Soldier's Pocket-Book for Field Service,* Third Edition, pp. 93, 97, 249. It is possible that the return comments on Lord Wolseley by the war correspondents themselves may have led to the elimination of these uncomplimentary remarks from later editions, although the paragraph on "retreat" appears in the fifth edition. See, *e. g.,* Archibald Forbes, *Memories and Studies of War and Peace,* pp. 353–354.

[20] *Memoirs of Henry Villard,* I, 209; II, 237–238.

ciations of press correspondents and of explanations why they regard him as the enemy of their class. "I announced," he writes in 1863, "that all such accompanying the expedition were and should be treated as spies. They are spies because their publications reach the enemy, give them direct and minute information of the composition of our forces, and while invariably they puff up their patrons, they pull down all others." And he continues: "The press has now killed McClellan, Buell, Fitz-John Porter, Sumner, Franklin, and Burnside. Add my name and I am not ashamed of the association. If the press can govern the country, let them fight the battles."

Again he writes John Sherman: "We have denounced their [the South's] tyranny in suppressing freedom of speech and of the press, and here too in time we must follow their example. The longer it is deferred the worse it becomes." And after an impassioned arraignment of the press for the information it has given the enemy, he adds, "I say with the press unfettered as now we are defeated to the end of time." To his brother's entreaties to be more moderate in his dealings with newspaper men, he only laments the more the freedom of the correspondents and adds, "Napoleon himself would have been defeated with a free press." [21]

Nor was General Sherman the only commander in the Civil War who anathematized the press. General Halleck's "famous war on the press" after the battle of Pittsburg Landing has been equally well-known and it has led to the comment that "the complaint was that correspondents praised some generals and did not praise others, and the complaint came from the parties not praised!" [22]

The neglect and the polite indifference of the Government at Washington to William Howard Russell and its consequent failure to appreciate the service he was able to render it through writing the absolute truth of military and political conditions both North and South are but too well remembered.[23]

[21] *The Sherman Letters*, ed. by Rachel Sherman Thorndike, Letters of February, 1863, pp. 187–188, 189, 191–193, 193–194.

[22] R. Cortissoz, *Life of Whitelaw Reid*, I, 89–91.

[23] W. H. Russell, *My Diary North and South*, and J. B. Atkins, *Life of Sir William Howard Russell*, 2 vols., give full details of the over-sensitiveness to criticism on the part of the officials involved that led to Russell's abrupt return to England.

The papers of governmental and military officials abound in illustrations similar to those that have been given showing the long-continued, deep-seated opposition of all in authority to all war correspondents individually and collectively.[24] The reasons for this are easily understandable. The conventional government likes secrecy and undoubtedly the war correspondent adds to its difficulties and embarrassment in times when secrecy seems absolutely necessary. Much of this disapproval on the part of the government seems wholly justified, for political, financial, and industrial questions are so interwoven with military operations that full publicity can not be accorded except under the sanction of the government and it naturally wishes to be its own medium of communication with the public.[25]

The government opposition to war correspondents reached its climax and new principles were introduced into their mutual relationships when in August, 1914, war correspondents were barred by the governments of Belgium, England, France, and

[24] The Editor of *The War Correspondence of the Daily News 1870* gives an excellent summary of the hostility of the French government towards war correspondents and of its unwillingness to authorize the presence of neutral observers within the lines.—I, chap. I.

H. Wagner enumerates twenty-one subjects forbidden press correspondents; photographs could be used only by special permission; all personal letters were subject to censorship; and personal freedom of movement was restricted. "It was categorically forbidden to send any news that was at all worth knowing, or to take any steps by which one could get possession of any such news."—*With the Victorious Bulgarians*, chap. XX.

[25] "The Crimean war was the first in which newspaper correspondents—called by Lord Wolseley 'the curse of modern armies'—were in the field; Lord Raglan and his immediate successors were the first, and last, commanders to conduct a campaign under the unchecked criticism of unofficial eye-witnesses. The correspondents, as I have already explained, were given no recognized status; they had to trust to their own wits, luck and daring, to maintain their position; but their proceedings and correspondence were otherwise unfettered."—Sir Edward Cook, *Delane of "The Times,"* p. 82.

"To echo Kinglake's criticism that the accounts from headquarters commissioned by Delane kept the enemy acquainted with all that was going on, is merely to say that the satisfaction of the public demand for war news may have dangers as well as its refusal."—T. H. S. Escott, *Masters of English Journalism*, p. 182.

Henry Villard, although he was himself a war correspondent, wrote that from what he had himself seen, "If I were a commanding general I would not tolerate any of the tribe within my army lines."—*Memoirs*, I, 209.

Similar opinions have sometimes been expressed by correspondents who have been able to see "the other side."

Germany,[26] and later by Italy.[27] The English press immediately raised a storm of protest against the banishment of correspondents from the field of war,[28] on the ground that if full reports were not given patriotism would be lessened,[29] recruiting hindered, interest decreased, distrust roused, indifference created, and nervous tension fostered. As a result of the protest the British War Office partly rescinded the order,[30] later only neutral correspondents were admitted,[31] and still later the rules were relaxed to permit three groups of six correspondents each by turns to visit the British front and each group to remain about six days each.[32] These statements, illustrating the variations in the policy of a single government, seem to justify the criticism made even before the war of 1914 that "war correspondence is more than ever a duel between an exasperated official called the censor and the correspondent." [33]

The War Office, as a special branch of the government, has shown a growing displeasure at the presence of war correspondents with the army. Not only have their numbers increased but many believe that the type has deteriorated. The elaborate

[26] In Belgium, only Belgian journalists were permitted to enter or to remain in the country; no war correspondents were allowed with the British or the French forces; in Germany, the war correspondent was forbidden, but the General Staff gave out news.—New York *Evening Post*, August 18, 1914.

[27] New York *Times*, May 24, 1915.

[28] "There will not be an unofficial, full, and independent account of any action fought in the war. . . . The Government's action would be starving the nation's interest in the greatest concern it has, and would deprive the future historian of his materials."—Cited from The London *Daily Telegraph*, August 19, 1914.

[29] "Graphic pictures of the life of the camp and incidents of the battle are the stuff that patriotism thrives on."—F. L. Bullard, *Famous War Correspondents*, p. 29.

[30] New York *Times*, August 19, 1914.
In America, Frederick Palmer represented the Associated Press and shared the news with all news associations in America.—New York *Tribune*, August 28, 1914.

[31] New York *Times*, November 16, 1914.

[32] The rules were relaxed about February 27, 1915. Press of that date.

[33] The German General Staff announced that no correspondent, artist, or photographer would be in future allowed at the German frontier.—Press of October 4, 1914.
The Department of State in Washington issued passports only to those writers regularly accredited to responsible journals or to press associations and to those whose neutral character was assured.—New York *Evening Post*, October 26, 1915.

outfit now considered indispensable demands highly trained officers to handle it and these are unwillingly detailed for such a purpose in a time of life and death struggle. But the War Office not only finds their presence a serious inconvenience but it finds them positively harmful. Why, it asks, if spies are shot for giving information to the enemy should war correspondents give the enemy gratuitous information in regard to the number and location of troops, strategic plans, food supplies, provision for hospitals, or any other matter of warfare? The question has apparently but one answer and the War Office, by whatever special name it may be known in the several countries, approves and even formulates the plans for the discomfiture of the war correspondent.

The army itself has come to dislike the war correspondent. In the early days, he was a man on horseback who shared the privations of the troops and was one of them. Now he travels with an elaborate outfit of cooks, grooms, interpreters, and assistants; a special train must be provided for tents, stores, cooking apparatus, provisions, photographers' outfit, horses, pack animals and fodder;[34] he rides in an automobile with a chauffeur and is accompanied by a photographer with a camera; the apparent luxury of his life and his extensive equipment tend to separate him from the rank and file of the army and he is equally unwelcome to the officers; he seems to be an onlooker rather than a participant in the war, and to feel himself somewhat consciously in the limelight; his own accounts of his hardships are not taken too seriously and may indeed seem somewhat spectacular [35] and they perhaps give color to the statement, "the high-priced war correspondent is a form of window-dressing." [36]

[34] See the enumeration of nearly seventy classes of articles regarded as indispensable by G. W. Steevens.—F. L. Bullard, *Famous War Correspondents*, p. 306.

The press quarters in Galicia were described in the New York *Tribune*, November 30, 1914.

Richard Harding Davis describes "A War Correspondent's Kit" in *Notes of a War Correspondent*, pp. 239–263.

Compare these accounts with the equipment in the Civil War.

[35] "The American correspondent who first scored an arrest was Captain Granville Fortescue."—Richard Harding Davis, New York *Tribune*, September 4, 1914.

[36] Francis McCullagh, New York *Evening Post*, January 11, 1913.

If the regular correspondent is in ill favor he is to the last degree objectionable when he carries a camera,—"camera and cinematograph have added the last straw." The army willingly endures privation and hardship in their most extreme form but it is averse to having these seemingly take the form of a dress parade. If collective defeat comes to the army, the individual members do not wish to have their personal misfortunes particularized, their forced retreat and consequent sufferings made a spectacle for the entertainment of others, their internment or imprisonment with the humiliation and disgrace they conceive is attached to it recognized on the screen by distant friends. The correspondent may write of impersonal defeat and disaster and justly find them characterized by heroism and extraordinary courage, but the camera can not show the hero with a halo, nor does it show him on a prancing charger waving his country's flag; it can show him only as he is externally,—unkempt, unshaven, and dejected, with none of the aspects of heroism that can be described by the pen. The camera is the most hated part of the outfit of the war correspondent.[37]

Editors and owners of newspapers have long felt the exhaustive drain made on their resources by war and the war correspondent and hence have not given him a sympathetic welcome. Just prior to the Boer War, Lord Glenesk had asserted that "a war was a great misfortune for a newspaper. The *Morning Post* must be supplied with the latest information and must employ the best correspondents, there could be no appreciable increase in the daily demand: the profit would be made by such of the evening papers as had no correspondents on the spot, and could rely on a brisk sale in the streets."[38] The newspaper expenses in the American Civil War were enormous.[39] Every war sends up the budget of the newspaper for expenses to be incurred for correspondence, photographs, news service, cable tolls, extra editions, increasing cost of paper and of wages, while revenues are

[37] Perhaps an explanation of the demand for the camera lies in a suggestion of Francis McCullagh's that while the earlier war correspondents like MacGahan and Forbes wrote for a highly educated class, the photographer caters to a public that either can not read or has no time to read.

[38] R. Lucas, *Lord Glenesk and the "Morning Post,"* p. 376.

[39] J. Francis, *Notes by the Way,* pp. 75–76.

decreased through the cutting down of advertisements.[40] Nor are these extra expenses met by the sale of papers even though the immediate effect may be, as in the Franco-Prussian War, that "the excitement caused by [it] has led to an increase of between fifty and seventy-five per cent. in the sale of the London daily papers." [41] The public quickly loses interest in the details of a campaign, spectacular descriptions of charges and combats and endurance of sieges soon pall, the center of continued interest shifts from the front to the conditions behind, below, and beyond the front, and the sales increased by a factitious interest quickly decline.

Other reasons seem also at times to have deterred editors from favoring war correspondents, but it is not always possible for the historian to go behind the face of the returns and to separate fact from motive.[42]

For the recent comparatively low status of the war correspondent he seems himself to have been in large part responsible. His chief equipment for the work may have been his own impelling desire to become a war correspondent.[43] He may have no knowledge of any language but his own. He may be entirely ignorant of horsemanship. He has frequently forgotten that he is the guest of the army and can claim no right to follow its operations. He often has virtually practiced espionage on his hosts. His complaints have sometimes seemed entirely baseless.[44] He has

[40] O. G. Villard, "The Press as Affected by War," *Review of Reviews*, January, 1915, 51: 79–83.

[41] The *Athenaeum*, July 23, 1870, 56: 117.

During the recent difficulties in Mexico an effort was made to meet the expenses entailed by war correspondence through syndicating the letters arranged for by a leading journal.

[42] M. B. Honan landed in Genoa, February 25, 1848, and says that not an Italian newspaper had a correspondent in camp. His own letters to the London *Times* explained that the disasters of the Italians were due to the weakness of Charles Albert. These letters, he states, were copied by the Italian papers and their contents approved by the army. But Italian editors were ambitious for office and therefore defended Charles Albert, although they published the *Times'* letters while assailing the writer. It seemed to him that the Italians were more desirous of suppressing than of aiding the efforts of the few who attempted to remedy the defect of lack of all intelligence from the camp.—*The Personal Adventures of "Our Own Correspondent" In Italy*, pp. 371–373.

[43] An interesting account of such an experience is well set forth by H. W. Farnsworth in *The Log of a Would-be War Correspondent*, 1913.

[44] E. N. Bennett, during the Balkan campaign of 1912, assisted the Turkish authorities in their censorship of the press. He writes, therefore,

often demanded privileges "on his honor" but not always maintained his honor. He has often evaded regulations through the use of private couriers and boats. His most serious preparation has sometimes seemed to be his plans for circumventing the censor.[45] He has written much of his personal experiences, his thrilling adventures, his hairbreadth escapes, his physical discomforts, the seizure of his papers, the loss of his camera, the breaking down of his motor car, and his arrest as a spy, but he often has seemed to write little in regard to the war. He has, indeed, been charged with circulating rumors,[46] and these make an imposing array. Among them have been those of concrete gun foundations in England and in France; the transfer of Russian troops around Archangel; the death of the Crown Prince stated in dispatches dated variously from Geneva, Athens, Rome, Stockholm, or The Hague; the illness of the German Emperor; the exact number of English casualties as reported from Copenhagen; the number of German troops transferred from the West to the East, or from the East to the West; the appearance of the Angel of Mons, and the blowing up of food wagons. So serious has the situation become that one of England's most distinguished historians has been at pains to show

---

from the point of view of the censor and gives a long list of instances of discourtesy and even contempt shown the Turks by the war correspondents. "The war correspondents with the Turkish forces had slender grounds for their grievances against the censor's staff," he writes, and adds that many of the rules of the government were quite justifiable and made for the benefit of the correspondents themselves. Few accounts of the ways of war correspondents have been written by censors; this is particularly outspoken.— "Press Censors and War Correspondents," *Nineteenth Century and After*, January, 1913, 73: 28–40.

[45] Perceval Landon notes the frank avowal by a daily paper of the way in which its representatives in South Africa had outwitted the censor by a pre-arranged code and published information that presumably the military authorities had thought it inadvisable to publish.—"War Correspondents and the Censorship," *Nineteenth Century and After*, August, 1902, 52: 327–337.

R. S. Baker gives a full description of the elaborate plans made for getting the news in the Spanish-American War, in spite of the censor, by using harmless-looking plain despatches that were, however, secret codes.— "How the War News is Reported," *McClure's Magazine*, September, 1898, 9: 491–495.

[46] F. B. Elser states emphatically that "this war has been largely a war of fake stories and misinformation."—"Reporting the War from Deskside," *The Outlook*, March 22, 1916, 112: 693–699.

that these rumors could easily be demolished by reference to a good map and Whitaker's *Almanac* and the use of average intelligence.[47]

Nor does this end the list of the war correspondent's sins of omission and commission. He has been charged with drawing on his imagination in default of facts, although "there is, after all," as E. N. Bennett observes, "a limit to war news based apparently on second sight and complete freedom from the fetters of time and space." Obvious "padding" has been one of the sins laid at his door,[48] the uncontrolled and irresponsible correspondent has affected detrimentally public opinion at home through unpleasant or inopportune truth-telling, or by deliberate falsehoods, he has produced discontent in the army in the field through shattering its confidence in army leaders, he gives information to the enemy, he parades officers' names for admiration and this without authority, and he indulges in sensational writing.[49] Even more subtle faults have been laid at his door and he has been held to be, as was said of G. W. Steevens, "somewhat too closely involved in the condition of the moment to see life steadily and to see it whole." [50]   W. T. Arnold protested against a new war correspondent who had had an erroneous idea of his work: "Z— is no use for war. I never saw a great opportunity so missed as in his . . . telegram. As if we wanted his noble sentiments . . . ! One wanted the *chose vue*—the detail which is the life and soul of all journalism . . . but, above all, of descriptive reporting, and one did not get it." [51] The recent war has fostered still other mischievous tendencies, and war cor-

[47] A. F. Pollard, "Rumor and Historical Science," *Contemporary Review*, March, 1915, 107: 321–330. The article was the annual address before the British Historical Association, January 8, 1915.

[48] "A journalist sees a battle for a quarter of an hour, talks to a few officers, fugitives, military attachés, wounded people, and then makes off in his motor car to cable four lines of fact and four columns of padding."— Francis McCullagh, New York *Evening Post*, January 11, 1913.
Many complaints of "padding" were made during the recent war. Especially in Canada complaint was made that one despatch might appear in several guises in the same paper.

[49] Viscount Melgund, "Newspaper Correspondents in the Field," *Nineteenth Century*, March, 1880, 7: 434–442.

[50] H. W. Boynton, *Journalism and Literature*, p. 18.

[51] Mrs. Humphry Ward and C. E. Montague, *William Thomas Arnold*, p. 85.

respondence has reflected the current interest in the short story. Many columns published as war news have been in reality stories or the writers' interpretation of news, and in no true sense news from the seat of war.

The past, present, and future of the war correspondent has been definitely passed on by one of the fraternity when he says, "The Russo-Japanese War killed the war correspondent; the conflict in the Balkans may be said to have buried him. He has become not merely a nuisance, but ridiculous." [52]

But the worm turns! The war correspondent believes that he holds the blue ribbon of the profession and that it is unfair and unreasonable to judge the experts in it by the bungling, bumptious amateurs who have crept in under the fence. He has a long list of the handicaps under which he suffers and he has enumerated many of them. He does his work under the greatest difficulties, only to have his copy "so scissored as to resemble Mexican drawn-work," [53] or absolutely rejected,[54] or cut down to an irreducible minimum of words,[55] or his best laid plans

[52] Sydney Brooks, "The Press in War Time," *Harper's Weekly,* December 21, 1912.

[53] E. Vizetelly relates that in 1882 he took a telegram for the *Daily News* to the press censor at the headquarters of Lord Wolseley's army, in which he stated that soldiers mortally wounded were dying in great agony because not a drop of morphia among medical stores there had been landed. The information was given him by a doctor of the Army Medical Staff Corps attached to the hospital, and was perfectly true, but the paragraph was removed because of objections raised by the censor and the Chief of Staff. The latter explained, "We can't have statements like this sent home, you know! A telegram of that description would cause endless trouble and annoyance."—*Reminiscences of a Bashi-Bazouk,* pp. 320–323.

[54] Archibald Forbes tells of an account written by J. A. MacGahan of the second battle of Plevna, but the Russian censor at the telegraph office in Bucharest refused even to look at it—"not a word to be despatched about any Russian mishap."—*Czar and Sultan,* pp. 78–81.

Dr. Harry Stuermer, the correspondent of the *Kölnische Zeitung* in Constantinople in 1915–16, sent to that paper, after the death of Prince Yussuf Izzedin under suspicious circumstances, an article in which he made "only very, very slight allusions to anything of a sinister character; but it did not find favor with the censor at the Berlin Foreign Office. The editorial staff reported: 'We have revised and touched up your report so as at least to save the most essential part of it:' but even the altered version did not pass the censor's blue pencil."—*Two War Years in Constantinople,* pp. 235–236.

[55] The official version of the first important Zeppelin raid on London was limited to fifty words. "Here was the biggest thing that had happened to London since the start of the war and even the Northcliffe press had to

thwarted by those higher up,[56] or to be at the mercy of a foreign government that by virtue of cable control edits all war correspondence, or to find his work considered a tool to be used for the benefit of the censor,[57] or that he is assumed to be a fakir who "writes home flat lies sent out by imaginative correspondents," [58] or that the censor is willing to pass untrue news if injurious to the enemy, or unwilling to pass true news if unfavorable to his side.[59]

He finds not only that his work is rejected but that the very spirit in which it is done does not win the sympathetic understanding he believes it merits. He considers it an honorable function of the war correspondent to stimulate the patriotism of those at home by narrating the deeds of valor of those at the front, but he finds his efforts coldly received by the government.[60]

---

dismiss it in three sentences."—F. B. Elser, "Reporting the War from Deskside," *Outlook*, March 22, 1916, 112: 693–699.

[56] "An Editor" gives an account of a wireless vessel organized by a newspaper correspondent in the Russo-Japanese War. In the Gulf of Pechili he impartially recorded the messages passing between the belligerent ships on both sides. "He closed his experiment without any illusions as to the future of his profession. After a polite intimation from both sides—by wireless—that they would sink him on sight, he felt constrained to abandon the cruise."—"A Newspaper in Time of War," *Littell's Living Age*, June 5, 1915, 285: 605–611.

[57] W. G. Shepherd says that early in the war (apparently in 1914) he wrote a harmless story and took it to the censor in Munich who greeted him effusively and handed back the copy without writing the word "censored." He started to write the word himself, but was told by the censor not to do so, "let it go as it is," thus to give the impression "that Germany was not hindering newspaper men in their expression of opinion." "The effort of the censorship system to use the reporters as tools in influencing neutral opinion was highly offensive."—*Confessions of a War Correspondent*, pp. 15–17.

[58] W. G. Shepherd gives a long series of "fake stories" thus sent out that give color to this charge.—*Ib.*, pp. 89–122.

[59] W. Maxwell, "The War Correspondent in Sunshine and Eclipse," *Nineteenth Century and After*, March, 1913, 73: 608–623.

Frank Fox wrote about the same time, "I suspect that at first the Bulgarian censorship did not object to fairy tales passing over the wires, though the way was blocked for exact information.

'Why not?' I asked the Censor vexedly about one message he had stopped. 'It is true.' 'Yes, that is the trouble,' he said."—"The New War Correspondent," *National Review*, June, 1913, 61: 769–778.

[60] Sydney Brooks writes that "It [the British Government] has been fully alive to the capacity of the Press for harm, but obstinately blind to its capacity for good," that "the whole business, in short, of stimulating popular enthusiasm by means of the Press has been scandalously mis-

War Correspondents' Monument

He believes that his government has no appreciation of the physical dangers he encounters,[61] or of the moral temptations he scornfully rejects;[62] that governments have no comprehension of the enormous difficulties under which the war correspondent does his work,[63] that the difficulties inherent in it are enhanced

managed," and that the Government has also failed "to grasp the importance of the Press as an influence on Imperial and neutral sentiment."—"The Press in War-Time," *North American Review*, December, 1914, 200: 858–869.

[61] Melton Prior tells of the surprise expressed by Gen. Willis in the Egyptian campaign of 1882 when he learned that war correspondents and artists actually ran the great risk of going to the front. Prior replied that unless he saw the actual fighting he could not make genuine sketches.— *Campaigns of a War Correspondent*, p. 172.

J. C. Francis gives from the *Daily Express*, June 6, 1900, a list of thirty-seven war correspondents who had suffered in the South African War.— *Notes by the Way*, pp. 74–75.

A tablet in memory of seven war correspondents who fell in the campaigns in the Soudan, 1883–1884–1885, has been erected in the crypt of St. Paul's Cathedral, London.

Another tablet was erected in memory of thirteen correspondents who lost their lives in the South African War, 1899–1902.

A special memorial tablet, with portrait bust, honors the memory of William Howard Russell; a portrait bas-relief in bronze, with appropriate inscription, commemorates Archibald Forbes; a tablet in memory of Melton Prior, "artist and war correspondent of the *Illustrated London News*," gives a list of the thirteen campaigns in which he was engaged, covering the years 1874–1903.

The recent death of Frederic Villiers has drawn renewed attention to the statement that "he had seen more fighting than any soldier alive."—*New York Evening Post*, April 6, 1922.

This opinion is confirmed by Villiers' account in *His Five Decades of Adventure.* 2 vols. 1920.

[62] W. J. Stillman, while the correspondent of the London *Times*, in Greece, 1877–1883, speaks of the critical condition of affairs in Athens and says "Comoundouros is buying up all the correspondents he can, and one of his emissaries told me two or three days ago that if I would help him out I could pocket 20,000 francs."—*Autobiography of a Journalist*, II, 228.

[63] See Archibald Forbes, "Ten Years of War Correspondence" and "War Correspondence as a Fine Art" in *Memories and Studies of War and Peace*, and "How I Became a War-Correspondent" and "MacGahan, the American War-Correspondent" in *Souvenirs of Some Continents; F. L. Bullard, Famous War Correspondents; Memoirs of Henri Stephan de Blowitz;* H. Labouchere, *Diary of the Besieged Resident in Paris;*—every volume written by or about the genuine war correspondent is filled with illustrations of the difficulties of the work and of the inventiveness and resourcefulness that always enable the war correspondent to surmount them. The situation is best summed up by Forbes when he writes: "Conditions are being so altered that it may be said, I fear, to have ceased to be the fine art into which zeal, energy and contrivance elevated it for a brief term. It is now an avocation at once simplified and controlled by precise and restraining limitations. In all future European wars, by an international arrangement the hand of the censor will lie heavy on the war-correspondent.

by the restrictions imposed on it by the government itself,[64] that it has disregarded his special fitness and preparation for the work and has preferred retired army officers to civilians as war correspondents,[65] that it has ignored his many services to the country,[66] and that it has contented itself with enumerating the various occasions when war correspondents have been taken to task for giving information to the enemy, although exonerated from the charge of wilfully so doing.

The war correspondent not only indignantly denies the justice of the criticisms of his work, but he points with pride to his achievements,[67] to his subordination of himself to his news-

---

He will be a mere transmitter by strictly defined channels of carefully revised intelligence liable to be altered, falsified, cancelled, or detained at the discretion of the official set in authority over him. . . . The new order of things has taken war correspondence out of the category of the fine arts."—"War Correspondence as a Fine Art," *Memories and Studies of War and Peace*, p. 216.

[64] M. Macdonagh gives an historic summary of the press regulations issued by different war departments in "Can We Rely on War News?", *Fortnightly Review*, April, 1898, 69: 612–625.

Lord Wolseley gives a complete statement of those in force during his command in *The Soldier's Pocket-Book for Field Service*.

G. Mason gives a summary of the restrictions in force at the opening of the war in 1914.—"American War Correspondents at the Front," *Bookman*, September, 1914, 40: 63–67.

Archibald Forbes, at white heat over the "degrading and intolerable" restrictions "that had been placed on war correspondents, especially the one authorizing the military censor to compel all communications to go through him,—should he deem the intelligence to be dangerous to the good of the army, he may stop it or alter it. In the case of telegrams the military censor will generally exercise this power,—" gave a scathing denunciation of the rules announced. "It is in his power," he writes, "if the correspondent perversely declines to lie, nevertheless to make a liar of him! Why not prescribe the torture till he lie at first hand? Why descend to the nefarious baseness of authorized forgery?—for virtual forgery it is thus to alter, to warp, to overturn."—"War Correspondents and the Authorities," *Nineteenth Century*, January, 1880, 7: 185–196.

[65] This suggestion has often been made, although the best correspondents have been civilians. M. Macdonagh, Note 64, *supra*.

[66] P. Landon suggests that a long list could be made of these services.— "War Correspondents and the Censorship," *Nineteenth Century and After*, August, 1902, 52: 327–337.

[67] An excellent account is given of the "brilliantly descriptive message from Metz" narrating the surrender of Marshal Bazaine,—"a message that was copied from the *Daily News* into nearly every other paper in England," in F. M. Thomas, *Fifty Years of Fleet Street*, pp. 176–177.

G. W. Smalley says that it was supposed in London to be the work of A. Forbes, but that the real author was in reality G. Müller, a correspondent of the New York *Tribune* who wrote his account in the London office

paper,[68] to his successful co-operation with his co-workers on other papers and to their organization of the entire field of war correspondence.[69] He insists that he realizes the costliness of war cor-

of the *Tribune*. It was at once cabled to New York, and a copy given to the *Daily News.—Anglo-Saxon Memories* (1911) pp. 216–217.

Viscount Melgund speaks of Forbes' Plevna telegram as "a personal triumph," while Forbes himself says of it that he neither spared blame nor stinted praise. It was accepted by the Russian military authorities and its publication authorized in the Russian papers.—"Newspaper Correspondents in the Field," *Nineteenth Century*, March, 1880, 7: 434–442, and A. Forbes, "War Correspondents and the Authorities," January, 1880, 7: 185–196.

Forbes later writes to a friend that "The mere writing of war letters and war telegrams is by no means the 'be-all-and-end-all' of the war correspondent's work. . . . A man does not do much good, however well and copiously he writes, if he has no means of getting his written or wired matter onto his editor's desk. The accomplishment of this, by dint of *a priori* organization, by sedulous arrangement, by constant watchfulness, and by frequent, severe, and prolonged personal exertion—that is the real material and effective triumph of the war correspondent. . . . I consider that in the Russo-Turkish war I went far to make something like a real science of the prompt forwarding of war correspondence."—Letter to W. H. Rideing, January 4, 1894, *Many Celebrities and a Few Others*, p. 272.

G. W. Smalley gives many important illustrations in *Anglo-American Memories* (1911), chaps. XXIII–XXV.

Excellent general articles on war correspondence are those by Charles Rieben, "Les Journaux et la guerre," *Bibliothèque universelle et revue suisse*, November, December, 1919, 96: 241–258, 408–428.

[68] In the war correspondence of the *Daily News* during the Franco-Prussian War, there is nothing to indicate the name of the "special correspondent" sending the letter, and in the letters themselves there is apparently only one letter where other correspondents are by name mentioned by their colleagues. In the war between Russia and Turkey, the *Daily News* had several correspondents in the field. No name was attached to any letter, each appearing with a different conventional sign or symbol (eight in all were used), although the title page states that the volume includes "the letters of Mr. Archibald Forbes, Mr. J. A. MacGahan, and many other special correspondents in Europe and Asia."

[69] An excellent account of the present organization of war correspondents is given by H. P. Robinson who, in commenting on the war front that is now so vast that no single man can cover it, says that all correspondents must collaborate and work in harmony, "each exchanging daily his news with all the others," thus securing substantial agreement of the despatches on all points and presumptive evidence in favor of their truth. "For the public good we have stifled that primitive instinct of the journalist to 'beat' the other man." Correspondents are now well informed of impending operations and they decide among themselves the best point of view from which to see them and after the attack is over, all meet at the press headquarters and exchange notes. "All that each man has learned is common property; each in rotation telling his story, generally from north to south of the battle-line;" then each writes his despatches. "It has taken us some time to organize this system. . . . And it has one transcendent ad-

respondence to his employers, but that he is not wilfully or unnecessarily extravagant,[70] that it is unfair to condemn the best of the profession for the sins of the irresponsible members of it and to compel all to suffer for the sins of the few, that, in spite of the fact that "the war correspondent practiced camouflage long before the present war introduced the word and the idea to readers of English," [71] his standards of truth and honor [72] as well as of his personal and technical qualifications for the work are the highest.[73] He is proud of the long list of distinguished men who have been war correspondents and he rejoices that he is one of the guild.

vantage. I do not believe that ever before has the public come so near to getting the full truth from the battlefield. The danger which besets all War Correspondents, when operating individually, is that they will give way to the temptation to embroider their accounts, adding trimmings of imagination to the facts, and using conjecture to supply deficiencies in things which they have not seen. No correspondent can do that here." "Of purposeful 'faking' there is none."—"A War Correspondent on his Work," *Nineteenth Century and After*, December, 1917, 82: 1205–1215.

[70] Winston Churchill wrote, "This advance into the Free State has cost you a lot of money. . . . I fear this war has been a great expense to you." R. Lucas, *Lord Glenesk and the "Morning Post,"* p. 386.

Melton Prior notes the enormous expense in mailing copy in the Transvaal War where he had to pay £70 for a runner.—*Campaigns of a War Correspondent*, pp. 296–297.

[71] S. Strunsky applies this term to all that form of correspondence where small defeats are promptly acknowledged in order to give an atmosphere of frankness while serious reverses are passed over in silence, retreats become "strategic retirements," and other accounts are "the capers of newspaper men who did not have enough to fill columns."—"War Notes from a Newspaper Desk," *Atlantic Monthly*, September, 1915, 116: 401–410.

[72] "The one lesson which a journalistic training teaches beyond all others is that of the ultimate invincibility of the truth. It is hardly to be expected that in training for war—wherein secrecy and the deceiving of the enemy necessarily play so large a part—the same lesson should be taught with anything like equal force.

"The conditions have immeasurably improved. But the Army has still some little way to travel in the directions, first, of understanding that nothing can ever be so powerful as the truth and, second, of trusting further to the discretion of Correspondents who know the use of the weapons which they wield much better than the Army can ever teach them."—H. P. Robinson, "A War Correspondent on his Work," *Nineteenth Century and After*, December, 1917, 82: 1205–1215.

[73] H. Wagner has an important chapter showing his own preparation and qualifications as a war correspondent in Bulgaria,—he was a linguist, he had lived among the Southern Slavs, he was familiar with the history of the Balkan peoples, he had had a military education, and he had founded a daily paper in Bosnia.—*With the Victorious Bulgarians*, chap. XX, "My Experiences as a War Correspondent."

And if at times the war correspondent is tempted to rebel at the entanglements in which he is enmeshed by governments, by war departments and by censors, he also remembers that he has profited enormously by inventions that make his work more intelligible, and that transmit it with all possible speed.[74] Mechanical devices enable him to accompany his letters with charts, maps, plans, outlines, and graphic sketches. He thus makes clear descriptions otherwise necessarily obscure, and material that was once reserved for books becomes a part of the daily newspaper.[75]

Even with the censor, the war correspondent is learning that there is "a more excellent way," and that instead of fighting him, it is better to try in advance to get his point of view since "it does not pay to try to beat the censor." [76]

If the war correspondent often finds himself in conditions that afford him little opportunity of writing about warlike matters, it must be remembered that he is not responsible for these conditions and that he, most of all, may ardently wish them otherwise than they are. The governments of the contending parties step in and practically assume control of the machinery of collecting and distributing news. Neutral governments consider news "contraband of war" and fear to become a party to the war by furnishing news. The War Office objects to his presence and is willing to do nothing for him. The official censor formulates rules he can not understand and may blue pencil his most apparently harmless statements. When his despatches have passed the censor there is intolerable delay in forwarding them.[77] The magnitude of military operations makes it difficult

[74] J. R. Robinson is credited with inaugurating telegraph service for the letters as well as for the despatches of war correspondents as far back as 1870.—F. M. Thomas, *Fifty Years of Fleet Street*, pp. 166–167.

But G. W. Smalley, in narrating how Holt White wrote the story of Sedan, reminds his readers "how alien from the mind of the British journalist at that time was the free use of the telegraph, which in America had become a thing of every day."—*Anglo-Saxon Memories* (1911), p. 213.

[75] C. K. Shorter, "Illustrated Journalism; its Past and its Future," *Contemporary Review*, April, 1899, 75: 481–494.

[76] W. G. Shepherd, *Confessions of a War Correspondent*, p. 30.

[77] The correspondent of the New York *Times* reported a delay of one hundred and thirty-two days in delivering a cablegram from New York to Paris. It was received by the censor December 22, 1914, and delivered to him May 3, 1915.—New York *Tribune*, May 17, 1915.

for a person untrained in military tactics to know what is taking place, and they are far too extended, too immense, too intricate for even the best trained correspondent to understand and interpret them. Battle flags, gay uniforms, and martial music have disappeared from the front and their place is taken by smokeless powder, khaki, trench warfare, and all the arts of concealment suggested by the word camouflage. The change from a desperate pitched battle of a few hours to a prolonged contest extending over weeks in the same locality makes it impossible to appreciate changes in situation. He can see and describe only isolated, local incidents and brief episodes, but these are subordinated to a great unified action, the purport of which he can neither see nor understand. He sees only "the emptiness of the battlefields," never any great, decisive event. Ignorance of the geographical features of the countries from which he writes confuses his accounts. Unfamiliarity with strange languages makes communication sometimes uncertain. Climate and weather conspire against him; and dust, smoke, wind, fog, rain, snow, blinding sun, and darkness may prevent him from receiving accurate news. Mental conditions growing out of hunger, sleeplessness, bewilderment, privation, illness, and over-exertion affect his attitude toward his work. When all has been said for and against the war correspondent, the one indisputable fact remains that there is to-day very little the war correspondent can see even if he were permitted to see it.

But in still greater measure it is undoubtedly true that the public is responsible for the meshes in which the war correspondent has become entangled.[78] The public has an insatiable appetite

---

Melton Prior complained, "making sketches is one thing but getting them away by post is quite another," while at one time in Turkey his sketches were not forwarded for six weeks.—*Campaigns of a War Correspondent*, pp. 264, 55–56.

"A [war] correspondent must not only collect his news; he must devise means for getting it through. In this branch of his art Forbes has never perhaps been equalled."—F. M. Thomas, *Fifty Years of Fleet Street*, p. 171.

Forbes himself says that while MacGahan was head and shoulders above him in descriptive power, he was superior to MacGahan in organization. His various volumes of war correspondence are filled with illustrations showing his remarkable ability in forwarding his despatches.

[78] "Primarily, of course, the public is to blame. Its craze for strong sensations has led to the present low status of war correspondence.

for war news and if none can be furnished substantially correct, description and comment are substituted, but this can not be called war news.[79]

What can the war correspondent do? He seems to face an *impasse*. Obstacles of every form prevent him from reporting genuine war news, and yet the demand for it exists. Little "local color" can be given since battles and sieges are much the same the world over. In the war of 1914, a prominent weekly of New York City cut the Gordian knot and installed its war correspondent in its city office with instructions to write the chronicle of the war, thereby but repeating an achievement attributed to the war correspondents of the seventeenth century as described by Shirley:

"Yet they may be called great spirits too, for their valour is invisible: these, I say, will write you a battle in any part of Europe at an hour's warning, and yet never set foot out of a tavern; describe you towns, fortifications, leaders, the strength of the enemies, what confederates, every day's march,—not a soldier shall lose a hair, or have a bullet fly between his arms, but he shall have a page to wait on him in quarto;—nothing

"The degradation of the war correspondent is due to a cause which has affected all the other departments of a modern newspaper—the craze for sensation. Archibald Forbes, Kinglake, and MacGahan wrote articles which could be re-published with very little alteration as serious history. At present the demand is for sensationalism which is worthless for historical purposes."—Francis McCullagh, New York *Evening Post*, January 11, 1913.

The war correspondence of the *Daily News* as collected and published in 1871 forms a continuous narrative of the war between Prussia and France, as the war correspondence of the *Daily News* in 1877 gives a continuous narrative of the war between Russia and Turkey.

[79] In the Spanish-American War the passenger steamer *Paris* left New York and was daily reported by a sensational daily as having been seized; the report was at once contradicted by the same paper, and then the contradiction denied. As the wireless telegraph was not then in operation, it was practically impossible for any one to know what happened to the *Paris* between ports.

The same daily maintained a bulletin-board on the top of a Broadway building. By means of a scaffolding a reporter constantly chalked bulletins concerning the war.

It often is impossible in such cases to separate cause and effect, demand and supply.

Hamilton Holt says that "to compare the history of the war as written in the headlines of certain American papers with the actual course of events would be an amusing though profitless occupation."—"Understanding the War News," *Independent*, January 31, 1916, 85: 146.

destroys them but want of a good memory, for if they escape contradiction they may be chronicled." [80]

But this plan can scarcely be generally adopted or if adopted it would not meet with universal acceptance.[81] In the presence therefore of all of these increasing difficulties in describing actual warfare, the war correspondent turns to new fields of interest, and a new form of war correspondence has been developed. Much of the correspondence now relates to the conditions and the questions growing out of the war rather than to war itself. International relationships and the duties and rights of neutrals; preparedness, standing armies, volunteer and conscript armies; the surroundings of military camps including all questions of morals, or recreation and instruction; the work of the Y. M. C. A., the K. of C.; all measures for ameliorating the horrors of war,— Red Cross work, hospitals, and nurses' training camps; plans for the rehabilitation of those maimed by war; the reconstruction of devastated territory; questions of how war is financed,— liberty loans, war taxation, taxes on incomes and excess profits; the part of the general public in food and fuel conservation, the high cost of living, new conditions of labor,—all the multiform ways in which normal life is compelled to adjust itself to abnormal conditions. All of these questions are what war means to-day and are the subject of letters from the army of special correspondents rather than war correspondents pure and simple.[82]

[80] *The Schoole of Complement*, I, 1.

[81] The advantages and disadvantages of this plan have been hotly contested on both sides. See S. Strunsky, "War Notes from a Newspaper Desk," *Atlantic Monthly*, September, 1915, 116: 401–410; "Skeletons in the Newspaper Closet," *Literary Digest*, September 18, 1915, 51: 592–93; Letter of Robert Herrick, and reply of Will Irwin who denies that the war correspondent must be discredited because he has not seen everything himself and indignantly reminds his opponents that "Gibbon never saw the Roman Army in action, and Taine was never received at the court of Louis XV."—New York *Tribune*, August 29, September 2, 1915. Walter Hale also retorts that the stories of "faking" come from disgruntled journalists who can not get to the front.—New York *Tribune*, September 2, 1915. The statement that "the best war stuff is the soldier's own letters home" seems to be contradicted by the planning of "the truth tour."—*Ante*, p. 191.

[82] The germ of this form of correspondence was of course found in the letters of W. H. Russell since the real importance of his letters from the front lay less in his descriptions of battles than in his accounts of camp and hospital conditions and in the effect that these descriptions had at home.

The "beat" and the "scoop" lose their importance in the presence of the vital problems of the future.

The war correspondent has defended himself against the charges brought against his work, but the historian can not accept this defence without further inquiry. The charge that the enemy profits by the excessive zeal of war correspondents has been so repeatedly made that it especially can not be dismissed without examination. The instances always cited are that Napoleon based his instructions to his lieutenants on information gained from that sent from the front to the English papers; that in the Peninsular War such information was gained by the enemy; that in the Crimean War the letters of W. H. Russell were valuable to the Russians; that Sherman's march to the sea was instigated by news supplied by the Southern press; that in the Franco-Prussian War, von Moltke, anxious to know the location of the French troops, saw in a London paper with a Paris date line the statement that they were concentrating near Sedan and, therefore, acting on this information, planned the Sedan campaign; that during the South African War letters from correspondents revealed important information to the enemy; that during the Spanish-American War every intended movement of the American forces was published in American journals.[83] These statements have become classic, the list is apparently never lengthened, and constant repetition has given it the force of authority.

It is difficult for the student of history to know how much weight to give to these oft-repeated statements. It seems unreasonable to believe that a military commander should, in

G. A. Townsend was one of the first of American war correspondents to describe not only the operations of the army but the country itself and its inhabitants.—*Campaigns of a Non-Combatant, passim.*

[83] Sydney Brooks, "The Press in War Time," *Harper's Weekly*, December 21, 1912; this article is elaborated and published under the same title in the *North American Review*, December, 1914, 200: 858–869.—William Maxwell, "The War Correspondent in Sunshine and Eclipse," *Nineteenth Century and After*, March, 1913, 73: 608–623.

C. R. B. Barrett, "Napoleon and the British Press," *Journal of the Royal United Service Institution*, November, 1916, 61: 814–879. The author raises the question how far Napoleon profited by information contained in the British press and decides that it is improbable that news received months late could have affected his plans. The article, however, supports Wellington in his censure of the press.

planning a campaign, rely on information that might have been sent out with the express purpose of deceiving him, since "sending out false rumors of intentions and even false news of events is the custom of warfare;" [84] that governments should rely on the war correspondents of the enemy when their own spies infest the enemies' country; that any leader would ever admit that he had received important information from this source. A war department is nothing if not omniscient as well as omnipotent, and not a single instance seems to have been recorded where it has itself acknowledged that the enemy was the authority for its knowledge of the military movements of the other side. On the other hand, it seems evident that war correspondence has sometimes been censored or suppressed "for political purposes only;" [85] that correspondents have been denied opportunities because governments and military officials have disliked criticism; that keeping military secrets from the enemy may be a pretext for controlling the news. These questions have been raised, not to decide them, but to indicate that the historian can not accept without further investigation these statements that may be *ex parte* and conventional.[86]

The quagmire in which the censorship of war correspondence may involve the historian is illustrated by the Spanish-American War. The American correspondents were prevented from writing

[84] Hamilton Holt, "Understanding the War News," *Independent*, January 31, 1916, 85: 146.

[85] "The military press censorship, originally established for the plausible purpose of guarding against the possibility of information, likely to prove of value to the enemy, being conveyed to their knowledge through the columns of the public press, was a weapon that a general in command of an army in the field, whether Oriental or European, did not fail to make use of against adverse criticism."—E. Vizetelly, *Reminiscences of a Bashi-Bazouk*, p. 320.

[86] An excellent discussion of this phase of the question is that of T. F. Millard, "The War Correspondent and his Future," *Scribner's Magazine*, February, 1905, 37: 242–248. The writer disapproves of the censorship of war news and of acquiescence in it. He believes publicity is war's most formidable opponent and that military censorship is a relic of barbarism. Other points raised by him have been incorporated above.

An important presentation of the *pros* and *cons* of the status of the war correspondent is found in the article of Archibald Forbes, "War Correspondents and the Authorities," *Nineteenth Century*, January, 1880, 7: 185–196, and the reply to it by Viscount Melgund, "Newspaper Correspondents in the Field," *Nineteenth Century*, March, 1880, 7: 434–442.

that fever was a serious factor and that the commissary and medical supplies were inadequate to cope with the situation, and thus it was complacently assumed that discouragement was prevented. On the other hand, the Spanish war correspondents, long before the fever broke out, represented the American troops as dying of fever by thousands and encouragement was thus spread abroad in Spain.[87]

In reading the war correspondence of the golden age of the war correspondent, in reading his own accounts of his experiences and his biographies that friends have written, and in comparing this material with the corresponding material of the present day, it seems clear that the historian finds its value affected by the personal equation of the correspondent, but still more that its authoritativeness must in large part be judged by the period in which he worked. In the early period, he waited for the issue of the battle and then wrote his account of what he had himself witnessed. If no favors were shown the early correspondent and no opportunities given him, he had at least the opportunity of making opportunity for himself.[88] The only censorship that he recognized was that of the newspaper he represented.[89] If he

[87] T. F. Millard, "The War Correspondent and his Future," *Scribner's Magazine*, February, 1905, 37: 242–248.

[88] "The war correspondent, it must be remembered, had in those days no recognized status. The fame which Russell attained was won, the national service which he rendered was done by him merely as a camp-follower, treated sometimes with less consideration than was shown to the T. G.'s, for so the army called the 'travelling gentlemen' who came out to the front. In such circumstances almost everything depended on the personal appeal made by the correspondent to those among whom his lot was cast. Kinglake, who as a T. G. himself met Russell at the front, admits us to some of the correspondent's secrets. His opportunity of gathering intelligence depended in great measure upon communications which might be made to him by officers of their own free will. Russell was so socially gifted that he evoked conversation."—E. Cook, *Delane of "The Times,"* pp. 75–76.

[89] W. H. Russell was once reprimanded by an army official for writing to *The Times* the exact condition of affairs in the Crimea, on the ground that the letters were regarded at the Conference of Diplomats at Vienna "as great impediments to peace." He replied, "I am here as a newspaper correspondent, not as a diplomatist. I am writing for the *Times*, and it is for the editor on the spot to decide what ought to be made public and what ought to be suppressed in my correspondence."—J. B. Atkins, *Life of Sir William Howard Russell*, I, 190–191.

Lord Raglan wrote the Duke of Newcastle, under date of November 13, 1854, "I do not propose to take any violent step, though perhaps I should

was left entirely alone by army officials,[90] and no provision whatever was made for his physical welfare,[91] he was at least free
from the expected obligation of currying favor with them.[92] He

be justified in doing so; but I have requested Mr. Romaine to endeavour
to see the different correspondents of the newspapers and quietly point
out to them the public inconvenience of their writings, and the necessity
of greater prudence in future, and I make no doubt that they will at once
see that I am right in so warning them.

"I would request that you should cause a communication to be made
to the editors of the daily press, and urge them to examine the letters
they receive before they publish them, and carefully expunge such parts
as they may consider calculated to furnish valuable information to the
enemy."—J. B. Atkins, *The Life of Sir William Howard Russell*, I, pp.
192–193.

Nothing in the conduct of a war would to-day seem more surprising than
that the censorship of the press should be exercised by the press itself.

Conditions were altered in the Civil War in regard to which W. H.
Russell sent letters to *The Times*. Under date of August 5, 1861, he writes
in his diary, "General M'Clellan invited the newspaper correspondents in
Washington to meet him to-day and with their assent drew up a treaty of
peace and amity, which is a curiosity in its way. In the first place, the
editors are to abstain from printing anything which can give aid or comfort
to the enemy, and their correspondents are to observe equal caution; in
return for which complaisance, Government is to be asked to give the press
opportunities for obtaining and transmitting intelligence suitable for publication, particularly touching engagements with the enemy."—*Diary*, p.
180. See also J. B. Atkins, *The Life of Sir William Howard Russell*, II, 67.

Subsequent restrictions, however, led to Russell's abrupt departure for
England.

[90] W. H. Russell once said to the Duke of Newcastle that Lord Raglan
had never spoken to him in his life, and when the Duke's "astonishment
was unbounded" he added: "I was regarded as a mere camp-follower,
whom it would be impossible to take more notice of than you would of a
crossing-sweeper—without the gratuitous penny."—J. B. Atkins, *Life of
Sir William Howard Russell*, I, 193.

[91] The letters of W. H. Russell are filled with accounts not simply of
the inadequacy of the provision made for press correspondents, but of the
absolute lack of all provision for them. "I was a very fly in amber."

[92] "I did not then grasp the fact that I had it in my power to give a
halo of glory to some unknown warrior by putting his name in type. Indeed, for many a month I never understood that particular attribute of
my unfortunate position, and I may say now in all sincerity and truth,
I never knowingly made use of it." His biographer adds: " 'Advertising'
was not then cultivated, nor had the art been developed of doing one's
fighting under the eyes of a special correspondent."—J. B. Atkins, *Life
of Sir William Howard Russell*, I, 162.

Much of the war correspondence of the recent war has obviously sought
to distribute praise impartially and equally to all contestants among the
Allies. Especially have the English correspondents given unstinted praise
to the Australians, Canadians, Irish, Scotch, Welsh, and to all troops
coming from the different parts of the British Empire. It was a disadvantage in the early part of the war that this policy led the English troops to
feel neglected and unappreciated.

gained such a knowledge of warfare as enabled him to give intelligent criticism of the military and the political policies represented in its conduct and this criticism seldom degenerated into petty fault-finding. He subordinated himself to the cause of the paper he represented, bore his privations lightly, became a part of the contest rather than a mere onlooker, and described what he saw in vivid and truthful pictures that rarely lapsed into mere fine writing.

During the second period, the social status of the war correspondent changed; he was honored and recognized as a person of importance and influence. William Howard Russell was the guest of Lincoln and he was a member of the party of the Prince and Princess of Wales on their tour in Egypt and the Near East. Social prestige could hardly fail to give additional weight to the words of the war correspondent,—Russell wrote to his eldest daughter that the Queen of Greece said to him, "Sir, I know England is governed by public opinion and that the *Times* makes a great deal of it. You make much of that public opinion for the *Times*, and believe me I shall ever remember you if you ever say a good word for Greece and the King." [93]

The inevitable result of this changed status of the war correspondent was that war correspondence came to be regarded as a stepping-stone to social preferment. Amateurs, millionaires, and mere sight-seers masquerading as journalists, were eager to go to the front, and, during the Boer War, the complaint was made that a multitude of correspondents was continually under foot wherever there was a field telegraphic wire, competing with Lord Roberts to send news home, tapping his wires, and magnifying their own importance. While there was a cable censorship at the front, there was none at home "and Fleet Street had a great time." [94] Troops went to war with bands playing and flags flying,—"we told the world exactly how many men and guns went in each ship, whence they sailed and whither they were bound." [95]

[93] J. B. Atkins, *The Life of Sir William Howard Russell*, II, 153.
[94] W. Maxwell, "The War Correspondent in Sunshine and Eclipse," *Nineteenth Century and After*, March, 1913, 73: 608–623.
[95] An Editor, "A Newspaper in Time of War," *Littell's Living Age*, June 5, 1915, 285: 605–611. From *The Cornhill Magazine. n. d.*

Similar conditions prevailed everywhere during this period. With much that is admirable in the war correspondence of the time, a larger proportion seems to be filled with the somewhat naïve accounts of the social attentions showered on the correspondents and with accounts of their personal adventures.

These conditions were recognized by the press itself and an interesting account is given of the efforts made, as a result of the ill-defined status of the war correspondent in the Spanish-American War, to work out a system that should eliminate "the free lance adventurers and news tipsters, responsible to nobody, always a nuisance, and sometimes a menace to the men in the field." The plan included among other points the guarantee that every correspondent should be an efficient, reputable working member of his profession, vouched for by his paper with a bond of $2,000 which would be forfeited if the correspondent violated the rules of the censor or misbehaved in any other way; that he must wear the clothes of the color of the uniform of an army officer and also wear a white arm band with a red letter C to indicate his status; that he must carry a pass properly countersigned; together with detailed provisions for securing correspondence expressed in clear, unequivocal language. The plan was worked out before the troubles with Mexico and was approved both by the army and the press.[96]

Somewhat similarly, as a result of the indiscretions of the war correspondent in the Boer War, individuals proposed plans for improving the service that included the proposals that only representatives of the great dailies, the illustrated weeklies, and certain recognized agencies should be allowed to go to the front, and only men of proved ability be recognized as correspondents; that correspondents should not have the use of the wire, since its use was a temptation to bribery, and it kept the correspondent in one place when he should be witnessing engagements; that the control of the wires should be in the hands of one man instead of being frittered away in lengths of fifty words; that the record of events should be given without comment by correspondents having both military knowledge and literary ability but without professional relations with those whose actions they

[96] New York *Evening Post*, April 25, 1914.

described,—that these daily dispatches should be distributed as the War Office thought fit to every newspaper that cared to pay its share toward the cost of the message.

The object of this plan was apparently to reduce to a minimum the friction with the censor, to lessen the expense of war correspondence, and to improve the service. The result, if carried out, would have been to make war correspondence an appanage of the War Office.[97]

Somewhat later a proposal was made by the *Morning Post*, the London *Outlook*, and a writer on the *Daily Mail* for a bill making it a penal offense to publish unauthorized news of naval and military movements, the bill to be passed in time of peace, but to lie dormant until needed and then to be made instantly operative by Order in Council. It was urged in favor of this proposed measure that the press needed to be protected against itself and protected against a liberty that in the nature of things it could not help abusing, while it also needed to be relieved of responsibility. But the inevitable result of such a measure would seem to an onlooker to be the transference of all responsibility for the authoritativeness of the press reports from the press itself to the Privy Council and thereby to reduce the press to a condition of nonage.[98]

The difficulties of the recent period are still too much in the foreground to have been as yet adequately dealt with by all the conflicting interests involved. If at times the war correspondent feels himself between the upper and the nether millstone, that the censor destroys his work while the government itself supplants it by installing official "war movies," he remembers the difficulties of his predecessors and takes courage.

[97] H. F. P. Battersby, "War Correspondents," *National Review*, November, 1900, 36: 420–429.

P. Landon emphasizes the importance of setting up a very high standard for those to whom licenses were in future to be issued and gives a series of important suggestions covering the future status of the war correspondent that had grown out of his experiences as a war correspondent in South Africa.—"War Correspondents and the Censorship," *Nineteenth Century and After*, August, 1902, 52: 327–337.

[98] A Journalist, "The Press in War Times," *Fortnightly Review*, March, 1906, 85: 528–536.

A footnote by the Editor states that steps to prepare such a bill were taken February 12, 1906, by a Committee of the Newspaper Society. No further information as to its fate has been available.

Any study of war correspondence must make clear the impossibility of formulating any all-inclusive generalizations concerning it. During the first period, the war correspondent was ignored, but he sent home letters crowded with news from the field; during the second, he was socially lionized, and his accounts were of thrilling events, embroidered by the press itself with stories of the difficulties of transmission; in the third, it was the correspondent personally who was in the limelight and much of the ostensible war correspondence reflects the personal achievements of the writers; the present period has seen the opportunities of war correspondents limited at every turn with the danger that war correspondence is reverting to type and becoming special correspondence,—in default of definite and exact military news, the correspondent gives his own interpretation of conditions brought about by the war. And again, as wars differ among themselves, so do war correspondents differ, and so therefore does war correspondence differ.

In probably most civil wars, an effort is made by both sides to secure advantageous foreign alliances and war correspondents are welcomed by the opposing factions in proportion as they are considered able to influence favorably public opinion at home. The power of the war correspondent who, while ostensibly sending news to his paper, writes at the same time in favor of one side or the other, is assuredly very great and correspondingly dangerous. The American Civil War is said to have created a corps of clever correspondents who reduced reporting in the field to something like a science.[99] But it also created a body of correspondents who were for the most part ardently either pro-North or pro-South.[100] At the close of the war, unbiased Northern correspondents rendered great service in reporting accurately the conditions produced in the South by the reconstruction legislation of Congress.[101]

In wars like that in South Africa where the war correspon-

[99] C. T. Congdon, *Reminiscences of a Journalist*, p. 275.
[100] See, for example, F. Ross, series of articles sent to *Blackwood's Magazine;* J. Williams, *The South Vindicated;* S. A. Goddard, letters to Birmingham and London newspapers; E. N. Hatcher, *Last Four Weeks of the War*.
[101] J. Pike, *The Prostrate State*.

dents were largely English, the war news given was almost inevitably colored by English sympathies. In wars of aggression, like the recent war, where the censorship rules are most rigorous, war correspondence becomes active propaganda for the aggressor,[102] or, on the other side, sympathetic descriptions of the harrowing results of aggression.

The type of war, whether civil war, rebellion against a home country, or a war of aggression, must always affect the type of war correspondence and therefore its authoritativeness.

As wars differ among themselves, so also do countries and readers differ, and the opinion has been expressed that war correspondence influences public opinion far more in England than it does in France or in Germany.[103]

These facts in regard to the war correspondent have been suggested to indicate that the historian is not only concerned with the authoritativeness of the material he presents but he is concerned with the character of the material. Fortunately, the future historian will not have to depend exclusively on the war correspondent for information concerning the actual conduct of wars,—"the last thing the historian wishes to know through war correspondence is the *events* of war"—these can be learned later from official documents.[104] But these documents will not give the impression the war makes on the public, or the influences that are at work for and against war. This the newspaper must give as well as the lights and shades of war. The effect of war on daily life, on business, on industry, on education, on manufactures, on social conditions,—all of this comes best, and indeed perhaps comes only, through the press. The real success of the war correspondent to-day depends on his ability to reconstruct these conditions rather than on his opportunity to give information in regard to military action.

If the place of the war correspondent seems somewhat less

[102] Sven Hedin, *With the German Armies in the West.*

[103] Viscount Melgund, "Newspaper Correspondents in the Field," *Nineteenth Century*, March, 1880, 7: 434–442.

[104] An important discussion of the relation that the accounts of war correspondents bear to other forms of historical material relating to wars is given by A British Officer, "The Literature of the South African War," *American Historical Review*, January, 1907, 12: 302–321.

important than it formerly was, the change is not due entirely
to an autocratic censor, to the disfavor of military commanders,
and to the sensitiveness of political leaders. The historian himself is changing his method of work in writing of war and he is
concerned with many other aspects of it besides the chronological
narrative of events. He finds material for his study of wars in
scores of places in the daily press where formerly he depended
on the war correspondent alone. International relations, discussions of preparedness, relief organizations, Red Cross work,
self-help for those disabled by war, the manufacture of munitions, the increased cost of living, the duties and the rights of
neutrals,—these are but a few of the many aspects of war with
which he is concerned. For knowledge of these conditions entailed by war and of the public opinion respecting them the
historian turns, not to the war correspondent, but to official
documents now speedily given to the press; to the reports of
great mass meetings held everywhere in the interests of war or
peace; to the accounts of associations formed to relieve the sufferers from war; to new plans of education whereby the lame,
the halt, the deaf, and the blind—all the victims of war—may
be taught to become self-supporting; to editorials that with
calmness or with fervor discuss the intricate international
phases of war; to advertisements that unconsciously reveal both
the sordid and the heroic characteristics developed by war. All
of this to-day means war quite as much as does the actual combat
of opposing forces.

The war correspondent must adapt himself to new conditions.
Barred from the field of war itself, little reporting or description
of actual warfare is possible. Little "local color" can be given
his reports, since all scenes of war are much the same. Descriptions of scenery and of places pall amid the tragedies and the
havoc wrought by war.

The new directions towards which the war correspondent is
turning, as seen in the time of the Great War, are those of
attempting to understand and report the causes of war as seen
at short range; of gathering up the separate lines and making
of them a coherent whole; of placing greater emphasis on his
own systematic intellectual and technical training for war

correspondence than on the assembling of his material equipment.[105] War itself is changing, histories of war are changing, and the war correspondent is changing with them. But until warfare ceases to be, it seems probable that the war correspondent will not pass.[106]

But it does not follow that all questions concerning his work or his qualifications for it will cease to be discussed. To some of these questions it seems, indeed, impossible to give a satisfactory answer. "Secrecy is of the essence of successful warfare. Publicity is of the essence of successful journalism. How is a common ground to be found or manufactured between these abrupt opposites?"—But again, until warfare itself ceases to be, common ground there is none.

And the ideal war correspondent? His picture has been drawn by one of the greatest of them all. "In my day dreams," says Archibald Forbes, "indulged in mostly when smarting under the consciousness of my own deficiencies, I have tried to think out the attributes that ought to be concentrated in the ideal war correspondent. He ought to possess the gift of tongues— to be conversant with all European languages, a neat assortment of the Asiatic languages, and a few of the African tongues, such as Abyssinian, Ashantee, Zulu, and Soudanese. He should have the sweet, angelic temper of a woman, and be as affable as if he were a politician canvassing for a vote; yet, at the same time, be big and ugly enough to impress the conviction that it would be highly unwise to take any liberties with him. The paragon war correspondent should be able to ride anything that chance may offer, from a giraffe to a rat; be able to ride a hundred miles at a stretch, to go without food for a week if needful, and without sleep for as long; never to get tired—never to feel the sensation of a slight sinking, you know; and be able at the end

---

[105] "Although the national judgment is much influenced by the reports of the press representatives from the seat of war, the need of systematically training such guides to public opinion in the performance of their responsible duties has not yet been accepted in democratic communities."—A British Officer, "The Literature of the South African War," *American Historical Review*, January, 1907, XII, 302–321.

[106] The best discussion of the work and the future of war correspondents that has been noted is that of J. B. Atkins, *Life of Russell*, II, chap. XXVIII.

of the ride—of a journey however long, arduous, and sleepless—
to write round-hand for a foreign telegraph clerk ignorant of
the correspondent's language, at the rate of a column an hour
for six or eight consecutive hours; after which he should, as a
matter of course, gallop back to the scene of action without an
hour's delay." [107]

[107] *Memories and Studies of War and Peace*, pp. 2–3.

CHAPTER X

THE INTERVIEW

"To be a good interviewer demands a knowledge and skill beyond the ready belief of a layman. The fundamentals of successful interviewing go down to the roots of human nature; its complex difficulties can be solved only by those that are willing to study life with enthusiastic and unflagging zeal."—*C. E. Russell.*

THE interview is a comparatively modern field of journalistic enterprise. Its first appearance was in America about the time of the Civil War, it was rare until about 1868, and the first formal notice of the practice of interviewing probably appeared in 1869.[1] It was at first looked at askance,[2] but it somewhat quickly established itself as an important and useful part of journalism, it came to be considered the most characteristic feature of American journalism, it was introduced into Europe where it was somewhat coldly received,[3] and after many ups and downs as well as many changes in form and in purpose, it has come to be recognized as a conspicuous, if not an indispensable part of the press, even though its function has materially changed.

In reality the interview is not so modern as it is credited with being,—the germ of it is found in all the conversations, real or imaginary, carried on between distinguished persons where a

---

[1] J. B. McCullough of the St. Louis *Globe-Democrat* has been called the inventor of the interview.—F. A. Burr, "The Art of Interviewing,"*Lippincott's Magazine,*—September, 1890, 46: 391–402.

E. L. Shuman finds its origin in 1859 when the New York *Herald* sent a reporter to see Gerrit Smith after John Brown's raid. The subject was freely discussed and the result was the interview in the modern sense.—*Practical Journalism*, pp. 47–48.

[2] "The 'interview', as at present managed, is generally the joint production of some humbug of a hack politician and another humbug of a newspaper reporter."—*The Nation,* January 28, 1869, 8: 66.

[3] R. Blathwayt says that he introduced the American interview into British journalism about 1890.—*Through Life and Round the World*, chap. VIII.

See also the chapter on "The Art of Interviewing," in his *Interviews,* pp. 347–354.

Boswell or a Landor has been present. No more famous interview has ever been reported than the one Dr. Johnson gave George III in the library of Buckingham House, in 1767, concerning the library resources of Oxford and Cambridge and general literary subjects.[4] It is probably the only instance recorded where a king has been the interviewer,—but the situation met with the entire satisfaction of the person interviewed. It is assuredly a far cry from that enjoyable library scene to a later day when the London press was reported to be irritated because American rather than English papers carried an interview with the King of Belgium that the Associated Press had obtained in December, 1914. "It never occurred to me that a king would see a reporter," was the rueful comment of the disconsolate would-have-been interviewer.[5] But the interview as it has come to be understood to-day implies a person to be interviewed for some specific reason and a reporter or correspondent detailed by a newspaper for this particular task.[6]

What is the attitude of the historian toward the interview? From his standpoint more or less discredit is attached to it. The interview is often sought with persons who are momentarily prominent and it is frankly sought for this reason, not because any weight is attached or, under other circumstances, would ever be attached to what is said by the person interviewed. If a person previously unknown is unexpectedly appointed or elected to an important office, the interview immediately gives his views on all subjects,— the weight of authority is attached to the office, in the opinion of the interviewer, rather than to the person filling it. The business man who becomes a college president *ipso facto* is interviewed on the work of the graduate or the professional schools; the coal

[4] Boswell's *Life of Johnson*, ed. by G. B. Hill, II, 37–48. A summary is given in the *Christian Science Monitor*, September 1, 1916.

[5] Detroit *Free Press*, April 13, 1915.

[6] Important accounts of interviewing and varying opinions as to its value from the point of view of the press are given by A. W. à Beckett, *The Modern Adam;* Frank Banfield, "Interviewing in Practice," *National Review*, November, 1895, 26: 367–378; E. L. Banks, *The Autobiography of a "Newspaper Girl;"* Raymond Blathwayt, *Through Life and Round the World;* A. Dunlop, *Fifty Years of Irish Journalism;* R. S. Durstine, "Appearing in Print," *The Outlook*, June 13, 1914, 107: 357–364; Ernest Foster, *An Editor's Chair;* A. F. Hill, *Secrets of the Sanctum;* J. Kilmer, "The American Interviewer," *The New Witness*, January 10, 1918, 11: 244–245; H. Leech, *Fleet Street from Within;* I. F. Marcosson, *Adventures in Interviewing;* R. Whiteing, *My Harvest;* C. F. Wingate, *Views and Interviews.*

dealer who is elected mayor is interviewed on the sanitary condition of the city; the mayor appointed to a cabinet position is interviewed on what his policy in the war department is to be; the editor who is made secretary of the navy is interviewed on the cost and number of dreadnaughts needed; the railroad president who has worked up from trainman is interviewed on the condition of the crops through which his railroad passes. In very many such interviews, the interviewer while presumably seeking information from the officer is really interviewing the office and hence the value of the interview is distinctly limited. Certain persons suddenly occupy a position which their previous training has not obviously fitted them to fill, the unusual circumstance calls for an interview, and the interview concerns itself not with what the officer has done in the lines of activity with which he is familiar but with what he purposes to do in an untried field. The office filled is an important one, the officer filling it is a successful man, the interview is sought concerning an unfamiliar subject, and it derives its importance from the individual giving it, not from the interview itself. Such is one form of the interview.[7]

The interview as historical material must be questioned by the historian because it is often prepared by a person desiring to be interviewed, given to his own secretary, prepared for publication in his own office, and given to the press in complete form. This might seem to guarantee the authoritativeness of the interview, but the prepared interview is often only a cloak used to hide the absence of ideas or thought on the part of the person giving it. A person conscious of waning influence, but on that account all the more desirous of keeping in the eye of the public, gives a prepared interview that is often but verbiage, and negation can not be considered authoritative. Neither the interview nor the interviewed are of importance and both are but shadows of a vanishing reality.

Next of kin to the prepared interview is the inspired interview. This serves but as a mask to conceal facts and situations that it is undesirable to have the public know, or it may be used to influ-

[7] One writer says that the interview is "more often asked for by persons to be interviewed than refused by people sought."—E. W. Townsend, "The Reporter," *Bookman*, August, 1904, 19: 558–572.

ence public opinion to support unpopular measures. The historian receives with caution the actual statements made, although he finds in the inspired interview a valuable record of the conditions that make it possible.

Men in authority are alert to notice changes in the public pulse and an interview given may be quickly repudiated, or disavowed if it is felt to be too divergent from public opinion. The repudiated interview may be true to fact, yet it can not stand as authoritative if it is denied by the person giving it. Officials are often dominated by "the man higher up" and compelled to repudiate interviews they have given in good faith. M. de Blowitz obtained an interview with Count Münster concerning the retirement of Bismarck, but a month after it had appeared in the London *Times* it was repudiated by the Count. He was attacked by the German press for granting the interview, although its facts seem not to have been questioned, and the attack led to the repudiation.[8]

At times information may reach the press that the interview that has been obtained is objectionable, unreasonable, or untrue, and hence it may be suppressed. But the suppressed interview may return to bring discredit to the person interviewed as well as confusion to the historian. In 1908, Emperor William gave to W. B. Hale a most outspoken interview *de omnibus rebus et quibusdam aliis*. The *Century Magazine* announced in its issue of November, 1908, the early appearance of the interview in its pages, but it did not appear, having apparently been suppressed at the insistent request of the German Foreign Office.[9]

The German Foreign Office was at that time particularly sensitive to the official indiscretions of the Emperor since he had recently given an impetuous interview to an English reporter who had written a flattering article about him. The interview was published in the *Daily Telegraph*, October 28, 1908, and was designed to conciliate England, but its chief result was to anger Germany where it led to innumerable controversies and investigations. In 1896, the Emperor had sent a congratulatory telegram

[8] H. de Blowitz, *Memoirs*, pp. 292-306.
[9] An account is given in the New York *Tribune*, December 17, 1917, and in following issues, to February 10, 1918. The final word seems to have been said by W. W. Ellsworth, "The Suppressed Interview with the German Emperor," *The Golden Age of Authors*, pp. 283-293.

to President Kruger, while in the interview of 1908 the same Emperor claimed the credit of having formulated the plans for the military operations in the Boer War on the identical lines as those actually adopted and successfully carried out by Lord Roberts. The interview was published in the official government organs and by the Wolff Bureau and it stands as one more interesting illustration of the inability of even the German Emperor to square the circle.[10] The patronizing attitude toward England assumed by the Emperor in the interview accorded in October, 1908, harmonized little with the general condemnation of England in the interview granted the previous July and the obvious discord undoubtedly explains the insistence of the German Foreign Office that the July interview granted to W. B. Hale should not be published in December.

The objectionable interview may not be suppressed, but it may be so edited, and its tone so tempered by "the man up stairs" to make it conform to his own ideas, that it loses all semblance to its original form, and the edited interview in its turn brings confusion to the historian

Positive misinformation may at times be purposely and consciously given interviewers by the officials interviewed. "The trouble is not to get 'fake' stories," writes an exasperated newspaper man, "but to detect them and keep them out of print. 'Official denials' have come to be, in the majority of instances, not worth the paper they are written on. They are of identical value with the maid's 'Not at home' to unwelcome visitors." [11] Historians and reporters suffer alike from these official denials of information given interviewers, and it is difficult for them to understand the reason for deliberate falsification since in the end the truth will be known.

[10] C. Gauss, *The German Emperor*, pp. 267–273; W. H. Dawson, *The German Empire*, II, 346–349. The text is given in D. J. Hill, *Impressions of the Kaiser*, pp. 329–335, and the explanation of Prince von Bülow made in the Reichstag, pp. 335–340.

[11] New York *Evening Post*, December 8, 1908.

It seems possible to class with the repudiated interview that given in New York and attributed to Lord Northcliffe by the *Daily Mail*, but given by H. W. Steed of *The Times*. The most important result of a situation that threatened international complications seemed to be the cancelling of a dinner engagement for Lord Northcliffe at the British Embassy in Washington.—Daily press, July, 1921.

The counterpart of the repudiated interview is the bogus, faked, or fictitious interview. Many persons do not wish to be interviewed, or they object to being interviewed on certain subjects, or it is inadvisable to give the interview at the time it is sought. But the reporter has been instructed to secure an interview and hence he has recourse to his own invention and imagination and the faked interview is published. At times the faked interview can be attributed only to desire for sensationalism or to paucity of genuine news items, and at such times every person deservedly prominent in the community or in public life seems to be at the mercy of irresponsible interviewers.[12] When the denial of the interview has been made, the interviewer may shield himself behind the statement that ignorance of a foreign language may have led him to misunderstand the person said to have given the interview,[13] or he may charge errors to the compositor,[14] or he may leave the field without apology. The explanation or the denial made by the one who has suffered from the fictitious interview may never overtake the published fabrication and the future historian is in grave danger of being led astray if he unwittingly accepts the bogus interview.[15] To the historian of the present it seems the most objectionable of all objectionable forms of the interview and in 1904 Goldwin Smith probably expressed the opinion of the guild in writing the president of the press club, Toronto, "There ought if possible to be some check to false re-

[12] New York *Evening Post*, December 8, 1908.

[13] An interviewer who understood only English and German cabled an interview purporting to have been conceded by Benedict XV who spoke only Italian and French. He apparently forestalled disavowal by using the saving clause, "if I understood His Holiness aright."—Daily papers, April 17-18, 1915.

[14] A prominent author was reported as having been called "an intellectual ass;" the person making the alleged statement said that he had called him "an intellectual asset."—New York *Times*, December 7, 1914.

[15] G. Stanley Hall states his experience with the manufactured interview in the New York *Evening Post*, September 10, 1910.

Similar experiences are given by George A. Coe, New York *Evening Post*, October 1, 1908.

See the press of August 12, 1914, for fabricated interview attributed to Philip Snowden, M.P., and the denial, August 26, 1916; the press of December 25, 1915, published an interview attributed to Mabel T. Boardman who denied it in the papers of December 27, 1915; the Danish press of January, 1916, published an interview purporting to come from Henry Ford which was immediately denied.

Numberless illustrations of this point could be given.

ports of interviews,"—a mild hope in view of the numerous illustrations he gives of the experiences of sufferers from interviews
incorrectly reported.[16]

"Interviewing by intuition" is a happy phrase characterizing
interviews "which comprise nearly everything except what the
commanders-in-chief said to the interviewer." An interview of
two columns with a famous man may contain from him the single
phrase, "Well, gentlemen, are you pleased with what you have
seen?" and the interview thus become "a matter of phrenological
and anatomical interpretation." [17]

The "reversible interview" has been facetiously described by
G. J. Holyoake who, after many trying experiences with interviewers who misunderstood him, says: "Once I tried the experiment of saying the opposite of what I meant, and next day it
came out all right." [18] But he is silent on the point of recom-
mending it for general adoption, though it might have commended itself to Hugo Münsterberg who complained bitterly of
his experiences with interviews distorted, manufactured, and
patched together from disjointed sentences.[19]

The "wooden interview," characterized by alternating ques
tions and answers, has happily disappeared, but the impression
of its artificiality has long remained and has unhappily been
carried over to the modern interview to its undeserved prejudice.[20]

The stolen interview enters the domain of ethics, but on the
side of history its value may be unimpeachable. The interviewer
is always specially desirous of securing information in regard to
proceedings done *in camera*. At the Second Hague Conference a
young English reporter who spoke French like a Frenchman was
very anxious to learn what had been said by a prominent delegate
from Belgium. He therefore went to him and casually remarked,
"We hear you made a strong speech in the Congress yesterday
against compulsory arbitration." The Belgian delegate, taken
unawares, replied in astonishment, "I, against compulsory arbi-

---

[16] *Correspondence of Goldwin Smith*, pp. 418–421.
[17] New York *Evening Post*, May 27, 1916.
[18] *Sixty Years of an Agitator's Life*, II, 156–157.
[19] "The Case of the Reporter," *McClure's Magazine*, February, 1911,
36: 435–439.
[20] A characteristic illustration of this type is "An Interviewer Interviewed," *Lippincott's Magazine*, November, 1891, 48: 630–638.

tration! Why, all my life I have fought for it. Here's my speech
to prove it." The reporter took it, memorized it while keeping
up a running talk with the author, went home and wrote it out
and the next day published it,—much to the discomfiture of the
author who never understood how his speech got into print and
accused an unknown person of stealing it.[21]

The interview may often be given to accomplish definite political ends. Prince von Bülow gave many interviews carefully
written in advance; sometimes they were given out through the
German Press Bureau, sometimes through representatives of a
favored paper that then submitted them to the Press Bureau,
sometimes they were personally handed to correspondents. The
interview was then well "played up," telegraphed around the
globe, and dissected and discussed in a dozen languages. This
form of communication with the public well suited his purpose
since through the interview he could give certain topics publicity
and could choose the time when his words would have the best
effect.[22] Baron von Bissing gave an interview, justifying the
deportations of Belgians, to the Berlin correspondent of the New
York *Times* and a French translation with the comment of the
North German Gazette was published in the Brussels papers.
The Baron "frequently gave out interviews all of them 'carefully
prepared,'" obviously thus expecting to explain the Germans to
the Belgians.[23]

Governor Whitman "took the public into his confidence" in
1916 and granted an interview that had as its keynote "what a
governor is up against," and it was thus of general application,[24]
although given to the press to meet a specific political situation.

The politician may refuse an interview to all papers except
those of his own party on the ground that they are hostile to him
and may ask him "embarrassing questions," or he may use the
interview as a means of "getting even" with his political opponents. But often the interview may be of real service to a public

[21] The account of this interview was given by a Belgian gentleman at a
semi-private meeting, May 15, 1916, but to my knowledge it has not been
published and hence printed citation can not be given.
[22] G. V. Williams, "The German Press Bureau," *Contemporary Review*,
March, 1910, 97: 315-325.
[23] Brand Whitlock, *Belgium*, II, 450-460.
[24] New York *World*, March 5, 1916.

man who suddenly finds himself misunderstood and misrepresented. Many circumstances arise where a man may wish to set himself right with his fellows "and in a large number of them he will find the interview more serviceable than any other form of newspaper publication." [25]

The interview is often sought and given "for domestic consumption only." If a person is socially or politically ambitious, the interview may be a ladder by which the ambition is realized, and on the other hand, local pride is gratified when citizens distinguished at home are made to seem equally distinguished abroad. A prominent weekly has a fine bit of satire on this form of interview:

"We confess to a particular fondness for this sturdy self-made gentleman from the West whom a single trip across the Atlantic renders an authority on the profoundest questions of contemporary interest. We read:

Mr. W. B. Sands of Milwaukee, who arrived yesterday on the Ruritania, after a two months' stay abroad, in the course of which he was introduced to the Grand Duke Michael at a luncheon at Monte Carlo, declares that never was the condition of the Russian Empire as satisfactory as it is at present. The Russian peasants all love the Czar and the Czar is constantly working for the welfare of the peasants. Mr. Sands declared that there is no basis for the rumors of a secret treaty of alliance between Russia and Japan.

"We read:

It is the firm opinion of Henderson W. Sloggs of Omaha, who arrived yesterday on the Cetacean, that Italy's measures in Tripoli are regarded with extreme dissatisfaction at Berlin and Vienna. At the same time, Mr. Sloggs insists that Italy was justified in acting as she did. Tripoli is a land of infinite promise and in the course of time can produce enough wheat to feed half the world. Mr. Sloggs' sojourn abroad was confined to Paris, London, and the Lakes of Killarney." [26]

[25] F. Banfield, "Interviewing in Practice," *National Review*, November, 1895, 26: 367–378.
[26] "The Fallible Interviewer," *The Nation*, December 28, 1911, 93: 622–623.

The English press has equally well satirized the social interview in proposing a series to be called "Half-hours with Nobodies" and "Ten Minutes with Persons of No Importance," [27]—a satire that may have had a basis of fact in the series entitled "Celebrities at Home" that its editor believed to be one of the most attractive features of *The World*.[28]

It must be evident that the interview from the very terms describing it has lacked authoritativeness,—it is most often characterized as prepared, inspired, repudiated, disavowed, suppressed, edited, officially denied, faked, padded, or a space-filler. The interview must also be questioned by reason of its source. The politician may use the interview to conceal his real opinions, or if he inadvertently expresses them, he may repudiate the interview. The author may readily grant an interview, but refuse to have it published as "it is taking the bread out of his mouth." The society leader may be anxious to give an interview, but may have nothing to say. The actor or professional musician may welcome the interview as a gratifying form of advertisement. The criminal may give a series of interviews all mutually contradictory. Persons who do not effusively welcome an interview are often described as snobs and aristocrats in return for the cool reception accorded the interviewer, and social climbers may be helped up by the publicity given by aspiring interviewers. Those from whom interviews are specially desired are unwilling to concede them and the views of those willing or anxious to grant them often carry little weight.

The interview is distrusted because of its form. It is given in the first person singular, but the interviewer takes no notes since "to use a note-book is to destroy the freedom of expression of the person attacked." The result in print, even when the interviewer has been most conscientious and has had the memory of a Macaulay, can scarcely, for the purposes of the historian, be considered an exact reproduction either of the language or of the opinions of the person interviewed. The dislike of both parties to the interview is probably best explained in saying that neither one realizes that the interview is not an address, a speech, or an

[27] A. W. à Beckett, *The Modern Adam*, p. 189.
[28] E. Yates, *Recollections and Experiences*, II, 330–333.

essay, but "an affair of two,"—if either of the two fails in collaboration, the interview is a failure.[29]

National prejudices doubtless account for much of the repugnance expressed for the interview. Much as the European press has ridiculed or condemned the interview, apparently because of its reputed American origin, it has adopted it, but in doing so it has varied somewhat its general characteristics. The interviewer thus becomes committed, perhaps unconsciously, to the type of interview characteristic of his own country and he defends it with a vigor equalled only by that with which he condemns the forms used in other countries.[30]

The interview is distrusted because of the frank avowal of journalists that the paramount idea of the interviewer should be to make an interesting story. While recognizing that the cut-and-dried, question-and-answer form of interview would probably be more authoritative on the side of information and definite facts, the journalist finds it dull and tedious and he considers that "the interview is a subtle, artistic piece of writing." The points of view of journalist and of historian must necessarily differ if to the one "generally speaking, the importance of the interview is gauged by the information it contains," while to the other the accuracy of the information must be a prime factor; they must differ, if to the one the interview "is a mental picture, a full-length portrait, a personal interpretation," while to the historian the personal interpretation of the interviewer seems negligible.

The interview is distrusted because the interviewer is sometimes sent out without reference to his special qualifications for the task,—a careless assignment may absolutely impeach the trustworthiness of what, under more favorable conditions, might have been an acceptable interview. The interviewer is sometimes bumptious and reports his own preconceived ideas as those of the person interviewed.[31] In the eyes of the citizen of the world, the

[29] The subtle characteristics of a good interview are best described by F. Banfield, "Interviewing in Practice," *National Review*, November, 1895, 26: 367–378.

[30] Edward Dowden, in "The 'Interviewer' Abroad," ridicules the interviews of French authors given by M. Huret and published under the title *Enquête sur l'évolution littéraire.—Fortnightly Review*, November, 1891, n. s. 50: 719–733.

[31] A peculiarly flagrant illustration of the distorted interview was given wide publicity by the press in December, 1918. Two distinguished English-

interviewer often makes a most unfavorable impression by his inexcusable insistence and even impertinence,—funeral processions are halted by the interviewer, he appears as an unbidden guest at wedding ceremonies, he rouses from sleep late at night a weary visiting foreigner that he may secure his impressions of the American press,[32] he asks gratuitously for what may have a very considerable commercial value to the person interviewed, and the greater the expert is the person interviewed the more time he must give the interviewer in order to avoid errors.

The interviewer may, indeed, have his own troubles that handicap his report. He may find that unconsciously to himself he has been the person interviewed rather than the one interviewing. The person interviewed may be self-conscious and the interviewer, therefore, be no more successful than is the camera in catching the spirit of the person before it. Henry James once said, "What is written about me has nothing to do with me, *my me*. It is only the other person's equivalent for that mystery, whatever it may be. Thereby if you have found anything to say about our apparently blameless little time together, it is your little affair exclusively," [33]—this baffling mystery must always face the interviewer. It is again Henry James who probably best expresses the opinions of persons who object to being interviewed, and therefore unconsciously discloses one phase of the difficulties that beset the interviewer. An interview granted in regard to his work as Chairman of the American Volunteer Motor Ambulance Corps is best described in the words of the interviewer: " ' I can't put,' Mr. James said, speaking with much consideration and asking that his punctuation as well as his words should be noted, 'my devotion and sympathy for the cause of our corps more strongly than in permitting it thus to overcome my dread of the assault of the interviewer, whom I have deprecated, all these years, with all the force of my preference for saying myself and

women visiting American colleges gave an interview to an undergraduate in a university open only to men. He stated to them his own views in regard to the undesirability of college education for women and then attempted to force their acquiescence in them. The distorted interview was indignantly denied, but truth seldom overtakes error. The entire story may be found in the *Vassar Miscellany News*, January 25, 1919.

[32] T. W. Reid, *Richard Monckton Milnes*, II, 314–315.

[33] W. H. Rideing, *Many Celebrities and a Few Others*, p. 335.

without superfluous aid, without interference in the guise of encouragement and cheer, anything I may think worth my saying. Nothing is worth my saying that I cannot help myself out with better, I hold, than even the most suggestive young gentleman with a notebook can help me. It may be fatuous of me, but, believing myself possessed of some means of expression, I feel as if I were sadly giving it away when, with the use of it urgent, I don't gratefully employ it, but appeal instead to the art of somebody else.' . . .

" 'It is very difficult,' he said, seeking to diminish the tension so often felt by a journalist, even at the moment of a highly appreciated occasion, 'to break into graceful license after so long a life of decorum; therefore you must excuse me if my egotism doesn't run very free or my complacency find quite the right turns.' . . .

"He explained his weighing of his words by telling an anecdote by which an Englishman explained the slight production of airships in England, 'Because the airship is essentially a bad ship, and we English can't make a bad ship well enough.' 'Can you pardon,' Mr. James asked, 'my making an application of this to the question of one's amenability or plasticity to the interview? The airship of the interview is for me a bad ship, and I can't make a bad ship well enough.' " [34]

The interviewer may find suspicion cast on his well-meant endeavors to give a deserved publicity to important subjects. Even in 1905 British physicians were reported to be discussing with much bitterness the propriety of granting interviews to newspapers on medical topics because such a policy seemed to them to savor of advertising.[35]

The interviewer may find that "talking for publication" becomes the equivalent of "talking for buncomb;" he may find his way blocked at every turn and realize that "it is much easier to interview the President of the United States than the assistant secretary of anything;" [36] he may be even more embarrassed in asking for important information than is a person in refusing it; he may be charged with killing journalism, as he is told that

[34] Preston Lockwood, New York *Times*, March 21, 1915.
[35] *The Globe*, July 19, 1905.
[36] R. S. Durstine, "Appearing in Print," *The Outlook*, June 13, 1914, 107: 357–364.

journalism has already killed literature; he often feels himself *persona non grata* among those whose society he naturally seeks, and he realizes that he is sought "for advertising purposes" by those whom personally he would avoid; he is told that persons are blamed for yielding to his requests for an interview,—T. W. Reid is quoted as saying that W. E. Forster was the first Englishman to be interviewed and that he "was fairly generally blamed at the time for having submitted to this interview;"[37] he may find even his own confrères comparing the faculty for interviewing "with a kind of twin faculty for shop-window dressing;"[38] he may frankly dislike interviewing,—"interviewing was ever an abomination to me," says Whiteing, "and I made a firm stand against it as soon as I could,"—[39] and he may be plainly told that the novelty of the interview has worn off and that since the public is no longer interested in interviews the best editors no longer wish to print them. The interviewer has his own difficulties and his own disappointments,—not the least of these are when the interview has been secured with much difficulty and prepared for the press with great pains and then the person interviewed positively prohibits its publication, or when the troubled conscience of the interviewer decides against the publication of an interview that he knows ought not to have been given.[40]

But in spite of all the adverse criticisms that may reasonably be brought against the interview, it still forms a part of the newspaper. But the function of the interview has changed in the fifty years since it was definitely introduced and naturally its relative importance has changed. At the height of its glory an exaggerated significance was attached to it,—"the history of the past thirty years could not be written without the interview," wrote one enthusiastic interviewer in 1890,—but it has now become a popular feature of the press rather than a corner-stone.

The interview is changing and it is changing for the better.

[37] H. Leach, *Fleet Street from Within*, p. 96.
[38] R. Blathwayt, *Through Life and Round the World*, p. 155.
[39] R. Whiteing, *My Harvest*, p. 98.
[40] These have been well stated by E. Foster, "Difficulties of the Interviewer," chap. X in *An Editor's Chair;* F. Banfield, "Interviewing in Practice," *National Review*, November, 1895, 26: 367–378; E. L. Banks, *Autobiography of a Newspaper Girl*, chap. XXIII, "The Story of a 'Failure'."

It is now less a description of the furniture of the room where the interview takes place, of the clothing worn by the person interviewed, of his mannerisms, of his personal tastes in cigars, automobiles, or color for neckties,—the interview over the telephone has brought at least this advantage. Specialists are now sent to interview specialists and often important information is secured and given publicity. The interview given to the press is often the medium of communication between public men and their constituents, rather than the lengthy personal correspondence of earlier days,—"What an editor wants," says Banfield, "is an interview that will be read with interest by those who have perfect faith in the honesty and accuracy of the information conveyed in his journal." [41]

It was Raymond Blathwayt who conceived the idea "that from interviewing individuals it might be well so to enlarge the scope of interviewing as to exploit great systems of thought or of practical work or of social effort and endeavour." He therefore interviewed the great public schools of England in a series of interviews called "The New Era and the Public Schools," and followed it by other series showing how different existing institutions could be modernized in their habit of thought or action.[42] It is to-day everywhere the group that is preferably interviewed. Any interesting activity is interviewed,—a new industrial plant, the work of the city engineer, the development of a new street, playgrounds, school gardens, the safe-guarding of machinery; all these activities are far more interesting subjects for interviews than are the comings and goings of local celebrities.

The converse of the group interview is the collective interview, where a large number of interviewers meet collectively an important person and gain from him the information desired. The collective interview thus becomes a safeguard against misinterpretation and elaboration, since both the person interviewed and the interviewers become mutual checks on wilful misstatements.

[41] F. Banfield, "Interviewing in Practice," *National Review*, November, 1895, 26: 367–378.
[42] *Through Life and Round the World*, chap. VIII.

The interview to-day is credited with having "more soul" than it formerly had and it still has enthusiastic supporters of its improved form and changed purpose.[43] It is probably not consciously either doctored or colored, its errors are reduced to a minimum, and the faked interview has no reputable supporters.

The interview has been a prolific source of error and has been the cause of more bitter complaints of the press than probably any other single cause,—errors that have seemed peculiarly exasperating because while made by the local press it has been difficult to secure retraction, correction, explanation, or apology from the papers publishing the incorrect interview. In exceptionally flagrant cases, the columns of rival papers may publish explanatory communications from those who have suffered; this, while of little service to the person immediately concerned, as explanations in other papers seldom reach those reading the original interviews, is of service to the historian in his final account of the questions involved. It must also be remembered that the press on its part suffers from those in public life "who feel no scruples about deceiving representatives of newspapers when it is their interest to tell half-truths or falsify absolutely."[44]

But after all has been said that can be said in favor of the interview, the historian must always question its absolute authoritativeness when he considers the designations attached to it, the objects for which the interview is sought and granted, the subjects of the interview, and the literary form given it.

[43] Joyce Kilmer, "The American Interviewer," *The New Witness*, January 10, 1918, 11: 244–245.

[44] See the newspapers' side of the question in the special Washington correspondence of the New York *Evening Post*, December 8, 1908.

CHAPTER XI

THE EDITOR AND THE EDITORIAL

"I am Sir Oracle and when I ope my lips let no dog bark."—*Shakespeare.*

"I have taken all knowledge to be my province."—*Bacon.*

"I can easier teach twenty what were good to be done, than be one of twenty to follow mine own teaching."—*Shakespeare.*

"Sir, I have often been contemplating with a particular Satisfaction, the eminent Station we Journal Writers, and the Printers of Journals stand in, and what high Characters we bear in the World."—*Defoe.*

"The newspaper editor writes in the sand when the flood is coming in. If he but succeed in influencing opinion for the present, he must be content to be forgotten in the future."—*Hugh Miller.*

" 'Tis the curse of an editor that he must always be right."—*Lowell.*

.THE newspaper historically has had three distinct functions; the first was to publish the news, the second was to interpret the news and thereby to influence public opinion, the third has been to gain success as a business enterprise. The editor and the editorial belong to that period in the history of the press when the chief interest of the public in reading the newspaper lay in knowing what opinions it was right and wise to hold in regard to the great questions of the day. It was practically a hundred years after the appearance of the first English newspaper before the editorial appeared even in shadowy form, and long after that before it assumed the responsibility of leading public opinion. Defoe introduced into *Mist's Journal* a "Letter Introductory,"—an essay written in the form of a letter on some subject of public interest. It is on the basis of this "Letter Introductory" that Lee claims "for Defoe that he first originated, and exemplified in his own person, those mighty agencies, in the formation and direction of public opinion, now comprehended in the words 'Editor' and 'Leading Article.' " [1]

[1] William Lee, *Daniel Defoe: His Life and Recently Discovered Writings,* I, 273.
This is also the opinion of W. P. Trent, *How to Know Defoe,* p. 150.

If Lee's identification of the authorship of these letters with Defoe be accepted, it must be evident how great a contribution Defoe made to the newspapers, the larger part of it to *Applebee's Journal*, between the years 1716 and 1729. They show not only that Defoe introduced new ideas into journalism,—"Defoe found time for the multitudinous activities which entitle him to be a great-grandfather of all modern journalism"—but through the wit and satire and good humor of what may be called the editorial columns they show how serious was the effort he made to influence public opinion. The records that these early editorials give of social, industrial, and political conditions that have long since passed away, and that they give of Defoe's part in effecting these changes, form a most important contribution towards a history of the press.[2] Defoe can not be called an editor, within the present meaning of the word, as Leslie Stephen has pointed out,[3] but that many of his contributions to the press can be justly characterized as editorials is not to be questioned.

It was apparently much later that in America the editorial emerged from the news proper as a distinctive feature of the newspaper. The character of an American paper down through the eighteenth century had in large part been gauged by the news furnished and by the "elegant selections" it provided.[4]

But the passage of the Alien and the Sedition Acts in 1798 had roused great opposition in all newspaper offices and thus gave great importance to the editorial.[5] It was in 1814 that Nathan Hale purchased the Boston *Daily Advertiser* and became "the first to assume the responsibility of expressing editorial opinions upon events of public interest and importance."[6] From that time on the editorial came to be the most important feature of the press, and the paper itself was identified with the editor. "Dana says so" or "Greeley says so" were equivalent to the opinions

[2] These contributions are comprised in Lee's *Daniel Defoe*, vols. II–III.
[3] Leslie Stephen, "The Evolution of Editors," *National Review*, February, 1896, 26: 770–785.
[4] E. C. Cook, *Literary Influences in Colonial Newspapers, 1704–1750.*
[5] F. Hudson states that out of two hundred newspapers in America at that time, from twenty to twenty-five were edited and controlled by aliens.— *History of Journalism in the United States from 1690 to 1872*, p. 159.
[6] S. K. Lothrop, "Memoir of Nathan Hale, LL.D.," *Massachusetts Historical Society Proceedings*, 1880–81, XVIII, 270–279.

of the *Sun* or the *Tribune* during the middle of the nineteenth century. The editor [7] and the editorial long had a growing influence as they were able to shape public opinion, but among other conventional generalizations relating to the press, none is more frequently heard than the one that the editorial has ceased to be an important part of the newspaper. The historian must therefore examine the editorial through a succession of years in order to determine how far these criticisms are justified.

How far the editor and the newspaper can be considered synonymous terms is one of the troublesome problems of the historian, but it is clear that they must be so considered during the period of personal journalism. The great age of the editor and of the editorial has been held to be the period dating from about 1830 to about 1890, although examples of them are still found. It was the period of "personal journalism" when the owner, editor, and publisher were one and the same person. The names of Bennett, Bowles, Bryant, Buckingham, Dana, Garrison, Greeley, Raymond, suggest a period when a man acquired a newspaper and it became his personal organ. In it he fought for the causes he gave his life to promote,—for abolition, for protective tariff, for political union, for western immigration; and he fought against all forms of political corruption as well as against all who opposed his personal policies. The business organization of the newspaper gave no opportunity for "amicable but irreconcilable difference of views" between publisher and editor.[8] Irreconcilable differences often indeed existed, but they were not amicable and they existed between the different editors of different papers, not between the different parts of the same paper. When Alaric Watts was the editor of the Leeds *Intelligencer*, one of the proprietors of the paper wrote him from London that the new editor should be careful to refer in very gentlemanly terms to everybody "except Mr. Baines,"— the proprietor and editor of the rival newspaper.[9]

[7] Roscoe C. E. Brown finds the first use of the title by an American paper in the *Boston News-Letter* of March 7, 1728. See his interesting letter in the New York *Times*, March 14, 1915.

[8] Correspondence between the publisher and the editor of the Philadelphia *Public Ledger*, daily press, January 1, 1915.

[9] A. A. Watts, *Life of Alaric Watts*, I, 163–164.

Much of this personal journalism has passed both in America and in England and its passing has been regretted, but the *Evening Post* notes that "laments over the passing of 'personal journalism' usually take no account of the personal rancor that went along with it. A defence of the lurid rhetoric that regularly resulted might be made on the ground of its unconscious humor, which was often better than our made-to-order sort." [10]

But exceptions even at an early time were found. An English traveler notes: "I have read a paragraph in a New York paper which announced the publication of another opposition paper which would take quite a different line in politics, and said, that the editor of the new organ was a man of so great ability, that it, the old established paper, could not doubt of the success it wished him. This was not the greeting which our established papers give to new adventurers." [11]

As a rule, however, the newspaper considered its own editorials white while those of its opponents were black,—no shadows mitigated the noonday brilliance of the one and no lights illumined the midnight blackness of the other. The editorial was a guarantee of the personal views of the editor, but it was not a guarantee that these same opinions were widely prevalent. How far they reflected public opinion can not be measured with any degree of certainty. Subscription lists are not an accurate gauge since so many influences induce subscriptions, nor can the votes cast on public questions accurately record public opinion since the exercise of the suffrage has always been limited by restrictions imposed by religion, property, residence, education, race, or sex.

During this period of personal journalism not only was the editor identified with the paper, but the paper was identified with the community. The dedication of two volumes of the editorial writings of Harvey W. Scott reads: "To the people of the Pacific Northwest who sustained the newspaper work of Harvey W. Scott, during forty-five years, for the spread of intelligence and

10 The New York *Evening Post* points its statement with "a specimen, rare in our time, of this style of composition," drawn from the Macon, Georgia, *Telegraph* and the Albany, Georgia, *Herald.*—September 26, 1914.
11 J. Richard Beste, *The Wabash: or Adventures of an English Gentleman's Family in the Interior of America.*—I, 289.

for a growing expression of the universal religious spirit, this collection of his writings is appreciatively inscribed."[12] This dedication expresses rarely well the intimate and cordial relationship between the editor and the community and the community reaching out through a large section of a great country, as it was exemplified in the work of this great editor.

The responsibility entailed by this identity of interest between editor and community may again be illustrated by the conception of it held by this same editor. It is seen in a letter of Harvey W. Scott to certain clergymen who had written him protesting that it was not the function of the editor of a secular newspaper to advocate or to attack the peculiar views of any church. The editor writes that he can not admit that it is not a proper province of a newspaper to touch a subject which some clergymen claim as their exclusive field, "more especially since, as a newspaper man, in active touch with the public mind during more than forty years, I have found no feature of *The Oregonian's* work more sought or approved than in the field from which you would bar it." . . . "*The Oregonian* is a newspaper whose function is discussion, as it thinks fit and deems just, of all subjects presented for consideration in the active life of our people—even the claims of dogmatic theology, on occasion." . . . "As a general newspaper, taking note of the movement of the thought of the world, *The Oregonian* cannot ignore a subject which has so large a part of the progressive world's attention."[13]

It was Thomas Carlyle who felt that in England the responsibilities of the editor were equally serious. "The true Church of England at this moment," he says, "lies in the editors of its newspapers. These preach to the people daily, weekly, admonishing kings themselves, advising peace or war with an authority which only the first reformers, and a long-past class of popes were possessed of; inflicting moral censure, imparting moral encouragement, in all ways diligently administering the discipline of the

---

[12] *Religion, Theology and Morals*, by Harvey W. Scott. Forty Years Editor-in-Chief *Morning Oregonian* of Portland. Edited by Leslie M. Scott, 2 vols., 1917.

This relationship is also indicated in the *Oregon Historical Society Quarterly*, June, 1913,—a Harvey W. Scott memorial number.

[13] *Religion, Theology and Morals*, I, 91–94; II, Appendix, 349–350.

Church." [14] It must be recognized, however, that Carlyle's approval at that time of the function of the press collectively, may have been colored by his strong admiration of Edward Sterling, then editor of *The Times*, of whose editorials he enthusiastically writes, "Let the most gifted intellect, capable of writing epics, try to write such a Leader for the Morning Newspapers! No intellect but Edward Sterling's can do it." [15]

It was of Lord Acton as editor that his biographer writes: "Few readers of these Letters but will rid themselves of prevalent opinions as to the ease with which a serious magazine may be conducted, or as to the levity with which grave articles are put into print. Probably no Minister of State ever performed his duties more conscientiously than Acton his as essayist or reviewer; none in any department of affairs could give to the details of office a more anxious attention, a more exhaustive care." [16]

It is also not always understood that the work of the editor extends far beyond the range of his own paper. As is so well illustrated in the editorial work of E. P. Clark,[17] the skilful conscientious editor is ever on the alert to detect signs of unusual ability in newspaper work in every section of the country, to discover "who is trying to find out the truth and tell it, in the face of absolute persecution from all the other papers in his State," and to encourage him by friendly personal letters, and by editorial commendation.

The social evolution of the editor has probably had no small effect on the influence of the editorial. The early writer for the press not only lived on Grub Street, but the nature of his work was not understood and was long held in ill-concealed contempt. The biographer of Alaric Watts, writing of journalism about 1822, says that it was not "held in high esteem as an occupation, and was indeed, save in few and exceptional instances in which the political influence of the particular daily newspaper had secured a corresponding influential recognition of the writer for it,

---

[14] Thomas Carlyle, "Signs of the Times," *Edinburgh Review*, June, 1829, 49: 439–459; republished in *Critical and Miscellaneous Essays*, English edition, II, 230–252.
[15] *Life of John Sterling*, pp. 228–229.
[16] Abbot Gasquet, *Lord Acton and his Circle*, p. 372.
[17] *A Soldier of Conscience*, pp. 13–15.

scarcely regarded as a literary occupation at all." But because the income derived from it was certain and regular, it was "accepted, not without some sacrifice of pride, as an occupation by literary men." [18]

Sir Wemyss Reid, writing of the press about 1857, says that "the Press—at all events in provincial towns—in those days was the reverse of respectable in the eyes of the world; and truly there was some reason for the low esteem in which it was held. The ordinary reporter on a country paper was generally illiterate, he was too often intemperate, and he was invariably ill-paid." [19] Conditions had not improved when Catling found a few years later that "no landlord or landlady would listen to the application of any journeyman for a decent house. Time after time I was refused as a tenant, even when payment of rent in advance was offered." [20]

When Lord Lyndhurst invited the editor of *The Times* to dinner it "made a great uproar," [21] but a recent journalist can facetiously remark that an "editor attends more public banquets than a cabinet minister." [22]

The wheel turns round and Moberly Bell is cited as saying, only twenty years ago, that it was an unheard-of thing for a member of the editorial staff of *The Times* to be seen talking with any member of the commercial department. Men working on the paper were forbidden to know each other. [23] In 1918 the wheel again turned when in Iowa the occupation was officially declared to be an unessential industry and its members therefore subject to the draft. [24]

A pendant to the social position of the editor is the very considerable number of editors who have been imprisoned—usually

[18] A. A. Watts, *Alaric Watts*, I, 156.
[19] S. J. Reid, *Memoirs of Sir Wemyss Reid*, p. 37.
[20] *My Life's Pilgrimage*, p. 81.
[21] *Greville Memoirs*, III, 159, 169.
[22] J. Pendleton, "The Humors of Newspaper Editing," *Littell's Living Age*, August 1, 1896, 210: 305–309.
[23] H. Simonis, *The Street of Ink*, pp. 4–5.
[24] New York *Times*, August 8, 1918; Secretary Baker on the status of newspaper men with reference to the draft, *ib.*, August 9, 1918.
See also ruling of United States immigration officials in Montreal that a newspaper man is a member of a learned profession.—*New York Evening Post*, March 4, 1922.

for debt, libel, or blasphemy—and have continued to edit their papers from behind prison bars.[25]

And the editor and journalist of every rank long sought his recreations in Bohemia. But thirty and more years ago, J. A. O'Shea wrote, "Bohemia is nearing the borders of Corinth," [26] —a change that has been attributed in America to the introduction of typesetting machines that have done much to render "the ancient Bohemianism of the composing-room distasteful to the modern editor and obsolete with the better class of printers." [27] Sir Francis Burnand gives a significant account of the change in England from the Bohemia of the journalists of the middle of the nineteenth century to the Bohemia that, in the words of Layard, "has been captured by men whose tastes and habits have been formed at the public schools, or who at least have had their three years at Oxford or Cambridge." [28] The change of standards is everywhere noticeable to-day in the absence of all allusion to Bohemia,—even twenty-five years ago it was customary to refer to it as a matter of course in accounts of the press.

Emerging from Grub Street, and Bohemia, the editor developed in England into a Delane,—the confidant of ministers and of royalty; or into a member of the House of Lords, commanding vast wealth and high social prestige; or into a recipient of birthday honors. "There is scarcely a large city in Great Britain," says Porritt, "in which there is not a titled journalist,"—a system practically begun by Lord Salisbury in 1885 and continued by his successors.[29] In America he has more than once left the editorial sanctum to represent his country at foreign courts.

It was probably a somewhat superficial view of the social position of the editor that led De Tocqueville to say contemptuously, "The personal opinions of the editors [of American papers] have no kind of weight in the eyes of the public: the only use of a journal is, that it imparts the knowledge of certain facts, and it is

---

[25] W. Lee, *Daniel Defoe*, I, 84–85; Theophila Carlile Campbell, *The Battle of the Press*.

[26] *Leaves from the Life of a Special Correspondent*, II, 179.

[27] J. A. Porter, *The Modern Newspaper*, p. 9.

[28] G. S. Layard, *A Great "Punch" Editor, Being the Life, Letters, and Diaries of Shirley Brooks*, pp. 250–251.

[29] E. Porritt, *The Englishman at Home*, p. 323.

only by altering or distorting those facts, that a journalist can contribute to the support of his own views." [30]

Undoubtedly the weight attached to the opinions of the editor has at times taken on new and greater importance by reason of the offices and honors conferred upon him. Delane somewhat quickly acquired a reputation for omniscience, and especially after announcing in *The Times* the abolition of the corn laws, "he acquired the reputation which he never afterwards lost of being the best informed man in England." [31] The opinions expressed by Delane in regard to the Civil War in America were apparently accepted without question by the readers of *The Times*. This readiness to accept his views, especially on a foreign situation, was undoubtedly due to the confidence felt in him because of his high social position, and the belief that this gave him authentic sources of information not available to others. But the disadvantage of omniscience is that it leads to over-confidence and an assumption of infallibility of judgment that does not always stand the test of time. In the case of Delane many of his intelligent contemporaries did not accept his judgment in regard to the Civil War. Leslie Stephen wrote with vehemence in an elaborate pamphlet: "My complaint against the *Times* is that its total ignorance of the quarrel and the presumption with which it pronounced upon its merits, led to its pouring out a ceaseless flood of scurrilous abuse, couched, indeed, in decent language, but as essentially insulting as the brutal vulgarities of the *New York Herald*. No American . . . could fail to be wounded, and, so far as he took the voice of the *Times* for the voice of England, to be irritated against England." [32]

How unerringly Leslie Stephen divined the effect of the attitude of Delane is seen in a letter of Lowell's to Leslie Stephen dated April 10, 1866, which he says "is the first one I have sent across the Atlantic since our war began." . . . "I confess I have had an almost invincible repugnance to writing again to England. I share with the great body of my countrymen in a bitterness (half resentment and half regret) which I can not yet get

[30] *Democracy in America*, I, 200–201.
[31] A. I. Dasent, *John Thadeus Delane*, I, 55.
[32] L. S. [Leslie Stephen], *The "Times" on the American War*, pp. 105–106.

over. . . . I cannot forget the insult so readily as I might the injury of the last five years." [33]

John Stuart Mill in turn felt it necessary to send out a warning against the editorial infallibility of *The Times* and he wrote Motley under date of January 26, 1863: "Foreigners ought not to regard the *Times* as representing the English Nation. . . . The line it takes on any particular question is much more a matter of accident than is supposed. It is sometimes better than the public, and sometimes worse. . . . Unfortunately these papers [the *Times* and the *Saturday Review*], through the influence they obtain in other ways, and in the case of the *Times* very much in consequence of the prevailing notion that it speaks the opinions of all England, are able to exercise great power in perverting the opinions of England whenever the public is sufficiently ignorant of facts to be misled." [34]

Even Englishmen grew restive under the editorial dominance of *The Times* and a long correspondence between Cobden and Delane followed the misrepresentations in a *Times* leader to the effect that John Bright had excited discontent among the poor, and had proposed "a division among them of the lands of the rich." Cobden called on Delane by name to withdraw the baseless imputation, and when Delane refused to publish the letter of Cobden's in *The Times*, the latter published the correspondence in the *Rochdale Observer*. The question at issue between the two was the refusal of *The Times* to admit that it had been in error, as it clearly had been, and Cobden's insistence it should apologize and retract its imputations.[35]

This attitude of infallibility and omniscience has almost inevitably been modified by the changes that have affected the paper as a whole. The principle of division of labor has entered the editorial columns as it has the business office, and the editor who himself once wrote on every subject now engages specialists to write editorials in their own special field and the editorial office may expand to include half a continent. William Lloyd Garrison became "Journalist at Large" after his work on the *Liberator*

---

[33] *Letters of James Russell Lowell*, edited by C. E. Norton, I, 358–359.
[34] *Correspondence of J. L. Motley*, edited by G. W. Curtis, II, 111–116.
[35] John Morley, *Life of Richard Cobden*, pp. 592–606.

ceased and the phrase well characterizes the place of many editorial writers. During the war the spirit of infallibility once more asserted itself to an extreme degree, but it seemed a passing phase and the close of the war is bringing a return of moderate judgments and a decrease in that spirit of omniscience which is a characteristic of ignorance.

As personal ownership of newspapers has been superseded by corporate ownership, the place of the editor becomes more and more conventional; as the personal owner continues to be the editor, he tends to consider more than formerly the commercial interests of his paper. These changes seem to create the impression, even among newspaper men themselves, that the editorial is declining in importance. "A newspaper is divided into three parts," says a recent novel dealing with the press. "News is the merchandise which it has to sell. Advertising is the by-product that pays the bills. The editorial page is a survival. At its best it analyzes and points out the significance of important news. At its worst, it is a mouthpiece for the prejudices or the projects of whoever runs it. Few people are influenced by it, many are amused by it. It isn't very important nowadays." [36]

To Porritt, it seemed "open to question whether the editorial writer is the power he once was in English journalism. He still helps to keep his party together; but nowadays it is doubtful whether the editorial columns of the daily press make many political converts." [37]

The explanation of these changes in England Porritt somewhat bluntly finds in the reform of the English civil service that has made it impossible for a Government to reward its journalistic supporters by quartering them on the civil establishment,—that there are no very substantial favors of any kind that a Government can confer on the editors or owners of journals; that about all it can do is to give a paper a share in official advertising and to

[36] S. H. Adams, *The Clarion*, p. 99.
A similar opinion has been expressed by H. W. Massingham who discusses the theory that the editor may disappear as the news side of the paper is more and more developed. "If nature has no further use for him, in Heaven's name let him go. The world did very well without him once, and will do so again."—"The Ethics of Editing," *National Review*, April, 1900, 35: 256–261.
[37] E. Porritt, *The Englishman at Home*, p. 319.

send it a few official communications sent out from State Departments, but "neither of these privileges is worth much;" that the number of tickets to the reporters' gallery at Westminster is limited; and that in general the Government can make little return to newspapers that support it.[38] But since Government has often been averse to conferring such favors, even when it has had the opportunity, the explanation is scarcely satisfactory. Canning indicated to William Jerdan under date of June, 1826, that he was most unwilling to make any appointments where the connection of the recipients with the press would make them objectionable.[39] The adoption of the policy of rewarding editors by gift of office that was adopted by Andrew Jackson and long continued by his successors never commended itself to any except to the often unworthy recipients.

Somewhat similar disaffection and complaint of lack of appreciation by government has been found in Germany where the newspapers have been called "poor international newsgatherers" and this has been in part explained by the personnel of the German newspaper office. It can seldom command men of the ability that represent the great London papers in foreign capitals, because of the inferior standing of journalists in Germany in comparison with those in Western Europe. Very few select journalism as an occupation because the social prestige belonging to the profession and professional pride among journalists are as undeveloped as when Freytag wrote *Die Journalisten.*[40] Why this has been so has sometimes been understood by the Germans themselves. Many years ago a writer on the operation of bureaucracy noted the great number of decorations distributed in time of war and acquiesces in it, but he can not refrain from adding, "But why, in time of peace, military exercise, good drill, good generalship, and the like, should count for more than solid judicial work, and the like, is not so easy to see." [41]

Whether Bismarck's attitude towards the press was cause or result is both uncertain and immaterial, but Bismarck himself

[38] E. Porritt, *The Englishman at Home,* pp. 320–321.
[39] W. Jerdan, *Autobiography,* IV, 160–164.
[40] R. H. Fife, Jr., *The German Empire between Two Wars,* p. 364.
[41] Friedrich von Schulte, "Bureaucracy and its Operation in Germany and Austria-Hungary," *Contemporary Review,* March, 1880, 37: 432–458.

spoke in contemptuous terms of the press, and foreign and German writers on the press of Germany during his time refer to the low social position of editors and press correspondents,—"no foreign correspondent can be received at the German court;" "editors are paid small salaries and are not in the highest social circles;" "journalists are a pack of fellows too lazy to work and too illiterate to be schoolmasters of children;" "journalism in the Fatherland is the calling for those who, for some reason or other, have never found another calling;" "it carries no dignity, offers no position, involves neither social, political nor literary distinction;" "it is an estate without a status." These characterizations of those connected with the press as given by Bismarck and his contemporaries indicate the difficulties the editor had to overcome in Germany during the Imperial régime.

The influences that justify a prominent paper of to-day in saying of a great metropolitan daily that "its editorial page is quite its least worthy part" [42] are not confined to a single paper, or to a single country, and they are more fundamental than the editor's desire to sit in high places. The influence of the editor and of the editorial has apparently been undermined by two important classes of changes that have come within the past fifty years.

The first class is connected with the internal conduct of the press. The relative importance of the editorial has been affected by the development of the great news-collecting agencies. Readers who once turned to the first leader in the London *Times* for information in regard to forthcoming ministerial decisions would to-day receive the news through the press agencies. The *Globe* once "foreshadowed more or less distinctly the intentions or the measures of the Government," but newspapers even in 1880 had become so much more powerful in debate than either of the Houses of Parliament that they roused a certain jealousy in official circles,—"Ministers instead of being anxious to prefigure their measures through the press, and so preparing the public mind for them, are jealous of being forestalled by it."[43] The introduction of the headline and the increasing dependence on it for

[42] "Endowing Newspapers," *The Nation*, July 20, 1918, 107: 60–61.
[43] "London Evening Newspapers," New York *Nation*, October 7, 1880, 31: 250–251.

the news of the day, together with the growing independence of readers, has also diverted interest from the editorial to the head-line. The relation of the leading article of the London *Times* to the news of the day is scarcely an extreme illustration of the change in importance that has taken place in the editorial. "The article was the place, and the only place, in which the best news was given. . . . There was, as a rule, no display of such political news elsewhere; there were no headlines. . . . Whatever may be thought of the new method from other points of view, it must be admitted that the old method gave peculiar power to the leading article. To-day a reader may skip the leading article and yet be sure of not missing any vital piece of news. In *The Times* of Delane the leading article was the thing which no politician could afford to miss, for it might contain early news nowhere else obtainable. . . . Thus in various subtle ways the opinion-forming power of the leading article obtained in *The Times* of Delane an almost pontifical influence." [44]

The publication of numerous signed articles written by experts or by special correspondents has added authoritativeness to the newspaper, but the custom has meant a decline in the influence of the editorial.[45] The apparently increasing migration of editors, sub-editors and reporters from one newspaper to another has given an impression of a certain instability in the conduct of the editorial page. The advertisement has come to be an important medium for conveying information and influencing public opinion [46] and has thus in large measure supplanted the editorial as the channel through which opinion is reflected, expressed, or moulded.

[44] Sir Edward Cook, *Delane of "The Times,"* pp. 288–289.

[45] "The collective expression of journalistic policy known as the 'leader' has been extensively superseded by the communication from the specialist or expert, vouched for by the signature of an individual."—T. H. S. Escott, *Masters of English Journalism*, p. 20.

"The new journalism means the organized co-operation of many trained workers, directed not to the expression of one person's thought, but to the interpretation of all the thoughts that agitate society."—R. E. Day, *Proceedings at the Unveiling of a Memorial to Horace Greeley*, 1914, p. 142.

[46] S. K. Lothrop says that the Boston *Weekly Messenger* was "the first weekly periodical in America published without advertisements, and depending for its support upon its political, historical, and literary interest and value."—"Memoir of Hon. Nathan Hale," *Proceedings of the Massachusetts Historical Society*, December, 1880, 18: 270–279.

The internal conduct of the press thus in part explains the apparently waning power of the editorial.

But a far more important group of causes has been put forth and has been vigorously upheld.

The decline of the editorial is most often attributed to the changes in the business administration of the newspaper. The substitution of the impersonal corporation for the personal owner has necessarily affected adversely the importance of the editorial. The frequent changes in policy that are inevitable when the editor becomes to a certain extent dependent on the corporation tends to uncertainty in the conduct of the editorial page. The growing importance of the business manager, the introduction of what has been termed "the department-store idea," the investment of large capital on which returns are expected—all combine on the business side to limit the influence of the editor.

Yet the problem of what should be the mutual relations between owner and editor and the complaint that each interferes with the other are probably as old as the periodical press itself. The owner may have been termed a patron, the press may have been controlled by a political party, the editor may have been called a hack writer,—whatever the designation applied to the party of either the first or the second part, the friction that has existed between those who hold the purse strings and those in their employ has been well understood. Defoe's difficulties with Fog, Applebee and Mist, have been set forth by all of his biographers. Addison and Steele strove for independence of their patrons, not always successfully. Walpole and his ministry worked through political pamphlets, the Opposition through newspapers.[47]

In the early nineteenth century, William Jerdan writes of his difficulties in conducting the *Aurora* under the management of a committee of fashionable hotel-keepers and the landlords of the principal inns and taverns at the West End of London,—one was ultra-Tory, one loyal but moderate, one favored the Church, and one the Roman Catholic Church; one was warlike, one a pacifist, one democratic, and one seditious. The editor was therefore al-

[47] Milton Percival, *Political Ballads Illustrating the Administration of Sir Robert Walpole*, p. xiii.

ways in perplexity in his efforts to effect a compromise between himself on the one side and all these discordant elements on the other side.[48] His *Autobiography* is filled with accounts of the wranglings of editors and of publishers and owners. The letters mutually exchanged are often abusive and personal to an extent that would not be tolerated to-day.

The lives and letters of John Murray, and of William Blackwood, are filled with accounts of the almost inevitable misunderstandings and disagreements among the owners, publishers, and editors of periodicals.[49]

James Macdonell was brilliant and able, a Liberal in politics and a vigorous opponent of all the policies that Disraeli stood for. "But the curb was put upon the enthusiastic leader writer, with his strong humanitarian views, and he had to see the paper with which he was identified taking a course of which he could not approve."[50]

J. A. Spender says that during his thirty-three years' connection with the press he has seen the power of the editor and writer constantly diminishing and the power of the proprietor constantly increasing. "Journalists can neither do justice to themselves nor serve the public honestly in a syndicated press producing opinion to a pattern designed by its proprietor."[51]

Similar statements have been recently made by Henry Watterson who declared that "he has seen many newspaper properties wrecked by internal dissentions and by the attempt of an ambitious business manager to dominate and control the editorial department."[52]

W. S. Robinson, the editor of the Boston *Republican* in 1848, found more than once that his editorial had been altered by one

[48] *Autobiography*, I, chap. XII.

[49] S. Smiles, *Memoirs and Correspondence of the Late John Murray*, 2 vols.; Mrs. Oliphant, *The Annals of a Publishing House; William Blackwood and His Sons*, 3 vols.

[50] S. J. Reid, *Memoirs of Sir Wemyss Reid*, p. 135; W. R. Nicoll, *James Macdonell*, pp. 294–295.

[51] "The Editor vs. the Proprietor," in the *Westminster Gazette*, cited by the *Literary Digest*, April 13, 1918, 57: 29–30.

The relations between editor and proprietor are discussed by A. W. à Beckett, *The à Becketts of "Punch,"* chap. X, "Advice Gratis," pp. 293–310.

[52] New York *Tribune*, June 26, 1917.

of the publishers and he was constantly annoyed throughout the presidential campaign of 1848 by the efforts made to bridle his pen. The *Republican* was reputed to be an anti-slavery paper, but its owners were more timid than its editor and hence this led to the wish to temper the outspoken, vigorous utterances of its courageous editor.[53] More than one instance, however, has been found where so-called disagreements between owners and editors have in reality been not disagreements as to policy, but incompatibility of temperament.[54]

Walt Whitman refers to "rows with the boss"—a leader in the "regular" Democratic organization,—but his recent editors find that "Whitman stood his ground, not only refusing to write what he did not believe but declining to refrain from expressing his strongly held convictions." [55] He remained on the Brooklyn *Daily Eagle* nearly two years, but left apparently owing to disagreements with the owner and proprietor on the question of the extension of slavery into the recently acquired territories.

So widely has it been assumed, and with apparent reason, that the owner of a paper attempts to control its editorial policy that assurances to the contrary have almost the appearance of ostentatious protests. When the London *Echo* changed owners, the statement was quickly made that "although Baron Grant was a Conservative in politics, he made no attempt to alter the Radical principles of *The Echo*." [56] James Grant gave nearly a chapter to "the unpleasant position of editors with newspaper proprietors and committees of management" [57] which Thomas Frost characterized as "rather ludicrous," saying that his experiences have not made him acquainted with "those extreme strains upon the consciences of leader-writers" and that he had been very little interfered with by the proprietors or chief editors of the papers

[53] "*Warrington*" *Pen-Portraits*, pp. 39–41.
[54] This seems to have been the case while Carl Schurz and E. L. Godkin were associated on the New York *Evening Post*, 1881–83.
Somewhat similar incompatibility between John Walter and Delane led to the vesting of full editorial control in Delane.
[55] C. Rodgers and J. Black, *eds.*, *The Gathering of the Forces*, by Walt Whitman, I, xxx.
[56] J. C. Francis, *Notes by the Way*, p. 30.
[57] *The Newspaper Press*, II, chap. XVII.

with which he had been connected with regard to his manner of dealing with the political and social questions of the day.[58]

G. C. Brodrick who wrote leaders in the London *Times* from 1860 to 1873 says, "One misgiving which haunted me at the outset proved entirely delusive. It was the fear that I should be expected to write strictly to order, and to advocate views opposed to my own convictions." But he found that if asked to write something he could not approve, another subject was promptly substituted by Delane.[59]

Differences of opinion in 1916 between the *New Republic* and its financial supporters in regard to candidates for the presidency led to an open letter from its chief financial supporter stating that its owners exercised no supervision over the editorial columns of the paper.[60] The recent transfer of ownership of the New York *Evening Post* was accompanied by a statement that the transfer would not affect in any way the editorial policy of the paper.[61]

The question in its entirety is closely allied to the fundamental problem of whether an editor should write at all or not,—a question to which E. T. Cook says "high authority, and probably the more general practice, are in favor of [giving] the negative answer."[62] But assuming that most editors do write, it leads to the question as to how far voluntarily and consciously the editor places his pen at the service of his employers, how far the theory prevails and is upheld "that the function of a political journalist resembles that of a barrister; the hired pleader paid to make the best of a case, good or bad; bound to his brief, and in no way held to compromise his honour by subordinating private opinions of his own."[63]

[58] *Reminiscences of a Country Journalist*, p. 133.
[59] *Memories and Impressions*, p. 130.
[60] Willard Straight, *New Republic*, October 28, 1916, 8: 313–314.
[61] New York *Evening Post*, August 1, 1918.
[62] *Edmund Garrett*, p. 84.
"A literary team is handled with the best results when the holder of the reins leaves the actual work to be done by those whom he directs."—T. H. S. Escott, *Masters of English Journalism*, p. 155.
[63] E. T. Cook, *Edmund Garrett*, p. 82.
The author cites an American journalist who told the story: "A political 'boss' noticing some able silver articles in a Chicago paper, said, 'Introduce me to that man; I should like to see him President of the United States'. Afterwards he was equally struck by some able gold articles in a New York paper, and said, 'Introduce me to that man; I should like to see him shot'. It was the same man."—*Id.*

The situation has seemed to others comparable to that of the stenographer who takes dictation and transcribes his notes on the typewriter,—a process that involves no ethical demand for an agreement between what he has written and his own personal beliefs. Certainly in the early days of the newspaper, when Grub Street flourished, writers for periodicals were considered in much this light. Men wrote with equal facility on both sides of a question, and they are condemned to-day. But inventions have not shifted the responsibility from the human to the metal machine and while the early editor was apparently not over-sensitive to a condition that demanded that his right hand should not know what his left hand wrote, he can no longer plead this justification. If he continues his connection with a paper whose policies have changed, he does so with a full realization of the principle involved. "*The Pall Mall Gazette* has always been more remarkable for its influence upon opinion than for its commercial success," was a general belief once expressed in print.[64] Its influence was undoubtedly explained, at least in large part, by the absolute certainty of its readers that its leaders expressed the personal convictions of its editors. While Frederick Greenwood was its editor, he had personally opposed the policies of Gladstone. This led to a rupture with the proprietor, and therefore to changes, and to demands that Greenwood could not meet and as a matter of personal honor he resigned.[65] When Zola, in addressing English journalists, "likened some journalists to mere writing-machines at the beck and call of a superior," he was reminded that "on two occasions when there had been a change in the proprietorship of the *Pall Mall Gazette* the editors and the bulk of their staff had quitted the paper to uphold their opinions elsewhere," while later "during the Boer war, various editors and others threw up their posts rather than write contrary to their convictions." [66]

The situation was reversed when Bernard Gillam drew caricatures of the Republican presidential candidate for *Puck* in 1884. Early in the campaign *Judge* was started by Republicans to counteract the influence of *Puck* "and Gillam went over to the

[64] "London Evening Newspapers," New York *Nation*, October 7, 1880, 31: 250–251.
[65] *Id.*
[66] E. A. Vizetelly, *Émile Zola*, p. 330.

younger journal to advocate with his pencil the candidate he had tattooed." [67]

How far then does the editor control the policy of the press, how far is it controlled by the owner? [68] The question, as has been seen, is a persistent one and no question connected with the press has been answered with more sweeping generalizations than this. Yet in this, as in every other question connected with the press, no one answer fits all cases. Editors and editorials differ in different countries, they differ at different times in the same country, and an editor does not always agree with himself.

In France the *article de fond* is often an expression of opinion by a well-known man and his views do not necessarily correspond with those of the paper itself,—the paper is perhaps most often read from an intellectual curiosity to see what the editor or a special writer may say on a somewhat academic question.

But in Germany "the fear of the law is the one great plague of the German editor's life," wrote Dawson in 1901. "So frequent are prosecutions of editors that many newspapers are compelled to maintain on their staffs what are known as 'sitting editors' whose special function it is to serve in prison the terms of detention that may be awarded for a too liberal exercise of the critical faculty." [69] The government does not own the press, but both editors and owners have in the past yielded to its superior power.

A volume would be needed to show how in England the editor and the editorial have changed from the days when Defoe was playing a double part and while openly in the employ of Mist, an ardent Jacobite, he was secretly in the service of the Government

[67] B. Matthews, "American Comic Journalism," *Bookman*, November, 1918, 48: 282–287.

[68] Bliss Perry gives an interesting sidelight on the opinion of publishers on this point in his account of the relations between the first publishers of the *Atlantic Monthly*, and "the editor who was never the editor," but who was alluded to by the head of the firm "in comfortable proprietary phrase" as "our literary man."—*Atlantic Monthly*, November, 1907, 100: 658–678; *Park Street Papers*, pp. 203–277.

[69] W. H. Dawson, *German Life in Town and Country*, chap. XIII, "The Newspaper and its Readers."

E. Poole, in "The Sitting Editor and the Russian Police," characterizes the custom as a trick common for decades from St. Petersburg to Siberia.— *World To-Day*, May, 1906, 10: 509–510; F. C. Trench, "The Russian Journalistic Press," *Blackwood's*, July, 1890, 148: 115–126.

and thus able not only to temper Mist's anti-Hanoverian bias, but also to give the Government secret information in regard to its opponents,[70] to the days when the aristocratic Londoner turned to the first leader of *The Times* to learn that Peel had determined to revoke the corn laws;[71] from the days when "the chief and sometimes the sole equipment needed for the discharge of the editorial duties was scissors and paste,"[72] to the days when it is said, "Leader-writing of a responsible journalist taxes every faculty. Judgment, fluency, accuracy, literary skill, all must be there; and they must be always *ready*. No waiting for the happy mood. Write with speed, write at once, write well: only so many hours lie between you and the most critical and competent audience in the world;"[73] from the eighteenth century remark, "I will make no comments of my own in this paper, as I assume that other people have sense enough to make reflections for themselves,"[74] to the twentieth century statement that "an editor has not only to supply his readers with the latest and truest information, he has to furnish them with ideas. . . . For the multitude the leading article is the obvious short-cut to convictions."[75]

[70] W. Lee gives six letters from Defoe to Charles De La Faye, April 12–June 13, 1718, that show this.—*Daniel Defoe; His Life and Recently Discovered Writings*, I, ix–xviii.
[71] E. T. Cook, *Delane of "The Times,"* p. 21.
[72] W. J. Couper, *The Edinburgh Periodical Press*, I, 115.
[73] Cited in W. R. Nicoll, *James Macdonell*, p. 281.
[74] Cited by John Pendleton, "The Humors of Newspaper Editing," *Littell's Living Age*, August 1, 1896, 210: 305–309.
[75] R. Lucas, *Lord Glenesk and the "Morning Post,"* p. 155.
    It is interesting to compare the editor of to-day with the ideal editor as he seemed to William Leggett. In an editorial on "Leading Public Opinion" he describes him at length.—*The Plaindealer*, January 21, 1837. Reprinted in his *Political Writings*, II, 167–170.
    Curiously enough, while elaborate qualifications have been listed for every other person connected with the staff of a newspaper, comparatively few have been noted in regard to the editor.—Gifford of the *Quarterly* believed "that inviolable secrecy was one of the prime functions of an editor." He therefore "never attempted to vindicate himself, or to reveal the secret as to the writers of reviews."—S. Smiles, *Memoirs and Correspondence of the Late John Murray*, II, 176.—"Mr. Jowett included in his 'Maxims for Statesmen and Others' Never Tell. Upon no others is the maxim more binding than upon editors. To respect confidences is with them a counsel of prudence as well as a law of honour; for no statesman is likely to run the risk of being betrayed a second time."—Sir Edward Cook, *Delane of "The Times,"* pp. 119–120.

It must be apparent that no off-hand statement that the editor controls the policy of the press or that he and the paper are both controlled by the owner is of weight unless it takes into consideration the factors of time and place. Equally necessary is it to remember the variations among editors and owners and even the variations in the moods and policies of individual editors. A singularly astute review of a life of Samuel Bowles clearly shows that his theory of journalism was not the same at all stages of his career, that he came to allow his regular correspondents to wreak their spite on his friends, that he allowed the *Republican* to give currency to charges of implication in the Crédit-Mobilier bribery on the part of Henry M. Dawes because he knew his readers would take an interest in them, not because he believed them,—"an evasion of personal responsibility, under the guise of a highly virtuous independence." [76]

But a very different problem is presented when the question is raised as to how far the editorial expresses public opinion and how far it carries in itself a guarantee that justifies the historian in making use of it. It must be obvious that here also no categorical answer can be given, since the answer must be conditioned by the time, country, and characteristics of the paper in which it appears. The function of the editorial differs much in different countries,[77] much at different times,[78] and much in different sections of the same country,[79] while the importance of the editorial and of other parts of the newspaper have varied at different times. If at one time the generals of an army trembled before the war correspondent,[80] it is the war department and the

[76] *The Nation*, December 31, 1885, 41: 553–554.
[77] In England the editorial has sought to influence public opinion, in France it seeks to act on the government, while in Germany it may be influenced by the government.
" 'The Times,' said Lord Clarendon, 'forms, guides, or reflects—no matter which—the public opinion of England.' "—Sir Edward Cook, *Delane of "The Times,"* p. 294.
[78] "The medium through which Delane wielded his influence was a journalistic instrument of which the force has in later days been somewhat blunted—the instrument of the leading article."—*Ib.*, p. 287.
[79] In the small country paper the editorial is almost disappearing, or has become stereotyped and conventional.
[80] "In his [W. H. Russell's] hands, correspondence from the field really became a power before which generals began to quail."—E. L. Godkin, cited in R. Ogden, *Life and Letters*, II, 101–102.

ministry as a whole that tremble before the editor and owner of a string of newspapers.[81]

The editorial has thus seemed to be drawn in opposite directions; one set of influences has tended to minimize its importance while another has given it a standing and a power it has never had before. It is the part of the historian in his use of the newspaper to weigh the influences behind the editorial and to measure its importance in his own work.

Yet when all has been said in regard to the declining influence of the editorial, it must be remembered that there is much to be said on the other side and that it is more nearly true to say that the position of the editorial has changed, and that its influence is being felt in new and other ways. The editor of the old school was born, not made, and, like the doctor and the lawyer, he believed that a person could learn the secrets of the profession only in a newspaper office. The editor of to-day has had a college or a university training; he probably was connected with one of the college papers, and he may have had the added training of a school of journalism. If he may not technically fulfil the specific requirements for an editor prescribed in a recent press law promulgated in China,—that he must be over thirty years of age, suffer from no nervous disease, been undeprived of civil rights, belong neither to the military nor the naval professions, and be neither an administrative or a judicial officer, nor a student,[82]—he conforms to them in effect. Maturity of years and of judgment, mental balance, upright character, freedom from official entanglements are the qualifications everywhere to-day demanded in an editor. Moreover, the individual editor is to-day not infrequently merged into an editorial board,—a change advocated in influential circles as assuring complete independence and impartiality in editorials, but by no means universally commended.

The country editor is changing as well as his city brother.[83]

[81] Cf. A. G. Gardiner, "The 'Times' and the Man who makes it," *Atlantic Monthly*, January, 1917, 119: 111–122, and Norman Angell, "The Problem of Northcliffe," *New Republic*, January 27, 1917, 9: 344–347.

[82] Special correspondence of the New York *Evening Post*, May 13, 1914.

[83] Some of the early country editors were pamphleteers rather than editors. F. W. Scott cites the case of J. B. Turner who in 1843 edited the *Illinois Statesman*. The Quincy *Whig* commented jocosely on one of his thirteen-column editorials and was gravely told in reply that the actual length was only eleven columns.—*Newspapers and Periodicals of Illinois, 1814–1879*, p. lxxiv.

The rural free delivery brings the city paper to farms and villages, but the city paper does not supersede the country paper. The country editor emphasizes still more the local news, and pushes ever farther back the frontiers of his dominion,—he becomes more and more the man of authority in the community because his opinions tend more and more to be based on knowledge. "Closest to the paper," says Harger, "nearest to their home life, its hopes and its aspirations, the country editor is at the foundation of journalism." [84]

It is inevitable that with the changing characteristics of the editor a change in the editorial should result. This change is manifest in the wider range of subjects chosen for editorial comment, in the greater breadth of treatment, and in the improvement in the method of treatment. The subjects chosen for editorials have infinitely broadened in scope. *The Spirit of the Public Journals; or, the Beauties of American Newspapers, For 1805*, a collection from "nearly one hundred vehicles of information" published in 1806, shows editorials or articles on "The Seasons," "Winter," "Return of Spring," "Autumnal Reflections," "Affection," "Love," "Hope," "Truth," "Modesty," "Deceit," "The Idler," "Begin in Time," "Fashion," "The Grave." Local topics were largely the subjects of editorials somewhat later in the century. William Leggett was most definite and concrete in his choice of subjects, but he did not wander from Washington, Albany, or New York City.[85] Much of the same type of editorial as regards both choice of local subjects, and style of writing, as is seen in the selected editorials of William Leggett, is found in a contemporary English work entitled: *Spirit of the Metropolitan Conservative Press: Being a Selection of the Best Leading Articles from the London Conservative Journals during the year 1839.* In sharp contrast to-day are editorials that consider every phase of human thought and activity the world over.

The subject of the editorial has broadened at the same time that its treatment of all subjects has notably improved. The editorial only somewhat recently recorded a tendency towards

[84] C. M. Harger, "The Country Editor of To-day," *Atlantic Monthly*, January, 1907, 99: 89–96.

[85] *A Collection of the Political Writings of William Leggett*, edited by Theodore Sedgwick, Jr., 2 vols., 1840.

the "snappy," scrappy, dialogue style of writing affected by many short-story writers,[86] but the reaction against it is coming and to-day the leading editorials in our leading papers have somewhat the character of the best magazine articles. A general survey of an important question, or an exhaustive comment on a single phase of a subject prominently in the public eye may cover the first three columns of a great daily, while in the care taken in the presentation of the subject it may vie with all that is best in literature.

At one time the "sixth column" and the "third leader" were exceptional and they were presumably the work of the regular staff, but to-day the editor calls upon a wide range of occasional editorial contributors with expert knowledge in many fields and this in part explains the broadening of the editorial page both in its interests and in its method of treating them. Modern editorials have been reprinted, as those from the London *Times*,— "third leaders" that "are meant to turn the reader from affairs and interests of the moment to a consideration 'of man, of nature, and of human life' in their larger, more permanent aspect. In one or another form they represent the daily demand and supply of material for thought. . . . They are journalism; but in them journalism is extending itself towards, is even becoming, literature." [87] The examination of a large number of editorials leads to the conclusion that never has there been so large a number of editorial columns so well written as can be found to-day.

An evidence of the permanent value of the editorial of to-day in contrast with the elusive, vague, and therefore temporary reflections of the early day, is seen in the growing tendency to collect them into book form. Charles T. Congdon was on the New York *Tribune* from 1857 to 1863 and his "editorials were so good that they received the unusual honor of republication in a book." [88] What was considered unusual in 1869 has now become the usual. A library might be collected of volumes made up of

[86] F. N. Scott gave timely warning that "our future managing editors will do well to set it down in their Tables that 'Punch,' 'Human Interest,' and 'Heart-Throbs' are not, in modern journalism, the 'Whole Thing'."— *The Nation*, July 25, 1917, 105: 91.

[87] J. W. Mackail, *Modern Essays*, p. x.

[88] W. H. Rideing, *Many Celebrities and a Few Others*, p. 49. Charles T. Congdon, *Tribune Essays*, New York, 1869.

editorials that have appeared since about 1880 and that give promise of being of permanent value from the nature of the subjects treated. Collected from the editorial columns of the press of different countries, they attest the permanent value as literature of much that appeared first in the so-called "ephemeral press." [89]

The editorial not only covers a wider range of subjects than ever before but it discusses them with a breadth and depth not known in the earlier editorial. This has been particularly noticeable during the recent war where the constant comparison between present and past conditions has been possible only because of the fund of exact information at command.[90] This information is made possible in part through the establishment in all great newspaper offices of special libraries under the care of trained librarians. It was considered noteworthy that the Boston *Daily Advertiser* in the time of Nathan Hale had command of a complete file of the London *Times* and of other important English,

---

[89] Many editorials have been collected by different journals and published collectively:—*Essays from the London Times*, 2 vols., 1852; *Mornings of the Recess*, from the London *Times*, 1861–64; *Casual Essays of the Sun; Seen by the Spectator, The Outlook; College Journalism*, J. Bruce, and J. V. Forrestal, *eds.*

One of the earliest, if not the first, of these republications was made in the latter part of the seventeenth century. John Dunton, his brother-in-law, Samuel Wesley (the father of John Wesley), and Richard Sault published the *Athenian Mercury* from March, 1691 until June, 1697. Dunton published in four volumes a selection from these Mercuries and issued it as the *Athenian Oracle*. John Underhill has recently collected into one volume "all that is most interesting and valuable in the four volumes of the *Athenian Oracle*." See introduction to the volume.

The counterpart of this is found in the practice of leading editors of collecting their own most important editorials:—E. L. Godkin, *Critical and Social Essays;* George Williams Curtis, *Ars Recte Vivendi;* Fabian Franklin, *People and Problems;* A. G. Gardiner, *Pillars of Society;* and *Prophets, Priests and Kings.*

These titles are but suggestive and illustrative of the very large number of works of this character.

[90] The New York *Times*, for example, compared the surprise victory of the British at Cambrai with the surprise victory of Stonewall Jackson over Hooker at Chancellorsville, "which has hitherto stood as a model."—December 3, 1917.

A mass of material on this point may be found in *The War from This Side,*—two volumes of editorials collected from the Philadelphia *North American*, July, 1914–July, 1916; *The Gravest 366 Days*, editorials collected from the New York *Evening Mail*, 1916; E. S. Martin, *The Diary of a Nation*, 1917; A. G. Gardiner, *War Lords;* and in numerous other volumes of collected editorials.

French, and German newspapers.[91] The development of "the morgue," or "the dead room" containing biographical material relating to every person even remotely connected with public life, and clippings in regard to every subject of public interest makes information instantly accessible.[92] The editor is and must be prepared for every emergency.

This improvement in the general standard of the editorial has in part been made possible by the great extension of the newspaper plant. Through modern invention and through news-collecting agencies, the whole world has been brought to the sanctum, and the time and energy of the office staff thus released has been turned in the direction of perfecting the various parts of the paper.

The early editorial might claim infallibility of judgment, but the editorial of to-day may with greater justice lay claim to omniscience. The slightest error of statement in regard to events brings on it the satire of its even more omniscient competitors while the danger of a libel suit lurks in every misstatement in regard to an individual. An examination of editorials covering a

[91] S. K. Lothrop, "Memoir of Nathan Hale," *Massachusetts Historical Society Proceedings*, 1880–81, 18: 270–279.
   The New York *Evening Post* opens its library to the use of students.—Advertisement, January 19, 1918.
   [92] L. E. Theiss, "The Morgue Man," *The Outlook*, September 14, 1912, 102: 83–88.
   "The morgue" is the clipping bureau of the newspaper, but individual workers use the same system in a limited way. See Robert Luce, "The Clipping Bureau and the Library," in *Special Libraries*, September–October, 1913, 4: 152–157.
   The New York *Evening Post* publishes, and frequently revises, a pamphlet giving the list of its obituaries in readiness, character sketches, and list of subject envelopes.
   The importance attached to the "morgue" by journalists themselves is indicated by the reply reputed to have been made by a city editor to a Japanese who had asked what constituted the most important element in the oft-repeated "power of the press." " 'Here is your answer,' said the city editor, taking him to the journalistic morgue. 'The newspaper keeps its fingers on the past and its eyes on the future.' In 'dead' news rest such important clues for the future as well as of the past, and such an infallible, indelible record and guide that the statement of the trained editor was well chosen."—G. J. Nathan, "Journalistic 'Morgues," *Bookman*, August, 1910, 31: 597–599.
   An exceptionally good account of the "morgue", is that of J. F. Kwapil, "The 'Morgue' as a Factor in Journalism," *Library Journal*, May 15, 1921, 46: 443–446.

long series of years leads to the conclusion, that no parts of the best newspapers of to-day are so free from errors of fact as are the editorial columns. Errors of judgment will always be found, yet the historian must regard these as personal and not to be attributed to the newspaper as such.

As the editorial has widened its scope from the early, almost exclusive consideration of political subjects, it has in so doing acquired an independence in treating all subjects. The early editorial was largely the expression of the personal opinions of the editor; the editorial to-day is the impersonal voice of the newspaper. This is in sharp contrast to the changes that have come in other parts of the newspaper. War correspondence was in its great days entirely impersonal,—the volume, *The War Correspondence of the "Daily News," 1887*, is made up of a very large number of letters, the authors of which can not be identified by any one who does not understand the cryptic symbol used by each, but the letters of war correspondents to-day are published, and later collected, under the name of each individual writer.

But it was the editor who may once have placed his initials under his editorial, as did Horace Greeley. The editorial to-day is impersonal and its authorship presumably unknown outside of the editorial office. Many illustrations of this, as also of the wide and accurate knowledge found in the best editorials, are seen in the volumes of editorials collected to-day that involve a knowledge of the conditions out of which the late war grew. As the editorial becomes more and more impersonal, it becomes for the use of the historian more and more valuable. It is of course inevitable that this very impersonality should bring with it a certain confusion growing out of the editorial "we,"—a custom almost contemporaneous with the origin of the newspaper press itself. It has been traced to the *Mercurius Politicus*, the official gazette the first number of which appeared June 13, 1650.[93] It contained letters from abroad and since "two persons were speaking, not only for themselves, but also for the Council of State," the form used was understandable. The plural form was

[93] "The British Newspaper," *Dublin University Magazine*, March, 1863, 61: 359–376.

carried on in the *London Gazette* after the Restoration [94] and has been generally accepted in spite of the obvious limitations in its use.[95] But even to-day distinctions must be noted in its use. The country editor uses "we," but often with a familiar, personal tone. Editorials on large, important subjects are often written with the home town in mind and in relation to local interests. In the great metropolitan dailies, the "we" that on the editorial page in the early days represented only a single voice has developed into the collective "we" that on the news pages, through the hundreds of significant passages collected by telegraph from editorials all over the country, justifies more than ever before the claim that the press is "the fourth estate."

The charge is often made that the editor has changed his position on important public questions and the implication is conveyed that the change has come from a desire to curry favor with those in authority, or from the still more ambitious plan of becoming the power behind the throne. The charge comes from other members of the press who with mirth resort to "the deadly parallel column" to prove their position,[96]—an effective weapon, but one which can be used in both directions and turned against the press. John Bright once said, "The *Times* says I repeat myself; the *Times* says I am guilty of what it calls tautology; the *Times* says I am always saying the same thing. What I complain of in the *Times* is that it *never* says the same thing." [97] Nor was John Bright alone in thinking that *The Times* never said the same thing. Greville found that "The 'Times' newspaper, always famous for its versatility and inconsistency, has lately produced articles on the Eastern Question on the same day of the most opposite characters, one warlike and firm, the next vehemently

[94] J. B. Williams, "John Milton, Journalist," *Oxford and Cambridge Review*, April, 1912, 18: 73–88.

[95] M. M'D. Bodkin finds that "The mysterious editorial 'we' is vaguely suggestive of an oracle kept tame on the newspaper premises and ready to deliver impromptu and infallible pronouncements on every subject under heaven, for the leader writer must know something of everything, or at least successfully assume a knowledge if he have it not."—*Recollections of an Irish Judge*, p. 245.

[96] It was undoubtedly with peculiar pleasure that the London *Nation*, of October 12, 1918, printed a selection in fulsome praise of Emperor William from the *Daily Mail* of June 20, 1910.

[97] Cited by G. M. Trevelyan, *Life of John Bright*, p. 250.

pacific by some other hand. This is of small importance, but it is indicative of the difference which exists in the Cabinet on the subject, and the explanation of the inconsistency of the 'Times' is to be found in the double influence which acts on the paper." [98]

While these editorial variations have often given rise to pungent criticism, very real difficulties are frequently presented to an editor, as has been recently suggested. An editor starts out to support a Mr. Jones whose intentions seem the best. His methods turn out to be a trifle shady. He makes enemies. Shall the editor continue to support him, pointing out his good qualities for the sake of the end in view, or shall he denounce Mr. Jones?—Every editor has to meet this situation. [99]

Other complications may arise as when editorials are written by persons at a distance who are not known to be connected with the papers for which they write. Kinglake says that Delane had once told him that while at Oxford he had supported himself "by writing leading articles for country newspapers." [100]   Jerdan considered that editing provincial papers in London was "just as effective as if the writer resided in the place of publication," [101] —an opinion that would not receive unanimous support.

The puzzling alternative in regard to policies to be followed is not the only one that confronts an editor. Is it one of his prerogatives to change a manuscript that has been accepted for publication? Editors have frequently assumed that it is,—much to the discomfiture of their contributors.

Leslie Stephen, writing of the period from 1856 to 1861, says: "I believe that the 'Edinburgh Review' still acted upon the precedent set by Jeffrey, according to which a contributor, especially, of course, a young contributor, was regarded as supplying raw material which might be rather arbitrarily altered by the editor." [102] How this was regarded by contributors is indicated in a

[98] *The Greville Memoirs*, VII, 74, July 12, 1853.—Lord Palmerston advocated a vigorous policy while Lord Aberdeen favored peace.
[99] "Editorial Dilemma," *New Republic*, October 23, 1915, 4: 299.
[100] A. W. Kinglake, *The Invasion of the Crimea*, IV, Appendix XV.
[101] *Autobiography*, I, chap. XV.—Jerdan says that, for a number of years, he thus edited the *Sheffield Mercury*, and also a Birmingham paper, an Irish journal, and other papers in various parts of the country. It seems possible that Jerdan has confused sending contributions to these papers with actual editorial work.
[102] *The Life of Sir James Fitzjames Stephen*, p. 162.

letter from Carlyle to Napier, November 23, 1830, in which he says: "My respected friend your predecessor [Jeffrey] had some difficulty with me in adjusting the respective prerogatives of Author and Editor, for though not, as I hope, insensible to fair reason, I used sometimes to rebel against what I reckoned mere authority, and this partly perhaps as a matter of literary conscience; being wont to write nothing without studying if possible to the bottom, and writing always with an almost painful feeling of scrupulosity, that light editorial hacking and hewing to right and left was in general nowise to my mind." [103] Napier also heard from Jeffrey who wrote, "I fear Carlyle will not do, that is, if you do not take the liberties and the pains with him that I did, by striking out freely, and writing in occasionally." [104] Macaulay was perhaps less sensitive; at all events, he wrote to Napier that he quite approved the alterations Napier had made in his article on Mackintosh.[105]

Mrs. Gaskell took umbrage at what she regarded as a reflection on Mr. Gaskell's ability as a critic. She wrote Dickens, objecting to "the purple patches with which he was anxious to embroider her work." All her work had been criticized by her husband, she wrote, and therefore she felt that what was good enough to pass his scrutiny was good enough for the public. She "keenly resented any alteration in her manuscript, and wrote off in great haste to Dickens," who had changed a complimentary allusion to *Pickwick Papers* in the first Cranford paper, "demanding the withdrawal of her sketch," but it was too late as it had already been sent to the printer of *Household Words*.[106]

Dickens apparently had little hesitation in altering the manuscripts of his contributors and his letters show the "delicate changes" and the rejection of titles that he made in them,[107] although himself indignant when the slightest change was made in his own manuscripts.[108]

[103] Macvey Napier, *Selection from the Correspondence of the late Macvey Napier, Esq.*, p. 96.

[104] *Ib.*, p. 126.

[105] *Ib.*, p. 173.

[106] Mrs. Ellis H. Chadwick, *Mrs. Gaskell Haunts Homes and Stories*, pp. 143–144, 184.

[107] R. C. Lehmann, *Charles Dickens as Editor*, pp. 51, 65, 70, 99–101, 126, 136, 188, 194, 319.

[108] *Ibid* , pp. 29–32.

Hazlitt found that "some Editors, moreover, have a way of altering the first paragraph: they have then exercised their privileges, and let you alone for the rest of the chapter;" that "Some Editors will let you praise nobody; others will let you blame nobody;" and that "Editors are a 'sort of *tittle-tattle*—' difficult to deal with, dangerous to discuss." [109]

It was to be expected that the fastidious Delane would make editorial emendations. "Much that appeared in *The Times* under the head of leading articles was so amended by his pen that it was in reality Delane's handiwork," acknowledges his biographer.[110] Henry Reeve, called by Delane "Il Pomposo," says that he rebelled against these editorial changes made in his leaders and he writes, "The moment an attempt was made to interfere with me and to garble my articles, I resigned [from *The Times*], and fell back on the 'Edinburgh Review'. " [111]

O'Shea found sub-editorial tinkering with his manuscript "an intolerable nuisance" and often thought "changes were made out of pure wantonness to show one's privilege of intermeddling." [112] Paris was probably infected with this feeling at that time, for Theodore Child wrote, "It is a common complaint on the part of the representatives of the English press in Paris that their letters are mercilessly mutilated in the editorial room in London." [113]

The benevolent Howells, in giving an account of his *Atlantic* stewardship, says that "sometimes it [the proof-reading] took the character of original work, in that liberal *Atlantic* tra-

---

[109] William Hazlitt, "A Chapter on Editors," *Men and Manners,* pp. 307, 309, 304.

[110] A. I. Dasent, *John Thadeus Delane,* I, 68.
"Bob Lowe wrote such an article upon Bright. It made my hair stand on end, and I have had to alter it almost beyond recognition."—*Ib.,* II, 159.

[111] J. K. Laughton, *Memoirs of Henry Reeve,* I, 339.—E. T. Cook puts the matter in quite a different light in *Delane of "The Times,"* pp. 192–195, as does A. I. Dasent, *John Thadeus Delane,* I, 213–223, where the correspondence is given in full.
H. Brackenbury frequently contributed to the *Athenaeum,* but when "a new editor, a very young man," altered his proof, he says, "this mechanical editorship was not to my taste, and I ceased contributing to the paper." —*Some Memories of My Spare Time,* p. 81.

[112] *Leaves from the Life of a Special Correspondent,* II, 168–169.

[113] "The Paris Newspaper Press," *Fortnightly Review,* August, 1885, n. s., 38: 149–165.

dition of bettering the authors by editorial transposition and paraphrase, either in the form of suggestion or of absolute correction." [114]

Even editors themselves are not immune from the blue pencil. When Blanchard Jerrold was the editor of *Lloyd's Weekly Newspaper*, Thomas Catling was sub-editor. At one time the latter told Lloyd that an article Lloyd had disapproved was written by Jerrold. "That," said the owner, "has nothing to do with it; I look to you to see that everything is kept right." "From that time onward," continues Catling, "though the editor's name appeared on the front page of the paper, his copy had to be closely supervised by the sub-editor." [115]

The troubles of editors with contributors do not end with the wrath expressed by them over the editorial changes made in their manuscripts. Often contributors claim that certain fields and subjects belong to them and that the editor should not allow others to poach on their preserves. To one such, Macvey Napier wrote with some asperity, "You think that I ought to have rejected an article on the Italian Economists by Spring Rice, on the ground that the whole province of Political Economy ought to be kept sacred for yourself. Now, it is impossible for me to agree to this. No man connected with the Review, none even of its founders, has ever claimed an exclusive right over any particular province." [116]

Brougham's infirmities of temper led Napier into frequent difficulties on the same score. "Pray send off your countermand to Macaulay," he wrote the harassed editor to whom Macaulay had offered an article on the politics of France after the Restoration, "I can trust no one but myself with it," and he plaintively adds, "Jeffrey always used to arrange it so upon delicate questions." Macaulay was naturally much vexed and so writes to Napier at some length, but he yielded to the imperious Brougham. [117]

[114] "Recollections of an Atlantic Editorship," *Atlantic Monthly*, November, 1907, 100: 594–606.

[115] *My Life's Pilgrimage*, p. 161.

[116] The correspondence on this point between Napier and J. R. M'Culloch is given in *Correspondence of Macvey Napier*, pp. 73–76.

[117] *Correspondence of Macvey Napier*, pp. 82–83, 88–94.

Another long controversy ensued over the question of whether Brougham or Macaulay should write an article on Chatham for the *Edinburgh*. Napier wrote Brougham who sent the article, "I know, however, I shall be blamed (but not by Macaulay himself) for taking the subject out of his hands, and that this article will be cited as another proof of what is frequently dinned in my ears,—my supposed subsurviency to your wishes." Brougham testily replied, "That he [Macaulay] has any better right to monopolize Lord Chatham, I more than doubt. That he would have done it better, I also doubt:" and he begs Napier "to pluck up a little courage, and not be alarmed every time any of the little knot of threateners annoy you. *They want to break off all kind of connection between me and the Edinburgh Review. I have long seen it.*" And he again fretfully writes Napier, "I thought the act of not letting Macaulay do an article on Lord Chatham, was nothing out of the way." [118]

Dickens was also a troublesome contributor and when a reviewer of his *American Notes* [119] had represented him as having gone to America in the cause of international copyright—at this distance in time a somewhat inadequate cause for rousing ire in celestial minds—he wrote to Napier in hot and voluble haste:

"I am at a loss to divine who its author is. I *know* he read in some cut-throat American paper, this and other monstrous statements, which I could at any time have converted into sickening praise by the payment of some fifty dollars. I know that he is perfectly aware that his statement in the Review, in corroboration of these lies, would be disseminated through the whole of the United States; and that my contradiction will never be heard of. And though I care very little for the opinion of any person who will set the statement of an American editor (almost invariably an atrocious scoundrel) against my character and conduct, such as they may be; still, my sense of justice does revolt from this most cavalier and careless exhibition of me to a whole people, as a traveller under false pretences, and a disappointed intriguer. The better the acquaintance with America, the more defenceless and more inexcusable such conduct is. For I solemnly declare (and appeal to any man but the writer of this

[118] *Correspondence of Macvey Napier*, pp. 259–268.

[119] "American Notes for General Circulation, by Charles Dickens. 2 vols.," *Edinburgh Review*, January, 1843, 76: 497–522.

paper, who has travelled in that country, for confirmation of my statement) that the source from which he drew the 'information' so recklessly put forth again in England, is infinitely more obscene, disgusting, and brutal, than the very worst Sunday newspaper that has ever been printed in Great Britain."[120]

The editor's troubles with contributors have not been confined to the comparatively harmless field of literary criticism. In an article for the *Edinburgh*,[121] Brougham severely criticized the Melbourne ministry and referred to the "secretaries," and "underlings" whom the ministry had allowed to "think for it." Brougham was disaffected towards the Whigs, yet expected his strictures on the party to be printed in the *Review*, although, as Napier wrote him, "The *Edinburgh Review*, I need not tell you, ever has been attached to the Whig Party." Macaulay later protested to Napier that Brougham, "not having a single vote in either House of Parliament at his command except his own, is desirous to make the Review his organ" and "he has begun to use the word *Whig* as an epithet of reproach." [122] When later Empson was consulted in regard to reviewing a recent book of Brougham's, he wrote with asperity: "His [Brougham's] position with the party, the *Review*, and you, is sufficiently notorious to make a review in the *Edinburgh* of any work of his one of the most delicate operations possible." [123]

With change of names and dates, the troubles between editors and contributors suggested by the history of the *Edinburgh Review* are those found everywhere in the periodical press.[124] The editor feels that he is limited by the temperament of his contributors and the contributor languishes under the heavy hand of the editor. The editor must not offend the public, and the contributor must not offend the editor. With exceptions almost equal in number to those that prove the rule, the student of history must find the editor of the periodical press essentially

---

[120] *Correspondence of Macvey Napier*, p. 417. The letter is dated January 21, 1843.

[121] H. Brougham, "Newspaper Tax," *Edinburgh Review*, April, 1835, 61: 181–185.

[122] *Correspondence of Macvey Napier*, pp. 165–171, 196–214, 261–265.

[123] *Ib.*, p. 463.

[124] See companion articles on the subject: A Contributor, "Editors," and An Editor, "Contributors," in the *National Review*, June and August, 1896, 27: 505–515, 793–801.

conservative, a man with his hand on the public pulse, an observer rather than a leader, a critic rather than an initiator. The controlling desire of a great modern newspaper is to give its readers the news, and the news therefore may show progressive action, the breaking of precedents, the activities of great organizations formed to uphold righteousness and peace. The editorial of the same paper, especially if scrutinized by an editorial board, may in the same issues show in spirit a tendency to lag behind the news, to be conservative and even timid and reactionary in expressing opinions concerning the effect of the news published in its own columns.

The important questions concerning the editor center, for the historian, around his reputed control by the proprietor, the influence exerted over him by governments on the one hand and on the other hand the influence he exerts over governments, and the decline in influence of the editorial while at the same time it has improved in accuracy and definiteness of statement, in good temper, in grasp of subject and breadth of treatment, and in its general authoritativeness.

But quite apart from these large phases of his work the position of an editor may involve situations that may bring many heart-burnings, much depression of spirit, and profound discouragement and questioning as to the real importance of his work. The conscientious editor may regret that he is not reaching certain classes in society, but he may himself find no adequate explanation for it; he realizes that his editorials are not read, but he does not know whether their tone is too aggressive, or too conciliatory, too laudatory, or too sarcastic. His divergence of opinion from the opinions of his subordinates may be as troublesome as is his divergence from the views of proprietors. He may cringe before the fear of offending local interests or high officials of state and cry out with the Pious Editor,

> " I du believe in Freedom's cause
> Ez fur away ez Payris is." [125]

He may be the champion of a dying cause as was Paul de Cassagnac who upheld the Empire and opposed the Republic until his death in 1904.[126] The editor may support an apparently

---

[125] J. R. Lowell, "The Pious Editor's Creed," *Biglow Papers*, Number VI.
[126] New York *Evening Post*, November 19, 1904.

hopeless cause and at last see it win, as Madame Adam long promoted the policy of *revanche* as a means of securing the return of Alsace-Lorraine to France.[127]

"The Editor is doomed," says a recent writer, "for the public will pay for news, and not for notions." [128]

The editor may be doomed, but his problems still persist and will not down. The names and the times of editors might at any period be exchanged for those quite otherwise and the same troubles would still confront him,—differences in degree and differences in constituencies would not alter the basic situation. Leslie Stephen has shown that in the eighteenth century Defoe considered that the journal "supplied the initiative and leverage for all movements of political and social reform;" that Addison and Steele tried to be independent of patrons and to reflect the opinions of those about them; that Steele believed in "strong writing;" that Swift was indifferent to patronage; that Cobbett appealed to the masses; and that Leigh Hunt made journalism literature.

But in 1810 the Reverend James Beresford wrote *The Twelve Labours of an Editor, separately pitted against those of Hercules.* The first three of these labors he found to be "beating the devouring critic," "overcoming innumerable errors," and "grasping the meaning of his author." He found that "the editor . . . is to be regarded as the Enemy, and Avenger of the anti-social Passions, under their two main divisions—those of *open, brutal, Fury;* and *deadly, poisonous malice.*" Another labor of the editor was pouring "his river of reformation through every contaminated stall and stye." He was to draw his "goose-quill upon the *men,* and welcome; but—*let* THE LADIES alone!" And his final labor was to expose evil.—Have the problems of the editor conspicuously changed since they were thus stated more than a century ago?

But the editorial at least is not doomed, and it takes on a new lease of life, although not necessarily of influence, as new forms of increasing its circulation are devised. Not only are the editorials of a single editor and the editorials from a single news-

[127] Winifred Stephens, *Madame Adam.*
[128] *Bohemian Days in Fleet Street,* p. 298.

paper collected and published in book form, but the editorials of one paper are reprinted on the editorial pages of other papers, they are reprinted as advertisements, they are copied in the news columns of the press, and they are collectively copied in an effort to secure a consensus of public opinion on important questions.

In a collection recently made of the editorials and various notes contributed to the *Syracuse Journal* during the years 1863–1865 by the late Willard Fiske, the editor of the volume expresses the hope that through them "incidentally a partial glimpse may be afforded of a standard American newspaper half a century ago." [129] Not only does this particular volume fulfil the hopes of its editor, but it shows that, in spite of all the transformations the editorial has undergone, to its readers the editorial is "the paper."

[129] H. S. White, *Memorials of Willard Fiske*, I, p. xv.

CHAPTER XII

CRITICISM AND THE CRITIC

"Apart from the publication of 'news' and reports, and occasional original articles of a descriptive and miscellaneous character, the chief function of a newspaper is criticism, whether of politics or other topics of the moment, or of the drama, art, music, books, sport or finance."— *H. Chisholm.*

The office of the critic "is mainly to ascertain facts and traits of literature, not to invent or denounce them; to discover principles, not to establish them; to report, not to create."—*W. D. Howells.*

"Literary criticism in France, by its catholicity, by the co-operation and continuity of its schools, has become the most authoritative and influential of the civilized world."—*E. Wright.*

"Telle que je l'entends et que vous me la laissez faire, la critique est, comme la philosophie et l'histoire, une espèce de roman à l'usage des esprits avisés et curieux, et tout roman, à le bien prendre, est une auto-biographie. Le bon critique est celui qui raconte les aventures de son âme au milieu des chefs d'œuvre."—*Anatole France.*

THE attitude the historian should assume towards criticism and the use he should make of the work of the critic in the periodical press is a troublesome problem. It is complicated by the varying and even contradictory standards of criticism that have prevailed in different countries at different times, and even in the same country at the same time. The historian is often confronted not only by an apparent lack of standards of criticism but he is also often met by a positive disbelief in the value of standards on the part of critics themselves. From the time of Aristotle down there has been no consensus of opinion as to the nature and functions of criticism,—a difference of opinion in part explained by different national ideals that have varied from generation to generation, in part by the develop-ment of schools of criticism in one country and by the entire lack of such schools in other countries, in part by the inevitable personal differences of opinion among the leaders of criticism.

One critic flings to the winds all previous standards of criticism,[1] while the belief that standards do and must exist is the leading thesis in the reasoned analysis of criticism given by another.[2] Carlyle believed that the critic's first and foremost duty is to make plain to himself, "what the poet's aim really and truly was, how the task he had to do stood before his eye, and how far, with such materials as were afforded him, he had fulfilled it," and he indignantly writes of the British reviewers of Goethe, "For what, after all, were their portraits of him but copies, with some retouchings and ornamental appendages, of our grand English original Picture of the German generally?—In itself such a piece of art, as national portraits, under like circumstances, are wont to be; and resembling Goethe, as some unusually expressive Sign of the Saracen's Head may resemble the present Sultan of Constantinople!"[3]

Matthew Arnold, with his fastidious distaste of everything savoring of Philistinism, writes of the *"aggressive* manner in literature" that prevails in newspapers, due to the provincial spirit that characterizes both literature and the press, and he explains it by saying: "The French talk of the *brutalité des journaux anglais.* What strikes them comes from the necessary inherent tendencies of newspaper-writing not being checked in England by any centre of intelligent and urbane spirit, but rather stimulated by coming in contact with a provincial spirit."[4]

Yet Matthew Arnold's theory of criticism as being "the art of seeing the object as in itself it really is" is a negative conception as compared with that of Irving Babbitt who finds that "to study the chief French critics of the nineteenth century is to get very close to the intellectual centre of the age,"[5] and that "the chief problem of criticism, namely, the search for standards to oppose to individual caprice, is also the chief problem of contemporary thought in general."[6]

[1] J. E. Spingarn, *The New Criticism*, 1911.
[2] W. C. Brownell, *Criticism*, 1914.
[3] "Goethe," *Foreign Review*, No. 3, 1828; *Critical and Miscellaneous Essays*, I, 198–257.
[4] "The Literary Influence of Academies," *Essays in Criticism First Series*, pp. 66–67.
[5] *The Masters of Modern French Criticism*, p. xi.
[6] *Ib.*, p. 368.

These variations and even positive disagreements as to the nature and function of criticism seem to indicate the tendency of each generation to discard the standards of previous generations.[7] The very title *The New Laokoon* given by Irving Babbitt to his recent work on criticism indicates that a change has come in standards of criticism since Lessing published his *Laokoon* in 1766,—a work that for more than a hundred years was read by successive generations of college students presumably as the final word in criticism. A further change is indicated in the spirit with which criticism is approached in that *The New Laokoon* is described by its author as "an inquiry into the nature of the *genres* and the boundaries of the arts" and as an effort "not to achieve a complete and closed system, but to scatter the *fermenta cognitionis.*" [8]

Bliss Perry is in fundamental agreement with D'Indy who considers it axiomatic that "tout art non basé sur la tradition est un art frappé de mort," and he upholds the discipline of tradition since it provides a "reasoned insight into some of the deeper laws of human life." [9]

The historian therefore in weighing the value for his purposes of the criticism found in the periodical press recognizes the instability of all criticism due to changing standards and the unconscious conflict carried on at all times, as Trent has pointed out,[10] between the conservative teachers of criticism and the individualistic methods of individual critics and reporters. He knows that criticism has always taken on the spirit of its age,— at one time it is impressionistic, at another academic; again it is ordered and reasoned, and again it is radical and revolutionary; and that in his search for the ideal critic he must accept the judgment of Irving Babbitt when he says that the ideal critic "would need to combine the breadth and versatility and sense

---

[7] D. Klein writes to prove that the Elizabethan playwrights rejected the authority of the ancients, that throughout the Elizabethan age there was a growth of a large critical consciousness among the dramatists, and that "the luxuriant overflow of Elizabethan dramatic literature was accomplished by a criticial consciousness which became more prevalent and definite as time went on."—*Elizabethan Criticism*, pp. 211, 220, 245.

[8] *The New Laokoon*, p. 252.

[9] "The Disciplined Heart," *Yale Review*, July, 1918, 7: 869–872.

[10] W. P. Trent, *The Authority of Criticism and Other Essays.*

of differences of a Sainte-Beuve with the elevation and insight and sense of unity of an Emerson. It might be prudent to add of this critic in particular what Emerson has said of man in general, that he is a golden impossibility. But even though the full attainment of our standard should prove impossible, some progress might at least be made towards tempering with judgment the all-pervading impressionism of contemporary literature and life." [11]

Must then the student of the periodical press sit idly down and say that as regards criticism it availeth not for the purposes of the historian? This conclusion does not necessarily follow from the foregoing brief statement of varying theories of criticism; it does follow that no part of the press demands a more careful analysis than do all the component parts that make up its body of criticism, no part stands in greater need of caution before accepting it without question.

A large part of the criticism of the press has always dealt with literature. The first English literary periodical appeared as far back as 1680, but it seems to have been scarcely more than a catalogue of books appearing from month to month. It was *The History of the Works of the Learned* that, for England, in 1699, ushered in the era of literary criticism, and it is of interest and profit to note its platform:

"We shall be very sparing of our Censures, as remembring our Province is that of Historians and not of Criticks: But at the same time, when any Books are published relating to our Civil Constitution or the Established Religion, and are so much taken notice of in the World, that an Account of them will be expected from us, we hope freedom may be allowed us to express our own Sentiments, so far as to show, that we are not Promoters or Incouragers of Works that tend to make Innovations in either.

[11] *The Masters of Modern French Criticism*, p. 392.
The author in this work gives a list of one hundred and thirty-four critics, with characterizations of many and the chief events in their lives, together with the titles of the works of each. The "list makes no claim to completeness" but is "aimed to record with some fulness the works of the more important writers who are primarily literary critics."—*The Masters of Modern French Criticism*, pp. 395–419.
J. E. Spingarn gives a chronological table of the chief critical works of the sixteenth century.—*A History of Literary Criticism in the Renaissance*, pp. 332–333.

We think fit likewise to assure the Reader, That we shall be so far from giving an Account of Books that are Trifling, or contrary to good Manners, that we will not so much as mention their Titles.

Then, as to the Management of the Work in general, it is our design to keep a Medium betwixt tedious Extracts, and superficial Catalogues, made up only of Title and Preface; the former being tiresom to the Reader, as well as injurious to the Sale of the Books; and the latter being a meer Imposition on the Publick. Therefore we shall take particular care to give such an Account of Books, as the Reader may thence be able to form a perfect Idea of the Design, Method and Principal Topicks insisted upon by the Authors." [12]

It is evident that this standard of perfection set up in 1699 includes principles of literary reviewing that have had a fluctuating acceptance, as it also suggests some of the stumbling blocks that have always been found in the path of both reviewer and publishers. The great English reviews in particular have in a measure been controlled by their publishers rather than by their editors; they have sometimes been concerned not to give offence to the authorities of church and state and they have noted the effect on sales of adverse criticism of books. Literary criticism is indeed not altogether the simple matter it is often assumed to be; it covers the whole field from advance notices sent out by publishers and continued on jacket covers [13] to the more permanent and more genuine criticism of the great critical quarterly reviews. It involves not only the points anticipated by the virtuous publishers of the *History of the Works of the Learned*, but it has a history of its own, the main points of which must be familiar to those using criticism and the book review as historical material.

[12] The Preface of *The History of the Works of the Learned: or, An Impartial Account of Books Lately Printed in all Parts of Europe. With a Particular Relation of the State of Learning In each Country.* Done by several Hands. For the Month of January, 1699.

Cave, some years later, in his Introduction to the *Gentleman's Magazine,* proposed "to give monthly a view of all the pieces of wit, humour, or intelligence, daily offered to the Public in the Newspapers," and to "join therewith some other matters of use or amusement that will be communicated to us."

[13] Louis Untermeyer, "Paper-Jacket Problems," *The Dial,* June 20, 1918, 65: 20–22.

The proposed rejection by an important periodical as early as 1699 of reviews that through their tediousness might interfere with the sale of books opened but did not close a question that still will not down. There has always been a suspicion that publishers look with kindly eye on all periodicals giving favorable notices of their publications,[14] and the suspicion becomes certainty in the case of publishers who are rivals. Walter Scott wrote to Sharpe, December 30, 1808, apropos of the *Quarterly* that was intended as a rival to the *Edinburgh* that "if it contains criticism not very inferior [to the *Edinburgh*] in point of talent, with the same independence of booksellers' influence (which has ruined all the English Reviews), I do not see why it should not divide with it the public favor." [15] Brougham was sure that his connection with the *Edinburgh Review* boded ill for a fair criticism of his recent book and he wrote to James Loch, June 19, 1803, "The reviews will all murder me on acct. of the *E. Rev.*, and it is unlucky enough that my connection with the latter prevents all possibility of justice being done me there." [16]

Henry Coburn, under date of December 31, 1827, wrote to William Jerdan, then editing the *Literary Gazette*, that he was about to be connected with the *Athenaeum* "in consequence of the injustice done to *my authors* generally (who are on a liberal side), by the '*Literary Gazette*'. I cannot any longer consent to see my best authors unfairly reviewed, and my own property injured, and often sacrificed to the politics of that paper." [17] Jerdan himself, although thus rebuked, questions whether any journal can be carried on with perfect freedom and uninfluenced by any outward circumstances,—personal regard and attachment, literary connections, and friendly interferences must have an effect in enhancing praise, and moderating blame; "and, in a baser manner, rivalry, envy, and malignity will, in some instances,

[14] Edward Bulwer says that Voltaire complained that booksellers in France and Holland guided the tone of the periodical reviews.—*England and the English*, II, 18. Note.

[15] *Letters from and to C. K. Sharpe*, I, 351.

[16] R. H. M. B. Atkinson and G. A. Jackson, *Brougham and His Early Friends*, II, 67–70.

[17] William Jerdan, *Autobiography*, IV, 68.

The courts have sometimes been called on to decide questions involving adverse criticism.

have the opposite effect in producing damning faint praise, or undue commendation, and abusive censure." [18]

The quarterly, the monthly, and the weekly were the accepted mediums for the review and it was apparently long before it found a permanent place in the daily press. Jerdan writes of "commencing a regular literary review of new publications in the pages of the 'Sun' (a pattern at length followed in every quarter)," and that "the war [with Napoleon] being again over, the 'Sun' Literary Reviews recommenced with increased energy" and he complacently hopes that his readers will not deny him the praise to which he aspires "of having most unequivocally led the way to these combinations in the periodical press, commingling the arts and literature with the news and politics of the hour . . . which [has] been the fruitful source of the universal newspaper system of the present day." [19] Even half a century later Catling, entrusted with the reviewing department of the *Daily Chronicle*, wrote that at first publishers were so shy that he "had to go round and ask for new books; some even then declined to send any but cheap publications." [20]

The first distinction that the historian must make is therefore between the characteristics of the reviews as found in the dailies, the weeklies, the monthlies, and the quarterlies.

Downey writes that in the early "eighties," the daily papers thought themselves fairly generous if they gave a column or two a week to notices of current literature. " 'Reviewing' (as a branch of journalism) used to be almost the last infirmity of noble mind." [21] The tendency to-day is for the dailies to give brief publishers' notices, not criticism in any true sense.

"The *rôle* of a weekly critic," *The Nation* in its early days found, "is, after all a very humble one. It is to examine the

[18] William Jerdan, *Autobiography*, IV, 82.
This complaint also will not down. Admiral Maxse says that Kinglake wrote him "a glowing tribute in a letter which I have by me," but that he himself "for one who sought distinction" did a foolish thing,—he criticized Kinglake's first two volumes rather severely in a magazine. "When he had occasion to mention me in his fourth volume the tribute had cooled down to a very commonplace reference. Of such stuff are historians made!"—"The War Correspondent at Bay," *National Review*, April, 1899, 33: 246–253.
[19] *Autobiography*, II, 22, 51–52.
[20] *My Life's Pilgrimage*, pp. 143–144.
[21] Edmund Downey, *Twenty Years Ago*, p. 279.

fields from which it finds the community drawing its mental food, and to point out, to the best of its ability, what those fields produce—what is bad and what is good; what had better be tasted, what digested, and what thrown away; to keep before the public the best standard in every department, and point out departures from it, according to the critic's understanding of it." [22]

The monthlies have for the most part paid comparatively little attention to criticism,[23] and it is to the quarterlies that in general, especially in the early days of serious reviewing, the historian must turn for information in regard to the reception accorded new works of literature. How far can he accept the contemporary verdict of the critic as authoritative and final?

It must be said that much of the criticism of the nineteenth century, especially that through the first half, and especially that of the quarterlies, was characterized by personal abuse and private hostility, and was lacking in nearly every characteristic that is now associated with genuine literary criticism. The critics indeed took themselves and their work most seriously. Sydney Smith gives the reasons that led him and other young enthusiasts to found the *Edinburgh Review* in 1802 and he explains that to appreciate its value "the state of England at the period when that journal began should be had in remembrance,"— all the manifold abuses and the thousand evils that were in existence in English political and social conditions were to be lessened or removed by the new review.[24] Yet even so, Harriet Martineau, in speaking of these young men who had projected the *Edinburgh Review*, feels that "there is no doubt that these young advocates of freedom indulged in much tyranny, and the most vehement denouncers of oppression inflicted dreadful pain," and she cites Romilly as saying: "The editors seem to

---

[22] "Our Literature and Our Critics," *The Nation*, March 1, 1866, 2: 266–267.
[23] *The Paisley Magazine*, for example, commented in 1828 on "the fierce invasion with which Magazines now threaten Reviews," and notes that "Magazines have been obliged thus to come into collision with Reviews,"— a situation to be deprecated since "reviewers are the caterpillars of literature. . . . Critics they are not."—"Magazines and Reviews," April, 1828, 1: 169–179.
[24] *Works of Sydney Smith*, Preface.

value themselves principally upon their severity; and they have reviewed some works seemingly with no other object than to show what their powers in this particular line of criticism are." [25] She elsewhere returns again to the subject and with deep conviction writes: "Neither its authors nor the public then perceived how false and dangerous is the very principle of such a work— of a small established corps of men undertaking to pronounce on works in regard to each one of which the reviewer is, probably, less competent than the author, who is most likely to know more of his subject than those who have studied it less. The failure to perceive this, and the virulence of tone natural to young men who felt themselves under a political and social ban, made the great Review a receptacle of unjust judgments and indefensible tempers." [26]

It was not in any sense a caricature of critics that Thackeray drew when he wrote, apropos of Pendennis, "The courage of young critics is prodigious; they clamber up to the judgment-seat, and, with scarce a hesitation, give their opinion upon works the most intricate or profound."

Unfortunately, the spirit of tyranny has not been confined to youth and the periodical reviews of the nineteenth century show how largely the personal element entered into the criticism of

[25] Harriet Martineau, "Lord Brougham," *Biographical Sketches*, pp. 392–402.

James Stephen wrote to Napier, December 26, 1842, "We have no right to be angry [over criticism] for, to this day, the blisters raised by Sydney Smith's caustic pen are unhealed."—*Napier Correspondence*, p. 414.

[26] *Introduction to the History of the Peace*, I, cccciii.

Lord Morley has aptly said that reviewers are in a position similar to that of a judge before whom is argued a patent right case or a suit about rubrics or vestments.—"Valedictory," *Fornightly Review*, October, 1882, n. s. 32: 511–521.

There may be some ground for the general feeling of authors that critics do not do them justice and often criticize the vestments rather than render a decision in the question involving their use. But Lord Morley himself gives an interesting illustration of the sympathy that may exist between author and reviewer. As a young man he had reviewed *Les Travailleurs de la Mer* in the *Saturday Review* and Victor Hugo wrote the editor a letter of warm appreciation in which he says: "C'est là une page de haute et profonde critique. Jamais livre n'a été analysé avec plus de pénétration. L'auteur de l'article s'est assimilé toute la philosophie de l'œuvre qu'il a si admirablement compris." Lord Morley's comment is,—"It is easy to believe how a young apprentice in criticism was encouraged in his new calling."—*Recollections*, I, 74.

the period. If at an earlier date the *Quarterly Review* mercilessly attacked Keats and Leigh Hunt, at a later period the *Saturday Review* turned its guns on all things American. If Macaulay found that Croker's edition of *Boswell's Life of Johnson* had "greatly disappointed" him; that it was "ill compiled, ill arranged, ill written, and ill printed;" if "nothing in the work has astonished [him] so much as the ignorance or carelessness of Mr. Croker with respect to facts and dates;" if he insists that the editor "shows almost as much ignorance and heedlessness in his criticisms as in his statements concerning facts;" if he laments that "the delicate office which Mr. Croker has undertaken he has performed in the most capricious manner;" [27] Macaulay learned later that Croker's memory was a long one. He found, in his turn, that Mr. Croker's hope of enjoying "unalloyed the pleasures reasonably to be expected from Mr. Macaulay's high powers both of research and illustration" "has been deceived;" that Macaulay's *History of England* [28] was "full of political prejudice and partisan advocacy;" that "there is hardly a page that does not contain something objectionable either in substance or in color;" that it is "impregnated to a really marvellous degree with bad taste, bad feeling, and" he is "under the painful necessity of adding—bad faith;" and that "Mr. Macaulay's pages are as copious a repertorium of vituperative eloquence as our language can produce." Macaulay has explained through forty pages why Croker's work has "greatly disappointed" him and Croker explains in eighty pages why his "hope has been deceived."

Such were the amenities of literary criticism in the *Edinburgh* and the *Quarterly* in the censorious "thirties" and "forties." Well may a publisher of many such reviews cry out in despair when writing of the "Magazine which has involved every one connected with it in alternate anxiety, disgrace, and misery." [29]

Contemporary criticism in America was scarcely more amicable

---

[27] *Edinburgh Review*, September, 1831, 54: 1–38.
[28] *Quarterly Review*, March, 1849, 84: 549–630.
[29] John Murray, Letter to Thomas Blackwood, Mrs. Oliphant, *Annals of a Publishing House*, I, 173.
R. B. Johnson, in *Famous Reviews*, pp. xi–xii, has collected some of the most caustic criticisms of criticism and critics.

or reasonable. The mutual relations of Poe and Griswold are still under discussion and the pros and cons of the controversy well illustrate how far that period was from a genuine theory of criticism.[30] The controversy must also illustrate of how comparatively little service to the historian is, in and of itself, the literary criticism of the periodical literature of that day. The situation was scarcely improved when later an eminent connoisseur of literature could imply that criticism is to be tempered by the temporal distress of the person whose work is to be reviewed.[31] Even in France where the high-water mark of criticism has been reached, it was possible for an eminent Frenchman to be credited with discriminating against Sainte-Beuve as a critic on the ground that "he was not a gentleman." [32]

It is evident that the historian must also take into account the personal characteristics of the periodical in which the review appears. The *Edinburgh Review* under the influence of Francis Jeffrey, who was its editor for twenty-seven years and contributed to it for nearly forty-six years, apparently made it a point of honor to find little worthy of commendation in any of the works submitted to it for review.[33] The *Quarterly Review* did not

[30] W. M. Griswold, *Passages from the Correspondence of Rufus W. Griswold; Graham's Magazine* during the editorship of both Griswold and Poe.

[31] J. T. Fields, "To a Malignant Critic,' *Poems*, pp. 119–120.—It is possible that this is only a legitimate protest against spiteful criticism, though the poem itself does not indicate it.
Akin to this is the implication that works by unknown authors are to be neglected. W. C. Bryant wrote R. W. Griswold in 1852 commending the poetry of a friend of Griswold's but adds, "Yet I doubt its success with the public if it appears as Mr. Hetherwold's. I fully believe that the best verses in the world published in a volume by an author not yet known to fame, would be inevitably neglected."—*Correspondence of R. W. Griswold*, p. 282.

[32] "Le hasard m'a fait un jour assister à une discussion animée entre gens qui comparaient, au point de vue de la valeur morale, Sainte-Beuve avec Mérimée. La controverse était vive: les uns tenaient pour Mérimée, les autres pour Sainte-Beuve. Tout à coup un des interlocuteurs, qui avait gardé jusque-là (et ce n'était guère son habitude) un profond silence, s'écria en commençant à arpenter la chambre à grands pas: 'Savez-vous la véritable supériorité de Mérimée sur Sainte-Beuve? Je vais vous la dire: Mérimée est gentilhomme, Sainte-Beuve n'est pas gentilhomme.' Je n'aurais jamais osé traduire ma pensée sous une forme aussi aristocratique, si je n'avais entendu tomber ce jugement de la bouche de M. Cousin."—G. P. O. d'Haussonville, *C. A. Sainte-Beuve—sa vie et ses œuvres*, pp. 334–335.

[33] Samuel Smiles says benignly of the *Edinburgh:* "In its early days the criticism was rude, and wanting in delicate insight; for the most part too dictatorial, and often unfair. . . . Jeffrey could never appreciate the merits

make matters much better for those whose works it reviewed and it condemned the works of Keats [34] and Leigh Hunt as scathingly as the *Edinburgh* had condemned another school of poets. Nor did *Blackwood's* spare its venom in dealing with those of whom it disapproved,[35] and it apparently justified its remorseless criticism on the ground that it was "good business" and lengthened the list of subscribers,[36] while in the same breath disclaiming the charge of personality in its criticism.[37]

The reviewer himself becomes the subject of review on the part of more or less unfriendly critics. "Jeffrey was twitted to

---

of Wordsworth, Southey, and Coleridge. 'This will never do!' was the commencement of his review of Wordsworth's noblest poem!"—*A Publisher and His Friends*, I, 91–92.

Jeffrey's contemporaries were not disposed to take the matter so calmly. Miss Seward wrote to Scott, "Jefferies ought to have been his name. Ignorance and envy are the only possible parents of such criticisms as disgrace the publication which assumes the name of your city."—*Ib.*, p. 92.

A long-distance view does not make matters better for the *Edinburgh* and Jeffrey. A recent critic finds that "he frequently treated authors very much as though they were guilty prisoners at the bar, and he the judge upon the bench, wearing the black cap and about to pronounce sentence of execution. . . . The solemnity and finality of his sentence of literary death pronounced upon Wordsworth, can hardly be surpassed."—E. L. Pearson, *Book-Reviews*, p. 18.

[34] Byron in *Don Juan* gave currency to the rumor that the adverse criticism of *Endymion* in the *Quarterly* caused Keats' death, and although informed to the contrary by Leigh Hunt, persisted in printing the statement. —S. Smiles, *A Publisher and His Friends*, I, 481–482.

[35] John Murray became half owner of *Blackwood's*, but from the first protested against its slashing criticisms and its personalities. This protest was unavailing and he finally severed his connection with the magazine on this ground.—S. Smiles, I, chap. XVIII.

S. Smiles entitles his memoir of John Murray *A Publisher and His Friends*, but Murray was so constantly harassed by his relations with the *Edinburgh*, the *Quarterly*, and *Blackwood's* through their acrimonious criticisms of writers and public men that the title seems a misnomer.

[36] The editor, John Wilson, in an article "An Hour's Tête-à-tête with the Public," boasted that while the *Quarterly* had a circulation of about 14,000 and the *Edinburgh* of upwards of 7,000, it was the intention of the editors not to allow the circulation of *Blackwood's* to go above 17,000.—*Blackwood's Magazine*, October, 1820, 8: 78–105.

[37] Blackwood had constantly replied to the expostulations of Murray that no one hated personalities more than he himself did, and that he had done his best to have the editors avoid them.

It is interesting to note that the late E. L. Godkin felt that before American criticism could merit the name it would have to pass through this stormy and belligerent stage like that of English criticism during the first quarter of the nineteenth century.—"Critics and Criticism," *Critical and Social Essays*, pp. 11–18.

the most tedious extent with his 'This will never do!'"—the "byword of critical cocksureness" with which he opened his review of Wordsworth's *The Excursion*;[38] Lockhart was called "the Scorpion which delighteth to sting the faces of men;" [39] Gifford attacked his contemporaries and was in turn read a well-deserved lesson thereon by Hazlitt;[40] Croker was known "above all, perhaps, as the wickedest of reviewers,—that is, as the author of the foul and false political articles in the *Quarterly Review*, which stand out as the disgrace of the periodical literature of our time," [41] although a recent critic awards to Gifford the first place for establishing the reputation of the *Quarterly Review* for scurrility;[42] Macaulay has been deemed "inhuman in insisting on the republication of poor Satan Montgomery's poems. It is a pity that he did not live to read Fitzjames Stephen's examination of his *Life of Warren Hastings*. It might have taught him mercy;" [43] Spedding through nineteen evenings criticizes Macaulay's review of Montagu's edition of the *Works of Francis Bacon*, taking up the review almost paragraph by paragraph in order to show how the ostensible review of Montagu is really made the excuse for an elaborate discussion of Bacon's career and that it suited Macaulay to use Montagu's facts in order to overthrow his theory.[44]

[38] *Edinburgh Review*, November, 1814, 24: 1–30.

[39] Mrs. Oliphant, *Annals of a Publishing House*, I, 194.

[40] "Letter to William Gifford," *Collected Works of William Hazlitt*, I, 365–411.

[41] Harriet Martineau, "John Wilson Croker," *Biographical Sketches*, 60–69.

[42] E. L. Pearson, *Book-Reviews*, pp. 20–21.

[43] Goldwin Smith, *Reminiscences*, p. 167.

Sir James Fitzjames Stephen speaks of his "affectionate admiration" for Macaulay who was his own friend, his father's friend, and his grandfather's friend, and that as he was also Macaulay's successor in office he was "better able than most persons to appreciate the splendour of the services which he rendered to India." Sir James is therefore anxious to repair if possible a wrong unintentionally done by Macaulay "because he adopted on insufficient grounds the traditional hatred which the Whigs bore to Impey, and also because his marvellous power of style blinded him to the effect which his language produced."—*The Story of Nuncomar and the Impeachment of Sir Elijah Impey*, I, 3.

Leslie Stephen in his life of his brother gives a full account of the publication of this work in which Sir James made "mince-meat of Macaulay's most famous essay."—*The Life of Sir James Fitzjames Stephen*, pp. 428–436.

[44] James Spedding, *Evenings with a Reviewer, or Macaulay and Bacon*, 2 vols.

These illustrations in the history of criticism have been suggested in order to indicate that distrust of criticism, especially as applied to current literature, has been deep-seated and of long duration. The historian in his use of criticism as found in the periodical press must seek the explanation of this distrust; he must attempt to ascertain how far this distrust is well founded before he is justified in using criticism in his efforts to reconstruct the past.

Several elements have discredited the criticisms of literature, and one of these is that the review has not always stood the test of time;[45] books of genuine merit have been passed by without notice, while "the best seller" has been extravagantly praised and then quickly forgotten. For this situation the publisher rather than the newspaper must largely be held accountable, yet a certain amount of blame must be attached to the press. The desire to secure and to keep the advertisements of publishing houses, as has been suggested, may quite unconsciously affect the reviews of the books coming from their presses and give to the author the benefit of the doubt in the case of mediocre works. The newspaper itself becomes uncritical of its own reviewers and throws upon them the responsibility of adverse or of favorable criticism, reserving to itself only the right of interfering when business interests are affected.

The review has been discredited because in the hands of some of the most famous reviewers it has been made the instrument of exploiting the superior knowledge of the reviewer. It has been discredited because excessive amiability on the part of an over-sympathetic reviewer has led to undue appreciation of the work of young writers or of personal friends, while, on the other hand, the vindictive review has been used as a means of "getting even" with writers with whose views or personal characteristics the reviewer is out of sympathy.

The book review is discredited because it is written on the

[45] "The *Quarterly Review* once despised everybody who could stop to notice Landor's faults, and eloquently described the process of the elevation of his fame, till it should become transcendent among the worthies of England; but it may be questioned whether the *Quarterly Review* has any more expectation than the *Edinburgh* that the writings of Landor will survive, except as curiosities of literature."—Harriet Martineau, "Walter Savage Landor," *Biographical Sketches*, pp. 121-129.

one hand in the language of the promoter or on the other in meaningless stock phrases that indicate poverty of ideas;[46] it is discredited because the reviewer is too often "garrulous, philosophical, opinionated, indolent, untrained, and poorly paid"; it is discredited because the reviews are often confessedly written in haste and bear internal evidence of the truth of the confession;[47] it is discredited because of the editor's shortness of memory;[48] it is discredited because often made an excuse of displaying the

[46] Some of these phrases are: "the book is welcome," "it is stimulating," "it is suggestive," "it furnishes capital reading," "it has the charm of Stevenson;" "the author is the American Maupassant," or "an American Dickens," or, "a new Mark Twain."—"Book Reviewing à la Mode," *The Nation*, August 17, 1911, 93: 139–140.

[47] "I have heard the editor of a scientific paper boast that he had dictated, in sixty minutes, reviews of eleven new scientific books, not one of which he had taken the trouble to read beyond the preface and the table of contents." —Bliss Perry, "Literary Criticism in American Periodicals," *Yale Review*, July, 1914, 3: 635–655.

"I reckon that on the average I review a book and a fraction of a book every day of my life, Sundays included."—Arnold Bennett, *The Truth about an Author*, p. 135. The author defends this on the ground that he is an expert and therefore able to do it.

H. S. Edwards says that when Edward Tinsley opened a second-hand book shop in London the proprietors of a morning paper arranged to send him all the books sent them for review "and to keep up their value the reviewers were specially cautioned not to cut the leaves!"—*Personal Recollections*, p. 136.

"The critical Reviewers, I believe, often review without reading the book through; but lay hold of a topick, and write chiefly from their own minds. The Monthly Reviewers are duller men, and are glad to read the books through."—S. Johnson, *Boswell's Life*, II, 24 (*Everyman's Library*).

The charge that reviewers do not read the books they affect to criticize was current when Gifford reviewed *Endymion* in the *Quarterly*, April, 1818.

[48] B. L. Gildersleeve notes the cases where the editor forgets to whom he has sent the volume of a book first published and sends the subsequent volumes elsewhere,—the reviews are necessarily different in tone.—"The Hazards of Reviewing," *The Nation*, July 8, 1915, 101: 49–51.

Walter Besant cites a novel that "was praised to the skies one week and slated pitilessly a few weeks later *in the same weekly!*"—*Autobiography*, p. 193.

J. M. Barrie reverses this incident and makes use of it in *When a Man's Single*.

The London *Times* within a few weeks gave two distinct reviews of a book of Felix Whitehurst's,—"the first review was not very good, but the second was very good indeed."—W. Tinsley, *Random Recollections*, I, 91.

R. Bagot says that a London paper published a "very flattering review" of one of his novels and a few days later another review of the same novel "than which nothing could have been more depreciatory."—"The Reviewing of Fiction," *Nineteenth Century and After*, February, 1906, 59: 288–297.

erudition of the critic;[49] it is discredited because it is too often
made the vehicle of personal ill will and even spite;[50] it is discredited because "the ordinary editor is blameworthy [in] that
he takes no care to keep out of his paper the personal element.
He allows the log-roller to praise his own friends and the spiteful
and envious failure to abuse his enemies;"[51] it is discredited
because many able journalists refuse to write reviews;[52] it is
discredited because of the presence on the press of "sham critics"
who use their position to serve their own ends;[53] it is discredited
because, in the general press, book reviews tend to be the work
of hack reviewers rather than of specialists as in the case of music
or of sports;[54] it is discredited because of the somewhat well-

[49] "He [Delane] would complain if a review were full only of small points
of detail and contained 'no such general summing up of the book as the
public would naturally expect.' He thought that the business of a daily
newspaper was to give news; that a book was a form of news; that a notice
of it should give the views of the author as well as those of his reviewer.
He had no use, in *The Times* at least, for the kind of review which aims
primarily at displaying the airs and graces of the critic."—Sir Edward Cook,
Delane of "The Times," p. 186.

[50] Harriet Martineau says of Croker's virulence: "That malignant ulcer
of the mind, engendered by political disappointment, at length absorbed his
better qualities. It is necessary to speak thus frankly of the temper of the
man, because his statements must in justice be discredited; and because
justice requires that the due discrimination be made between the honorable
and generous-minded men who ennoble the function of criticism by the
spirit they throw into it, and one who, like Croker, employed it at last for
the gratification of his own morbid inclination to inflict pain."

He declared, when Lord Grey came into office, . . . that he should make
his income by "tomahawking" liberal authors in the *Quarterly*. "He wrote
articles about them, but also interpolated other persons' articles with his
own sarcasms and slanders, so as to compel the real reviewers, in repeated
instances to demand the republication of their articles in a genuine state and
a separate form."—Harriet Martineau, "John Wilson Croker," *Biographical
Sketches*, 60–69.

[51] Sir Walter Besant, *Autobiography*, p. 194.

[52] Francis Power Cobbe writes: "The pain and deadly injury I have seen
inflicted by a severe review is a form of cruelty for which I have no predilec-
tion. It is necessary, no doubt, in the literary community that there should
be warders and executioners at the public command to birch juvenile
offenders, and flog garrotters, and hang anarchists; but I have never felt
any vocation for those disagreeable offices."—*Life*, II, 400.

[53] "The difference between the sham critic and the real critic is that the
latter shows the reader how to look first for the intention of the book, and
next how to examine into the method employed in carrying out that intention."—Sir Walter Besant, *Autobiography*, p. 182. The general subject of
"Critics and Criticasters" is considered, *ib.*, pp. 180–197.

[54] R. C. Holliday, "The Hack Reviewer," *The Unpopular Review*, April–
June, 1916, 5: 379–391.

grounded suspicion of the connection between the business manager and the reviewer.[55]

This is indeed a veritable Homeric catalogue of the ships, but it is far from being all that must be said in regard to the review as trustworthy historical material. The contemporaneous review, even the best, must fail to note the elements of a book that may have the greatest value for the historian. Dickens was read and criticized by his contemporaries for the sake of the story, the descriptions, the interest in the characters, and the problems of life that he presented. But the critic of Dickens to-day would be concerned with the priceless record that he unconsciously gives of the manners and customs, social and political, of his own day. The contemporaneous review and the later review must necessarily differ, not simply because the tastes of critics and readers differ from generation to generation, but chiefly because of the varying values placed on different features. The contemporaneous review may or may not be better than the subsequent one, but it is necessarily different.[56] It is not necessarily to the disadvantage of the historian that time changes the

[55] "No publishers' advertising, no book reviews, is the policy of nearly every newspaper."—R. C. Holliday, *Unpopular Review*, April, 1916, 5:379–391.

" 'In the name of common sense, Mr. Pendennis,' Shandon asked, 'what have you been doing—praising one of Mr. Bacon's books? Bungay has been with me in a fury this morning, at seeing a laudatory article upon one of the works of the odious firm over the way.'

"Pen's eyes opened with wide astonishment. 'Do you mean to say,' he asked, 'that we are to praise no books that Bacon publishes: or that, if the books are good, we are to say they are bad?'

" 'My good young friend, for what do you suppose a benevolent publisher undertakes a critical journal,—to benefit his rival?' Shandon inquired.

" 'To benefit himself certainly, but to tell the truth, too,' Pen said— *'ruat coelum*, to tell the truth.' "—Thackeray, *Pendennis*, p. 344.

[56] Carl Becker draws an interesting comparison between M. Brunetière's criticism of Taine's *Origins of Contemporary France* written when the book first appeared and that of M. Aulard written twenty-five years later. This intervening period gave M. Aulard opportunity relentlessly to catalogue presumably all of Taine's sins of commission, but the result is after all but a caricature of Taine,—it is in M. Brunetière's essay that is found "some comprehensive estimate of the work, some dispassionate yet profound and searching criticism of it, which is at the same time an illuminating discussion of the Revolution itself and of its principles."—"The Reviewing of Historical Books," *Annual Report of the American Historical Association for 1912*, pp. 127–136.

See also, Hilaire Belloc, "Ten Pages of Taine," *International Quarterly*, January, 1906, 12: 255–272.

contemporaneous valuation put on a book, since the book itself remains and its value may always be re-tested, and thus ultimately the author rather than the critic holds the field.

It must be evident that literary criticism has its own history; that the prevailing tendency in England in the early nineteenth century was to indulge in slashing personalities; that the criticisms of the middle of the century were characterized by an overwhelming display of the erudition of the critic; while to-day many reviews resemble tables of errata, so punctiliously has the critic focused his microscope on every line; that while the tendency of the English reviewers has been towards undue censure, that of American reviewers has of late been towards undue praise. Matthew Arnold notes the fundamental differences between the French and the German critics. In Sainte-Beuve he found an unrivalled guide to a knowledge of the French genius and literature and that to the "merits of mental independence, industry, measure, lucidity, his criticism adds the merit of happy temper and disposition. Goethe long ago noticed that, whereas Germans reviewed one another as enemies whom they hated, the critics of the *Globe* reviewed one another as gentlemen." [57]

These are but suggestions of the wide range of time and of nationalities involved in criticism; theories of the functions of criticism have varied; standards of criticism have differed at different times; criticism has changed from age to age. But back of all criticism lies the critic and he too changes, as also does the opinion of the public towards him. The contemptuous verdict of Mr. Phoebus in *Lothair*,—that "critics are the men who have failed in literature and art,"—was probably Disraeli's own. Nadal credits no author as appearing "to think that a critic has a soul, or that it is a matter of the least consequence what becomes of it." [58] Hazlitt wrote to Gifford: "When you say that an author cannot write common sense or English, you mean that he does not believe in the doctrine of divine right . . . Your praise or blame has nothing to do with the merits of a work, but with the party to whom the writer

[57] Matthew Arnold, "Sainte-Beuve," *Essays in Criticism*, III, 137–150.
[58] E. S. Nadal, "Newspaper Literary Criticism," *Essays at Home and Elsewhere*, 261–281.

belongs." [59] Saintsbury quotes, "They also serve, who only stand and—whip," but adds, "it is better to have a soul above mere whipping." [60] Boynton pleads that "the great critic is born *and* made," [61] while Gertrude Buck looks into the future of the critic and finds that his reading "must be a process indefinitely progressive," that "it will continually arrive at valuations of particular books and authors, but must never regard these valuations as having, even for the critic himself, more than a present validity and a relative truth;" each opinion "becomes to him, not a final truth in which to rest, but a point of departure for further reading and criticism." [62] The earlier conception of the critic as one who has been thrown to the discard is assuredly yielding to the hopeful view that finds in him capacity for growth and an inclination to improve this opportunity. If, as Saintsbury says, "there certainly has been more bad criticism written in the nineteenth century than in any previous one,—probably more than in all previous centuries put together,—it is quite certain that no other period can show so much that is good," [63] the verdict must be encouraging for the general progress of criticism in the twentieth century. In the last analysis, it is always the critic, rather than the author, whose authority is paramount in the mind of the contemporaneous general reader, but not in the mind of the historian. It is, indeed, impossible to agree with O'Shea who doubts whether the public reads literary criticism at all and believes that "to secure an appreciative public the temptation to be cynical and evolve caustic epigrams [is] very strong." [64] He has himself pointed out that when *Lady Audley's Secret* appeared as a serial it passed unnoticed, but in book form it was reviewed by *The Times*, and "a column of a review in *The Times* made the success of the most successful of modern English

---

[59] *Collected Works of William Hazlitt*, I, 366.

[60] *History of Criticism*, III, 428. A. C. Benson says that reviews are often "written in the spirit of a schoolmaster correcting a boy's exercise."— "The Ethics of Book-reviewing," *Putnam's Monthly*, October, 1906, n. s. I: 116–122.

[61] H. W. Boynton, "Reviewer and Critic," *Journalism and Literature*, pp. 215–226.

[62] "The Function of the Critic," *The Social Criticism of Literature*, pp. 47–60.

[63] *History of Criticism*, III, 421.

[64] J. A. O'Shea, *Leaves from the Life of a Special Correspondent*, II, 171.

lady novelists." [65] It is probably true that "the days when post-card notices from Gladstone secured a record in sales are over; and, from whatever combination of causes, we hear no more of famous reviews." [66] But it has been seen that reviews may be famous without thereby being admirable—Saintsbury speaks of Macaulay's criticism being "choked by its own parasitic plants"—and that reviews may, like Macaulay's, be admired "for their vivid eloquence, extensive learning, and splendour of illustration," without in the slightest degree conforming to the canons of literary criticism.

Literary criticism and the book review have thus far been considered as if the two terms were equivalent terms, yet Robert Lynd points out that "a review should be, from one point of view, a portrait of a book," and that "book-reviewing is something different from criticism." [67] The "something different" is best stated by R. B. Johnson who makes the distinction between the review,—that introduces the reader to a book, offers comment and analysis, and leaves him to form his own opinion of the merits of the work,—and the criticism that assumes some familiarity with the work on the part of the reader and thus discusses and illumines a judgment already formed. The reviewer hazards prophecy and is only interesting as a sign of the times. The critical essay is a permanent contribution to literature. The review thus seems more congenial to the daily press, the critical essay to the weekly, monthly, or quarterly,[68] and each type of periodical is prone to believe that it is best adapted for presenting to the public the merits or demerits of literary works.[69]

[65] J. A. O'Shea, *Leaves from the Life of a Special Correspondent*, II, 173.
[66] R. B. Johnson, *Famous Reviews*, p. ix.
[67] R. Lynd, "Book-Reviewing," *British Review*, April, 1915, 10: 92–106.
[68] *Famous Reviews*, pp. vii–viii.
[69] "The review that, with fairness and simple directness, handles 'books as news' is far more apt to convey a just idea of the author's purposes and actual achievement than a review that is either a learned presentment of its writer's ideas on art or a clever essay at the expense of the book that is being slaughtered."—New York *Times*, February 18, 1917.
"There are probably a hundred newspapers in the United States which pay more or less attention to books, and a few of them include surprisingly good book reviews."—E. L. Pearson, *Book-Reviews*, p. 33.
It is probably true to say that these book notices serve as a sieve,—sifting out those that are worthless, so that only those works that are fairly good reach the monthlies and the quarterlies.

Some of the pitfalls in the path of the reviewer have long been recognized and efforts have been made to avoid them. In the early days of the *Athenaeum*, the editor, James Silk Buckingham, had issued a warning against the prevailing custom of seeking favorable reviews,[70] but the editorship quickly passed into the hands of Frederick Denison Maurice who apparently had little sympathy with either reviews or reviewers.[71] It remained for Charles Wentworth Dilke, to whom again in quick succession the editorship passed, to set himself so resolutely against the practice [72] as to win the support of the press, although he did so

The recent significant development of news about books and of book reviews in the daily press of both England and America has recently been noted.—*Publishers' Weekly*, February 4, 1922; *New York Evening Post*, May 1, 1922.

[70] "To Authors and Publishers.—It having been discovered that applications are sometimes made by individuals to Authors and Publishers for Books to be Reviewed in the *Athenaeum*, and this practice not being authorized or sanctioned by the Editor, it is particularly requested that all Works intended for Review in these pages be sent directly to the Editor himself at the Office of Publication."—J. C. Francis, *John Francis, Publisher of the Athenaeum*, I, 30.

The minute book of the *Athenaeum* a few months before the paper was acquired by J. S. Buckingham gave this curious instruction in regard to the reviewing of books: "In reviewing, only a brief analysis, with extracts, should be given, without much praise or censure, to avoid giving offence to other publishers."—J. C. Francis, *Notes by the Way*, p. 180.

Walt Whitman wrote: "A new book was sent us the other day with a highly eulogistic written notice, to be inserted as editorial. We can't do *such things*."—"Criticism—New Books," editorial, Brooklyn *Daily Eagle*, November 9, 1846, cited by C. Rodgers and J. Black, *The Gathering of the Forces*, II, 278–280.

[71] "It is very gratifying to think that the influence of reviewers upon society is every day becoming more and more limited. In nine cases out of ten it is a question of no material consequence to the public, or to any individual member of it, whether the verdicts which they give are carelessly uttered, or are the result of mature and conscientious deliberation. The most perseveringly impartial and earnest critic will find that he has some power of strengthening the foundations of his readers' opinions, but very little in forming those opinions, or changing them, while the most indefatigable of the scribes of darkness can scarcely flatter himself that he has done any single act of successful mischief, and must console himself with the reflection that, in the silent work of lowering the tone of public feeling and morality, his labours have not been wholly in vain."—Frederick Maurice, *The Life of Frederick Denison Maurice*, I, 83–84.

A later critic differs from this arraignment: "That it [the periodical] has multiplied criticism itself is a truism; that it has necessarily multiplied bad criticism is maintainable; the question is whether it has actually multiplied good. I think it has."—G. E. B. Saintsbury, *History of Criticism*, III, 420.

[72] "He determined to break down once and for ever the system of publishing puffs, whether the publishers sent or did not send their books or

at no small sacrifice, some publishers refusing to sell the paper and others refusing to send it advertisements.[73]

The stern *Saturday Review* went even farther and a foot-note to its prospectus states that the conductors "decline to receive books, prints, &c., gratuitously for review, as the limits of no periodical admit of a proper notice of all new publications. The conductors will provide for themselves the works which they may select for criticism." [74]

Yet publishers and editors might well hesitate to interfere with the sale of books through adverse criticism, were all to meet the fate that befell Gifford. The *Quarterly Review* attacked Hazlitt and thus "stopped the sale of his writings for a time and blighted his credit with his publishers." It led to Hazlitt's "Letter to Gifford," [75] in which he showed himself even more abusive and malignant than his critic has been.

To-day the added suspicion comes that not only does the publisher demand favorable reviews in return for books sent, but that the publisher of reviews looks still farther ahead and publishes favorable reviews in return for the anticipated advertising of the favored firms. "No man," says Bliss Perry, "can grow from a young reviewer into an old one without coming into prompt and humiliating contact with the system of control which the advertiser of books tends to exercise over the literary columns of the periodicals which print his advertising and review

---

advertisements. This great fraud upon the public was to be put an end to, or, failing sufficient support, the journal should be abandoned. There should be no attempt at any compromise with the unclean thing. In justice to those then engaged in the publishing trade it must be remembered that they were merely continuing an old-established system. There had never been a newspaper started upon the principles of free and independent literary criticism. Authors had always been accustomed to laudatory notices, and resented strongly anything like fault-finding, considering, when they handed a work to a publisher, that it was a part of his business to secure it favorable reviews."—J. C. Francis, *John Francis*, I, 35–36.

[73] "This principle is now so fully recognized that it is difficult to believe what a hard-fought struggle was required to establish it, and that it was only owing to the thorough independence of all connected with the *Athenaeum* that this position was attained. It is pleasant to record that the public press gave most generous and efficient support, and warmly and zealously came forward to serve the cause."—*Ib.*, I, 36–37, 41.

[74] J. C. Francis, *Notes by the Way*, p. 201.

[75] *Collected Works of William Hazlitt*, I, 365–411.

his books." [76] The more cynical aspects of the situation are bluntly put by another reviewer who writes, "The business office exerts not a direct but a moral influence, so to put it, upon the literary department. Business tact must be recognized. A hostile review already in type and in the plan of the next issue may be 'killed' when a large 'ad' announcing books brought out by the publisher of this one so treated, comes in for the next paper; and then search is made for a book from the same publisher which may be favorably reviewed. Or a hostile review may be held over until a time more politic for its release, say following several enthusiastic reviews. And there is no sense in noticing in one issue a disproportionate number of books published by one house." [77] A more hopeful view is presented by Bliss Perry who believes that "misleading advertising of books must be left to defeat itself, as it ultimately will. But in the meantime it produces wide-spread demoralization of the critical sense, and creates an atmosphere highly unfavorable to accuracy of judgment and honesty of record." [78]

But many probably will believe that "the Silent Bargain has been decorously struck [between the publisher of books and the publisher of reviews];" publishers demand reviews that puff when they should demand reviews that interest, and the critic

[76] "The American Reviewer," *Yale Review*, October, 1914, 4: 3–24.

An anonymous writer says that Volume 114 of the *North American Review* in the Widener Library has the word "suppressed" at the top of one page,—the proof sheet of a review of Bayard Taylor's translation of *Faust*. At the end of the review the writer found the note: "This notice, written originally by a strong admirer of Mr. Taylor, but much changed by me in tone, led to a protest from the author, and a request from Mr. Osgood that the notice be suppressed. Which was done. HENRY ADAMS." Mr. Adams was at that time the editor of the *North American Review*, then published by Mr. Osgood who also published Bayard Taylor's translation of *Faust.*— "Harvard Calm and Henry Adams," in Contributors' Club, *Atlantic Monthly*, January, 1921, 127: 140.

[77] R. C. Holliday, "The Hack Reviewer," *The Unpopular Review*, April, 1916, 5: 379–391; republished under the title "That Reviewer 'Cuss'," in *Walking Stick Papers*, pp. 87–107.

This statement can not pass unchallenged. *The Nation*, for example, has always had an unusual proportion of publishers' advertisements, but its reviews are noted for their fairness and there is no apparent influence on its advertisements unless it be to induce publishers to advertise in it even though *The Nation* may review its books unfavorably.

[78] "Literary Criticism in American Periodicals," *Yale Review*, July, 1914, 3: 635–655.

must choose between admirable conduct and admirable criticism.[79]

Yet these strictures on the deplorable effect of "the silent bargain" on literary criticism are not new. Poe, nearly eighty years ago, sent out the same warning, though with a note of hope. "If our editors," he says, "are not as yet *all* independent of the will of the publisher, a majority of them scruple, at least, *to confess* a subserviency, and enter into no positive combinations against the minority who despise and discard it. And this is a *very* great improvement of exceedingly late date." [80]

A variant of the advertisement is the log-rolling by which works written by unknown authors are exploited by equally unknown but ambitious author-critics. "Once upon a time," *The Nation* caustically remarks, "people believed that a Dickens or a Thackeray comes once in a hundred years. To-day they come at least twice a year in the spring and autumn publishing season." [81]

The net result of all of these interrelations of publishers, editors, authors, and critics is that the hands of the press often seem tied and that it vitiates the taste and lowers the standards of the reading public.

Charles Miner Thompson has indicated clearly that five distinct groups are interested in literary criticism,—publishers of books, authors, publishers of reviews, critics, and the reading public.[82] The interest of all of these groups, except the reading public, as he so clearly shows, is obviously a financial one; the publisher of books is interested in reviews because they are gratuitous advertising;[83] the publisher of reviews hopes they

[79] C. M. Thompson, "Honest Literary Criticism," *Atlantic Monthly*, August, 1908, 102: 179–190.

[80] "Exordium," *Graham's Magazine*, January, 1842, 20: 68–69.

[81] "Book Reviewing à la Mode," August 17, 1911, 93: 139–140.

E. L. Pearson suggests that if a librarian writes a book, "we may feel fairly certain that out of a feeling of fellowship for us as librarians the *A. L. A. Booklist* will duly recommend it, showing that however stern and uncompromising they would have the professional literary critic, when it comes down to their own case librarians prefer the milk of human kindness to the corrosive acid of outspoken criticism."—*Book-Reviews*, p. 35.

[82] "Honest Literary Criticism," *Atlantic Monthly*, August, 1908, 102:179–190.

[83] The importance that publishers and booksellers attach to the mere bulk of the reviews is indicated by the announcement in a recent catalogue of books,—"within ten days of the publication of this important work fifty columns of reviews appeared in the Press."

will lure advertising to his columns; the critic depends on reviews for his livelihood, and the author for reputation. The reading public alone has no financial interest in reviews, but desires adequate service, which it does not get and is, therefore, dissatisfied as are the commercial interests involved because the returns are incommensurate with the efforts expended. Between the upper and the nether millstone the review is crushed.

Yet other grounds besides the financial ones explain the dissatisfaction with the review on the part of these various groups. The opinions of certain publishers have already been indicated. Authors have been far from agreeing in regard to the desirability of criticism. Walter Scott flung magnificent defiance to the tribe of critics in writing to James Ballantyne, apropos of a letter of William Blackwood's, suggesting certain changes in the *Black Dwarf:*—"Tell him and his coadjutor that I belong to the Black Hussars of Literature, who neither give nor receive criticism." [84] George Eliot, in a letter to John Blackwood, confessed her belief that "reviewers are fellowmen towards whom I keep a Christian feeling by not reading them." [85] William Black, like many another author, felt that the criticisms of reviewers were always either obvious or foolish and steadily maintained his rule not to read the reviews of his books.[86]

The critics themselves have their own troubles,—troubles with which the historian must sympathize even when realizing that they militate against the absolute reliability of criticism. Some of these troubles come from within. One is what Collins calls "the increasing tendency to regard nothing of importance compared with the spirit of tolerance and charity. An all-embracing philanthropy exempts nothing from its protection. Every one must be good-natured." [87] Yet this good nature has its defenders. "The good reviewer," says R. C. Holliday, "does go easy with most books. It is a mark of his excellence as a

[84] J. G. Lockhart, *Memoirs of Sir Walter Scott*, I, 22.
[85] Mrs. Oliphant, *Annals of a Publishing House*, III, 393.
[86] Wemyss Reid, *William Black*, pp. 204–206 (English Edition). This letter of Black to Reid is of special interest when taken in connection with one written by him to the *Daily Graphic* in which with fine irony he describes the work of the reviewer, from Black's point of view.—*Ib.*, 301–308.
[87] J. C. Collins, "The Present Functions of Criticism," *Ephemera Critica*, pp. 13–44.

reviewer that he has a catholic taste, that he sees that books are written to many standards, and that every book, almost, is meet for some. It is not his business to break things on the wheel; but to introduce the book before him to its proper audience; always recognizing, of course, sometimes with pleasant subtle irony, its limitations." [88]

But if, on the other hand, this temptation to excessive leniency were to be resisted and "I were to tell the truth," says one member of the guild, "as forcibly as I could wish to do, about the books sent to me for review, in six months my proprietors would be in the bankruptcy court." [89] And the sympathetic reviewer with fair intent may in turn justly claim the sympathy of his readers, as does Lord Acton in his statement of his position,[90] and Mrs. Lynn Linton in her indignation over what she deemed the unfairness of an author to the subject of his biography.[91] The reviewer himself sometimes pleads for his craft as does Boynton in discussing the reviewer "whose critical integrity finds itself wavering under, it may be, the fourfold pressure of author, editor, publisher, and the public. He is not a judge, or a mere fabricator of book notices. It is not his business to help the sale of books, or to coddle sensitive writers, or to make everybody feel comfortable about everything; discrimination is always offensive in one quarter or another; and the reviewer, like other critics, discriminates, or is lost." [92]

[88] "The Hack Reviewer," *The Unpopular Review*, April–June, 1916, 5: 379–391.
[89] J. C. Collins, *op. cit.*, p. 23.
[90] "If books are to be noticed at all, it must be done uprightly and with even scales. I sat down with the best resolution of speaking favorably of Robertson, who had begged for a notice, but I found so little good to say that I am afraid he will hardly be grateful and that we have not much assisted the sale of his book."—Abbot Gasquet, *Lord Acton and His Circle*, p. 131.
[91] Dickens sent Forster's *Life of Landor* to Mrs. Lynn Linton to review for *All the Year Round*. In it Forster had seemed to her to show a despicable "want of loyalty to the man, dead, whose feet he had kissed while living" and she began her review, "The Life of Walter Savage Landor has yet to be written." This offended Dickens who returned the article with a letter in which he says it could hardly be otherwise than painful to Forster that he should insert in his magazine an account of Landor without a word of commendation for a biography that had cost a world of care and trouble.— G. S. Layard, *Mrs. Lynn Linton*, 160–162.
[92] "Reviewer and Critic," *Journalism and Literature*, pp. 217–226.

It is possible that the best solution of the difficulty is found in the *Rhymed Reviews* of writers like Arthur Guiterman who "in them has said merrily what another reviewer could only say heavily." [93]

Critics are often misled by reprints, by lack of information in regard to the interval between the date of writing and the date of publication, or the date of publication and that of republication.[94] They may be the victims of jest or hoax;[95] they may be called on to review forged literature,[96] or books that have not been published;[97] they may be the victims of personal assault, or of actions for libel.[98]

[93] E. L. Pearson, *Book-Reviews*, p. 36.

[94] H. B. Wheatley, *Literary Blunders*, pp. 44–46.

[95] Henry Vizetelly gives an account of a review of nearly three columns by the London *Times* and of six columns by the *Athenaeum* of a book purporting to be by J. Tyrwhitt Brooks, entitled *Four Months Among the Goldfinders of Alta California*, but in reality a hoax perpetrated by Vizetelly himself, when the news of the discovery of gold in California reached England. Other papers also reviewed the book, it was reprinted in America, translated into several foreign languages, and "for years it held the position of chief authority on the subject."—*Glances Back Through Seventy Years*, I, chap. XVIII. J. C. Francis quotes the *Athenaeum* review in *John Francis*, I, 146–149.

As late as 1902, a prominent American critic writes of it: "A rare and very striking pamphlet published as 'The result of actual experience, which it doubtless was, being taken from letters sent home by the author. It was very widely circulated in the Atlantic states, in 1849, and has been more or less utilized by all careful students of the period to which it relates."—Annotated notice of J. Tyrwhitt Brooks, *Four Months Among the Goldfinders in California* in J. B. Larned, ed., *Literature of American History*, No. 2021.

Firmilian, purporting to be the work of a new writer of a new school, was reviewed in *Blackwood's*, May, 1854, 75: 533–551. The story of the hoax is given by H. Maxwell, "Firmilian," *Rainy Days in a Library*, pp. 33–42.

A similar recent hoax was the volume called *Spectra*, ostensibly written by Emanuel Morgan and Anne Knish, but in reality a satire on futurists and cubists written by Witter Bynner and Arthur Davison Ficke. For two years it was reviewed by the critics as serious work, but the acknowledgment of the hoax by the authors "banished into ignominy many of the bearded prophets of verse in America."

[96] H. G. Hewlett, "Forged Literature," *Nineteenth Century*, February, 1891, 29: 318–338.

[97] *Blackwood's Magazine* contained reviews "of a professedly first edition" of *Peter's Letters to His Kinsfolk*, "but in fact there was no first edition at all, the first actual publication being called the 2nd edition."—Mrs. Oliphant, *Annals of a Publishing House: William Blackwood and His Sons*, I, 219–222; *Blackwood's Magazine*, February, March, 1819, 4: 612–621, 745–752.

[98] A long abusive review, written by Dr. Maginn of Grantley Berkeley's novel, *Berkeley Castle*, was published in *Fraser's Magazine*, August, 1836. This led to an attack on Fraser, in Fraser's shop, by Berkeley and his brother; then to a duel with Maginn; then to a justification of the original

Occasionally a writer has taken the reviewers less seriously and has had a jest at their expense, as did Maria Jane Jewsbury in her "First Efforts in Criticism," [99] a humorous parody on current criticism and critics,—a parody that had in its turn its own amusing sequel.[100] Others, like Harriet Martineau, have been scandalized by the tricks of the trade.[101] Only occasionally per-

review by Maginn in *Fraser's Magazine;* then to further assailing by Berkeley; and finally to an action for assault by Fraser who was awarded £100, and to an action against him for libel which was settled for 40s damages, without costs.—H. Vizetelly, *Glances Back Through Seventy Years,* I, 124–126.

Thomas Moore challenged Jeffrey who had written a denunciatory review of a volume of Moore's poems, but the police interrupted the affair. The review is found in the *Edinburgh Review,* July, 1806, 8: 456–465.

[99] *Phantasmagoria,* I, 233–347.

[100] The critic, as described by the author, purports to be reviewing certain imaginary books on mathematics, gives an essay on the advantages of the study of arithmetic, and then, the author adds, "Here follows a disquisition of twenty pages on things in general, with particular mention of the Brazils, the Peninsular War, and Church History." This was a sly hit at Southey of whom Macaulay wrote to Napier, December 6, 1844, "Southey used to work regularly two hours a day on the history of Brazil, then an hour for the Quarterly Review, then an hour on the life of Wesley, then two hours on the Peninsular War, then an hour on the Book of the Church."—*Selection from the Correspondence of the Late Macvey Napier,* pp. 476–477; also, p. 425.

To jest at Southey was, to a contemporary, comparable to "Sydney Smith's man who had been heard to speak disrespectfully of the Equator." But Wordsworth, to whom Miss Jewsbury had dedicated her volumes, with an entire lack of a sense of humor, sent the volumes to Southey to review for the *Quarterly,* and when Southey "responded to this overture with some austerity" and left the author "wholly unnoticed," Wordsworth "must have wondered what it all meant."—A. A. Watts, *Alaric Watts,* I, 184–186.

[101] "Even through these liberal and honourable publishers [Messrs. Saunders and Otley], however, I became acquainted with one of the tricks of the trade which surprised me a good deal. After telling me the day of publication, and announcing that my twenty-five copies would be ready, Mr. Saunders inquired when I should like to come to their back parlour, 'and write the notes.'—'What notes?'—'The notes for the Reviews, you know, Ma'am.' He was surprised at being obliged to explain that authors write notes to friends and acquaintances connected with periodicals, 'to request favourable notices of the work.' I did not know how to credit this; and Mr. Saunders was amazed that I had never heard of it. 'I assure you, Ma'am, — — does it; and all our authors do it.' On my emphatically declining, he replied, 'As you please, Ma'am: but it is the universal practice, I believe.' I have always been related to the Reviews exactly like the ordinary public. I have never inquired who had reviewed me, or known who was going to do so, except by public rumour. I do not very highly respect reviews, nor like to write them; for the simple reason that in ninety-nine cases out of a hundred, the author understands his subject better than the reviewer."—*Autobiography,* I, 404.

Probably a similar custom is alluded to in a letter to R. W. Griswold from Epes Sargent who, in writing of his "little book," says, "Please keep the

haps has the honest, capable reviewer had the satisfaction of knowing that his adverse criticism has produced good results.[102]

One of the difficult problems connected with literary criticism and book reviewing is that of the comparative merits of the signed and the unsigned review. There is, and can be, no middle ground,—the review is signed or it is anonymous, and it is equally true that there is, and can be, no compromise between two hostile camps that defend or attack anonymity in criticism.

The abuses of anonymous criticism were much in evidence in the early years of the nineteenth century,—personal spite, rancor, and revenge were all indulged in under the cover of anonymity. In protest against these evils, Richard Cumberland in 1809 founded the *London Review* "of which the distinguishing feature was to be that each writer should put his name to the article." [103] "It was this last terrifying clause," his biographer says, "which hindered and finally put an end to the new magazine." [104] Cumberland himself, in the Introductory Address to the *London Review*, explains that his real object was to correct a prevailing abuse. "Booksellers of all degrees had purchased the magazines, and behind the bulwark of anonymity dealt terrific blows at their opponents' publications, while they lavished praises upon their own." [105] Walter Scott had noted the danger of the plan, for he wrote to Charles Kirkpatrick Sharpe of "the extraordinary proposal that each contributor shall place his name before his article, a stipulation which must prove fatal to the undertaking." But Scott himself had always liked the cover of anonymity and wrote to Sharpe concerning the *Quarterly*

---

authorship a secret, and if you can get the accompanying notices published, one in the North American, and the other in the Evening Journal, without betraying it, do so."—*Passages from Correspondence*, p. 107.

[102] B. L. Gildersleeve gives an account of a review of an edition of a Greek author edited by a man "who transcended everything I had ever known or imagined in the way of incompetence." The result of the review was that the textbook was withdrawn by the publishers, and therefore the review was not published.—"The Hazards of Reviewing," *The Nation*, July 8, 1915, 101: 49–51

[103] Henry Crabb Robinson, *Diary*, I, 189.

[104] S. T. Williams, *Richard Cumberland*, p. 272.
Williams states that only two numbers were published, but Robinson says, "Four half-crown quarterly numbers were published." *Diary*, I, 189.

[105] S. T. Williams, *Richard Cumberland*, p. 273.

Review: "You have yet to learn the magic virtue of calling yourself *we*. I never knew the emphatic force of the pronoun till I became a reviewer, and then I no longer wondered at its being a royal attribute." [106]

On the other hand, Schopenhauer was even more emphatic in denouncing anonymity as "the refuge for all journalistic rascality,"—a remark to have been anticipated from one who had written that his "remarks on the critical faculty are chiefly intended to show that, for the most part, there is no such thing." "Every article," he goes on to say, "even in a newspaper should be accompanied by the name of its author; and the editor should be made strictly responsible for the accuracy of the signature." [107] Harriet Martineau felt that Croker "carried the license of anonymous criticism to the last extreme." [108]   Edward Bulwer explained that without signature "the critic can thus take certain liberties with the author with impunity; that he may be witty or severe without the penalty of being shot," that he can review books more on their merit and without personal feeling, but on the whole he apparently favors signature.[109]

Howells, in recalling the remorseless criticism in the early English quarterlies, of Keats, Wordsworth, and other writers, is indignant that "this savage condition still persists in the toleration of anonymous criticism, an abuse that ought to be as extinct as the torture of witnesses." [110]   Brander Matthews finds that "anonymous reviewing might readily put it in the power of a personal enemy to attack a writer from the ambush of half-a-dozen journals." [111]

[106] *Letters from and to Charles Kirkpatrick Sharpe*, I, 351, 353.
[107] "On Criticism," *Essays*, Translated by T. B. Saunders, pp. 337–347.
[108] "John Wilson Croker," *Biographical Sketches*, 60–69.
[109] "View of the Intellectual Spirit of the Time," *England and the English*, II, 7–76.
[110] W. D. Howells, *Criticism and Fiction*, p. 50.
[111] He draws his conclusion from what may be an exceptional case. He gives an account of a favorable review in the *Academy* of a book on the epic songs of Russia signed by "the leading British authority on Russian literature," and equally favorable unsigned reviews of the book in the *Athenaeum* and in the *Saturday Review*. The critic stated he had written all three, but did so because the book was good and no one in England but himself was interested in Russian literature, and the book would have gone without notice if he had not written these reviews.—*These Many Years*, pp. 297–298.

The far-reaching discussion of anonymity that was precipitated by Zola's address in 1893 to the congress of the English Institute of Journalists ranged over the entire field of literary, dramatic, and political criticism, but it apparently changed little the current opinion in regard to literary criticism. Traill took the address as his text for a plea for the continuance of anonymity,—a system that the critic found in possession and conformed to it,—although he recognizes that the question is not *causa finita;* the public and literature are best served by anonymous criticism, even though the critic at times prefers signature.[112]

Literary criticism has apparently often left something to be desired and this failure to reach an ideal has, as has been seen, been variously attributed in turn to perverted standards of criticism, to the critics themselves, to the editor, to publishers, to the business manager, and equally to the signed and to the unsigned review. It is Bliss Perry who with keen insight finds "a public which is genuinely interested in stock-market criticism, in baseball criticism, in political, social, and economic criticism, and, in a few cities, in musical and dramatic criticism, but which is not very eagerly interested in the criticism of books. To put it concretely, the 'financial' page of a New York, Chicago, or Boston newspaper is likely to be more expertly edited and more expertly read than the 'literary page'." [113] It seems probable that "the decline of the reviewer" so often lamented [114] must be explained by this failure of the public to demand genuine literary criticism,

[112] H. D. Traill, "The Anonymous Critic," *Nineteenth Century*, December, 1893, 34: 932–943.

English periodical literature shows no subject that has engaged writers more frequently than has that of anonymous criticism. Among the most important may be noted T. Hughes, "Anonymous Journalism," *Macmillan's Magazine*, December, 1861, 5: 157–168; A. Trollope, "On Anonymous Literature," *Fortnightly Review*, July 1, 1865; 1: 491–498; the best statement noted in favor of anonymity is that of G. C. Lewis, *On the Influence of Authority in Matters of Opinion*, pp. 236–249.

American writers have apparently been less interested in the subject. Poe favored signed criticism. Bliss Perry discusses the relative value of the signed and the unsigned review, but gives no decision. "And no one knows, possibly not even these critics themselves."—"The American Reviewer," *Yale Review*, October, 1914, 4: 3–24.

[113] "Literary Criticism in American Periodicals," *Yale Review*, July, 1914, 3: 635–655.

[114] New York *Evening Post*, January 18, 1919.

—a failure that has in its turn led to instability in all criticism.[115] Given an ideal public trained to demand and to appreciate genuine literary criticism, the question of book reviewing may be summed up in the words of Robert Lynd who says, "What seems to be wanted, then, in a book-reviewer is that, without being servile, he should be swift to praise, and that, without being censorious, he should have the courage to blame." [116]

The companion question of criticism may be summed up in the words of J. C. Collins who concludes that "Criticism is to Literature what legislation and government are to States. If they are in able and honest hands all goes well; if they are in weak and dishonest hands all is anarchy and mischief." [117]

Yet for the historian who seeks to use criticism as one means of reconstructing the past the book review is but the initial step. He must still look for that larger criticism that in the opinion of Carl Becker has to do with the entire intellectual activity of the time and is therefore concerned with books only as they aptly illustrate some aspect of this larger subject.[118]

Dramatic criticism in the press is a comparatively recent development. "The production," says John Underhill, "of a new play by a Dryden or by an Etherege, interesting as it was to a playgoer like Pepys, does not appear to have been thought sufficiently important to merit a single line in any contemporary news-sheet." [119] In the eighteenth century present conditions

[115] R. Bagot deplores the lack of an organized system of criticism in the press and proposes a body chosen from the most capable critics to sift the tares of fiction from the wheat and become in effect a clearing-house for fiction.—"The Reviewing of Fiction," *Nineteenth Century and After*, February, 1906, 59: 288–297.

Many practical difficulties would seem to prevent the organization of such a body, while a perverse novel-reading public would probably object to the overthrow of a system that has produced "the six best sellers."

Two opposing views of the subject are given by William Knight, "Criticism as a Trade," and A. J. Church, "Criticism as a Trade. A Reply," *Nineteenth Century*, September, November, 1889, 26: 423–430, 833–839.

Archdeacon Farrar somewhat ostentatiously disclaims that he is himself a reviewer and attacks literary criticism in "The Nether World," *Contemporary Review*, September, 1889, 56: 370–380.

[116] "Book-Reviewing," *The British Review*, April, 1915, 10: 92–106.

[117] J. C. Collins, "The Present Functions of Criticism," *Ephemera Critica*, pp. 13–44.

[118] "The Reviewing of Historical Books," *Annual Report of the American Historical Association for 1912*, pp. 127–136.

[119] *Athenian Oracle*, p. xiii.

were reversed and "one London newspaper paid as much as £200 a year for early intelligence of what was to be presented at the theatres." [120] But, while dramatic criticism has now come to be an important feature of the press, it furnishes the historian one of his most troublesome problems. This is in part owing to the difficulties inherent in such criticism. The critic is limited by the policy of the editor towards the theater, by his assumed tacit obligation to theater managers, by his personal relations with actors, and frequently by his own efforts in playwriting and in acting.

There has long been a feeling on the part of theater managers that the receipt of complimentary tickets by a newspaper carries with it an implied obligation to give a favorable notice of the play seen.[121] "We are on no new ground," says Lucas, "when we find an actor-manager quarreling with a dramatic critic," and he cites the case of Charles J. Mathews, the actor, who in 1853 wrote to the *Morning Post* that, after admitting its representative as usual, he had met with what he deserved in consequence. Last season, he says, he had protested against what he considered unfair criticism. Now, with "every respect and goodwill" towards the editor personally, he can not allow his critic to be admitted again. A caustic letter from the editor says, "You meant that you would never give him free tickets. Frankly, I do not see that that matters one straw. I should as soon dream of uttering a 'threat' to induce you to give him a free ticket as I would to oblige you to take off your hat to him." [122]

But when a newspaper has refused complimentary tickets and instructed its critic to purchase them, the theater manager has sometimes refused to sell them to any representative of the paper. The result has more than once been prolonged litigation, with decisions unfavorable to the newspaper. The case of *Life vs.* Klaw and Erlanger in 1907 turned on the refusal of the theater

---

[120] Thomas Catling, *My Life's Pilgrimage*, p. 356.

[121] C. T. Congdon complains of the amusement mongers who think that newspapers are specially printed for their use. "The whole bad business of puffery was upon a much lower basis not a great many years ago; and the manager of a theater, for the consideration of a free admission, thought himself entitled to the occupation of as many columns as he cared to fill."— *Reminiscences of a Journalist* (1880), p. 312.

[122] R. Lucas, *Lord Glenesk and the " Morning Post,"* pp. 164–165.

managers to admit the dramatic critic of *Life* to their theaters, and in 1915 the dramatic critic of the New York *Times* was refused admission to the Shubert theaters. In both cases, the final court of appeal ruled that the managers had a right to exclude a dramatic critic from their theaters whenever they pleased. These decisions have been rightly called "a blow to honest dramatic criticism," [123] since they stand for the right of all theatrical managers in New York State to bar from their theaters those who have criticized unfavorably their productions, or any one who is displeasing to them, providing the exclusion is not on grounds of race, color, or creed.

In all lawsuits attempting to exclude dramatic critics from theaters, the real object of theater managers is obviously to attempt to control newspaper opinion and to that extent it is a menace to the freedom of the press; wherever freedom of the press prevails, the answer to such judicial decisions is inevitably the introduction of legislative measures intended to strengthen the law on the side of freedom of expression and thus make impossible similar decisions in the future.[124]

But the principle is not new. L. Bamberger cites a somewhat parallel case in Germany, prior to 1890, where a court of law decided that a writer could be refused admission to a theater subventioned by the public money, even though he had paid for his ticket, because he had criticized the actors so sharply that he had spoilt the pleasure of the public in the performance.[125] Assuredly the effect of decisions of this character must be to leave the historian entirely in the dark as to the real merits of dramatic presentation in theaters that virtually permit the publication of only favorable criticism. "Henceforth we shall not have independent criticism, but compulsory commendation," and theatrical managers "by excluding the critics who found

[123] *The Independent*, March 6, 1916, 85: 329; *The Outlook*, March 15, 1916, 112: 596; *Literary Digest*, March 18, 1916, 52: 715–716.
The full text of the arguments and the decisions in the *Times* suit is given in its issues of April 8, May 19, May 25, June 19, July 10, 1915, and February 23, 1916.

[124] A bill was introduced into the New York State legislature, April, 1915, to prevent the intimidation of dramatic critics by making it a misdemeanor to exclude any person from a theater without cause.

[125] "The German Daily Press," *Nineteenth Century*, January, 1890, 27: 24–37.

fault with their plays, have destroyed the last vestige of faith which the public has placed in dramatic criticism."

The advertiser in his turn is offended by adverse criticism. Bussey relates that many years ago the proprietor of a Brighton theater did a good printing business in addition, and if a theatrical company visited Brighton and did not order its bills and posters from him, their performances were not likely to be favorably criticized. On one such occasion, he wrote a severe criticism of the part of the leading actor. But illness compelled a change of piece at the last moment. The printer's apprentice filched a proof and gave it to the manager who read from the stage the notice of the piece that had not been played. The editor did not know till morning what had happened, and by that time the whole of the week's issue had been put in circulation.[126]

It is to-day the fear of the advertiser that is the skeleton in the closet of the dramatic critic.[127] Kenneth Macgowan says that not more than half a dozen newspapers east of the Mississippi give their dramatic critics a free hand or protect him "from corruption by innuendo as well as intimidation." And he gives a long list of instances where the dramatic critic of a newspaper has been its advertising solicitor; where in the salary of the dramatic critic is figured a percentage on the receipts from theatrical advertising; where the dramatic editor inspects the list of Sunday advertisers before making up the advertising page; where the dramatic critic is required to write a fixed number of lines about every new opening, paying for a corresponding size of advertisement; where notice is sent to a theatrical manager, "if you will send on Saturday full copy for our paper, we will be glad to help your show along when it opens;" where the weekly notices from a large theater bear the penciled message, "30 line

[126] H. F. Bussey, *Sixty Years of Journalism*, pp. 40–41.
Catling says that "The nineteenth century saw the development of another curious custom: newspaper proprietors printing their own press tickets, with which some dozen or more persons were sent to a theatre each night. . . . This system was in use when I commenced in the sixties. Charles Mathews and Benjamin Webster at length protested against it, and it gradually fell into disuse."—*My Life's Pilgrimage*, p. 356.
[127] The minute book of the London *Globe* for April 4, 1827, directed that "admission tickets for places of entertainment be as much as possible at the command of those who advertise most largely and steadily."—J. C. Francis, *Notes by the Way*, pp. 180–181.

ad. Saturday," "two column ad. tomorrow," or "150 lines next week." [128] These are indeed the "secrets of the critics' prison house."

Dramatic criticism has been hampered not only by theater managers and by advertisers, but also by the social conditions surrounding critics. Leigh Hunt says that "it was the custom at that time [1805] for editors of papers to be intimate with actors and dramatists. They were often proprietors, as well as editors,—and, in that case, it was not expected that they should escape the usual intercourse, or wish to do so. It was thought a feather in the cap of all parties; and with their feathers they tickled one another. The newspaper man had consequence in a green-room, and plenty of tickets for his friends; and he dined at amusing tables. The dramatist secured a good-natured critique in his journal, sometimes got it written himself, or according to Mr. Reynolds, was even himself the author of it. . . . What the public took for a criticism on a play was a draft upon the box-office, or reminiscences of last Thursday's salmon and lobster-sauce." [129]

Catling relates that E. P. Hingston, a theater manager of about 1840, during the intervals of a play, mingled freely with the audience, "and several of us enjoyed his hospitality. Suddenly a voice cried, 'Ah, Hingston, at your old game, trying to nobble the Press!' 'Yes,' replied the manager, 'and I've squared three of them for tenpence.'" "It is absurd to suppose," he goes on to say, "that such an incident had any effect on what was written, but the free-and-easy method did much to lighten labour and make the evening pass pleasantly." [130]

But A. W. à Beckett writes with emphasis still later that "the great difficulty with which a professional 'first nighter'

[128] "Corrupted Dramatic Critics," *Dial*, January 3, 1918, 64: 13–15.

An important editorial in the *Outlook* condemned a prominent New York daily for dismissing its eminent dramatic critic at the instigation of its theater advertisers.—"The Newspaper and the Theater," September 4, 1909, 93: 12–13.—*The Independent* discussed the report that three prominent dramatic critics had been retired from three New York papers at the instigation of the theatrical syndicate.—"The Dramatic Critic and the Trust," September 30, 1909, 67: 770–771. "A Theatrical Press Agent's Confession and Apology" may be found in *The Independent*, July 27, 1909, 59: 191–196.

[129] *Autobiography*, I, 181–182.

[130] *My Life's Pilgrimage*, p. 359.

has to contend is the tie of personal friendship." The dramatic critic, he maintains, "should avoid knowing actors and actresses, dramatic authors and theatrical managers. He should be chary of accepting what may be termed 'professional' hospitality. He should have a prior engagement when asked to 'celebrate' anything in the 'customary fashion' by anybody. He should train himself to hate 'chicken,' to loathe 'champagne'." While suppers became the rule at a certain class of entertainment the best critics avoided the feasts,—"the moment it was felt that the suppers were intended for favours to be paid, those invited to the banquets absented themselves *en masse.*" Subsequently, he waives aside all suggestion of the relations between critic and manager as being necessarily harmful to dramatic criticism and says, "So long as the scholar is linked with the gentleman there is no fear of corruption," and that since two persons have to be squared in matters of this kind,—the dramatic critic and the editor,—between the two the freedom of the press is fairly protected.[131]

The temptation of the critic is strong and the anxiety of both playwright and players is understandable,—William Archer says that producing a play and waiting for the opinion of the critics is comparable to the sensation of a felon waiting for the verdict. A play that is condemned remains condemned, while a work of art or of literature "remains to give the lie to an unjust judgment." It is this that leads Archer to say that "there are in the literary world few more responsible positions than that of the dramatic critic of an influential daily paper." [132] The actor in particular knows that his "labour is forever lost if it miss instant recognition." But this very instant recognition is fraught with danger since "the mistaken kindness of his friends by indiscriminate praise robs the player of his best encouragement to strive to a high mark, win definite appreciation for himself, and honour for his calling." [133]

These differences of opinion between critics and actors did not

---

[131] *The Modern Adam, or How Things are Done,* pp. 163, 166–167, 216–217.
[132] "The Duties of Dramatic Critics," *Nineteenth Century,* February, 1885, 17: 249–262.
[133] Henry Morley, *The Journal of a London Playgoer,* p. 7.

begin yesterday and they will not end to-morrow,[134] and it is this
that has led Archer to propose "A Critical Court of Honour" [135]
competent to decide disputes where players and playwrights
believe they have been too harshly dealt with by critics. These
disputes have sometimes been decided by courts of law, but
Archer deems them incompetent to render judgment on such
technical questions.

Occasionally the press has been the victim of a jest at the
hands of a dramatic critic and these jests must add a cheerful
tone to the somewhat depressing aspects of dramatic criticism.[136]

It is probably because there have been so many critics who
"came short of rendering the best service to the public because
of counting-room pressure in favor of liberally advertising
theatres, or against the theatres whose patronage was less valuable," because sometimes actors were friends or foes of editor or
owners, and "the critic was bidden to be 'a respecter of persons'" [137] that an eminent dramatic critic has raised the question
"Is dramatic criticism necessary?" [138]

The historian has but one answer to the question,—dramatic
criticism is absolutely essential if he is to reconstruct the dramatic
representation of the past, and it is this that leads him to change
slightly an opinion expressed by Henry Austin Clapp and to say,
"The qualities of Master Samuel Pepys which made him a
dangerous neighbor in 1670 make him valuable to an historian in
1901."

But press criticism of the drama is much more than the simple
question of a favorable or an unfavorable judgment. There is
as yet no consensus of opinion as to what principles should

[134] René Doumic, "La Querelle des auteurs et des critiques au théâtre,"
Revue des Deux Mondes, September 15, 1906, Per. V, 35: 446–457.

[135] *Fortnightly Review*, April, 1903, n. s. 73: 698–705. The suggestion of
such a court grew out of the exclusion of A. B. Walkley from the Garrick
theater. Henry Arthur Jones wrote "An Appeal to the Press" claiming
that Walkley's criticism had shown personal animus.

[136] A. W. à Beckett wrote for the *Oriental Budget* a criticism of an amateur
theatrical performance given for a charitable purpose and in it criticized
severely the part he had taken himself. The editor sternly rebuked him and
characterized the notice as libellous, but was relieved when told, "The
actor I went for was myself! I always try to be impartial."—*Recollections
of a Humorist*, pp. 81–82.

[137] H. A. Clapp, *Reminiscences of a Dramatic Critic*, pp. 23–24.

[138] Brander Matthews, *Bookman*, September, 1915, 42: 82–87.

govern dramatic criticism and yet in no form of criticism are so many complex factors involved. The play is first of all a work of literature and it is naturally reviewed as such. But the play acted on the stage becomes something entirely different and it must be criticized as such.[139] These entirely different and even contradictory characteristics in a play to be read as literature and to be acted as drama explain why certain admirable works of literature as Tennyson's *Harold* and *Queen Mary* and Browning's *Strafford* have failed on the stage, as they explain why the Greek drama and Shakespeare survive. "The play," says Clapp, "which never passes into literature; the play, which in 'the cold permanency of print' cannot endure reading and re-reading, has the sure seed of death within it." [140]

The critic may regard the play as literature and give the outline of the plot,—this is useless to those who have seen the play; it may be disconcerting to those who wish to see it; but it is even more disappointing to the historian who can read the play as literature. The nominal critic may be in reality a reporter and hence regard the play as a piece of news to be written up entertainingly. The critic may be the man in the office who is willing to spend his evenings at the theater, and he may be paid by space and hence criticize all plays by procrustean methods. The critics may disagree among themselves, as when one dramatic critic recently wrote of a first night that the actors had made the play, while another wrote of the same performance that a good play had been spoiled by bad acting. Personal criticism may be written of the actors in the play, rather than of their acting, still less of the drama as acted. The confessions of dramatic critics themselves often give interesting revelations of their qualifications to act as such and of their conception of the duties involved.[141] From Aristotle to the present day there has been

[139] Edmund Yates while dramatic critic for the *Daily News* once utterly condemned a play of his own. He had thought the play very good in manuscript, but when he saw it on the boards, he changed his mind and felt bound to condemn it.—J. McCarthy and J. R. Robinson, *The Daily News Jubilee*, pp. 83–84.

[140] *Reminiscences of a Dramatic Critic*, p. 45.

[141] C. T. Congdon says that when Rachel began her season in Boston, he wrote for his paper all the articles on her acting without knowing a word of French. "A really good journalist," he adds, "never betrays his ignorance of anything."—*Reminiscences*, p. 315.

no consensus of opinion as to whether criticism should deal with the drama as literature, or with literature as interpreted through dramatic representation.

Contemporaries are everywhere prone to regard the dramatic criticism of their own age, as a recent writer has said it is still regarded in America,—as "ephemeral, unprincipled, jejune." [142] An occasional oasis is sometimes found and the student of history rejoices for coming historians when he reads of the work of the late William Winter, "The amount of sagacious, instructional, and descriptive comment in his total output is amazing. Much of it, in its general shrewdness, competency, and accuracy, is of great and permanent historical value—a living picture of a theatrical era." [143]

But the real difficulty is not in finding the ideal dramatic critic, but in limiting and describing the functions of dramatic criticism. His task is to bring to his criticism a sympathetic and adequate knowledge of the drama, an understanding of the technical machinery of the stage, an appreciation of the effect of the drama upon the audience, and a comprehension of the problems of the playwright and of the actors. The question has been well put by H. N. MacCracken who considers that:

"The function of drama is precisely that contained in the literal meaning of the word,—doing. Doing in the technical dramatic sense means impersonation, and from the earliest times actors have spoken of 'doing' parts or roles. The function of the dramatic critic is, then, primarily, to consider how successful in the rendition is the public performance of a play. The critic as a reporter of dramatic news should furnish an outline of the program and note whatever of news value attaches to the performance. His prime question should be, however,—was the

---

John Oxenford, a dramatic critic on the London *Times,* used to boast that he never wrote a word in the *Thunderer* that could do professional damage to an actor, or take the bread out of the mouth of an actress.— *Bohemian Days in Fleet Street,* p. 84.

The author of *Bohemian Days in Fleet Street* speaks of Joseph Knight as "a sort of pluralist in dramatico-critical benefices, representing at one time three or four daily and weekly publications."—p. 91.

[142] T. H. Uzzell, "A Diagnosis of Dramatic Criticism," *The Unpopular Review,* July–September, 1915, 14: 96–109.

[143] J. Rankin Towse, New York *Evening Post,* July 2, 1917.

impersonation artistic? Today impersonation requires accessories such as scene, music, costume, ensemble, plot, and the like. There can be little doubt that the audience which reads dramatic criticism and which then formulates its governing principles, asks of the critic primarily, How good is this drama as drama? The art of impersonation is precisely that imitation of life, that creation of the illusion of life, for which Aristotle contended. Its values as a form of art have not changed since the days when theatres like those of Epidaurus were made large enough to contain the population of the entire city, and every man was his own critic. Good acting will bring people to a play no matter how bad it is as a life lesson, as plot, as scene; plays fail almost in proportion to the quality of the acting. Unfortunately, dramatic critics are nearly always more interested in the rules governing the accessories of their art, and in the dramatist's philosophy of life, than in the art itself."

The historian looks to the dramatic critic to give him informing criticism on those points rather than a review of the play as literature, yet it is in all of these matters that he will as a rule find dramatic criticism lacking and he will be unable to disentangle pure criticism from the confusing questions of complimentary and purchased tickets, reporter playwrights, theatrical advertising, the possibility of perverted morals and questionable taste on the part of the audience, good acting spoiled by inadequate stage setting and admirable stage setting wasted on inartistic acting.

It was many years ago that G. H. Lewes felt that to ensure good dramatic criticism more was necessary than good plays, good acting, and good critics. "There must be," he says, "not only accomplished artists and an eager public; there must be a more enlightened public. The critical pit, filled with play-goers who were familiar with fine acting and had trained judgments, has disappeared. In its place there is a mass of amusement-seekers, not without a nucleus of intelligent spectators, but of this nucleus only a small minority has very accurate ideas of what constitutes good art. . . . The drama is everywhere in Europe and America rapidly passing from an art into an amusement, just as of old it passed from a religious ceremony into an art." [144]

[144] *On Actors and the Art of Acting*, p. 182; *cf.* A. B. Walkley, "The Ideal Spectator," *Dramatic Criticism*, pp. 7–45.

The same situation is found to-day by Clayton Hamilton. The theater, he writes, suffers from the lack of patronage by persons of intelligence and taste. The public that patronizes music, painting, sculpture, dancing, all other forms of art has ceased to patronize the theater, and this has led to a decadence of dramatic criticism.[145]

Thus in dramatic criticism, as in literary criticism, the critics hold the public rather than the press ultimately responsible for the short-comings of criticism. It is apparently G. B. Shaw who alone among critics places the responsibility frankly on the press.[146]

Art criticism, as found in the press, is in its turn open to many serious criticisms. It often serves as a text for a discussion of the nature of art, for cursory histories of art, for an analysis of art at different periods, for criticism of art exhibitions as such,— a recent critic plaintively asks, "if it is impossible to keep out the pictures that should not be in, why not substitute ground glass for clear glass in framing?" It often shows a pronounced tendency to become simply fault-finding and it seldom indicates the impression made by art on the public. But since the works of art themselves remain, the defects of art criticism must give the historian less difficulty than do those of dramatic criticism.

Musical criticism presents, for the historian, somewhat the same fundamental problems as does the criticism of the drama and of art. The advertiser, the business manager, the friend, the social circle, the technical language that may conceal poverty of thought, the lack of constructive listening, the absence of standards,—all these combine, as they do in similar forms of criticism, to perplex the historian in his efforts to reconstruct the music of an era from the contemporaneous criticism of music.[147]

[145] "The Public and the Theater," Bookman, November, 1916, 44: 252–257.
[146] The Author's Apology, with Introduction by John Corbin on "The Tyranny of Police and Press," pp. 5–19.
[147] Even baser aspects are suggested by H. F. Chorley who gives an account of the efforts of an opera manager to revive his sinking fortunes through the aid of journalists who lent themselves to his sensational advertising schemes.—Thirty Years' Musical Recollections, I, 271–274.
H. G. Hewlett gives an account of money offered Chorley by a foreign composer of eminent genius who apparently believed that every musical critic had his price, and he gives more than one illustration of attempts to

The historian, for his final estimate of the value of present criticism in all its forms may well turn to Bliss Perry and read: "Musical criticism in this country has made a steady advance, always a little ahead of the musical education of the public, but constantly gaining in authority and courage as the standard of public appreciation of music has risen. The progress of architectural and art criticism has likewise corresponded to the development of public taste, always in advance of it, yet always being overtaken by it. Dramatic criticism has seemed to move in our day in a circle; the criticism of poetry and fiction seems just now to be retrograding as the public taste for poetry and fiction has grown less refined." [148]

If it be true that the chief function of a newspaper is criticism, it is also true that there is a widespread skepticism as to the trustworthiness of newspaper criticism and it is with this skepticism that the historian is concerned. Is this all but universal doubt justified, is it grossly exaggerated, is it entirely negligible?

It must be recognized that there are certain general limitations on all criticism that must invalidate it for the historian. One of the most important of these is the tendency of the public to take more kindly to censure than to praise and it is doubtless this that explains why the very word criticism has come to connote adverse judgment. Lord Palmerston who, Sir Edward Cook says, "knew most things that are to be known about the Press (except that here and there a paper may have a soul),"

---

secure favorable criticism from Chorley. But "alike to the bribery of managers, the venality of journalists and *claqueurs*, the extravagant assumptions of composers, and the insolent vanity of singers and instrumentalists, he showed himself a bitter, almost a remorseless enemy."—Henry Fothergill Chorley: *Autobiography, Memoir, and Letters*. Compiled by H. G. Hewlett, I, 289–290.

In editing Chorley's *Autobiography* in 1873, Hewlett says that "it would be affectation to assume that thirty or forty years ago the critical press, either in this country or the Continent, occupied the same honorable position in public estimation that it occupies now, or to ignore the discredit of venality and sycophancy which then attached to organs of wide circulation and influence."—I, 285.

C. A. Cooper notes that about 1850 the Pyne and Harrison Company— "the chief exponents of English opera"—"carried their musical critic with them when they were on a provincial tour. Possibly this was a measure of self-protection."—*An Editor's Retrospect*, p. 61.

[148] "The American Reviewer," *Yale Review*, October, 1914, 4: 3–24.

has put the matter concisely when he says, apropos of certain criticisms of *The Times* made by Queen Victoria:

"The profit of the newspaper arises from the price paid for advertisements, but advertisements are sent by preference to the newspaper which has the greatest circulation; and that paper gets the widest circulation which is the most amusing, the most interesting, and the most instructive. A dull paper is soon left off. The proprietors and managers of *The Times* therefore go to great expense in sending correspondents to all parts of the world where interesting events are taking place, and they employ a great many able and clever men to write articles upon all subjects which from time to time engage public attention; and as mankind takes more pleasure in reading criticism and fault-finding than praise, because it is soothing to individual vanity and conceit to fancy that the reader has become wiser than those about whom he reads, so *The Times*, in order to maintain its circulation, criticises freely everybody and everything."[149]

What was true of *The Times* of Delane's day has apparently been true of the press everywhere and the historian must take this into account in turning to it for reliable criticism of contemporaneous events. The tendency to omniscience often displayed by the press makes it unduly censorious of persons holding responsible public positions and often the most unreliable of sources for estimating justly the work of prominent leaders.[150]

In a memoir of William Thomas Arnold, after his nearly twenty years' connection with the Manchester *Guardian*, M. Filon wrote in the columns of the *Débats:*

"In the continuous effort to understand public questions, Arnold was himself guided by the spirit and method he had acquired through his Roman History ·research. . . . Does not the whole secret of good journalism depend upon the application to the men and events of the passing hour, the same critical

[149] *The Letters of Queen Victoria*, III, 590.

[150] See, *e. g.*, contemporary accounts of Washington, Jefferson, Lincoln, and Cleveland collected by the *Outlook* and given in the number for August 19, 1911, 98: 861–863.

The contemporary London press for the most part failed to understand the question at issue in the American Civil War and was equally fallible in its criticism of current events connected with it and in its prophecies as to its outcome. See Leonard Courtney, "The Making and Reading of Newspapers," *Contemporary Review*, March, 1901, 79: 365–376, and Leslie Stephen, *The "Times" on the American War.*

processes which we apply to the men and events of two thousand years ago? " [151]

Must not the historian apply to all criticism as found in the periodical press the same principles that were used by the great journalist-historian of the Manchester *Guardian?*

[151] Mrs. Humphrey Ward and C. E. Montague, *William Thomas Arnold,* p. 123.

CHAPTER XIII

THE ADVERTISEMENT

"The man who first took advantage of the general curiosity that was excited by a siege or a battle, to betray to the Readers of News into the knowledge of the shop where the best Puffs and Powders were to be sold, was undoubtedly a man of great sagacity, and profound skill in the nature of Man."—*Samuel Johnson.*

"In no manner can we so well obtain, at a rapid glance, a view of the salient points of generations that have passed as by consulting those small voices that have cried from age to age from the pages of the press, declaring the wants, the losses, the amusements, the money-making eagerness of the people."—*Quarterly Review,* 1885.

"Advertising is to business what steam is to machinery, the grand propelling power."—*Macaulay.*

"The newspaper is a microcosm of the national life. This is as much the case in regard to the advertisements as to the letter-press. A glance over the advertising columns of a large morning paper shows reflected, as it were in a mirror, the whole of the active life of the people."—*W. Stead, Jr.*

ADVERTISING has been called the process of purchasing publicity and no phenomenon in the modern world has seemed so remarkable as has its development.[1] Yet in the beginning the ad-

---

[1] Material on the history of advertising may be found in Henry Sampson, *History of Advertising,* 1875; W. Stead, Jr., *The Art of Advertising;* J. B. Williams, "The History of Advertising to 1659," *History of English Journalism,* chap. IX; J. B. Williams, "The Early History of London Advertising," *Nineteenth Century and After,* November, 1907, 62: 793–800; Montaigne discusses the origin in *Essays,* Bk. IV, chap. 24; A. Hayward, "The Advertising System," *Edinburgh Review,* February, 1843, 77: 1–43; "Advertisements," *Quarterly Review,* June, 1855, 97: 183–225; H. J. Palmer, "The March of the Advertiser," *Nineteenth Century,* January, 1897, 41: 135–141.

J. B. Williams finds the first newsbook advertisement in *Mercurius Britannicus's* Coranto, February 1, 1625–26.—*History of English Journalism,* p. 160. He also notes that two advertising offices were started in 1611 by Sir Arthur Gorges and by Sir Walter Cope.—*Ib.,* pp. 158–159.

J. Underhill considers that the first newspaper advertisement in England appeared in the *Impartial Intelligencer* in 1648.—*Athenian Oracle,* p. 251.

An exhaustive bibliography of advertising, complete to date, has been compiled under the direction of H. H. B. Meyer and is published in *Special Libraries,* April, 1916, 7: 61–76.

vertisement was scarcely more than an announcement of runaway apprentices, articles lost, auctions, and the hours of stage-coach departures. Even after the great London fire of 1666, the offer of the *London Gazette* to publish the new business locations of those who had been burned out met with little response.

It was long before the advantages of advertising were realized,—the advertiser was at first humble and obsequious in craving the patronage of those who read his announcement. Even as late as the middle of the nineteenth century he "solicits a call," "respectfully informs," "has the honor to announce," and considers that "thanks are due his customers." Not until about 1890 do we find the beginnings of the enormous volume of advertising matter that has threatened to overwhelm both periodical and reader. The advertisement to-day, from the briefest "want ad" to the single and double page daily advertisement of "big business" is the great instrument used for securing business. Everything bought or sold is advertised, wants of every description are advertised, and it has apparently come to be generally accepted that the newspaper is the best medium for advertising a large number of well-defined classes of business.

Of this situation the newspapers themselves are quick to take advantage. They advertise their own supremacy as advertising mediums and the extravagant claims of some are kept in check only by the sworn statements of audit bureaus of circulations.[2] They indicate in what lines of advertising they specialize and show by figures, charts, and every form of graphic illustration that they lead all competitors in carrying the largest number of advertisements of art, automobiles, department stores, dry goods, finance, bonds and securities, foodstuffs, hotels and restaurants, legal matters, lost and found articles, the publishing business, real estate,[3] pleasure and health resorts, recreation and amuse-

---

[2] It is interesting to note the early opposition to this check, now universally welcomed by the press as one of its chief business assets and advertised by it as such. In 1869 a contributed article in the New York *Nation* opposed strongly the "advertisers' bill" introduced at Albany compelling newspapers (but not magazines) to declare in each issue the number of copies printed of the preceding issue.—April 1, 1869, 8: 252.

[3] Parke Godwin, connected with the *Evening Post* from 1836 to 1881, states that he originated the real estate advertisements in that paper. He went to the leading real estate dealers in New York City and induced the

ment, schools of every description, the theater, "wants," Christmas advertising, general advertising, display advertising, national or international advertising, and they are true to their newspaper colors in sometimes indicating a preference for advertisements having news value.[4] They display by graphic illustration and indicate by figures the percentage of increase in their advertisements over their own best previous record and over the best records of their competitors; they publish the aggregate number of advertising lines, columns, and pages printed in a year, and give the total number of columns carried in a single number,— in one case, 609 columns in the issue of September 22, 1919. They publish the number of columns of advertisements they are compelled to omit for lack of space and the number of advertisements of "wants" cancelled because the needs have been immediately filled. They print the names of advertisers that have used their columns or pages ten years or more, state that they themselves advertise in more than four hundred weeklies, and announce that their circulation is not only large but of the best quality and that their advertisers "move in the best society." Since their circulation is greatest among the monied classes, the returns to advertisers, they feel, will be correspondingly large. They announce the daily delivery of the paper by airplane, and state where copies may be obtained in other cities and what news stands are open until late at night. They carry advertisements in different languages, and they republish in book form the advertisements that have appeared in their columns. The newspapers themselves seem to have caught the spirit of those who advertise in their columns and to have taken on something of the department-store methods of advertising themselves.[5]

---

firm to let him print their advertisements free for one year. "After that they were very glad to pay for their advertisements."—*The Evening Post Hundredth Anniversary*, p. 43.

[4] "Owing to the great demand for advertising space in The New York Times it has frequently been necessary to omit many advertisements. This demand promises to continue and forces discrimination in assigning space, i. e., preference will be given to advertisements having news value and to those for which copy is delivered before 6 P. M. on the day previous to publication."—New York *Times*, October 25, 1916, and subsequently at intervals.

[5] One paper conducts a "music in the home" page and under its auspices advertises popular priced home symphony concerts; others advertise contests,

In all of the appeals that the newspaper makes to its varied classes of readers, through its own published advertisements of itself, the paramount one is made to its advertisers. It is seldom to-day that the newspaper in its advertisements of itself appeals to the general reader, or to its priority in news-gathering, or the excellence of its editorials. It may advertise that its photograph patrol is constantly visualizing the daily events for its readers, it may print a table of contents for the guidance of readers, though even so it adds a special guide to the kind of advertising in which it specializes; but it never fails in the large cities to note the arrival of out-of-town buyers and to give their hotel address, and to emphasize in every way its own supremacy as a medium of communication between buyer and seller.[6]

It was the commercial advertisement that first came to the forefront and that in the opinion of many has now come to control the policy of the periodical press. But to the historian the interest of the commercial advertisement lies not so much in its ubiquity, its obtrusiveness, its cleverness, and its ingratiating manner as it does in the appeal it unconsciously makes to its readers, in the changes that have come in this respect, and in the revelation of itself and of current conditions that are thus made.

The early commercial advertisements were largely haphazard in their form and hence in their appeal. In the middle of the last century, Hayward noted that pain or the fear of pain was the most active stimulant to advertising and that this resulted in the supremacy of patent medicine advertising. Since vanity made

---

in infinite variety, by which they hope to profit; others use flattery,—"you like to form your own opinion;" some maintain a "better job bureau;" others open their libraries to the public. The greater number of these devices are seemingly used to increase circulation.

[6] It is interesting to note the wide divergence in self-advertising of the monthly magazine and of the daily newspaper. The monthly makes its appeal on the ground that it carries "no gloom and no filth," but is good-natured and practical; that it is not hitched to any cause; that it believes in families and in decent life; and that "its stuff is not long and tedious,"— "no story ever has more than 4,000 words;" that it is not a fighting magazine, but it has infinite variety and is journalistic in form; and it is prone to advertise how much of various commodities its families of readers buy. Its general appeal is to the somewhat sentimental side of human nature.

The publishers of various monthlies often carry inconspicuously in their own small advertisements in the daily press the names of well-known business houses whose advertisements are carried in their monthlies.

the next strongest appeal, the advertisers of beauty producers followed hard after quack doctors.[7] But anaesthetics and science have found "a better way" for the relief of suffering, while the balance has been shifted from interest in personal beauty to the more vital things in life. Conditions of life have greatly changed since that day and advertisements with them. Under the influence of experimental psychology they developed enormously in extent and in effectiveness, and their appeal was centered on the product, the nature of the finished article to be sold. But to-day the commercial advertisement in its appeal reverts to first principles and more and more it runs its roots far back into a remote past. Greece and Rome, banished from the editorial columns of the periodical press, live on in perpetual youth in the advertising pages. Classical mythology advertises automobile tires, cement, horseshoes, lead pencils, stoves, hats, and mineral waters; ancient geography and history advertise rubber companies, shoes, and cigarettes; the Greek and Latin languages advertise special brands of soap, oil, and ready-made clothing. The Sphinx, the Pyramids, and notable Egyptian columns form the background of illustrated advertisements. Caravans from India and argosies from Venice, the streets of Cairo and of Constantinople, and tales from the Arabian Nights advertise modern products. Even a representation of a man of the stone age advertises a variety of chewing-gum, and the tower of Babel a history of the world. Historical structures, portraits of men eminent in the past, buildings and bridges erected by famous architects, accounts of historic events,[8] and descriptions of historic scenes all make their contribution to the commercial advertising of to-day. One of its strongest appeals is thus found in this universal, though probably unconscious, desire to connect the immediate present with a remote antiquity. The newer is the commodity to be put on the market the more insistent is the appeal to the past. The more an industry realizes that a large part of the community holds it in disfavor, the more it associates with its advertisements the names

[7] A. Hayward, "The Advertising System," *Edinburgh Review*, February, 1843, 77: 1–43.

[8] An important automobile company carried as an advertisement in the daily press of November 27, 1918, two double columns of the history of the Pilgrim Fathers.

of the great men of history. Psychology has given the form to the commercial advertisement while history has given the substance; the one represents the cross-cut section, the other the longitudinal view of commercial advertising.

Commercial advertising often appeals not only to history but to the imagination. Pegasus and Pygmalion, the Sistine Chapel, da Vinci, and Benvenuto Cellini and every great character and important association in history are conjured up by the imagination and become a part of the daily newspaper.

The commercial advertisement was long content with exploiting the products of industry,—silks, woolens, laces; bicycles, motorcycles, and automobiles. But to-day it concentrates its appeal on bridging the distance between producer and consumer and on the processes of production. Time and space are annihilated when products are "sold everywhere" and "can be found everywhere," and when the consumer has only to "ask your grocer," or to "inform us if you can't get it."

The advertiser of furs takes readers to the far North and describes the various steps by which furs, through trapping, trading, and shipping, are brought from remote places and peoples to great metropolitan centers. The advertisers of pearls explain the pearl fisheries in Oriental seas and the steps that intervene between the shell as it comes from the hand of the diver and the pearls as they reach Fifth Avenue. The process of shoe manufacture and the preparation of milk for the market; the textile mill that shows every process in the manufacture of cotton, woolen, silk, and knit goods; the advertisement of a complete exhibit of the textiles used in the army and the navy; the advertisement giving an insight into the extent that the manufacture of by-products plays in a great industry; the description of the equipment of a great electric company,—everywhere, whether it be a tool, a screw, an implement, the construction of an automobile tire, or a factory in full operation, it is the process of production that is advertised as an appeal in the sale of commodities.

In many forms of business, the advertising appeal is made to the conditions under which work is performed,—to the abundance of fresh air and sunshine, the short hours of labor, the holidays and summer vacations, rest rooms and lunch rooms, medical attendance, clubs and classes, to the general high standards of physical and intellectual conditions maintained.

The banking house and the insurance company make their appeal to authority and to precedent, to evidence of law and to court decisions, to guarantees of safety and security. They state the points at issue in cases that have come before the courts and give the court decisions made, together with specific reference to volume and page where the decisions are recorded; they appeal to age, to the high standing, and the distinction of their officers during their long history.

The advertising world is peopled with characters as well known as are those of the real world [9] and even the animals assume a semblance of real life.[10]

But the development of advertising has reached far beyond the confines of business. While commercial advertising as yet takes up the greatest space in the press, it is by no means the most important of all classes of advertising. The advertisement is used to solicit contributions to all charitable causes, and this in addition to the older and more familiar advertisements of balls, bazaars, concerts, and other forms of entertainment for the benefit of specific causes. The numerous associations for the relief of sufferers from fire, flood, earthquake, famine, disease, and war reach the philanthropic through the advertisement. Relief during the recent war was sought through advertisements for the Armenians, Belgians, French, Germans, Greeks, Hungarians, Irish, Italians, Persians, Poles, Roumanians, Russians, Serbians, Syrians, Ukrainians, and probably other nationalities; for war orphans, fatherless children, widows, the wounded, the sick, men blinded in battle, and cripples; for artists, musicians, university professors, and clergymen; for Jews, Roman Catholics, and various other religious denominations, and for the United War Workers; for contributions of money, food, clothing, books, periodicals, toys,

[9] Sunny Jim, Phoebe Snow, and the nameless but equally well-known cream-of-wheat chef, Baker's chocolate lady, the Armour boy, Uneeda biscuit boy, Jello girl, Fairy Soap child, Gold Dust twins, Campbell kids, and a score of others are all familiar friends.

[10] Victor dog, Bon Ami chicken, Horlick cow, Borden eagle, borax mules, tobacco bull, dates of dromedary fame, are but suggestions of the wide use of animals in advertising.

The contributions of vegetable and plant life are much less numerous.

chairs for free kindergartens, "patriotic yarn," and Thanksgiving dinners; for homes for consumptives, foundling hospitals, the promotion of proper housing for girls, improving the condition of children brought before the children's court, and for various missions, cults, and fraternal organizations; for victims of infantile paralysis; bandage material for lepers; boys' clubs; the Christmas Fund for Belgian Children; the Royal Blind Asylum and School, Edinburgh, Scotland; the British Red Cross and the Order of St. John of Jerusalem; for Belgian relief.[11]

The American Ambulance hospital of Paris advertised for contributions and forestalled criticism of the expense thereby entailed by stating that "no part of any contribution is used to pay expenses of postage, printing, advertising, salaries, or anything else." Every number after the first in the series of appeals headed "Message to Jews" was followed by some variation of the statement, "A friend has paid for and donated this advertisement." The advertisement of the Federation for the Support of Jewish Charitable and Philanthropic Societies of New York City contains an interesting record in the statement that "the modern, tested and proper method" is to give through a federated organization.[12]

In all of these philanthropic advertisements and appeals for contributions to various good causes it is evident that the appeal is largely made to the emotions. Funds are desired for "suffering Belgians," "French orphans," "starving Poles," "milk for babies," but little evidence is given in the advertisement of exact

[11] The manager of this fund stated, "Newspaper advertising has been our strongest asset, and more than $500,000 has come in with blanks and coupons clipped from our advertisements in the newspapers. Another $250,000 can be traced to newspaper advertising."—New York *Times*, March 31, 1915.

[12] New York *Evening Post*, November 23, 1916.

These illustrations have been taken from New York dailies, but they are typical of the appeals found in other metropolitan papers. These appeals have been specially numerous at Thanksgiving and at Christmas.

Among the most significant requests have been those in the announcements of deaths. One was followed by the statement, "It is earnestly requested that no flowers be sent, but that those who so desire make a donation in memory of the deceased to the Montefiore Home for Aged and Infirm Hebrews or to similar institutions."—September 5, 1916.

Another reads: "It is most earnestly requested that instead of sending flowers, those who wish to do so, send contributions in his memory to the American Red Cross for war relief work."—December 6, 1916.

information in regard to actual conditions or the precise needs of special places or districts; no information is given, comparable to what is found in commercial advertising, as to the methods by which the funds collected are administered, or the results that have followed from the efforts made. Enormous sums for relief work have been collected through advertising, but since the appeal has been so largely emotional, it is not surprising to learn through the press that the funds raised have sometimes been dissipated in extravagant expenditure.[13]

Governments have entered the lists and have extensively used the advertisement to secure recruits,[14] to further government loans, and to carry on their commercial and industrial activities. But although a government may be behind all of these classes of advertising, the appeal made through each class differs and hence they are in reality fundamentally unlike.

Since war is always war, the inducements held out for entering the regular army have never varied in principle since the days when Paul Jones issued his broadsides inviting "gentlemen seamen" to join his expedition,[15] to 1919 when the Federal

[13] Reports of the Army and Navy Bazaar, daily press, October, 1917. The profits were "amazingly small," since agents and promoters of the bazaar had received enormous fees.

[14] At a meeting of the American Luncheon Club in London, June 11, 1915, H. Le Bas (later Sir Hedley), who had been directing the great advertising efforts to raise British armies, said that nothing had ever demonstrated so clearly the usefulness of advertising.—New York *Tribune*, June 12, 1915. More than a year later he stated that the British government had been carrying on an advertising campaign of such a nature and extent as had never before been undertaken by any nation. It comprised not only pleas for army volunteers and loans of money, but also condemnation of extravagance in every form. Display advertisements were kept running in 1500 newspapers and spread on myriads of billboards. He estimated that by this means 5,000,000 recruits had enlisted and "billions of dollars raised in loans." The working classes turned over to the Government £100,000,000 from their savings during the first two years of the war and Sir Hedley believed that the advertisements had been responsible for the deposit of a large proportion of this amount.—Correspondence of the Associated Press, New York *Times*, August 6, 1916.

The number of recruits secured through advertising was apparently overestimated by Sir Hedley. See statements made a year later, *infra*, p. 343.

Advertisements for recruits in America seemed to be less successful, and in at least one town the advertisements were torn down.—New York *Evening Post*, August 15, 1916.

[15] "A very rare broadside inviting enlistment under Paul Jones, 1777," is headed "Great Encouragement for Seamen" and announces that for

Government widely advertised for army and navy recruits.[16] War is represented only on its defensive, never on its aggressive side, and the advertisements have never suggested the hardships, privations, and suffering that are inevitable in all war, nor have the advertisements carried any guarantee that the inducements held out will ever be fulfilled. Unfortunately, the universal fear of incurring the charge of disloyalty and of lack of patriotism casts a heavy shadow over the press. Scarcely an indication is given anywhere that the government advertisements for recruits for the regular army and navy are misleading and that that class of advertising is antiquated and far inferior to the commercial advertising of the day,—antiquated and inferior in view of the campaigns everywhere carried on for honest advertising. War is brutal and a brute remains a brute whether wearing evening dress, a golf suit, or khaki, but the government advertisement

---

"all gentlemen seamen and able-bodied landsmen who have a mind to distinguish themselves in the glorious cause of their country, and make their fortunes, an opportunity now offers on board the Ship Ranger . . . where they will be kindly entertained, and receive the greatest encouragement. . . . Any gentlemen volunteers who have a mind to make an agreeable voyage in this pleasant season of the year, may, by entering on board the above Ship Ranger, meet with every civility they can possibly expect, and for a further encouragement depend on the first opportunity being embraced to reward each one agreable to his merit."—In December, 1776, the Continental Congress, "for the Encouragement of those that shall Inlist in the Continental Army," had announced by broadside the payment of twenty dollars bounty and a suit of clothes annually to each soldier who should enlist for a term of three years, and in addition one hundred acres of land to those serving to the end of the war.

A handbill sent among the British troops on Bunker Hill offered "seven dollars a month, fresh provisions and in plenty, health, freedom, ease, affluence, and a good farm."—C. K. Bolton, *The Private Soldier under Washington*, pp. 46, 66, 90.

Much important information is given throughout the book in regard to the promises held out and the difficulty of fulfilling them.

[16] The inducements advertised were:—"the chance of a life time to see the battlefields of France and the Rhine," "healthy out-of-doors life," the volunteer "will have the best physical care with the best food and clothes that money can buy," "the army gives you the only real companionship in the world," "opportunities innumerable for advancement," "free education," "training in a skilled trade," "good pay and money in the bank," "plenty of liberty," "lots of entertainment," "you go to shows, dances, movies, you meet agreeable people in the hostess houses, you get acquainted with nice girls, in fact you have a better time than most civilians," "Men, it's a great life!"—Daily press, June, 1919.

gives no hint of this when "guaranteed advertisements" are in the forefront in all business advertising.

The various liberty and victory loans were entirely different and had a definite educative value. The appeal made by them was largely to honor, duty, patriotism, loyalty, hatred of the enemy; to history,—"Columbus was in quest of a liberty loan," while Washington, Franklin, Jefferson, Lincoln, and Grant were all commandeered, and a description was given of the invasion of France by the Huns in the fifth century. But the appeal was also made to discouraging the enemy, shortening the war, and preventing greater bloodshed. Most of all, the advertisements emphasized the investment character of the loans and they became a text for many a sermon preached against waste and extravagance and in favor of thrift, saving, and the rainy day. "As safe as a government bond" had for the first time a meaning to millions of small investors. The advertisements themselves were definite and exact,—one manufacturing company donated an advertisement "expressing its idea of exactly how Liberty Bonds should be advertised to make those who are unaccustomed to bond investments know what a bond is." Other advertisements gave forms of bonds, illustrated the blanks to be filled out in subscribing to the loan, discussed the important points to be kept in mind in making investments, and gave a mass of expert advice on securities, investments, and business methods and principles never before so readily available to the general public. Precisely what a fifty dollar bond would buy and the extent to which the loan would help the government was explained, and then the shield was turned and the advantage of the loan as an investment also shown.

The advertisements of the loan illustrated, better than had ever been done before, the value of collective advertising,—hundreds of forms of business, from art dealers and automobile manufacturers to the tobacco trade and upholsterers, combined to contribute advertising space where the advantages of the loan as a business investment were definitely stated.

The industrial and commercial advertising of the government during the war assumed various forms. The government control of the railroads led to a decline in national advertising since the different lines were forbidden to claim superior service, or to publish extraneous matter of any sort,—"folders must be purely informative." But later the department of labor carried an advertisement urging all to advertise who had anything to sell. The government itself acted on this advice and sold alien property, surplus army supplies, and complete industrial communities,—and the love of a bargain became the general appeal.

The great force wielded by advertising in the hands of a national government is best summed up in a statement of the indispensable aid it rendered the British government during the war. In June, 1917, it had already been the means through which the ministry had enlisted 3,000,000 volunteers, had secured "countless billions in loans," had discovered more than a million men who were transformed into skilled munition workers, had persuaded more than a million women to take up work that thus released men for the army and that had taught the people to work harder and to produce more.[17]

States and cities have widely explained their advantages and sought settlers through advertisements,[18] and they have carried on business propaganda in urging that every one eat the products

[17] J. M. Allison, New York *Tribune*, June 6, 1917.

[18] Arkansas, Georgia, and other states have arranged railway trains, organized land exhibits, and in other ways sought to influence immigration to these states. The newspaper advertising of these efforts has been indirect but not the less important.

The Southern Commercial Congress in 1917 urged a wide publicity campaign through the press in the interests of the South.

The Chamber of Commerce of Kansas City in the summer of 1919 advertised extensively in Eastern papers the advantages of Kansas City from the standpoint of business, transportation facilities, climate, and health.

This too is not a new device. The New York *Tribune* for November 6, 1872, called attention on its editorial page to a compilation published on another page of letters from various states inviting immigration. "Florida, Texas, California, and Oregon each have special advantages to advertise; and the adventurous pilgrim who seeks a new home and wider field of industry is sure to meet welcome and good words from these and many other bidders for more population."

In 1922, the governor of Nebraska stated that publicity through advertising had made the State prosper. — New York *Times*, May 2, 1922.

Tourists have been sought in every quarter of the globe through extensive advertising campaigns.

of certain states on a specified date, as apples, onions, oranges, raisins; or to use American products.[19]

It was in 1916 that a widespread appeal began to be made through advertisements as a means of influencing public opinion, especially in regard to industrial conditions. Both sides of disputes were presented through advertisements and occasionally a third side was advertised. The conviction that reliance could be placed on the public to decide in favor of the right side, when once acquainted with the facts, had probably never before been so much in evidence as it was at that time.

In the disagreements between the Cloak, Suit and Skirt Manufacturers' Protective Association and their employees, the Citizens' Committee advertised the points at issue in the controversy and their reasons for supporting the side of the workers. The manufacturers also advertised their side of the question, and "an unbiased citizen" advertised a plan for the immediate settlement of the strike. The case of the railroads was set forth through advertisements at the time of an anticipated railroad strike, and the Railway Investors' League conveyed through advertisements its desire "to protect the interests of investors in the crisis which threatens railroad credit and national prosperity." The New York Railways Company, the Third Avenue Railway Company, the Interborough Rapid Transit Company, and the Brooklyn Rapid Transit Company all stated their position through advertisement at the time of the street car strike, and through the same means assured the public of their determination to run cars in spite of the strike. After the strike at the Bayonne, New Jersey, refinery, the Standard Oil Company (New Jersey) stated its position in the matter through a solid three column advertisement. An important business house in New York City whose drivers had struck, not for higher wages but for a closed shop, announced through advertisements its determination not to accede to the demand and stated to the public its general business policy. In the

[19] The Silk Association of America discussed fully in an advertisement the question of the relative difference in the amount spent on clothes by men and by women, and in the course of an elaborate argument urged that all tailored suits should be sewed with silk.—New York *Times*, November 13, 1916.

controversy between the producers and the distributors of milk during the summer and autumn, exhaustive advertisements in all the New York papers set forth the position of the distributors and gave a mass of important information in regard to the scientific and hygienic handling of milk as well as the industrial questions involved. The anthracite coal operators explained the demands of the operatives and their reasons for not granting them. A series of bulletins issued by the Bethlehem Steel Company advertised in the summer of 1916 the advantages of having armor plate manufactured by privately owned companies rather than by Government-owned plants.

That this conviction of the value of the advertisement in acquainting the public with both sides of a controversy has had a basis in fact seems borne out by the great acceleration in this form of advertising since 1916. Late in 1918, and in 1919, public opinion was appealed to through the advertisements of both sides in the hotel waiters' strike, the harbor strike, the building industries controversy, the international ladies' garment workers union dispute, the printers' strike, the disputes involving the publishers' printing companies, theater managers and actors, and various other industries and occupations. Among the most persistent of all advertisers have been the Dairymen's League and the various individual and collective milk producers' associations. All the questions at issue in the milk drivers' strike in 1921 were presented through advertisements, while both sides of the question of trading stamps and coupons have been presented through advertisements.

But industrial relations involve much besides strikes and controversies and the advertisement often appeals to the public or to definite classes through information given, and points out their co-operative or contributory responsibility. In 1916, the Illinois Railroad Committee advertised the comparative risks from railway trains incurred by motor vehicles, horses, and teams, and pedestrians in crossing railway tracks; gave the percentage of each class that looked neither way, both ways, or one way only; and showed which should stop and why. The Long Island Railroad advertised a long series of "Life-Saving Bulletins" asking the public to use every reasonable caution on approaching grade crossings and explaining the precautions taken by the railroad. In 1918, a campaign against death and disability by accident was carried on in New York City during four months by thirty-five manufacturing interests, financial institutions, public service corporations, insurance companies, firms, and individuals, under the general heading, "Take Care!"

But other questions, as well as those of industry, have two sides and after 1914 the questions of war and peace, of preparedness, of universal military training, of thrift and savings, were all argued or stated through advertisements,—not always with extreme good nature, for an advertisement of the Emergency Peace Federation was answered with an advertisement that was a biting parody of itself.

The advertising campaign urging the conservation of food, fuel, and travel for pleasure was apparently universal. Special campaigns in favor of thrift and conservation were carried on by the lines of business that had suffered most from the thoughtlessness of their patrons. The telephone companies through advertisements urged their patrons not to call "information" unnecessarily, to avoid curiosity calls, not to have telephones moved, to pay bills promptly, and they issued a series of "Don'ts" of universal application. They took advantage of the situation and incidentally advertised the business and personal advantages of courtesy, politeness, good manners, correct habits, and etiquette in the use of the telephone, and parallel principles for the guidance of telephone operatives were widely advertised. The department stores urged their customers not to return merchandise, to carry small packages, not to ask for special deliveries, to shop in the morning, and in many other ways attempted to indicate fundamental business principles for the benefit of thoughtless shoppers. "Conservation chats" through advertisements were widely popular, but the distinction between legitimate conservation and unwise saving was not always clearly made and this led to responsive advertising. "An Open Letter" to several named gentlemen "and other well-meaning patriots" begged them to "please soften this extreme save, save, save, talk;" other advertisements warned of "misdirected economies," of the "curtailment of consistent expenditures," and urged that "it is just as wrong to give and not spend as it is to spend and not give." No more troublesome questions were argued by the embattled advertisers than those of expenditure and of saving.

Advertisements to influence personal action merge imperceptibly into those intended to actuate collective action. Arguments for and against proposed legislation have been widely circulated through newspaper advertisements and they have often proved distinctly serviceable in presenting facts to a heedless, ignorant, or prejudiced public.[20] Where the comparative strength of the two sides has been in doubt, as in the questions of equal suffrage and prohibition, the pros and cons have been vigorously stated. Where authority has felt its strength, it has not troubled to answer the advertising appeals of its opponents. The postal zone law was ably and widely opposed through advertisements. Direct appeals against entrance into war and against preparedness were practically answered, not by facts and argument, but by indirect appeals to loyalty, patriotism, and honor. Where the advertisers have been upholding a losing cause, as in the case of compulsory vaccination, and vivisection, their advertisements have been ignored by their opponents. Advertisements that have assumed an unproved thesis, as those of the Association to Resist English Domination of American Commerce, have also apparently been ignored. But a movement to save the retail trade district of New York was carried on through advertisement and met with surprising success.[21]

Many of these advertisements have represented not only

[20] The first instance noted was the advertisement of oleomargarine; it was used to urge the repealing of an objectionable law and the passage of a better one.—*Outlook*, November 30, 1912, 102: advertising section.

In a western state, a bill before the legislature to increase the number of trainmen on every railway train was referred back to the voters of the state. Advertisements were published in the press telling in a clear, definite way how the proposed law was a menace both to the people and the roads, and the bill failed.—New York *Evening Post*, March 6, 1916.

The Railway Investors' League advertised an "Open Letter to All Investors in American Railway Securities in regard to the Newlands Joint Congressional Committee."—Daily press, November 21, 1916.

A more questionable illustration has been noted where a state institution in the Middle West bought editorials in the country press at advertising rates for the purpose of influencing the state legislature to make it a larger appropriation.—H. Holt, *Commercialism and Journalism*, p. 25.

[21] Daily press, September, 1916.

current opinion but they have unconsciously recorded the survival in our own time of primitive instincts of mankind. The language of the mediaeval personal combat was perpetuated in the full page advertisement of many citizens of a Western city bearing foreign names published in a newspaper of Washington, D. C., calling on their representatives in Congress "to take prompt and vigorous action for the protection of the honor and dignity of the nation." The selfishness of the unselfish was recorded in the advertisement signed by several distinguished citizens protesting against the entrance of America into the war on the ground that "What we can achieve on that field [of war] will win nothing for humanity, and for us neither profit or glory, for our adversaries have nothing that we want, and their strength is already gone." [22]

It is again a hair line that marks the separation between modern propaganda and old-fashioned politics. Whether or not political parties took their cue from the propagandists is immaterial, but it is certain that the presidential campaign of 1916 saw an extraordinary development of political advertising and the transference of interest to it from the editorial and from political rallies. The side to be presented by the editorial was almost a foregone conclusion, while rallies had been most expensive and they had been attended only by the partisans of the party arranging them. The political advertisement carried a new appeal and quickly outstripped in interest and effectiveness all the old-time forms of political campaigning. It was carried on not only by the publicity committees of the great party organizations, but by independent leagues, by fusion committees, by non-political associations interested in non-political legislation, by partisan associations formed to secure a specific end or to defeat an undesired policy, by non-partisan leagues for good government, and by every organization that had not a special "organ" at its command. It reached its climax in the advertisements supporting or opposing candidates or parties that appeared over the signature of private individuals and presumably at their personal expense,[23] and in the formation

[22] New York *Times*, February 5, 1917.

[23] Henry Ford advertised under the caption "Humanity and Your Vote" the reasons that led him to support President Wilson, and placed the

of advertising clubs pledged to the slogan, "the truth in politics."[24] Within the various states political advertising was effectively used.[25]

It was significant that national political advertising in 1920 was much less extensive than it had been during the preceding presidential campaign,—significant in that the result of the election seemed a foregone conclusion and advertising therefore unnecessary for both of the two great parties.

One of the most significant campaigns involving political action, although economic in the nature of the question at issue, was carried on in 1917 between George W. Perkins as chairman of the New York City food supply committee and the agricultural societies of New York State. Through advertisements of Saturday, August 18, the chairman gave definite information to the citizens of the city concerning the food bill advocated by Governor Whitman and directed his advertisements against unscrupulous food speculators and other selfish interests. These were followed on Monday by advertisements addressed to the citizens of the state and appealing especially to the up-State

---

advertisement in five hundred newspapers in all sections of the country.—New York *Times*, October 31, November 5, 1916. John Wanamaker was stated by the Democratic National Committee to be responsible for a full page advertisement appearing in the leading papers in the largest cities of Pennsylvania, New Jersey, New York, Connecticut, Delaware, and West Virginia.

Advertisements appeared over the signatures respectively of George Harvey, Thomas W. Lawson, George W. Perkins, and Amos Pinchot.

These all appeared in New York dailies.

[24] The advantages of such clubs were set forth by a group of Chicago advertising men who declared that they "would give to the Republican party a permanent organization of trained publicity experts who will for the first time apply to politics the same merchandizing principles that are applied to successful business enterprises."—New York *Tribune*, July 23, 1916.

[25] In New York a series of nearly thirty advertisements issued by the Non-Partisan League for Good Government brought detailed and exhaustive charges against the administration of Governor Whitman. These ran from October 9 to November 7, 1916, and constitute the most explicit arraignment of a public official through advertisement that has been noted.—The omission of one in the numbered series seemed to indicate a fear on the part of the advertisers that it carried libellous matter.

In Ohio the Republican candidate for governor carried on his campaign by means of display advertising and with the help of "one of the greatest advertising men in America. This man has made a certain paint a household word. We're advertising to the people of Ohio my brand of politics."—United Press despatches, July 6, 1916.

farmers to support the proposed bill. Later, a number of the farmers' organizations through a speech at a county fair opposed the confirmation of Mr. Perkins as president of the state food commission, and when their representative was asked why they did not give their objections publicity through the press, he replied that "Mr. Perkins was able to purchase space in the press, but that farmers had no money for such purpose." Mr. Perkins at once offered to pay for an advertisement in every morning and afternoon paper in the State giving the reasons against his own confirmation by the Senate that had been advanced by the representative of the agricultural societies. The offer was accepted and the advertisement appeared.

The episode is significant not only as illustrating the belief in the efficacy of the advertisement as a means of securing desired legislation and of defeating a plan of a state governor, but also as showing supreme confidence in the ability and the willingness of the voters to decide between two opposing sides after both have been presented by advertisement and most of all the willingness to make "the trial by advertisement" at the expense of the person opposed. Reliance on the advertisement as a means of settling political controversy can scarcely be carried further.

The domestic political advertisement in its turn leads into the advertisement that has its international aspects [26] or that may lead to international complications. The advertisement was used in an effort to prevent the sale of arms and ammunitions to the Allies,[27] and residents of other countries have used the advertisement to influence public opinion in times of emergency,[28]

[26] The Republican National Publicity Committee, in the interests of protective tariff, reproduced in American papers a poster issued by the Tariff Reform League of London; the Association to Resist English Domination of American Commerce issued an advertisement addressed to the Secretary of State in regard to the black list published by the British government; the appearance of the *Deutschland* gave opportunity to direct advertisements against the Administration. The hyphen in disguise often appeared in political advertising.

[27] Advertisements signed by the editors of four hundred and thirty-two out of the five hundred and seventy-five papers belonging to the American Association of Foreign Language Newspapers; the appeal was published in two hundred newspapers scattered throughout the United States, April 5, 1915.

[28] This cable message sent the Belgian Consul-General in New York appeared as an advertisement in the press: "News from Belgium describes

to secure the recognition of independence of disaffected or revolutionary states or to win popular support of national causes.[29] Stern rebukes were administered by cabinet officers to firms that in their advertisements of poisonous, acid-loaded shells "draw a picture of human misery as a means of earning a profit through the sale of machines to produce it." [30] To the advertisement has been given the credit of so influencing public opinion in Germany as to bring about national unity.[31]

Even the domestic advertisement is not exempt from the danger of libel suits incurred through its statements and from misstatements and misunderstandings that call for explanation and apology.[32]

situation horrible. Over forty thousand men already deported for military works, amid awful scenes. Number proposed three hundred thousand. Please get influential friends start strong campaign opinion which might prevent extensive slave raid. I implore your help in name humanity and honour mankind."

(Signed) Chevalier Carton de Wiart.

[29] The recognition of Lithuania and of Ukrainia was sought through advertisements; the Friends of Irish Freedom and the Russian Economic League appealed for support through advertisements.

The Japan Society was organized in 1907 and in 1916 advertised in the New York papers its desire to give the public "a proper conception of the aims and ideals, the inspirations and aspirations of this newly 'westernized' island empire whose social, industrial and economic progress has amazed the world."

[30] Letters of Secretary Redfield, daily press, July 19, 20, 1915.

The advertisement as it appeared in the *American Machinist*, May 6, 1915, threatened to lead to international entanglements, but the investigations of the Department of Commerce showed that the advertisement related, not to the manufacture of poisonous shells, which would have been a contravention of the Hague convention, but to that of machinery to be used in such production.—New York *Times*, June 25, 1915.

The advertisement was included, without apparent appropriateness, by F. Avenarius in his *Das Bild als Verleumder* and attention was directed to the peculiarly offensive features of the advertisement, while the complementary illustration of the machine itself was omitted. P. 56

[31] C. H. Whitaker, in an article under the headlines, "Great advertising man led Germany to war. By an unparalleled publicity campaign, using many mediums, he advertised Germany to the Germans until they held views he wished," describes the use of the advertisement in influencing public opinion in Germany.—New York *Times Magazine*, September 5, 1915.

[32] *The New Republic*, March 25, 1916, carried an advertisement of *Harper's Weekly* that asked leading questions in regard to a recent American Ambassador and promised the answers to them in a forthcoming article. In its issue of July 22, 1916, the editors copy the original advertisement and add: "The foregoing was published as a matter of business routine. It is needless to say that it was not intended by *The New Republic* as a reflection in any way upon the official or personal conduct of Mr. . . . *The New Republic*

The advertisement is sometimes used as a means of "getting even" with business or political opponents,—a device not new. Cave complained in the *Gentleman's Magazine* in 1783 of "fallacious advertisements to set the Publick against this Magazine," and Vizetelly writes of the insertion of a spitefully worded advertisement in London morning papers of February 26, 1856, intended to injure the parliamentary prospects of Herbert Ingram.[33] To-day such advertisements do not pass unanswered but take on a distinctly strophic and antistrophic character.[34]

The advertisement of churches and advertising campaigns to promote church attendance have not as yet met with universal favor, and the proposal so to use the advertisement has given rise to the charge that the churches are becoming sensational and to heated discussion as to whether church advertising is ethical. But it is significant of the dependence of the public on advertising, and therefore of the apparent necessity of using this means to secure a desired end, that each year apparently sees a more and more extensive use of advertising by the churches, and that a conference on advertising as a means of stimulating church attendance was held in connection with the Convention of the Associated Advertising Clubs of the World in Philadelphia in 1916.[35] The question of whether the churches shall advertise

---

regrets that any one should have found in the foregoing advertisement anything derogatory to Mr. . . ."

"Only the other week a big magazine refused to print an advertisement which in its copy reflected upon the business methods of competitors of the advertiser, resisted a suit at law to maintain its position—'and won'."— G. French, Report of Sagamore Sociological Conference, 1912.

". . . the Abgeordneten Fest, or dinner to the Liberal Members to be given at Cologne and here on Saturday and Sunday. The Government have forbidden it, and the newspapers are filled every day with letters of notice to this and that person, from the Cologne police authorities warning them not to attend, and the answers. Yesterday the *Cologne Gazette*, the chief German paper, was seized, because it contained an advertisement to the effect that the dinner would still take place."—Matthew Arnold, *Letters*, I, 338.

[33] *Glances Back Through Seventy Years*, I, 424.

[34] New York daily press, April, 1915; August, 1919;—illustrations are not infrequent.

[35] It is interesting to note that in October, 1916, an advertising convention to promote church attendance was held in New Haven, Connecticut, under the joint auspices of the leading clergymen of the city and the Publicity Club of the Chamber of Commerce.

In July, 1921, the press carried the statement that two important con-

or not is apparently being superseded by the discussion of what are the most effective means of advertising them.[36]

Active campaigns in the interests of health and safety, of better conditions of living and of working are everywhere carried on through advertising by great permanent organizations like the Life Extension Institute, by individuals, and by collective industries. The importance of a rational diet and of the proper care of all parts of the body, with corresponding information of the harmful effects of incorrect habits of living; the announcement of offices to let "with lots of healthy sunshine;" of the closing of cigar stores on Sundays for the benefit of employees; the caution that all applying for work in assembling orders "must be able to work standing,"—all of these but illustrate the widespread belief in the efficacy of advertising to convey lessons of health and a belief in the importance of health in every line of business.

The advertisement has been urged as an effective means of teaching world brotherhood;[37] it has even been suggested that the friendship between the Entente Alliance and the United States has been the result of business relations established many years ago,[38] while an equally strong case could be made out

ferences of the Protestant Episcopal Church had unanimously endorsed the use of the advertising columns of daily newspapers for general church publicity as well as for evangelistic purposes.—New York *Tribune*, July 18, 1921.

[36] "The daily newspaper is without any question the best advertising medium for the Church . . . for general publicity, the newspaper is unexcelled for our purpose."—C. Stelzle, *Principles of Successful Church Advertising*, p. 72; C. F. Reisner, "Paid Newspaper Advertising," *Church Publicity*, pp. 119–147; A. G. Turner, "Display Advertising for Newspapers," in W. B. Ashley, *Church Advertising*, pp. 45–52.

[37] "If one-tenth of the cost of the European war had been put into well-directed publicity and advertising to teach the people of the world that they were brother citizens of the world, instead of patriotic and partisan Germans, Frenchmen, English, or Turks, the war would never have come."—J. B. Powell, as reported in the New York *Evening Post*, January 28, 1916.
This is prophecy, not history,—no one knows what the situation would have been had other factors been introduced into it. But it is an interesting illustration of the recognition that public opinion is influenced to-day by the advertisement rather than by the editorial.

[38] *The National Magazine*, cited by the New York *Evening Post*, November 11, 1916.
Many English products, as soaps, teas, sauces, jams and marmalades, are widely advertised in America, as are French mineral waters, perfumes, and toilet articles. American food products and inventions have been widely advertised not only in England and France, but in other European countries.

showing that the friendship between America and the countries of Northern and Central Europe has been fostered by the mutual exchange of advertisements. Even the introduction of American methods of advertising into England, difficult as it was in the beginning, has probably done much to cement the friendship between the two countries.[39]

The advertisement, rather than the news columns or the editorial, is often the medium for making announcements to the public, and in so doing it but reverts to its original character, as indicated by its first appellation, "advice."[40] This use of the advertisement has also had an extraordinary development since 1914. The Imperial Government of Germany conveyed information through advertisements placed in the most prominent newspapers of America warning all travelers that those sailing in the war zone on ships flying the flag of Great Britain, or any of her allies, did so at their own risk,[41] and it thereby considered itself absolved from all further responsibility. Neutral ship owners and brokers advertised in 1916 their positive refusal to act as intermediaries for the forwarding or re-despatch of letters from persons belonging to neutral or belligerent nations and intended for third persons.[42] Announcement was made early in the war in the advertising columns of the official English *Gazette* that the names of certain persons of Teutonic descent but who were British subjects by birth or naturalization had been legally Anglicized. Announcement was made by advertisement that the German socialists were planning to interpellate Chancellor von Bethmann-Hollweg in regard to the allegation that 200,000,000 marks had been spent the first two years of the war for newspaper propaganda.[43]

A caution against "fake stories" concerning the ships of the Norwegian American S. S. Line was conveyed through advertise-

[39] J. M. Richards, *With John Bull and Jonathan*, gives much important information on this point.

[40] The word advertisement in the modern sense was not used until about 1660.—J. B. Williams, "The Early History of London Advertising," *Nineteenth Century and After*, November, 1907, 62: 793–800.

[41] Advertisements in the daily press, May 1, 1915.

[42] Advertisement of Wm. H. Muller & Co. of Rotterdam, The Hague and Amsterdam.—New York *Evening Post*, August 26, 1916.

[43] New York *Times*, October 12, 1916.

ments.[44] False stories were circulated in regard to the American Transatlantic Line and an announcement was made by advertisement of a reward of $10,000 for the conviction of the offenders.[45]

Long advertisements have been used to acquaint the public with the absolute acquittal by the courts of persons who had been wrongly accused.[46]

Industrial firms announce to the public that agreements satisfactory to both parties have been reached and that strikers have voted to return to work. Others make the announcement that they are inaugurating a system of group life insurance for all connected with the company both on the selling and on the manufacturing sides.[47]

The Packard Motor Car Company believed that its position in regard to the payment of its employees during absence on military duty had been misstated by a Detroit daily in a leading article and a leading editorial. It, therefore, published an elaborate advertisement containing the original order issued by the directors of the company, stating fully its position, giving in detail its own contributions to the patriotic movement, and showing the trade sacrifices made in order to give preference to Government orders.[48]

The Central Hudson Gas and Electric Company used the advertisement to explain to its customers that an exceptionally severe storm had so damaged its power station as to make it advisable to avoid the risk of further damage by withdrawing its service for less than two hours on the previous day. The nature of the accident was described in detail and regret expressed for the inconvenience caused.[49]

Announcement of a coming shortage of coal was made by advertisement as was the later welcome news that anthracite coal was available for all purposes in any quantity,[50] and also the

[44] New York *Tribune*, August 9, 1917.
[45] New York *Evening Post*, May 11, 1917.
[46] New York *Tribune*, November 14, 1918; New York *Times*, March 17, 1919.
[47] Daily press, June 13, 1919.
[48] New York *Tribune*, July 30, 1916.
[49] Poughkeepsie *Eagle-News*, July 14, 1916.
[50] February, 1918.

probably equally welcome announcement to many that all restrictions on the use of platinum for jewelry had been
removed.[51]

The New York Telephone Company carried advertisements
giving specific information in regard to the use of the telephone
when summoning help in cases of fire, lawlessness, or accident.[52]
This, to the New York *Times*, indicated on the part of the Company a "determination not to let 'system', or the desire always to
have its instruments manipulated in the regular and appointed
manner, stand in the way of meeting irregular and unappointed,
but real and important, emergencies," and it adds, "This is
not as often as it might be the attitude of great corporations." [53]

Apologies to patrons from advertisers who have themselves
been misled by manufacturers who have misrepresented their
merchandise,[54] and apologies by the press for accidents to type;
thanks to officials for performing their duty,—that may be a ruse
for advertising a new play; congratulations to competitors,[55] and
recognition of distinguished services;[56] self-laudation of "What X
papers have done to help win the war;[57] warnings against fakers
asking for contributions to charitable causes in the name of the
newspaper;—all of these matters of varying importance are
announced through press advertisements.

It must be evident from these illustrations,—they could be
multiplied indefinitely in number and in variety,—that reliance

[51] New York *Times*, December 5, 1918.

[52] New York dailies, November, 1916.

[53] November 17, 1916.

[54] New York *Tribune*, January 30, 1919.

[55] *The Christian Science Monitor* notes from a Georgia paper that one
business firm congratulated another firm "across the way" on the latter's
completion of fifty years of continuous service to the community. The congratulations were printed in bold type in a prominent place.—October 13,
1916.

[56] The New York Edison Company carried, October 21, 1916, an advertisement saying: "In appreciation of Mr. Edison's great work, to-day, the
birthday of the incandescent lamp, is receiving recognition throughout the
land. The New York Edison Company gladly acknowledges its lasting
indebtedness to the man whose name it bears."—This in one form or another
is repeated every year on "Edison Day."
   The personal birthday of Mr. Edison is annually recognized by advertisement, February 11.

[57] New York *Times*, June 1, 1918.

is to-day placed on the paid advertisement for conveying to the public a mass of announcements obtainable in no other way. They transmit important information, explanations, and apologies, correct misapprehensions, announce policies, improvements planned, and public hearings on them, give public notice of exoneration by courts, and point out opportunities of a noncommercial character.

Many of the side lines of advertising are no less important to the historian than are these large, more conspicuous classes. The connection between advertising and manners may at first thought seem remote, yet that good manners may be inculcated through the advertisement is believed by at least one great business corporation,[58] and that bad manners may nullify the advantages of advertising was made clear at a recent convention of American bankers.[59]

The agile advertisement sometimes squares the social circle,[60] and it not infrequently assumes a proprietary right in individuals in any way conspicuous in official or business life and politely appropriates them in the interests of business firms.[61]

Advertisements of auction sales of important art collections, as that of the Davanzati Palace, contain detailed descriptions of works of art and of collections often not elsewhere accessible in print outside of expensive catalogues, while the daily press through

[58] The New York Telephone Company carried a series of advertisements giving suggestions in regard to the correct use of the telephone and stating that they "are published at the request of a number of large business houses that are interested in developing pleasing telephone manners among their employees."

It announces that one of the most important rules that has been developed and adopted by a number of large business houses is: "Take a personal interest in every telephone call you handle."

[59] "A teller or a cashier with a grouch will waste a whole year's advertising appropriation. . . . What does it avail you to advertise that the man with the dollar is as welcome as the man with a thousand if the man with a dollar finds that it isn't so?"—E. G. McWilliams, *Report of Convention of American Bankers at Kansas City, Missouri, 1916.*

[60] The Clyde Steamship Company advertises that "class restriction aboard ship is now eliminated by the inauguration of an exclusive 'One Class' cabin service," but it is secured through a $19 rate on Wednesdays and Saturdays and a $24.90 rate on Tuesdays and Fridays.—New York *Times,* November 14, 1916.

[61] An advertising agency in 1916 ran a series of open letters to men of national and international prominence in the interests of a certain brand of cigarette.

its own advertisements gives the latest information in regard to fashions.[62]

The advertisement records the high price of living and also the means used to combat it,[63] and the same antiphonal character is seen in the advertisements for and against the use of articles of consumption.[64] It is used to remind the public that it has a responsibility for the success of business enterprises it has wished to see undertaken,[65] and at times through the advertisement the public is taken into the confidence of great corporations and given information, perhaps inadvertently, in regard to the speculative character of business.[66]

The advertisement is extensively used to give information to the public that may or may not redound to the benefit of the advertiser. Financial advertisements give important information on matters often obscure and not easily obtainable even by intelligent readers;[67] and they

---

[62] "The Mediaeval in Fashions Supersedes the Russian. Secure a FREE Copy of The New York Evening Post's Fall and Winter Fashion Guide," October 25, 1916.

[63] The general baking companies advertised that the continued high price of raw materials together with the increased cost of almost every item of expense connected with the manufacture of bread compelled them to readjust the prices of their products.—Answering advertisements came from gas companies "showing conclusively that by baking bread at home in a gas range you can save one and eight-tenths cents a loaf over a baker's loaf of the same weight."

A great packing company advertised that "In the face of the high cost of living" it "keeps faith with consumers."—Daily press, November, 1916.

[64] The advertisements of postum having apparently had an effect on the sale of coffee, the coffee dealers replied by advertisements showing the beneficial effects of coffee.

[65] The Black and White Cab Company advertises, "The Black and White cab is purely an experiment. If the people of New York want it, it will stay and multiply. If they don't want it, it will be abandoned. It is entirely up to YOU. If you people of New York decide, after six months' trial, that the Black and White cab fills 'the long-felt want' and is your deliverer from inefficient, unreliable and unsanitary taxi-cabs, you will say so with your patronage."—Daily press, November 1, 1916.

[66] A New York firm advertised the profits to be made by the Union Bag and Paper Company through the advantage it was able to take of the scarcity of paper.—New York daily press, October 19, 1916.

[67] The Columbia Trust Company published in 1916 and subsequently in the New York *Times* and the *Evening Post* a series of messages answering everyday questions concerning a Trust Company's business. These number to date 472, December, 1922.

The Metropolitan Trust Company in 1916 showed through advertisements the difficulties that beset inexperienced executors and administrators

give reports of financial conditions in distant cities and countries.[68]

One of the most important uses to which the advertisement has been put has been that of combating crime,[69] and in sharp contrast, is the use of the advertisement in simplifying the choosing of Christmas gifts.[70]

The beneficial effects that "advertising good works" would have on the general body of public officials have been ably presented through the press,[71] while the advertisement plays a large part to-day in all welfare work.[72]

It must be evident that scarcely a single field of human thought or activity has not been entered by the advertiser,[73] and that the

---

of estates, indicated by citations from court decisions why they were or were not legally liable for losses sustained, and explained how these losses to estates, to executors, or to administrators could have been avoided.

The Harriman National Bank has advertised the benefits of life insurance as a credit factor, has recognized the increasing importance of women in the field of business by making a special feature of women's accounts, and advertises the reasons why it advertises.

[68] A single issue of a New York daily advertised reports from seven Canadian banks and from twenty-five different banks of Albany, Buffalo, Chicago, Cleveland, Milwaukee, New Orleans, Philadelphia, and Pittsburgh. —New York *Evening Post*, November 25, 1916.

Another daily advertises that of the sixty-three statements published in response to the last call of the State Superintendent of Banks, it has published forty-three, while the next New York paper published thirteen.— New York *Times*, December 3, 1916.

[69] A campaign for this object was begun in New York City in 1916 and was placed in charge of the Advertising Club. Advertising was to be the sole medium of the crusade.—Daily press, December, 1916.

[70] "The Gift-Plan Bureau. 1. You ask the Bureau to inquire of a definite person what gifts are desired. 2. The Bureau asks this Person by letter for the information, keeping your name secret. 3. This Person tells the Bureau what gifts are desired by listing them on the form sent by the Bureau. 4. The Bureau then tells You when the list is returned what are the desired gifts."—New York *Evening Post*, December 4, 1916.—The success of the plan was apparently not sufficient to justify its repetition in subsequent years.

[71] "Many a worthy and deserving and able public official has failed because he did not get his case across to the public through the newspapers." —Fire Commissioner Adamson (New York City), cited by the New York *Tribune*, June 16, 1916. The *Tribune* adds: "Is it not about time to stop laying all the blame on the poor voter for his lack of interest and turn our attention toward making politics as direct and forceful and appealing as, say, a box score or the automobile advertisements?"

[72] See report of conference on Publicity and Public Welfare, by G. French, L. S. Richard, W. C. Freeman, and A. W. McCann, Sagamore Sociological Conference, 1912.

[73] The medical code of ethics as yet prevents advertising by reputable physicians. But with the elimination of advertisements of fake doctors and

most significant features of newspaper advertising to-day are that the advertisement is used to influence public opinion quite as much as it is to sell commodities, and that it is the advertisement rather than the editorial that is used as the most effective means of influencing public opinion.[74]

This use of the advertisement for other purposes than for the exchange of commodities has apparently been a very recent development and it has grown to such proportions that it is possible that the present zeal of the advertiser to have his copy set up "next to reading matter" may in time be rivaled by the desire of authors to have their articles printed "next to advertising matter."[75] "Short stories" often become in reality long stories and are apparently spun out in order to hold together the advertisements.

The natural sequence of this extraordinary development of advertising has been the introduction of educational courses to teach how to write advertisements,[76] the development of the

---

of patent medicines, as a result of the campaign for honest advertising, there would seem to be no objection to the expansion of the card now permitted so as to include facts that the public reasonably wishes to know, as office hours, and Sunday hours.

Authors do not personally advertise, but they are advertised by their publishers. Members of the theatrical profession often find that indirect means of advertising themselves are more effective than are direct advertisements.

[74] A striking illustration of the relation between the editorial and the advertisement is seen in the republication as an advertisement in the Philadelphia *Public Ledger*, November 1, 1916, of an editorial that had appeared in the Chicago *Daily News*, October 25, 1916. Illustrations of this are frequent.

G. J. Holyoake says that Joseph Cowen's first speech in Parliament, March 23, 1876, contained three things never heard in Parliament before,— that "the divine right of kings perished on the scaffold with Charles I," that "the superstition of royalty had never taken any deep hold of the English people," and he described Napoleon III, the ally of England, as "a usurper." These statements so accorded with popular sentiment that some persons paid for their publication as an advertisement in the *Daily News* and other newspapers.—*Bygones Worth Remembering*, II, 54.

The speech as given in *Hansard* does not give the statement concerning Napoleon III.

[75] The advertisement has already invaded the editorial page and heads the editorial columns. See series running in the New York *Evening Post*, November, 1916, and continuously for some weeks afterward.

[76] The success of these has been such as to give rise to the pleasantry that the "cereal advertisements in the magazines are far more interesting than the serial stories;" to the rebuke, attributed to Kipling, of a friend who

advertisement signed and copyrighted by its author, or copyrighted by the business advertised; the publication of a mass of technical, scientific, and popular books, on the subject of advertising; the enormous development of advertising agencies, the formation everywhere of advertising clubs, the organization of national advertising associations; the erection of buildings for their accomodation; the holding of national conventions addressed by the leading men of the country, including its President,[77] and the establishment of a National Newspaper Window Display Week.[78]

To this extraordinary development the student of history can not be indifferent. How is he to regard the advertisement as historical material? His first feeling is one of lack of confidence growing out of what writers of advertisements have written in regard to their own methods and their own conception of the relative importance of the advertisement and the other parts of the paper.[79] He sees the charge that "As is well known, instead of papers controlling their advertisers, practically all the news-

had sent him a periodical from which all the advertisements had been cut,— "I can write stories myself;" to the tribute said to have been paid by Gladstone,—"that he bought American rather than English magazines because he liked to read the advertisements they published;" and to the opinion expressed, apropos of the commendation of American advertising by an English visitor, "Not for nothing have our schools of advertisement-writing and our advertising agencies wrestled with the English language. The delight that the Elizabethans found in experimenting with the sonnet and other forms of verse, we obtain by inventing novel and catchy advertising phrases."—New York *Evening Post*, October 15, 1913.

[77] President Wilson addressed the Associated Advertising Clubs of the World at their annual meeting in Philadelphia, June 29, 1916.

[78] Daily press, October, 1914.

[79] "Not even the publisher will openly acknowledge that he is publishing a magazine for the advertisers, even though he is perfectly well aware of the fact that he couldn't pay for raw paper and literary talent without them. The reader must be flim-flammed with the idea that the publisher is really printing the magazine or newspaper for him."—T. A. De Weese, *Book on Advertising*, p. 18.

"The owner or editor of a paper may maintain the beautiful and impressive bluff of running a journal to influence public opinion, to purify politics, to elevate public morals, and to reorganize the social structure in general. If he is in earnest he may soon sink a million. If he is using the editorial page as a cloak for a legitimate commercial enterprise and not to put politicians in office or to tell the people how to think and how to vote he will not have to issue bonds to meet his obligations."—*Ib.*, p. 62.

[80] Frederick Dwight, "The Significance of Advertising," *Yale Review*, August, 1909, 18: 197–205.

papers and periodicals are in their power," [80] and he sees this repeated on all sides. Moreover, he realizes that the most severe arraignments of the influence exerted by the advertiser on journalism have come, not from the critics of the press, but from the members of the press itself.[81] The press has also given wide publicity to the often conflicting interests of business manager and of editor.[82] He finds the advertisements themselves often specious

There is much, however, to disprove the sweeping character of this statement. The complaint was made to the editor of the New York *Tribune* that certain advertisers threatened to cancel a large contract unless an adverse criticism was repudiated. "Reid's answer was to instruct his critic to return at once to the charge, with redoubled energy."—R. Cortissoz, *Life of Whitelaw Reid*, I, 159.

[81] "The advertiser, rather than the subscriber, is now the newspaper bogie. He is the person before whom the publisher cowers and whom he tries to please, and the advertiser is very indifferent about the opinions of a newspaper. What interests him is the amount or quality of its circulation. What he wants to know is, how many and what class of persons see it, not how many persons agree with it. The consequence is that the newspapers of largest circulation, published in the great centres of population where most votes are cast, are less and less organs of opinion, especially in America. In fact, in some cases the advertisers use their influence—which is great, and which the increasing competition between newspapers makes all the greater —to prevent the expression in newspapers of what is probably the prevailing local view of men or events. There are not many newspapers which can afford to defy a large advertiser."—E. L. Godkin, *Unforeseen Tendencies of Democracy*, pp. 195–196 (1898).

See Hamilton Holt, *Commercialism and Journalism, passim* (1909).

"With the increasing expenses of modern newspapers under the stress of competition the necessity of swelling the advertising revenue of a paper becomes of paramount importance. So the courting of prominent advertisers is every day more and more the preoccupation of a newspaper manager and he is apt to listen too favourably to any representations made by strong monied interests and himself to exercise a corresponding pressure on the editorial side of the enterprise."—G. B. Dibblee, *The Newspaper*, p. 166 (1913).

"The department store advertiser continues to assert his right to dominate the news columns, and it is only a brave and powerful newspaper like the New York *World* which can answer the demand of an advertiser that a murder or an accident in his store be omitted from its columns by printing it on its first page with most conspicuous headlines. The weaker newspaper to whom that contract is vital is very apt to overlook the necessity of presenting this particular piece of news."—O. G. Villard, "Some Weaknesses of Modern Journalism," in Merle Thorpe, *The Coming Newspaper*, p. 60 (1915).

[82] The editor of *Collier's Weekly* who resigned in 1912 stated that it was because the advertising manager had had too much to say concerning the editorial policy of the publication.—New York *Evening Post*, October 19, 1912.

[83] Advertisements on the eve of a state election for governor in 1914 read: "President Wilson asks you to elect Martin H. Glynn. Whitman increased

and misleading [83] even when not absolutely false, as has often been the case in regard to medical panaceas.

But while the pernicious effects of advertising are often lamented, although not always proved, it must be remembered that there is another side to the question and that the beneficial effects of advertising on the business administration of the press may have been even more important. An examination of the autobiographies, recollections, lives, and other forms of personal records of men connected with the press in the past shows that a happy-go-lucky spirit has often prevailed in the setting up of a new newspaper with little or no capital, credit, or business experience.[84] A man with a gift for writing but with little interest in business started a new venture in the newspaper line, failure swiftly followed, another newspaper was started, and there followed a constant repetition of ambitious hopes and subsequent disaster.

But the advertiser of to-day demands business stability in the newspaper that carries his advertisements. Audit bureaus of circulations must guarantee circulation and the best advertisers demand in addition a circulation among the classes in society and in business that they desire to reach.[85] No paper on the verge of bankruptcy and no paper that has a shady reputation in a

---

the expenses of one office $150,000. Glynn reduced state expenses $10,000,-000. A vote against Glynn is a rebuke to the President."

Even the newspapers themselves sometimes advertise their own merits in a misleading way. A flagrant illustration of it was the case of the advertisement, "The Staats-Zeitung Leads them All! First in Circulation, First in Advertising." At the end of the advertisement, it is evident that *all* refers to the German newspapers published in New York City.

[84] Merle Thorpe notes the inefficient business management of many papers,—general carelessness prevails, debts are not collected, bills are not paid, and credit is poor. In Kansas, in 1912, eighty-two per cent. of the publishing business was mortgaged. "The country paper, speaking generally, stands at the foot of credit ratings."—*The Coming Newspaper*, pp. 12–13.

The indifference of the editor to the business side of the newspaper is probably best illustrated in the case of Henry Labouchere. See A. L. Thorold, *The Life of Henry Labouchere*, especially chap. XVIII, "Mr. Labouchere as a Journalist," by R. Bennett.

[85] The New York *Evening Post*, August 11, 1916, showed by a map of New York City that its circulation covered almost exactly the distribution of greatest wealth in the city; it publishes in graphic form the headings of different publishing houses whose advertisements it carries; it gives an analysis of its advertising showing the ratio of each kind of advertising to the total volume of advertising carried.

business way can hope to have the patronage of responsible advertisers, for no business house will make an advertising contract with a newspaper that may at any time suspend publication. It is as necessary for a first-class business house to carry its advertisements in a medium of unquestioned business integrity as it is for a newspaper to carry only advertisements it can guarantee.[86]

The general strengthening of all newspapers in a business way is in large part due to the wholesome effect the advertiser has had on its business management. If the somewhat recent establishment of the office of business manager has seemed to result in the subordination of the press to its business interests, it must not be forgotten that the business manager has often brought order out of previous financial chaos.

The development of national advertising has done much to develop the local and provincial press. If the subscription lists of the country papers drop off through the competition of the press of the neighboring city, their advertising columns, carrying national as well as local advertising, strengthen their business credit.

The student of history finds, moreover, in these very questionings of the power of the advertiser an important record of changes that have come in the business management of the press. If the advertiser has unduly influenced the press to suppress news unfavorable to special business interests, it has been the press itself that has set the danger signal. If the advertiser has been unfair in his dealings with the public, it has been the press that has led the campaign for honest advertising and that has found its great

---

[86] The New York *Evening Post* inquired under the caption ASSOCIATES: "Do you prefer to walk arm in arm in the street with a person whose appearance would indicate that he was headed for a free lunch counter rather than with a person of character? Do you prefer to live next door to a shark? Do you prefer to patronize the cheapest places without regard to the quality of what you buy? As an advertiser do you want your good name associated with houses of questionable business repute or merchandising reputation? You buy more than actual space when you use The New York Evening Post. You get association of prestige, character, and responsiveness to legitimate appeal. As a man is known by the company he keeps, a newspaper is known by the advertising it carries as well as by its honesty of purpose in its news and editorial columns."—November 18, 1916.

Another aspect of the same question is presented in the advertisement, "The character and standing of the New York Times readers is such that Lost and Found advertisements appearing in its columns are productive of a high percentage of results."—New York *Times*, November 25, 1916.

allies among the advertisers themselves. In all of these changes he finds records of an awakened business conscience and of higher standards of business and of newspaper morality. Even if he can not accept the statements that many advertisers have made in the past, in that fact he finds encouragement through the realization it brings of growing intelligence and higher morality. It is not simply the advertisement itself with whose authoritativeness he is concerned, he is even more concerned with all the influences that have made it what it is. These influences are the primeval bed rock and as such they are his chief records.

The influences at work to secure honest advertisements are therefore of primary importance. These have been the newspapers and magazines themselves with the slogans, "First to last—the Truth—News—Editorials—Advertisements," and "Only Advertisements Fit to Print;" their guaranteed advertisements,[87] and rewards offered for information leading to the arrest and conviction of any one who may have obtained money through false or misleading advertisements printed in their columns; their rejection individually and collectively of large classes of advertisements;[88] the Advertising Men's League; the

[87] See pamphlets published by The Tribune Association,—*How it Works*, 1915; *The Adams Articles*, 1916; "*Keeping the Faith*," 1916.
[88] The New York *Times* declines advertisements involving fraudulent or doubtful financial offerings, attacks of a personal character, large guaranteed dividends, offers of something for nothing, guaranteed cures, matrimonial offers, fortune tellers, objectionable medical advertising, offers of extravagant salaries, and it offers $100 reward for information leading to the arrest and conviction of any person publishing an advertisement in the *Times* containing false or misleading information.
It announces that advertisements submitted for insertion in its automobile exchange are subject to censorship and that information is welcomed from readers of doubtful or misleading announcements; that satisfactory bank and business references are required before the acceptance of any advertisement for insertion in its Business Opportunities columns.—Advertisements, April, 1922.
Others have included advertisements of patent medicines, massage, palmists, traps for purchasers or investors, loan sharks, questionable schemes, fraudulent or doubtful financial offerings, bucket shops, large guaranteed dividends, want advertisements that request money for samples or articles, home sewing, addressing envelopes, suggestive books, matrimonial offers, personals, attacks of a personal character, and whiskey and other liquors.
The Associated College Newspaper Publishers, representing thirty-nine institutions, voted unanimously at their annual meeting, August, 1915, to bar liquor advertisements from their papers and re-affirmed their regulation banning proprietary advertising.—New York dailies, August 28, 1915.

National Association of Advertisers' Clubs;[89] the national associations formed in different lines of business; boards of health and health officers; protective bureaus and vigilance committees; bureaus of weights and measures;[90] voluntary associations of local merchants; penal laws in nearly a score of states making intentionally false or misleading advertising a misdemeanor;[91] legislation preventing disguised advertising and requiring that the word "advertisement" be printed with all reading matter for which money or other valuable consideration is paid, accepted, or promised; laws preventing the advertisements of lotteries; the consideration of laws to prevent the advertisement of real estate where offers are made of prizes, gifts, rewards, distinctions, or puzzle methods are used; laws forbidding the advertisement of liquor in newspapers printed or sold in states that prohibited the manufacture or sale of intoxicating liquor; government prosecution of those who violate the laws; decisions of courts upholding the legality of laws restraining advertising, as also decisions affirming the right of a newspaper to decline an advertisement deemed objectionable, even if submitted under a yearly contract; the publication of books like *The Clarion* showing the iniquity of fake advertisements; the establishment by newspapers of bureaus to report fraudulent or misleading advertisements; the investigation of advertisements that seem to demand legal attention, as of "pure silk" ties and "gold mesh" bags,—all this is but a

[89] At its annual meeting in 1914, its 11,000 members made a plea for "truth in advertising," and urged newspapers to reject fraudulent advertisements, to state their circulation truthfully, to maintain their advertising rates as published, to combat discounts, and to oppose free publicity.

[90] One Bureau began an interesting campaign against fraudulent advertising with the double object of teaching the consumer how to detect such advertisement and of getting advertisers to give up misrepresentations.— New York *Evening Post*, August 29, 1914.

[91] That this law is not a dead letter is indicated by the recent fine of $250 imposed on a prominent merchant for violating it.—New York *Tribune*, August 24, 1918.
A clothing corporation was fined $150 for inserting a misleading advertisement in the newspapers.—New York *Tribune*, December 30, 1921.
It is, however, sometimes difficult to enforce the law. In October, 1917, five hundred and twenty-three mechanics went from Newark, New Jersey, and the vicinity to Baltimore in reply to an advertisement that seven hundred and twenty men were wanted there. Each paid $3.00 to the agent, and his railroad fare, but the advertisement proved a hoax. Although every effort was made to locate the agent, it was apparently impossible to do so.

suggestion of the dykes and barriers that have been erected to protect the readers of the periodical press from mischievous and even criminal advertising.[92] The effect of this campaign for honest advertising has been seen in the reports of the post office department that show a decrease in fraudulent advertising;[93] in the great decrease in the sale of patent medicines by drug-stores and the consequent development by them of departments for the sale of confectionery, cigars, magazines, newspapers, stationery, and similar lines of business; and in a voluntary relinquishment by the press of more than one line of remunerative advertising.

The student of history finds in this campaign for honest advertising records that show how widespread have been dishonest business methods,—a dishonesty due in part to ignorance of better methods, in part to lack of a sensitive conscience, in part to sheer carelessness and indifference; he finds a record of the study of psychology on the part of the seller of commodities, while the study of psychology on the part of the buyer has been as yet but imperfectly developed; he finds records of the influence of the advertiser on the press, but also by a turning of the tables of the influence of the press on the advertiser; and he sometimes finds records of the presence on the same paper of what has been termed "Editorial Dr. Jekyll and Advertising Mr. Hyde."

[92] Newspapers now vie with each other in showing their efforts made for honest advertising. The Philadelphia *North American* in 1913 advertised that within the five years previous it had excluded from its columns advertising matter to the amount of $250,000.—Editorial in *The Dry Goods Economist*, November 28, 1914, republished in New York *Tribune*, December 3, 1914. C. F. Reisner gives many detailed classes of advertisements rejected by the *North American.*—*Church Publicity*, pp. 125–126.—The New Orleans *Item* threw out in a single day $30,000 worth of advertising,—A. G. Newmyer, Convention of Advertising Clubs of the World, June 23, 1915.—The New York *Evening Post*, March 26, 1918, stated that the previous week it had rejected nine different financial advertisements and that it had "turned away thousands of dollars in financial advertising."—The New York *Times* states that all its advertisements are censored and selected.—May 25, 1919. —The *Times* still later developed the point that "the exclusion of suspicious offers makes the Business Opportunities advertisements in The New York Times worth consideration."—January 18, 1921.

In 1921, the budget of the Associated Advertising Clubs of the World included the item of $70,000 to be used in the further promotion of truth in advertising.—New York *Tribune*, July 30, 1921.

[93] Report of the Solicitor of the Post Office Department, December 26, 1915.

With the development of advertising in the directions now opening up, the chasm between the advertising pages and the editorial columns must be bridged and the newspaper acquire a new sense of unity and harmony it has heretofore entirely lacked. The great business corporations, especially those controlling industry and transportation, have heretofore not taken the public into their confidence and hence have laid themselves open to censure. If this censure has been administered by the press and the corporations have been "pounded," the result has been to intensify, not to ameliorate, an unfortunate situation. If, on the other hand, the press has been silent, it has thereby brought odium upon itself through the charge so easily made, so wearisomely disproved, that it is "owned by capital." Within an almost incredibly short space of time the whole character of advertising has been changing, apparently in large part through the efforts of the press itself. In its campaigns for honest advertising and in weeding out a large part of the objectionable advertising previously carried, the press has raised the whole standard of advertising. Advertisers have been quick to note the change and have been ready to meet the press more than half way. Campaigns of "good will" advertising on the part of great corporations now explain in great detail their methods of conducting their business and in thus enlightening the public they have done much to change hostility into sympathetic interest.

The student of history therefore finds in the very processes of advertising valuable records of the changing business standards of the press as well as a raising of general business standards. What records he finds in the advertisements themselves must be considered elsewhere. Meantime it must be remembered that the temper of the advertiser always differs from the temper of the editor, as the function of each differs with reference to its relation to the press. Optimist and pessimist are both honorable gentlemen yet neither is nor can be the other. The impassable chasm that often is found between advertising pages and editorial columns is felicitously expressed by the New York *Evening Post*, when it says:

"The hypothetical and somewhat overworked visitor from Mars, who should pick up a copy of one of our magazines, could not help being struck by the difference in spirit between the literary and the advertising sections. If he concludes that the earth is inhabited by two races of men, a race of stumbling, bungling, unhappy failures and pessimists, and a race of vigorous, successful, radiant optimists, we can scarcely blame him. In the literary pages the world is the worst of all possible worlds; in the advertising supplement it is the best of all conceivable worlds. In the magazine proper everything goes askew. The railroads cheat us and kill us. The food manufacturers poison us. The liquor dealers destroy our moral fibre. The army is depleted. The navy has its armor-belt in the wrong place. Workmen go about without work. Lack of sanitation kills its thousands. Automobiles do their share—the list is endless. But what a reconstructed world of heart's desire begins with the first-page advertisement. Here, no breakfast food fails to build up a man's brain and muscle. No phonograph record fails to amuse. No roof-paint cracks under cold or melts under the sun. No razor cuts the face or leaves it sore. Illness and death are banished by patent medicines and hygienic shoes. Worry flees before the model fountain pen. Employers shower wealth upon efficient employees. Insurance companies pay what they promise. Trains always get to Chicago on time. Babies never cry; whether it's soap or cereal, or camera or talcum, babies always laugh in the advertising supplement. A happy world, indeed, my masters." [94]

These efforts to secure honest advertising have been of late so much in evidence that it is natural to think that they have been a product of our own high standards. But the ubiquitous Cobbett when he started the English *Porcupine* in 1800 announced his intention of refusing questionable advertisements,—"not a single *quack* advertisement will on any account be admitted into the *Porcupine*. Our newspapers have been too long disgraced by this species of falsehood, filth and obscenity." "I am told," Cobbett continues, "that, by adhering to this resolution, I shall lose five hundred a year, and excite the resentment of the numerous body of empirics," but apparently he did not abandon it. [95] The London *Times* threw away $30,000 a week in advertisements during the railway mania in 1846, and "made money by the loss.

---

[94] New York *Evening Post*, May 7, 1909.

[95] Lewis Melville, *Life and Letters of William Cobbett in England and America*, I, 123–124.

The *Porcupine* ran only from October, 1800 to November, 1801 and it is possible that one of the contributory causes of its short career may have been its pioneer policy in regard to advertising.

It could not have afforded not to throw the money away."[96]
G. W. Holyoake recalls that at one time he wrote advertisements
for a firm whom he persuaded that "to tell the truth in them
would be the greatest novelty out."[97] The editor of the *Glasgow
Herald* writes of many advertisements refused from quack doctors,
and baby farming, personals, and "agony" advertisements. He
gives an important side-light on the number and the dangerous
character of such advertisements in stating that the editing required the services not of one but of several men.[98]

When Arthur Tappan started the *Journal of Commerce* in 1827,
he wished it to exert "a wholesome moral influence, abstaining
particularly from publishing immoral advertisements,"[99] and
when Lewis Tappan took over the paper the following year he
announced that "it will refuse to derive emolument from advertisements that are at war no less with the political and commercial prosperity, than with the innocence, integrity, and moral
weal of the community," and he exercised a censorship in regard
to quack medicines.[100] *The American*, started in Lowell, Massachusetts, in 1849, "published no advertisements demoralizing
to the community or to the home."[101] Henry Ward Beecher
signalized the beginning of his editorship of the *Christian Union*
by shutting down "once and for all upon a large class of profitable
business, in excluding medical advertisements and in ordering a
strict censorship upon whatever might offend the taste or impose
upon the credulity of readers."[102]

[96] Whitelaw Reid, *American and English Studies*, II, 221.
The influence of the railway mania on advertising is best seen in the case
of the London *Gazette* that made large profits from its advertisements,—
about 1835 "it made above 15,000*l* a year by advertisements, and the whole
of its working expenses did not amount to half that." But "its busiest time
was during the railway mania, when all railway projects had to be advertised
in the *Gazette* by a certain day, for otherwise Parliament would not recognize
them. The ferment this caused is now inconceivable. As the limit of time
approached, the advertisements increased, till, on one November day, the
paper was enlarged to 583 pages! It required nearly 150 stamps and was
sold at something more than half-a-crown."—Cited from the *Athenaeum*,
by J. C. Francis, *John Francis*, II, 239.
[97] *Sixty Years of an Agitator's Life*, I, 132.
[98] A. Sinclair, *Fifty Years of Newspaper Life*, pp. 10, 11.
[99] *Life of Arthur Tappan*, p. 91.
[100] J. P. Thompson, *Memoir of David Hale*, pp. 48, 50.
[101] Mrs. W. S. Robinson, "*Warrington*" *Pen-Portraits*, p. 44.
[102] Cited from John Howard, the publisher of the *Christian Union*, by
A. Tassin, *The Magazine in America*, p. 275.

The real campaign for honest advertising and for protecting readers from fraudulent advertising apparently began when the *Farm Journal* for October, 1880, went one step further and promised to "make good to subscribers any loss sustained by trusting advertisers that prove to be deliberate swindlers. . . . No publisher in the United States had ever made such an offer."[103]

That the result of the plan was satisfactory was indicated by the statement: "Over twenty-five hundred dollars' worth of advertising of a doubtful character was refused admission to these columns [those of the *Farm Journal*] through 1880 and 1881, and we think this ought to be a pretty good endorsement of those who are now in."[104]

But it was probably ten years later[105] that these early and somewhat isolated attempts gathered a collective momentum and have resulted in the present widespread opprobrium incurred by misleading, dishonest, and objectionable advertising.[106] In the mutual congratulations of press and public on the success of the campaigns for honest advertising it must never be forgotten that this success has been the culmination of many long-continued, though spasmodic, efforts to bring it about and that its beneficial results have extended far beyond the immediate object of protecting the public from unscrupulous advertisers.

But the interest of the student of history in advertising also extends far beyond the uses made of it by commerce, philanthropy, government, and all the varied activities of modern life, and far beyond the questions involved in honest advertising. He is

[103] Wilmer Atkinson, *An Autobiography*, p. 180.

[104] *Ib.*, p. 184.

[105] J. A. Thayer dates from 1892 the beginning of the refusal of patent medicine advertisements by the Curtis Publishing Company.—*Astir*, pp. 87–89. In chap. X, "The fight for clean advertising," he gives an account of the effort to eliminate all fraudulent and objectionable advertising.

[106] It is interesting to note a certain timidity that still prevails in some localities. In 1917, a leading paper advertised that it printed "more advertisements than any other evening paper published in Boston, although nothing of a doubtful or unpleasant character is accepted," and that it "does not accept highly speculative advertising."—Advertisement in New York *Evening Post*, January 10, 1917. In view of the active campaigns carried on in New York and Philadelphia, this seems a conservative statement of disapproval.

fundamentally concerned in the records it presents, in the evidence it gives of conditions not elsewhere made known, in the revelations unconsciously made of social and business ideals and of the deviations from them. The advertisement has developed from the mere simple announcement of articles lost, apprentices disappeared, and auctions to take place, into elaborate publicity agencies covering every field of human endeavor. The individual commercial advertiser is being absorbed in collective advertising, the local advertisement has become national, and the national has developed into the international advertisement. The immediate psychological reaction of the advertisement on the individual prospective buyer is being supplanted by the appeal to the remote past; the simple object of putting before the public the merits of commercial articles is being superseded by complex competitive advertising that has all of the characteristics of a race. Much of the present commercial advertising, begun in the interests of efficiency, has so far overreached itself as to have developed into such an extreme inefficiency, that "an advertiser is willing to spend $500,000 in advertising if his balance sheet shows a gain of $5,000;" more than one business has been wrecked by over-advertising rather than by over-production or under-selling. Advertising appeals to thrift and economy are side-tracked by wasteful competitive advertising.[107]

[107] Many times the question is asked, "How much is spent for advertising?" Robert Mackay, in *Success*, under the heading "How $1,284,000,000 Was Spent for Advertising in 1920," gives the following figures:

How the Money Was Divided

Newspapers	$600,000,000
Direct Mail	300,000,000
Magazines	150,000,000
Trade Papers	70,000,000
Novelties	30,000,000
Electric and Painted Signs	30,000,000
Farm Papers	27,000,000
Demonstrating and Sampling	24,000,000
Window and Store Display	20,000,000
Bill-Posting	12,000,000
Street-Car Cards	11,000,000
Programs	5,000,000
Motion Pictures	5,000,000

From the *Publishers' Weekly*, September 17, 1921, 100: 780.

The historian finds in all commercial advertising a perfect record of the conditions out of which it has grown. He is not immediately concerned with the question whether competitive commercial advertising is beneficial or extravagant,[108]—it is a condition that he finds and he is concerned only in examining the record it thereby presents. He finds in it a record of waste and extravagance everywhere tolerated by a wasteful, extravagant society. He finds a record of sordid influences behind the enormous expansion of advertising during the war, both in its volume, and in its costliness, since it has been possible to deduct the sums expended for advertising from the profits on which income and excess profits taxes were payable. He finds conversely a record of high-minded business houses that have scorned to take advantage of this situation. He finds a record of the short-sighted business policy that accepts questionable advertisements on the plea that it can not do without them, while he again finds conversely the record of an honorable press that can not be tempted, and of a discerning press that has grown in wisdom.[109] He finds a record of the primitive instincts towards conquest not held in check by other higher primitive instincts towards mutual aid and co-operation; of economic conditions that have had as yet but superficial examination.

He finds in philanthropic calls for help made through advertising an appeal to the emotions that records an all but universal tendency to appeal to the feelings,—a tendency as yet little restrained by reasoned inquiry into conditions below the surface. In all advertising by government agencies, he finds in the foreground the ideas of loyalty and patriotism, but no suggestion as to whether the patriotism is that defined by Dr. Johnson as being "the last refuge of a scoundrel" or that described by Admiral Decatur in

[108] J. R. Tinkham, in *Advertising is Non-Essential*, has fully considered the various forms of competitive commercial advertising.

[109] A newspaper in the Middle West somewhat recently accepted the well-paying advertisements of an affluent firm putting a patent medicine on the market. Its other advertising at once fell off and it then banished the advertisement of the patent medicine,—to find that within a month it had more than recouped itself for the loss thereby entailed.

"You can never get circulation for the paper whose editorial policy is run from the business office."—J. Daniels, cited by Wilmer Atkinson, *Autobiography*, p. 159.

his toast "Our Country! In her intercourse with foreign nations may she always be in the right; but our country, right or wrong." And he also sees this appeal to patriotism unconsciously controverted by other appeals to the citizens of other countries though the advertisements carried in foreign languages,—French, Italian, Spanish, German, Greek, Hebrew, Persian, Chinese, Esquimo, and Cree, have all appeared in American papers.[110]

In all advertising the historian finds a record of conditions which the press as a whole has not made, which the advertiser has not made, but which unerringly give evidence of fundamental conditions of society. It is a truism that the stream can not rise higher than the source. Neither the press nor the advertiser can in or of itself change these conditions. The advertisement, more perfectly than any other record at his command, reveals to the student of history the hidden springs of the social order, it shows him the forces that for good or evil move mankind to thought and action.

The "ad-less newspaper" so often urged as a remedy for all the evils laid at the door of the press would not only not prove a panacea, but it would deprive society of the most flawless mirror of itself and the historian of the most unimpeachable class of evidence at his command. Such a newspaper was started in Chicago in 1911, but given up in 1917,—nominally on account of the high cost of paper. But such a paper must carry in itself the seeds of dissolution, not because "the advertisements pay for the news," but because news is ephemeral, while the advertisements fundamentally record the mainsprings of human action.

Nor is the proposal to increase the postage on the advertisements carried by newspapers and magazines other than a claim for the pound of flesh. It is a fatal error to consider the sole function of the advertisement that of promoting the financial side of the paper,—for good and for evil the advertisement is today an integral part of the periodical press and it can not be separated from it without doing violence to the periodical press as a whole. Competitive commercial advertising is an anachronism in an age that boasts of its efficiency; emotional appeals

---

[110] A recent collective advertisement of thirty Chinese restaurants seems to show that the opposition to the Chinese is at least not gastronomic.

in advertising are survivals of an unintelligent and unscientific age; governmental appeals to an undefined patriotism and loyalty are out of harmony with the inquiring spirit that seeks to know how it may best serve its country. But all of the misdirected zeal in advertising is but a tithe of the total effort that has been put into advertising to make it honest, effective, and representative of the highest ideals. For better and for worse the advertisement unconsciously records our imperfections as well as our highest attainments; our sordid motives and our spiritual aspirations; our criminal tendencies and our conscientious lives. As is the world to-day, so is the advertisement.

Dr. Johnson wrote in the *Idler*, in 1759, "The trade of advertising is now so near to perfection, that it is not easy to propose any improvement." Although not in the Johnsonian meaning, it is still true, and must always be true, that "it is not easy to propose any improvement" in the advertisement as a record of our complex daily life.

The advertisement therefore serves the historian in every part of his effort to reconstruct the past. If the advertisement is true, the facts it states are of value. If the advertisement is not true, that in and of itself is a record of the low moral standards that are tolerated but not acknowledged by the press and by the public. The tests that the historian applies to the advertisement to determine its accuracy are simple, and moreover it is usually unnecessary to apply them since the press of late has pledged itself to the reliability of the advertisements it publishes. Even more than that, the advertisement, true or false, is an invaluable record in the reconstruction of the normal life of the past,—invaluable, because in large part unconsciously made and recording not only material conditions but even more clearly the intellectual and moral conditions from which they have sprung.

CHAPTER XIV

THE ILLUSTRATION AND THE GRAPHIC PRESS

"Picture journalism furnishes the most available and the most valuable materials for the historian of manners."—*C. Knight.*

"When the history of our own age comes to be written the pictorial newspapers will form an inexhaustible storehouse for the historian."—*Mason Jackson.*

"The works of Gillray preserve an entire social revolution."

"Art deals in *illusion*. Literal accuracy, even when possible, is art's undoing."—*J. L. Lowes.*

"Journalism is the criticism of the moment *at* the moment, and caricature is that criticism at once simplified and intensified by a plastic form."—*Henry James.*

ILLUSTRATIONS are to-day a conspicuous feature of the daily press and of the weekly and the monthly periodicals. Their use was coincident with the invention of printing, but the illustration that in the early history of printing was a prominent feature of the title page of the book has, in the periodical,[1] been transferred to the cover, or it has become an important part of the text, or a still more important part of the advertising column.

The attitude of the press itself towards illustrations has greatly changed; once in a state of amiable but passive receptivity,[2] it has now become an active competitor for the best work of the

[1] The *Mercurius Civicus* was the first regularly illustrated periodical.—J. B. Williams, *History of British Journalism*, p. 44.
The first number appeared May 4–11, 1643, and it was published Thursdays until December 10, 1646. *Ib.*, p. 233. A reproduction of the first page of No. 8 is given in Williams, p. 45.
[2] The early attitude of the press towards illustrations is indicated by this announcement: "*Harper's Weekly* has already reached a regular issue of more than sixty thousand copies and the editions printed are steadily increasing. The proprietors beg to say that they will be happy to receive sketches or photographic pictures of striking scenes, important events, and leading men from artists in every part of the world and to pay liberally for such as they may use."—*Harper's Weekly*, June 13, 1857.
The Gentleman's Magazine of 1750 has a "List of Embellishments to the Volume."

best illustrators. Great dailies command to-day the entire time and work of more than one eminent illustrator.[3] The omission of illustrations from the columns of some of the leading representatives of the press may be due to the theory that the illustration cheapens the text,—a few influential dailies and important monthlies have thus far resisted the pressure to introduce illustrations that accompany the text, although admitting them freely into advertising columns and pages. Other periodicals do not carry illustrations because of the large disbursements involved and they prefer to turn their expenditures into other channels.[4] With a few conspicuous exceptions the use of the illustration by the daily press has become almost universal, while the weeklies that are founded primarily for the sake of their illustrations continue to multiply.[5] It may be true to say that the newspaper uses the cartoon and the caricature to teach and to influence public opinion, while the magazines use various forms of reproduction to entertain their readers and either to illustrate a text or to form a connected story having a running thread of comment.

The attitude of artists towards illustrating for the press has also changed. Once considered beneath the dignity of an artist of standing to have his work appear in a daily newspaper, famous artists are now represented in all the great dailies and other periodicals not only in cartoons but also in the advertising pages.[6]

[3] "Many of the great dailies retain a permanent staff of from ten to twenty men. . . . Each man of the staff is a specialist in some line—portrait, society, yachting, naval, military, sport, or humor."—W. Jenkins, "Illustrations of the Daily Press in America," *The International Studio*, March, 1902, 16: 254–262; October, 1902, 17: 281–291.

J. Pennell describes and gives a history of the use of the illustration by the daily press in "Art and the Daily Press," *Nineteenth Century*, October, 1897, 42: 653–662.

[4] At least one periodical having a large circulation is reputed to have narrowly averted a financial disaster that had been imminent because of extravagant outlay for illustration.

[5] "Our artistic skill has led us into temptation, and by degrees engendered a habit of making pictures when we ought to be recording facts. We have thus, through our cleverness, created a fashion and a demand from the public for something which is often elaborately untrue."—H. Blackburn, "The Illustration of Books and Newspapers," *Nineteenth Century*, February, 1890, 27: 213–224.

[6] Louis Baury in an interesting paper on "Art in Publicity" gives an historic account of illustrated advertisements.—*The Bookman*, October, 1912, 36: 128–147; E. Knaufft, "Art in Advertising," *Review of Reviews*, June, 1922, 65: 625–634.

M. Liotard drew upon himself the disapproval of his brother artists for painting *La Belle Chocolatière* at the behest of a great industrial house, but the original hangs in the Dresden gallery. To-day the advertising pages of our illustrated magazines carry the signed work of artists of fame and distinction. It is to them that lovers of art turn for examples of the classical school of art rather than to the reading pages where the experiments in the new art are frequently "tried out."

The attitude of the public in its turn has also greatly changed if Wordsworth's sonnet on "Illustrated Books and Newspapers"[7] may be taken as a criterion of public opinion.

As a result of this changing attitude of both press and artist and the growing demand of the public for illustrations of every description in every department of the newspaper the illustration has become an epitome of the press as a whole. The part is not equal to the whole, but an examination of the illustration and of the graphic press must show that in and of itself it has independently the same characteristics as has the press considered collectively; it has the same problems to meet and its relation to the public is the same. This is not true of other parts of the paper. News, reports, correspondence, editorials, criticism are all incomplete parts of the press, but the illustration is a wheel within a wheel, complete and self-contained.

The illustration has its own distinct personality as has each representative of the press and this is expressed not so much by epithets and nicknames as in graphic form. *Life, Puck, Punch,*

[7] This was written in 1846 and was probably apropos of the founding of the *Illustrated London News* in 1842.

"Discourse was deemed Man's noblest attribute,
And written words the glory of his hand;
Then followed Printing with enlarged command
For thought—dominion vast and absolute
For spreading truth, and making love expand.
Now prose and verse sunk into disrepute
Must lackey a dumb Art that best can suit
The taste of this once-intellectual Land.
A backward movement surely have we here,
From manhood,—back to childhood; for the age—
Back towards caverned life's first rude career.
Avaunt this vile abuse of pictured page!
Must eyes be all in all, the tongue and ear
Nothing? Heaven keep us from a lower stage!"

Kladderadatsch each has its own appropriate, distinctive, recognizable symbol. Different artists even more than different writers have their own distinguishing characteristics.[8] In turn they have created distinctive national characters like John Bull and Uncle Sam, they have symbolized political parties by the donkey, the elephant, and the moose, or one wing of a political party by the tiger. They have created hundreds of well-known characters not only in advertising columns and in comic supplements but in the regular news and editorial columns of the daily press, and they have thus widely extended the acquaintance of all classes of society. The personality of the illustrated press and of the illustrations within the daily press is even more clear-cut and recognizable than is that of the paper of which it may form a part.

Each class of illustration is often a counterpart of another feature of the press—"our special artist" is twin brother to "our own correspondent;" the illustrated advertisement, like the advertisement itself, is to-day concerned with the processes by which results are achieved;[9] the cartoon of the day illustrates the same changes that have come in news and in editorial column,— they appeal to the rank and file rather than to the exceptional person; the cartoonist elected to Congress may find the paper for which he drew barred from the mails;[10] another cartoonist may, like an editor, find his political views, his patriotism, and his Americanism called in question by ever-watchful, self-constituted guardians of the existing order;[11] the illustrator, like the news-

---

[8] *Life* represented Lincoln after the manner of ten different artists.—February 4, 1918.—A page in Spielmann gives thirty-six different representations of Gladstone drawn for *Punch* by several of its artists.—*History of Punch*, p. 207.—The New York *Times*, January 10, 1919, gave on a double page two hundred and ninety-two pictures of Roosevelt.

[9] The illustration of a concrete steel company shows a factory in process of construction; asbestos roofing is being laid; sectional furniture is being put together; parts of automobiles are being assembled.

The customs of the so-called upper classes are discovered through the illustration of the butler serving a well-known brand of soup, the double-handled bouillon cups illustrating a variety of beef extract, the waitress carrying a tray with coffee service and coffee pot containing coffee of a special brand, and boys playing in an exclusive park rather than on the street advertise the clothing of a high-priced dealer in boys' clothing.

[10] New York *Sun*, July 14, 1917.

[11] The discussion of the political views of "Ding" filled many columns of the New York *Tribune*, October, 1919.

contributor, may be "edited" and thus his meaning be qualified;[12] the illustrator, like the interviewer, may find himself *persona non grata*;[13] the illustration may be used to further international hatred or friendship,[14] or to perpetuate sectional ill will,[15] or to minister to national glory;[16] it may bring danger of persecution to the illustrator,[17] or unintentionally bring undeserved discredit to the person illustrated;[18] it may be used for propagandist purposes, as effectively as is the text.[19]

[12] It was rumored that Raemaekers' cartoons in the New York *American* were thus edited, in spite of the contract that no captions or drawings should be changed.—New York *Tribune*, August 26, October 12, 1917.

Differences of opinion between Th. Nast and G. W. Curtis are discussed by A. B. Paine, *Th. Nast*, pp. 214–220.

[13] H. Vizetelly was commissioned by Vincent Dowling to make sketches of the coronation of Queen Victoria for *Bells' Life in London* and *The Observer*. He made preliminary sketches of Westminster Abbey and Dowling then asked permission of the Duke of Wellington to allow him to make a sketch from the roof of Apsley House of the royal procession passing along Picadilly. The answer ran:

"F. M. the Duke of Wellington has received a letter signed Vincent Dowling.

"The Duke has no knowledge of the writer of the letter, neither is he interested in any way in 'the Observer' newspaper. Apsley House is not a public building but the Duke's private residence, and he declines to allow any stranger to go upon the roof.

"Apsley House,
"June 21, 1838."

Henry Vizetelly, *Glances Back Through Seventy Years*, I, 156.

[14] The frequent ridicule by Germany of America's sympathies with England was answered by *Life* in a cartoon called "Our Nursery Days."—Cited by the New York *Times*, August 5, 1917.

[15] "The Fate of the Carpetbagger and the Scalawag," W. L. Fleming, *Documentary History of Reconstruction*, Vol. I, Frontispiece, reproduced from the *Independent Monitor*, Tuscaloosa, Alabama, September 1, 1868.

[16] The recent war gave rise in America alone to forty-seven thousand official photographs and one hundred and sixty-five miles of motion-picture negatives.—New York *Evening Post*, August 16, 1919.

[17] It was charged that the fires in Paris in 1871 were started by the Communard and the Petroleuses, that there were two thousand of the latter at Satory, that they were in regiments and well drilled, and every woman taken prisoner was called a "Petroleuse." Only one or two so-called "Petroleuses" were brought to trial, the evidence was ridiculous, and the trial was abandoned. But Paris believed it and "a photographer tried to earn an 'honest penny' by its means. He published portraits of the Petroleuses. For this purpose he utilized some old negatives of female faces that chanced to be unprepossessing, but at last he was prosecuted by a citizen for using in this way the portrait of his mother-in-law or some other near relative."—W. Simpson, *Autobiography*, pp. 267–268.

[18] In 1866, William Simpson was sent to Russia to make sketches for the *Illustrated London News* of the marriage of the Czarevich and a sister of the

The illustration may serve political as well as artistic ends, as the text may have a primary political end and a secondary literary one and it may have its counterpart in a corresponding form of literature, as the illustrated satires of *Life* find their counterpart in the descriptions of the same conditions given by the gentle satire of George William Curtis in the *Potiphar Papers*. The intellectual lineage of both pictorial and written satire has been traced to classic Greece by a recent writer in reminding us that "In nineteenth, if not twentieth century England, cartoons like those of Sir John Tenniel or Sir F. C. Gould, and the best political writing by prose satirists in the weekly journals have produced impressions closely akin to those that Aristophanes made it his business to create."[20] Yet the advantage must be held to lie with the illustration rather than with the writer. "For the 'Biglow Papers' and the best of Mr. Dooley's political satire there have been dozens of notable cartoons."[21]

The illustration, like the press as a whole, has its own distinguishing national traits. "The spirit of French comic art," says Bunner, "turns distinctly—and delightfully—to caricature. The French cartoon—the pictorial lampoon, that is—has but to exhibit in an exaggerated form the objectionable characteristics of an individual, to serve its purpose and to touch its public." The French nature, he finds rather observant than deductive,

Princess of Wales. After the ceremony, the Prince of Wales and the artist spent two days in Moscow where they witnessed as spectators a dance of Russian gypsies. The artist sketched the scene and introduced inconspicuously in a corner the figures of the Prince of Wales and Prince George of Denmark. Some years later, a lady was criticizing the Prince of Wales to the artist, saying, among other things, "Yes, and see how he went on in Russia, among a parcel of gipsy dancing-girls." The only evidence she could have had was the illustration of the dance, witnessed by the artist and the Prince of Wales because a member of the suite of the Prince had informed them that the dancing much resembled an Indian nautch.—W. Simpson, *Autobiography*, pp. 179–181. The illustration is given in the *Illustrated London News*, December 15, 1866.

[19] "I was frequently called to the Minister's room [Bismarck's] to receive instructions. Our illustrated papers were to publish pictures of the charge at Spichernberg, and also to deny the statement of the *Constitutionnel* that the Prussians had burnt down everything on their march, leaving nothing but ruins behind them. We could say with a clear conscience that we had not observed the least signs of this."—M. Busch, *Bismarck: Some Secret Pages of his History*, I, 82–83.

[20] T. H. S. Escott, *Masters of English Journalism*, p. 26.

[21] New York *Evening Post*, December 14, 1912.

while the English spirit is more deliberately logical and "asks something beyond this of the man who tries to reason with it in a picture." Hence the artist approaches his subject "by means of a fable, a parable, an allegory, something that will stand the test of argument and comparison." In America, the idea of the cartoonist long "was simply to express in drawing a figure of speech—and the more realistically the better." The characteristic of the German school has been that it "carries the art and mystery of cartooning far beyond any of its rivals."[22]

An examination of the typical illustrated periodicals that are synchronous and comparable in purpose must show that these conclusions are justified. *Le Journal amusant* and *L'Illustration*, the *Illustrated London News*, *Harper's Weekly*, and *Kladderadatsch* all show distinct national traits. The French have emphasized the caricature, the English the cartoon, Americans the illustration pure and simple, and the Germans a special form of cartoon. Similar distinctions are found in the corresponding classes in different countries,—*Puck* and *Life*, *Punch*, and the *Fliegende Blätter* are all combinations of the cartoon and the caricature, but it would be impossible to mistake the illustrations of any of them and attribute them to another source.

During the recent war these national characteristics were specially pronounced. They show national differences in workmanship, in object, in method of treatment, and in underlying spirit. The German cartoons have shown most prominently the spirit of hatred towards England, the English cartoons have seemed to indicate a "grin and bear it" spirit, the Dutch cartoons show a hatred of oppression, while the French disposition has been indicated by calm endurance.[23] Corresponding national characteristics and differences are evident in the cartoons, caricatures, and illustrations that have been collected from every nation on the globe.

Yet all illustrations of the war have had certain features in common,—all have caricatured the caricatures of other countries; all have at times satirized themselves; all have exalted the same

---

[22] H. C. Bunner, Introduction to *A Selection of Cartoons from Puck by Joseph Keppler*.
[23] Compare H. P. Adam, *ed.*, *International Cartoons of the War*.

virtues and claimed their own national pre-eminence in them; all bemoan the enormous financial burdens of war; all proclaimed immediate political revolutions in the enemy's country; all the Allies and all neutrals united in finding Achilles' heel in the expectation of the Germans of their speedy entrance into Paris, in their prophecy of the conquest of the British fleet by the submarines,[24] in their missionary zeal for spreading *kultur*, and in their attribution of fear and cowardice to the Allies.

All use of the illustrations of the war period must be tempered by these national characteristics and it is in this respect but duplicating the experience of the press as a whole.

The illustration, like the press, may tell a plain unvarnished tale, it may present a series of unadorned facts, it may give an embroidered story, it may represent a picture in artistic form, it may give information in regard to existing conditions, it may have a purely commercial object, it may be intended to interpret situations little understood, it may be used to influence public opinion in both an open and a secret way. Some illustrations may be intended to make readers see, others to make them think.

The illustration is everywhere therefore a parallel or a complementary medium of expression, working in the same fields, under much the same handicaps, having practically the same ends in view as the printed or the spoken word. Its métier is biography, narrative and topical history, description of contemporary society, and every field open to the medium of type. It may run the gamut of human emotions and cover a wide range of intellectual achievement. It may be witty, humorous or serious, dull, inspiring, or colorless, but whatever the field it selects or the spirit in which it works, it is collectively and in miniature a replica of the press as a whole.

The illustration as found in the daily paper and in the periodical is of great variety, including initial letters, tail pieces, vignettes,

---

[24] These conclusions have been largely drawn from an examination of several collections of illustrative war material, but they are the same that have been drawn by many others. See R. de la Sizeranne, "La Caricature et la Guerre," *Revue des Deux Mondes*, June 1, 15, 1916, 6. Période, 33:481–502, 806–841. The general statements, however, are made with the consciousness that, like all general statements, many individual exceptions to them may be found.

decorated borders, cartoons, caricatures, photographs or sketches of persons, places and commercial articles, charts, plans, working drawings, puzzles, rebuses, photogravure special sections, and the decorative cover. Graphic representation is usually confined to the weekly, monthly, or quarterly periodicals, although occasionally it is found in the daily paper.[25] Maps that illustrate military campaigns, explorations of previously unknown territories, and new boundary lines arranged by treaties are being given great space. All of these forms of illustration are coming to be a more and more important part of the newspaper in that they make the text clearer, tell a story independently of the written text, give specific information on technical matters that would otherwise be incomprehensible to the laity, clarify obscure situations, and elucidate complex subjects. But they may be considered subsidiary forms of illustration and they are therefore of less importance to the historian than are the four great classes of illustrations that may be grouped by the method of making them and the use to which they are put. He is specially concerned with the drawing or sketch, the photograph, the caricature, and the cartoon.

The sketch is now practically limited to illustrating fashions in clothing and furniture or other objects that can not be protected by copyright or patent, and it is also often used where specially artistic effects are desired. It is thus most frequently found in the advertising columns.

The photograph is largely used to show distant places, individuals prominent for any and every reason, animals or objects conspicuous in exhibitions, machinery or scientific apparatus and it is thus most often used in the news columns or on the pages devoted to society affairs.

The caricature [26] has always been an instrument of satiric,

[25] Charts showing weather indications have come to be an important feature. H. Blackburn says that the first weather chart in an English daily paper was printed in *The Times* in 1875. "The Illustration of Books and Newspapers," *Nineteenth Century*, February, 1890, 27: 213–224. But see *supra*, p. 11, Note 30.

A good discussion of the value of the graph to business men may be found in the New York *Times*, September 11, 1921.

[26] The literature of caricature is extensive. M. H. Spielmann gives a general bibliography of the subject in connection with his article on "Caricature," *Encyclopaedia Britannica*, 5: 331–336.

spiteful, even malignant attack and a great modern daily considers that "it perhaps speaks well for modern manners that caricature is almost a lost art."[27] By comparison with "the polite cartoon," it may be considered a coarse, vulgar, even brutal way of conveying ideas or administering rebuke. But caricature in its very nature must deal with coarse, brutal subjects and inevitably the style is adapted to the subject,—it is impossible to caricature in a courteous, gentlemanly way since caricature and politeness are mutually exclusive terms. Yet even so the caricature becomes for the historian an unimpeachable record of a hard, brutal society of which it has been an outgrowth. If the caricatures of Gillray seem on a low social plane,[28] it is because the lives of lords and ladies of high degree of that day left much to be desired and because much was acceptable to the public of his time that would not be tolerated to-day, however true to life it might be. If, as M. Gaultier has so well shown,[29] caricature is essentially pessimistic; if it represents, while it distorts but always with an ulterior motive; if it is exaggerated, grotesque and extravagant as well as brutal, it is because in society itself there exist these same elements of pessimism, exaggeration, and brutality.

The "characteristic portrait" is a variant of the personal caricature and, as a softened modification of it, may be of greater service to the historian in his search for personal material than is given by conventional portrait, or by caricature.[30]

J. Grand-Carteret in 1885 in *Les Mœurs et la caricature en France* gave an extended bibliography and history of journals of caricature, pp. 555–618, and biographies of caricaturists, pp. 619–673; in *Les Mœurs et la caricature en Allemagne* he gives a bibliography of journals of caricature, pp. 427–449, and a list of caricaturists, pp. 451–482.
These illustrate fairly well the extent of the material available.
[27] New York *Tribune*, November 8, 1916.
[28] T. Wright, *ed.*, *The Works of James Gillray, the Caricaturist*.
W. S. Jackson cites a contemporary of Gillray who wrote: "The period of dread of foreign and domestic enemies has passed away, and we verily believe it is due to the satiric pencil of Gillray." He himself points out that "a Gillray, tremendous as he was, could become the valued ally of a Pitt and the particular joy and encouragement of a nation in its struggle."—"Wanted—a Gillray," *Nineteenth Century and After*, September, 1910, 68: 522–531.
[29] P. Gaultier, *Le Rire et la Caricature*, 1911.
[30] Leslie Ward developed this form of illustration in an interesting way. His *Forty Years of 'Spy'* has nearly two hundred of these telling portraits that "without the same qualities as the caricature, are sometimes more

Political caricature at first was used exclusively by the great weeklies, like *Punch*[31] and *Harper's*, but later it was taken up by the daily press. Each has its special caricaturist and cartoonist, "process" methods simplify and expedite reproduction,[32] and thus the caricature and the cartoon minister to the desire for the illustration that expresses in concrete form political theories and abstractions, industrial conditions that are little understood, and social spheres that are far removed from the reader. It must be remembered, however, that poor paper and rough printing often frustrate the plans of both artist and editor and complicate the result for the historian, and that it is often difficult for the artist to unite historical accuracy with artistic expression and produce a sketch with the speed required.

As historical material, the historian must accept the caricature with many qualifications. It represents abnormal conditions in war and in politics, it suggests the extremes in society, it is frankly used as a weapon to defeat an end regarded by the caricaturist as undesirable. More than any other form of illustra-

---

successful." He adds later: "It is extraordinary how deeply-rooted the idea is that a big head and miniature body make a caricature, whereas, of course, it does not in the least." He believes that "the genuine caricaturist combines a profound sense of character with such a gift of humour as will enable him to rise above the mere perception of idiosyncrasy or foible, and actually to translate into terms of comedy a psychological knowledge unsuspected by those who uncritically perceive and delight in the finished caricature."—Pp. 114, 115, 110-111.

The caricatures of Caruso contributed to *La Follia di New York* "embody and show a distinctive, personal psychology: they present the individual in his entirety and completeness."—L. Roversi, "Introduction," Enrico Caruso, *Caricatures*.

In this respect, therefore, they may be considered character sketches rather than caricatures in the usual sense.

[31] Athol Mayhew, in a chapter "Follow my Leader," lists very many comic journals—most of them short lived—started in imitation of *Punch.—A Jorum of Punch*, pp. 132-150.

M. H. Spielmann, in "The Rivals of 'Punch'," names a dozen periodicals incorporating the name in their title.—*National Review*, July, 1895, 25: 654-666.—Some of these rivals had comparatively few illustrations and no cartoons, and evidently grew up in conditions that afforded little material for genuine satire, either of the pen or pencil, such as was found in the original *Punch*. See *Punch Staff Papers*, from the *Sydney Punch*.

[32] "When I saw the drawings of Burne-Jones coming off the press at the rate of over twenty thousand copies an hour, I knew I was assisting at a revolution in art which would be as wide reaching as that started by Dürer or by Bewick."—J. Pennell, "Art and the Daily Paper," *Nineteenth Century*, October, 1897, 42: 653-662.

tion it shows the excesses and the defects of its time; more than any other form, especially when it takes the form of political caricature, it may become vindictive or malicious [33] and thus fail to distinguish between the legitimate and the illegitimate fields open to it.

It has been well shown that while the essential principles of caricature were as well understood in the eighteenth as in the nineteenth century and the means used were the same, the results were radically different. Modern caricature is essentially journalistic, and it appears regularly in special weeklies and as a daily cartoon in the newspaper. It thus often shows the effect of haste and speed with a resulting tendency to expend itself on the local and ephemeral. Caricature of the eighteenth century was spasmodic and was given publicity through print shops. It was essentially personal in its conception and remained a one-man effort.[34] The cartoon of *Punch* has been the result of the conference of the entire editorial staff and it is thus in accord with the settled policy of the paper as a whole.[35]

[33] In the political campaign of 1872 the personal appearance and the personality of Horace Greeley lent themselves to caricature particularly well, and the caricaturists of the day so improved their opportunity that it was popularly believed the caricatures were contributory causes to the death of Mr. Greeley in November, 1872.

The *World* printed at the height of the Burchard-Blaine incident, 1884, a cartoon entitled "Belshazzar's Feast" that "portrayed the Republican chiefs in the robes of ancient revelers at the banquet of privilege with Blaine himself in close conference with Jay Gould, Commodore Vanderbilt and others. The newspaper cartoon was then an innovation in New York, and the 'feast' caused a well-remembered sensation."—J. L. Heaton, *The Story of a Page*, pp. 32–33.

Harvey's Weekly, during the presidential campaign of 1920, contained a cartoon, based on the Immaculate Conception, that gave great offense not only to the Roman Catholics but to all who deprecated the use of religious subjects in a political campaign.—Daily press, October, 1920.

It has been well said that two generations ago American cartoons tried to mould public opinion, to make political capital, and to win votes, but that they only resulted in personal abuse.

Maurice and Cooper maintain that the success of caricature depends on its timeliness, its seizure of critical moments, and its grasp of the important question of the hour. The best caricature therefore does not merely reflect public opinion, but guides it.—*History of the Nineteenth Century in Caricature*, pp. 1, 2.

[34] A. A. Maurice and F. T. Cooper, "The Influence of Journalism," in *The History of the Nineteenth Century in Caricature*, pp. 278–288.

[35] The policy of co-operation and the subordination of the individual to the collective paper has undoubtedly been one of the chief factors in its long

The historian must recognize these limitations and he must use the caricature as itself a record of the existence of this temper in contemporary life, but without accepting it at its face value. The caricature is an intellectual and artistic rash that appears when the body politic is out of order, and the historian can regard it only as a symptom of the existence of unhealthy conditions. It flourishes best amid disordered conditions of politics, when ill-gotten wealth is a festering sore, when in times of war every man's hand is against every man. Its value to the historian lies in his ability to measure by it the degree to which society has departed from the normal and to diagnose the particular nature of the disease that afflicts it.[36]

The cartoon tells a story, points a moral, assumes knowledge, intelligence, judgment, and imagination on the part of its readers, and it is in effect "a leading article transformed into a picture."

and successful career. Accounts of the Wednesday dinners where the cartoon of the ensuing week has been decided on as well as the general policy of the paper may be found in M. H. Spielmann, *The History of Punch;* A. W. à Beckett, *The à Becketts of Punch,* and *Recollections of a Humorist;* G. S. Layard, *A Great "Punch" Editor Being the Life, Letters and Diaries of Shirley Brooks;* F. C. Burnand, *Records and Reminiscences,* 2 vols.; W. P. Frith, *John Leech,* 2 vols.; H. Furniss, *Confessions of a Caricaturist,* 2 vols.; Walter Jerrold, *Douglas Jerrold and Punch;* W. M. Thackeray, "The Mahogany Tree," *Ballads and Tales.*

[36] Addison notes that "politicians can resolve the most shining actions among men into artifice and design; others, who are soured by discontent, repulses, or ill-usage, are apt to mistake their spleen for philosophy; men of profligate lives . . . are for pulling down all appearances of merit which seem to upbraid them; and satirists describe nothing but deformity. From all these hands we have such draughts of mankind, as are represented in those burlesque pictures which the Italians call caricaturas; where the art consists in preserving, amidst distorted proportions and aggravated features, some likeness of the person, but in such a manner as to transform the most agreeable beauty into the most odious monster."—*The Spectator,* No. 537, November 15, 1712.

This has been noted as the second known instance of the use of the word *caricature,* even in its Italian form, the first being found in a work on *Christian Morals* written more than a hundred years earlier by Sir Thomas Browne.

It would be difficult to give a better description of caricature than that of Addison's.

Augustin Filon in discussing Hogarth cites the well-known anecdote of Charles Lamb who as a child visited a cemetery and said to his sister, "They are all good here; where are the wicked buried?" He makes the application to Hogarth's work and remarks, "All are wicked here; where are the good?"—*La Caricature en Angleterre,* pp. 73–74. This is the most searching summary noted of the limitations of caricature as historical material.

Since it is most frequently used to influence public opinion, it is often found in immediate proximity to the editorial columns, although often placed on the front or the back page where it can be easily seen without turning the paper.

It partakes somewhat of the nature of the caricature,[37] but it lacks the caustic features that distinguish the latter,[38] it is genuinely good-natured, and it usually represents group interests and activities rather than prominent individuals. Even the caricature, until the outbreak of the war of 1914, was being more and more confined to its legitimate field of depicting objectionable principles or abstractions and was seldom directed against individuals unless they consciously and perniciously represented base principles of action.[39] Indeed, the process of

[37] There has been much confusion in the use of the two terms since they have often been used synonymously, but they are essentially different.

Robert de la Sizeranne notes that the word *caricature* is used in three different and sometimes contradictory senses: it may denote sketches of exaggerated and grotesque figures, without legend and without moral intent; it may be used of scenes intentionally ironic, but without grotesque figures; it may represent figures neither grotesque nor ironic, but accompanied by the symbols of glory, or depicting scenes of horror. Many caricatures seem to him to be simply the genre scenes of the painter, differing only in that they evoke thought while the genre painting simply acts upon superficial vision. —"La Caricature et la Guerre," *Revue des Deux Mondes*, June 1, 15, 1916, 6. Période, 33: 481–502, 806–841.

The word *cartoon* as at present used in America apparently is an amplification of caricature in the third sense as noted by de la Sizeranne.

The difference between *caricature* and *cartoon* is perhaps best suggested by M. H. Spielmann who implies that caricature has been a weapon of venomous attack, used as an instrument for the manufacture of public opinion, while the cartoon "has come to be regarded as a humorous or sarcastic comment upon the topic uppermost in the nation's mind." He has also defined the cartoon as "a pictorial joke," but his definition would assuredly not cover the cartoons of Cesare, Forain, and Raemaekers. He has also defined it as "a leading article transformed into a picture," but in this case it is not a joke.

See also an editorial, "Caricaturist and Cartoonist," New York *Tribune*, November 9, 1916.

The word *cartoon*, as distinguished from *caricature*, was first applied to a drawing of John Leech's in No. 105 of *Punch*, 1843. M. H. Spielmann, *The History of "Punch*," chap. VIII; also his articles on "Caricature" and "Cartoon" in *Encyclopaedia Britannica*, 5: 331–336, 434–435.

[38] "The large consensus of opinion is that the artist must shoot folly as it flies with arrows that do not fester in the wound. He must be able to make his attack so witty and laughable that even his victims will be unable not to smile."—New York *Evening Post*, October 8, 1910.

[39] "The element of caricature in the political cartoon has been disappearing. Instead of personal caricature, we have symbols of parties, movements, and issues."—New York *Evening Post*, May 3, 1912.

change had been carried so far that complaint was made that
"our good-natured cartoons on bosses and their legislative
henchmen are the reflection of our criminal good nature to evils
in public life. A sharper civic consciousness should make the
cartoonist's pen dig in deeper." [40]

Thus the cartoon, like the photograph, the sketch, and the
caricature, carries with it its own limitations, for the cartoonist
shows in his work the same personal characteristics as are shown
by those who express their ideas through words. If he is by
nature a fighter, he does his best work under high tension; if
he is an onlooker in life, his work shows detachment; if he is a
satirist, the sting points his pencil. All of these personal equations
the historian must consider and weigh in the newspaper artist
as well as in the writer.[41]

What is to be the attitude of the historian towards the illustration considered collectively as well as by its various classes?
If it is an epitome of the press as a whole, it must follow that the
same general tests for authoritativeness must be applied to it
as are applied to the various parts of the press, although they
must vary somewhat since they must be applied both to the
means by which the illustration is made and also to the subject
of the illustration.

The illustration is a most prolific source of error, but many
of the minor errors, like those made by the local reporter, are
amusing in themselves, and do not seriously militate against
their general reliability. Some of them are due to carelessness,[42]

[40] New York *Evening Post*, June 30, 1913.—It seems probable that the
writer was in reality referring to the caricature rather than to the cartoon.
The same point has been elaborated by W. S. Jackson who finds much
embroidery but few ideas in the work of contemporary artists.—"Wanted—
a Gillray," *Nineteenth Century and After*, September, 1910, 68: 522–531.

[41] A penetrating discussion of "The Art of Political Cartoons" is found in
the Literary Supplement of the London *Times*, March 4, 1920.

[42] A cartoon in *Punch*, April 12, 1845, was entitled "Who's Afraid? or the
Oregon Question;" the drawing on the block had not been reversed so that
every actor in it appeared to be left-handed.—M. H. Spielmann, *The Hitherto
Unidentified Contributions of W. M. Thackeray to "Punch,"* pp. 11–12. The
drawing is there reproduced.

John Leech in speaking of W. P. Frith's *Derby Day* could not understand
how in so careful a work he had missed one of the most notable facts at such
places,—not a person in the crowd was represented as smoking a pipe or a
cigar.—The Brothers Dalziel, *A Record of Fifty Years' Work*, p. 44.

others to ignorance,[43] and still others to inadvertence to which no blame could be attached.[44] Other errors must be explained by the mechanical difficulty of making corrections after the block has left the hand. Some errors are due to the temptation of the illustrator to see an event as he wishes it to be seen or as he thinks would produce a striking or artistic effect,[45] and others can only be explained by the mental slovenliness that is willing, in deference to a real or supposed popular demand for illustration, to make pictures from insufficient data.[46] At an

[43] "He [X. Khan] was amused at Pan-Islamic agitation made in Germany, and described a proclamation lately sent to India with a photogravure portrait of the Skeikh-ul-Islam, clad in a stiff shirt and wearing a starched collar; the idea of this seemed ludicrous, as both the image and the dress were anathema to true believers."—Lewis Einstein, *Inside Constantinople During the Dardanelles Expedition*, p. 65.

After the Republican party in 1884 nominated J. G. Blaine for the presidency, the Independents supported Cleveland. *Judge* in a cartoon, July, 1884, figured Roosevelt as one of the Independent Army, but incorrectly since he supported Blaine. The cartoon is reproduced in A. Shaw, *A Cartoon History of Roosevelt's Career*, p. 12.

[44] William Simpson was sent to Rome to illustrate the meeting of the Vatican Council in 1869. At the opening of the Council, each Bishop, as he walked up the nave of St. Peter's, knelt at the confessional of St. Peter before the high altar. This the artist introduced into the picture and represented the Bishop shown as wearing his mitre on his head. But on account of the crowd, he could not see the Bishops when on their knees, and as they passed into the Chamber afterwards they had their mitres on. After the sketch was published, he was told that a rule of the Church required every one to uncover his head, since the Blessed Sacrament was exhibited at the time on the high altar and that it was to it they knelt and prayed.—*Autobiography*, p. 232. The illustration is given in the *Illustrated London News*, December 25, 1869.

[45] Leech drew for *Punch*, November, 1849, a representation of the opening of the coal exchange in which Queen Victoria figures as being presented with a "black diamond." The Queen, however, was not present.—H. W. Lucy, *The Queen and Mr. Punch*, No. XIV.

[46] A popular book of illustrations of the war, dated 1914, has nearly two hundred illustrations selected from a pictorial newspaper. They are variously described as photographs, paintings, drawings, impressions, sketches, visions, drawings from notes, drawings from photographic material and notes, drawings from notes by an eye witness, drawings from descriptions, drawings from sketches on the spot, drawings by A roughly finished by B, drawings by C from sketches by D, and paintings from descriptions by eye witnesses. It is almost inevitable that material thus hurriedly gathered and published should be filled with errors.

The New York *Daily Graphic* for Tuesday, March 15, 1881, had an illustration purporting to be of "the sixth and successful attempt on the life of the Emperor of Russia last Sunday afternoon," and notes that it is "from a telegraphic sketch by our special correspondent in St. Petersburg."

Still earlier, the New York *Tribune* had an illustration of a shooting match in Dublin, between an American rifle corps and English volunteers,

earlier date, when less rigorous standards were accepted than have since prevailed and when the methods of mechanical reproduction were cruder and slower, many illustrations were drawn in this spirit.[47]

The illustration like the text often suffers from the necessity of having to anticipate conditions and events that may belie anticipations. In 1892, B. Gillam drew for *Judge* a cartoon to be used in anticipation of the expected victory of Harrison over Cleveland. It was a double page cartoon representing the elephant riding over Cleveland. At the last moment, it was evident that Harrison had been defeated and the cartoon was changed by retouching the face of Cleveland and giving him a Harrison beard, putting a patch over the eye of the Republican elephant, and changing legends.[48]

Punch, in anticipation of the success of the expedition sent out to relieve General Gordon at Khartoum, published a cartoon

---

"sent by cable" and printed the morning after the event.—*Tribune*, June 30, 1875.

"Thus *The Times* and all other papers were distanced by the *Tribune*."—H. Blackburn, "The Illustration of Books and Newspapers," *Nineteenth Century*, February, 1890, 27: 213–224.

[47] "In the first number of the *Illustrated London News*, there was not a single picture that was drawn from actual sight, the factor which is the most essential element of the illustrated journalism of to-day. Sir John Gilbert has stated that not one of the events depicted by him—a state ball at which the queen and the prince consort appeared, the queen with the young prince of Wales in her arms, and other incidental illustrations—was taken from life."—C. K. Shorter, "Newspapers," *Encyclopaedia Britannica*, XIX, 550–551.

H. Vizetelly says that the only authorities the artist had to guide him were scanty scraps of information concerning the guests and the costumes as they appeared from time to time in the *Morning Post* and *The Times*, and that in general "the system pursued [in the *Illustrated London News*] with regard to the majority of engravings of current events—foreign, provincial, and even metropolitan when these transpired unexpectedly—was to scan the morning papers carefully, cut out such paragraphs as furnished good subjects for illustration, and send them with the necessary boxwood blocks to the draughtsmen employed."—*Glances Back Through Seventy Years*, I, 232.

The opening address of the first editor, F. W. N. Bayley, "was little else than an amplification of the prospectus, couched in the writer's customary high flown style, only he sought to hoodwink the public by saying that, 'should the pen ever be led into fallacious argument the pencil must at least be oracular with the spirit of truth'. And this, too, with not even a single engraving in the opening number derived from an authentic source!" —*Ib.*, I, 237.

[48] The cartoon is reproduced in Maurice and Cooper, *History of the Nineteenth Century in Caricature*, pp. 310–313.

representing the meeting of General Stewart and General Gordon, calling it "At Last." But Khartoum had fallen two days previously and the cartoon a week later was named "Too Late!" [49]

The illustration may also, like the text, sometimes suffer from other forms of "previousness," but these are not necessarily disconcerting.[50] The versatile cartoon may turn its coat and serve to illustrate equally well entirely different situations.[51]

These have been suggestions of a variety of errors frequently found in the illustrations of periodicals. They are due to a variety of causes and while they detract from the strict accuracy of the illustration, they are for the most part unimportant in themselves and they are readily corrected.

Another very large class of errors in the illustration is due to deliberate misrepresentation, but all such errors are explained away by their authors in the spirit of "no one knows any better and it doesn't matter." In the end, however, some one often does know better, or the illustration itself may prove its own undoing.[52]

[49] The cartoons are in the issues of February 7 and February 14, 1885.

[50] *The Independent*, February 7, 1916, gives a portrait of Louis D. Brandeis with the caption "Mr. Justice Brandeis." The nomination of Mr. Brandeis was not confirmed by the Senate until June 1, 1916.

[51] The New York *Evening Post* made effective use of one of Cesare's cartoons representing Wilson and Hughes standing near the chair of state. Election eve it was published over the caption "The Anxious Seat" and three days later over the caption "Watchful Waiting."—November 6, 9, 1916.

[52] October 31, 1914, the New York *Evening Sun* and the New York *Mail* both published the same picture on their front pages. One labelled it "Sinking of the Cressy, Aboukir and Hogue by a German submarine," and the other called it "Sinking of two German destroyers by British cruiser in the North Sea."—W. R. Page in the New York *Evening Post*, November 7, 1914.

The Sunday gravure section of the New York *Tribune*, March 26, 1916, gave an illustration of Nahr-el-Kelb, Syria, and named it Boyap Junction. "The place pictured is on a sixteen mile branch line along the sea coast and in no way connected with the Bagdad railway which was the subject of the page of photographs. There is no 'Boyap Junction'. A glance at the map would have shown the name of the junction, and the map would also have shown that it is in the midst of a broad level plain, and not a rocky gorge like that at Dog River or Nahr-el-Kelb where the picture printed was taken." —Personal letter from M. O. Williams, a former resident of Syria.

"At the time of the Benjamin Franklin bicentenary there appeared in one or more papers a reproduction of 'Franklin chez lui, à Philadelphie' illustrating Manasseh Cutler's letter describing Franklin with others, seated in his garden. A little investigation proved that the picture had been painted about 1876 by Henry Bacon and was therefore a purely imaginary depiction of something that might indeed have taken place."

The photograph lends itself specially well to this form of deception. It may have been made at a date much earlier than that of the paper where it appears and hence give a wrong impression,[53] or the artist may "fake" a portrait or a scene as a reporter may fake an interview,[54] although there is a growing intolerance of wilful deceptions of this nature.[55]

The general newspaper-reading public apparently has little

A one-issue "blanket-sheet" published in New York in 1847 had "an amusing mixture of bona-fide portraits of American generals and French and other foreign cuts, appropriated to do duty as delineations of Mexican life." French cuirassiers and Italian brigands, posing as Mexican soldiers and civilians, were mingled with the others.—Frank Weitenkampf, "Pictorial Documents as Illustrating American History," *The History Teacher's Magazine*, February, 1917, 8: 48–51.

After the San Francisco earthquake and fire in 1906, a newspaper published a panoramic photograph of the city, "ingeniously reduced to ruin by means of brush-work and embellished by flames and smoke of similar origin," but inadvertently left in place the notice that the photograph was copyrighted more than a year before the fire had taken place.

The Chicago *Tribune*, August 2, 1921, published a four-column photograph sent by its Paris correspondent. It purported to represent an attack in the streets of Moscow by Soviet leaders who turned machine guns on a mob of men, women, and children demanding food.—The following day the *Tribune* stated that it regretted to learn that this photograph was a misrepresentation; that it had been printed in the *Tribune* nearly four years previously; and that it represented a street scene in Petrograd during the war.

[53] This is frequently the case where photographs of individuals are used. A person suddenly becomes prominent, a recent photograph is not available, and one of an earlier date is used. This explains the frequent comments, "He is much younger than I supposed," or "He looks too young for the office."

Photographs of very young men purporting to be those of Theodore Roosevelt and Charles E. Hughes were published in the *Barbadoes* (*W. I.*) *Weekly Illustrated Paper*, October 14, 1916, accompanied by the explanation, "From the present indications it appears that either Roosevelt or Hughes will secure the nomination for president from the Republican Convention."—New York *Tribune*, November 15, 1916.

[54] This has often been done in the case of foreigners where identification is difficult for readers.

[55] The press of January 7, 1912, contained descriptions of the making of fake photographs that represented tourists in Washington hobnobbing with President Taft,—greeted by him at a White House reception, received by him in private audience, taken out by him for a walk, or shown through the White House by him,—a fabrication that went on until stopped by the District Attorney. The account of the deception was copyrighted by John Elfreth Watkins.

The illustrated advertisement is a frequent sinner of this type. Psychology has taught scientific advertisers how to misrepresent goods for their purpose, —a certain brand of lead pencils, for example, may be illustrated and announced as sold at a low rate, but the illustration does not show that they are only one-half the ordinary length of pencils.

appreciation of art and does not encourage higher standards, and events themselves, like fire, flood and earthquake, sudden death and accident, may encourage deception of a more or less grave nature, even though at times the essential truthfulness of the spirit may be retained.[56]

It is but a step from this form of deception to a deliberate misrepresentation conceived with the definite idea of proving that black is white.[57] In view of the large number of supposititious

[56] H. Leach writes of one block that with chipping, smudging, and other artifices has done duty as a view of Port Arthur, the battle of Santiago, a scene in the West End of London, a railway accident, and massacres in Africa.—*Fleet Street from Within*, p. 37.
In sketching the death-bed of Gladstone, the artist by making a few changes used a sketch originally made for the death-bed of Bismarck.— K. L. Smith, "Newspaper Art and Artists," *Bookman*, August, 1901, 13: 549–556.
[E. V. Lucas,] *All the Papers* has many clever satires on the way the same illustration may be made to serve a dozen different ends.
Sir Mark Sykes and Edmund Sandars have given in *D'Ordel's Pantechnicon* a clever skit on the production of the illustrated magazine,—it includes "directions exposing the whole manual art of the trade" and is "a perfect model for the guidance of students."

[57] Sidney Whitman states that he had seen an illustrated paper giving harrowing pictures of women and children being massacred in a church. Such pictures were drawn by artists who arrived in Constantinople after the news of the outbreak on the Ottoman Bank in 1896 had spread to Western Europe and they were commissioned to supply the demand for pictures of atrocities. The demand could be met only by inventing what they could by no possibility have witnessed.—*Turkish Memories*, p. 29.
"German war-photographs are supplied to various Italian newspapers, which being provided with Italian text, can be printed as they are, and, according to the intention of the German enlighteners, should serve to give the Italian reader an appropriate and sympathetic picture of our army and our method of warfare. The Italian newspapers accept the material for illustration, which is supplied gratis, with joy, and print it. But sometimes after altering the explanatory text! Thus, for example, the following swindle was perpetrated by a Roman newspaper. A photograph, which, according to the Italian text appended, represents the transportation of a flying-machine by Germans of the *landwehr*, appeared in print with the legend, 'A captured German flying-machine being taken in triumph to Petrograd'."— *Kölnische Zeitung*, December 9, 1914, in *A Month's German Newspapers*, selected and translated by A. L. Gowans, pp. 122–123.
"A reliable correspondent of the New York *Times*, Mr. Charles Selden, sends to his newspaper a story told him by an American army officer recently back from Italy. As an instance of superior intrigue the story seems almost too Machiavellian to be true. 'In [Fiume],' says this American officer, 'the Italian government officials recently got the populace together at a great open-air meeting for the distribution of food. After the supplies had been given out, the crowd was asked if they wanted a further distribution of food, and, if so, to indicate their desire by raising their hands. All hands in that immense crowd went up. Photographs were taken that instant, and later

illustrations that the historian meets with, he must agree with
a prominent newspaper when it says, "The temptation to
'fake' pictures is considerably stronger than the temptation to
'fake' news itself, and it is yielded to with proportionately greater
frequency by those papers that make the pretence that their
pictorial chronicle is anything like as complete as their news
service."[58]

The illustration has often been a convenient medium for
influencing political policy. In time of peace the photograph
may be so manipulated as to magnify the walls of snow that
line the streets of a city and thus the illustration may be used
to oust a street commissioner objectionable to the politicians in
control, or it may reduce in height the piles of accumulated
street refuse and thus help to keep in office an inefficient deputy
commissioner; it may magnify and distort the cracks in the walls
of a building and thus turn a building inspector out of office.

Political caricatures and cartoons have been most effective
weapons in times of national and of international controversy,
and the general rules for the cartoon "have now been worked
out in experience. One upon which nearly all are to-day agreed
is that it must be predominantly good-natured. It may be

---

widely distributed throughout Italy with a caption to indicate that they were
pictures of citizens of Fiume voting in favor of annexation to Italy.' "—*The
New Republic*, May 10, 1919, 19: 33; New York *Times*, April 30, 1919.

F. Avenarius evidently published *Das Bild als Verleumder* with the object
of showing the Germans and the neutral countries the misrepresentations in
the illustrated papers of France, England, and Russia. The seventy-two
illustrations included in it seem to sustain his contention that these misrepresentations were deliberate and not infrequent. But when he challenged
friends or enemies of Germany to show him similar misrepresentations in
German newspapers he might have expected the gauntlet to be picked up.—
The answer to *Das Bild als Verleumder* was *L'Imposture par l'Image*. The
book gave seventy-eight illustrations,—sixty-one collected from seventeen
German papers and eleven from three Austrian papers,—showing that the
legend of pictures had been changed; negatives had been retouched and
"improved;" illustrations used many years before appeared with new names;
illustrations of the defeat of the French in 1870 were made to serve for the
war of 1914; signatures were erased; names of places were exchanged; a
French attack was transformed into a retreat.—It seemed to be, in homely
phrase, a case where the pot called the kettle black.

Charge and counter-charge are discussed by Dr. Lucien-Graux, "La
fausse nouvelle et l'image," *Les fausses nouvelles de la grande guerre*, II,
175–199.

[58] New York *Evening Post*, February 17, 1908.

as earnest as you please in intent, but it must be smiling in method." [59]

But they have not always been "good-natured," especially the caricature.[60] This gives essentially a distorted view, and it has a distinctive purpose. Its main object is not simply to create a laugh,—an ulterior motive lies beyond the laugh. It must thus be classed with the editorial as a means of influencing public opinion,[61] and even of rousing international hatreds.[62]

[59] New York *Evening Post*, October 8, 1910.

[60] Augustin Filon gives an interesting account of political caricature, particularly of the exchange of caricatures between the Whigs and the Tories at the time of the Revolution of 1688. The Whigs having called to their aid the Dutch caricaturists, the Tories used their sketches to their own ends by slightly changing the figures. The Dutch caricaturists rendered efficient service against the pretender and his family.—*La Caricature en Angleterre*, chap. III. The political caricatures of Hogarth and his quarrel with his quondam friend, John Wilkes, are discussed by Filon in chap. VII. The entire work deals almost exclusively with political caricature.

[61] The caricatures of *Punch* undoubtedly influenced public opinion in England at the time of the American Civil War and it is frequently said that Sir John Tenniel's cartoons did much to tighten the strain between England and America.

It is a question not yet decided as to what was the real opinion of England in regard to the Civil War in America, but there is not a shadow of doubt as to what was the attitude of the London *Punch*. This is conveyed not only by the text, but even more by the cartoons and caricatures that cover the period of the war. If the first cartoon of Lincoln (May 11, 1861) represented him as strong and intelligent, he quickly became in its pages "the bearded ruffian, a repulsive compound of malice, vulgarity and cunning."

The *amende honorable* made after Lincoln's death—"Britannia Sympathizes with Columbia"—May 6, 1865, and the poem of Tom Taylor's on Abraham Lincoln scarcely atoned for the years of caricature preceding, especially since it has recently been shown how divided was the sentiment of the *Punch* staff.—G. S. Layard, *A Great "Punch" Editor Being the Life, Letters, and Diaries of Shirley Brooks*, pp. 245–248. That these facts were not forgotten and that an effort was made to make use of them in stirring up strife between England and America is seen in a facsimile issue of *Punch* made up of cartoons that had appeared in *Punch* during the Civil War and the years immediately following and bore on the cover the inscription "As England sees U. S. shown in Punch." It was offered for sale in October, 1915.—An account is given in the New York *Evening Post*, October 22, 1915.

Full accounts of the original cartoons are given in G. S. Layard, *A Great "Punch" Editor Being the Life, Letters, and Diaries of Shirley Brooks*, London, 1907. M. H. Spielmann in his *History of Punch* barely alludes to the subject.

The cartoons, comments, and poems relating to the Civil War that were published in *Punch* have been collected and edited by W. S. Walsh under the title *Abraham Lincoln and the London Punch*.

[62] "The art of newspaper caricature as carried on abroad is savage to an extent that we, on this side of the Atlantic, neither practice nor even under-

It is again but a step from an open, legitimate use of the illustration to influence public opinion to the secret use of the illustration for propagandist purposes. More than ever before propaganda has been thus carried on during the recent war,[63] and the effort to combat it by one side has led to renewed activity by the other side. Difficult as it is in time of peace to deal with the illustration as historical material, it is manifoldly greater in time of war.[64]

These difficulties grow in part from the very nature of these forms of expression. The venom inherent in the caricature becomes even more intense, and the humor of the cartoon jars amid scenes of destruction. The use of the caricature and of the cartoon is limited in time of war by their inherent contradictions,—in all countries the cartoonists extol the same virtues and condemn the same faults, and each cartoonist is prone to

stand. In the first place, the Continental artist ranges much wider for his game."—New York *Evening Post*, June 30, 1913.

Francis Stopford states that "The Cologne *Gazette*, in a leading article on Holland, threatens that country that 'after the War Germany will settle accounts with Holland, and for each calumny, for each cartoon of Raemaekers', she will demand payment with the interest that is due her'," and he adds: "A Teuton paper has declared that Raemaekers' cartoons are worth at least two Army Corps to the Allies."—Francis Stopford, "Introduction," *Louis Raemaekers' Cartoons*, 1916.

[63] The plan for a campaign by caricature was communicated to the German press by the Wolff News Bureau,—"It would, therefore, be important from a patriotic point of view, for the daily papers also to occupy themselves by means of caricatures with the principal events of the day." This was specially urged in view of the caricatures of the Kaiser, the Crown Prince, and alleged German militarism and the special inducement was held out that the blocks would be supplied free of expense.—From the *Berner Bund*, cited by the *Literary Digest*, November 3, 1917, 55: 16.

"The camera with a purpose" has come to be ubiquitous.

[64] Collections of the cartoons and caricatures of all the warring countries and of neutrals can be found in the great public libraries; they have been reproduced in the American and the English weekly and monthly periodicals,—*A History of the War in Cartoons* has been published by the New York *Times*,—Robert de la Sizeranne has made an exhaustive study of them under the title "La Caricature et la Guerre," in *Revue des Deux Mondes*, June, 1916.—A discriminating article on the short life of war cartoons is found in the London *Times*, October 26, 1916; it was written apropos of an exhibition opened in the Whitechapel Art Gallery of the war cartoons of all nations.

See also André Blum, "La Caricature de guerre en France," *Gazette des beaux-arts*, April, 1921, 5. Période, 3: 235–254.

In striking contrast to the cartoons of the Great War are the *Pictures of Many Wars* as given and described by Frederic Villiers, in a volume published in 1902.

attribute the virtues to his own country and the faults to the country of his enemies. Their use is limited by their deliberate misrepresentations,—"how often have the Germans sunk our fleet and starved us out in their cartoons,—" says an English writer; "how often in ours has the Kaiser confessed that he was beaten." These misrepresentations may in a sense be said to be one of the very objects of the cartoon,—"Cartoonists, for the most part, are uproariously cheerful, whatever may happen. They seem to be cheering victories all the time,"—but the object in view in no way minimizes the deliberate falsification.[65] Their use is limited by their tendency to "make the wish the father to the thought" and to "fake" outrageously the news presented.[66] Their use is limited by the suddenness of the war that found the cartoonists of the Allies as unprepared as were the politicians and the financiers; the Kaiser and the Crown Prince were familiar to them, but they were ignorant of the physical features and of the personal history, the habits and customs of Bethmann-Hollweg, of Hindenburg, of Bernhardi, and of other chief actors in the war on the German side,—"they heard the steps of the horse, but saw not the horseman." A

[65] "On War Cartoons," The London *Times*, October 26, 1916.

[66] Many misleading illustrations have been given, especially by the Continental papers, of places destroyed by the war, or where the war was going on, but taken before the war began.

The German illustrated papers show Belgian towns before the war.

Many illustrations have been given of the sinking of unnamed ships, evidently with the intention of cheering the public at home.

Many illustrations of the war have been "drawn from memory," since the use of the camera has been forbidden in the places illustrated.

R. de la Sizeranne notes how perverted would be the history of the war based on the cartoons that represent England invading France and attacking Belgium; hordes of negroes roaming over Europe and threatening Germany with fire and sword; America conspiring against Germany; the French, Russians, and English overthrowing their governments and perishing like Samson in the ruins of the revolution they have wrought.

He also notes that it would be difficult to discover from the cartoons that Germany was at war with France since the German cartoons are so generally directed against England and are especially vindictive against Sir Edward Grey; he is represented in a score of different ways and for the most part in a repulsive manner.—*Revue des Deux Mondes*, June 1, 15, 1916, 6. Période, 33: 481–502, 806–841.

This study by de la Sizeranne bears out the contention of the New York *Evening Post* that caricature in Europe is a matter of personalities, in America a matter of symbols. The form the illustration is to take necessarily varies with time and place.

new symbolism had to be devised and this, almost of necessity, was changed from time to time during the war.[67]

The historian can but find in the cartoons and the caricatures of the war the flotsam and jetsam of shipwrecked nations,—a record for the most part, as regards cartoons, of forced gaiety and humor under the most appalling conditions. Transient as they are in themselves, they will remain a psychological record of the havoc wrought by war.

Considered collectively it must be obvious that the illustration has many limitations as historical material. This is not by any means due to downright errors found in it,—these are many, but like the innumerable minor errors found in the daily news they are easily detected, they seldom matter, and they are quickly forgotten.

A more important limitation is found in the language used. The early periodical illustrations in America, especially caricatures, show how imperfectly developed was the technical side of the art and how crude was the direct method of using it. Every character was labeled, and often represented as half animal, sentiments were enclosed in loops, and nothing was suggested or left to the imagination.[68] In Europe a language of symbolism was quickly developed and this has become standardized while receiving constant additions as new conditions demand new symbols. Henderson has noted the extraordinary number of symbols, personifications, and emblems that were developed during the French Revolution.[69] The recent war has given rise to a large addition of new symbols, each of the contending parties having its own set of symbols. America has gradually developed a symbolic language, probably less complete than that used abroad.

Much of this symbolism has been both interesting and significant. America is represented by the double symbolism of an

---

[67] A writer in the London *Times*, noting that the cartoon is made for the moment, adds, "One can tell from the cartoons exactly what was the official formula at the date when they were published."—October 26, 1916.

[68] *American Caricatures Pertaining to the Civil War*, 1856–1872.
The use of the loop enclosing the sentiment of the figure depicted was abandoned in Europe where artists drew pictures that told their own story.
—J. B. Bishop, *Presidential Nominations and Elections*, p. 148.

[69] E. F. Henderson, *Symbol and Satire of the French Revolution*, 1912.

abstract Columbia and Uncle Sam, Great Britain by Britannia and John Bull, while Germany has been symbolized by the Kaiser. In the case of Uncle Sam, it was long before the present accepted figure was finally evolved,[70] but while it now varies in proportions and in the fit of the clothes, it is everywhere unmistakably Uncle Sam. But in the characteristic features of prominent individuals the illustration is prone to exaggerate. Napoleon's tri-cornered hat, Wellington's large nose, Louis Philippe's pear-shaped face, Disraeli's forehead curl, Bismarck's three hairs on the top of his head, the Kaiser's moustaches are all recognized as having a reasonable element of truth behind the trifling exaggeration, but when *Punch* always represented John Bright, even after he had adopted the more ordinary coat and collar of the day, as wearing the Quaker coat he had once worn, in the broad-brimmed hat he had never worn, and with an eye-glass that he never wore and never would have dreamt of wearing,[71] the wilful exaggeration becomes historically misleading.

Much of the conventional symbolism quickly becomes outworn and ceases to represent the types for which it was originally conceived;—the symbol of the farmer as at first created, of the grandfather or the grandmother of an earlier day, no longer represent the twentieth century persons of these classes and since they continue to be used they are misleading and uncritical.[72] The symbolism developed by the recent war, as illustrated by Belgium represented as a prostrate or fainting woman; Germany by a dachshund with helmet and in arrogant attitude; the Kaiser with halo in armed automobile, has all been significant of contemporaneous opinion among the Allies, but with the close of the war it has become obsolete.[73]

On the other hand a symbol may in part remain basic while

---

[70] Even as late as 1860, Uncle Sam was figured as Franklin,—"Stephen Finding His Mother," *American Caricatures Pertaining to the Civil War;* M. Sherwood, "Uncle Sam," *Atlantic Monthly*, March, 1918, 121: 330–333; V. Barbour, "Uncle Sam," *MS.*

[71] G. M. Trevelyan, *John Bright*, p. 107, *Note.*

[72] Longfellow in the picture with "grave Alice, laughing Allegra, and Edith with golden hair" is represented as an elderly man, presumably because he is usually so represented and would not otherwise be recognized.

[73] *Life* and *Punch* seemed especially prolific in creating symbols representing situations growing out of the war.

adding accessories that bring it down to the present moment. Santa Claus was developed by Nast from the Pelze-Nicol, "the fat, fur-clad, bearded old fellow" of his childhood, and "the world has accepted [it] as the popular portrayal of its favorite saint." [74] But he now arrives by searchlight instead of by moonlight, he is called up by telephone, and his reindeer have in recent years been transformed into an automobile and still more recently into an aeroplane.

The illustrator may be limited by the psychological conditions of those for whom he illustrates when he understands that their thoughts have not kept pace with modern invention. If the majority of persons can not think of a battle without smoke or of military heroes without a uniform, the artist feels compelled to draw battles showing smoke, although smokeless powder has been used, and to depict soldiers in gay uniform, although uniforms have become sombre and inconspicuous, and soldiers may fight stripped to the waist. [75] The illustration, obviously incorrect in itself as regards the actual condition illustrated, may be an interesting record of the successful effort of the artist to adapt his work to the mental condition of those for whom he illustrates. The historian is much less interested in the sketch of the battle as such than he is in the condition that makes it necessary to convey a true impression of an event through a false representation of it. However exaggerated and however untrue in themselves the details may be, there may be no question that the picture is true in essentials.

In this aspect, the illustration shows its affinity on one side with poetry, since this demands illusion rather than scientific fact,—fact often dispels the illusion and thereby destroys poetry, as J. L. Lowes has so convincingly shown in *Convention and Revolt in Poetry*. The illustration, however, is of two varieties,— one leads to concrete, scientific, absolute fact, while the other leads to illusion that is equally true but is reached by a different route. It is at times a troublesome problem for the historian

[74] A. B. Paine, *Th. Nast and his Friends*, pp. 6, 96.
[75] This has been suggested by Burges Johnson from the experiences of Lester Ralph, who was illustrating the Boer War for the *Illustrated London News*.—"Impression and Expression," *The Well of English and the Bucket*, pp. 73–74.

to discriminate between the technical error, consciously made, that results in truth and the deliberate error that results in falsehood.

The illustration is becoming more and more a feature of the advertisement and hence is increasing in value as historical material. When it was first used as an accessory of the advertisement, it was a simple conventional cut of *a* house, irrespective of the actual house offered for sale, or whatever could be readily standardized in a printing impression; while to-day the demand is for an illustration of the specific house or building offered for sale.[76] But it is noteworthy that the New England newspapers very early recorded the regional interest in shipping since specific forms of ships were indicated in connection with the sailing lists printed.

The illustration as now used in connection with the advertisement often purposely varies from the article nominally illustrated. The complaint is frequently made by business houses that rival firms copy their patterns that are unprotected by patent, adopt their styles, or steal their fashions, and hence the illustration is used to suggest general lines rather than the specific details of the articles advertised, artistic sketches take the place of the too-accurate photograph, and picturesque hints that appeal to the imagination are substituted for the matter-of-fact representations of articles advertised.

Since the illustration is thus used in the advertising pages or columns of periodicals to give specific information intended to persuade readers to purchase the articles

---

[76] J. Richard Beste describes the illustrated advertisements in the *Daily Indiana State Sentinel* and among others those "of the railroads that preface their notices by little prints of smoking engines, which show, by the by, the driver, as everywhere on American lines, standing under a shade to protect him from the sun and the rain."—*The Wabash: or Adventures of an English Gentleman's Family in the Interior of America*, I, 284.

That the illustrated advertisement has ever been quick to avail itself of whatever new interest is uppermost in the mind of the public is seen in the descriptions he gives of the illustrated advertisements in the *Daily Indiana State Sentinel*, including one "of a great boot upon wheels, smoking like the funnel of a steam engine, and followed by four shoes of different sizes racing after it on wheels, while 'Fairbanks' exclaims, 'Clear the track' and bids you 'call and examine for yourself' his supply of boots and shoes."—*The Wabash*, I, 285.

advertised, it necessarily is thereby limited for the use of the historian.[77]

The editor has his difficulties with the artistic temperament. When several artists withdrew from a well-known weekly journal because they believed it should be free not only from any journalistic influence but also free from the influence of an editorial art, the genial editor euphemistically explained the situation in saying, "They wished to sacrifice the symmetry, completeness, order, timeliness, unity in variety, and so forth, of the magazine as a whole to the ideal of unconditioned individual expression," and this too when the paper, its editor believed, was "the only illustrated magazine in America which habitually declines to conciliate its readers, or to consider either the advertisers or the subscription lists in deciding what art and what writing it shall publish." [78]

The illustrated press of political parties must be used with qualifications. Each political party has its own political organ, and every paper has its own political bias. The result is that all political cartoons are one-sided but not necessarily unfair,[79] although their target may think them so.[80] It is also often difficult for cartoonists to deal successfully with political conditions outside of their own country,[81] while at home their work may be popular, as Thackeray said of one of his contemporaries, not because it is witty but because it deals with well-known and easily recognized public characters.

Still another limitation in the use of illustrations is found in the censorship exercised in regard to them in time of war,—a censorship over photographs and all illustrations that is as strict

[77] The illustrations used in connection with plant and seed advertisements are interesting examples of the discrepancy between roses and cabbages grown by experts and by amateurs,—the first class are illustrated, the latter are not.

[78] Max Eastman, *Journalism versus Art*, pp. 10–12.

[79] F. C. Gould, *Political Caricatures*, 1903, 1904, 1905, 1906. These have been reproduced from the *Westminster Gazette* and are an excellent record of the political questions of the day, of governmental action on them, and of the effect of this on the voters.

[80] *Richard Croker as he is and as the Cartoonist Makes him* is a collection of about five hundred and sixty cartoons, really caricatures, "gathered by their target" mainly from the press of New York City and State, but with examples from many other states. They cover the period from 1893 to about 1901.

[81] John Leech, *Later Pencillings from Punch*.

as that in regard to despatches. But the extent to which the cartoon is used may thereby record the degree of freedom or of censorship of the press where it is found. It flourishes in every country where there is freedom of the press, while its field of action is limited where restrictions are placed on the press, except as these cartoons are directed against conditions elsewhere.[82] The cartoon is less prominent in countries where a risk is incurred in printing cartoons of the monarch, or of political parties that do his bidding, or of the court life by which he is surrounded. The historian in his use of the cartoon must therefore understand the conditions under which it has been produced.

In the early days of newspaper illustration "the mechanical difficulties of reproduction subjected the artist's work to a sort of censorship which at least gave it a certain amount of deliberation and responsibility,"[83]—but the very speed with which illustrations are to-day reproduced invites the censorship of governments, especially in time of war.[84] They are often deprecated in times of peace and under conditions less easily reached by censorship.[85]

[82] This has been notably seen in the cartoon used during the war of 1914. The cartoons of each country have been in great part directed against conditions in the enemy's country, and it has thus become in a sense a weapon of attack.

[83] New York *Evening Post*, Feb. 17, 1908.

[84] Photographs illustrating the spoliation of places, and the distribution of illustrated periodicals containing such pictures were forbidden in Antwerp by the proclamation of the German governor.—Cable to the New York *Times*, from Amsterdam, December 6, 1914.

The proprietors of the *Bystander*, the former editor, and a cartoonist were fined sums ranging from £100 to £50 for publishing a cartoon considered prejudicial to military discipline and to recruiting.—Cablegram of February 18, 1916, New York *Times*, February 19, 1916.

The New York papers of February 19, 1916, contained an illustration showing the effect of a Zeppelin raid upon Paris, but the censor would not permit the publication of the exact location of the apartment house bombarded.

The publication of an illustration of a biplane school was permitted, with the understanding that the photographer was not to mention the location of the school. But the censor forgot that the name of the school appeared prominently on some of the hangars.—*Leslie's Weekly*, December 21, 1916.

[85] The British Ministry was asked in the House of Commons, February 29, 1916, whether it was aware that the friendly relations between the United States and Great Britain had been injured by offensive articles and cartoons published in England reflecting on American diplomacy and whether steps should be taken to counteract this influence. Sir Edward Grey replied that while it was very desirable that published articles, cartoons,

What then are the limitations of the illustration in all its forms, in so far as it is available for the use of the historian?

It must be obvious that illustrations, both those intended to make others see and thus reproduce other scenes and other times, as well as those designed to provoke thought and thus influence opinion are of the greatest value to the historian. But this value is modified or affected by the mechanical difficulties of reproduction, by the standards of taste on the part of both artist and reader, by the varying grades of intelligence among those for whom the illustration is made, by the degree of artistic ability shown by the illustrator, and by the amount of jurisdiction over it exercised by editorial or governmental authorities. It is limited by its numerous accidental and intentional errors, by the inherent characteristics of certain great classes like that of caricature, by the language it employs, and it is also limited by the insatiate demand of the public for daily cartoons from the same popular artist. The daily cartoon encourages mediocre ideas and even absence of ideas; it is often slovenly in workmanship, and it may become even more ephemeral than do other parts of the newspaper.

The personal equation and the reputed artistic temperament that render the illustration vivid and telling may detract from its strict accuracy; an overpowering sense of humor may lead the artist to perpetrate a "fake;" the process by which the illustration is made, as the camera or the pencil, may carry its own special temptation; the caricature is by its very nature an exaggeration; the cartoon may have an even more definite purpose to engender hatred in time of war than has the literary side of the press, since it seems possible to say in the form of

---

moving pictures, etc., should not give offense to friendly nations, they could not be prevented unless they contravened the law.—Daily press, February 29, 1916.

The Democratic National Committee sent out a cartoon that was published in the daily press of November 5, 1916. It represented Mr. Hughes tearing from a book the record of Democratic achievement under President Wilson, the Republican candidate's arm being guided by a hand labeled Wall Street. Beneath was a quotation attributed to Mr. Hughes, "The whole Democratic accomplishment must be wiped off the books."

The Chairman of the Republican National Committee protested that the cartoon was "false and malicious in every line and word."—Daily press, November 5–7, 1916.

an illustration what one might shrink from saying in words; the argus-eyed censor may suppress many illustrations in whole or in part, and thus render the record incomplete or defective.

The illustration apparently carries in itself fewer guarantees of unimpeachable accuracy than do many other parts of the press, the very vividness of impression that it creates may be its own undoing, and the tests of usefulness that must be applied to it are specially numerous and important in comparison with those demanded by other parts of the periodical.

But the illustration has for the historian certain very definite concrete advantages not shared by the body of the paper. The illustration is complete in itself; it has no last paragraph that can be lopped off in an emergency or when space is otherwise needed, and since it has a limited space it can not run over on the next page, be "continued in our next," or be dismembered for the sake of floating the advertising pages. Thus the illustrator can give his work a definiteness and exactness of form denied the copy writer whose work too often is amputated to meet space requirements, to the ultimate confusion of the historian.

The illustration is often purposely faked, but it must not be forgotten that the illustration may become a corrector of erro-. neous statements. Lord Palmerston, in opposing the Suez Canal, had affirmed that the sand of the desert would fill up the Canal as fast as it was made, and this was believed. When the illustrations of William Simpson, in 1869, together with the letters of W. H. Russell to *The Times* and of J. Fowler, a civil engineer, showed that the Canal was a success and that the sand of the desert was a myth, public opinion changed.[86]

The illustration also serves as an ally of "the higher criticism." At the end of the first Afghan War, Lord Ellenborough issued a proclamation stating that he had restored to India the so-called gates of Puttun Somnath, carried away by the Mohammedans. When William Simpson, nearly fifty years later, sat down to sketch these famous gates, he at once realized that the ornament was purely Mohammedan, and in no sense Hindu,— "not a vestige of the Hindu mythology was visible." Subsequent examination of the wood under a microscope showed that it was

[86] W. Simpson, *Autobiography*, pp. 204–205.

not sandalwood but Deodar pine. The apparent trustworthiness of an official document was thus overthrown by the unimpeachable evidence of a style of art confirmed by the use of the microscope.[87] Somewhat later, sketches made by Simpson of the sword, spur, and cross used in the investiture of Lord Bute as a Knight of the Holy Sepulchre, said to have been those used by Godfrey of Bouillon, showed that the claim was without foundation as the spur sketched had a roulette, while the spurs of the time of Godfrey had only spikes.[88] Thus the illustration becomes of value in exposing the falseness of claims made through ignorance or pretense.

The close alliance between the illustration and poetry explains why the illustration in the periodical press and the graphic press as a whole have the quality of interpretation less often found in other parts or forms of the press. The artistic insight of the illustration enables it not only to interpret the present but also often gives it a prophetic character not found elsewhere. The cartoons of *Puck* from 1876 to 1893 show an understanding and appreciation of the character of Bismarck and Emperor William II that subsequent events have proved correct;[89] they did much to interpret to his own generation, as well as to the following, the aims and achievements of President Cleveland. "No history of Napoleon is quite complete which fails to recognize Gillray as a potent factor in crystallizing public opinion in England."[90] The success of Gillray was the more noteworthy since it is often difficult for a foreign illustrator to interpret correctly the characteristics of the leading personages of other countries,—Albert Shaw has shown the failure of foreign cartoonists, even friendly ones, to have a correct understanding of Roosevelt as depicted either by his admirers or by unfriendly critics; they give at best but a nondescript creation.[91] If "Du

[87] William Simpson, *Autobiography*, pp. 126–128.
[88] *Ib.*, pp. 212–213.
[89] J. Keppler and H. C. Bunner, *A Selection of Cartoons from Puck*.
An interesting European cartoon in 1890 showed the Kaiser rocking the boat in which the European powers were sitting, but saying to him, "Don't go on like that, or you'll upset us all."—*Cartoons Magazine*, November, 1914, p. 621, from *Punch*, May 10, 1890.
[90] *Cartoons Magazine*, November, 1914, p. 580.
[91] *A Cartoon History of Roosevelt's Career*.

Maurier's picture of Society was largely falsified," it was due to his "inability to appreciate variety in feminine genius,"[92] but his insight did not otherwise fail him.

The illustrations of the recent war have been invaluable for the historian, less on account of their representations of what men and women have been doing, as for their interpretation of what they have been thinking and feeling. It is difficult to find illustrations in the past that give the depth of understanding of fundamental contemporaneous thought as many of those of the present time have given.

It is in the pages of the *Kladderadatsch* that the steps are seen by which Bismarck in the public eye changed from a Prussian into a German.[93] It is in the pages of the *Fliegende Blätter* that the slow acceptance of this change in Southern Germany may be noted. It is M. Grand-Carteret who has shown the far-reaching influence of Bismarck for good and for evil as shown in the caricatures of all nationalities.[94] Nowhere else as in cartoon and caricature can it be so clearly understood that the opposition to Napoleon was to an individual;[95] that Bismarck was caricatured as a public man while he was respected as a private citizen; that the Kaiser was regarded as a typical German and that the attitude of the English people towards him was at first one of good-humored curiosity to see what he would do next, but ultimately one of aversion and horror.[96]

Considered from every point of view, the illustration thus becomes in itself a record of the increasing public demand for

[92] T. M. Wood, *George Du Maurier*, p. 18.

[93] The establishment of *Kladderadatsch* was almost coincident with the appearance of Bismarck in public life. The *Bismarck-Album des Kladderadatsch* gives the representations of Bismarck contained in it from his first appearance as a Prussian deputy in the Frankfort parliament in 1847 to his dismissal in 1890.

[94] J. Grand-Carteret, *Bismarck en Caricature*, 1890; *Crispi, Bismarck et la Triple-Alliance en Caricatures*, 1891.

[95] A. M. Broadley, *Napoleon in Caricature*, 2 vols.

[96] It is an interesting study to note the attitude of both *Punch* and *Life* towards the Kaiser before, during, and since the war. "Dropping the Pilot" expressed surprise at his policy, while "Wilful Wilhelm" well shows the feeling of the Kaiser towards *Punch* as indicated in the cartoon "Take the Nasty *Punch* Away." The German censor cut out both cartoons before *Punch* was allowed to circulate in Germany. The Kaiser later becomes Mephistopheles in *Punch*, while in *Life*, during the war, he became a dachshund.

illustrations and of the business competition that has made it necessary to meet the demand. It is a record of the development of the art of illustrating as it has grown through invention, discovery, and experiment from the first crude efforts to the high degree of excellence it has attained to-day both in regard to the illustration itself and to the accuracy, speed, and facility with which it is reproduced. The illustration, better than any other record outside of the patent-office, shows the stage reached by inventions at any specified time,—the development of aerial and of submarine navigation, as of all other modern inventions, can be followed through all of their steps. It is a record of changing but diverging tastes that at one extreme have insisted on higher artistic standards and that at the other faithfully reflect the vitiated taste and low standard that demand the Sunday comic supplement.[97] It is an equally faithful record of the changing tastes in the subjects chosen for illustration. If at one time the illustration catered to the morbid taste for pictures of accidents, hairbreadth escapes, encounters with wild beasts, and cannibalism;[98] if it found humorous, and therefore illustrated, the movements of the insane and the feebleminded, the victims of hysteria, epilepsy, alcoholism, torture, and all forms of human suffering, it to-day revels in depicting crimes, criminals, and the work of detectives, and in purveying to the vulgarity, the ignorance, and the low moral and artistic standards of those interested in the comic supplement.

If the evil influence of illustrations of crime and of criminals has often been noted, scarcely less to be deprecated is the exaggerated idea of their own importance given themselves and their families by the illustrations of school-boys prominent in school athletics, of society debutantes, of prize-winning babies, and contestants for the honors in school gardens and farm crops. The illustration thus records the same tendencies as are found in other forms of news to represent the abnormal, the conspicuous, and the unusual. In itself it is an interesting record of an educa-

[97] "The most dangerous influences at work against the art of the future are the comic supplements of the Sunday papers."—W. S. Perry, New York *Times*, March 5, 1916.
[98] Many illustrations of this are given by Mason Jackson, *The Pictorial Press Its Origin and Progress*, London, 1885.

tional theory that illustration may often convey information and point a tale more perfectly than can the printed word.

With all of its limitations and its advantages as historical material, the illustration probably more than any other single feature of the press gives the historian a conspectus of contemporary thought and action.

CHAPTER XV

AUTHENTICITY OF NEWSPAPERS

"So common an object as a newspaper is seldom the subject of serious reflection."—*Dibblee.*

THE question of the authenticity of the material available for his use is of primary importance to the historian. But it is a question that in the very nature of the case can rarely arise in connection with the newspaper,—general forgery of complete newspapers is precluded by the expense involved, by ease of detection, by lack of sufficient motive for attempting it. Yet a few such instances are known and they have aroused interest commensurate with their rarity.

The term forgery implies a criminal intent on the part of the forger, but the so-called "forged newspapers" can not all be classed as such within this meaning of the word. Some of these so-called forgeries are to be attributed to ignorance or to carelessness, some have been fabrications growing out of the love of jesting, others have been in the strictest sense deliberate forgeries, others have been reprints of well-known numbers circulated for advertising purposes, while still others have come into existence for reasons not as yet evident. Partial forgeries have not been uncommon, but they have usually been confined to special letters issued for a special purpose.

The first important instance of a fabricated newspaper is probably the transcriptions of some alleged fragments of the *Acta Diurna* of 168 B. C. These were given general publicity through their publication in the *Gentleman's Magazine*,[1] where the origin of the transcription is attributed to the *Annales* of Pighius published in 1615 and their genuineness vouched for by the learned Dodwell in 1692. Dr. Johnson seems to have pinned his faith, as regards their authenticity, on the lineage ascribed to them by their sponsors, but he confesses he finds

[1] 1740, 10: iii–viii.

them uninteresting,—"they want that sprightly Humour and diffuse Kind of Narration, which embellish the Compositions of our modern Diurnal Historians. The *Roman* Gazetters are defective in several material Ornaments of Style. They never end an Article with the mystical Hint, *this occasions great Speculation.* They seem to have been ignorant of such engaging Introductions, as *we hear it strongly reported;* and of that ingenious, but threadbare, Excuse for a downright Lie, *it wants confirmation.*—It is also very observable, that the Praetor's Daughter is married without our being told, *that she was a Lady of great Beauty, Merit and Fortune."*

Later readers have pardoned their lack of inherent interest, but have found them spurious.[2] The acceptance of their genuineness, however, long persisted and recent writers have found it necessary to say with decision, as does Jebb, "we have no genuine fragments of the Roman gazettes."[3] From this verdict there can be no appeal.

A claimant for the honor of being "the earliest newspaper known" was made by George Chalmers[4] on behalf of *The English Mercurie,* dated 1588. He directed attention to its supposed priority of publication over all other newspapers in existence and says that he was filled with patriotic joy that the first newspaper published was, as he supposed, British in every respect.

[2] Le Clerc shows that the first seven articles were printed in Pighius who gives his source as a manuscript found among the papers of Louis Vives. Lipsius, in his notes on Tacitus, had already cited some lines in 1581, and Mark Welser, in 1596, had spoken of them as vouched for, not by himself, but by Ortelius or Vives. Welser thought them forged; Lipsius thought them genuine.—Dodwell, in the appendix to his *Praelectiones Camdenianae,* added to the seven days already given three days of the Roman year 691 and one of the year 698, from a copy of Adrian Beverland's, of a copy of Isaac Vossius', made from a copy belonging to Paul Petau who was not a critical collector. Dodwell followed Pighius in calling them *diarium, Urbis diurna,* commented on them at great length in his appendix, and in his treatise *De Veteribus Cyclis* persisted in regarding them as authentic.

Le Clerc gives the text of the journals, after Pighius and Dodwell, and a French translation, following it with an analysis proving them forgeries, from internal and other evidence. The material, he shows, was taken from Livy and he believes the forgery dates from the sixteenth century.—J. V. Le Clerc, *Des Journaux chez les Romains,* Part II, "Discussion sur de faux journaux romains," pp. 261–341.

[3] R. C. Jebb, "Ancient Organs of Public Opinion," *Essays and Addresses,* p. 160.

[4] *Life of Thomas Ruddiman,* pp. 106–108.

It was probably natural that his statements in regard to his discovery should be repeatedly copied; all accounts of *The English Mercurie* and all allusions to it are to be traced directly to this account.[5] But in 1839, in a slender pamphlet of sixteen pages entitled *A Letter to Antonio Panizzi on the Reputed Earliest Newspaper, "The English Mercurie, 1588,"* Thomas Watts conclusively showed, by exhaustive proofs, that the newspaper was not genuine. He returned to the same subject in 1850 and in an article entitled "Authorship of the Fabricated 'Earliest English Newspaper',"[6] he showed that the fabrication was evidently the work of Philip Yorke, second son of Lord Hardwicke.

It still further remained for D. T. B. Wood [7] to give the final history of the fabrication—it can not in any sense now be called a forgery—and to show that the long-famed English Mercuries were the youthful pranks of two young Englishmen [8] who found diversion in this form of literature, as college students are to-day wont to find diversion in writing parodies and imitations, and they had themselves probably not expected to be taken too seriously.

An interesting modern illustration of the same spirit was found when the Harvard *Lampoon* issued a fake number of the Harvard *Crimson,* "delicately enough caricatured to fool all

[5] Isaac Disraeli gives more than a page to *The English Mercurie* for which "we are indebted to the wisdom of Elizabeth and the prudence of Burleigh." *Curiosities of Literature,* I, pp. 155–160. After eleven editions of the work had been published, a foot-note nearly as long as the original notice explains the forgery. Benjamin Disraeli gives the note "that it may remain a memorable instance of the danger incurred by the historian from forged documents; and a proof that multiplied authorities add no strength to evidence, when all are to be traced to a single source."

[6] *Gentleman's Magazine,* May, 1850, n. s., 33: 485–491.

[7] "The True History of the Fabrication of the 'Armada Mercuries'," *Nineteenth Century and After,* February, 1914, 75: 342–354.

[8] The proof rests on the correspondence between Philip Yorke and Thomas Birch between 1740 and 1745. The letters are in the British Museum.

The author makes the interesting suggestion that the publication in 1740 of the so-called *Acta Diurna* may have given the young authors the idea of fabricating an early English newspaper.

Much interesting and valuable information in regard to early newspapers, especially the fabricated "Earliest English Newspaper," is given in *Bibliographical Notes,* edited by A. C. Bickley, in the *Gentleman's Magazine Library* edited by G. L. Gomme.

but the observant reader."[9] A fairly long list of such jests in college journalism could be made.

The love of jesting is universal and this was undoubtedly the spirit behind the *Figaro* that led it one morning apparently about 1869 to come out "in perfect facsimile of the official journal, containing a number of governmental decrees in orthodox style, and in the exact typography of the genuine *Moniteur*, appointing some of the bitterest enemies of the *régime* to portfolios." The jest was "so successful that the editor of *Galignani's Messenger* positively handed slips of it for translation to his colleagues," but Paris soon "broke into one huge Homeric explosion of laughter."[10]

And the love of jesting has been perennial. It was in May, 1787, that one number of the *London Gazette* was forged, but "no police acuteness was acute enough to lay hand on the inimitable rogue who played that perilous joke."[11]

"A clumsy modern forgery," the object of which has not as yet been shown, is found in *The Commonwealth Mercury*, purporting to have been printed in 1658.[12] That it is a forgery has been shown conclusively by J. B. Williams [13] who states that its true date must be one later than 1852, since it contains an account of Cromwell's funeral but is not quoted by Carlyle whose *Oliver Cromwell* appeared in that year. That it is a fictitious paper is indicated by its title, since the Commonwealth was not in favor in 1658, while Mercury, as a term for a periodical was then almost unknown,—it was applied to women hawkers of newsbooks, the form Mercurius being invariably applied to periodicals. Moreover, a short title or catchword was not then in use, the front page has a black border which was never used at that time, a part of the title is printed in Gothic type while Roman type was then always used, while periodicals appeared twice a week and were given two titles

[9] L. G. Price, "American Undergraduate Journalism," *Bookman*, March, 1903, 17: 69–82.
[10] J. A. O'Shea, *Leaves from the Life of a Special Correspondent*, I, 259–260.
[11] J. C. Francis, *John Francis*, II, 239.
[12] The New York Public Library has a copy of this "Mercury" and even to a casual observer its origin is mid-Victorian.
[13] "The Commonwealth Mercury," *Notes and Queries*, June 1, 1912, 11S, 5: 432.

down to the time of the *Oxford Gazette*, November, 1665,—the Monday issue, for example, having one title and the Thursday issue another. A second proof of its spuriousness is its date,— Cromwell suppressed licensed periodicals in 1655; and still another evidence comes from its contents and phraseology. The parts of the paper that are true can be traced to other papers that appeared much later, while the language used is not always that of the Cromwellian period.[14]

Altogether different in character and purpose was an unquestionable forgery apparently executed "to fill a long-felt want." No contemporary newspaper giving an account of the Mechlenburg Declaration of Independence had been known, and it had long been a desideratum, but what purported to be a facsimile of the *Cape-Fear Mercury* bearing the date of June 3, 1775, and giving the Declaration was published in 1905. It was quickly pronounced a forgery that had been accomplished by making up a paper from a photograph of an original heading of a *Cape-Fear Mercury* and at least two other distinct and separate pieces of paper put together and photographing the whole. The forgery was clumsily executed, easily detected, and quickly exposed by two historical experts.[15]

These detailed illustrations are given to show how extremely difficult it is to forge or to fabricate a newspaper so successfully that its spuriousness escapes the eye of the trained observer. In this very difficulty lies, in a measure, the protection of the historian. It is clear that in the case of the *English Mercurie* and probably in that of the *Commonwealth Mercury* the object of the fabricators could only have been the love of a jest or the desire to lay a harmless trap for unsuspecting readers.

The recent war gave an opportunity for issuing newspapers that had been forged and were then circulated as propaganda. A facsimile of a local Italian newspaper, "so adroitly done as to defy detection," was circulated among the Italian troops

---

[14] This evidence is summarized from the article of J. B. Williams.

[15] The photograph was first published in *Collier's Weekly*, July 1, 1905.

The forgery was exposed by A. S. Salley, Jr., in a pamphlet, *The True Mechlenburg Declaration of Independence*, and by A. S. Salley, Jr., and Worthington C. Ford in the *American Historical Review*, April, 1906, 11: 548–558.

near the frontier. Its obvious intention was to stir up disaffection and discouragement through reports of serious reverses of the Allies and of the impossibility of America being able to send troops to France before 1919.[16] But the ultimate exposure of the real character of the newspaper undoubtedly acted as a boomerang against the inventors of the scheme.

In the opinion of *The Nation and The Athenaeum*, it was well known that the Russian "Whites" issued and circulated forged numbers of the Russian communist newspapers. These were circulated clandestinely in Russia and they supplied sympathetic correspondents in "White" centers with damaging "quotations" from the Russian official press to be telegraphed back to London.[17]

But if the forged newspaper as such has been almost unknown, forged letters printed innocently by the press have not been uncommon, although naturally the greatest care is taken to prevent their acceptance,—if for no other reason, on account of the risk of libel suits involved.

Among the most famous of these forged letters was the one concerning Charles Parnell and the London *Times*. *The Times* published April 18, 1887, a facsimile letter purporting to have been written by Parnell nine days after the Phoenix Park murders apologizing for his attitude in regard to them. Mr. Parnell declared in the House of Commons that evening that the letter was a forgery. A commission appointed to investigate this and other charges began its sittings September, 1888, and reported February, 1890, that they found the letter to be a forgery. The self-confessed forger committed suicide and Mr. Parnell recovered £5,000 damages from *The Times* in an action for libel, the matter being settled out of court.[18]

[16] Caspar Whitney, New York *Tribune*, February 3, 1918.

[17] The London *Daily Herald* reproduced in reduced facsimile a part of one of these forged newspapers. At the bottom of the page was the name of a London printer.—*The Nation and The Athenaeum*, March 5, 1921, 28: 767.

[18] Full accounts of the forgery are given in John Morley, *Life of Gladstone*, II, Bk. X, chap. III; A. L. Thorold, *Life of Henry Labouchere*, chaps. XIII–XIV; G. A. Sala, *Life and Adventures*, II, chap. LXI; John Macdonald, ed., *Diary of the Parnell Commission, Revised from "The Daily News,"* 1890; *Hansard*, vols. 313, 341; *The Times* reprinted in pamphlet form the alleged Parnell letters and its leaders on the subject.

Apparently *The Times* took no precautions and applied no tests to ascertain the genuineness of the letter published. It was after the retirement of

A conspicuous case of a forged letter printed by an American paper purported to have been written by ex-President Cleveland in advocacy of the election of W. H. Taft in 1908, but the forgery was quickly detected and the punishment of the forger swiftly followed.

A forged letter of even more serious bearing had some years earlier been planned to shipwreck the candidacy for the presidency of J. A. Garfield. A letter that purported to have been written by him to a certain H. L. Morey had opposed restriction on Chinese immigration and thus contradicted one plank in the Republican platform. It seemed probable that these views would seriously endanger his hope of election and that this was the intention was evident from its being produced just prior to the election, although dated January 23, 1880. Mr. Garfield quickly denounced the letter as a base and very clumsy forgery and this denial of its genuineness was accepted as final.[19]

A forged proclamation that involved serious consequences to several members of the press and to different individuals was one purporting to come from President Lincoln in May, 1864. It called for 400,000 additional troops between the ages of eighteen and forty-five and it appointed a day of fasting and prayer. Its design was to upset the stock market, advantage of which could be taken by the promoters of the forgery. It was apparently regular as regards its source and it was published by the *Journal of Commerce* and the *World*, other New York papers almost by accident escaping the trap set for them. These two papers did everything possible to rectify the wrong done,[20] but

Delane, and Escott contrasts the carelessness of *The Times* in the matter with the infinite pains taken by Delane in ascertaining the facts behind a letter sent him by his Paris correspondent in 1875.—*Masters of English Journalism*, p. 184.

[19] The New York *Herald* was specially active in securing the denial; see issues of October 23 and October 26, 1880, and broadside issued by it. Full accounts are given in all the papers of the time.—The forger was arrested and held for trial.

[20] Under date of May 23, 1864, Manton Marble wrote President Lincoln explaining that the proclamation arrived late at night; that in the morning when the facts were known every effort was made to retrieve the error; declared that the explanation exculpated the *World* and that the suppression of the *World* and the *Journal of Commerce* was arbitrary, illegal, and unconstitutional; and made a strong defense of the constitutional right of freedom of the press.

their publication was suspended for four days, the editors and owners were arrested though quickly released, and the self-confessed forger was imprisoned. But the matter long haunted the papers that had originally published it, or had reprinted it, like the New Orleans *Picayune*,—an offense that in the eyes of General Butler merited the suspension of that paper from May 23 to July 9, 1864.[21]

Forged documents have for centuries been a favorite device for attacking a weak or an unpopular minority, but such documents have had comparatively little relation to the newspaper press, except as this press has been a convenient means for establishing their spurious character.[22]

Not uncommon are reprints of entire or of single pages of the

---

The letter was subsequently privately printed without the knowledge of the author, by persons two-thirds of whom did not know him or belong to his political party, "as a frank, fearless, and manly protest against a gross act of tyranny."

A full account of the episode is given in Appleton's *Annual Cyclopaedia*, 1864, pp. 389–393.

[21] Brief accounts are given in J. M. Lee, *History of American Journalism*, pp. 297–299; J. L. Heaton, *The Story of a Page*, pp. 2–3. The death, July 24, 1917, of Manton Marble, the editor of the *World* at the time of its suspension, has recalled the story to the daily press of that date.

Only part of the edition of the *World* of May 18 contained the proclamation,—an indication of its honest effort to retrieve its error.

[22] The Sisson documents were intended to discredit the Soviet government by showing that it was having improper dealings with Germany. The authenticity of a part of the documents was seriously questioned in Paris, as also by the head of the American Red Cross mission in Russia, and by the head of the Finnish Information Bureau in New York, but through the Committee on Public Information they were published widely in American newspapers.—The chief service rendered in the affair by the American press, notably by the New York *Evening Post*, was to point out their glaring inconsistencies and to pave the way for an examination of their authenticity. This examination was made by a committee of scholars, but its report did not meet with unanimous acceptance. With the close of the war the subject passed into oblivion.—New York *Evening Post*, September–November, 1918; *The Nation*, September 28, November 23, 1918, 107: 334, 616–617.

The series of documents known collectively as the "Protocols of Zion" was intended to show the existence of a conspiracy between the Jews and the Freemasons to support Bolshevism. A committee of learned Jews gave the Protocols an exhaustive examination and published an elaborate report in which they declared the documents to be "a base forgery" and the evidence given in support of this conclusion seemed indisputable. The daily press gave wide publicity to the report. It may be found in full in the New York *Times*, December 1, 1920, and further evidence in the same journal of February 25, 1921. The report was also published in pamphlet form under the title "*The Protocols,*" *Bolshevism and the Jews*. 1921.

original issues of newspapers on the anniversary of some note-worthy events. These have often been circulated by enterprising business firms through a desire to attract attention to their products, but the publicity desired for the articles to be sold prevents deception as to the means used.

Another reprint with deliberate intent to deceive was an issue of *Punch* put on the market in October, 1914, through German influence. It purported to be the current issue, but its cover reproduced a cartoon of the Civil War that at the time had justly given great offense to the North. The evident intention was to revive old animosities between America and England and thus prevent America from supporting the cause of the Allies.

It is difficult to class with any of the illustrations given the *Ulster County Gazette* of January 4, 1800, containing an account of the funeral of George Washington,—"Without doubt the most widely known literary relic in this country." [23] The *Ulster County Gazette* was established at Kingston, New York, in 1798, the only known original issue of the year 1800 is that of May 10, and "in the thousands of copies issued of this interesting paper, a copy of the original issue has never come to light." The first so-called reprints were made in Kingston in 1846 or 1847, at the time of a local celebration; "since then there have been published no less than twenty-one differing reprints of that issue." The Library of Congress has listed all these reprints and checked the variations in them. It has also published a circular of information, giving a brief history of them and suggesting some of the evidences of spuriousness that characterize them all. But in spite of all the careful study given the paper, the object of the reprint is yet to be explained; a still further explanation is needed of the large number of successive and varying reprints.[24]

---

[23] A. J. Wohlhagen, "The Spurious Ulster County Gazette of January 4, 1800," *The New York Historical Society, Quarterly Bulletin*, April, 1917, I, 15–17.

[24] These facts have been largely taken from the article of A. J. Wohlhagen, cited above. He adds the following interesting list of other old newspapers that have been reproduced: *New England Currant*, February 4–11, 1723; *New York Gazette*, March 28, 1726; *New England Weekly Journal*, April 8, 1728; *Boston Gazette and Country Journal*, March 12, 1770; *New York Morning Post*, November 7, 1783; *The Sun*, September 3, 1833.

ULSTER COUNTY GAZETTE.

ULSTER COUNTY GAZETTE.

ULSTER COUNTY GAZETTE.

U'LSTER COUNTY GAZETTE.

ULSTER COUNTY GAZETTE.

ULSTER COUNTY GAZETTE.

ULSTER COUNTY GAZETTE.

ULSTER COUNTY. GAZETTE.

Ulster County Gazette.

Published at KINGSTON (Ulster County) By SAMUEL FREER and SON

VOL. II. SATURDAY, JANUARY 4, 1800. NUM. 88

AMERICAN CONGRESS
TUESDAY, December 10.

ULSTER COUNTY GAZETTE.

Published at KINGSTON, Ulster Co., N.Y., By SAMUEL FREER and SON.

[Vol. II.] SATURDAY, January 4, 1800. [Num. 88]

ULSTER COUNTY GAZETTE.

Published at KINGSTON, (Ulster County,) By SAMUEL FREER and SON.

SATURDAY, January 4, 1800. [Num. 88]

ULSTER COUNTY GAZETTE.

Published at KINGSTON, (Ulster County,) By SAMUEL FREER and SON.

[Vol. II.] SATURDAY, January 4, 1800. [Num. 88]

AMERICAN CONGRESS
TUESDAY, December 10.

ULSTER COUNTY GAZETTE.

Published at KINGSTON, (Ulster County,) By SAMUEL FREER and SON.

[Vol. II.] SATURDAY, January 4, 1800. [Num. 88]

AMERICAN CONGRESS
TUESDAY, December 10.

ULSTER COUNTY GAZETTE.

Published at KINGSTON, (Ulster County,) By SAMUEL FREER and SON.

[Vol. II.] SATURDAY, January 4, 1800. [Num. 88]

AMERICAN CONGRESS

ULSTER COUNTY GAZETTE.

Published at KINGSTON, (Ulster County,) By SAMUEL FREER and SON.

SATURDAY, January 4, 1800. [Num. 88]

ULSTER COUNTY GAZETTE.

Published at KINGSTON, (Ulster County,) By SAMUEL FREER and SON.

[Vol. II.] SATURDAY, January 4, 1800. [Num. 88]

AMERICAN CONGRESS
TUESDAY, December 10.

Fabricated newspapers, forged newspapers, reprints of newspapers for unknown or for evident reasons have not given the historian serious concern, however much they may have deceived the uncritical.

A still further variant of the forged newspaper is the alleged 'reprint'. This is illustrated in the volume called *Reprints of* The Times *and other early English Newspapers*. It is found somewhat frequently in England and in America, and the various parts are also believed to have been sold separately. It comprises eighteen articles, ten of them documents such as the "Declaration of American Independence," and eight purporting to be reprints of various numbers of *The Times*, ranging from 1793 to 1821. A careful examination that has been made of these documents shows that they are neither reprints nor facsimiles, but altered copies of original documents, papers purporting to be copies of original newspapers that never existed, and compilations from genuine newspapers but in no sense reprints.[25]

Important information is given in a circular issued by the Kingston, N. Y., *Daily Freeman*.

H. M. Lydenberg has written an important article on the subject. He gives in it a very useful analytical list of seven issues of four types of reprints. By reference to this article any copy of any reprint can be readily identified.—New York *Times Saturday Review of Books*, August 27, 1904, p. 580.

Joseph Gavit has noted the curious fact that the *Ulster County Gazette* of January 4, 1800 was reproduced in J. C. Larkin's *Practical Drapery Cutting* published in Minneapolis in 1897. "The reprint varies from all the full sized reprints in that it is entirely reset. The author offers no explanation for including it."

A recrudescence of interest in the spurious *Ulster County Gazette* comes periodically. Two corner-stones of churches in Dutchess County, New York, were recently opened, each containing a copy of the paper and giving rise to much local discussion.—In March, 1921, the daily press carried full accounts of the paper, based on an interview with the librarian in charge of the collection of old newspapers in the University of Chicago. He finds the ultimate test of its spuriousness in the quality of the paper used.

Other papers reproduced at intervals are the first number of the Philadelphia *Public Ledger*, and the Vicksburg *Daily Citizen* of July 2, 1863,— originally printed on wall-paper.

[25] "Alleged 'Reprints of *The Times* and other Early English Newspapers'," *Notes and Queries*, May 29, 1920, 12S, 6: 247.—One set of documents examined bore the imprint "Presented by John Pigott, 'my Tailor,' 116 Cheapside, London, E. C." The set in the Vassar College Library is entitled "Head's Reprints."

These so-called "reprints" were obviously an elaborate advertising plan quite crudely executed but they apparently had wide circulation.

Closely allied to the question of the authenticity of periodical literature is that of the identification of the authorship of letters published in the press. The controversy over the authorship of the "Letters of Junius," published in the *Public Advertiser* from January 21, 1769, to January 21, 1772, has been one of the most remarkable on record, the literature of identification has been almost inexhaustible, and it is still coming from the press.[26]

Scarcely less in importance is the identification of various numbers of *The Federalist*,—that the letters were the work of Hamilton, Jay, and Madison has been unquestioned, but to which of the three authors certain letters are to be attributed has been a question often settled, often re-opened.[27]

A collateral rather than a lineal kinsman of the forgery is the hoax,—of which the public is sometimes the victim at the hands of the newspaper, while sometimes the newspaper itself is the prey of designing or of jesting contributors. The "moon hoax" that appeared in the columns of the New York *Sun* in 1835 was the work of R. A. Locke.[28] It professed to give an account of the inhabitants of the moon, based on discoveries reported as made by Sir John Herschel at the Cape of Good Hope. But it seems uncertain whether it was intended as a deliberate hoax or as a satire.[29] The chief results were to secure to the *Sun* "the largest circulation of any daily in the world," to "firmly establish the 'penny system' throughout the country," to divert for the time being the minds of its readers "from the contemplation of political

[26] The latest edition noted is dated 1906, and the latest work relative to Junius, 1917.

A manuscript bibliography of Junius, edited by Robert F. Pick, in the Vassar College Library, lists one hundred and fifty-nine different editions of Junius, one hundred and forty-three titles of works relative to the subject, and sixty-two names of persons for whom the authorship of the letters has been claimed.

[27] See P. L. Ford, *Introduction to the Federalist;* E. G. Bourne, *Essays in Historical Criticism*, pp. 113–145.

The literature relating to *The Federalist* is scarcely less extensive than that relating to the letters of Junius.

[28] The story of the hoax has recently been published by F. M. O'Brien, *The Story of the Sun*, pp. 64–102. An interesting early work (1852) is that of W. N. Griggs, *The Celebrated "Moon Story."* It gives the life of the author, together with the story of the affair and a reprint of the articles that appeared in the *Sun*.

[29] W. N. Griggs, p. 30.

apples of discord," and to throw several other apples of discord into literary and scientific circles.

The hoax is sometimes planned to teach "a high moral lesson." The New York *Courier and Enquirer,* "in order to expose those who were guilty of appropriating news without credit," once printed a small edition, specially intended for the morning papers, denying the fall of Warsaw announced a few days before. The later news purported to have been gleaned from papers brought by the ship *Ajax,* but "there was no Marjory Daw." Other papers announced the news, without giving credit to the *Courier and Enquirer,*—the trap set for them had sprung.[30]

But far more troublesome to the historian than questions of authenticity, fabrication, identification of anonymous articles, or correct attribution of signed articles must be that of the real authorship of newspaper articles signed by noted names but written by persons whose names do not appear. The tendency has been more and more away from anonymity and more and more towards measuring the importance of an article by the name attached to it. This has resulted in extraordinary pressure on persons of distinguished reputation and those occupying high official position to contribute articles to the press of every degree of periodicity. It is absolutely impossible for these demands to be met by those on whom they are made and hence the writing of the articles has been delegated to others, but it appears under the signature desired.

This is not indeed a new device,—it has long been a well-known custom in official circles for secretaries and clerks to prepare public documents that are subsequently signed by the official higher up. This is done, not with intent to deceive, but through the application of the principle of division of labor and from the necessity of economizing the time of those on whom unusual demands are made.[31] But it is the wide extension of this principle

[30] A Journalist, *Memoirs of James Gordon Bennett and his Times,* p. 135.

[31] Washington's farewell address is attributed to Alexander Hamilton.— The phraseology of the Monroe Doctrine has been ascribed to John Quincy Adams.—Webster was asked just prior to the inauguration of President Harrison the reason for his unusual weariness and he replied that he had that day "killed seventeen Roman proconsuls as dead as smelts, every one of them." The anecdote is given by Peter Harvey, *Reminiscences of Daniel Webster,* pp. 160–163. Many of Harvey's anecdotes are given first hand, but

to the writing and signature of articles outside of routine documents that must in future perplex the historian. It is to-day unfortunately impossible to trust the name attached to a newspaper article, if it is that of a public officer, as indicating, beyond peradventure of a doubt, its true authorship. The name signed presumably means that the ostensible writer assumes the responsibility for it, yet this can not always be true since articles are hurriedly read, or possibly not read at all by those purporting to write them. Confusion and perplexity must at every turn await the historian compelled to depend in any degree upon this class of material.[32] Such material is authentic in the sense that it is not forged, much of it is undoubtedly authoritative, as regards its content, but it is also true that the real authorship of much of it will never be known.

this is not, since Harvey was apparently not in Washington at the time. It does not, indeed, indicate Webster's authorship of the inaugural address, but certainly a radical revision of it.

[32] One illustration will suffice as representing many that could be given. An important document in 1918 came from Washington supporting a great popular movement. It was signed with the name of a very prominent member of the Administration and it was at once quoted in a textbook with the comment that if so very busy a man as the writer was known to be could take the time to write this article all persons ought to give the movement their support. The article was in fact not written by the official in question, but by a distinguished scholar who had offered his services to the government.

CHAPTER XVI

THE AUTHORITATIVENESS OF THE PRESS

"Straight through the mighty Libyan folks is Rumour on the wing—
Rumour, of whom nought swifter is of any evil thing:
She gathereth strength by going on, and bloometh shifting oft!
A little thing, afraid at first, she springeth soon aloft;
Her feet are on the worldly soil, her head the clouds o'erlay.
Earth, spurred by anger 'gainst the Gods, begot her as they say,
Of Coeus and Enceladus the latest sister-birth.
Swift are her wings to cleave the air, swift-foot she treads the earth:
A monster dread and huge, on whom so many as there lie
The feathers, under each there lurks, O strange! a watchful eye;
And there wag tongues, and babble mouths, and hearkening ears up-
stand
As many: all a-dusk by night she flies 'twixt sky and land
Loud clattering, never shutting eye in rest of slumber sweet.
By day she keepeth watch high-set on houses of the street,
Or on the towers aloft she sits for mighty cities' fear!
And lies and ill she loves no less than sooth which she must bear."—
Virgil, translated by *William Morris*.

"I have been so cheated with false relations i' my time, as I ha'.
found it a far harder thing to correct my book, than collect it."—
Ben Jonson, *News from the New World Discovered in the Moon* (1621).

"The difference between a journalist and a diplomatist is that the
latter must not tell what he knows, and that the journalist must talk
about what he doesn't know."—*De Blowitz*.

Is the newspaper an authoritative source for the study of
history? In attempting to answer the question the student of
history must hesitate before giving a final and definite statement.
He realizes that for the most part historians have not availed
themselves of it. He knows not only that the press has ever been
held in ill favor by men in public life whose actions have been
criticized by it or whose political policy has been attacked by it,
but he knows that men of probity have questioned its value, and
he recalls a letter of Jefferson's written under date of June 14,
1807, in which he says to a correspondent:

"To your request of my opinion of the manner in which a
newspaper should be conducted, so as to be most useful, I should

answer, 'by restraining it to true facts & sound principles only.' Yet I fear such a paper would find few subscribers. It is a melancholy truth, that a suppression of the press could not more compleatly deprive the nation of it's benefits, than is done by it's abandoned prostitution to falsehood. Nothing can now be believed which is seen in a newspaper. Truth itself becomes suspicious by being put into that polluted vehicle. The real extent of this state of misinformation is known only to those who are in situations to confront facts within their knowledge with the lies of the day. I really look with commiseration over the great body of my fellow citizens, who, reading newspapers, live & die in the belief, that they have known something of what has been passing in the world in their time; whereas the accounts they have read in newspapers are just as true a history of any other period of the world as of the present, except that the real names of the day are affixed to their fables. General facts may indeed be collected from them, such as that Europe is now at war, that Bonaparte has been a successful warrior, that he has subjected a great portion of Europe to his will, &c., &c.; but no details can be relied on. I will add, that the man who never looks into a newspaper is better informed than he who reads them; inasmuch as he who knows nothing is nearer to truth than he whose mind is filled with falsehoods & errors. He who reads nothing will still learn the great facts, and the details are all false." [1]

He realizes that Jefferson was probably still rasping under the Sedition Act passed by the Federalists and the prosecutions that had been directed under it against the journalists and hack writers of his own party and that his own confidence in some of these men, like Callender, had been misplaced, yet Jefferson's words carry weight. The Duke of Wellington had held in no higher favor the English press of the same period. [2] In the hundred and more years that have passed since these judgments were given, men in public life have expressed opinions no more favorable to the veracity of the press.

It was not alone Matthew Arnold who nearly forty years ago found the American papers below par, [3]—similar criticisms were

---

[1] *Writings of Jefferson*, ed. by P. L. Ford, IX, 73–74.

[2] J. H. Stocqueler, *supra*, p. 198, note.

[3] "They [the Americans] are excellent people, but their press seems to me at present an awful symptom."—Matthew Arnold, *Letters*, I, 271.

"The great relief will be to cease seeing the American newspapers. Here one must read them, for through them only can one get the European news;

later passed on them by leading American journalists.[4] Nor have the American papers alone been the recipients of adverse criticism. It has been a habit everywhere to affect a critical attitude towards the press from the time of Ben Jonson to the present day.[5]

It has been inevitable in our own day that with the enlarging sphere of influence of the press corresponding distrust should arise. Everywhere and at all times there has been this distrust and it has been manifested alike by governments that have attempted to suppress, to regulate, and to control the press, and by its increasing millions of readers who have had no share in the production or the distribution of the news, who have passively

---

but their badness and ignobleness are beyond belief. They are the worst feature in the life of the United States, and make me feel kindly even to the *Pall Mall Gazette* by comparison with them."—*Ib.*, II, 404.

[4] E. L. Godkin wrote to C. E. Norton, January 12, 1895: "But with a villainous press—venal and silly,—and a somewhat frivolous and distinctly *childish* public, it is difficult to be sure of more than a few years [of good city government], . . . the practice of reading trivial newspapers begets, even among men of some education, a puerile habit of mind."—Rollo Ogden, *Life of E. L. Godkin*, II, 199.

He writes again, December 29, 1895, apropos of the Cleveland-Venezuela-Great Britain difficulty: "The press is the worst feature in the situation, and yet the press would not be what it is without a public demand for it as it is."—*Ib.*, II, 203.

[5] George Crabbe in his Preface to *The Newspaper* says: "It must, however, be confessed, that these things [newspapers] have their use; and are, besides, vehicles of much amusement; but, this does not outweigh the evil they do to society, and the irreparable injury they bring upon the characters of individuals." . . . "That in writing upon the subject of our Newspapers I have avoided everything which might appear like the opinion of a party, is to be accounted for from the knowledge I have gained from them; since, the more of these instructors a man reads, the less he will infallibly understand: nor would it have been very consistent in me, at the same time to censure their temerity and ignorance, and to adopt their rage."

Two provisions in the will of Dr. Rush should be remembered: "Temperate, sincere, and intelligent inquiry and discussion are only to be dreaded by the advocates of error. The truth need not fear them, nor do I wish the Ridgway Branch of the Philadelphia Library to be encumbered with the ephemeral biographies, novels, and works of fiction or amusement, newspapers or periodicals, which form so large a part of the current literature of the day."—*Provisions of the Last Will and Testament of Dr. James Rush, Relating to The Library Company of Philadelphia*, p. 13.

"Let it be a favor for the eminent works of fiction to be found upon its shelves; but let it not keep cushioned seats for time-wasting and lounging readers, nor places for every-day novels, mind-tainting reviews, controversial politics, scribblings of poetry and prose, biographies of unknown names, nor for those teachers of disjointed thinking, the daily newspapers, except, perhaps, for reference to support, since such an authority could never prove the authentic date of an event."—*Ib.*, pp. 27–28.

accepted it or blindly protested against it, who have not understood the operation of its invisible machinery, the impersonal character of its pages, or the source of the power it wields.

The uncertainty in regard to what is the function of the press and the blind distrust of the press find expression in the phrases used with reference to it. The newspaper has been called an advocate, a broker, an entertainer, an informant, an interpreter, a solicitor, a teacher, and a tribune. It is spoken of as the gutter press, the sensational press, a jackal press, an inspired press, a capitalistic press, a reptile press, a prostituted press; the news it presents is said to have been elaborated, embroidered, garbled, colored, cooked, doctored, padded, improved, distorted, truncated, faked, perverted, juggled, censored, exploited, spiced, falsified, poisoned, camouflaged; its accounts are called red, yellow, drab, gray, melodramatic, impressionistic, or tabloid; its manner of narration has, on the other hand, been termed dull, stupid, trivial, commonplace, unattractive, heavy, ponderous, monotonous, disjointed, and its general policy is alluded to as a newspaper game. These general expressions of distrust and disapproval tend to become more specific and the press is accused of "unblushing exaggeration," of being misleading, mendacious, venal, truculent, crude, shallow, coarse, vulgar, brutal, boorish, ill-natured, flippant, impertinent, meddlesome, insolent, intemperate, scurrilous, unscrupulous, corrupt, dishonest, false, insincere, irresponsible, imbecile, ignorant, ill-informed, absurd, self-seeking, outrageous, reckless, cowardly, partisan, unfair, unjust, illiberal, untrue, unreliable, vicious, malevolent, malicious; it is charged with suppressing the news, shaping the news, "hushing up" the news, misrepresenting the news, distorting the news, falsifying the news, creating news, misconstruing the news, with misleading the public, feeding private grudges, meddling in private affairs, with craving sensation, with general deterioration, and those contributing to it are said to be "indebted to their memories for their jests and their imaginations for their facts;" it is arraigned for being controlled by capitalists, by Wall Street, by the trusts, by the interests, by corporations, by its advertisers, by politics, or by commercialism.

If these charges are to be accepted as stated, the historian must assuredly discard the press as an authoritative source in his reconstruction of the past. But it must be noted in connection with this blanket arraignment that it is through the press itself that these charges are circulated and that this must discount their value,—were the press guilty of all these high crimes and misdemeanors, it would hardly spread abroad the news of its own shame. It must be put to the credit of the press that the very papers that expose these conditions, as far as they really exist, are helping to improve them through the publicity the discussion of them gives. And it must be remembered that it is easy to judge the press by its worst representatives, that a few conspicuous illustrations of its rampant errors serve, in the eyes of many, as a sufficient basis for a sweeping condemnation of the press as a whole, and that standards of perfection are raised for the press collectively that never could be applied to individuals. It is, indeed, easy to fall into the habit of criticizing the press,— it is the expected thing and often not to be taken more seriously than are generalizations about the weather of the past. There is a tendency to include all papers, of all times, and of all countries in these blanket charges. But while they may be partially true of certain papers at certain times in certain countries, wholesale denunciations are as false and as pernicious as are the corresponding panegyrics of the press.

The criticism of the press most frequently heard and that, if true, most limits its authoritativeness is that the press does not give the news, but wilfully suppresses it through fear of offending its advertisers, or prominent citizens to whom it is beholden, or for other unspecified reasons.

The statement that the papers do not give the news is probably as old as the newspapers themselves and in and of itself is not to be taken more seriously than did the *Massachusetts Centinel*, in reporting, June 29, 1785, "The general complaint in the coffee-houses for some time has been that *there is nothing in the papers* . . . in short, all is dead, and *there is nothing in the papers*,"— much to the disappointment of all as expressed by the politicians, old women, and "those who are curious in physic and philosophy," and the *Centinel* adds, "all patients are in perfect health." [6]

[6] J. T. Buckingham, *Specimens of Newspaper Literature*, II, 35–36.

But the charge that the press intentionally suppresses the news can not be so lightly dismissed. It has been made repeatedly by the press itself, although never in the form of a confession, and it has been scarcely less frequently made by individual journalists both in public and in private. In 1905, Greenwood wrote to Goldwin Smith: "In England the character of journalism is certainly falling. . . . But where, I think, the newspaper press sinks lowest is in its dealing with news. There is far more selection, repression, maiming, and focussing of news than was thought decent forty years ago." [7] So often has the statement been iterated and reiterated that it has come to have somewhat the authority of an axiom.

Does the press suppress news? Unquestionably it does, and it may be added, equally unquestionably, it ought to suppress much more than it does. Does it suppress the news that the public ought to have, does it suppress it knowingly, and through fear of diminishing its revenues? That is another question and one to be more cautiously answered. It is always easy for the critics of the press to make the worse appear the better reason and *vice versa*. If news that the critic thinks important does not appear in his morning paper, the impulse is to assume that it has been wilfully suppressed.

But this condemnation fails to recognize the variations in judgment and in interest that make one set of conditions seem vastly important to one person and entirely negligible to another. A class in journalism was recently asked to select the most important news item on the first page of a great metropolitan daily, —practically every item on the page was selected by some one, with the exception of the one that had seemed most important to the instructor in charge. The selection of the one hundred best books of all time, or of the past year, or of the current week, or for a shelf of any length must always vary infinitely,—even the Bible and Shakespeare would presumably not be listed by Chinese or Brahmin scholars, and in some quarters doubts in regard to Shakespeare have arisen since the reminder that it was German scholarship that discovered his rank. During an important trial involving labor and capital, the charge was made that "the

[7] *Correspondence of Goldwin Smith*, pp. 439–440.

jackal press has 'hushed up' or perverted utterly the story of the I. W. W. trial. Publicity could not help but win the case for the 'wobblies'; and so the great prostituted newspapers ignore the most dramatic legal battle since Dred Scott—one whose implications are as serious, and whose sky is banked with thunder heads." [8] But while to many everything connected with the I. W. W. is of supreme interest, to others it has not as yet become so. The press may not grasp the dimensions the movement has already attained and hence miscalculate the proportion of space to be given it. It has been clearly shown that the press can not give space to news that does not interest more than a third of its readers and omniscience is needed to determine what this is.[9]

Extraordinary conditions necessarily change proportions. During the war everything was subordinated to that and the press gave comparatively little space to subjects that prior to it had filled many columns,—education, municipal government, tenement house reform, and all the questions that had agitated society gave way to the war and to conditions growing out of it. News of this character was not "suppressed," but public interest in it was in a state of suspended animation and could not be revived until the war had closed.

The steel strike in 1919 dropped out of the press, not necessarily because news concerning it had been suppressed, but because, after it had been running some weeks and the situation was apparently unchanged, information concerning it ceased to be news. The mass of readers lose interest in a prolonged controversy and the press holds to the principle of printing as news only what interests a definite proportion of readers. The declaration of war against Germany and the declaration of the armistice were received by the public with equal demonstrations of rapturous joy because each furnished a new sensation. The sustained effort required to follow the development of a situation from beginning to end is lacking and "what the public wants" is news pure and simple. A society once existed to secure in the Constitution of the United States the recognition of the existence of God. But

[8] A. Young and J. Reed, "The Social Revolution in Court,". *Liberator*, September, 1918.
[9] G. B. Dibblee, *The Newspaper*, p. 72.

the omission from this document does not necessarily mean the denial of such existence. The question must at least be raised whether the omission of news by the press must always be attributed to wilful suppression.

But it must be recognized that it is in the selection of material that one of the great limitations on the authoritativeness of the press is found. Standards in the readers of the press are as essential as are standards in the newspaper itself and when the press gives as much space to a would-be assassin "who delights in being the most talked of man in the country to-day" as it gives to his victim, it is presumably in deference to the standards of its readers.

The charge is often made that the newspaper does not give the news and that it suppresses the news, yet the news desired by the public is often what the press is legally prevented from giving. If a great brokerage firm fails, involving hundreds of clients in financial loss, the public demands to know the cause and to know what has become of the money; yet to print even one of the score of tales current on the street, before official investigations are completed, would be to prejudge a case and render the press liable to an action for libel. If a fire is suspected as having had an incendiary origin, the public demands to know who caused it, yet to give the news desired and indicate the offender before an indictment had been presented would again be to print libellous matter. If a death occurs under suspicious circumstances, the public demands all the news, yet to point to any individual as having been criminally concerned in it is to invite an action against the press so reporting the crime. If the press does not always tell all things to all men, it is not always because the news is suppressed, but because the press, like all individuals, is justly controlled by the laws made for the protection of the innocent.

The position of the press in regard to all matters of scandal is a troublesome one; if it suppresses news of this character, it seems at least entitled to the defense always accorded an individual,— that a man is innocent until he is proved guilty. It may or it may not be true that in such cases "the silence of the press was due to a cowardly fear of the money of the other side." [10] Until it is

[10] Caro Lloyd, *Henry Demarest Lloyd*, II, 145. Mr. Lloyd cites a conspicuous case where appearances indicated suppression of news, but other reasons might be assumed besides the one inferred.

possible to settle the question by evidence rather than by opinion, the press, like an individual, seems entitled to the benefit of the doubt.

The suppression of the news that is often attributed to personal hostility, class interest, or premeditated plan, may have been due entirely to accident. Lord Houghton was greatly interested in the conduct of business in the House of Lords and at one time wrote an important letter on the subject to *The Times*. It was not inserted, but neither was it "suppressed,"—the editor was in Paris when the letter had been received, his mail was not opened during his absence, and no explanation could be made prior to his return.[11]

Press notices may be desired because the persons interested in a subject may deem them all-important, and yet they may be omitted without obvious or sinister reason. The Queen of Holland wrote Lord Houghton, September 26, 1869: "Our [Statistical] Congress has passed unobserved and unnoticed. Can you account why the *Times* has not deigned to mention it? Have we undergone the bad will of Mr. Delane? Why? And in what manner? Pray tell me if you can discover it."[12] *The Life of Lord Houghton* does not disclose why the notice did not appear, but other letters from the Queen of Holland indicate an oversensitiveness to the remissness of correspondents.

The different hours at which papers go to press often explains the absence of news of an important event in one paper while another paper may give it half a column. The difference in time explains why an event may receive a few lines in an Eastern paper and adequate notice in a Western paper.

The press may tell the truth, but it may not necessarily tell all the truth about everything. Newspapers have the privilege of selection as do private individuals in private conversation and need not be charged with wilfully suppressing news if various subjects honestly seem to them inconsequential. A newspaper may not report a meeting of socialists, or of Mormons, or of equal suffragists, not because it wishes to supress the news, but because

[11] T. W. Reid, *The Life, Letters and Friendships of Richard Monckton Milnes, First Lord Houghton*, II, 204.
[12] *Ib.*, II, 204.

it honestly believes that the public is not interested in any of these matters. When a half dozen national learned societies hold their meetings in the same city during the same week, the press gives extensive reports of the societies whose deliberations are presumably of interest to its readers while it may barely mention the meetings of other organizations no less important.[13]

The fear of the advertiser is a common explanation for the so-called supression of news, and the conventional illustration is the elevator accident in a department store carrying large advertising. It seems altogether reasonable, however, to assume that no reporters are at hand to send the news and that the press does not learn of it until the accident has ceased to have news value;[14] that if known, the report is not published through a desire to prevent fear in the use of elevators; that the inconspicuousness of the individuals concerned gives the accident little interest in the eyes of the general public. Even so, it is easy to show the incorrectness of the initial assumption, and to cite more than one illustration of elevator accidents in department stores carrying full page advertisements that are given full and adequate reports in the city papers. The fallacy lies in the general statement, "the press,"— the truth being that the press of large cities, in the multiplicity of news at its command, does not report elevator accidents, while the press of small cities, with less local news to report, does report them.[15]

Here, as elsewhere, publicity is the wholesome corrective. If a newspaper is known to suppress news that the public has a right to know, or has that reputation even if it is wholly undeserved,

---

[13] Much interesting material on this point is given in a series of contemporary letters of Henry Redhead Yorke, edited by J. A. C. Sykes under the title *France in Eighteen Hundred and Two*, especially in the section on "Newspapers," pp. 213–225. The writer, in an effort to secure for a London daily authentic information in regard to what was passing in France, was offered much concerning the opera, plays, "and all the other equipage of folly and pleasure," but his informants could not understand his desire for "*facts* and *facts only.*"

[14] An eminent journalist once said that the ideal reporter was one who knew something important was going to happen and was on hand to report it.

[15] A serious elevator accident occurred in Poughkeepsie, New York, May 10, 1918. The daily city papers gave long and detailed accounts of it, although both were carrying full page advertisements of the department store where it occurred. See Poughkeepsie *Eagle-News* and *Star-Enterprise* of that date.

it is fatal to it. The public demands the news, the press is organized to meet the demand, and such papers as fail to do this, fall by the wayside. Some papers undoubtedly suppress the news, but in so doing they run great risks and in the end pay a heavy price for it. To attribute the suppression of the news to malicious design on the part of the press as a whole is to charge the press with suicidal intent.

But has the public an inherent right to demand the publication of all or any news? The newspaper, like the hotel, is a private enterprise dependent on the public for support, but notwithstanding this, like the hotel it has the right to exercise selection; like the church, each newspaper ministers to its own constituency and makes little attempt to please all,—the Presbyterian clergyman does not expect Episcopalians to attend his services and his sermons presumably do not meet the wishes and beliefs of Roman Catholics,—one newspaper constituency clamors for one kind of news, and another one is grossly offended by its publication; like the college, it is free to admit what conforms to its standards and, like the college, its standards are multifarious; like the private school, it may exclude certain sects, races, or occupations from its corps of teachers as well as from its body of pupils. The newspaper has the universal prerogative of selection; the public has the moral right to know whatever concerns the public welfare, but it has no moral or legal right to compel the press to be the medium through which it acquires this knowledge. If the newspaper selects its news wisely, the public supports it; if it makes an injudicious selection, if it suppresses what ought to be printed in the interests of the public welfare, the public withdraws its support and the newspaper goes to the wall. Wherever the evil exists, it quickly cures itself without the exercise of compulsion.

News may sometimes be "colored," it is said, even when not suppressed. This is specially true when news dispatches give a complexion to a subject not warranted by the real facts of the case. In 1917, the lower house of the Swedish Parliament passed by an overwhelming majority, without a division, a bill giving suffrage to women; in the non-representative upper house, the question remained as before, but the majority was so small that the change in only a few votes would have turned an adverse into a favorable decision.[16] The American press reported that equal suffrage for women in Sweden had been defeated,—a statement technically correct, but more unfavorable to the cause of suffrage for women than the facts themselves justified. It is possible that the report may have been colored by a prejudice against equal suffrage; it is also probable that it may be explained by ignorance of the character of the Swedish Parliament, by interference with cablegrams in time of war, by failure to realize the interest in the question here, or by other less obvious explanations. The press here, as in similar cases, seems entitled to the benefit of the doubt.

Intimately connected with the suppression of the news, is the question of venality. The price of a newspaper, even with a large subscription list, yields inadequate returns, and if the revenues derived from the advertising are small, other sources of income must be found. The newspaper that is inherently weak or dishonest may yield to temptation, as sometimes does the individual, and withhold news disadvantageous to its chief advertisers, print spurious news, or attempt a "sensation." Yet with the newspaper, as with the individual, dishonest and even questionable practices work in the long run to its disadvantage,—not to put the question on higher grounds. It is impossible in the case of a newspaper to conceal evidence of guilt for any length of time and ultimate disclosure is always sure.

But while in normal times newspapers are not bought and sold in the crude sense of the term, it is often said that editors, business managers, and the upper class of journalists are well paid, that they meet at social clubs and associate with capitalists, bankers, and men of wealth, and that they therefore unconsciously reflect the views of this class; to this extent they do not represent the masses of the people. But quite as unconsciously the newspaper is written for the masses and it appeals to them through cartoons, through choice of subject for interviews, reports, special letters, and discussion of questions uppermost in the public mind. The coal situation, conservation of food, school accommodations are subjects that respect neither social clubs nor tenements.

[16] *The Woman Citizen*, June 23, 1917.

If opinions may be considered near kinsmen of news, a possible explanation for the absence of news in the press may be found in the blunt statement made many years earlier by Edward Bulwer that new opinions were not popular. The *Quarterly Review*, he says, puts forth the fewest new opinions and sells the most copies; the *Westminster*, the most and sells the fewest. "*The Edinburgh*, hovering between, rather modifies opinion than changes its form, and it sells accordingly, a little less than the first-named journal, and greatly more than the last." [17] Somewhat similar reasons have been given for the absence of a radical press in America.[18] If the opinions of the press tend to be colorless, the news may tend to be colorless without the press necessarily being open to the charge of suppressing the news. The tendency of news-collecting agencies is to standardize the news; the tendency of chains of papers and of press syndicates is to standardize the interpretation of news. The standardization of both news and interpretation does not necessarily connote the suppression of either.

The charge is often made that the press can not be trusted because of the contradictory elements in its composition. A dyed-in-the-wool Republican paper may carry a full page political advertisement of the Democratic party; a paper may advertise an obviously questionable financial project, report in its news column a suicide due to unwise investments, and editorially declaim against gold bricks; it may editorially urge its readers to patronize home industries while advertising the bargains offered in the nearest city, and the special trolley service arranged to take advantage of them. But these discrepancies and contradictions deceive no one. All political advertisements are labeled as such,—it would be a work of supererogation for any political party to advertise exclusively in papers of its own complexion since its business is to convert its opponents. Reputable papers no longer admit the advertisements of questionable concerns and editorial virtue in declaiming against them, while carrying them in its own columns, illustrates the ostrich

[17] *England and the English*, II, 14.
[18] C. E. Russell, "The Radical Press in America," *Bookman*, July, 1919, 49: 513–518.

with its head in the sand. The conventional advice to "shop at home" carries no more and no less weight than do other conventions and is seldom misunderstood. The authoritativeness of the press is not necessarily impeached by reason of its mutually contradictory parts.

The newspaper, like the individual, is open to the charge of generalizing from insufficient data. On Thanksgiving Day, 1915, approximately twelve hundred clergymen preached in Greater New York. A leading New York paper gave two columns to extracts from eleven sermons out of the twelve hundred preached. Of the eleven quoted, three sermons seemed to urge some form of military preparation; the others were silent or definitely opposed to the plan. Yet the headlines of this paper read, "Preparedness from Many Pulpits. Thanksgiving Sermons Justify War for Defense of American Liberty and Ideals." [19] Pernicious as is the oral general statement of an individual, the printed general statement of the press is infinitely more destructive of the truth. Yet in both the private individual and the individual speaking through the press it is an evidence of mental immaturity and untrained mind rather than an illustration of deliberate falsehood.

A serious limitation on the usefulness of the press to the historian is found in its failure to give continuous news; it gives full information on any subject only in times of crises. This is evident to any one making a collection of clippings on any current question. Many links are always lacking in the chain of evidence and these must be supplied from other sources. Continuity of narration is found in the newspaper through the letters of correspondents permanently attached to national capitals or assigned to report at length on important, prolonged questions, but these letters can not always be considered news. Continuity is found in the serial advertisements that are often complete and continuous; they are numbered with each appearance and indicate when the next advertisement in the series may be expected. But apart from these two sources, continuity of material is not found in the press.

[19] "The Falsification of the News," *The Independent*, December 13, 1915, 84: 420.

A limitation on the press is found by the historian in what may be termed the seasonal character of the news. Many years ago Samuel Foote observed in *The Bankrupt*, "The conductor of a newspaper, like a good cook, should always serve up things in their season: who eats oysters in June? Plays and parliament-houses are winter provisions," while a writer of to-day finds that "what in May or June would scarcely be worthy of a four-line paragraph, in September is considered entitled to half a column." Yet it may be in May or June that the historian is most anxious to secure detailed information.

The specific adverse criticism has been made that where the press falls short is, not in failing to give the news, but in failing to report correctly public opinion. Sir Wemyss Reid, in speaking of the overthrow of the Conservative party under Beaconsfield in 1880 and the success of the Liberals under Gladstone, held the London press distinctly responsible for failing to interpret correctly English opinion outside of London—"The amazement approaching to consternation," he says, "with which the Liberal uprising at that time was regarded in London, and by society of all ranks, from its most illustrious personages downwards, affords sufficient proof of the fact that the people who might reasonably be supposed to be the most intelligent and the best-informed in all public affairs, had been kept in the profoundest ignorance of what was happening all round them in the country." Men read *The Times*, he says, "not so much to learn what may be the opinions of its Editor upon any particular question, as to discover what, according to his judgment, is the prevailing opinion of the public upon that question." [20]

But the very nature of the press prevents it from representing public opinion, even in the imperfect way in which it may be said to be represented by its regularly chosen delegates in a legislative body. Each paper may have its own constituency, but as a rule it ignores, and perhaps to a certain extent must ignore, public opinion outside of that constituency. The instability of the claim of any paper to represent public opinion is evident from an examination of its basis; the judgment of the press can not be

[20] T. W. Reid, "Public Opinion and its Leaders," *Fortnightly Review*, August, 1880, n. s. 28: 230–244.

regarded as final, and it is not altogether reasonable to hold it responsible for not doing what, from its very nature, it can not do.

In all of these adverse criticisms of the press, it must be remembered that it is through the press itself that they are given circulation,—an indication that the press itself is most responsive to the criticism directed against it. "Nowhere is a newspaper so criticised as among those who create it," said Charles T. Congden,[21] and in this it shares the experience of all other occupations and professions. It is from schools and colleges that come the most severe criticisms of educational systems. No one is so severe a censor of the failings of the Church as is the Church itself. Politicians and statesmen are everywhere the severest critics of the political system.

But while other occupations and professions must wait on the printed word to carry abroad their strictures on themselves, the press is ever prepared to act against itself. It was in 1795 that Charles Whittingham started *The Tomahawk! or Censor General*, with the motto "*Pro rege saepe, pro patria semper*," and it ran for one hundred and thirteen numbers. *The Tomahawk* professedly avoided news and its main object was "to expose the daily lies in the newspapers, . . . but the tax-master came and clapped on the newspaper stamp, daily killing and exposing lies being pronounced *news*," [22] and it was discontinued. In Austria only recently *Fackel*, a periodical pamphlet of Vienna, "biting, stinging, sometimes scurrilous," has kept "a vigilant eye upon the follies and failings of daily journalism and pillories them mercilessly." [23] If the sins of omission and of commission on the part of the press are not widely known, it is not because of lack of publication through the columns of the press itself.

If there has been frequent anxiety expressed of the dangers of the press from commercial interests, it has been Fleet Street itself that has been "alarmed at the encroachments made by a few wealthy men." [24] It is the editor who holds out encouragement and finds that "Large capital in newspapers, and their

[21] *Reminiscences of a Journalist*, p. 268.
[22] J. C. Francis, *John Francis*, II, 364–365.
[23] H. W. Steed, *The Hapsburg Monarchy*, p. 192.
[24] Correspondence of the New York *Evening Post*, December 10, 1904.

heightened earning power, tend to steady them. . . . Just because a great sum is invested, it can not be imperiled by allowing unscrupulous men to make use of the newspaper property; for that way ruin lies, in the end." [25]

The press itself has never been backward in expressing its strictures on others. In time of war, it is prone to measure all citizens by its own standard of patriotism and to pronounce anathemas on all who do not conform to these particular standards. In time of peace, it is equally prone to scent evil where no evil exists and in some cases it has relentlessly persecuted innocent persons and driven them into exile. It is ever prone in war and in peace to accuse those whom it opposes of being "in the pay" of some objectionable faction. Carl Schurz was forty years ago accused by the press of being "in the pay" of the Prussian government, of being a spy on the German political refugees in America, and of receiving fabulous sums for his political speeches.[26] The judgment then meted out to a distinguished citizen of America by political opponents represented on the press has had many counterparts both before and since that time. It has to many seemed a righteous judgment on the press that it has in turn been "hoist by its own petard" and that it has so often been charged by its critics with being "in the pay of" Wall Street, or of the "interests," or of being owned by corporations.

Troublesome as is the question of the general authoritativeness of the press under normal conditions and in time of peace, it becomes infinitely complicated in time of war. There exists a rigorous censorship not only of actual war news but of much that in ordinary times would be published without question. Much news is suppressed lest it bring discouragement alike to civilians and to the troops. "When will French Governments understand," writes Henry Labouchere in despair, "that it is far more productive of demoralization to allow no official news to be published than to publish the worst?" [27] The opposite habit of

[25] Rollo Ogden, "Some Aspects of Journalism," *Atlantic Monthly*, July, 1906, 98: 12–20.

[26] Carl Schurz, *Reminicences*, II, 133, *et seq.*

[27] *Diary of the Besieged Resident in Paris*, p. 12, September 19, 1870. The *Diary* is made up of the letters sent by Labouchere from Paris to the London *Daily News*.

publishing false or highly colored news is equally confusing. "The newspapers," writes Labouchere, "are still pursuing the very questionable policy of exaggerating every little affair of the outposts into a victory, and assuring those who read their lucubrations that powerful armies are on the march to raise the siege." [28] He writes later: "Nothing new has passed at the front since yesterday. I learn from this morning's papers, however, that Moltke is dead, that the Crown Prince is dying of a fever, that Bismarck is anxious to negotiate, but is prevented by the obstinacy of the King, that three hundred Prussians from the Polish provinces have come over to our side, and that the Bavarian and Wurtemberg troops are in a state of incipient rebellion." [29] Despair must indeed come to the historian when he finds both press and government mutually questioning the reports given by the other. Labouchere again writes: "The *Débats* and some other journals contain extracts from the English newspapers up to the 22nd ult. I observe that everything that tells against France is suppressed, and what is published is headed with a notice, that as the source is English the truth is questionable. Thus does the press, while abusing the Government for keeping back intelligence, fulfill its mission." [30] A few days later he comments: "Yesterday morning the *Journal Officiel* contained an announcement that the Government knew absolutely nothing of these negotiations [reported by the press as going on at Versailles for peace]. The newspapers are, however, not disposed to allow their hopes of peace to be destroyed in this manner, and they reply that 'it being notorious that no member of the Government can speak the truth, this official denial proves conclusively the contrary of what it states'." [31]

In time of war accounts given by the press do not always tally with what other observers note. When a premature announcement of the taking of Sebastopol had been made, Dickens wrote to Wills from Boulogne, October 4, 1854: "It is extraordinary to know through the evidence of one's own senses, however, that

[28] *Diary of the Besieged Resident*, p. 43, September 27, 1870.
[29] *Ib.*, p. 103, October 11, 1870. — Labouchere's pages are filled with illustrations of this point.
[30] *Ib.*, p. 188, November 8, 1870.
[31] *Ib.*, p. 193, November 14, 1870.

the *personal* enthusiasm and devotion of the Troops, is enormously exaggerated in the London papers. Their coldness was, to me, astonishing—so much so, as to be, under all the circumstances, almost irritating." [32]

Adverse criticism, even wholesome criticism, is tacitly avoided by the press itself or is suppressed by government regulation. Criticism of government action that in times of peace would be deemed entirely legitimate is considered in time of war pernicious and destructive. "Not a paper in the East printed an elaborate communication to Congress from a lawyer, Amos Pinchot, who had collated big concerns' reports of war profits. He was called a pro-German pacifist and his researches suppressed." [33] The critical faculty itself is held in abeyance and the press may accept as authoritative, documents that, under normal conditions, would not bear close scrutiny,[34] and publish reports whose accuracy has not been investigated. Labouchere writes that a Paris paper contained "a wonderful account of what Mr. Lynch had seen when with the Prussians. Meeting him this evening, I asked him whether it was true. He told me that he had already been to the newspaper to protest against its appearance, as every statement in it was destitute of foundation. He could, however, get no redress; the editor or his *locum tenens* told him that one of their reporters had given it to him, and that he knew nothing more about it. This is an instance of the reckless mode in which the business of journalism is conducted here." [35]

The numbing of the critical faculty has its counterpart in the general attitude of suspicion that prevails. The press in time of war becomes the channel through which suspicions and rumors find an outlet and in the absence of authentic facts these are widely circulated and in turn lead to hysteria, as this again leads to suspicion and rumor—and thus the vicious circle is completed.

But the limitation on the authoritativeness of the press in time of war does not stop here. A singularly astute analysis of

[32] R. C. Lehmann, *Charles Dickens as Editor*, p. 153.

[33] An Ex-City Editor, "Newspapers in Wartime," *The Public*, March 16, 1918, 21: 334–337.

[34] In September, 1918, the press in general accepted the so-called Sisson documents issued by the Committee on Public Information, but the New York *Evening Post* questioned the authoritativeness of a part of them.

[35] *Diary of the Besieged Resident*, pp. 117–118, October 13, 1870.

the situation has been made by an English writer [36] who has found the press despondent,—irrespective of party, proprietorship, or other obvious bias. He finds an explanation in comparing the development of a nation with the mental development of the individual who from birth passes through the stages of emotion, discrimination, co-ordination, and intellect. "When a nation goes to war," he observes, "it behaves exactly as does its 'mean' man when forced into a quarrel—viz., the intellect practically ceases to work. Co-ordination and discrimination (except in scientifically-trained boxers or fencers) becomes weak, and emotion—whether of hatred, rage or fear—becomes the dominating element." When the most physically active twenty-five per cent. of the adult population is segregated out and sent across the seas, the "mean" of the remainder sinks below the normal in self-control and falls a ready prey to the lower emotions. "When a crowd has for the time being suspended intellectual activity it is no use appealing to its reason—it can only be reached through its emotions; hence, if the Daily Press fails to provide emotional headlines, alternating between extremes, its circulation will rapidly dwindle," and bankruptcy result,— "unless the headlines are calculated to make the flesh creep their sales will certainly fall."

A press dispirited and temporarily below the normal in its intellectual development; dependent on headlines to create a momentary factitious interest on the part of its readers; irritable instead of critical; and unable to co-ordinate warring movements both at home and on the field unquestionably can not be considered unimpeachably authoritative. It is true that this opinion of the effect of war on the press must be expressed subject to many limitations,—undoubtedly the press of America has been less affected by pessimism than has the European press, but it is a question of degree rather than of one of fundamental difference.

These are suggestions of the general criticisms of the press that as far as they are supported by evidence must militate against the authoritativeness of the press. But other possible limitations must be recognized.

[36] F. N. Maude, "Pessimism in the Press and its Causes," *Contemporary Review*, May, 1918, 113: 495–498.

It is difficult for the press of to-day to overcome its long inheritance and to violate the traditions of its past. More than two hundred years ago Defoe rebuked unprincipled journalists, satirized their love of scandal, gave them many a friendly caution and much good advice, commented genially on the tricks and contrivances incidental to journalism where there is "a severe, cruel Scarcity of Intelligence," proposed remedies for a dearth of news, took a cheerful view of the political and religious dissensions of his time, discussed solemnly but with a twinkle in his eye the duty of journalists towards the Government, advocated independence in journalism, was free from personal abuse of his opponents, and was in every sense of the word the most modern of journalists. The journalist of to-day who believes that "'yesterday' has almost ceased to exist for the newspaper man" may well take counsel of Defoe.

The press is hampered, and its authoritativeness for the historian thereby modified, by the existence in society of formulated political and social creeds and ready-to-wear opinions. These are often accepted by the press, but how far acceptance is at the behest of unseen and unknown powers, how far it is in response to hidden pressure, how far it reflects public opinion, how far it is the result of an inherited, ingrained aversion to genuine independence, how far it represents a desire for conformity, how far it results from genuine conviction on the part of the press it is impossible for the historian to determine. Yet without such knowledge he is relying on the blind for guidance.

A conspicuous member of the press has, perhaps inadvertently, disclosed a secret of the sanctum in saying that "teaching is the most important and the most difficult" of the editorial writer's opportunities.[37] This statement, that has in effect frequently been made by others, must create misgivings in the mind of the historian. The distrust comes from the confusion of "teaching" with "giving information,"—a confusion widespread and difficult to disabuse the public of when university presidents advocate five foot shelves as royal bridges leading to education. The dis-

---

[37] A. Brisbane, "The Editorial Writer's Opportunity," New York *Evening Journal*, November 12, 1912, cited by J. W. Cunliffe and G. R. Lomer, *Writing of To-day*, pp. 153–155.

trust also comes because the teacher must himself learn, and the public must desire to be taught; but there is little evidence of an overwhelming desire on the part either of the press to learn or of the public to be taught.

For this confusion the press itself is not altogether to be blamed. Our educational system is still in its essential ideals founded on the principle of authority rather than on that of research. The press can not rise higher than its source. As long as knowledge, as interpreted by this system, is something kept in a closed chest containing the accumulations of the years and is to be handed down from generation to generation, the press will continue to conceive its function to be teaching rather than learning and thereby incur distrust. The present clamor of the press against the so-called radical press is significant in that it overlooks the original meaning of "radical" and thereby voices its own unwillingness to get at the root of questions it discusses.

Another limitation on the authoritativeness of the press is that its own interest in itself seems to begin and end with outstripping a neighbor in the rapidity with which it gets news. Enormous expense is incurred in getting news in advance of competitors, but no evidence is shown that equal expense is incurred in getting authoritative news. That deference is paid to the abstract principle is indicated in the frequency with which statements are qualified by the phrases "it is said," "it is reported," "it is rumored," but these modifying terms are dropped as other newspapers copy the information and thus rumor becomes crystallized as fact.

This unquestioning acceptance of information has been of long duration. "During the eighteenth century," Couper writes, "the Edinburgh journals were almost parasites on the newspapers of London and the continent. . . . Everything was admissible so long as it appeared in some accredited journal." [38] In America but little effort was made by the early press to substantiate the information received, the facilities for doing so were inadequate even had the wish been present, little interest was shown in local news, and news from a distance came slowly and irregularly.

Necessity, tradition, convenience, and long practice have

[38] W. J. Couper, *The Edinburgh Periodical Press*, I, 117.

everywhere been on the side of not examining too scrupulously the sources from which news is derived. Schools of journalism could make no greater contribution to the authoritativeness of the press than the development of the perfect news circle from the opposing forces of speed and reliability.

A dead weight that the press is forced to carry is the skepticism of its readers. Years ago Albany Fonblanque commented as an editor on "the greatness that never descends to read newspapers." Roosevelt and Bryan, only somewhat recently, were both quoted as saying that the great mass of daily papers had ceased to deserve confidence.[39] A person conspicuous in the public eye has recently remarked that outside of baseball scores and stock reports the general public should no longer believe in the press. [40] "The wickedness that isn't so" has been the editorial protest against such a conception of the press. [41] John Bright was credited with saying that the newspaper should be divided into four compartments,—"one for truth; a second for the probable; a third for the possible; and a fourth for lies." [42] George Russell seriously inquired, "How could people, who never read anything but newspapers, have any genuine knowledge of any subject on earth or much imagination of anything beautiful in the heavens?" [43]

The press is justly criticized for making general statements unsupported by facts. The critics of the press are equally open to just criticism for making on their part general statements concerning the press that are unsupported by facts, for reversing rule and exception and generalizing from the exception, for bringing sweeping charges against the press unsupported by evidence. The press, the college, the school, the church, and every institution is open to the charge of failing to attain the ideals of its most intelligent and most honorable representatives, but it is another matter to bring the indiscriminate charge that all members of these or other institutions are wilfully negligent of their duties and ever ready to sacrifice honor to gain.

[39] "The New Periodical Virtue," *The Nation*, April 20, 1911, 92: 392–393.
[40] *The Survey*, January 9, 1915, 33: 410–411.
[41] *The Independent*, September 17, 1903, 55: 2240–2241.
[42] "The British Newspaper: the Penny Theory and its Solution," *Dublin University Magazine*, March, 1863, 61: 359–376.
[43] *The National Being*, p. 5.

Public opinion of the press has vacillated between the weight attached to it in the proverb "four hostile newspapers are more to be feared than a thousand bayonets" and the contemptuous phrase "it is mere newspaper talk." Newspaper men themselves have written on the waning power of the press [44] and the student of history can but ask, assuming that it is true to speak thus of the press, how far this declining influence vitiates its serviceableness as historical material.

But the student of history realizes that in the last analysis the answer to the question as to how far the newspaper can be authoritatively used in writing history can not come from noting what historians have or have not done in the past; it can not be answered by considering how prominent and intelligent men have regarded the press; it can not be decided by the popular opinion of the press; it can not be determined even by what newspaper men themselves think of their own profession; the question can be answered only by a study of the press itself. Does this study of the press show how far it can be used to reconstruct the past, does it show what are its own limitations in such reconstruction, can the sources of errancy be isolated, and can principles be deduced that will enable the historian to determine what are the conditions that justify his use of the press as historical material?

If the analysis of the press thus far given is reasonably correct, it must be evident that a large part of the newspaper is concerned with giving information of very definite concrete nature for the authoritativeness of which governments, known organizations, associations, and individuals are fully responsible, and in effect guarantee. These guarantees are as absolute as it is possible to find, and they affect the permanent parts of the newspaper and much of the news proper except local news.

Another large portion of the newspaper is in the twilight

[44] Francis E. Leupp, *Atlantic Monthly*, February, 1910, 105: 145–156. He attributes it to the transfer of policies and properties from personal to impersonal control; the rise of the cheap magazine; the tendency to specialization; competition in the newspaper business; the demand for larger capital, "unsettling the former equipoise between the counting-room and the editorial room;" the mania for hurry; the development of the news-getting at the expense of the news-interpreting function; the remoulding the narration of facts to confirm office-made policies; the disregard of decency in the choice of news to be specially exploited; the scant time given by men of the world for reading journals of general intelligence.

realm where only a partial guarantee is afforded by the press itself and where the material must be considered "on its merits." These limited guarantees are connected with the business administration of the press and the office management; the desire for news in order to increase the circulation and the desire to increase the circulation in order to attract advertisers make a distinct limitation in both directions. At one extreme is the tendency to over-emphasize sensational news and to "play it up" to such an extent that all sense of proportion is lost. [45] At the other extreme is the important indirect limitation that concerns the source of news. In every community there are individuals who are occasional sources of news,—they may be trustees of colleges about to elect a new president; or members of a board of public works looking for a new superintendent; or delegates to a religious association that may decide to try a local clergyman for heresy; or leading politicians who are to determine the incorporation in party platforms of certain much discussed planks; but whatever the important items of news in their possession, they are persons to be conciliated. Every local paper wishes to be the first to announce the important decision, and hence it is extremely careful to say nothing against these individuals or against their interests. The press is thus limited by its own desire for news.

There is also, especially in the press of small places, the tacit understanding that certain news affecting certain families will not be published. Here, as at various other points, the question enters the realm of ethics. The suppression of much news is often a genuine advantage to the historian since its publication can add nothing of importance to a study of the period or of the community. Moreover, while the modern newspaper may often seem cruel to the living in its fierce denunciations of men who differ from it, it usually adheres to the spirit and the letter of the old injunction *de mortuis nil nisi bonum.*

[45] In a recent poison case one large daily had twelve reporters at work on it, while another paper in the same city gave it but half a column. One paper was charged with "sensationalism" and the other with "suppressing the news." Neither charge was apparently true. The sense of proportion in the two papers varied, and the event proved that the paper giving the less space to it had the better judgment.

A partial limitation is found in the work done by the special correspondent. He is often paid by space and thus is always open to the temptation, to which he sometimes yields, of making "a good story." Details are elaborated, and unnecessary features are enlarged upon; the errors of the special correspondent are not so much those of commission and omission as they are those of an apparent lack of a sense of proportion. Here again the criticism is not of to-day. Defoe wrote in 1719, "We must confess these People's Way of Writing is a Keen Satyr upon the credulity of the Age; and they take care to let the World know, that the English Nation are all BELIEVERS; for did they not think we were credulous to a degree beyond all the POPERY that ever we pretended to quarrel with, they could never impose such Trumpery for News, and such Forgeries for Intelligence," [46] and one of his biographers writes that "scarcely a week elapsed in which he did not complain of the contradictory and unreliable character of the pretended foreign News Letters, with which he was compelled to deal." [47]

Another limitation on the authoritativeness of the press is that exerted by the advertiser. This is often thought to be a serious limitation, and several well-known examples seem to bear out the contention. Yet the very publicity given such cases is an indication that they are exceptional. An examination of the press itself seems to lead to the same conclusion and it shows where the pitfalls lie. The supposed limitation exerted by the advertiser does not prevent the curious anomalies found in political advertising. It is not unusual to find in editorial columns scathing denunciations of a political party or organization whose advertisements are found in the same issue. It does not prevent the best representatives of the press from expressing an honest opinion adverse to the merits of new books and at the same time carrying the advertising matter of the firms publishing these very books. The campaign carried on by the press itself for honesty in advertising is a clear indication that whatever the limitations imposed by the advertiser have been in the past these limitations are on the wane. The guaranteed advertisement is not only a

[46] W. Lee, *Daniel Defoe*, I, 305.
[47] *Idem.*

guarantee of the article advertised, but it is even more a guarantee of the emancipation of the press from the control of the advertiser.

It has been seen that the press is handicapped by many conditions. The fundamental one is that it is a business enterprise. That the newspaper, therefore, has regard for its advertising columns is a natural business consequence, as business is now conducted. It may in its editorial columns remember its advertising pages; it may assume the semblance of virtue and exclude liquor advertisements while showing editorially that "prohibition does not prohibit;" it may be silent in regard to local conditions that demand moral surgery to preserve the life of the community; it may promote new federal buildings and improvements of an as yet undiscovered watercourse in its congressional district and therefore support its representative in Congress for the sake of the loaves and the fishes. The press is indeed handicapped by conditions that the historian can not disregard.

The historian, however, finds similar restraints on all other means of expressing or of influencing public opinion. The politician and even the statesman not infrequently remember the coming election; the clergyman has in his congregation men and women of questionable business and private morality; the leading citizen does not always in time of danger press on to the front. The restraints on the individual are many and serious, and often perfectly legitimate. One property owner may wish to take down a division fence while his neighbor may wish to keep it up; the citizens on one side of a residential street may wish asphalt pavement while those on the other side may advocate macadam; one-half a community may support municipal ownership of all public utilities and the other half advocate private ownership.

These self-evident conditions are noted to suggest that the press shares with every other known human activity, collective or individual, the restraints inherent in human society, and probably to no greater or less a degree. This is only stating that the press is a part of a most complex organization and that it can not be singled out either by itself as suffering peculiar hardships by reason of its limitations or by others as yielding to temptations unknown in other occupations. The historian recognizes, without extenuating, these conditions. He finds in them, however, records of conditions that are world-old and that whether of good or evil form part of the warp and woof of his material.

Whether these criticisms of the authoritativeness of the press are justified by fact or not, they can not be ignored and the historian must ask what precautions have been taken by the press itself to minimize them or to prevent their future occurrence.

An important means used by the press itself to insure as far as possible the authoritativeness of its statements is found in the building up of special libraries in connection with every great newspaper, in the organization of systems of newspaper exchanges, in the formation of enormous collections of clippings and illustrative material, and in advance preparation of much biographical material to be available in any emergency.

More than a hundred years ago Jerdan began the collection of newspapers in connection with his editorship of the *Literary Gazette* and lists various German, French, and Austrian journals for which he subscribed, together with some twenty-six German, Belgian, Dutch, French, Spanish, and Portuguese journals that were "ransacked for intelligence" "so as to furnish a better-culled and far more ample mass of continental intelligence, than had ever been dreamed of before (or probably since) for English readers." [48] History is a safer field than prophecy and Jerdan could not have anticipated the remarkable development that has come in newspaper offices in the collection of this material.

The press itself realizes that the distrust with which it is regarded springs largely from its own inaccuracy and carelessness and that it must itself remedy this condition if it is to have the confidence of its readers. A considerable number of great metropolitan dailies have initiated measures intended to stamp out this inaccuracy as far as it is possible to do so.[49]

[48] *Autobiography*, II, 370–371.

[49] The New York *World* established, July, 1913, a Bureau of Accuracy and Fair Play. During the first two years of its existence it considered seven hundred and eighty-seven cases involving accuracy or fair play in the news and editorial columns. Every complaint received was carefully inquired into, the complaints sustained numbered four hundred and ninety-eight, and the corrections published two hundred ninety-one. In addition there were sixty-eight publications in the interests of fair play where the *World* had not been at fault.—I. D. White, *Biennial Report of Bureau of Accuracy and Fair Play*, 1915.

More than fifty years ago Sir Charles Wyke wrote J. T. Delane from Copenhagen, July 9, 1869, proposing that abuse of liberty of the press should be regulated by the press itself rather than by the government since "this same abuse of liberty degenerating into license is more hurtful to the healthy portion of the Press than to any other element in the State." He suggested that a committee should be chosen and elected among the leading journalists who should be empowered to prosecute, and enabled to do so by a fund specially set apart for that purpose from the revenues of the country, in order to punish and put down what was at once discreditable to their profession and hurtful to the community at large. This committee would be changeable from time to time, and in its operation, backed by public opinion, would have far more power than could ever be exercised by a Government prosecution.

The suggestion of Sir Charles arose out of a proposal to pass a law in Hanover regulating the press; the Government, while anxious to give all due liberty to the press, wished to control its excesses. The Minister of the Interior consulted with him and the result was this suggestion. It was received with favor, but before it could be acted on Hanover had become a Prussian province. Sir Charles evidently questioned the feasibility of carrying out the idea in England, but felt that something ought to be done to check the license of the press, as he regarded it. [50] Public opinion may in the long run be relied on to disapprove of flagrant cases of inaccuracy that miss by a hair's breadth action for libel, and the defect of the plan of Sir Charles was that it was punitive, not preventive.

A plan looking directly to prevention rather than to cure has

---

Aside from these results, the Bureau has "had a beneficial and bracing effect upon out-of-town correspondents and news agencies and [has] brought to light and weeded out several habitually careless men and fakers."

[50] A. I. Dasent, *John Thadeus Delane*, II, 241–242.

It is interesting to note that only a few months before *The Nation* had complained bitterly of a maliciously padded interview of a New York daily, and adds, "The lesson that there are limits to people's endurance of printed impudence is one that should be taught the conductors of the press by their own sense of moral responsibility for all the damage done by anything to which they give publicity."—"Interviewing," *The Nation*, January 28, 1869, 8: 66–68.

been that of licensing reporters.[51] This plan has not as yet received the unqualified support of the press itself, but from the point of view of the student of history it has much to commend it. He believes that the newspaper man needs not only an instinct for news, but such previous training as will enable him to sift his material, to weigh evidence, and not to accept at its face value every statement made, deterred from doing so only by fear of libel suits. The license is now everywhere required in the interests of the physical health and well-being of the public and its extension to cover other fields of danger would to many persons seem most desirable. If one great source of error is found to lie in the work of the local reporter, if the newspaper-reading public naturally reasons that if so many errors are made in regard to matters that are familiar, an even greater number must be made in regard to subjects more remote and unfamiliar, it would seem to follow that greater confidence in the general reliability of the press would be secured by the guarantee afforded by a license.

A variant of the license has been the suggestion of an entrance examination to be demanded of all persons before going into journalism. Inasmuch as similar examinations are demanded by other professions this seems not unreasonable.[52]

If the press gains a reputation for inaccuracy through the carelessness of reporters, it also suffers from the lack of positive knowledge on the part of many of its members. In the fields of music and art, the drama and literature, sports and athletics, markets and finance, the work of reporting and of criticism is done on the large dailies by persons who have the technical knowledge demanded by these subjects. Reporters now have considerable training in politics and in court matters and there-

[51] This has been ably supported by Barratt O'Hara in "A State License for Newspaper Men," M. Thorpe, ed., The Coming Newspaper, pp. 148–161.

Percy S. Bullen describes "The English Substitute for the License Plan," Ib., pp. 162–170. The object, however, of the Institute of Journalists of Great Britain has been the professional advancement and improvement of its members,—"to accomplish for [the] profession what the American bar societies have accomplished for lawyers and the medical councils for doctors," —rather than the end suggested by the license plan.

[52] The State Editorial Association of Pennsylvania has urged the adoption of this plan and it was considered by the Canadian Press Association at its annual meeting in Toronto, 1914.—Talcott Williams, New York Tribune, October 9, 1915.

fore there are fewer errors in these accounts. But specialization has as yet been but imperfectly developed in other fields and in these, many errors almost unavoidably arise.

In reporting crime, reporters who have been trained in psychology would avoid many of the errors now found,—the understanding mind is quite as necessary as the facile pen. Reporters with a knowledge of the elementary facts of medical science would presumably write of medical questions more understandingly than is now possible. In the discussion of every subject, an introduction to the study of it would qualify reporters to discuss it more intelligently and thus reduce the probable area of errancy.

A troublesome source of errancy lies in the censorship of the press in time of war. The reporter presumably knows nothing of war and the censor presumably knows nothing of reporting,—the present arrangement for censorship exasperates the press, the public, and the war department. But skilled newspaper men instructed in the art of war and military strategy and then given the responsibility of censoring the news would reduce to a minimum the chances of error.[53]

The authoritativeness of the press is limited by its own desire for news, but the press itself is coming to appreciate that it there-

[53] The city editor of a New York daily has kindly given this outline of a plan already discussed:

A prominent newspaper man in New York has served as an army manoeuvre expert. Every time he covered a mobilization he realized that the average reporter on the ground was unable to comprehend the finer points of the manoeuvres because of more or less dense ignorance of military tactics. This led him to talk over with a number of staff officers a plan for improving the situation. The main points, as he outlined it, were that the Government should choose every year a certain number of skilled reporters with a military trend, who were to be officially accredited to staff headquarters during manoeuvres. Every man was to be properly certificated, so that in case of a sudden war the Government could, automatically, draw on experienced reporters who would be unlikely to make any blunders, either through ignorance or semi-misinterpretation. The same general scheme could be followed in the case of the navy. This plan would, of course, provide a constantly renewable brigade of correspondents who would be practically fit to censor their own material, but would, of course, work under an official censor. Under such a working agreement with the Government, blunders necessitating censorship would be reduced to a minimum. The plan would stimulate competition in excellence among the various staffs of great dailies, and the commission attached to manoeuvre headquarters would be regarded as a signal honor. The plan has been talked over with many army and naval officers, and in each case the general plan of procedure has been heartily approved.

by lays itself open to criticism and it is changing its policy accordingly. "The dictum," says G. B. Dibblee, "of a leading London manager about news is, that he will not print anything that interests less than a third of his readers and such a policy is beginning to cover the whole field and to narrow news down steadily only to those things which are next door to the daily pre-occupation of the majority of readers." [54]

Errors have come through over-zeal to secure "beats" and "scoops," but newspapers to-day show a growing respect for each other's rights and are learning that they thereby gain in a growing reputation for authoritativeness. [55]

The many volumes coming from the press that treat of newspaper reporting, advertising, and the more technical phases of journalism are in themselves some indication of how far the press can be considered authoritative, and of a desire on the part of those connected with newspaper work to remove just causes of criticism.

An obvious limitation of the press lies in the headline. The desire to attract attention gives it a prominence out of all proportion to its real value as news. The headline often does not fit the article for which it serves as a caption, or it misplaces the emphasis, or it may be satirical and thus express "the headline's personal relation to the article." The historian can not trust to the authoritativeness of the headline but must know the details of the article itself. That this, too, is understood by the writers for the press is evident from the explicit directions given in all technical works on journalism for the composition and arrangement of headlines.

Other limitations are found in trade journals, in the religious

[54] *The Newspaper*, p. 72.
[55] It seems improbable that a reputable journal would to-day boast of a feat described by G. B. Dibblee: "Sir William Russell was sent on a special mission for the *Times* to Dublin to report the trial of O'Connell in 1844. He came back in a specially chartered steamboat well ahead of any one else and as he was entering the *Times* office among a group of shirt-sleeved men, whom he took to be compositors of his own paper, one came up, touched his hat and said, 'We are glad to hear, sir, they have found O'Connell guilty, at last.' 'Oh yes!' replied Russell innocently, 'all guilty but on different counts.' This individual turned out to be an emissary of the *Morning Herald*, who stole Russell's secret from him in the very jaws of the rival office."—*The Newspaper*, p. 57.

press, in papers printed in foreign languages, in all special papers of every description. Here again the limitation arises from the absence of proportion and of perspective that is imposed by the design and purpose that the paper has chosen for itself. Such limitations are so apparent that they not only can never be misleading, but they in effect become guarantees of the reliability of such newspapers within the limited field occupied.

The two most widely discussed plans for securing greater reliability in the press have been the establishment of schools of journalism and the founding of endowed newspapers.

The proposal to give courses in journalism in colleges and universities, as also to found special schools of journalism, has only comparatively recently become an accomplished fact, but the idea goes back at least to June 9, 1864, when *The Independent* printed a letter on "A College for the Training of Editors," [56] gave it editorial comment, but withheld its judgment on the plan until the writer had elaborated it, and opened its columns for discussion of the subject, but nothing apparently came from the suggestion

Willard Fiske was called in 1868 to a professorship in Cornell University and the introduction to his collected writings states that "among the courses which he conducted [there] was one on journalism, which contained material of much practical value." [57]

Somewhat later President R. E. Lee of Washington College submitted, on behalf of the faculty, to the board of trustees, certain recommendations looking to the establishment of fifty scholarships for young men proposing to make printing or journalism their profession. The catalogue for the year ending June, 1869, announced the general plan,[58] and a circular letter concern-

[56] *The Independent*, June 9, 1864, vol. 16. The author is unknown; the letter is reprinted in *The Independent*, June 15, 1914, 78: 481–483.

[57] H. S. White, *ed., Memorials of Willard Fiske*, I, xiv.

[58] "The Board of Trustees have authorized the Faculty to appoint to Scholarships a number of young men intending to make practical printing and journalism their business in life. These Scholars are to be free from tuition and college fees, on condition that when required by the Faculty they shall perform such disciplinary duties as may be assigned them in a printing office, or in other positions in the line of their profession, for a time equal to one hour in each working day."—*Catalogue of Washington College, 1869.*

The resolutions as presented by the faculty to the board of trustees have

ing it was issued August 19, 1869. "This curious document" stated that candidates must be over fifteen years old, and of unimpeachable character. The scholarships were to be held two years, were to include tuition and all college charges, and each holder was to "labor one hour per day in the line of his profession." The typographical unions in the Southern States were asked to nominate the candidates, but the request evoked little response "and the newspapers became facetious over a programme which was inherently absurd. . . . The practical journalists, who had worked their own way upward by diligent application, knew the impossibility of learning the lessons of Journalism within the walls of a collegiate institution." [59]

But at least one practical journalist thought he knew otherwise and Whitelaw Reid in an address before the faculty and students of New York University, April 4, 1872, urged preparation for journalism as the most effective means of raising the standard of the profession.[60]

For the most part the idea was received by the press itself with scant favor if not with positive derision,—there was something of the feeling that the journalist, like the poet, is born, not made and "that if a higher power does not endow him with [the necessary qualities] he may apply himself in vain in an effort to acquire them." But no school of journalism ever dreamed of educating as journalists those who have no aptitude for the profession,—artists do not apply for admission to schools of medicine, or lawyers seek training in schools of engineering. This conventional objection, however, long carried weight and it was not until 1893 that the first courses in journalism were given in this country,[61] while in 1894, courses in journalism were given at the University of Lille and in 1895 a course of lectures on the "History of the Press and Journalism in Germany" was given at

recently been reprinted by Washington and Lee University, *Bulletin*, Vol. XX, No. 8, April 15, 1921.

It is hoped to re-establish the school in September, 1923.—Letter from President Henry Louis Smith, April 20, 1922.

[59] A. Maverick, *Henry J. Raymond and the New York Times for Thirty Years*, pp. 355–356.

[60] "Journalism as a Career," *American and English Studies*, II, 193–227.

[61] J. M. Lee, *Instruction in Journalism in Institutions of Higher Education*, pp. 10–11.

the University of Heidelberg,—the first of the kind ever delivered in any German university.[62] The work at Lille, it is interesting to note, dealt with the press rather more than with the technical side of journalism and included courses on the great journalists of England, the press laws of France, and the history of the French press, including also the practical duties of a journalist. The comment of a French writer was: "The Americans have established a school for journalists—the thing is possible with their conception of a journal— . . . Days, Months and Years, however, will pass before this dream materializes [in France]." [63]

But a great cosmopolitan journalist had already gone far beyond anything as yet suggested in America in advocating a national school of journalism in every country. De Blowitz outlined a long and extensive course for the training of journalists in the highest sense of the word,—not simply seekers after news, but men with breadth of view and depth of knowledge. He then urged the establishment in every capital of a paper to be called *The Judge* and a federation of all national schools of journalism. "It would in the end," he says, "succeed in forming, with the help of *The Judge* in other countries, a universal justice, to redress all errors, to chastise bad faith, to make public opinion more wholesome and sane, and by the high and impartial severity of its judgments, it would force those who enjoy the terrible and responsible honour of holding the pen, to remember their duty as well as their interest, and to bow before an enlightened public opinion, at last protected against the poison which was formerly poured out for it." [64]

British writers have been less enthusiastic both as to the theoretical importance and the practical value of such schools. Goldwin Smith in writing of the proposal to found a college for the training of journalists finds it "doubtful whether the pro-

[62] E. P. Oberholtzer, "Courses in Politics and Journalism at Lille," *Annals of the American Academy of Political and Social Science*, September, 1896, 8: (342)–(349).

One course of six lectures was given by M. E. Tavernier on "The Duties and Practice of Journalism." These lectures, probably somewhat extended, have been published under the title *Du Journalisme*, 1902.

[63] *Ib.*, p. (347).

[64] H. de Blowitz, "Journalism as a Profession," *Contemporary Review*, January, 1893, 63: 37–46.

posal is feasible." [65] Others have shown a mild interest in the establishment of such courses in London and in the provincial universities, while disapproving of them for Oxford and Cambridge. [66] The wishes of both circles were probably met when an independent school of journalism was opened in London in 1921 under the patronage of an impressive list of titled journalists and the personal directorship of Max Pemberton.

But in spite of scepticism and even ridicule, courses in journalism have been established and have increased with astonishing rapidity both in numbers and in attendance. [67] A great school of journalism has been founded through the benefaction of a prominent editor, [68] students trained in such schools are found in many newspaper offices, annual conferences are held by those giving instruction in journalism and attended by men and women from every section of the country, and the far-reaching results of these conferences is suggested in the numerous volumes now coming from the press. Achievement has not only silenced doubt, but it has created enthusiasm for the professional aspects of journalism.

[65] Letter to the President of the Press Club, Toronto, October 10, 1904, *Goldwin Smith's Correspondence*, pp. 418–421.

[66] J. C. Collins, "The Universities and a School of Journalism," *Nineteenth Century and After*, February, 1908, 63: 327–340.

The general conventional opposition to such schools is expressed by "A Journalist" in *Bohemian Days in Fleet Street*, pp. 18–19.

[67] In 1915, courses in various phases of journalism were given in forty-one universities and colleges and several maintained schools of journalism. Talcott Williams, *World Almanac*, 1916, p. 566.

In 1918, the secretary of the American Association of Teachers of Journalism, gave lists of eighty-six institutions offering work of some character in journalism.—J. M. Lee, *Instruction in Journalism in Institutions of Higher Education*, pp. 15–16.

In view of this success, it is interesting to read the strictures passed on the idea in 1888 by C. A. Dana, in *The Art of Newspaper Making*, pp. 12–18, and H. White, "The School of Journalism," *North American Review*, January, 1904, 178: 25–32.

[68] The School of Journalism in Columbia University on the Pulitzer Foundation opened in September, 1912, with an endowment of $1,000,000. See Talcott Williams, "The School of Journalism," *Columbia University Quarterly*, June, 1912, 14: 235–248, and his annual reports as Director of the School of Journalism; also, "Teaching Journalism in a Great City," *The Independent*, August 7, 1913, 75: 313–315.

The reasons that led to the establishment of the School are fully stated and the questions and objections of doubters and opponents are answered by Joseph Pulitzer, "The College of Journalism in Columbia University," *North American Review*, May, 1904, 178: 640–680. See also J. L. Heaton, *The Story of a Page*, pp. 292–293.

But the school of journalism, as it has thus far been developed, has emphasized the process of producing a newspaper, and it has therefore taught the technical side of collecting news, and of presenting it in "crisp," "breezy," "snappy" form and its curriculum therefore has as yet apparently left something still to be desired.[69] There is little indication in it of a desire to look beyond the immediate effect that the "story" is expected to have on the reader, and to weigh the evidence in regard to the reliability of the material collected. A wide acquaintance with the facts of history is regarded as essential for the journalist, but apparently there is little appreciation of the importance of an acquaintance with historical method. The value of economic study is conceded, but for the most part the school of journalism seems contented with conventional economic theories past and present and makes little effort to show their inadequacy in the present industrial order. Existing political and social institutions are accepted, but without investigation as to their sufficiency in time of need. The school of journalism has as yet shown more interest in the technical process of producing a newspaper than it has in the press as a resultant of this process and it has thus seemed to fall short of the success possible to it. It has helped to standardize forms and processes, and it has made definite contributions to journalism, but its contributions to the press have been slight. It has not been an investigator, its foundations have seemed insecure, and as yet it has occupied but a half-way house.

Books dealing with the various parts of journalism—the editorial, the advertisement, the work of the reporter—are coming from the press in ever increasing numbers, but the appeal made in them all is to the present and they deal only with the mechanism of journalism. In this intensity of its concern with the present, the school of journalism might well take counsel of the modern writers of advertisements who recognize the strength of the appeal to the past,—writers who have apparently been trained for their work through their studies in psychology rather than in schools of journalism.

The general effect of this concentration on the present is an

[69] See Hammond Lamont, "The Curriculum of the School of Journalism," *Educational Review*, November, 1903, 26: 325–331.

apparent self-consciousness and a straining after effect that is, however, less noticeable than it would otherwise be since such writing is assimilated by the newspaper with other material. The old motto of *Niles' Register*,—The Past—the Present—for the Future,—must become that of the school of journalism if it is to make an enduring improvement in the authoritativeness of the press.

An explanation of this lack of complete success has been offered by a recent writer who protests against all schools of journalism on the ground that their professorships are filled with "out-dated newspaper men capable by the old standards and traditions, but more or less completely out of tune with the aggressive, resourceful methods which prevail in metropolitan offices" and that they "are recruited from the ranks of editorial wool-gatherers instead of reportorial news-gatherers." [70] This generalization will not stand the test of an examination into its fidelity to fact, but even were it otherwise, it would be an inadequate explanation of the short-comings of the school of journalism as it has thus far been developed. Its imperfections are not superficial, but deep-seated, its range of vision has been short, it has suffered from its incorporation into a scheme of education where education and information have been considered synonymous, and the key to its short-comings is found in its appropriate name,—school of journalism. To the extent that it has brought together students and instructors actuated by a common desire to standardize and then to raise the ordinary standards of journalism, it has made already a contribution to the authoritativeness of the press. Its usefulness will be still further increased when it extends its boundaries and incorporates among its activities more serious investigation into the history of the press, an application of methods of work used in other fields, considers more completely the press as the resultant product of its journalistic activities, and develops from its present immature curiosity the spirit of intellectual research.

The endowed newspaper has often been urged as a corrective of the defects found in the press, and such endowment would be in harmony with the tendencies of the day. Endowments have

[70] *Dial*, September 20, 1919, 67: 259.

been made not only for the church, for school and college, for philanthropy of every form and description, for research in scientific and social fields, but even hotels and private individuals have been endowed. An endowed newspaper, many have believed, would be independent of subscription lists, of advertisers, of party politics, and of all the millstones that hang on the neck of the newspaper. Relieved of the necessity of printing only "what will sell," of suppressing what would discredit its advertisers, of currying favor with local magnates and party managers, the endowed newspaper would seem to occupy the serene heights from which it could authoritatively survey society.

But while the endowed newspaper has been long, widely, and persistently advocated, there has been no consensus of opinion as to the nature of the endowed newspaper and there has been much confusion in regard to what such a paper really means.

Newspapers have been classed, as regards ownership, under the three heads of proprietary or self-supported, endowed or subsidized, and state-supported.[71] Under endowed or subsidized newspapers and journals are classed many scientific and scholarly periodicals published at the expense of learned societies. But while these give the reports of scientific and technical discoveries, they give no news in the usual acceptance of the term and can not in any sense be considered newspapers. Others are given extra support by those interested in the special cause the paper was founded to promote, but such papers are thus not newspapers, but rather organs of a propaganda, of a trade, or of a single idea, and often are excellent illustrations of missionary zeal in the cause of Church or State.[72]

"A very urgent necessity—the reform of the newspaper press," had appealed to Goldwin Smith and he wrote to Gladstone, May 2, 1855, proposing "a new Joint Stock Newspaper." "It should

[71] E. E. Slosson, "The Possibility of a University Newspaper," *The Independent*, February 15, 1912, 72: 351–359.

[72] *The Northern Chronicle* was started in Inverness in January, 1881, by shareholders who "looked upon the money they put into the concern as money dedicated to the purpose of giving the Highlands one organ of Conservative opinion in affairs of State and Church," and they would have been satisfied if it simply paid its own working expenses. Incidentally, its editor states, it paid five per cent. on the investment.—D. Campbell, *Reminiscences and Reflections of an Octogenarian Highlander*, pp. 529–531.

have," he says, "a capital sufficient to contend with advantage against any private newspaper, and this capital should be raised in £5 shares, which should all be paid up at once, which would give at once a large circulation and a large advertising medium."[73] But a joint stock company, operating a newspaper, and looking to profits, can not be considered as providing an endowed newspaper and as safe-guarding the public from the control of its policy by the business administration. It seems questionable whether an endowed newspaper in the true sense of the word has ever existed,—in the opinion of some, "the endowed newspaper is an impossibility," and "endowment of brains rather than of money is what is needed."[74]

This lack of enthusiastic support of the idea of an endowed press must be in part explained by the inherent difficulties in the way of carrying it out. In spite of its name, the function of the newspaper "to give the news" is only a temporary one. Its permanent function, perhaps not yet fully recognized by the press itself, is to record contemporary conditions. Any endowed institution seems predestined to be conservative rather than progressive and an endowed newspaper would almost inevitably fail to record progressive movements,—that its failure to do so would be unconscious on its part does not alter the probability. Every newspaper is as truly published for a definite constituency as is a technical trade journal[75] and an endowed newspaper, it may reasonably be assumed, would quickly take on protective coloring. It would not necessarily lessen the inaccuracies and ignorance

[73] *Goldwin Smith's Correspondence*, collected by A. Haultain, pp. 7–9. Apparently nothing resulted from this earliest proposal.
[74] W. M. Payne, "An Endowed Newspaper," *Little Leaders*, pp. 178–185. The endowed newspaper has been advocated by C. H. Levermore, "A Plea for Endowed Newspapers," *Andover Review*, November, 1889, 12: 485–490; W. H. H. Murray, "An Endowed Press," *Arena*, October, 1890, 2: 553–559; "An Endowed Newspaper," *Dial*, January 16, 1893, 14: 35–37; Hamilton Holt, *Commercialism and Journalism*, pp. 99–101, and "A Plan for an Endowed Journal," address before the First National Newspaper Conference, Madison, Wisconsin, August 1, 1912; E. A. Ross, "The Suppression of Important News," *Atlantic Monthly*, March, 1910, 105: 303–311. —Articles opposed to it are, F. H. Page, "Endowments for Newspapers: A Rejoinder," *Andover Review*, January, 1890, 13: 25–31; W. P. Hamilton, "The Case for the Newspapers," *Atlantic Monthly*, May, 1910, 105: 646–654.
[75] C. M. Harger, "The Country Editor of To-day," *Atlantic Monthly*, January, 1907, 99: 89–96.

that are so largely responsible for the unauthoritativeness of the press, it would be responsive to the demands of the community where it was published and be as susceptible as is the unendowed press to conditions that militate against its prosperity, such as industrial methods and disease. Inspiring as is the idea of an endowed press that does not cater to the public, that is not compelled to print "what will sell," that can speak to the public as it ought to be spoken to, rather than as it wishes to be spoken to, its realization seems inherently improbable. Since it has not as yet been realized, it is impossible to speak of it except in terms of the subjunctive.

Whether the endowed press would in and of itself be more authoritative than the present proprietary press must therefore remain a purely academic question. It seems clear that less pressure for it is exerted to-day than formerly,—an indication that the adverse conditions it was relied on to redress have been alleviated through other means. It is also evident that while schools of journalism have everywhere succeeded in spite of the early opposition to the idea, the endowed newspaper has made little or no headway. Had there been at any time a well-grounded belief in the efficacy of the endowed press as a panacea for the admitted evils of the press, such a press would have been established.

State supported newspapers have in turn been urged as a means of avoiding the evils of a proprietary press. But the periodicals already published under government auspices [76] can not always be given a clean bill of health. Some of these do not technically give news, but others, like the *Congressional Record*, that ostensibly give official records and are, therefore, presumably authoritative, are in reality open to grave doubt on that score. "Leave to print" has long been an open scandal in connection with the official report of the deliberations of Congress, and the unofficial *Searchlight*, published by the National Voters' League, has given a needed corrective in listing month by month under the caption "Speechless Speeches" the undelivered speeches printed in the *Congressional Record*.

[76] E. E. Slosson gives the number published in 1912 as thirty-nine. It has been impossible to ascertain the exact number for which the government stood sponsor during the recent war.

The municipal papers that have recorded the business transactions of various cities apparently have been free from many of the temptations that beset the reports of the national legislative body, but they can be considered "endowed" only in the sense that they are considered a part of current municipal expenditures.

Newspapers published under or by any form of governmental [77] authority can not be deemed to obviate the errors found in the proprietary press to any greater extent than can a regularly endowed press.

The attempt has been made to show that the material of the newspaper, as regards its authoritativeness, may be classed under three heads,—the first class carries with it an absolute guarantee of its reliability, the second class carries with it only a partial but a fairly presumptive guarantee of its trustworthiness, the third class carries with it no guarantee of its reliability. This is the class where the largest number of errors are found, but it is also the class where the errors are presumably of least importance. It seems reasonable, therefore, to connect the source of errors in the press with the causes giving rise to them and to apply a remedy to suit the case. If many errors found in the press spring from inaccuracy, ignorance, lack of observation, and similar causes, they must be explained by the inadequacy of the reporter, and the remedy would seem to lie in securing reporters who have had better training, giving them greater responsibility, and holding them to higher standards. In so far as errors come from sensationalism, the cause may be found in the poor taste of the newspaper-reading public, and the remedy may lie in educating the taste of the public through offering them newspapers of improved character. Where errors have their source in premature release of copy, in untimely haste to secure news, or in office difficulties, they may be explained by a defective organization of the newspaper staff and the remedy may be found in a re-organization of both the editorial and the business side of the newspaper. If errors come through a censorship imposed on the press by authority in any form, it is authority that must be so re-constituted as to make possible complete freedom of the press.

[77] C. R. Woodruff, "Municipal Newspapers," *The Survey*, August 19, 1911, 26: 720–723.

These are but slight intimations that, in homely phrase, the shoe must fit the foot. If the causes for such elements of unauthoritativeness as are now found in the press can be fairly well located, it seems reasonable to believe that they may be removed by applying a remedy to suit the case. Granting freedom of the press to a previously shackled press would seem to hold out little hope for improving the work of careless reporters. The establishment of schools of journalism would seem an ineffective way of coping with office mismanagement. Campaigns for honest advertising do much to raise the ethical standards of the press, but they do not necessarily improve the intellectual standards of newspaper readers. The endowed newspaper would not in and of itself remove the evils arising from press competition. All blanket arraignments of the press are arrows sped at a venture. All panaceas applied to the press are as futile as are the patent medicines denounced in its columns.

The development of the periodical press has everywhere partly caused, partly resulted from, a change in the mental attitude of its readers. To the universal demand for news has been added the demand on the part of a limited but constantly increasing number of readers that news must be authoritative. The historian in his use of the press must therefore recognize the differences in the press that have resulted from its own evolution. If the demand for news has apparently been constant from the beginning of time, the demand that what is presented as news shall be authoritative has had an ever-widening angle. Many of the questionable characteristics of the press are disappearing and it seems possible to accept the verdict of Bliss Perry when he says, "No one can watch the development of our current journalism without becoming aware that this sense of responsibility to the public is raising the whole level of the American press." In the final analysis, it is not what direct information the newspaper gives, but what the newspaper *is*, that determines its authoritativeness in the eyes of the historian.

CHAPTER XVII

HOW FAR CAN THE PAST BE RECONSTRUCTED FROM THE PRESS?

"Avant que ce siècle soit fermé, le journalisme sera toute la presse, toute la pensée humaine. Depuis cette multiplication prodigieuse que l'art a donnée à la parole, multiplication que se multipliera mille fois encore, l'humanité écrira son livre jour par jour, heure par heure, page par page; la pensée se répandra dans le monde avec la rapidité de la lumière; aussitôt conçue, aussitôt écrite, aussitôt entendue aux extrémités de la terre, elle courra d'un pôle à l'autre, subite, instanée, brûlante encore de la chaleur de l'âme qui l'aura fait éclore; ce sera le règne du verbe humain dans toute sa plénitude; elle n'aura pas le temps de mûrir, de s'accumuler sous la forme de livre; le livre arriverait trop tard: le seul livre possible dès aujourd'hui, c'est un journal." —*Lamartine, 1831.*

"I look upon the common intelligence in our public papers with the long train of advertisements annexed to it, as the best account of the present domestic state of England, that can possibly be compiled: nor do I know any thing, which would give posterity so clear an idea of the taste and morals of the present age, as a bundle of our daily papers."—*The Connoisseur, 1850.*

"If I desired to leave to remote posterity some memorial of existing British civilization, I would prefer, not our docks, not our railways, not our public buildings, not even the palace in which we now hold our sittings; I would prefer a file of *The Times* newspaper."—*Edward Bulwer-Lytton, 1855.*

"I do not think there will be any novels or romances, at all events in volume form, in fifty or a hundred years from now. They will be supplanted altogether by the daily newspaper. . . . As historic records the world will file its newspapers. Newspaper writers have learned to color every-day events so well that to read them will give posterity a truer picture than the historic or descriptive novel could do."—*Jules Verne, 1902.*

"The man who writes about himself and his own time is the only man who writes about all people and about all time."—*G. B. Shaw, 1918.*

THE attempt has been made to show to what extent the press can be deemed authoritative, but essential as is authoritativeness

in all material used by the historian, other considerations must
enter in if the periodical press is to be used as historical material.
Nothing is more persistently urged on the press in season and out
of season than the injunction to "tell the facts," but the belief
that the press can not be used to reconstruct the past because of
its manifold inaccuracies, is not well founded. It is true that the
press may claim accuracy for itself, but in the very nature of
things it is and must be inaccurate. But it must be remembered
that it is possible to make a fetish of accuracy. Literal accuracy,
as has been seen in the case of verbatim official reports, interviews,
and illustrations, may often be misleading and in essence un-
truthful; a specious accuracy is perfectly compatible with a
genuine fundamental misconception of an existing situation and
with ignorance of the real truth. On the other hand, it is perfectly
possible for an inaccurate report to be fundamentally authoritative. The press does for the most part give the facts faithfully
and well, as has been indicated in the numerous direct and indirect guarantees, voluntary and compulsory, given in, by, and
for the press. But for the purposes of the historian something
more is needed. Edward Dicey points out that if "a foreigner
were to read the *Times*, and half a dozen other English newspapers,
daily for years, his knowledge of English life and politics would
be extremely incomplete and erroneous, unless he had actually
lived enough in England to have acquired what may be called
the key to the English press," and while the "Hieroglyphics
contain the history of Egypt . . . to understand the history,
you must be able to read the characters." [1] It is not sufficient "to
tell the facts,"—all the facts may be accurately and truthfully
told in regard to any event and yet the account of it may give
little understanding of its real meaning,—the mind of the seer,
the poet, the philosopher is needed to interpret these facts, for
without interpretation they are but dry bones. This power of
interpretation may come to a periodical through the force of
a single dominating character, or it may come through the
absolute suppression of all personalities to such an extent that
the resulting paper is altogether impersonal, but through what-

[1] Edward Dicey, "The American Press," *Six Months in the Federal States*,
I, 27–50.

ever channel it comes, it must be the breath of life that vivifies the press. This does not mean that the editor, the reporter, and the correspondent must express their personal opinions on all subjects brought forward in the press,—far from it. It does mean that the newspaper as a whole must itself so understand and so convey to its readers a sense of relationships, so respect values and relative proportions, and so discern the meaning of the times that its value will be rendered permanent. In spite of its name, the chief function of the newspaper is not to give the news, it is not even exclusively to reflect public opinion,—important as this is,—but it is to record all contemporaneous human interests, activities, and conditions and thus to serve the future. What the historian wishes from the newspaper is not news,—that always ultimately comes to him from other sources,—but a picture of contemporary life.

But not only must the newspaper interpret the events that it consciously reports,—it must in its turn be interpreted by those who use it in a reconstruction of the past. It must be evident that not all of the parts of a newspaper are of equal value to the historian, or will be of equal value,—the proportion shifts from year to year, even in the same paper; the country weekly has one value in a reconstruction of the past, a quite different value is attached to the metropolitan daily. Much that passes as news and fills the foreground of the present will later on lapse into obscurity and be of no service whatever to the historian. The reader on his part must have the seeing eye and the understanding mind.

The parts of the press that are most obviously of immediate service in reconstructing the past are the editorial, the illustration and the advertisement.

The editorial serves in a measure to reconstruct current opinion, yet its value is somewhat lessened by the tendency of some editors "to keep an ear to the ground," a tendency that must in part vitiate the value of editorials on political questions and other mooted subjects, like preparedness. Lamartine spoke of the scum that rises to the surface when the nation boils and the editorial sometimes reflects the superficial rather than fundamental public opinion. But no part of the press has been so frequently reprinted as has the editorial column. Various collections selected from leading London papers "present in a new light a series of occurrences that have in their day been subjects of public recognition and journalistic record," [2] and they thus give an almost complete collection of material for the study of certain phases of nineteenth century English history. The editorials in American newspapers while perhaps less significant must still be reckoned with by the historian. James Ford Rhodes has written, "I can emphatically say that if you want to penetrate into the thoughts, feelings, and grounds of decision of the 1,866,000 men who voted for Lincoln in 1860, you should study the New York weekly *Tribune* . . . it was the greatest single journalistic influence in 1854 with a circulation of 112,000." And again he writes, "The story of the secession movement of November and December, 1860, can not be told with correctness and life without frequent references to the *Charleston Mercury* and the *Charleston Courier*. The *Mercury* especially was an index of opinion and so vivid is its daily chronicle of events that the historian is able to put himself in the place of those ardent South Carolinians and understand their point of view." [3]

The illustration is the most conspicuous feature of the press that suggests present or past conditions and it is of special value as an interpretative record. The cartoon in particular through its insight into the past interprets the present for the future; the cartoonist and the historian are thus kindred spirits. Since the newspaper in its illustrations tends to the form of the caricature, the cartoon, and the photograph, it has as a rule greater value for the historian than have the illustrations of the magazines that, outside of the advertising pages, tend to the purely ornamental.

One of the greatest values of the illustration to the historian is its comparative freedom from authority. In political cartoons especially, much is tolerated and even welcomed that would probably not be permitted in the text. *Punch* has more than once shown weak spots in the methods of canvassing at a general election and it has thus been an ally on the side of purity of elections. The cartoon in Germany has seemed to be under less

[2] H. F. Bussey, *Sixty Years of Journalism*, Preface.
[3] "Newspapers as Historical Sources," *Atlantic Monthly*, May, 1909, 103: 650–657.

restriction than have other parts of the press. In *Bradley's Cartoons* there is much interpretation of the widespread aversion to war and of the conviction that war was futile as a solvent of the world's troubles. The same freedom of expression in other parts of the press would at least have been deemed "indiscreet." It has been said that "the cartoon thrives best in the fertile soil of democracy" and this may perhaps be accepted even in the face of the great uncertainty as to what democracy really is and whether it has anywhere ever been achieved. The illustration certainly often guides rather than merely reflects public opinion and it does it through the power of interpretation that gives it a prophetic character.

If, as has been seen, it seems possible to reconstruct from the pages of *Punch* the attitude of at least a part of England towards America during the Civil War,[4] the rule works both ways and *Harper's Weekly* well indicates the reciprocal feeling of America towards England. The press discloses little effort made in either country to remove prejudice and to arrive at a better mutual understanding. If *Punch* during the recent war showed an impatience with America for not earlier entering the war, but threw the blame of it on the president, *Life* showed America and England smoking the pipe of peace.

The press has sometimes been accused of being "anti-social" in its tendencies and influence because readers on trains and trolleys are absorbed in their newspapers and do not converse with their neighbors. But it is rather to be said that the newspaper enlarges the social circle and that readers thousands of miles apart are by the newspaper brought into oneness of mind or ranged in opposing columns far more effectively than they would be through the chance conversation or the monologuing of those in their immediate physical proximity.

It is the illustration in particular that enlarges the social circle and that shows everywhere the tendency towards luxury,— views of spacious homes, summer residences, city hotels; distant countries reached by luxurious railway trains and steamer service;

[4] Two members of the *Punch* staff have shown the still more extensive use that may be made of *Punch* in reconstructing the past. See F. C. Burnand and A. à Beckett, "History in Punch," *Fortnightly Review*, July, December, 1886, n. s. 40: 49–67, 737–752, April, 1887, 41: 546–557.

the automobile in infinite variety, elaborate clothing, household equipment,—a thousand and one illustrations in the daily press and in weekly and monthly periodicals all show prosperity and the ability on the part of many to gratify every desire, whim, or caprice. These are all the unconscious representations of the life of the wealthy, illustrated through the appeals of business houses for the patronage of the rich. If "we make the thing we buy," the illustration shows infallibly the enormous production of everything that contributes to a life of ease on the part of some members of society. It shows with equal clearness the development of the similar appeal made by all transportation companies, —speed, comfort, luxury, amusements, strange sights, unusual scenery, opportunities for business, "safety first," politeness and consideration for both employees and passengers. The limousine in its turn is always illustrated in appropriate surroundings.

But just as unerringly the illustration shows the opposite extreme. This, however, it does consciously,—no one seeks through illustration the patronage of tenement-house dwellers. The illustration is used, not to sell to those who can not buy, but to show overcrowding of tenements, lack of space, air, and light, the unwarranted use of fire escapes, unsanitary conditions in passage-ways, areas, and back yards, and violations of decency, order, and law. The illustration becomes a conscious co-operator with the forces in every community that make for righteousness through its service in showing negatively undesirable, positively objectionable conditions of life. The illustration presses upwards into the homes of the rich to seek their patronage, but it also presses downwards into the homes of the poor to show to the rich conditions they have it in their power in part to relieve and prevent. Both extremes are abnormal, the illustration faithfully depicts each class, but each from opposite motives.

The great middle class is more normal in its conditions and its interests and these the illustration also faithfully represents. It is interested in time-saving inventions, in ready-made clothing, in prepared foods, in victrolas and piano-players, in bicycles and runabouts,—all of these interests are standardized and represented through the illustration.

But the illustration shows far more than passive conditions of living,—it shows the enormous development of new interests, the changing relationships between different elements in society, the quickening of the social conscience, and the widening sense of responsibility for all conditions that can be improved. New interests are seen in the illustrations of baseball crowds, college "bowls," golf links, open-air theaters, folk dances, playgrounds, and all conditions that show the development of out-of-door life and wholesome recreation. With equal clearness the illustration shows the dividing line between those who take their amusements vicariously, as in the views of opera houses with capacity audiences, and those who find their recreations in active participation with others in community singing and in other forms of collective activity.

But with this somewhat superficial jolting of society out of its traditional grooves through the development of new interests, the parallel illustration shows how other conditions move with glacier slowness towards perfectibility. The illustrator who satirizes modern society shows how universal and apparently fundamental are certain human characteristics; the braggart, the snob, the tuft hunter, the flunkey, the poseur, the social climber, the miser, the spendthrift, the slacker in peace as well as in war, know neither time nor country. Is it strange that this form of social satire has its complement in the illustrations that everywhere show the prevailing social and industrial unrest?[5]

The prevailing feeling, often however contradicted, that the relative position of children in society has changed, finds confirmation in the illustration. Once inconspicuous in the illustration, represented as dressed like their elders, evidently restrained in their actions, the newspaper now gives children their own illustrated pages, illustrates their own special fashions in dress, in toys, in amusements, in books; it represents the part they take in fashionable society, and shows them everywhere in the limelight.[6]

[5] The *Survey*, July 4, 1914, has an account of Michael Biro, the Hungarian cartoonist of social unrest. With change of names, this form of illustration is well-nigh universal.

The *Liberator*, 1918–1922, has many cartoons of this character.

[6] The illustrations of fifty, or even of ten years ago probably show nothing comparable to the exploitation of a child of ten in the collection of money for a battleship.

FETRIDGE AND COMPANY'S PERIODICAL ARCADE

That this is the woman's age the illustration unerringly shows. The early illustration did not represent women outside of the fashion magazine or ballroom and society scenes. To-day it shows her engaged in every form of professional, business, and industrial activity; in all enterprises for the promotion of public welfare; taking a prominent part in out-door sports and recreations; putting her housekeeping on a scientific basis; gaining her training for every occupation through colleges, universities, technical, and professional schools.

The illustration shows the changes in fashions not only in clothing and in architecture, but in the accessories of life. The large dog once illustrated as guarding the lonely farm house, or drawing a cart for village children, has been supplanted on the farm by the telephone and in the village by the bicycle; in the restricted space of the city apartment he has become a toy and plaything,—the illustration shows the fashionable breed of dog of each generation, a fashion changing not simply with whim and caprice but necessitated by changes in manner of living.[7] And it is the illustration again that reconstructs the services rendered by the dog in time of war where he is trained to act as scout and rescuer.

The tendency towards specialization is clearly seen in the illustration,—specialization not only in all industrial and educational lines, but even in the smaller matters of every day life. The jeweller in the advertising columns illustrates a dozen varieties of forks, of knives, of spoons; the department store illustrates a score of different articles of china and silver; the housekeepers' column illustrates their use and shows the development of an elaborate table service with special dishes for each particular article of food.[8]

The illustration also shows the changes that have come in the temper of the public mind, the effect of the interest in psychology,

---

[7] Suggested by E. Coatsworth.—An incidental confirmation is seen in the names given dogs,—Rover, Fido, and Sport are no longer appropriate and such names disappear in favor of fancy names or those taken from popular personages.

[8] The advertisements of beef extracts illustrate the bouillon cup; of teas, coffees, and of chocolate preparations the different varieties of cups used with each. Thus through the illustration every person may enter every social circle.

and the widening of the circle of interest from the individual to the community, while the individual becomes concrete. Illustrations of games and of athletic contests are now from photographs that show the whole event, both players and spectators; individual athletes are shown rather than drawings of any man running, or playing ball, or with wings on his feet; the symbolic and the conventional has changed to the specific and the individual illustration, while the individual is shown in relation to a larger whole.[9] A single periodical like *Life* shows within the range of a few years the decline in the use of fabulous and prehistoric animals and the use made of representations of the devil.[10]

The illustration in its own character shows the cleavage between those to whom an appeal is made by the crude humor of the comic supplement and the sporting page and those attracted by artistic effects both of process and of scene. Thus the illustration shows the change in fashions of humor as unerringly as it records the changes of fashion in material things.

The illustration reflects the prevailing interest in all questions of sanitation and of public health. It shows the plans and the interior arrangement of hospitals, the uniform of surgeons, physicians,and trained nurses,and it spreads far and wide specific knowledge of sanitary conditions.

The illustration serves the investigator in disclosing the conditions of tenement house life where piecework is done, in showing the peculiar features of casual occupations like those of berry-picking and the canning industries, in making known the effects of overwork, of child labor, and of occupational diseases.

The illustration may also serve the cause of justice through enabling the officers of the law to detect and to identify those who have violated the law. The snapshot may have great value in the courts. Often it is so clear that no person could prove an

[9] Suggested by A. Rogers.

[10] Early magazines show initial and marginal decorations of dragons, sea serpents, griffins, and various grotesque animals. *Life* in 1901 shows a mermaid as a collector of water rents, the submarine is an octopus, the devil tortures the beef trust,while later the trusts are represented as a dragon about to devour liberty. In 1905 the devil in Hades caricatures modern society; by 1909 the fabulous animals disappear and the humorous devil appears; in 1915 the devil is apparently first represented in the character of a particular person.—Suggested by M. K. Brown.

alibi if represented by the camera as forming one of a group of strikers, or taking part in mob violence, or disturbing the peace. It may show incontestably that many of the participants in strike riots have been mere boys, presumably encouraged by their elders to take part in them.[11] The illustration is thus of service not only in reconstructing the past but also in reconstructing the present.

Nothing shows so conclusively as does a comparison of illustrations through a series of years the changes that have come in the way in which holidays are celebrated. The "safe and sane" Fourth of July with its appeal to a new nationalism and internationalism is far removed from the flamboyant, bombastic celebrations illustrated fifty years ago. The early illustrations of Christmas depict family scenes, later come the illustrations showing the results of late Christmas shopping, while to-day Christmas sales have become the conspicuous feature of December advertising. "What is Easter?" or what is the popular conception of the meaning of Easter, is perhaps better answered by the illustration and by the advertisement than it is by the Church, and sectional differences may be seen in the much greater influence of Easter on the illustrations and advertisements in the New York than in the Boston press.[12] Nothing more clearly indicates how widespread is the love of luxury to which particularly the advertisement appeals than do the advertisements of expensive clothing for men and women, gifts, jewelry, flowers, confectionery, restaurants, music, amusements, and excursions to all expensive resorts arranged for the Easter season. War, here as elsewhere, is utilized as a motive for commemorating the day,—"Easter services are to reflect loyalty," "we are mobilizing the serried ranks of Easter's army." To the child the differences between Christmas and Easter are specially illustrated in the gifts for them advertised at that time,—if one brings dolls and drums, the other brings chickens and rabbits.

The extent to which the illustrations of the press may be used to reconstruct the past may again be tested through using the press printed in a foreign language. Much may be gleaned in

[11] The New York *Times*, July 24, 1915.
[12] Suggested by J. C. Coburn.

regard to business, social, military, and political conditions in contemporary Greece through an examination of a file of Athenian newspapers by one not familiar with modern Greek. The language of the illustration, unless it is that of a not self-explanatory symbolism, is a universal one.[13]

The most significant change in illustration has been its introduction into advertising. An examination of the illustrated papers extending over a series of years shows the ingenuity used in combining the illustration with the advertisement and its increasing use in every field of business enterprise; both advertisement and illustration take advantage of current interests and profit by them. The current interest in athletics has been constantly utilized to illustrate and to sell innumerable articles. Twenty-five years ago the bicycle was illustrated, but only later was the figure of a woman introduced and then shown on the wheel; men and women were later shown riding wheels and the illustration used to advertise a brand of soap; men starting on a race or putting shot illustrate a patent medicine; a sailor in uniform advertises a smoking tobacco; a horse jumping a hurdle illustrates a camera advertisement and is one of the first illustrated advertisements to use the photograph itself; the automobile appears, but without occupants; later, the automobile appears with women seated in it, and still later, with a golf course in the background, with picnic parties in the foreground, with parties of elegantly dressed women appearing from palatial residences, all, not simply to advertise automobiles and their accessories, but to advertise quite different articles.[14] But not only is the interest in athletics utilized to advertise and to push the sale of articles that may be but remotely connected with them, but the prevailing interest in athletics and sports of every

[13] The extent to which social conditions can be reconstructed through the illustration is specially evident in the works of J. Grand-Carteret, *Les Mœurs et la Caricature en Allemagne en Autriche en Suisse; Les Mœurs et la Caricature en France.* It must be noted, however, that illustration tends naturally to humor and caricature, and that it is often more difficult to find material for a reconstruction of simple, normal life.—See also G. Paston, "The Illustrated Magazine of the Georgian Period," *Side-Lights on the Georgian Period,* pp. 57–75.

[14] A special make of shoes is advertised through an illustration of a man wearing them and sitting in an automobile.

kind, in all their wide ramifications, can be completely reconstructed from the illustrated and the unillustrated advertisement.

The agile advertisement everywhere is in the van in anticipating new demands, in creating new interests, in realizing new conditions, and in being prepared to meet them. The prevailing weather and the climate of a particular section may be reconstructed from the advertisements of articles for sale adapted to every degree of temperature, atmospheric conditions of wind, moisture, dust, and even a knowledge of the state of the highways and of a particular road may be gained from noting the advertisements of articles offered for sale adapted to these conditions.

The object of the advertisements of a great department store is obviously to sell its merchandise, yet if the advertisements of a single such establishment are examined day by day throughout a year in a single metropolitan daily it will be found that they have done far more than set before possible customers the advantages of purchasing goods at this particular store. Quite incidentally and unconsciously they have narrated much of the history of the business, they have shown the extent of the business, the foreign and domestic markets from which and to which goods are shipped, the business methods employed, the spirit that actuates it, and its relations to both employees and patrons. It is possible to gain from such advertisements a wide knowledge of foreign and of American geography, as also of many of the facts of ancient, mediaeval and modern history and of current events; to become acquainted with the names of the great masters of all time in the fields of music, art, and literature and with the names of their chief works; to understand somewhat the nature of the industries, occupations and professions that occupy men; to gain an introduction into the social life and customs of the very rich, and to know the conditions of the average household; to realize the progress made for the householder and housekeeper in matters of sanitation and hygiene; to come into contact with the great problems of education; to acquire much information in regard to the natural resources of the country and many facts of natural history,—much is given in regard to weather and climatic conditions, different varieties of woods and their uses, fruit, flowers, vines, shrubs, trees, birds, animals, leather, and furs,—and finally to have an insight into the qualifications needed in the writers of advertisements in order to produce successful advertising.

How do these advertisements fail to reproduce the life of the time? The advertisement of the great department store in its appeal to persons of wealth and leisure looks out on a world where all is fair and smiling,—it has no hint of disaster, of hard times, low wages, lack of employment, poverty, sickness, misfortune, political struggles, tariff controversies; for it, crime, evil, and sin are non-existent; fire and flood, tornado and earthquake, the horrors of war pass unnoted.

Yet the advertisement records unerringly all of these conditions. Fire destroys a great building and within twenty-four hours advertisements referring to it appear. They concern insurance and safe deposit companies; fireproof buildings, vaults, cabinet safes, and floorings; metallic doors and interiors; automatic sprinklers; bonds covering burned securities; office rentals with immediate possession; offers of free rooms for limited periods; removal notices; night and day service for the furnishing of offices of those burned out; new addresses of former tenants asked; club privileges extended to the members of a club burned out, and library privileges offered those whose professional libraries have been destroyed.

Do the advertisements of great establishments ignore strikes and all labor troubles? The advertisements of others lay bare their difficulties and disclose their methods of dealing with strikes. The advertisements "we break strikes" show the frequency of strikes, the necessity felt of breaking strikes promptly, the inability to cope with a strike situation unaided, the hostile attitude towards trade unions, violence attending strikes, the attempt to establish the open shop, and the difficulty suggested of lodging and boarding imported workmen.[15]

Are men and women out of employment? The "want ad" columns answer the question,—"willing to work at anything," "unfortunate, without work, good worker," "well-educated man needs work," "carpenter, wants any kind of work," "man, 40,

[15] Suggested by G. L. Price.

former steamer steward, wants any kind of a job,"—so the list lengthens into column after column, day after day, throughout the year.

Why are men and women out of work? The "help wanted" column in part answers the question,—"thoroughly competent bookkeeper wanted," "experienced salesman, willing to go on the road," "ambitious man, not tired of life, can get permanent position," "hustlers only need apply," "office-boy, willing and ambitious," "best of references demanded," "applications considered only from sober men," "no boozers need apply," "applicant must dress well and have good personal appearance," "small capital needed,"—and so this list, too, goes on, suggesting in every line the difficulties employers have in securing the help of well-trained, competent, ambitious workers.

Is war menacing the world? All articles advertised for sale are urged on buyers with the statement that they are to be used in some way connected with the war,—sewing machines will make garments for soldiers, and piano-players will play martial music; "personals" are used to communicate with absent friends or to locate wounded relatives; [16] Kurt Schwarz in London advertises that he has changed his name to Curtis Black, while Schmidts become Smiths, and Müllers, Millers; "want ads" in English papers are printed in the French, Dutch, and Russian languages; newspapers offer to translate foreign advertisements into English, and the reverse; "situations wanted" become "situations needed," and they indicate that the loss of occupation is most felt at first in what the English call the middle class,—"stranded Englishman, expelled from Germany needs work;" innumerable sales are advertised of clothing, jewelry, furniture, automobiles, pianos, houses, and of pets of every description; firms advertise that they look for lost luggage, and others that they will discover the secret of making articles hitherto made in Germany; books are advertised describing the

[16] It was estimated that early in September, 1914, the *Petit Parisien* was printing advertisements to the amount of $4000 per week that were used by families separated by the war to get into communication with each other. Cable from Paris to New York *Times*, September 25, 1914.

Many advertisements for news of relatives lost in the war appeared in American papers.

countries at war, as are also maps, photographs, and plans of cities; advertisements call for cooks for the army and electricians for the navy.

The advocates of war urge that it develops courage, manliness, and all the cardinal virtues, but the advertisements of the press record quite different developments and they reflect the very worst traits in human nature,—every opportunity is improved to take advantage of the necessities of others, and every necessity is magnified in order to impose on the generosity of others; gifts of motor-cycles are solicited in order that the recipients may join the motor-cycle corps, and the gift of an aeroplane is desired; loans of harriers or beagles to be used by officers until ordered abroad are asked for; an agency announces to clergymen that it will supply them with sermons every week, "new, fresh, simple, and drawing lessons from the war;" "A Continental chaplain unable to return to his work on account of war would be grateful for temporary hospitality for Wife and Himself;" "Gentleman, Austrian by birth, but naturalized British subject since 1908, debarred through present war from use of his club (a leading West End Club) would like to join a club offering similar conveniences;" many bare-faced advertisements asking for personal gifts of all kinds are signed *Pro Patria*. Even more sordid conditions are recorded in the advertisements for the return of stolen goods and offers from legal owners to buy at full value stolen surveying instruments or other implements of a profession or trade. Numerous fortune tellers ply a lucrative trade in time of war, hedge lawyers offer their services on all "war questions," and "fences" seem immune in advertising columns.

But it is the advertising that also unconsciously reveals the very real sufferings and privations entailed by war. The Swiss boarding-schools for boys that advertise in Berlin papers and hold out as a special inducement for patronage "abundant food;" the photographers who furnish life-size photographs of those who have fallen; the compulsory auction sales of household goods; the small business for sale cheap because the husband is at the front; the insurance against explosion, bombardment, and riot, and life insurance without restriction or extra premiums,—a thousand and one similar advertisements from European papers indicate the genuine misery and sorrow that follow in the wake of war. They are in striking contrast to the light-heartedness of the advertisements in countries less immediately concerned with the war where deftness of phrase may veil the real meaning of war while using its language for commercial purposes.[17]

The press has everywhere been a potent witness to the transformation wrought through war in industrial society. The messages from the governors of twelve states calling on women to enter industrial and business service indicate a significant change from the somewhat recent time when the slogan was "woman's place is home."[18] Advertisements of fashionable hotels for waitresses to take the place of waiters whose services had been requisitioned by the government "for essential industry" have given an insight into important changes in the industrial world.[19]

Not less significant are the changes in social conditions recorded in the announcements of births, engagements, annulment of engagements, marriages, and deaths. During the war it was noticeable that into the notices of engagements and marriages there was incorporated much information in regard to the military affiliations of the contracting parties. The army rank of one was given in detail and the Red Cross or training camp activities of the other were mentioned; the distinguished lineage of both parties was noticed; details given in regard to probable delay in the wedding,—"Lieutenant X has been called to the colors;" the plans for the honeymoon and for future residence, as well as the occupation of the bridegroom, were stated, as was also the college of the young man, his college fraternities, his social clubs, and his business connections. Since the close of the war much of this information in regard to ancestry, previous life, and future plans has been retained.[20]

[17] "Present Arms! Our soft cuff shirts fit them all," "Health and Safety at Mountain Lakes," "Sever relations with inefficient accounting,"—the list could be indefinitely extended.

[18] New York *Tribune*, November 10, 1918.

[19] New York *Times*, October 29, 1918.

[20] Recent birth announcements have included much information in regard to the ancestry of the child and the distinguished public services these ancestors rendered.

Advertising columns give one of the best records of the progress of the temperance movement, even before the adoption
of the Eighteenth Amendment. Men sought work and stated
that they were sober, or total abstainers, and one of the leading
demands in the "help wanted" column was for men who were
sober. Through the advertisement information is given in
regard to legislating liquor out of Canada [21] and on the other
hand the advertisement has been used to combat the further
spread of the prohibition movement,—liquor firms increased
the number and size of their advertisements in such papers
as did not exclude liquor advertisements; in covertly advertising
beer as the best temperance drink, they recognized the progress
made by the Anti-Saloon League; and they used the advertisement as propaganda to promote in every way their private
business interests.

The newspaper is not necessary to reconstruct the books
printed, the works of art produced, the new music written,—these
presumably survive and the historian can examine them himself.
But the newspaper records the impression made on the public
by the appearance of new works of literature, art, and music.
It reflects even more perfectly than do statements of the number
of editions issued and copies sold to what extent the impression
left has been purely ephemeral, how far it has been relatively
permanent, how far a work has at first apparently been a failure
but later has come into its own.

The press, considering all of its departments collectively, may
be used to reconstruct in a measure the daily life of different
classes in society,[22] though the lack of proportion in the conscious
description and the unconscious reflection of these classes must
somewhat impair its usefulness in this direction,—the life of one
class must seem to be filled with weddings, dances, dinners,
charity balls, and of another with drunken brawls, murders,

[21] Philadelphia *Public Ledger*, November , 1916.
[22] Suggestive articles on advertising of an earlier day are found in H.
Friedenwald, "Some Newspaper Advertisements of the Eighteenth Cen-
tury," American Jewish Historical Society, *Publications*, 1897, 6: 49–59;
W. P. Trent, "Gleanings from an old Southern Newspaper," *Atlantic
Monthly*, September, 1900, 86: 356–364; A. B. Slauson, "Curious Customs
of the Past as Gleaned from Early Issues of the Newspapers in the District of
Columbia," *Records of the Columbia Historical Society*, 1906, 9: 88–125.

crime of every description, while the life between these two extremes passes unnoted.

These differences are evident in the country press and in the metropolitan press. They are illustrated by a comparison of the society columns in these two classes of papers. The country weekly gives both relatively and sometimes absolutely a larger proportion of its space to purely social events than does the daily of the large city. Every trifling event is chronicled and its importance magnified, yet while its exaggerations are prone to be excessive, they are easily detected and discounted. All weddings are described as pretty, all brides are beautiful, all bridegrooms are successful, both are always popular in the community, the wedding repast is sumptuous or elegant, and the presents received are numerous and valuable. The facts may often be precisely the reverse, but in a small community the rhetorical descriptions deceive no one and presumably will not mislead the future historian.

These elaborate descriptions of social events are found in the metropolitan dailies only in exceptional cases,—the vast majority of weddings and of social events go unchronicled by the press. In such as are chronicled, a different set of conventional phrases is used. Barring change in names, the society columns vary little from one social season to another. The historian is rarely concerned with the names that fill these columns, the inaccuracies that inevitably creep in do not vitiate his use of them in his reconstruction of the past since this reconstruction must concern itself less with the individual than with the type. The dinner party or the theater party may supplant the ball, skating may take the place of *thé dansant*, new experiments in social entertainment may be introduced to whet the jaded appetites of the professional social classes,—it is with this that the historian is concerned in his reconstruction of social life rather than with the individuals through whom they are carried out. The genial editor who describes in florid language the social events of a country village is in effect not so much describing these events as he is recording his own natural characteristics, the family ties that bind together all parts of the village, the common desire to give every one "a good send-off," the intimate relationships that prevent the naked truth from being told in public places, the concealments that do not conceal,—all of these conditions are faithfully portrayed by descriptions that in themselves are wholly unreliable, yet are absolutely trustworthy records of the state of mind, the intellectual interests, the friendly relationships of the rural community. It must also be remembered that conditions in a poor, backward community can also be in part reconstructed from what the paper does not contain as well as from what it publishes. The country press as an interpreter of rural and village life is best described by William Allen White who says:

"Therefore, men and brethren, when you are riding through this vale of tears upon the California Limited, and by chance pick up the little country newspaper with its meager telegraph service of three or four thousand words—or, at best, fifteen or twenty thousand; when you see its array of countryside items; its interminable local stories; its tiresome editorials on the waterworks, the schools, the street railroad, the crops, and the city printing, don't throw down the contemptible little rag with the verdict that there is nothing in it. But know this, and know it well: if you could take the clay from your eyes and read the little paper as it is written, you would find all of God's beautiful sorrowing, struggling, aspiring world in it, and what you saw would make you touch the little paper with reverent hands." [23]

The reconstruction through the newspaper of the life of the small community seems simple,—the reconstruction of the life of a great city is a more complex matter. The rural community knows itself, it is interested in reading about itself, and it makes the necessary modifications of all local accounts given. But a huge city does not know itself,—"the people in one part read with eagerness about the other part of which it knows not. The society debutante will read of the temptations of the Bowery and of Chinatown, while the shop girl pores over the descriptions of Mrs. K's jewels and the latest entertainment or the newest scandal in the upper set." [24] Yet as one star differeth

[23] "The Country Newspaper," *Harper's Magazine*, May, 1916, 132: 887–891.
    See also E. A. Start, "The Country Newspaper," *New England Magazine*, November, 1889, 7: 329–335; C. M. Harger, "The Country Editor of To-day," *Atlantic Monthly*, January, 1907, 99: 89–96.
[14] Suggested by M. H. Besser.

from another in glory, so the metropolitan press of different countries and of different sections of the same country have their own variations. A historian of the press finds that "the local news in Berlin and other large cities is written with the minuteness and the familiarity of style of a village chronicle, and gives the impression that every one is occupied in observing the doings of his neighbor." [25] An England reconstructed from the advertisements of the *Spectator* [26] of Addison is a very different England from the England that it would be possible to reconstruct from the advertisements of to-day.

Many extracts from early Australian newspapers make it possible to reconstruct social and industrial life in Australia during the first part of the nineteenth century, although not political conditions since "there were but two classes, those who ruled and those who obeyed." Although the first fleet for Australia carried out a printing press in 1787, no one in the colony was able to set type and when the first paper was issued in 1803 it was found that Australia had not only inherited all of the press disabilities of the mother country but it had added to them the trouble of securing paper and ink as well as compositors since ships were sent out but once or twice a year. "Being under the strictest censorship," the Sydney *Gazette* "did not attempt to discuss public matters. Officials of all grades, when mentioned at all, were spoken of in terms of the most fulsome flattery." [27] The press is the limelight that illumines, as do no other sources, the hardships of frontier life as well as the courage with which they are met.

The newspapers that come to-day from Australia, the Fiji Islands, Hawaii, and the Philippines are invaluable in reconstructing present-day life there,—even to the extent of showing how long the advertisements linger of patent medicines announced as cures for cholera.

In *The Voice of the Negro*, R. T. Kerlin, through a compilation from the negro press of America for the four consecutive months

[25] Hugh Chisholm, "The German Press," *Encyclopaedia Britannica*, XIX, 579.

[26] Lawrence Lewis, *The Advertisements of the Spectator;* "The 'Spectator' as an Advertising Medium," *Atlantic Monthly*, May, 1909, 103: 605–615.

[27] James Bonwick, *Early Struggles of the Australian Press*.

immediately succeeding the Washington riot in 1919, has shown how the negro feels in regard to national affairs, what his own grievances are, as well as what are his hopes and his aspirations.

The contemporary accounts of the battle of the Yser that have been collected from the press of England, France, Russia, Holland, Switzerland, and Austria, in the opinion of the editor, "deserve to be presented for the edification of future generations." [28]

The reconstruction of the exploits of Paul Jones in English seas during 1778–1780 has been made from the contemporary accounts collected from English newspapers.[29]

These various reconstructions of the past and the present that have been made indicate the great opportunities afforded by the press for an insight unconsciously given into conditions seldom consciously described.

The press itself is the best refutation of the conventional judgments passed on America, and presumably of those passed on other countries. The advertisement everywhere rebukes the assertion that Americans are superficial,—it records to-day precisely the opposite tendency. A genuine desire to reach foundations is recognized by the advertiser who shows the construction of the automobile engine and illustrates the inmost foldings of the tire. Tools, implements, instruments with which work is done are portrayed as evidence that work is thoroughly done. Laws are cited in advertisements showing that banks are permitted to act as executors, administrators, guardians, and testamentary trustees. The statements made that in filling such positions preference should be given the impersonal bank are supported by citations in advertisements from court decisions showing that estates have often been squandered through the mismanagement of the private executor. Recognition of a desire "to know the law" is given in the information frequently conveyed through the advertisement of the latest legislation on important matters. Extracts from debates in Congress are given in advertisements to satisfy a desire to know tendencies in legislation proposed. The advertisement repeatedly gives un-

---

[28] Leon van der Essen, *The Invasion and the War in Belgium*, p. 351.
[29] Don C. Seitz, *Paul Jones*, 1917.

conscious testimony to the universal desire to get at the bottom of things, to have guarantees of the reliability of statements made, to ask for evidence and proof that things are as they seem to be.

The press gives indisputable evidence of the growth of the principle of co-operation. During the war different industries co-operated in raising war loans, and in promoting the sale of war stamps. "Working with Uncle Sam" became a persuasive slogan and wide circulation was given the phrase of Secretary Franklin K. Lane's,—"We are but beginning to learn the art of co-operation in the United States." [30] Kipling's lines,—

> "It is not the guns or armament
> Or the money they can pay,
> It's the close co-operation
> That makes them win the day,"—

recorded the universal belief in the effectiveness of co-operation.

The sentences carried by the press,—"This is heatless Monday," "This is meatless Tuesday," "This is wheatless Wednesday,"—were illustrative of the efforts toward national co-operation as well as privations entailed by the war, and they are more impressive in reconstructing the conditions of the time than would have been a statement of the request to forego the use of coal, meat, and wheat.

The press everywhere announced the formation of scores of alliances, councils, federations, leagues, societies, and unions,— all formed to co-operate with the government in the prosecution of the war, as similar alliances to-day exist to promote peace.

Collective advertisements [31] and international advertisements are again significant illustrations of the growing spirit of co-operation.

The value of certain parts of the press to the future historian may be tested by an examination of the accounts given by different reporters of any contemporaneous signal event in a community. How far is it possible to reconstruct from the press

[30] New York *Tribune*, October 24, 1917.
[31] An interesting advertisement illustrating this was that of thirty New York City Chinese restaurants that combined on a page advertisement in the city press, May 3, 1921.

a series of events, running through several days, attended by thousands of persons from different sections of the country and by delegates from foreign countries? Such reports, to those who have taken an interested and sympathetic part in the events, must often bring depression and discouragement. If the reporters are instructed to send in "snappy stuff," the instructions are assuredly literally obeyed. With every possible opportunity to gain information in advance and at the time, often no preparation whatever has apparently been made, and the reports show not only ignorance of the events to be commemorated but a general rudimentary ignorance. Errors innumerable are made due to a failure to understand the significance of the event, to a lack of knowledge of local conditions easily obtainable, and to a perverted notion that every report must be "a good story." Attempts at reconstruction from such reports encounter at one end innumerable but needless inaccuracies of statement, exaggeration, flippancy, frivolity, sensationalism, and many positive errors of omission and commission. At the other end, they encounter a failure to see the general plan of the events, the unifying principle that binds together all parts of it, the subordination of the individual to the whole and the spirit of co-operation that has made it a success, and a lack of appreciation of the dignity and seriousness of the occasion. The resulting report, in spite of a straining after the spectacular, is a prosaic, unbalanced account that might well serve as an illustration of Buckle's "golden age of successful mediocrity." It fails to provide material for an adequate reconstruction of an important series of events, but in so doing it unconsciously records the tendency of even reputable journals to encourage reporters to add their own personal views to their reports of news; it records a belief on the part of the press, that the reading public wishes only to be amused and that therefore it must be amused at any cost; it is an unconscious kodak of the standards of that part of the press that "follows the crowd," that "gives the public what the public wants" and that thereby fails to interpret the times in which it lives.

The analysis of the periodical press that has been made, it is hoped, may indicate that the actual value of the newspaper is far beyond all that could have been anticipated when the presses close, the papers have passed into the hands of their readers, and have then been cast aside as having served their purpose. The suggestions that have been made of its ultimate value to the historian through the infinite range of reconstructions of past time made possible by the press have presupposed a press under normal conditions. A press regulated or censored by authority, a press under governmental control, a press used by governments to promulgate its special doctrines is not a free press, and a society reconstructed from a press thus limited by external conditions is but a caricature of what should be a normal society.

For this study of normal life the newspaper,—abnormal as it itself may seem with flaring headlines and blurred pages of illustrated advertisements, with all of its limitations, its inaccuracies, its unworthy representatives, its lack of proportion, its many temptations—not always resisted—to throw prismatic colors instead of the white light of truth on its accounts of the day, the periodical press still remains the most important single source the historian has at his command for the reconstruction of the life of the past three centuries.

APPENDIX I

BIOGRAPHICAL NOTES *

NAME	BORN	DIED	OCCUPATION
A'BECKETT, A. W.	1844	1909	*humorist*
ABERDEEN, G. H. GORDON, Earl of	1784	1860	*statesman*
ACTON, Sir J. E., first Baron	1834	1902	*historian*
ADAM, H. Pearl (Mrs. George)	1882		*journalist*
ADAM, Juliette	1836		*editor*
ADAMS, F. P.	1868		*columnist*
ADAMS, Henry	1838	1918	*historian*
ADAMS, S. H.	1871		*author*
ADAMSON, Robert	1871		*editor, writer*
ALDEN, W. L.	1837	1908	*author, journalist*
ALDRICH, T. B.	1836	1907	*author, editor*
AMBLER, C. H.	1876		*university professor*
AMES, Fisher	1758	1808	*statesman*
ANGELL, Norman	1874		*author and special corre-spondent*
ARCHER, William	1836		*critic*
ARNOLD, Matthew	1822	1888	*poet and critic*
ARNOLD, Thomas	1795	1842	*educator*
ARNOLD, W. T.	1852	1904	*author and journalist*
ASHLEY, Evelyn	1836	1907	*author*
ASQUITH, H. H.	1852		*statesman*
ATKINS, J. B.	1871		*editor*
ATKINSON, Wilmer	1840	1920	*newspaper proprietor*
AULARD, F. V. A.	1849		*historian*
AVENARIUS, Ferdinand	1856		*author*
AYER, N.W., and Son, founded, 1869			*advertising agency*
BABBITT, Irving	1865		*university professor*
BACHAUMONT, L. P. de	1690	1771	*memoir writer*
BACON, E. M.	1844	1916	*editor*
BACON, Henry	1866		*architect*

* These biographical notes it is hoped may be of service in showing the approximate period of the writers who have been cited. The attempt has been made to characterize, as far as possible, the occupation in the terms used by the persons themselves.

It has not been possible to secure information in regard to every person mentioned, and in spite of much care taken to avoid errors, doubtless many have been made.

NAME	BORN	DIED	OCCUPATION
BAGOT, Richard	1860	1921	*novelist*
BAINES, Edward	1774	1848	*newspaper proprietor*
BAINES, Sir Edward	1800	1890	*editor*
BAKER, Alfred Z.	1870		*illustrator and writer*
BAKER, R. S.	1870		*author and editor*
BALLANTYNE, James	1772	1833	*publisher*
BAMBERGER, L.	1823	1899	*political writer*
BAMFORD, Samuel	1788	1872	*poet and weaver*
BARRETT, J. P.	1852		*clergyman*
BARRIE, Sir J. M.	1860		*author*
BATE, Henry (Sir Henry Bate Dudley)	1745	1824	*editor*
BAYLEY, F. W. N.	1808	1853	*editor*
BAZAINE, A. F.	1811	1888	*Marshal of France*
BEACONSFIELD, see Disraeli			
BEATTY-KINGSTON, Wm.	1837	1900	*foreign correspondent*
BEAUMONT, Gustave de	?	1868	*diplomat*
BECKER, Carl	1873		*university professor*
BEECHER, H. W.	1813	1887	*preacher*
BEERBOHM, Max	1872		*caricaturist*
BELISLE, Alexandre	1856		*publisher*
BELL, C. F. Moberly	1847	1911	*managing director of The Times*
BELL, E. P.	1869		*special correspondent*
BELLOC, Hilaire	1870		*author*
BENJAMIN, L. S. (Lewis Melville)	1874		*author*
BENNETT, (E.) Arnold	1867		*author and editor*
BENNETT, E. N.	1866		*war correspondent*
BENNETT, J. G.	1794	1872	*editor*
BENNETT, J. G.	1841	1918	*newspaper proprietor*
BENNETT, R. A.	1855		*editor*
BENSON, A. C.	1862		*author*
BERESFORD, James	c 1764	1840	*clergyman*
BERGENGREN, R. W. A.	1871		*cartoonist and critic*
BERKELEY, G. C. Grantley	1800	1881	*writer, sportsman*
BERNHARDI, Friedrick von	1849		*soldier, writer*
BESANT, Sir Walter	1836	1901	*novelist*
BESTE, J. R.	1806	1885	*traveler and editor*
BETHMANN-HOLLWEG, Theobald von	1856		*statesman*
BEVERLAND, Adrian	1654	1712	*jurist and philologist*
BEWICK, Thomas	1753	1828	*wood-engraver*
"BILLINGS, JOSH," see Shaw, H. W.			

NAME	BORN	DIED	OCCUPATION
Birch, Thomas	1705	1766	scholar
Biré, E.	1829	1907	author
Bishop, J. B.	1847		journalist, author
Bismarck, O. E. L. von, Prince	1815	1898	statesman
Bissing, M. F., von	1844	1917	soldier
Black, John	1783	1855	editor
Black, William	1841	1898	novelist and war correspondent
Blackburn, H.	1830	1897	artist and editor
Blackwell, H. B.	1825	1909	editor, merchant
Blackwood, John	1818	1879	editor and publisher
Blackwood, William	1776	1834	publisher
Blaine, J. G.	1830	1893	statesman
Blathwayt, Raymond	1855		special correspondent
Bleackley, H. W.	1868		author
Blennerhassett, Sir Rowland	1839	1909	political writer
Bleyer, W. G.	1873		university professor
Bloomer, Amelia	1818	1894	editor, reformer
Bloomer, D. C.	1816	?	lawyer
Blowitz, H. S. de	1832	1903	special correspondent
Bluysen, Paul	1861		editor
Bodkin, M. M'D.	1850		judge
Boissier, Gaston	1823	1908	classicist
Bolton, C. K.	1867		librarian
Bonwick, James	1817	1906	archivist
Borrow, George	1803	1881	author
Borthwick, Algernon, see Glenesk			
Boswell, James	1740	1795	biographer
Bourne, E. G.	1860	1908	university professor
Bowles, Samuel	1779	1851	editor
Bowles, Samuel, Jr.	1826	1878	editor
Bowles, Samuel	1851	1915	editor
Boynton, H. W.	1869		author, critic
Brace, C. L.	1826	1890	philanthropist and author
Brackenbury, Sir Henry	1837	1915	soldier
Bradley, Will	1868		artist
Brandeis, L. D.	1856		jurist
Bright, John	1811	1889	statesman
Brisbane, Arthur	1864		editor
Broadley, A. M.	1847	1916	author, collector
Brodrick, G. C.	1831	1903	political writer
Brooks, J. Tyrwhitt, nom-de-plume of H. Vizetelly			

NAME	BORN	DIED	OCCUPATION
BROOKS, Shirley	1815	1874	*author and editor*
BROUGHAM, H. P., Baron	1778	1868	*statesman, author*
BROWN, John	1800	1859	*abolitionist*
BROWN, R. C. E.	1867		*editor, university professor*
BROWNE, E. G.	1862		*university professor*
BROWNE, Sir Thomas	1605	1682	*author*
BROWNELL, W. C.	1851		*author, critic*
BROWNING, Robert	1812	1889	*poet*
BRUNETIÈRE, Ferdinand	1849	1906	*critic*
BRYAN, W. J.	1860		*editor, politician*
BRYANT, W. C.	1794	1878	*poet, editor*
BÜCHER, Carl	1847		*economist*
BUCK, Gertrude	1871	1922	*college professor*
BUCKINGHAM, J. S.	1786	1855	*editor*
BUCKINGHAM, J. T.	1779	1861	*editor*
BUCKLE, H. T.	1821	1862	*historian*
BUELL, D. C.	1827	1894	*soldier*
BÜLOW, B. E. von	1815	1879	*statesman*
BÜLOW, B. H. K. M., Prince von	1849		*statesman*
BULLARD, F. L.	1873		*editor, author*
BULLEN, P. S.	1868		*special correspondent*
BULWER-LYTTON, Edward, First Baron Lytton	1803	1873	*novelist and editor*
BUNCE, J. T.	1828	1899	*editor*
BUNNER, H. C.	1855	1896	*editor*
BURCHARD, S. D.	1812	1891	*clergyman*
BURGES, Gelett	1866		*humorist*
BURKE, Edmund	1729	1797	*statesman*
BURLEIGH, William Cecil, First Baron	1520	1598	*statesman*
BURNAND, Sir Francis C.	1836	1917	*humorist and editor*
BURNE-JONES, Sir Edward	1833	1898	*painter*
BURNEY, Charles	1757	1817	*classical scholar*
BURNSIDE, A. E.	1824	1881	*soldier*
BURR, F. A.	1843	1894	*author*
BUSCH, J. H. M.	1821	1899	*publicist*
BUSSEY, H. F.	?	1919	*journalist*
BUTLER, B. F.	1818	1893	*soldier and politician*
BUTLER, Sir William F.	1838	1910	*soldier*
BYNNER, Witter	1881		*poet and playwright*
CALLENDER, J. T.	1758	1803	*journalist*
CAMPBELL, Duncan	1824	1890	
CAMPBELL, John, fl. c. 1700			*newswriter*

NAME	BORN	DIED	OCCUPATION
CANNING, George	1770	1827	statesman
CANNING, Sir Stratford	1786	1880	diplomat
CARLILE, Richard	1790	1843	printer, editor
CARLYLE, Thomas	1795	1881	essayist
CARTON DE WIART, Edmund	1876		diplomat
CASSAGNAC, Paul de	1843	1904	editor
CATLING, Thomas	1838		editor
CAVE, Edward	1691	1754	printer and editor
CELLINI, Benvenuto	1500	1571	artist
CHALMERS, George	1742	1825	antiquary
CHAMBERLIN, W. J.	1866	1901	special correspondent
CHAMBERS, Robert	1802	1871	publisher
CHENERY, Thomas	1826	1884	editor, foreign correspondent
CHESTERTON, G. K.	1874		author, journalist
CHILD, Theodore	1846	1892	author, journalist
CHIROL, Sir Valentine	1852		editor and foreign correspondent
CHISHOLM, Hugh	1866		editor Encyclopedia Britannica
CHORLEY, H. F.	1808	1872	musical critic
CHURCH, A. J.	1829	1912	author
CHURCHILL, Winston	1874		war correspondent, statesman
CLAPP, H. A.	1841	1904	dramatic critic
CLARENDON, G. W. F. Villiers, fourth Earl	1810	1870	
CLARK, Champ	1850	1921	congressman
CLARK, E. P.	1847	1903	editor
CLARK, V. S.	1868		economist and editor
CLEAVELAND, Moses	1754	1906	pioneer
CLEMENCEAU, Georges	1841		editor and statesman
COBBE, F. P.	1822	1904	philanthropist, editorial writer
COBBETT, William	1782	1835	essayist, editor
COBDEN, Richard	1804	1865	statesman
COE, G. A.	1862		theological seminary professor
COLBURN, Henry	?	1855	publisher
COLCHESTER, First Baron	1757	1829	
COLERIDGE, S. T.	1772	1834	poet
COLLIER, R. J.	1876	1918	editor and publisher
COLLINS, J. C.	1848	1908	author

NAME	BORN	DIED	OCCUPATION
CONGDON, C. T.	1821	1891	*journalist*
CONNELLEY, W. E.	1855		*author*
COOK, Sir Edward T.	1857	1919	*editor*
COOK, F. A.	1865		*explorer*
COOK, JOSEPH	1838	1901	*clergyman*
COOK, Waldo L.	1865		*editor*
COOPER, C. A.	1829	1916	*editor*
COOPER, F. T.	1864		*author*
CORBIN, John	1870		*author, dramatic critic, editorial writer*
CORTISSOZ, Royal	1869		*art critic and literary editor*
COURTNEY, Leonard H., first Baron	1832	1918	*political economist*
COUSIN, Victor	1792	1867	*philosopher*
COWEN, Joseph	1831	1900	*editor and proprietor*
COWPER, William	1731	1800	*poet*
CRABBE, George	1754	1832	*poet*
CREELMAN, James	1859	1915	*author, journalist*
CRISPI, Francesco	1819	1901	*statesman*
CROKER, J. W.	1780	1857	*essayist, secretary to the Admiralty*
CROKER, Richard	1843	1922	*politician*
CROMWELL, Oliver	1599	1658	*statesman*
CUMBERLAND, Richard	1732	1811	*dramatist*
CUNLIFFE, J. W.	1865		*editor, university professor*
CURTIS, G. W.	1824	1892	*author, editor*
CURTIS, C. H. K.	1850		*publisher*
CUTLER, Manasseh	1742	1823	*clergyman*
DAGUERRE, L. J. M.	1789	1851	*inventor*
DALZIEL, George	1815	1902	*wood-engraver*
DALZIEL, T. B. G. S.	1823	1906	*artist*
DANA, C. A.	1819	1897	*editor*
DANBY, Thomas Osborne, Earl of	1631	1712	*statesman*
DANIELS, JOSEPHUS	1862		*editor*
DARLING, J. N. ("Ding")	1876		*cartoonist*
DASENT, A. I.	1859		*author*
DAVIS, Elmer	1890		*editor*
DAVIS, R. H.	1864	1916	*author and correspondent*
DAWES, H. L.	1816	1903	*statesman*
DAWSON, W. H.	1860		*author*
DAY, R. E.	1852		*editor, author*
DECATUR, Stephen	1779	1820	*naval commander*
DEFOE, Daniel	1661?	1731	*journalist and novelist*

NAME	BORN	DIED	OCCUPATION
DE LA FAYE, Charles, fl. c. 1720			*official*
DELANE, J. T.	1817	1879	*editor*
DELL, Robert	1865		*foreign correspondent*
DE WEESE, T. A.	1860		*editorial writer*
D'EWES, Sir Symonds	1602	1650	*antiquarian*
DIBBLEE, G. B.	1868		*editor*
DICEY, Edward	1832	1911	*editor*
DICKENS, Charles	1812	1870	*novelist and editor*
DILKE, C. W.	1789	1864	*critic and editor*
D'INDY, Vincent	1851		*composer*
DING, J. N., see DARLING, J. N.			
DISRAELI, Benjamin, first Earl of			
Beaconsfield	1804	1881	*statesman and author*
DISRAELI, Isaac	1766	1848	*author*
DITHMAR, E. A.	1854	1917	*editorial writer*
DODWELL, Henry	1641	1711	*scholar and theologian*
DOESTICKS, see THOMSON, Mortimer			
DOOLEY, Mr., see Dunne, F. P.			
DOUMIC, René	1860		*critic*
DOWDEN, Edward	1843	1913	*critic*
DOWLING, Vincent G.	1785	1852	*editor*
DOWNEY, Edmund	1856		*editor and novelist*
DRAKE, J. R.	1795	1820	*poet*
DRUMMOND-WOLFF, Sir H.	1830	1908	*diplomat*
DRYDEN, John	1631	1700	*poet*
DU BOIS, W. E. B.	1868		*author and editor*
DÜRER, Albrecht	1471	1528	*artist*
DU MAURIER, George	1834	1896	*illustrator and author*
DUNNE, F. P. (Mr. Dooley)	1867		*humorist*
DUNTON, John	1659	1733	*bookseller*
EASTMAN, Max	1883		*author and editor*
EDISON, T. A.	1847		*inventor*
EDWARDS, H. S.	1828	1906	*war correspondent and editor*
EGGLESTON, G. C.	1839	1911	*author*
EINSTEIN, Lewis	1877		*diplomat*
ELLENBOROUGH, Edward Law, first Earl of	1750	1818	*judge*
ELLIOT, H. R.	1849	1906	*editor*
ELLSWORTH, W. W.	1855		*publisher*
ELTZBACHER, Paul	1868		*political writer*
EMERSON, R. W.	1803	1882	*philosopher*
EMPSON, William	1791	1852	*editor*

NAME	BORN	DIED	OCCUPATION
ERLANGER, A. L.	1860		theatrical manager
ESCOTT, T. H. S.	1844		editor and author
FARRAR, F. W.	1831	1903	clergyman
FAVRE, Jules	1809	1880	statesman
FICKE, Arthur D.	1883		author
FIELD, Eugene	1850	1895	poet and journalist
FIELDING, Henry	1707	1754	novelist, editor
FIELDS, J. T.	1817	1881	publisher, editor
FIFE, R. H., Jr.	1871		university professor
FILON, Augustin	1841		author
FISKE, Willard	1831	1904	scholar, foreign correspondent, librarian
FITZPATRICK, E. A.	1884		educator
FLEMING, W. L.	1874		university professor
FONBLANQUE, Albany	1793	1872	editor
FONBLANQUE, E. B. de	1821	1895	author
FOOTE, Samuel	1720	1777	actor-dramatist
FORAIN, J. L.	1852		caricaturist
FORBES, Archibald	1838	1900	war correspondent
FORD, P. L.	1865	1902	author and editor
FORD, W. C.	1858		historian and editor
FORNEY, J. W.	1817	1881	journalist
FORSTER, John	1812	1876	biographer
FORSTER, W. E.	1818	1886	statesman
FORTESCUE, Granville R.	1875		author, special correspondent
FOSTER, Ernest	1852		editor
FOWLER, Sir John, first Baronet	1817	1898	civil engineer
FOX, C. J.	1749	1806	statesman
FOX, Frank	1874		war correspondent
FOXCROFT, Frank	1850		editor
F. P. A., see Adams, F. P.			
FRANCE, Anatole	1844		author
FRANCIS, John	1811	1882	publisher
FRANCIS, Sir Philip	1740	1818	reputed author of the Letters of Junius
FRANKENBERG, T. T.	1877		dramatic critic, author
FRANCKLIN, Thomas	1721	1784	scholar
FRANKLIN, Benjamin	1706	1790	statesman
FRANKLIN, Fabian	1853		editor
FRANKLIN, Sir John	1786	1847	explorer
FRANKLIN, W. S.	1824	1886	soldier
FRASER, James	?	1841	publisher

NAME	BORN	DIED	OCCUPATION
FREEMAN, W. C.	1860		*advertising manager*
FRENCH, George	1853		*advertising counselor*
FREYTAG, Gustav	1816	1895	*novelist and editor*
FRIEDENWALD, Herbert	1870		*author*
FRITH, W. P.	1819	1909	*artist, author*
FROISSART, Jean	1338	1410?	*chronicler*
FROST, Thomas	1821	1908	*journalist*
FUNCK-BRENTANO, F.	1862		*author*
FURNISS, Harry	1854		*caricaturist*
GALIGNANI, J. A.	1796	1873	*publisher*
GARDINER, A. G.	1865		*editor*
GARRETT, Edmund	1865	1907	*editor*
GARRISON, W. L.	1805	1879	*reformer, editor*
GARRISON, W. P.	1840	1907	*editor*
GARTH, T. R.	1872		*psychologist*
GASKELL, Elizabeth C.	1810	1865	*novelist*
GASKELL, William	1805	1884	*clergyman*
GASQUET, F. A., Cardinal	1846		*historian*
GAULTIER, Paul	1872		*author*
GAUSS, Christian	1878		*university professor*
GAVIT, J. P.	1868		*editor*
GAYLORD, F. A.	1856		*Y. M. C. A. Secretary*
GIBBON, Edward	1737	1794	*historian*
GIBBS, Sir Philip	1877		*war correspondent, author*
GIFFORD, William	1756	1826	*editor*
GILDERSLEEVE, B. L.	1831		*philologist*
GILBERT, Sir John	1817	1897	*illustrator*
GILLRAY, James	1757	1815	*caricaturist*
GLENESK, Sir Algernon Borthwick, first Baron	1830	1908	*foreign correspondent, newspaper proprietor*
GLYNN, Martin H.	1871		*ex-governor, editor*
GODKIN, E. L.	1831	1902	*war correspondent, editor*
GODWIN, Parke	1816	1904	*author*
GOETHE, J. W., von	1749	1832	*poet and philosopher*
GOLDBERG, Isaac	1887		*translator, author*
GOMME, Sir G. L.	1853	1916	*scholar*
GORDON, Charles	1833	1885	*administrator, soldier*
GORGES, Sir Arthur	?	1625	*poet and translator*
GOULD, Sir F. C.	1844		*caricaturist and editor*
GOULD, Jay	1836	1892	*financier*
GRAND-CARTERET, John	1850		*author, collector*
GRANT, Albert, Baron	1830	1899	*company promoter*

NAME	BORN	DIED	OCCUPATION
GRANT, James	1802	1879	*editor*
GRAUX, Lucien	1878		*author*
GRAY, David	1836	1888	*editor*
GREELEY, Horace	1811	1872	*editor*
GREENWOOD, Frederick	1830	1909	*editor*
GREGORY, T. W.	1861		*Attorney-General, 1914–1919*
GREVILLE, C. C. F.	1794	1865	*politician, author*
GREW, E. S.	1867		*author, astronomer*
GREY, Charles, second Earl	1764	1845	*statesman*
GREY, Edward, first Viscount	1861		*diplomat*
GRISWOLD, Rufus W.	1815	1857	*editor and compiler*
GRISWOLD, W. M.	1853	1899	*indexer*
GROTE, George	1794	1871	*historian*
GUITERMAN, Arthur	1871		*poet*
GUTHRIE, William	1708	1770	*author*
HALE, David	1791	1849	*journalist*
HALE, Nathan	1784	1863	*journalist*
HALE, Walter	1869	1917	*illustrator*
HALE, W. B.	1869		*editor and correspondent*
HALL, G. Stanley	1846		*educator*
HALLECK, H. W.	1815	1872	*soldier*
HAMILTON, Alexander	1757	1804	*statesman*
HAMILTON, Clayton	1881		*author, critic*
HAMILTON, W. P.	1867		*editor*
HAPGOOD, Norman	1868		*editor and diplomat*
HARCOURT, Sir William Vernon	1827	1904	*statesman*
HARDWICKE, Philip Yorke, first Earl of	1690	1764	*Lord Chancellor*
HARDWICKE, Philip Yorke, second Earl of	1720	1790	*author*
HARGER, C. M.	1863		*editor*
HARMSWORTH, see NORTHCLIFFE			
HARRINGTON, H. F.	1882		*university professor*
HARRISON, Frederic	1831	1923	*historian*
HARVEY, George	1864		*editor and diplomat*
HARVEY, Peter	1810	1877	*merchant*
HASKELL, D. C.	1883		*librarian*
HASTINGS, Warren	1732	1818	*administrator*
HATCHER, E. N.	1849		
HATIN, E.	1809	1893	*historian*
HAULTAIN, Arnold	1857		*author*
HAUSSONVILLE, O.B.G., Count d'	1843		*author*

NAME	BORN	DIED	OCCUPATION
HAWKINS, Sir John	1719	1789	author
HAYWARD, A.	1801	1884	critic
HAZLITT, William	1778	1830	essayist
HEARD, F. F.	1825	1889	jurist
HEARST, W. R.	1863		newspaper proprietor
HEATON, J. L.	1860		editorial writer
HEDIN, Sven	1865		traveler and author
HEINE, Heinrich	1797	1856	poet
HENDERSON, E. F.	1861		author, historian
HEPWORTH, G. H.	1833	1902	clergyman
HERRICK, Robert	1868		author
HERSCHEL, Sir John	1792	1871	astronomer
HETHERINGTON, Henry	1792	1849	printer and publisher
HEWLETT, H. G.	?	1897	author
HILL, D. J.	1850		diplomat
HILL, G. B.	1835	1903	author
HINGSTON, E. P.	1823	1876	theatrical manager
HOBSON, J. A.	1858		economist
HODGKIN, Thomas	1831	1913	historian
HOE, R.	1812	1886	inventor
HOGARTH, William	1697	1764	painter and engraver
HOLLIDAY, R. C.	1880		author, editor
HOLMES, O. W.	1809	1894	poet
HOLST, H. E. von	1841	1904	historian
HOLT, Hamilton	1872		editor
HOLYOAKE, G. J.	1817	1906	co-operator and secularist
HOOKER, Joseph	1814	1879	general
HOUGH, C. M.	1858		judge
HOUGHTON, Lord (see R. M. Milnes)			
HOUSE, E. M.	1858		politician
HOWARD, J. R.	1837		publisher
HOWELLS, W. D.	1837	1920	novelist and editor
HUDSON, Frederic	1819	1875	editor
HUGHES, T.	1822	1896	author
HUME, Joseph	1777	1855	radical politician
HUNT, J. H. Leigh	1784	1859	essayist and poet
HUNT, Henry ("Orator")	1773	1835	radical politician
HURET, Jules	1864		editor
HYACINTHE, Père (Charles Loyson)	1827	1912	theologian
IMPEY, Sir Elijah	1732	1809	Chief Justice of Bengal
INGRAM, Herbert	1811	1860	newspaper proprietor
IRWIN, W. H. ("Will")	1873		war correspondent, author
JACKSON, Mason	1819	1903	wood-engraver, art editor

NAME	BORN	DIED	OCCUPATION
JACKSON, T. J. ("Stonewall")	1824	1863	soldier
JAMES, Henry	1843	1916	novelist
JAY, John	1745	1829	statesman
JEBB, Sir R. C.	1841	1905	scholar
JEFFREY, Francis, Lord	1773	1850	critic, editor, and judge
JELLALCHICH, Josef, Count	1801	1859	statesman
JENNINGS, L. J.	1836	1893	special correspondent and editor
JERDAN, William	1782	1869	editor
JERROLD, Blanchard	1826	1884	author, editor
JERROLD, Douglas	1803	1857	author and editor
JERROLD, WALTER	1863		editor and author
JEWSBURY, Maria Jane	1800	1833	author
JOHNSON, R. B.	1867		author
JOHNSON, Samuel	1709	1784	lexicographer
JONES, Henry Arthur	1851		dramatist
JONES, John Paul	1747	1792	naval officer
JONSON, Ben	1573?	1637	dramatist and poet
JOWETT, Benjamin	1817	1893	scholar
JUNIUS, pseudonym, see Francis, Sir Philip			
KATKOFF, M. N.	1818	1887	editor
KENNAN, George	1845		special correspondent, author
KENYON, Lloyd, first Baron	1732	1802	Lord Chief Justice
KERLIN, R. T.	1866		educator, author
KILMER, Joyce	1886	1918	poet
KING, Rufus	1755	1827	political leader
KINGLAKE, A. W.	1809	1891	historian
KINNEAR, A.	1841	1912	war correspondent
KIPLING, Rudyard	1865		author
KLAW, Marc	1858		theatrical manager
KLOPSCH, Louis	1852	1910	"knight of mercy"
KNIGHT, C.	1791	1853	editor and publisher
KNIGHT, Joseph	1829	1907	dramatic critic
KNIGHT, W. A.	1836	1916	university professor
KOSSUTH, Louis	1802	1894	patriot
LABOUCHERE, Henry	1831	1912	politician and journalist
LAMONT, Hammond	1863	1909	editor
LA FOLLETTE, R. M.	1859		editor, senator
LAMB, Charles	1775	1834	essayist
LAMARTINE, A. M. de	1790	1869	poet, author
LANDIS, K. M.	1866		judge

NAME	BORN	DIED	OCCUPATION
LANDON, Perceval	1869		*special correspondent, dramatist, author*
LANDOR, W. S.	1775	1864	*author*
LANE, F. K.	1864	1921	*statesman*
LARNED, J. N.	1836	1913	*librarian*
LASKI, Harold J.	1893		*political writer*
LAUGHTON, J. K.	1830	1915	*biographer, university professor*
LAWSON, T. W.	1857		*broker*
LAYARD, Sir A. H.	1817	1894	*archaeologist*
LAYARD, G. S.	1857		*author and reviewer*
LEACH, Henry	1874		*journalist*
LE BAS, Sir Hedley F.	1868		*publisher*
LE CLERC, J. V.	1789	1865	*philologist*
LEE, J. M.	1878		*editor*
LEE, R. E.	1807	1870	*soldier, college president*
LEECH, John	1817	1864	*cartoonist*
LEGGETT, William	1802	1839	*author, journalist*
LEHMANN, F. W.	1853		*lawyer*
LEHMANN, R. C.	1856		*editor*
LESSING, G. E.	1729	1781	*critic and dramatist*
LEUPP, F. E.	1849	1918	*editor and author*
LEVERMORE, C. H.	1856		*educator*
LEWES, G. H.	1817	1878	*author and editor*
LEWIS, A. H.	1857	1914	*author*
LEWIS, Sir G. C.	1806	1863	*statesman*
LIEBER, Francis	1800	1872	*educator, publicist*
LINTON, Eliza (Mrs. Lynn)	1822	1898	*novelist and correspondent*
LIOTARD, J. E.	1702	1789	*artist*
LIVINGSTONE, David	1813	1873	*explorer*
LLOYD, Edward	1815	1890	*newspaper proprietor*
LLOYD, H. D.	1847	1903	*author, editor*
LOCH, James	1780	1855	*economist*
LOCKE, D. R. (Petroleum V. Nasby)	1833	1888	*humorist*
LOCKE, R. A.	1800	1871	*editor*
LOCKHART, J. G.	1794	1854	*critic and editor*
LOMER, G. R.	1882		*librarian*
LONG, R. C.	1872		*special correspondent*
LOTHROP, S. K.	1804	1886	*clergyman, author*
LOUGHBOROUGH, Alexander Wedderburne, first Baron	1733	1805	*Lord Chancellor*
LOW, Sir A. Maurice	1860		*author and special correspondent*

NAME	BORN	DIED	OCCUPATION
Lowe, Charles	1848		*special correspondent*
Lowe, Robert, first Viscount Sherbrooke	1811	1892	*politician*
Lowell, J. R.	1819	1891	*author and editor*
Lowes, J. L.	1867		*university professor*
Lucas, Reginald J.	1865	1914	*author*
Luce, Robert	1862		*lawyer, president press cutting bureau*
Lucy, Sir Henry ("Toby")	1845		*special correspondent and editor*
Lucien-Graux, see Graux			
Ludendorff, Eric	1865		*soldier*
Lynd, Robert	1879		*editor, critic*
Lyndhurst, J. S. Copley, Baron	1772	1863	*Lord Chancellor*
Macaulay, T. B.	1800	1859	*historian*
MacCracken, H. N.	1880		*college president*
Macdonagh, Michael	1882		*special correspondent, and reporter*
MacDonald, William	1863		*special correspondent, author*
Macdonell, James	1842	1879	*editor, special correspondent*
MacGahan, J. A.	1844	1878	*war correspondent*
Mackail, J. W.	1859		*author*
Mackay, Charles	1814	1889	*author, journalist*
Mackintosh, Sir James	1765	1832	*philosopher*
Maginn, William	1793	1842	*poet and editor*
Manning, H. E.	1808	1892	*Cardinal-priest*
Marble, Manton	1834	1917	*editor*
Marcosson, I. F.	1877		*editor, author*
Martin, E. S.	1856		*editorial writer*
Martineau, Harriet	1802	1876	*author, editorial writer*
Mason, Gregory	1889		*writer, lecturer*
Massingham, H. W.	1860		*editor*
Mathews, C. J.	1803	1878	*actor, dramatist*
Matthews, Albert	1860		*author, bibliographer*
Matthews, Brander	1852		*author, critic*
Maude, F. N.	1854		*military writer*
Maupassant, Guy de	1850	1893	*novelist*
Maurice, A. B.	1873		*author*
Maurice, Frederick (Sir John F.)	1841	1912	*author*
Maurice, Frederick Denison	1805	1872	*divine*
Maxse, F. A.	1833	1900	*admiral and political writer*

NAME	BORN	DIED	OCCUPATION
MAXWELL, Sir Herbert	1845		author
MAY, Sir T. E.	1815	1886	constitutional jurist
McCABE, Joseph	1867		author and lecturer
McCARTHY, Justin H.	1830	1912	author
McCARTHY, J. H., Jr.	1860		novelist, dramatist
McCLURE, S. S.	1857		editor
McCULLAGH, Francis	1874		war correspondent
M'CULLOCH, J. R.	1789	1864	economist, editor
McKENZIE, F. A.	1869		war correspondent
McMASTER, J. B.	1852		historian
McMURRAY, DeWitt	1866		"newspaper man"
MEDILL, Joseph	1823	1899	journalist
MEISTER, Aloys	1866		historian
MELBOURNE, William Lamb, Viscount	1779	1848	statesman
MELGUND, Viscount, Gilbert, fourth Earl of Minto	1847	1914	Governor General (war correspondent 1873)
MELVILLE, Lewis, pseud., see Benjamin, L. S.			
MÉRIMÉE, Prosper	1803	1870	novelist
MERRIAM, G. S.	1843	1914	author
MÉTRA, Le bonhomme,	c. 1714	1786	news gatherer
MEYER, H. H. B.	1864		bibliographer
MIALL, Edward	1809	1881	politician, editor
MILL, J. S.	1806	1873	philosopher
MILLARD, T. F. F.	1868		war correspondent
MILLER, Hugh	1802	1856	man of letters, geologist
MILNES, R. M., Baron Houghton	1809	1885	poet, politician
MIST, Nathaniel	?	1737	printer
MITCHELL, Maria	1818	1889	astronomer
MOLTKE, H. C. B., Count von	1800	1891	soldier
MOMMSEN, Theodor	1817	1903	historian
MONTAGU, Basil	1770	1851	writer
MONTAGUE, C. E.	1867		author, journalist
MONTALEMBERT, C. F. de	1810	1870	historian, editor
MONTGOMERY, Robert ("Satan")	1807	1855	poetaster
MOORE, F. F.	1855		novelist, dramatist
MOORE, Thomas	1779	1852	poet
MORLEY, Christopher	1890		columnist
MORLEY, Henry	1822	1894	author
MORLEY, John, first Viscount	1838		statesman, author
MORRIS, William	1834	1896	poet, artist, manufacturer

NAME	BORN	DIED	OCCUPATION
MOTLEY, J. L.	1814	1877	*historian*
MÜNSTER, Count (Prince Münster von Derneburg)	1820	1902	*diplomat*
MÜNSTERBERG, Hugo	1863	1916	*psychologist*
MURPHY, Arthur	1707	1805	*actor, author*
MURRAY, John	1778	1843	*publisher*
MURRAY, W. H. H.	1840	1904	*clergyman, author*
NADAL, E. S.	1843		*author*
NAPIER, Macvey	1776	1847	*editor*
NAPIER, W. F. P.	1785	1860	*soldier, historian*
NASBY, Petroleum V., see Locke, D. R.			
NAST, Thomas	1840	1902	*caricaturist*
NATHAN, G. J.	1882		*editor, dramatic critic*
NETTEMENT, Alfred	1805	1869	*editor, author*
NEVINS, Allan	1890		*editor, author*
NEWCASTLE, Henry Pelham, Duke of	1811	1864	*statesman*
NICHOLS, John	1745	1826	*printer and author*
NICOLL, Sir William R.	1851		*editor*
NILES, Hezekiah	1777	1839	*editor*
NORTHCLIFFE, A. C. Harmsworth, Baron	1865	1922	*newspaper proprietor*
NORTON, C. E.	1827	1908	*university professor*
NOTESTEIN, Wallace	1879		*university professor*
NOYES, F. B.	1863		*editor*
NYE, Edgar W. ("Bill")	1850	1896	*humorist*
OBERHOLTZER, E. P.	1868		*author*
O'BRIEN, F. M.	1875		*journalist*
O'BRIEN, William	1852		*journalist*
OCHS, A. S.	1858		*newspaper proprietor, publisher*
O'CONNELL, Daniel	1775	1847	*politician*
OGDEN, Rollo	1856		*editor*
OLIPHANT, Margaret	1828	1897	*author*
O'RELL, Max, pseud. of Paul Blouet	1848	1903	*author and special correspondent*
O'SHEA, J. A.	1839	1905	*special correspondent*
PAGE, F. H.	1860		*clergyman, editor*
PAINE, A. B.	1861		*author*
PALMER, Frederick	1873		*war correspondent*
PALMERSTON, H. J. Temple, Viscount	1784	1865	*statesman*

NAME	BORN	DIED	OCCUPATION
PANIZZI, Sir Anthony	1797	1879	*librarian*
PANMURE, Fox Maule, second Baron	1801	1874	*secretary-at-war*
PARNELL, C. S.	1846	1891	*political leader*
PASTEUR, Louis	1822	1895	*chemist*
PATERSON, James	1805	1876	*antiquary, journalist*
PAYNE, W. M.	1858	1919	*critic*
PEARSON, E. L.	1880		*author, librarian*
PEBODY, Charles	1839	1890	*editor*
PEEL, Sir Robert	1788	1850	*statesman*
PEMBERTON, Max	1863		*novelist*
PENNELL, Joseph	1860		*artist*
PENNYPACKER, S. W.	1843	1916	*author*
PEPPER, C. M.	1859		*special correspondent*
PEPYS, Samuel	1633	1703	*diarist*
PÉRIVIER, Antonin	1847		*editor*
PERKINS, G. W.	1862	1920	*financier*
PERRY, Bliss	1860		*editor, university professor*
PERRY, W. S.	1855		*art director*
PHILLIPS, Wendell	1811	1884	*orator*
PIKE, J. S.	1811	1882	*political writer*
PINCHOT, Amos	1873		*lawyer*
PITMAN, Sir Isaac	1813	1897	*inventor*
PITT, William, Earl of Chatham	1708	1778	*statesman*
PITT, William, the younger	1759	1806	*statesman*
POE, E. A.	1809	1849	*poet, critic*
POLLAK, Gustav	1849	1919	*editor*
POLLARD, A. F.	1869		*historian*
POOLE, Ernest	1880		*novelist*
PORRITT, Edward	1860	1921	*editor, author*
PORTER, Fitz-John	1822	1901	*soldier*
PORTER, J. A.	1856	1900	*editor*
POWELL, J. B.	1886		*editor*
PRIOR, Melton	1845	1910	*artist, war correspondent*
PULITZER, Joseph	1847	1911	*editor, founder school of journalism*
PULITZER, Joseph	1879		*editor*
RACHEL, Elizabeth Felix	1821	1858	*actress*
RAEMAEKERS, Louis	1869		*cartoonist*
RAGLAN, J. H., Baron	1788	1855	*soldier*
RALPH, Julian	1853	1903	*foreign correspondent*
RAYMOND, Henry J.	1820	1869	*editor*
RAYMOND, H. W.	1847		*editor and proprietor*

NAME	BORN	DIED	OCCUPATION
REDFIELD, W. C.	1858		*ex-secretary of commerce*
REED, A. Y.	1873		*educator*
REED, John	1887	1820	*war correspondent*
REEVE, Henry	1813	1895	*editor*
REID, Sir Thomas Wemyss	1842	1905	*editor and biographer*
REID, Whitelaw	1837	1912	*editor and diplomat*
REINACH, Joseph	1856	1921	*author*
REISNER, C. F.	1872		*clergyman*
RELF, F. H.	1874		*historian*
RENAUDOT, Théophraste	1586	1653	*physician, editor*
REUTER, Herbert, Baron de	1852	1915	*director news agency*
REUTER, P. J. Baron de	1821	1899	*news collector*
REYNOLDS, Frederic	1764	1841	*dramatist*
RHODES, Cecil	1853	1902	*imperialist*
RHODES, J. F.	1848		*historian*
RICHARDS, J. M.	1841	1918	*business man*
RICHMOND, M. E.	1861		*social worker, author*
RIDEING, W. H.	1853		*editor*
RITCHIE, Thomas	1777	1854	*editor*
ROBERTS, Frederick S., Earl	1832	1914	*soldier*
ROBERTSON, J. C.	1813	1881	*canon*
ROBERTSON, J. M.	1856		*editor, author*
ROBINSON, H. Crabb	1775	1867	*special correspondent*
ROBINSON, H. P.	1859		*editor, war correspondent*
ROBINSON, Sir John R.	1828	1903	*editor*
ROBINSON, W. S.	1818	1876	*editor*
ROBINSON, Mrs. W. S. (Harriet Jane Hanson)	1825	1911	*author*
ROCHEFORT, Henri	1830	1913	*editor, politician*
RODGERS, Cleveland	1885		*editor*
ROGERS, Lindsay	1891		*university professor*
ROMILLY, Sir Samuel	1757	1818	*law reformer*
ROSS, E. A.	1866		*university professor*
ROVERSI, Louis	1859		*editor*
ROYALL, Anne	1769	1854	*editor*
ROYCE, G. M.	1850		*clergyman*
RUDDIMAN, Thomas	1674	1757	*librarian*
RUSH, James	1786	1869	*physician*
RUSSELL, C. E.	1860		*editorial writer, author*
RUSSELL, Lord Charles	1832	1900	*Lord Chief Justice*
RUSSELL, G. W.	1867		*man of letters*
RUSSELL, G. W. E.	1853		*author*
RUSSELL, John, Earl Russell	1792	1878	*statesman*

NAME	BORN	DIED	OCCUPATION
RUSSELL, Sir W. H.	1820	1907	war correspondent
SAINTE-BEUVE, C. A.	1804	1869	critic
SAINTSBURY, G. E. B.	1845		critic
SALA, G. A.	1828	1895	editor, author
SALISBURY, Robert Cecil, Marquis of	1830	1903	statesman
SALLEY, A. S., Jr.	1871		author
SALOMON, Ludwig	1844	1911	editor, author
SAMPSON, Henry	1841	1891	editor
SARGENT, Epes	1813	1880	editor
SAULT, Richard	?	1702	mathematician and editor
SAUNDERS, T. B.	1860		author
SAUNDERS, William	1823	1895	news collector
SCHIERBRAND, Wolf von	1851	1920	foreign correspondent
SCHLESINGER, A. M.	1888		university professor
SCHOPENHAUER, Arthur	1788	1860	philosopher
SCHURZ, Carl	1829	1906	statesman
SCOTT, F. N.	1860		university professor
SCOTT, F. W.	1877		university professor
SCOTT, H. W.	1838	1910	editor
SCOTT, Leslie M.	1878		writer
SCOTT, Sir Walter	1771	1832	novelist and poet
SCOTT-JAMES, R. A.	1878		editor
SEDGWICK, Theodore, Jr.	1811	1859	lawyer
SEITZ, D. C.	1862		journalist
SELDEN, C. A.	1870		special correspondent
SENIOR, Nassau W.	1790	1864	economist
SEWARD, Anna	c. 1747	1809	poet
SHADWELL, A.	1854		author, journalist
SHAND, A. I.	1832	1907	journalist and critic
SHARPE, C. K.	1781?	1851	antiquary
SHAW, Albert	1857		editor
SHAW, G. B.	1856		dramatist
SHAW, H. W.	1818	1885	humorist
SHEPHERD, W. G.	1878		war correspondent
SHEPHERD, W. R.	1871		university professor
SHERIDAN, R. B.	1751	1816	dramatist and orator
SHERMAN, John	1823	1900	statesman
SHERMAN, W. T.	1820	1891	soldier
SHERWOOD, Margaret	1864		college professor
SHIRLEY, James	1596	1666	dramatic poet
SHORTER, C. K.	1857		editor
SHUMAN, E. L.	1863		editor

NAME	BORN	DIED	OCCUPATION
SIMPSON, William	1823	1899	artist and war correspondent
SISSON, T. U.	1869		member of congress
SIZERANNE, R. de la	1866		author, editor
SLAGLE, R. L.	1865		college president
SLOSSON, E. E.	1865		editor, author
SMALLEY, G. W.	1833	1916	foreign correspondent
SMILES, Samuel	1812	1904	editor and reformer
SMITH, Elias	1769	1846	editor
SMITH, George	1840	1876	Assyriologist
SMITH, Gerrit	1797	1874	reformer and philanthropist
SMITH, Goldwin	1823	1910	author, historian
SMITH H. L.	1859		college president
SMITH, J. E. ("Shepherd")	1801	1857	clergyman
SMITH, Munroe	1854		university professor
SMITH, Sydney	1771	1845	canon, editor
SMITH, W. A.	1842		author
SMITH, W. H.	1825	1891	news distributor
SMOLLET, T. G.	1721	1771	novelist
SNOWDEN, Philip	1864		member of Parliament
SOUTHEY, Robert	1774	1843	poet
SPEDDING, James	1808	1881	critic, essayist
SPEED, J. G.	1853	1909	editor, author
SPENDER, J. A.	1862		editor
SPIELMANN, M. H.	1858		editor
SPINGARN, J. E.	1875		critic
SPRING-RICE, Thomas, Baron Monteagle	1790	1866	statesman
START, E. A.	1863		educator, editor
STANLEY, A. P.	1815	1881	clergyman
STEAD, W., Jr.	1874	1907	journalist
STEAD, W. T.	1849	1912	editor
STEED, H. Wickham	1871		foreign correspondent, editor
STEELE, Sir Richard	1672	1729	author and editor
STEEVENS, G. W.	1869	1900	special correspondent
STELZLE, Charles	1869		sociologist
STEPHEN, Sir James	1789	1859	colonial under secretary
STEPHEN, Sir James Fitzjames	1829	1892	judge
STEPHEN, Sir Leslie	1832	1904	editor, man of letters
STEPHENS, Winifred	b. England		writer and lecturer
STERLING, Edward	1773	1847	war correspondent, editor

NAME	BORN	DIED	OCCUPATION
STERLING, John	1806	1844	author, editor
STEVENS, G. W.	1866		art director and editor
STEVENSON, R. L.	1850	1894	author
STEWART, Sir Herbert	1843	1885	major-general
STILLMAN, W. J.	1828	1901	special correspondent
STOCQUELER, J. H.	1800	1885	war correspondent, author
STOKES, H. P.	1887		special correspondent
STOKES, I. N. P.	1867		architect, author
STONE, Lucy	1818	1893	reformer
STONE, M. E.	1848		journalist
STOPFORD, F. P.	1861		editor
STRACHEY, J. St. L.	1860		editor, proprietor
STRAIGHT, Willard D.	1880	1918	consul-general, press correspondent
STREET, Julian	1879		dramatic critic
STRUNSKY, Simeon	1879		editor
STUART, Daniel	1766	1846	editor
STUBBS, William	1825	1901	historian, bishop
SUMNER, E. V.	1797	1863	soldier
SWEM, E. G.	1870		librarian
SWIFT, Jonathan	1667	1745	satirist
SYKES, Sir Mark	1879	1919	author
TAINE, Hippolyte	1828	1893	critic and historian
TALMAGE, T. De Witt	1832	1902	preacher and editor
TAPPAN, Arthur	1786	1865	merchant, philanthropist
TAPPAN, Lewis	1788	1873	merchant
TASSIN, Algernon	1869		author, university professor
TAYLOR, Bayard	1825	1878	author, foreign correspondent
TAYLOR, Tom	1817	1880	dramatist, editor
TENNIEL, Sir John	1820	1914	artist
THACKERAY, W. M.	1811	1863	author, editor
THAYER, J. A.	1861		publisher
THIERS, L. A.	1797	1877	statesman, historian
THOMAS, E. S.	1775	1845	editor
THOMAS, Isaiah	1749	1831	printer
THOMPSON, C. M.	1864		editor
THOMPSON, J. P.	1819	1879	Egyptologist
THOMSON, Mortimer ("Doesticks")	1832	1875	humorist
THOROLD, A. L.	1866		author and editor
THORPE, Merle	1879		editor
TINGUY, Marquis de	1813	1881	politician

NAME	BORN	DIED	OCCUPATION
TINSLEY, William	1831	1902	*publisher*
TOCQUEVILLE, Alexis de	1805	1859	*political writer*
TOWNSEND, E. W.	1855		*author*
TOWNSEND, G. A.	1841	1914	*author, war correspondent*
TOWSE, J. R.	1845		*dramatic critic*
TRAILL, H. D.	1842	1900	*editor, author*
TRENCH, F. C.	1805	1886	*soldier*
TRENT, W. P.	1862		*university professor*
TREVELYAN, G. M.	1876		*historian*
TREVELYAN, G. O.	1838		*historian*
TROLLOPE, Anthony	1815	1882	*novelist*
TURNER, G. K.	1869		*author, editor*
TYLER, M. C.	1835	1900	*historian, university professor*
UNTERMEYER, Louis	1885		*author*
VANDERBILT, F. W.	1856		*capitalist*
VAN VLIET, Morris	1839	1918	*compositor*
VERNE, Jules	1828	1905	*novelist*
VEUILLOT, Louis	1813	1883	*editor*
VILLARD, Henry	1835	1900	*editor, war correspondent, financier*
VILLARD, O. G.	1872		*editor, author*
VILLEMESSANT, J. H. A. C. de	1812	1879	*journalist, editor*
VILLIERS, Frederic	1852	1922	*war artist and correspondent*
VIZETELLY, E. A.	1853	1922	*war correspondent and editor*
VIZETELLY, Henry	1820	1894	*artist and editor*
WADE, John	1788	1875	*author and leader writer*
WALKLEY, A. B.	1855		*dramatic critic*
WALPOLE, Horatio	1717	1797	*author*
WALPOLE, Robert	1676	1745	*statesman*
WALSTON, Sir Charles	1856		*archaeologist*
WALTER, John	1818	1894	*newspaper proprietor*
WARD, Artemus (C. F. Browne)	1834	1867	*humorist*
WARD, Mrs. Humphry (Mary A.)	1851	1920	*novelist*
WARD, Leslie	1851	1922	*caricaturist and portrait painter*
WARD, Susan H.	1838		*author*
WARNER, C. D.	1829	1900	*editor and essayist*
WATKINS, J. E.	1875		*journalist, syndicate manager*
WATTERSON, Henry	1840	1921	*editor*

NAME	BORN	DIED	OCCUPATION
WATTS, Alaric Alexander	1797	1864	editor, poet
WATTS, Alfred Alaric	1825	1901	biographer
WATTS, Thomas	1811	1869	librarian, bibliographer
WEBSTER, Benjamin N.	1797	1882	actor and dramatist
WEEKS, L. H.	1851		author, genealogist
WEITENKAMPF, Frank	1866		librarian
WELLINGTON, Arthur, first Duke of	1769	1852	field marshal
WHEATLEY, H. B.	1838	1917	bibliographer
WHEELER, H. D.	1880		editor
WHITE, A. D.	1832	1918	educator
WHITE, Bouck	1874		author
WHITE, Horace	1834	1916	editor
WHITE, H. S.	1852		university professor
WHITE, I. D.	1864		journalist
WHITE, R. G.	1822	1885	scholar, editor
WHITE, W. A.	1868		editor and author
WHITE, W. H.	1831	1913	author
WHITEING, Richard	1840		writer and editor
WHITLOCK, Brand	1869		author and diplomat
WHITNEY, Caspar	1864		editor
WHITTINGHAM, Charles	1767	1840	printer and founder of Chiswick Press
WHITTY, E. M.	1827	1860	journalist
WILBERFORCE, William	1759	1833	philanthropist
WILCOX, Delos F.	1873		franchise expert
WILKES, John	1727	1797	politician
WILLIAMS, S. T.	1888		author
WILLIAMS, Talcott	1849		editor, university professor
WILLIAMS, Walter	1864		university professor
WILLIAMSON, Sir Joseph	1633	1701	statesman, editor
WILLIS, Sir G. H. S.	1823	1900	soldier
WILLS, W. H.	1810	1880	editor
WILSON, John	1785	1854	editor
WINDHAM, William	1750	1810	statesman
WINGATE, C. F.	1848	1909	editor and sanitary engineer
WINTER, William	1836	1917	dramatic critic
WOLFF, H. D.	1830	1908	politician, diplomatist
WOLSELEY, G. J. W., first Viscount	1833	1913	soldier
WOODFALL, William ("Memory")	1746	1803	parliamentary reporter
WOOLER, T. J.	1786	1853	printer and editor
WOODRUFF, C. R.	1868		lawyer, editor

NAME	BORN	DIED	OCCUPATION
WRIGHT, Thomas	1810	1877	*archaeologist*
WYKE, Sir Charles	1815	1897	*diplomat*
YATES, Edmund	1831	1894	*novelist and editor*
YORKE, H. R.	1772	1813	*publicist*
YORKE, Philip, second Earl of Hardwicke	1720	1790	*author*
YOUNG, Arthur	1741	1820	*agriculturalist, author*
ZOLA, Émile	1840	1902	*novelist, critic*

APPENDIX II

BIBLIOGRAPHICAL NOTES

The great source for the study of the newspaper must be the newspaper itself. The bulk of long runs of the daily paper must, however, always prevent the usual public or college library from having on its shelves more than a very limited number of bound volumes of newspapers. But great collections extending over many years and covering every part of the world are found in the Library of Congress, in the library of the State Historical Society of Wisconsin[1] at Madison, in the library of the American Antiquarian Society at Worcester, Mass., in the Boston Public Library, and in the New York Public Library. For all ordinary purposes, however, the exchanges found in any newspaper office, even the smallest, will repay careful study.

Books written in regard to the press are surprisingly few and nearly all are of recent date.[2] They can, in general, be grouped into two classes,—the recollections of newspaper men, and the lives of eminent editors, correspondents, critics, cartoonists, and other persons connected with the press.

Personal memoirs are often random recollections, often garrulous, sometimes censorious, and, especially the earlier ones, usually written so carelessly and so lacking in a sense of order and system as to give rise to the constant query how such work could come from professional journalists. Possibly the explanation is unconsciously given by the author of one of these works when he says: "Although I had many other things to do, I knocked off the present volume within the space of little more than a fortnight." Their value *per se* is often the slightest and is found for the most part in the revelation they give of the financial "hard luck" that has often attended the founding of new papers and the consequent reaction of this on the private fortunes of those connected with them.

Lives of editors, correspondents and cartoonists as a rule suffer from the temptation of their authors to make excursions into contemporaneous politics and to explain the criticisms directed against the subjects of the biography. Very few biographers of journalists have been able to make the persons of whom they are writing take on flesh and blood and become living men. It must be said in extenuation of this defect that biography is the

---

[1] The annotated catalogue of the files of the collection fills, with the Index, 591 pages. Edition of 1911.

[2] Hubert W. Peet, *A Bibliography of Journalism*, London, 1915, gives but six titles prior to 1820.

most difficult of all forms of literature, although often in the past relegated to hack writers on the theory that it is a simple form of composition for any one who wields a facile pen. Yet even so, very able writers, in full sympathy with the men whose biographies they are writing, with a fearless determination to write impartially even while writing sympathetically, in possession of all needed material for writing such biographies, have somehow or other often failed to make editors live again in their pages.

It is probable that the difficulty is inherent in the nature of the subject. Many years ago a great publishing house planned a series of volumes dealing with American statesmen, and so successfully were these men discussed in their public capacity that a companion series quickly followed. But the series of American commonwealths was less successful since it is impossible to separate the life and history of a state from that of the larger political unit of which it forms but a part. The editor, or "newspaper man," is in large measure the counterpart of the commonwealth. The more successful he is as an editor the more his individuality is merged in that of the newspaper with which he is connected. Delane was always "Delane of *The Times*." With the passing of personal journalism and the merging of the individual journalist into the composite board, it becomes still more difficult to individualize the editor. It is true that many of the "stories" and special departments of the paper bear the names of individual writers, but this becomes rather a means of identifying the authorship of articles than a clue to the individuality of the writer.

The biographical material dealing with the press has thus, considered as a whole, something of an external character in its relation to the press, and it gives comparatively little help in discovering the secret of the success or the failure of those who have been a very vital part of the press.

Technical works on journalism form a new but comparatively large class of works. Collectively they give an insight into the evolution of methods that are changing the press on its literary side; individually and separately they vary little. They give minute directions for the construction of copy, especially for writing the "story," the headline, advertisements, and the editorial, and for the advantageous display of all features of the newspaper on its mechanical side. But since they concern the form rather than the spirit, their use to the historian is comparatively slight.

The works treating of the business administration of the press are concerned in the main with the subject of advertising in all of its ramifications,— psychological, ethical, literary, and commercial. They probably form the numerically largest single class of works connected with the press and they are of importance in showing the development of the powerful alliance between the business management and the editorial side of the newspaper.

The newspaper press has long been a favorite subject for articles in reviews and magazines. They are roughly classified into the descriptions of the newspaper press of other countries, accounts of war correspondents and their work, and occasional discussions of general press problems. Singularly enough the newspaper press itself rarely writes of these subjects which are comparatively favorite ones with contributors to reviews. The editor who travels abroad apparently leaves his professional interests behind and writes of European scenery, art galleries, and politics, but seldom of the newspaper press of other countries.

Histories of the press are comparatively few. Those that have been written are for the most part practically chronicles rather than interpretative histories. Occasional histories of individual newspapers have been of value, but as they are usually written in commemoration of some special event they have had distinct limitations. In spite of M. Hatin's monumental works on the history of the newspaper press in France and the careful history of J. B. Williams of the Early English press, the history of the newspaper press has yet to be written.

The chief sources used in this work have been found in the Justice collection of material relating to the press. This collection has been made possible through the bequests of the late Anna Justice, Vassar College, Class of 1901, and of the late Henry Justice of Philadelphia. It now numbers approximately two thousand titles and forms a part of the Vassar College Library.

INDEX

INDEX

A'Beckett, A. W., on dramatic critics, 322–323; criticism of himself, 324 n.; joint author, articles by, cited, 472 n.; works by, cited, 234 n., 242 n., 264 n., 388 n.
Aberdeen, Lord, 278 n.
Aboukir, sinking of, 393 n.
Academy, review in, 316 n.
Acorn (Burr Oak, Mich.), 48.
Acta Diurna, 2, 3 n.; forged transcripts from, 412–413, 414 n.
Acta Senatus, 2.
Acton, Lord, Catholic press and, 19, 20; letter to *The Times*, 57 n.; Abbot Gasquet on, 254; on book reviews, 312, 312 n.
Adam, H. P., *ed.*, work by, cited, 382 n.
Adam, Madame, 25; Stephens's biography of, cited, 26 n.; her policy of *revanche*, 285.
Adams, Henry, note by, quoted, 309 n.
Adams, John Quincy, Monroe Doctrine and, 423 n.
Adams, S. H., on the newspaper, 259.
Adamson, Fire Commissioner, on public officials and press, 359. n.
Addison, 103, 104, 487; mottoes selected by, 46 n.; Spectators and Freeholders of, 107; on news-writers, 141–142; patrons and, 263; Stephen on, 285; on caricaturas, 388 n.
Adirondack Tourist, emblem of, 51.
Adolphus, Gustavus, war correspondence from army of, 196 n.
Advance, 48.
Advertisements, 11, Chap. XIII; patent medicines, xli–xlii, 95, 95 n., 96, 335, 359 n., 371 n., 373 n., 487; historian and, xli–xlii, 335, 361–363, 364–365, 367, 368, 371–375; appeal to past made in, 32, 336–337, 342; rates of, 43, 81; newspaper mottoes and, 45; liquor, 57, 86, 365 n., 451, 484; press guarantees of, 82, 364, 365, 450–451; church, 83, 92, 92 n., 94, 352–353; financial, 83, 358–359; government, 87, 89, 90, 340–343, 373–374; quack doctors, 95, 336, 359 n.; educational institutions, 101; plate service does not carry, 134; ready-print service carries, 134; of books in syndicated newspapers, 135; effect of, on book reviews, 135, 303 n., 308–311, 450; advertisers careless in running,

146; editorials and, 262, 348, 353 n., 354, 360, 360 n., 368–369, 450, 451; bibliography of, 332 n.; slow growth of, 332–333; of newspapers themselves, 333–335, 363 n., 364 n.; circulation and, 334, 362 n., 363, 373 n.; commercial, 335–338, 358, 372–373; charitable and relief, 338–340, 373; honest, 341–342, 360 n., 364–371, 450; collective, 342, 348, 349, 374 n., 489; of states and cities, 343–344; of industrial disputes, 344–345, 480; "safety," 345–346; controversial, 346–348; social habits and, 346, 357, 358, 359, 472–475; political, 348–352, 359, 450; libel and, 349 n., 351; for health, 353; for good will, 353–354, 368; origin of the use of the word, 354 n.; announcements conveyed by, 354–357; of art, 357; high cost of living and, 358; crime combated by, 359; welfare work and, 359; recognized importance of, 360–361; De Weese on, 361 n.; Dwight on, 361; Godkin on, 362 n.; Dibblee on, 362 n.; Villard on, 362 n.; proprietary, banned, 365 n.; Holyoake on, 370; competitive, 372–373; in foreign languages, 374; Johnson on, 375; illustrations in, 376, 377–378, 379, 384, 394 n., 403–404, 478–479; suppression of news and, 434; serial, 438; specialized, 475; Easter, 477; as historical material, 478–484; in time of war, 481–483; prohibition, 484; propaganda in, 484; of the *Spectator*, 487; disprove Americans are superficial, 488–489. See *also* Newspaper as a business enterprise.
Advertiser, Boston, Holmes' "Old Ironsides" in, 106.
Advertising Men's League, 365.
Advocate, 48.
Aegis, 47.
Affiches, used in Brussels during war, 7 n.
Afghan War, first, 407.
Africa, South. *See* South Africa.
Afro-American press. *See* negro press.
Agitator, 48.
Ajax, ship, 423.
A. L. A. Booklist, Pearson on, 310 n.
Albert, Charles, defended by Italian press, 208 n.